DATE DUE

AUG 3 1 2011			

THE OXFORD SHAKESPEARE

General Editor · Stanley Wells

For Sam Neill

THE OXFORD SHAKESPEARE

Othello, the Moor of Venice

EDITED BY MICHAEL NEILL

CLARENDON PRESS · OXFORD
2006

OXFORD
UNIVERSITY PRESS

Great Clarendon Street, Oxford OX2 6DP

Oxford University Press is a department of the University of Oxford.
It furthers the University's objective of excellence in research, scholarship,
and education by publishing worldwide in

Oxford New York

Auckland Cape Town Dar es Salaam Hong Kong Karachi
Kuala Lumpur Madrid Melbourne Mexico City Nairobi
New Delhi Shanghai Taipei Toronto

With offices in

Argentina Austria Brazil Chile Czech Republic France Greece
Guatemala Hungary Italy Japan South Korea Poland Portugal Singapore
South Korea Switzerland Thailand Turkey Ukraine Vietnam

Published in the United States
by Oxford University Press Inc., New York

© Michael Neill 2006

British Library Cataloguing in Publication Data

Data available

Library of Congress Cataloging in Publication Data

Data available

ISBN 0-19-812920-3   978-0-19-812920-2
ISBN 0-19-281451-(pbk)   978-0-19-281451-7

10 9 8 7 6 5 4 3 2 1

Typeset by SNP Best-set Typesetter Ltd., Hong Kong
Printed in Great Britain
on acid-free paper by
Biddles Ltd., King's Lynn, Norfolk

ACKNOWLEDGEMENTS

THE list of those who have helped me since I began work on this edition in 1997 has become a long one. I am indebted to the generosity of the Folger Shakespeare Library and of Trinity College, Cambridge, for visiting fellowships, to the New Zealand Marsden Foundation for a research award, and to the University of Auckland through grants of leave in 1997–8, 2002, and 2005. I received unstinting assistance from the staff of the libraries whose resources I have quarried, including the University of Auckland Library, the Auckland City Library, the Harvard Theatre Collection, the Library of Congress, the library of the Shakespeare Centre in Stratford-upon-Avon, the library of the London Theatre Museum, the archives of the Royal National Theatre of Great Britain, Cambridge University Library, and above all the Folger Shakespeare Library. My gratitude to the Folger includes the kindness of a long list of resident and visiting scholars, including Barbara Mowat, Gail Paster, Georgianna Ziegler, Peter Blayney, Leslie Thomson, Linda Levy Peck, the late Susan Snyder, Jeff Masten, Meredith Skura, Albert Braunmuller, and Linda Austern. I am especially indebted to Professor Austern for her excellent appendix on the music in the play.

Elsewhere, Edward Pechter, Patricia Parker, Anne Barton, Jean Howard, Janet Adelman, John Kerrigan, Jocelyn Harris, Jyotsna Singh, and Graham Bradshaw have done their best to inform my critical judgement, while Paul Werstine, Tom Berger, and Mac Jackson have offered invaluable textual expertise. With exceptional consideration, Ernst Honigmann ensured that I received an advance copy of his new Arden edition; Louise Noble shared the fruits of her research into early modern medicine; and Charles Edelman was equally helpful in military matters. I am grateful above all to my colleague Bruno Ferraro for his meticulous translation of the source *novella* from Giraldi Cinthio's *Hecatommithi*.

I have learned a great deal from the insights of theatre professionals, among them Patrick Stewart, Lisa Harrow, and Bruce Purchase. I owe a particular debt to Jude Kelly and her cast from the Washington Shakespeare Company for allowing me to sit in on rehearsals for her 'photo-negative' production; and to the staff of the Brooklyn Academy of Music who made certain that I received tickets for Sam Mendes's National Theatre production when it reached Brooklyn.

Needless to say, I owe much to the patience and learning of the General Editor, Stanley Wells, as well as to the professionalism of staff at Oxford University Press, especially Frances Whistler, Sophie Goldsworthy, Tom Perridge, and my copy-editor, Christine Buckley, whose sharp eye and scholarly acumen have been invaluable. As always I am grateful to colleagues at the University of Auckland for numerous kindnesses—especially Sebastian Black, Judith Binney, Albert Wendt, Terry Sturm, Ken Larsen, Sophie Tomlinson, and Margaret Edgcumbe. Finally, I must thank Kubé Jones-Neill, whose ungrudging support included more proof-reading than any wife should be asked to undertake.

MICHAEL NEILL

CONTENTS

List of Illustrations   ix

Introduction   I
Reception   I
Sources   16
  Setting, Characters, and Plot   18
  The Time Scheme   33
The Play in Performance   36
  Playing Black   40
  Othello and Iago   71
  Desdemona   100
  Emilia and Bianca   106
  Cassio and Roderigo   111
Interpretation   113
  Reading Blackness   113
  '*Othello*' and Discovery   130
  '*Othello*' and the Monstrous   138
  Place, Office, and Occupation   147
  Love, Service, and Identity   158
  The Place of Women   169
  Conclusion   177

Editorial Procedures   181
Abbreviations and References   183

THE TRAGEDY OF OTHELLO, THE MOOR OF VENICE   195

APPENDIX A
The Date of the Play   399

APPENDIX B
The Texts of the Play   405
  The Textual Problem   405
  Quarto and Folio   406

Contents

The Scholarly Debate   411
Conclusion   430

APPENDIX C
*Giraldi Cinthio: 'Gli Hecatommithi', Third Decade, Seventh
Novella* Translated by Bruno Ferraro   434

APPENDIX D
The Music in the Play by Linda Phyllis Austern   445

APPENDIX E
Alterations to Lineation   455

APPENDIX F
Longer Notes   461

Index   469

LIST OF ILLUSTRATIONS

1. James Earl Jones as Othello, Christopher Plummer as Iago
   (Stratford, Connecticut, 1981)   4
   (HARVARD THEATRE COLLECTION)

2. Map illustrating Ralegh's *Discoverie of . . . Guiana,* from
   Theodor de Bry, *America pars VIII* (Frankfurt, 1599)   21
   (FOLGER SHAKESPEARE LIBRARY)

3. German reliquary statue of the black St Maurice, 1525–7
   (*Heiltumsbuch,* fol. 227^v)   27
   (HOFBIBLIOTHEK, ASCHAFFENBURG)

4. The bedchamber scene: engraving by François Boitard (?)
   in Nicholas Rowe's edition of Shakespeare's *Works* (1709)   38
   (FOLGER SHAKESPEARE LIBRARY)

5. The bedchamber scene: engraving by George Noble from
   a painting by Josiah Boydell for the Boydell Gallery, 1800   39
   (FOLGER SHAKESPEARE LIBRARY)

6. The burlesque tradition: the wooing of Desdemona.
   Illustration from *Othello: An Interesting Drama, Rather*
   (London, [*c.*1850])   43
   (FOLGER SHAKESPEARE LIBRARY)

7. Moors, from C. Vecellio, *De Gli Habiti Antichi et Moderni*
   (Venice, 1590)   46
   (FOLGER SHAKESPEARE LIBRARY)

8. Sir Herbert Beerbohm Tree as Othello, Phyllis Neilson-Terry
   as Desdemona (His Majesty's Theatre, London, 1912)   48
   (VICTORIA AND ALBERT MUSEUM)

9. Ira Aldridge as Othello   51
   (FOLGER SHAKESPEARE LIBRARY)

10. Paul Robeson as Othello, with Peggy Ashcroft as Desdemona
    (Savoy Theatre, 1930)   53
    (VICTORIA AND ALBERT MUSEUM)

11. Edmund Kean as Iago (1814)   73
    (HARVARD THEATRE COLLECTION)

12. Edwin Booth as Iago   76
    (PHOTOGRAPH BY SARONY; FOLGER SHAKESPEARE LIBRARY)

13. Edmund Kean as Othello   81
    (FOLGER SHAKESPEARE LIBRARY)

14. William Charles Macready as Othello   82
    (FOLGER SHAKESPEARE LIBRARY)

15. Sir Laurence Olivier as Othello, Frank Finlay as Iago
(National Theatre, London, 1964)   87
    (PHOTOGRAPH BY ANGUS MCBEAN. © THE HARVARD THEATRE COLLECTION.
    THE HOUGHTON LIBRARY)

16. Simon Russell Beale as Iago (Royal National Theatre,
London, 1997)   97
    (PHOTOGRAPH BY MARK DOUET)

17. The Temptation Scene: Paul Robeson as Othello, José Ferrer
as Iago (Shubert Theatre, New York, 1943)   141
    (HARVARD THEATRE COLLECTION)

INTRODUCTION

Reception

'*Othello*', in the words of Edward Pechter, 'has become the tragedy of choice for the present generation.'[1] If the existential 'prison' of *Hamlet* was the place in which generations of post-Romantic intellectuals, following the example of Goethe and Coleridge, found the angst-ridden image of their own alienation; if, in the wake of World War II, it was the wasteland of *King Lear* that provided a mirror for humanity living under the shadow of holocaust and nuclear devastation; then, towards the close of the twentieth century, it was *Othello* that began to displace them both, as critics and directors alike began to trace in the cultural, religious, and ethnic animosities of its Mediterranean setting, the genealogy of the racial conflicts that fractured their own societies. *Othello*, the black protagonist of Murray Carlin's play *Not Now, Sweet Desdemona* had declared in 1969, '[was] the first play of the Age of Imperialism': written (as this 'Othello' reminds his white interlocutor) just ten years after the Portuguese consolidated their control of the East African littoral with the establishment of Fort Jesus in Mombasa, it necessarily also became a play about that most malign legacy of empire, colour—'the first play about colour that ever was written. . . . *Othello* is about colour, and nothing but colour'.[2] Carlin's reworking of Shakespeare's tragedy now has a prophetic look to it, for it is as a foundational document in the history of 'race' that much recent criticism has treated the play.

Yet *Othello* was not always approached in these terms: perhaps the most striking thing about the very earliest responses to the tragedy is that they pay no attention to what, from a modern perspective, seems its most conspicuous feature—the interracial love affair at the centre of the action. In his brief comments on the performance he saw at Oxford in 1610, the academic Henry Jackson did not even trouble to notice 'race' as an issue in the play; and his

---

[1] Edward Pechter, *Othello and Interpretive Traditions* (Iowa City, 1999), p. 2.
[2] Murray Carlin, *Not Now, Sweet Desdemona* (Nairobi, 1969), pp. 31–2.

I

seeming indifference was shared by a mid-century reader of plays, the clergyman Abraham Wright, whose notebooks praise the characterization of 'Iago for a rogue and Othello for a jealous husband', but make no mention of the protagonist's colour.[1] Indeed, the contention of Carlin's white antagonist that *Othello* is first and foremost a tragedy of jealousy would probably have caused little demur before the last third of the twentieth century—even if from the end of the seventeenth century, as we shall see, the hero's colour was capable of generating the most intense anxiety amongst viewers and critics alike.

However, although controversy over matters of race has played an increasingly significant role in the play's reception history, there are other, more strictly dramaturgical reasons why that history has been unusually vexed and contradictory. From the time of its first performance, somewhere between 1601 and 1604 (see Appendix A), the romantic cast of the story made *Othello* one of Shakespeare's most popular and frequently performed plays; yet its claim to rank amongst the greatest tragedies has been challenged by critics who have found its plot too strained, its characters too improbable, and its tale of marital jealousy and murder too meanly domestic to challenge comparison with *Hamlet, King Lear, Macbeth*, or even that saga of tragic infatuation, *Antony and Cleopatra*. In the theatre—despite its long dependence on the fundamentally implausible pretence that the white actor playing the hero was a black man—*Othello* has proved remarkable for its ability to overwhelm audience disbelief and to compel extraordinary identification with the suffering of its central characters.

In the Jacobean and Caroline periods *Othello* seems to have enjoyed widespread popularity and admiration, inspiring numerous dramatic imitations, and attracting more contemporary allusions than any other Shakespeare tragedy.[2] It seems clear that it was equally well liked at the Globe, where it was probably first performed, and at the more exclusive Blackfriars, which

---

[1] British Library Add. MS 22608, fol. 84ᵛ, cited in Sasha Roberts, 'Shakespeare's Tragedies of Love', in Richard Dutton and Jean E. Howard (eds.), *A Companion to Shakespeare's Works: The Tragedies* (Oxford, 2003), 108–33 (p. 121).

[2] See G. E. Bentley, *Shakespeare and Jonson, Their Reputations in the Seventeenth Century Compared* (Chicago, 1945), p. 113; and cf. Marvin Rosenberg, *The Masks of Othello* (Berkeley, Calif., 1961; repr. Newark, Del., n.d.), pp. 258–9 n. 2.

Shakespeare's company used as a winter house from about 1609. We know of revivals in 1610 (at the Globe), in 1629 and in 1635 (at the Blackfriars); but in a period of scanty records, there are likely to have been many performances for which no documentation survives. *Othello*'s appearance at Oxford in 1610 indicates not only that it was popular enough to be taken on tour, but that it was expected to appeal to an elite university audience as well. Evidently it was just as highly regarded at Court, which was the site of its first recorded performance, at the Banqueting House in Whitehall on 1 November 1604. It was brought back as one of the entertainments for Princess Elizabeth's wedding to the Elector Palatine in the winter of 1612/13, and performed again for Charles I and Henrietta Maria in 1636. The play's frequent revivals may help to account for the fact that it has been preserved in two distinct versions, the Quarto of 1622 and the Folio of 1623, whose differences reflect the exceptional fluidity of performance texts in the early modern theatre (see Appendix B).

Othello's early popularity was maintained after the Interregnum, when it was probably the first of Shakespeare's tragedies to grace the re-established London stage; and it enjoyed continuing favour throughout the Restoration period. This was, however, also the period that witnessed the earliest systematic critique of the play—one that set the terms for a great deal of subsequent debate. In his *Short View of Tragedy* (1693), Thomas Rymer prefaced a blistering attack on Shakespeare's dramaturgy by admitting the high esteem in which this work was held: noting that '[f]rom all the tragedies acted on our English stage, *Othello* is said to bear the bell away', he identified Iago's temptation of Othello (3.3) as 'the top scene, the scene that raises *Othello* above all other tragedies on our theatres' (pp. 86, 118). But he denounced the play for the rank implausibility of its characterization and plotting: '[n]othing', he wrote, 'is more odious in nature than an improbable lie; and, certainly, never was any play fraught, like this of *Othello*, with improbabilities' (p. 92). No sensible audience, Rymer believed, could possibly be taken in by the absurdities of its design: even were they to overlook the unlikelihood of the central relationship between a supposed 'blackamoor' general and an aristocratic Venetian woman, and to ignore the gross indecorum of presenting a soldier as the conniving villain of the piece (pp. 91–4), the palpable inconsistencies of the time scheme meant that playgoers 'must deny their

3

1. 'The Tragedy of the Handkerchief': James Earl Jones as Othello, Christopher Plummer as Iago (Stratford, Connecticut, 1981).

senses, to reconcile it to common sense'.[1] Moreover, in view of the ludicrous device chosen to trigger the hero's jealousy, he declared that the play had better have been 'called *The Tragedy of the Handkerchief*':

Had it been Desdemona's garter, the sagacious Moor might have smelt a rat: but the handkerchief is so remote a trifle, no booby on this side Mauretania could make any consequence of it. . . . Yet we find it entered our poet's head to make a tragedy of this trifle.[2]

Everywhere he looked, Rymer found monstrous breaches of tragic decorum in the treatment of fable and characters: arguing that Othello's 'love and . . . jealousy are no part of a soldier's character, unless for comedy', he concluded that while 'There is in this play some burlesque, some humour, and ramble of comical wit, some show, and some *mimicry* to divert the spectators . . . the tragical

---

[1] Rymer, p. 123, and cf. pp. 115, 120, 126–7, 132.
[2] Rymer, pp. 114–16, 139–40, 145. Rymer's sneer is remembered in the title of Paula Vogel's feminist reworking of *Othello, Desdemona: A Play about a Handkerchief*, in Daniel Fischlin and Mark Fortier (eds.), *Adaptations of Shakespeare* (London and New York, 2000).

4

is plainly none other than a bloody farce, without salt or savour'; even the widely admired temptation scene reminded him of *commedia dell'arte*—'such scenes as this have made all the world run after *Harlequin* and *Scaramuccio*'.[1]

Recent work examining the 'comic matrix' of the play's design,[2] like the long-running debate over its use of so-called 'double time',[3] show that, however obtuse Rymer's overall response, his complaints about plot and decorum were not as foolish as they have often been made to appear. Shakespeare himself sometimes appears to draw deliberate attention to his juggling with comic convention: even in the tragic catastrophe, when Emilia denounces Othello as a 'murderous coxcomb' (5.2.234), her oxymoron makes scornful play with the traditionally ridiculous figure of the jealous cuckold. Nor is Rymer the only critic to have questioned the fundamental believability of *Othello*: many of his criticisms were to be echoed two centuries later by no less a critic than Bernard Shaw, who not only denounced the fable for its 'police-court morality and commonplace thought', but excoriated the plot for 'its farcical trick with a handkerchief'.[4] Reviewing a production

[1] Rymer, pp. 93, 146, 118–19; cf. also pp. 110, 112.

[2] Contemporary criticism has been more sympathetic to what it sees as Shakespeare's deliberate manipulation of comic conventions: see Susan Snyder, *The Comic Matrix of Shakespeare's Tragedies* (Princeton, 1979), pp. 70–4; Stanley Cavell, *Disowning Knowledge in Six Plays of Shakespeare* (Cambridge, 1987), pp. 132–3; Michael Bristol, 'Charivari and the Comedy of Abjection in *Othello*', *Renaissance Drama*, NS 21 (1990), 3–21, and repr. in Linda Woodbridge and Edward Berry (eds.), *True Rites and Maimed Rites: Ritual and Anti-Ritual in Shakespeare and His Age* (Urbana, Ill., 1992), 75–97; Peter J. Smith, ' "A good soft pillow for that good white head": *Othello* as comedy', *Sydney Studies in English*, 24 (1998–9), 21–39; Robert Hornback, 'Emblems of Folly in the First *Othello*: Renaissance Blackface, Moor's Coat, and "Muckender" ', *Comparative Drama*, 35 (2001), 69–99; and Stephen Orgel, '*Othello* and the End of Comedy', *SS 56* (2003), 105–16.

[3] See below, 'Sources', pp. 33–6.

[4] Edwin Wilson (ed.), *Shaw on Shakespeare* (New York, 1961; repr. Harmondsworth, 1969), p. 252; Bernard Shaw, *Our Theatres in the Nineties*, 3 vols. (1948), iii. 315. More recently, the negative side of Shaw has been echoed by the black actor Hugh Quarshie, who argues not only that the play presents an entirely conventional portrait of an African 'with little in the way of plausible psychological motivation', but that the coincidences of the plot strain the credulity of the audience, while 'Shakespeare's attempts to tie up the loose . . . threads at the end of the play invite derision' (*Second Thoughts About Othello*, International Shakespeare Association Occasional Paper 7 (Chipping Campden, 1999), pp. 8, 19). See also Herbert Kretzmer's description of the play, when reviewing the 1964 Dexter/Olivier production, as 'a surface-scratching melodrama' that nevertheless 'remains sublime', given an Othello of sufficient 'largeness, mystery and . . . human vulnerability' (*Daily Express*, 22 Apr. 1964).

in 1897, he called *Othello* 'pure melodrama'; yet even Shaw found himself reluctantly moved by the power of its language, admitting that for all its 'superficiality and staginess, [*Othello*] remains magnificent by the volume of its passion and the splendor of its word-music, which sweep the scenes up to a plane on which sense is drowned in sound. The words do not convey ideas: they are streaming ensigns and tossing branches to make the tempest of passion visible. . . . Tested by the brain, it is ridiculous: tested by the ear, it is sublime.'[1]

The force of Rymer's and Shaw's complaints about the plot is well illustrated by the fate of various attempts to rewrite the play in alternative genres. In the case of Verdi's *Otello*—as we might expect from Shaw's remarks about the opera-like qualities of *Othello* itself and the seductiveness of its word-music—the sheer power of the score is enough to overwhelm any reservations about the plausibility of the action. But in the case of two recent screen versions, the effect of translating the play into a contemporary idiom was to reduce it to banal risibility. Tim Blake Nelson's 2001 film *O* turns Othello into 'Odin James' (Mekhi Phifer), the black star and captain of an otherwise white high-school basketball team, who falls for the principal's beautiful daughter, Desi (Julia Stiles), only to be destroyed by the machinations of his envious friend Hugo (Josh Hartnett), the son of coach Duke Goulding; despite its knowing

---

[1] Wilson (ed.), *Shaw on Shakespeare*, pp. 171–2. In his later essay on Verdi (1901), Shaw was rather less complimentary about the play's word-music: 'the truth is that instead of Otello being an Italian opera written in the style of Shakespear, Othello is a play written in the style of Italian opera. . . . Desdemona is a prima donna, with handkerchief, confidant, and vocal solo all complete . . . Othello's transports are conveyed by a magnificent but senseless music which rages from the Propontick to the Hellespont in an orgy of thundering sound and bounding rhythm; and the plot is a pure farce plot: that is to say, it is supported on an artificially manufactured and desperately precarious trick with a handkerchief which a chance word might upset at any moment. With such a libretto, Verdi was quite at home: his success with it proves, not that he could occupy Shakespear's plane, but that Shakespear could on occasion occupy his, which is a very different matter' (pp. 174–5). Rymer similarly acknowledged the pleasing 'sound' of Shakespeare's verse (p. 124), but thought it largely empty of sense: 'In the *neighing* of an horse, or in the *growling* of a mastiff, there is a meaning, there is as lively expression, and, may I say, more humanity, than many times in the tragical flights of *Shakespeare*' (pp. 85–6). For two usefully complementary essays exploring the ways in which Verdi and his librettist, Boito, adapted Shakespeare's tragedy, see Frank Kermode, 'Shakespeare and Boito', in *Pieces of My Mind* (New York, 2003), 357–73, and Graham Bradshaw, 'Metaferocities: Representation in *Othello* and *Otello*', *Shakespearean International Yearbook*, 3 (2003), 336–56.

allusions to Shakespeare ('I thought he wrote movies,' says Hugo) and to Verdi's *Otello* (Nelson opens with the 'Ave Maria', and ends with the 'Credo' as Hugo is led away by the police), the unrelievedly pedestrian screenplay and the telescoping of the action to ninety-one minutes reduce the play to precisely the improbable melodrama described by Shaw. Little more can be said for Andrew Davies's television play, *Othello*, misleadingly subtitled, *A Modern Masterpiece*: here Shakespeare's Moor becomes 'John Othello' (Eamonn Walker), London's first black Police Commissioner, whose promotion—together with his marriage to the upper-class Dessie Brabant (Keeley Hawes)—provokes the bitter resentment of his deputy, Ben Jago (Christopher Eccleston), a closet racist whose pretence of loyal friendship is complicated by frustrated homosexual desire. Like *O*, Davies's play is full of self-conscious homages to the original, including a bed decorated in Venetian Gothic, as well as an epilogue spoken by Jago in which he paraphrases a familiar critical debate about *Othello*: 'Don't talk to me about race, don't talk to me about politics: it was love—simple as that.' A perfect index to the banality of Davies's conception is the replacement of Desdemona's magically imbrued handkerchief with a falsified DNA test.

For Shaw's contemporary, the critic A. C. Bradley, *Othello* remained 'the most painfully exciting and the most terrible' of all Shakespeare's tragedies; yet he was forced to concede that for many readers the meanness of its subject, 'sexual jealousy', rendered the play 'not merely painful, but so repulsive that not even the intense tragic emotions which the story generates can overcome this repulsion'.[1] It may well be, however, that for most audiences it is precisely this combination of the mean and repulsive with the most tragic intensity that accounts for the play's exceptional power to move. This at least is what is suggested by the response of an anonymous Romantic critic to the play's yoking of opposites: on the one hand, its emotions seem almost painfully familiar:

Othello is a faithful portrait of the life with which we are daily and hourly conversant; love and jealousy are passions which all men, with few exceptions, have at some time felt; the imitation of them, therefore, finds an immediate sympathy in every mind; Othello has no feelings that we should not ourselves have in his situation.

[1] A. C. Bradley, *Shakespearean Tragedy* (1904; repr. 1961), pp. 143, 148–9.

On the other hand, it endows these feelings with an awful, super-human sublimity:

it resembles a thunderstorm, which awes by its magnificence of terror; in fact it is grand beyond loveliness; the word beauty might as well be applied to the terrors of an earthquake, or the heights of the Andes.[1]

The emotional force of Shakespeare's poetry, especially in the last three acts, can indeed be devastating: for the normally sober Dr Johnson, even the experience of editing the play was almost more than he could bear: 'I am glad I have ended my revisal of this dreadful scene,' he wrote of *Othello*'s ending, 'it is not to be endured';[2] while the Variorum editor H. H. Furness, reflecting on the 'unutterable agony' produced by the scene, wished 'that . . . this tragedy had never been written'.[3]

The play's performance history provides ample testimony of its continuing power to move onlookers—sometimes to an extravagant degree. The French novelist Stendhal recorded an extraordinary event during an American performance in 1822: 'a soldier who was on guard duty inside the Baltimore theatre, seeing Othello . . . was about to kill Desdemona', intervened to protect her: ' "It will never be said that in my presence a confounded Negro has killed a white woman!" he shouted, and then fired his gun . . . breaking the arm of the actor who was playing Othello.'[4] 'A year does not go by', Stendhal claimed, 'without the newspapers reporting similar stories.' Such absolute surrender to the power of Shakespeare's theatrical fiction would have astonished Rymer; yet the most conspicuous feature of the play's theatrical life has been precisely this extraordinary capacity to swamp aesthetic detachment—even to the point where (as in the case of the Baltimore guard) the boundary between fiction and reality has sometimes

---

[1] Cited from the prefatory 'Remarks' in *Othello* 'As it is performed at the Theatre Royal' (1819).

[2] Quoted in James R. Siemon, ' "Nay, that's not next": *Othello*, V.ii in Performance, 1760–1900', *SQ* 37 (1986), 38–51 (p. 39).

[3] Furness, p. 300.

[4] Stendhal, *From Racine to Shakespeare* (1823), in Jonathan Bate (ed.), *The Romantics on Shakespeare* (1992), 218–37 (p. 222). Only slightly less extravagant was the interjection of an audience member responding to Edwin Forrest's Iago in 1825: 'You damn'd lying scoundrel, I would like to get hold of you after the show is over and wring your infernal neck'—cited in Julie Hankey (ed.), *Plays in Performance: Othello* (Bristol, 1987), p. 1.

appeared to dissolve altogether.[1] This has reputedly been true not only for audiences, but for performers: according to a persistent theatrical legend, famously exploited in Marcel Carné's film *Les Enfants du Paradis*, as well as in George Cukor's *A Double Life*, actors playing Othello and Iago are especially liable to carry over their roles into their offstage lives.[2] This is precisely what seems to have happened after a performance by British officers and their wives in Freetown, Sierra Leone, in 1857: the commanding officer, who played Othello, shot his Cassio in cold blood, provoking a public scandal over heavy drinking and sexual promiscuity amongst the garrison community. In 1942 Paul Robeson's adulterous affair with Uta Hagen, his second Desdemona and wife of his Iago, José Ferrer, made it seem as if 'the actors were taken over by their roles'.[3]

From the very beginning playgoers have recorded the emotional impact of *Othello*: in his note on the 1610 Oxford performance, Henry Jackson wrote of its power to move the onlookers to tears, especially in the scene where 'the celebrated Desdemona, slain in our presence by her husband . . . entreated the pity of the spectators by her very countenance'.[4] Numerous later anecdotes confirm Jackson's testimony to the work's disturbing emotional effect. Samuel Pepys remembered that when he saw it performed at the Cockpit in 1660 'a very pretty lady that sat by me cried out to see Desdemona smothered'.[5] Eighteenth- and nineteenth-century audiences often wept openly during the performance; beginning in

---

[1] On *Othello's* capacity to overwhelm the audience's (and even the actors') capacity for disbelief, see Pechter, pp. 11–14, 108; A. C. Sprague, *Shakespeare and the Actors* (Cambridge, Mass., 1948), p. 199, and Elise Marks, ' "Othello/me": Racial Drag and the Pleasures of Boundary-Crossing with *Othello*', *Comparative Drama*, 35 (2001), 101–23.

[2] See Lois Potter, 'Unhaply for I am white', *TLS*, 5 Mar. 1999, 18–19, and Potter, *Othello* (Manchester, 2002), pp. 135–9. A similar plot-device was employed in two other films, *Carnival* (1921)—a silent movie, remade as a talkie in 1931—Walter Reisch's *Men are not Gods* (1936). Another version of the fatal triangle appears in Theatre at Large's play *Manawa Taua/Savage Hearts* (Auckland, New Zealand, 1994) in which a Maori chief, commanded by Queen Victoria to play Othello in a tour of his home country, finds himself playing out an uncanny version of the story in real life.

[3] Christopher Fyfe, *A History of Sierra Leone* (Oxford, 1962), pp. 304–5; and Potter, pp. 124, 134.

[4] Cited in Hankey, p. 18; Jackson's original note is in Latin.

[5] Robert Latham and William Matthews (eds.), *The Diary of Samuel Pepys*, 11 vols. (1970–83), i. 264 (11 Oct. 1660).

1746, Spranger Barry's electrifying Othello 'invariably' caused 'the females . . . to shriek' in the murder scene;[1] half a century later, the fierce pathos of Edmund Kean's Moor was enough to make even Byron cry, whilst 'old men leaned their heads upon their arms and fairly sobbed' at the catastrophe.[2] In revolutionary France such was the effect of Joseph Talma's 1792 performance that the killing of Desdemona provoked '[t]ears, groans, and menaces . . . from all parts of the theatre', while 'several of the prettiest women in Paris fainted in the most conspicuous boxes and were publicly carried out of the house'. So alarmed was Talma's translator, Jean-François Ducis, that he feared 'for his tragedy, for his fame, and for his life', and felt bound to revise his version of the play, equipping it for several performances with a happy ending.[3] In 1829 according to Alexandre Dumas *père*, Alfred de Vigny's translation was equally overwhelming in its impact on his Paris contemporaries, who 'shook [and] shuddered' at Othello's 'roars of African jealousy'.[4] In mid-nineteenth-century London, even the relatively restrained oriental Moor of William Charles Macready produced so 'thrilling' an effect that when, after the murder, he thrust 'his dark, despairing face through the curtains of the bed', a female spectator is said to have 'hysterically fainted' at the sight.[5] In another of his performances, at the point when Macready seized Iago by the throat in the temptation scene, a gentleman 'started up and exclaimed, loud enough for all around to hear, "Choke the devil! Choke him!"'[6] The response of later nineteenth-century audiences to such notable Othellos as Ira Aldridge and Tommaso Salvini was often equally intense.

---

[1] John Bernard, *Retrospections of the Stage*, 2 vols. (1830), i. 28; and cf. Virginia Mason Vaughan, *Othello: a contextual history* (Cambridge, 1994), p. 120; Rosenberg, pp. 45–6.

[2] Rosenberg, p. 61; G. H. Lewes, *On Actors and the Art of Acting* (1875), p. 5, cited in Hankey, p. 59.

[3] See Rosenberg, p. 32.

[4] Hankey, pp. 78–9.

[5] Westland Marston and John Forster, cited in Hankey, pp. 64, 317.

[6] Sprague, p. 199. For a modern production in which the audience shouted at Othello in the murder scene, see Pechter's discussion of Peter Zadek's *Othello* at the Deutsches Schauspielhaus, Hamburg, in 1976 (p. 56 and n. 5, pp. 203–4). The action of Pier Paolo Pasolini's film *Che Cosa Sono Le Nuovole* (1967) is built around the performance of a puppet-play *Othello* in which the audience not only call out warnings to Othello in the eavesdropping scene (4.1), but finally invade the stage in Act 5 to rescue Desdemona and kill both Iago and the Moor.

Twentieth-century playgoers generally proved rather less suggestible: as early as 1905 we find a reviewer complaining that '[t]here have been many successful Hamlets, but no Othello seems to have satisfied critics in like degree';[1] and by 1948 Ruth Ellis recorded that '[t]his tragedy, so overwhelming to read, has lately proved one of the most difficult to stage to complete satisfaction'.[2] But some performances could still produce extraordinary reactions: Laurence Olivier's 1965 Moscow season is said to have generated storms of emotion reminiscent of those that greeted Aldridge a century earlier;[3] and in 1979 (more predictably perhaps) when the first black actor to play Othello in the southern United States kissed his Desdemona, it was enough to produce 'audible gasps' from the audience and a string of hate letters.[4] A decade afterwards the reviewer John Peter confessed that the effect of Trevor Nunn's claustrophobic Stratford production was to make him 'want to reach out and stop Othello before it's too late'.[5]

Difficult as it may appear to reconcile this history of emotional surrender with the cool derision of the play's detractors, the two phenomena are related, for (as Bernard Shaw implicitly recognized) *Othello* is a play whose designs on the audience can only succeed when there is a collapse of aesthetic distance. In its most extreme form, illustrated by the soldier's attack on the unfortunate Baltimore Othello, this absolute suspension of disbelief can express itself as an irrational compulsion to intervene in the action of the play. But a more sophisticated version of the same response manifests itself in the aggressive rhetorical challenges to Shakespeare's protagonist issued in a number of twentieth-century reworkings of the play. So in Carlin's postcolonial drama, where two actors—a

---

[1] *Stratford Herald*, 12 May 1905; the critic repeated the same complaints verbatim when reviewing another Benson performance on 9 August 1911, suggesting that '*Othello* is a tragedy of almost unattainable ideals, towards which the realities of performance, as far as the chief character goes, and also perhaps Iago, must show some disparity.'

[2] *Stratford Herald*, 30 July 1948.

[3] See Marks, pp. 103–5. The play's unusual capacity to possess the imagination of its audiences is clearly related, as Marks indicates, to the exceptional degree of self-abandonment that the central role seems to elicit from the actors who play it—a phenomenon acknowledged by Othellos from Macready to Paul Robeson and Ben Kingsley (pp. 101–12).

[4] See Suajata Iyengar, 'White Faces, Blackface: The Production of Race in *Othello*', in Philip C. Kolin (ed.), *Othello: New Critical Essays* (New York, 2002), p. 112.

[5] *Sunday Times*, 27 Aug. 1989.

white South African and a black West Indian—debate the significance of the tragedy for contemporary race politics, 'Desdemona' at one point attacks her fellow performer as though he were indeed Shakespeare's Moor:

You wouldn't let go of the colour problem—not if they gave you a million pounds and made you the King! Othello! The thicklips! As if you'd give them up. The colour of your skin's your most precious possession. That's your role. [1]

In Charles Marowitz's agitprop drama *An Othello* (1974)—a rewriting of Shakespeare's play in the context of the Black Power movement—it is Iago (now cast as a black radical) who is made to challenge Othello as the model of all blacks who, by capitulating to the values of the white world, offer themselves as scapegoats to racial bigotry:

Do you feel it, General—that crazy little shiver in the blood—a little like speed—a little like cum—a warm, spikey, liquid glow lightin' through all the back-alleys of the body? That's what a black man feels when he scourges the whiteness in him. . . . Now the best half of your work's done and they're nestlin' in the wings—cosy in the stalls—waitin' for their high; the joy of seein' the black man pay his dues, purge his soul, drive three inches of steel into his regret and his remorse, so's he makes his final bloody apology for risin', mixin', makin' it and thinkin' he could carry it off despite all the odds. Look at 'em all, General, sittin' cool and quietly pantin' for what they know's already theirs—your rich-red, routine-and-predictable blood. Pause brother . . . and reflect before you feed those hyenas what four centuries of black generals have given them without reflection . . . without one moment's pause. [2]

Similarly in Caryl Phillips's novel *The Nature of Blood* (1997), the narrative voice harangues Othello as a sexual and political sell-out:

And so you shadow her every move, attend to her every whim, like the black Uncle Tom that you are. Fighting the white man's war for him / Wide-receiver in the Venetian army / The republic's grinning Satchmo hoisting his sword like a trumpet / You tuck your black skin away beneath their epauletted uniform, appropriate their words (Rude am I in my

[1] Carlin, pp. 42–3.
[2] Charles Marowitz, *An Othello*, in *Open Space Plays*, selected by Charles Marowitz (Harmondsworth, 1974), pp. 307–8.

speech), their manners, worry your nappy woollen head with anxiety about learning their ways. . . . O strong man, O strong arm, O valiant soldier, O weak man. You are a lost, a sad black man, first in a long line of so-called achievers who are too weak to yoke their past with their present; too naïve to insist on both; too foolish to realize that to supplant one with the other can only lead to catastrophe. Go ahead, revel in the delights of her wanton bed, but to whom will you turn when she, too, is lost and a real storm breaks about your handkerchiefed head? My friend, the Yoruba have a saying: the river that does not know its own source will dry up. You will do well to remember this. . . . My friend, an African river bears no resemblance to a Venetian canal. Only the strongest spirit can hold both together.[1]

The political implications of Othello's marriage to Desdemona are once again at issue in Djanet Sears's *Harlem Duet* (1998), which displaces the action of the play to Harlem in 1860, 1928, and 1998. The antebellum Othello's subservient passion is denounced by his black lover: 'O? O? Othello . . . why you trying to please her? I'm so tired of pleasing her. I'm so tired of pleasing White folks.'[2]

The strident tone of these examples reflects the extent to which racial controversy dominated late twentieth-century responses to the play. From another point of view, however, they—like a number of other dramatic and novelistic reworkings[3]—merely give a

---

[1] Caryl Phillips, *The Nature of Blood* (1997), pp. 181–3.

[2] Djanet Sears, *Harlem Duet*, in Fischlin and Fortier (eds.), *Adaptations of Shakespeare*, p. 302. For an analysis of the way in which Phillips and Sears 'displace . . . the action of Shakespeare's play into broader con-texts', see John Thieme, *Postcolonial Con-texts* (2001).

[3] Apart from the texts already cited, these include three other novels—Tayeb Salih's *Season of Migration to the North* (1969) as well as two by Salman Rushdie, *The Moor's Last Sigh* (1995) and *Fury* (2001)—and at least four other plays—C. Bernard Jackson's unpublished *Iago* (Los Angeles Inner City Cultural Center, 1974); Anne-Marie Macdonald's *Goodnight Desdemona (Good Morning Juliet)* (Toronto, 1990); Caleen Jennings's unpublished 'Playing Juliet/Casting Othello' (Washington Theatre Festival, 1996; Folger Theatre, 1998); and David Geary's and Willie Davis's unpublished *Manawa Taua/Savage Hearts* (Auckland, Watershed Theatre, 1994; see above, p. 9, n. 2). Mythili Kaul's critical collection, *Othello: New Essays by Black Writers* (Washington, DC, 1997), includes a contribution by the African American poet and novelist Al Young entitled 'Hello, Othello', which takes the form of an imaginary interrogation of Shakespeare's protagonist. For other postcolonial reworkings and appropriations of the story, see Ferial Ghazoul, 'The Arabization of *Othello*', *Comparative Literature*, 50 (1998), 1–31; Paromita Chakravarti, 'Modernity, Postcoloniality and *Othello*: the Case of *Saptapadi*', and Poonam Trivedi, 'Reading "Other Shakespeares"', in Pascale Aebischer et al. (eds.), *Remaking Shakespeare: Performance Across Media, Genres, and Cultures* (Basingstoke, 2003), 39–55, 56–73;

contemporary political accent to a long-established way of dealing with the imaginative challenge of this tragedy: for it is a testimony to the peculiar power of *Othello* that, of all the dramatist's works, it has been the most extensively interrogated, appropriated, and rewritten in other fictions. The habit of rewriting began early in the seventeenth century with the character of 'honest' De Flores in Thomas Middleton's and William Rowley's *The Changeling* (*c*.1622), a treacherous servant transparently indebted to Iago, and continued with John Ford's *Love's Sacrifice* (1632)—a drama that transforms the original plot by imagining a guilty Desdemona who bears the name of Shakespeare's courtesan, Bianca. Further imitations followed after the Restoration in the form of Thomas Porter's *The Villain* (1662), and Henry Nevil Payne's *The Fatal Jealousie* (1673);[1] and in the eighteenth century the play won the attention of European dramatists, producing German and French adaptations by Schröder (1776) and Ducis (1792), which gave the play a happy ending,[2] as well as Voltaire's tragedy *Zaïre* (1732), in which the French *philosophe* attempted a neoclassical refurbishment of Shakespeare's 'barbarous' work.

What most attracted these imitators and adaptors seems not to have been the dramatist's strikingly unconventional choice of tragic protagonist, so much as his pathos-laden treatment of jealousy and temptation, Desdemona's martyred goodness, and the splendid dignity of Othello. The persistence of the 'noble Moor' sobriquet indicates the extent to which Othello's heroic self-image tended to dominate responses to the play, helping to explain (among other things) its extraordinary popularity amongst military officers in the eighteenth and nineteenth centuries.[3] The

Ania Loomba, 'Local-manufacture made-in-India Othello fellows: Issues of race, hybridity, and location in post-colonial Shakespeares', in Ania Loomba and Martin Orkin (eds.), *Postcolonial Shakespeares* (1998), 143–63; and Jyotsna Singh, 'Othello's Identity, Postcolonial Theory and Contemporary African Rewritings of *Othello*', in Lena Cowen Orlin (ed.), *Othello: Contemporary Critical Essays* (Basingstoke, 2004), 171–89.

[1] On these plays, see Vaughan, pp. 101–2, 107–12.

[2] Rosenberg, pp. 31–3, and Hankey, pp. 75–7.

[3] See Brian Southam, *Jane Austen and the Navy* (2000), p. 265 n. 93. According to Southam, 'articles and reports in the Navy's professional journal, the *Naval Chronicle*, are larded with quotations from . . . *Othello*'; and officers of the Gibraltar garrison (perhaps capitalizing on its garrison setting, and story of Mediterranean naval triumph) staged a production of the play shortly before the battle of Trafalgar in 1805. *Othello*'s popularity in military circles extended to the United States, where

imaginative power of the tragedy's romantic aspects continued to influence nineteenth-century stage versions, its emotive potential being exploited to particular effect in the operas by Gioachino Rossini (1816) and Giuseppe Verdi (1887), as well as in Salvatore Viganò's 1818 ballet, all of which played down the issue of racial *mésalliance* in order to concentrate on the pathos of jealous obsession and love destroyed.[1]

As early as 1688, however, an alternative direction had been suggested by Aphra Behn's novel *Oroonoko*, subsequently dramatized by Thomas Southerne. Loosely influenced by Shakespeare's tragedy, and written as English participation in the slave trade moved towards its peak, Behn's fiction capitalized on *Othello*'s racial dimension by inventing a new history for the princely African hero, whose enslavement now belonged not to the Mediterranean conflict with Islam, but to the horrors of the Atlantic triangle. Three decades later, Edward Young's *The Revenge* (1721), perhaps influenced by Rymer's strictures on Shakespeare's violations of decorum, would reverse the colour values of the original, by creating a black Iago in the swagger-part of Zanga, and making the victim of his temptation a white man.[2] In Behn's and Young's reworkings, as in Rymer's invective, we can see the beginnings of the process by which Othello's colour would come to be identified as the key to his tragedy; and by the beginning of the next century, the racial assumptions implicit in Young's transformation of the villain would reach their nadir in the succession of 'burlesques' and 'travesties' that brought Rymer's sneers at the 'blackamoor' general to vicious theatrical life. From this point on, although *Othello* would continue to be discussed primarily as a drama of sexual jealousy, its theatrical and critical history would be increasingly

one of the more extraordinary records is of a production in 1846 at Corpus Christi, Texas, by troops engaged in the Mexican war, starring the young Lieutenant Ulysses S. Grant as Desdemona.

[1] For a useful summary of the plot adaptations in the two operas, see Sanders's introduction to his Cambridge edition, pp. 49–51. The overwhelmingly domestic focus of Verdi's librettist, Arrigo Boito, is indicated by his excision of Act 1's Venetian scenes. Twentieth-century adaptations have included a third opera (A. Machavariani, 1963). In contrast to the operatic versions, the 1974 rock musical, *Catch My Soul!* (subsequently filmed by Patrick McGoohan) starring the soul singer Richie Havens as Othello, placed strong emphasis on the story's racial themes.

[2] See Hankey, pp. 57, 75, 78. The great Ira Aldridge—the first black actor to play Othello—did so in repertory with the part of Zanga, implying a complementarity between the two roles.

inflected by racial ideas—ideas to which pseudo-Darwinian theories in due course gave spurious intellectual support.

Until the last quarter of the twentieth century, understanding of the part played by colour in the play was fraught with contradiction. In so far as it appeared problematic, it was as an accident of plot—something whose import needed to be minimized or explained away, just as in performance it was frequently diminished by the transformation of 'black Othello' into a light-skinned North African. At the same time it was generally assumed that 'race' and 'colour' were in themselves unproblematic categories whose significance remained constant through time. The advent of so-called 'new historicist' criticism in the 1980s challenged such anachronistic assumptions, by demonstrating the unstable nature of the categories that defined human difference in Shakespeare's time—a period that had yet to evolve anything like a coherent language of 'race'. Nevertheless, as critics have also been aware, it is impossible to read texts from the past in absolute isolation from intervening history, including the history of their own reception. In the case of *Othello*, the play as we read it today is inevitably marked by its long implication in the development of racial thought; and later sections of this introduction will examine the ways in which the critical and performance histories reflect changing responses to the tragedy's racial dimension. It is important to recognize that Shakespeare's role in this historical process has not been a purely passive matter: for good as well as ill, the play's involvement in the white world's construction of 'blackness' has been to some extent a formative one; and it has been so because of the dramatist's own deep imaginative engagement with the meaning of 'colour'. We can track this engagement through the striking way in which Shakespeare reshaped his principal source material, giving to the hero's blackness a prominence and significance it had not had in the original.

Sources

Before discussing Shakespeare's adaptation of his 'sources', some definitions need to be established, since the term can be a dangerously elastic one: some modern editors, concerned to stress the importance of broader cultural contexts in the shaping of literary works, have sought to collapse the old distinction between 'sources' and 'influences', arguing that the latter can sometimes be just as important in determining the final shape of a work as the texts of which the writer can be shown to have made direct use. It is quite possible, for example, to think of *Othello* as a reworking of Christopher Marlowe's tragedy of damnation, *Dr Faustus* (*c*.1589). Just before his death, confronted with the stupefying evidence of Iago's treachery, Othello craves an explanation for his ensign's inexplicable malice: 'Will you, I pray, demand that demi-devil | Why he hath thus ensnared my soul and body?' (5.2.299–300). It is the moment at which, more explicitly than any other, we are made aware of the model upon which the fearful intimacy between the protagonist and his tempter has been based—the damnable symbiosis through which a literally demonic servant contrives to deliver his master 'body and soul' into Lucifer's possession: 'O what will I not do', gloats Mephostophilis, as Faustus indites the fatal deed of gift, 'to obtain his soul?' (2.1.73).[1] Throughout Shakespeare's tragedy 'honest' Iago seems to be at the Moor's side, pouring insinuations in his ear, just as 'sweet' Mephostophilis shadows the Wittenberg magician, confiding his diabolical persuasions: so close is their bond that some critics have seen them as aspects of a single personality, locked in a combat that, like Faustus's, replays the *psychomachia* of the medieval Morality drama, in which the battle for possession of man's soul was fought out by allegorical representations of vice and virtue.[2] Marlowe's influence on *Othello* seems obvious enough; yet *Dr Faustus* is not in any exact sense a 'source' for the later tragedy: Shakespeare had a remarkably absorptive intelligence; and in *Othello* (as elsewhere) it is possible to trace numerous literary and dramatic influences: these include popular travel literature, Italian romance,[3] and a whole range of plays—notably a group of turn-of-the-century domestic dramas featuring the suffering of abused wives, as well more exotic

[1] Cited from Christopher Marlowe, *Dr Faustus and Other Plays*, ed. David Bevington and Eric Rasmussen (Oxford, 1995). For parallels with a number of other double-protagonist plays by Ben Jonson, see Potter, p. 7.
[2] This in fact was how the actor Ben Kingsley, who played Othello in Terry Hands's 1985–6 production for the RSC, approached his relationship with Iago: 'Othello and Iago are almost two faces of the same man', he declared. 'They are both suffering from the same psychological disturbance' (*Observer Colour Magazine*, 22 Sept. 1985).
[3] On the possible influence of the epic romances of Ariosto and Tasso, see Honigmann, pp. 245, 368, and Potter, p. 9.

tragedies such as Peele's *Battle of Alcazar* (*c.*1588–9), the anonymous *Lust's Dominion* (1598–9), and Shakespeare's own *Titus Andronicus* (*c.*1589–94) to whose conventionally villainous Moorish characters Othello and Iago provide a kind of riposte.

The problem with such an approach is that the number of 'sources' credited to a particular play becomes limited only by what we can conjecture about the extent of the author's reading and theatrical experience; and because it is in principle almost impossible to set manageable boundaries to influence of this kind, I have thought it better to confine the term 'sources' to material that Shakespeare appears certain—or at least likely—to have consulted in the course of writing the play.

Setting, Characters, and Plot Scholars have uncovered extensive traces of Shakespeare's contextual reading in *Othello*, especially in the play's historical and geographical detail. For information about the political and social organization of the Venetian republic, he evidently turned to Sir Lewis Lewkenor's translation of Cardinal Contarini's *The Commonwealth and Government of Venice* (1599);[1] while (as indicated in my discussion of the play's date in Appendix A) he may have derived information about the Venetian struggle to defend Cyprus against the Turks from Richard Knolles's *Generall Historie of the Turkes* (1603), as well as from James I's *Lepanto* (*c.*1585), a poem celebrating the Christian naval victory that temporarily saved Cyprus from the Turks in 1571.

As we shall see, the choice of a Moorish hero was determined by the novella on which his plot was based; but the source makes no real effort to explore the nature or significance of the character's difference. Shakespeare, by contrast, sought to flesh it out with ethnographical material garnered principally from Leo Africanus' encyclopedic *Geographical Historie of Africa*—presumably in the translation by John Pory (1600).[2] Not only did Leo stress the 'venery' of African peoples and their propensity for jealousy; but his own biography, as a North African who was captured by Venetian pirates and enslaved before converting to Christianity and acquir-

---

[1] See Muir, pp. 187–8, and Commentary, 1.1.181, 1.2.43, 3.3.178, 5.2.338.

[2] For details of possible borrowings, see Lois Whitney, 'Did Shakespeare know Leo Africanus?', *PMLA* 37 (1922), 470–88, and Geoffrey Bullough, *Narrative and Dramatic Sources of Shakespeare*, 8 vols. (1957–75), vii. 208–11.

ing the patronage of Pope Leo X, has been proposed as a likely model for Othello's 'travailous's history' (1.3.129–45). In the introduction to his translation, Pory writes of Leo's 'exceeding great travels' in terms that seem to anticipate the exotic wonders of Othello's great speech to the Venetian Senate:

> had he not at the first been a Moor and a Mahometan in religion. . . . I marvel much how ever he should have escaped so many thousands of imminent dangers. . . . For how many desolate cold mountains, and huge, dry and barren deserts passed he? How often was he in hazard to have been captived, or to have had his throat cut by the prowling Arabians and wild Moors. And how hardly many times escaped he the lion's greedy mouth, and the devouring jaws of the crocodile. . . . But not to forget his conversion to Christianity, midst all these his busy and dangerous travels: it pleased the divine providence. . . . to deliver this author of ours . . . into the hands of certain Italian pirates. . . . Being thus taken the pirates presented him and his book unto Pope Leo the tenth, who, esteeming of him as of a most rich and valuable prize, greatly rejoiced at his arrival, and gave him most kind entertainment and liberal maintenance, till such time as he had won him to be baptized. (Book 1, p. 6)[1]

Leo himself exhibits a moving self-consciousness about his conflicted identity as a Christianized Moor, whose life resembled that of the strange fish-birds he calls *Amphibia* (1.41–3); and it was perhaps this that prompted Shakespeare to ponder the destructive double allegiance expressed in Othello's suicide, where he is at once the 'malignant' infidel, the 'circumcisèd dog' who 'beat a Venetian and traduced the state', and the heroic Christian avenger of that outrage (5.2.351–5).

In addition to what he may have gleaned from Leo, Shakespeare's knowledge of Africa was coloured with exotic details culled from one of the oldest of all geographies, Pliny's *Natural History*, translated by Philemon Holland in 1601: Othello's response to the accusation that he has used magic charms on Desdemona is closely modelled on the protestation of a defiant former bondslave in Pliny; and Othello's famous Pontic Sea trope, like his lyrical description of Arabian trees that weep 'medicinable gum', derives from the same source.[2] Pliny was also the first to describe the

---

[1] See also Commentary, 1.3.140, 340–1, 349; App. F(iv).
[2] See App. F(ii); Commentary, 1.3.169, 5.2.349–90. For other apparent debts to Pliny, see also 2.1.153, 3.3.331, 5.2.101–3, 143.

monstrous people known as *Blemmyae* or *Acephali,* the 'men whose heads do grow beneath their shoulders' who feature in Othello's traveller's tales, along with the 'Anthropophagi' whom Pliny had located in Ethiopia (1.3.144–5). While he seems to have known Pliny at first hand, Shakespeare is likely also to have been acquainted with the *Travels of Sir John Mandeville,* a much reprinted fifteenth-century fantasy, in which numerous Plinian monsters appear, including eaters of human flesh and men whose eyes and mouths are in their shoulders. But Othello's reference to 'Cannibals' (l. 143) suggests that he had more recent travels in mind, since 'Cannibal' (a derivative of Carib) was used to designate particular peoples of the New World. Sir Walter Ralegh's *Discoverie of Guiana* (1595) contains an extended description of the headless '*Ewaipanoma*'—a people with 'eyes in their shoulders, and their mouths in the middle of their breasts, and . . . a long train of hair . . . backward between their shoulders' (p. 178), of whom he claimed to have heard reports along the Orinoco, and whose existence seemed to prove the truth of Mandeville's 'incredible' fables.[1] Among other tribes in the region, Ralegh encountered 'a great nation of *Canibals*';[2] and the appearance of the legend 'Canibales' close to an illustration of an acephelous warrior in Theodor de Bry's map for his 1599 edition of the *Discoverie* in *America pars VIII* suggests that the dramatist may even have seen de Bry's compendium (fig. 2).

Whilst his main plot closely follows Giraldi Cinthio's novella, Shakespeare's handling of the murder scene seems to have been influenced by a story from Geoffrey Fenton's *Certaine Tragicall Discourses* (1567), a translation (via Belleforest's expanded French version) of a collection of Italian *novelle* by Bandello. Discourse 4 tells the story of an insanely jealous captain who murders his loving and obedient wife in order that no one shall enjoy her after his death. Although Don Spado is an Albanian rather than an African, he is credited with a 'rage and unnatural fire, far exceeding the *savage and brutish* manner of the tiger, lion, or leopard, *bred in the deserts of Africa, the common nurse of monsters and creatures cruel*

---

[1] Sir Walter Ralegh, *The Discoverie of the Large, Rich and Bewtiful Empyre of Guiana,* ed. Neil L. Whitehead (Manchester, 1997), p. 178.

[2] Ralegh, p. 179.

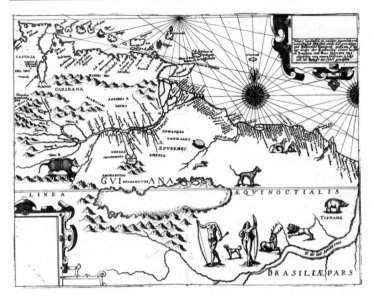

2. 'The cannibals that each other eat . . . and men whose heads │ Do grow beneath their shoulders', from Theodor de Bry, *America pars VIII* (1599).

without reason'.[1] Like Othello, Don Spado murders his wife in bed, and kisses her ('in such sort as Judas kissed our Lord') before he kills her; and like Othello too he stabs himself and falls dead on his wife's body. Like Desdemona she in turn revives long enough to 'pardon . . . her husband with all her heart'.[2] Daniel Vitkus has also noted some parallels with the widely disseminated story of the Sultan and the Fair Greek, in which an Ottoman tyrant, in order to prove his manly resistance to intemperate desire, murders the Christian captive with whom he has become infatuated.[3]

So far as the main outline of the plot and many of its details are concerned, however, only one significant source has been discovered: *Othello* is closely based on Story 7 in the Third Decade of Giovanni Battista Giraldi Cinthio's *Gli Hecatommithi* (see Appendix

[1] Bullough, p. 260; emphases, unless otherwise indicated, are my own.
[2] Bullough, pp. 261–2.
[3] Daniel Vitkus, *Turning Turk: English Theater and the Multicultural Mediterranean, 1570–1630* (Basingstoke, 2003), p. 99.

C), which Shakespeare almost certainly read in the original. Although Giraldi's compilation of *novelle* was first published in 1565, no English translation is known to have existed before the mid-eighteenth century; and while a French translation by Gabriel Chappuys appeared in 1584, verbal parallels overwhelmingly favour the Italian version.[1] Giraldi's collection is framed as the product of a conversation between a group of travellers who seek to alleviate the tedium of a sea-voyage by debating a series of amatory topics, each of which they illustrate with appropriate tales. In the opening conversation, Fabio, the leader of the group, announces a thesis which becomes an overriding theme of the ensuing tales—namely 'that peace can be found only in the love that comes of counsel and chooses well. For in such a love appetite is ruled by reason.'[2] The Third Decade illustrates the perils of unreasonable love and unbridled appetite with stories of '[t]he infidelity of husbands and wives', among them Story 7, which recounts the fatal jealousy of a Moorish captain, who, whilst on garrison duty in Cyprus falls prey to the envious machinations of his *alfieri* (ensign).[3] This officer, though 'handsome' and 'much loved by the Moor', is described as harbouring 'the most wicked disposition', which, however, he so conceals with his 'lofty and proud words and manner . . . that he appear[s] to resemble a Hector or an Achilles'. By exploiting his plausible appearance, he is able to convince the Moor that his Venetian wife is conducting an adulterous affair with one of his subordinates, a *capo di squadra* (corporal).

The novella supplied Shakespeare not only with all the salient features of his plot, but with much of its incidental detail: the virtuous Disdemona (as Giraldi calls her) insists on sharing the perils of her husband's life by accompanying him to Cyprus; Disdemona treats the subordinate officer with particular kindness because she knows he is 'very dear to the Moor', and the *alfieri* exploits their friendship to plant suspicion in the Moor; the villain makes his insinuations more persuasive by feigning reluctance to speak, insisting that only his 'loving service', his profound sense of duty, and his care for the Moor's honour compel him to reveal the truth.

---

[1] See Bullough, p. 194; Muir, pp. 182–3; Honigmann, pp. 368–9; and cf. Commentary 1.3.342, 2.1.16, and 3.3.361–5.

[2] Bullough, p. 239.

[3] Citations from this tale are to Bruno Ferraro's translation: Appendix C, below.

Like Iago, he manipulates the Moor's racial unease by suggesting that '[t]he woman has come to dislike your blackness'. The Moor for his part demands some visible proof of the adultery, which (as in the play) is supplied partly in the form of a purloined handkerchief, and partly through a carefully staged conversation between the *alfieri* and the supposed adulterer, which the Moor is allowed to witness and persuaded to misinterpret. Disdemona, like Shakespeare's heroine, expresses her anxieties about her husband's altered demeanour, first to the Moor himself, and then to her confidante, the villain's wife. The Moor meanwhile conspires with his subordinate to kill both Disdemona and her alleged lover. The latter is ambushed by the villain, who (as in the play) only succeeds in leaving him severely wounded in the leg. Then, after a discussion between the conspirators on the best method of dispatching her, Disdemona is murdered in her bedchamber. The wronged wife dies, begging heaven to witness her innocence; and the Moor, realizing too late the villainy of the *alfieri*, is distracted with grief. In Giraldi, however, the Moor's remorse does not drive him to suicide: instead, he is arrested, tortured, and (when he refuses to confess) condemned to perpetual exile, after which he is hunted down and killed by his wife's relatives. His subordinate is subsequently arrested on a different charge and tortured so severely that he later dies of his injuries.

Observing the extensive parallels between the two versions of the story, one senses that Shakespeare must have been drawn to Giraldi's story partly because of its wealth of circumstantial material. Readers will be struck by how many of the play's scenes derive their theatrical liveliness from the elaboration of some unusually vivid detail in the source. Just as important, perhaps, was the uncharacteristically matter-of-fact style of the novella—the accumulation of realistic and sometimes pedestrian details which suggest that its origins may lie in some sixteenth-century police report.[1] Not surprisingly, much of this detail tends to cluster around the devious machinations of the villain on which the plot depends: for example, the almost pedantic care with which the narrative specifies the number of blows with a sand-filled stocking needed to break Disdemona's skull, or the meticulous fashion in which it explains just how it was that the villain, having 'with very deft . . . fingers' stolen

---

[1] See Bullough, p. 195.

the handkerchief from Disdemona's girdle, was able to use it to incriminate her. The flat documentary quality of Giraldi's narrative might seem to be at odds with a play whose distinctive 'music' makes it the most lyrical—the most operatic even—of the mature tragedies ;[1] but it seems to have contributed significantly to the reductivism of Iago, a character so resistant to the play's music that he can hear only 'bombast' in the swell of Othello's oratory, whilst his own verse is often barely distinguishable from the informal prose that marks his bluff exchanges with Cassio and Roderigo. It is precisely the prosaic realism of Iago's stories, his instinctive eye for commonplace detail, that makes them so persuasive: consider, for example, the way in which his concocted account of Cassio's amorous sleep-talking, is carefully anchored in the banal circumstance of his own sleeplessness ('being troubled with a raging tooth') and the scrupulously catalogued physical embarrassments that ensue: 'And then, sir, would he gripe and wring my hand . . . then kiss me hard . . . then laid his leg | Over my thigh, and sighed, and kissed' (3.3.416, 422–6); or observe how brilliantly Iago reinforces the adulterous suggestiveness of the stolen handkerchief with a piece of seemingly offhand observation: 'such a handkerchief . . . did I today | See Cassio wipe his beard with' (3.3.438–40). Othello's desperate longing for 'ocular proof', his repeated insistence that Iago 'Make me to see' what he most dreads seeing (3.3.362, 366) is at once stimulated and fed by autoptic detail of this kind, dependent as it is (or appears to be) on the kind of dogged scrutiny that the ensign urges on the Moor himself:

> Do but encave yourself,
> And mark the fleers, the gibes, and notable scorns
> That dwell in every region of his face.
> For I will make him tell the tale anew:
> Where, how, how oft, how long ago, and when
> He hath, and is again to cope your wife.
> I say, but mark his gesture . . .
>
> (4.1.77–83)

If Iago were given his reductive way, *Othello* would be no different from Giraldi's squalid tale of jealousy and wife-murder. Indeed, for Thomas Rymer it was not, since the moral he extracted from the

---

[1] On this aspect of the play, see G. Wilson Knight's celebrated essay, 'The *Othello* Music', chap. 5 of *The Wheel of Fire* (1930; repr. 1954).

play ('This may be a caution to all maidens of quality how, without their parents' consent, they run away with blackamoors'; p. 89) was precisely that announced by Giraldi's Disdemona ('I shall be held up as an example to young girls who wish to marry against their family's wishes, and to Italian girls so that they may learn not to choose a man whom nature, God, and manner of life make so different from us'). This passage is echoed by Iago himself when he persuades Othello that to ignore 'clime, complexion, and degree' is to marry against 'nature' (3.3.233–7). Shakespeare, however—while retaining not only the broad outline of the narrative, but a surprising amount of incidental detail from Giraldi—reworked it in ways that gave the story a completely different colouring. Some of the changes he made, especially those involving the characters, are substantial; others, particularly those affecting the plot, may appear relatively insignificant; but their combined effect is momentous.

To begin with, nearly all the first act is of Shakespeare's invention. Here he not only lays an entirely new groundwork for the Ensign's scheming against his commander, but by greatly elaborating a couple of small hints in Giraldi, turns Othello's elopement into a matter of public import. In *Gli Hecatommithi* Disdemona's family are simply said to have 'tried all they could to make her wed somebody else'; in *Othello* her enraged father is a powerful senator who seeks to have the Moor arraigned for seducing his daughter with forbidden arts, and whose suit appears to fail mainly because a military crisis takes priority with the Venetian state.[1] Shakespeare dignifies the story by translating its main action from Giraldi's apparently peaceful island to a Cyprus that has become the strategic focus of Christian–Islamic conflict in the Mediterranean. The Moor himself is no longer the mere 'Commandant' of a relief detachment (*Capitano de' soldati*) but general of the Venetian forces, and military governor of the island.

Whilst the public dimension of the play becomes less conspicuous once the providential destruction of the Turkish fleet has removed any immediate threat to the island, the framework of

---

[1] Technically, Brabantio's case collapses when Desdemona answers his challenge by admitting that she was indeed 'half the wooer' (1.3.175–97); but the Duke's speech at ll. 171–4 makes it clear that he has already decided to acquit the man he means to employ 'Against the general enemy Ottoman' (l. 50).

momentous public events lends gravity to what might otherwise seem a mere domestic tragedy, little different from bourgeois dramas like Heywood's *A Woman Killed with Kindness* (1603) with which it has sometimes been associated.[1] Giraldi's Moor is never seen in the public role that helps to shape the audience's view of Othello in the first two acts. He is described as 'a very valiant Moor' who was dear to the Venetian lords 'because he was very brave and had given proof of his courage and prudence in warfare'. But Giraldi makes no effort to substantiate this bald assertion; and his Moor is a long way from Shakespeare's supremely self-possessed commander, whose confidence rests equally upon pride in his illustrious ancestry and awareness of the unmatched service he has done the state (1.2.18–24). In his re-invention of Giraldi's anonymous and thinly described Moor not only as a Christianized black African, but as a princely warrior who boasts of fetching his 'life and being | From men of royal siege' (1.2.21–2), Shakespeare may have been influenced by two well-established iconographical traditions—one that habitually represented Balthasar, one of the three Magi in the Nativity story, as a splendidly attired black king,[2] and another that represented the soldier–martyr, St Maurice, as a Negro clad in rich European armour (see fig. 3).[3] Since medieval times, Europeans had been excited by rumours of a black Christian monarch named Prester John, who might prove a valuable ally in the struggle against Islam; and Lois Potter has suggested that Shakespeare could also have known about the Kongo kingdom, 'ruled for over a hundred years by Christian kings who could have been the "men of royal siege" from whom Othello claims descent'.[4]

---

[1] See Honigmann, p. 349.

[2] See G. K. Hunter, 'Othello and Colour Prejudice', *Proceedings of the British Academy*, 53 (1967), 139–63 (pp. 154–5). From the ninth century onwards the Magi were customarily interpreted as representing the three continents of Europe, Asia, and Africa, though traditions varied as to whether Balthasar or Melchior should be identified as the black king.

[3] There appears to be no historical foundation for the representation of St Maurice as a black man, beyond his name, which derives from the Latin *Mauros* = a Moor, or a swarthy, dark-complexioned man (see also Commentary, 2.1.221, 5.2.224). On the iconographic tradition, see Jean Devisse, *The Image of the Black in Western Art*, 3 vols. (1997–2005), II.i; Part III, 'The Sanctified Black: Maurice', 149–205.

[4] See Potter, p. 9.

3. The noble Moor: reliquary statue of St Maurice, 1525–7.

In Giraldi, we are left uncertain as to what kind of Moor his protagonist is supposed to be; indeed, for most of the novella his ethnicity appears to be of relatively minor significance. Although Disdemona accuses the Moor of being hot and jealous by nature, while the Ensign at one point suggests that she has come to hate her husband for his colour, these imputations appear to have no particular effect on the Moor himself.[1] Shakespeare, however, seizes on such small hints as a key to the insecurities that Iago is able to arouse and then exploit (3.3.231–42). Othello, moreover,

---

[1] This is in line with Giraldi's general lack of interest in the psychology of his tale: he registers, for example, the paradox of the Moor's jealous longing 'to get more proof of that which he did not wish to discover', but it is left to Shakespeare to explore the psychological consequences of this painful contradiction.

proves vulnerable to Iago's insinuations that there is something 'unnatural' about his match, not merely because of his alien identity (of which blackness is the most conspicuous sign), but also because the dramatist has made him significantly older than his wife, so that Othello comes to fear that—as in so many of the jealousy-plots of Renaissance comedy—his may be a misalliance of age as well as kind (3.3.266–9).

Other important characters, such as Desdemona, Iago, Emilia, Bianca, and Cassio are similarly worked up from their underdeveloped prototypes in the novella, while still others, such as Roderigo and Brabantio, are entirely of Shakespeare's creation. In Giraldi Disdemona is a somewhat colourless figure, a pattern of wifely devotion and patience, whose role is partly glossed by the 'unfortunate name that she had been given by her father' (Disdemona = 'The Unfortunate' in Greek), and who remains a model of courtesy and humility in the face of the gravest provocation; but Shakespeare endows his heroine with a vocal independence of spirit that makes her ultimate submissiveness in the face of Othello's murderous jealousy seem at once more moving and more shocking than her counterpart's routine goodness. He provides an occasion for her to demonstrate her mettle through the addition of a despotic father-figure, Brabantio, whose previous patronage of Othello has given way to bitter hatred at the news of his daughter's elopement. Desdemona's defiance of her father before the Senate looks forward to Cordelia's resolute refusal to co-operate in Lear's public spectacle of filial devotion. But where Cordelia's resistance may initially seem like mere obstinacy, Desdemona's is so framed as to make it appear both courageous and admirable; for, as Susan Snyder has shown,[1] the first act of *Othello* draws heavily on the conventions of romantic comedy, in which patriarchal tyrants figure prominently amongst the obstacles to erotic fulfilment that lovers are expected to overcome.

If Brabantio is a figure whose antecedents can be traced back through Italian *commedia dell'arte* to Roman New Comedy, the same is true of Roderigo, the gullible and ineffectual rival who serves as Othello's foil, as well as a necessary interlocutor and dupe for Iago, enabling him to display his vicious intentions to the audi-

---

[1] Snyder, *Comic Matrix*, pp. 70–4.

ence without constant recourse to soliloquy and aside.[1] In a similar fashion, Shakespeare makes use of the plain-spoken waiting-woman or nurse from the comic tradition to work up the character of Emilia from her anonymous counterpart in Giraldi. Thus, where the Ensign's wife is simply a close friend whom Disdemona often visits, in Shakespeare she becomes Desdemona's intimate confi-dante—albeit one whose servant-role establishes a suggestive par-allel between this relationship and that which ties her husband to Othello. In Giraldi she plays no part in the theft of the handkerchief (though Iago purloins it during one of Disdemona's visits to her), but she is made privy to all her husband's schemes, which she dares not disclose to Disdemona, confining herself to the warning that her friend should give the Moor no occasion for suspicion and do everything to reassure him of her love and loyalty. Emilia, by contrast, remains ignorant and largely unsuspecting of Iago's wickedness until after the murder, concealing from Desdemona only her complicity in the theft of the handkerchief. Emilia's refusal to doubt her husband, in spite of his offhand treatment, helps (along with Cassio's trusting attitude, and Roderigo's com-plaisance) to make Othello's belief in Iago's 'honesty' seem less improbable than it otherwise might. But perhaps her most impor-tant function is to act as a kind of second self for Desdemona, pro-viding a voice for that sturdy resistance to patriarchal tyranny that she exhibited in the confrontation with Brabantio, but which her love for her husband forces her to suppress.

The interest in gender issues highlighted by Emilia's powerful denunciation of abusive husbands (4.3.81–98) is further developed through the character of Bianca, who is an amalgam of two women mentioned in Giraldi—the servant whom the *capo* orders to copy the Moorish embroidery on Desdemona's handkerchief, and the courtesan whose house he has been visiting on the night of the Ensign's ambush. But although her part remains a minor one, Shakespeare gives Bianca a structural function well beyond her importance in the plot: she is linked with the 'fair' Desdemona both by her name (which means 'white') and by the accusations of whoredom which are levelled at her by Iago (5.1.115), just as they are levelled at Desdemona by Othello in the so-called 'brothel

---

[1] See Bernard Spivack, *Shakespeare and the Allegory of Evil* (New York, 1958), pp. 441–2.

scene' (4.2). At the same time, her jealousy of Cassio's supposed infidelity establishes an unexpected kinship with 'black' Othello; while her seemingly guileless love for the offhand Cassio mirrors both Desdemona's self-sacrificial adoration of Othello, and Emilia's stubborn loyalty to her misogynistic husband.

But as far as the characters are concerned, perhaps the most significant transformation of the source material (leaving aside the psychological development of the Moor himself) occurs in the handling of Cassio and Iago; and a key component in this change involves the question of rank. In both versions of the story, the villain is an ensign. 'Ancient' is Shakespeare's preferred spelling of the word, but that the two forms must have been pronounced more-or-less identically is indicated by Iago's wry punning: 'I must show out a *flag and sign* of love— | Which is indeed but *sign*' (1.1.155–6; italics added). As his standard-bearer, an ensign was in fact the public 'sign' of his commander's honour; but Iago's sardonic word-play identifies his hypocritical service as a form of hollow signification. It was perhaps Shakespeare's recognition of the neat ironic symbolism in the rank of Giraldi's villain that caused him to reconsider the rank and function of the Moor's other officer. In Giraldi, Disdemona's supposed seducer is a mere *capo di squadra*—usually considered roughly equivalent to corporal. In Shakespeare he becomes Othello's lieutenant—not the lowly subaltern denoted by the term today, but his second-in-command, a 'lieutenant-general' as it were. Probably the dramatist felt that a corporal would hardly seem plausible as the lover of a general's wife; but in elevating the *capo* to officer status, he also decided to make him Iago's superior, thereby immediately complicating the villain's motives; and in making him 'lieutenant', he chose a term beautifully calculated to inflame the wound of displacement.[1]

---

[1] See below, '*Interpretation*', pp. 152–4. The choice of 'lieutenant' (a relatively uncommon rank in Shakespeare) must have been a pointed one, since although the word had existed in the broad sense of 'deputy' or 'second' since the fourteenth century, it did not appear as an English military designation before the late sixteenth— *OED*'s earliest example being 1578. As military manuals of the time make clear, it was a controversial innovation, because the lieutenant assumed duties that formerly belonged to the ensign; commentators also observed that the rank was not only without precedent in admired 'Roman discipline', but had not been adopted by the Spanish—a fact which may point to an additional source of resentment in Iago, if we take his name to point to a Spanish origin—see Commentary, 'The Persons of the Play'.

In Giraldi the Ensign's plotting is driven entirely by his desire for the Moor's wife and by his mistaken belief that her failure to reciprocate his passion is caused by her being already in love with the *capo*. This conviction turns his love for her to hatred, so that the Ensign's anger is directed almost entirely against Disdemona, leaving the Moor and even the *capo* as largely incidental victims of his spite. In Shakespeare, by contrast, while Iago admits in an almost casual way to frustrated desire for Desdemona (2.1.282–5), he confesses to a bewildering array of other motives that make Cassio and (above all) Othello the primary objects of his revenge. These include: (ironically in view of his own Spanish name) prejudice against foreigners, including the 'Florentine' Cassio (1.1.19); disgust at the military and sexual triumphs of a black man (1.1.32, 88–91, 110–16); the suspicion that both Othello and Cassio have cuckolded him (1.3.375–9; 2.1.285–90, 298); and (most conspicuously of all) resentment at Cassio's promotion to become Othello's second-in-command, together with bitterness at the servile nature of his own office (1.1.7–60). It was the sheer variety of the villain's professed motives that led Coleridge to accuse him of 'the motive-hunting of a motiveless malignity';[1] and other critics have expressed similar scepticism at the apparently fleeting and heterogeneous nature of his complaints, pointing out that the anger Iago professes at being bilked of the lieutenancy is never mentioned again after the indignant tirade with which he opens the play (1.1.7–39).[2] However, it is telling that Emilia's slowly awakening suspicion of her husband is intimated by her conjecture that Desdemona has been slandered by 'Some cogging, cozening slave, to get some office' (4.2.132); and closer attention to Iago's language will show that the lost promotion never ceases to rankle with Iago: he harps on his rival's new rank with an insistence shown by no one else in the play—fifteen of the twenty-five occurrences of 'lieutenant' are in his mouth, where it begins to sound more and more

---

[1] S. T. Coleridge, *Coleridge's Shakespeare Criticism*, ed. T. M. Raysor, 2 vols. (1930), i. 49.
[2] For an account of Iago that sees Iago's motives as fundamentally 'divorce[d] . . . from his dramatic personality and his actions', and accounts for them as a naturalistic veneer disguising his fundamental nature as a reworking of the medieval Vice figure, see Spivack, chaps. 1, 12 (p. 58).

like a sardonic caress that anticipates and celebrates his own usurpation of Cassio's 'place'; he continues (with barely veiled sarcasm) to address Cassio as 'lieutenant' after he has been cashiered (2.3.250, 299, 318), and even after he himself has been promoted in his rival's stead (4.1.99; 5.1.57). Moreover, just as Iago uncovered a punning licence for deceit in his own rank, so his remorseless iteration of Cassio's title draws attention to the etymological insult concealed in 'lieutenant'—literally 'one holding [another's] place' (French *lieu tenant*). Dis-placement, after all, is the unifying theme of Iago's resentments—whether social, sexual, or psychological. By the symmetrical logic of retribution, of course, it is also the organizing principle of Iago's revenge, ensuring that his gnawing conviction that Othello and Cassio have 'done my office' (1.3.377 and cf. 2.1.286–7, 298) will find an exact equivalent in the Moor's agonized 'Cassio shall have my place' (4.1.253).[1]

Whatever conclusion one reaches about his motives, Shakespeare's Ensign is certainly a more consistent and purposive schemer than his counterpart in Giraldi. What in the original are merely convenient accidents, in *Othello* become the products of his cunning: it is Iago who engineers Cassio's drunkenness, sets up the brawl with Roderigo, and then urges the cashiered Lieutenant to use Desdemona as an intercessor with his general. Desdemona's loss of the handkerchief may now be a matter of chance, but it is used to emphasize Iago's improvisational genius; so that like Richard III, or Marlowe's Barabas, or Jonson's Mosca, the actor–hypocrite also emerges as a kind of surrogate dramatist, relishing the cleverness of his own plot in shameless appeals for the approbation of the audience:

---

[1] 'The captain being absent,' wrote Edward Davies in *The Art of War* (1620), 'the lieutenant possesseth the principal and chief place' (sig. O2): the logic of the tragedy's paranoid word-play ensures that, in so far as Othello imagines Desdemona's body precisely as the 'chief place' he has 'occupied', the Senate's order must come as a confirmation of his deepest fears. For detailed analyses of how the tropes of lieutenancy, place, and office work in the play, see Michael Neill, 'Changing Places in *Othello*', *SS* 37 (1984), 115–31 (repr. in *Putting History to the Question: Power, Politics and Society in English Renaissance Drama* (New York, 2000), 207–36); and Julia Genster, 'Lieutenancy, Standing In and *Othello*', *ELH* 57 (1990), 785–805. An additional pun may be suggested by the alternative spelling 'lieftenant' (ancestral to the modern British pronunciation, 'leftenant'), which occurs in Q1 *Henry V*, 5.5.95, and which *OED* suggests was influenced by lief = love, desire; sweetheart, mistress.

And what's he then that says I play the villain,
When this advice is free I give, and honest,
Probal to thinking, and indeed the course
To win the Moor again?

(2.3.321–4)

The Time Scheme Of all the changes that Shakespeare made to
the original, perhaps the most notorious involves his radical
rearrangement of Giraldi's generally non-specific time scheme,
which he subjected to a rigorous and uncharacteristic tightening.
In Giraldi, the Moor's jealousy seems the more inexplicable
because, unlike his Shakespearian counterpart, he has lived with
Disdemona for some time in marital 'harmony and tranquillity'
before receiving the summons to Cyprus; not only that, but Giraldi's repetition of such phrases as 'one day' and 'soon after' makes it
seem that events in Cyprus take place over an extended period of
time—prompting questions as to why his Moor makes no effort to
determine the veracity of the Ensign's allegations by questioning
either his wife or her supposed lover. In Shakespeare, by contrast,
events take place with such dizzying rapidity that even the question
of whether their marriage is consummated remains clouded in
uncertainty:[1] the couple are summoned before the Senate on the
first night of their elopement, and are required to depart for Cyprus
immediately; barely are they reunited on the island than they are
once again roused from their bed by the brawl that leads to Cassio's
disgrace (2.3); Act 3 evidently begins on the following morning,
and the murder of Desdemona (5.2) appears to take place that
same night. It is a scheme of almost neoclassical rigour—as if
Shakespeare, setting aside the lengthy dramatized prologue of Act
1, were determined to observe the traditional unities of time, place,
and action, which (except in the case of *The Comedy of Errors* and
The Tempest) he elsewhere disregarded.

Yet there are moments at which a much more extensive time
scheme can seem to be implied. It is, for example, difficult to understand why Venice should send an order recalling Othello, and
appointing Cassio in his place (4.1.227–9) when news of the Turkish fleet's destruction cannot possibly have reached them; furthermore, the relationship between Cassio and Bianca appears to be of

---

[1] See below, 'Interpretation', pp. 136–8.

much older standing than his arrival in Cyprus would allow, since she complains that he has neglected her for an entire week (3.4.168–71); and finally there are a whole series of remarks which appear to suggest that Othello and Desdemona have been married far longer than the time scheme will in fact allow—notably Othello's claim that Desdemona 'with Cassio hath the act of shame | A thousand times committed' (5.2.209–10), and Emilia's repeated claim that Iago 'hath a hundred times | Wooed me to steal [the handkerchief]' (3.3.295–6; 312, 317–18). The cumulative effect of such detail has been to encourage some critics to speak of an elaborate 'double time scheme', according to which Shakespeare's 'astonishing skill and judgement as a practical craftsman' enables him to play an elaborate 'trick' on the audience, persuading them to accept the simultaneous operation of a 'short time' that makes possible the successful execution of Iago's plot, and a 'long time' that renders plausible Othello's extravagant conviction of Desdemona's infidelity.[1] However, the apparent inconsistencies on which this theory is based are almost never noticed in performance; and it is telling that it should have been Rymer who first drew attention to them, since his entire critique was founded on a neoclassical notion of 'probability'[2] quite alien to Shakespeare's practice. By the same token the elaborate theory of double-time, invented to account for the temporal inconsistencies about which Rymer is so sarcastic, belongs originally to the mid nineteenth century, arising out of assumptions grounded in the realistic staging practices of Victorian theatre, and encouraged by reading habits associated with the emergence of literary scholarship.[3] In fact, as Graham Bradshaw has demonstrated, it is possible to account for

[1] See Ridley's introduction, pp. lxvii–lxx.

[2] See above, 'Reception', pp. 3–5.

[3] For useful summaries of the problems, see the introductions in the editions by Ridley, pp. lxvii–lxx, Sanders, pp. 14–17, and Honigmann, pp. 68–73. The double-time theory was first advanced by John Wilson in *Blackwood's Magazine* (Nov. 1849, Apr. and May 1850). Like Rymer, Wilson argued that, while the events of the play appear to occur in a rapid and continuous sequence (except for the time taken to sail from Venice to Cyprus between Acts 1 and 2), the probability of the plot depends on our assuming the much longer stretch of time between marriage and murder. The scattering of temporal references in the dialogue encouraging such an assumption persuaded him that Shakespeare had deliberately engineered a 'double-time scheme', in which the 'short time' framework helped to create a sense of events crowding towards disaster, whilst the 'longer time' helped to preserve the plausibility of Iago's insinuations and Othello's jealous fantasies.

almost all of the 'long time' references by assuming that they refer to events that occurred in Venice, during Othello's extended courtship, or (in some cases) on the voyage to Cyprus.[1] There is, for example, no obvious reason to presume that Bianca is a denizen of Cyprus; and if indeed she is to be recognized as a courtesan, then Shakespeare's audience would probably have assumed that her 'custom' belonged originally to Venice, the proverbial capital of European prostitution. Perhaps indeed she is even to be seen as the object of Iago's sarcasm in the opening scene, when he speaks of Cassio as 'almost damned in a fair wife' (1.1.20). Moreover, Othello's increasingly frenzied conviction of Desdemona's repeated infidelities is only a problem if we assume that it must refer to the period after their marriage; but since we know that Cassio was party to their love affair from the beginning (3.3.96–7), 'came a-wooing' with Othello (3.3.71–2), and even seems to have engaged in private conversation with Desdemona about him (3.3.72–4), there has clearly been ample opportunity for them to make the Moor a cuckold before the fact.[2] It is really only the strange revocation of Othello's commission that creates a problem; and an audience might easily ascribe even that to the influential manoeuvring of Brabantio's faction back in Venice.[3]

In the end, however, such speculation is probably pointless, since Elizabethan dramatists were accustomed to treating time rather as their stage encouraged them to treat space: just as a speaker might be made, when a particular scene demanded it, to identify the normally neutral platform stage with a particular location, so the needs of the plot might require him to tie a particular set of events to a specific time scheme—even while the action as a whole remained floating in a kind of temporal limbo. The so-called

---

[1] See Graham Bradshaw, *Misrepresentations: Shakespeare and the Materialists* (Ithaca, NY, 1993), pp. 148–68.

[2] Of course, as Bradshaw points out, Othello's suspicions will seem more probable if (as may be the case) the marriage is never consummated, so that the question of Desdemona's virginity remains moot. But, given that the devices used by whores to fake their own virginity were well known, that need not be decisive—especially since in any case the utter irrationality of jealousy is part of Shakespeare's dramatic point.

[3] Interestingly even Rymer, with his nose for inconsistencies, explained it in this way, declaring that Brabantio (whose death from mortification at Desdemona's marriage he seems to have forgotten) 'gets the Moor cashiered, [and] sends his kinsman, Signor Ludovico, to Cyprus with the commission for a new general' (p. 133).

'double-time' produced by the acceleration of key elements in Giraldi's plot required no ingenious sleight of hand on the play-wright's part: it is no more than a particularly striking side-effect of the general indifference to naturalistic handling of time and space that Shakespeare shared with other dramatists of the period.

The Play in Performance[1]

As a practical man of the theatre, actor as well as playwright, Shakespeare seems to have conceived his dramatic designs as much in visual as in narrative terms. The great tragedies, in particular, stamp themselves on the imagination through a series of powerful theatrical images in which the whole meaning of a play can some-times seem to be compacted: the graveyard in *Hamlet*; the storm-lashed heath in *King Lear*, the weird sisters huddled about their cauldron in *Macbeth*—these, not surprisingly, are among the scenes that illustrators have chosen again and again to epitomize the plays from which they come. In the case of *Othello*, it was the pathetic spectacle of Desdemona 'slain in our presence by her hus-band . . . lying in her bed' that etched itself on the memory of the play's first recorded viewer, Henry Jackson, to the exclusion of any other scene; and although other commentators singled out Iago's temptation of Othello (3.3) as the 'top scene' of the tragedy,[2] it was the shockingly expressive image of the dark-skinned murderer standing over his unconscious wife, stretched out on their nuptial

---

[1] For more thorough and detailed accounts of the play's life in the theatre, see Rosenberg, Hankey, and Potter. Vaughan's Part 2, 'Representations', offers accounts of representative productions from the Restoration through to Trevor Nunn's 1989 RSC *Othello*; while Pechter's *Othello and Interpretive Traditions* links per-formance and critical history with outstanding skill. Martin L. Wine's *Othello: Text and Performance* (Basingstoke, 1984) confines itself to an overview of produc-tions between 1943 and 1982, paying particular attention to the Othello/Iago/Desdemona teamings of Paul Robeson, José Ferrer, and Uta Hagen (1943), Laurence Olivier, Frank Finlay, and Maggie Smith (1964), Brewster Mason, Emrys James, and Lisa Harrow (1971–2), and James Earl Jones, Christopher Plummer, and Dianne Wiest (1981–2). In *Shakespeare in Performance: An Introduction through Six Major Plays* (New York, 1973), John Russell Brown prints a full text of the play, with an extensive commentary describing stage business, rhetorical delivery and interpreta-tion, together with details of outstanding nineteenth- and twentieth-century performances.

[2] The phrase is Rymer's (see above, p. 3); but the commonplace book of Abra-ham Wright, Vicar of Okeham, had made a similar claim in 1637 (see Hankey, p. 19).

bed, that long dominated the illustrative tradition.[1] The disturbing power of the spectacle seems to have been increased rather than diminished by the systematic bowdlerization of Shakespeare's script in the eighteenth and nineteenth centuries, which purged the play not only of its explicit sexual language, but of every reference to the marriage bed.[2] For generations of readers, beginning with François Boitard's engraving for Rowe's 1709 edition (fig. 4), the eroticism and latent violence of the image served to highlight the centrality of the tragic love affair between Desdemona and the Moor, and (not least through the symbolic chiaroscuro favoured by Romantic artists) to highlight the scandal of their racial *mésalliance* (fig. 5).

In the twentieth century, however, when the photographic documentation of stage and screen productions largely replaced commissioned engravings in the visual record, the balance of visual representation showed a marked change. The murder scene continued to receive its share of attention; but more often than not it was the temptation scene that was now chosen to represent the tragedy (fig. 17). Thus the painting by Peter Blake, conceived for the 1979 paperback cover of Ridley's long-lived Arden edition, showed Iago hovering at Othello's shoulder, ready to pour the poison of suspicion in his ear. The striking recurrrence of such images reflected the increasing dominance of Iago in performance, and the consequent displacement of the relationship between Othello and Desdemona in favour of that between tempter and victim as the principal focus of the play's tragic concerns.[3]

Needless to say, the possibility of such displacement had always been inscribed in the text itself: as befits a play about fantasies of adultery, two competing relationships sit at the centre of *Othello*, linked by the ugly symmetries that are pointed up in the language

[1] For an extended analysis of the significance of this image, see Michael Neill, ' "Unproper Beds": Race, Adultery and the Hideous in *Othello*', *SQ* 40 (1989), 383–412, reprinted as chap. 9 (pp. 237–68) of *Putting History to the Question*; all references to this essay are to the latter version.

[2] See Neill, ' "Unproper Beds" ', p. 240.

[3] By contrast the cover of Honigmann's New Arden shows a photograph of a floating handkerchief, picking up Iago's reference to 'trifles light as air' (3.3.323), and constituting a kind of silent homage to Rymer's dismisssive 'tragedy of the handkerchief' that accords with this editor's tendency to play down the play's social and racial concerns.

4. The bedchamber scene (Rowe's edition, 1709).

of the temptation scene. At the climax of that episode, Othello recognizes that he is 'bound to [Iago] for ever' (3.3.216), and their exchange ends in a mock-wedding through which Iago symbolically takes the 'place' of the Moor's 'fair warrior', Desdemona, even as he usurps that of his military second, Cassio: 'Now art thou my lieutenant' (3.3.478). The play's tragic effect depends partly upon the performers' ability to achieve a proper balance between the two relationships; but this has not always been easy to achieve. This is partly because, to modern sensibilities at least, the character of Desdemona, unless very carefully handled, can seem too flatly and monotonously conceived to offset the theatrical magnetism of Iago: thus as early as 1770 we find Francis Gentleman suggesting that Desdemona's 'unvarying gentleness' makes hers 'a

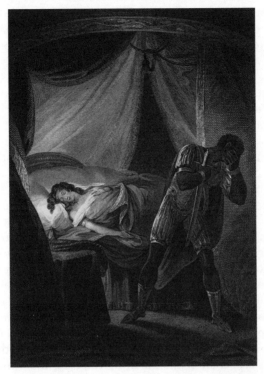

5. Racialized chiaroscuro: the bedchamber scene as imagined
by Boydell, 1800.

part of no shining qualifications';[1] and by the end of the nineteenth century Iago had begun to establish an increasing ascen-
dancy over the imagination of theatregoers. Just as commentators
have typically divided themselves into 'Othello critics' and 'Iago
critics',[2] so stagings of the play have a marked tendency to become
either Othello-productions or Iago-productions; and if the actor
playing Othello falls short of the heroic scale demanded by his role,
then Iago—who is, after all, given more lines than the hero—can

[1] [Francis Gentleman], *The Dramatic Censor* (1770), p. 154, cited in Potter, p. 48.
[2] For this distinction, see Carol Thomas Neely, 'Women and Men in *Othello*',
in Carolyn Lenz, Gayle Greene, and Carol Thomas Neely (eds.), *The Woman's Part:
Feminist Criticism of Shakespeare* (Urbana, Ill., 1980), 211–39 (p. 211).

all too easily become the animating spirit of the whole performance. A. C. Bradley's celebrated analysis of the play (1904), which
set the terms for so much twentieth-century criticism, significantly divides into two essays—one largely devoted to the nominal
hero, the other almost entirely to his antagonist; and Bradley's
Iago is an almost Nietzschean figure whose astonishing 'lordship of
the will' makes him 'great, almost sublime', to the point where he
threatens to usurp the protagonist's centrality—for 'the tragedy of
Othello is . . . his tragedy too. . . . [the tragedy of] a thoroughly bad,
cold man, who is at last tempted to let loose the forces within him,
and is at once destroyed.'[1]

If the post-Victorian performance history of *Othello* has been
characterized by the growing dominance of Iago, from the last
quarter of the twentieth century it has also been marked by an
increasingly urgent preoccupation with Shakespeare's treatment
of colour and its implications for casting. There may indeed be a
connection between these two developments, since productions
that focus on Othello's tragically mistaken jealousy of Desdemona
necessarily tend towards an unconscious endorsement of the traditional moral symbolism of black and white, inviting at least a partial acceptance of Emilia's judgement—'the more angel she, and
you the blacker devil' (5.2.131). In contrast, productions that focus
on Iago's seduction of the Moor, by reversing the conventional
valencies, necessarily problematize the significance of colour, and
invite a more probing response to the play's treatment of 'race'.
Because the resulting controversies are so closely related to the critical debate that emerged at the same time over the nature of *Othello*'s implication in the history of racial thinking, I have chosen—at
the risk of some structural clumsiness—to devote a separate section of my performance history to the vexed issue of the protagonist's colour and how it should be represented on the stage.

Playing Black

> I cannot go on stage and give audiences a black man who is a
> dupe.
>
> Sidney Poitier[2]

---

[1] Bradley, pp. 178–9.
[2] Quoted in James Earl Jones and Penelope Niven, *James Earl Jones: Voices and
Silences* (New York, 1993), p. 298.

> I remember the first time I saw my husband and I caught
> a glimpse of his skin, and, oh, how I thrilled. I thought—
> aha!—a man of a different color. From another world and
> planet. I thought if I marry this strange dark man, I can leave
> this narrow little Venice with its whispering piazzas behind—
> I can escape and see other worlds.
> (Pause)
> But under that exotic façade was a porcelain white Venetian.[1]
>
> Paula Vogel, *Desdemona: A Play about a Handkerchief*

Anxieties about the treatment of race in *Othello* are a recurrent feature of both its critical and performance histories: where they once focused on the supposed scandal of miscegenation, they are nowadays more likely to address the play's complicity in racial stereotyping. Indignation and disgust at the union of Othello and Desdemona were clearly among the driving motives of Rymer's derisive attack: he returns repeatedly to the impropriety of the match between a senator's daughter and a 'blackamoor' in terms that recall the racial slurs of Iago; and, citing Horace on the unnatural commingling of species—*non ut | Serpentes avibus geminentur, tigribus agni* ('snakes do not mate with birds, or lambs with tigers') implies a consonance between the 'monstrous' nature of the match and the monstrousness of the play's mixed design as a 'bloody farce'.[2] There is clearly a connection between Rymer's contemptuous attitude towards Africans and the rapid acceleration of British involvement in the slave trade at the end of the seventeenth century; yet oddly enough the eighteenth century seemed, for the most part, to find the idea of a black hero relatively unproblematic. In this it was perhaps assisted by Behn's and Southerne's romanticization of the slave predicament, as well as by a discreet bowdlerization that purged the text of much of its sexual suggestiveness.[3] However, concern with Othello's colour re-emerged strongly during the years of political turmoil that followed the French Revolution as abolitionism gathered strength.[4] In France itself, Ducis,

[1] Quoted from Fischlin and Fortier (eds.), *Adaptations of Shakespeare*, p. 242.
[2] Rymer, pp. 88, 146. On critical denunciations of the play's 'monstrosity' and their relationship to horror of miscegenation, see Neill, ' "Unproper Beds" ', esp. pp. 260–2, and below, pp. 138–47.
[3] See 'Unproper Beds', pp. 240, 464 n. 8.
[4] On the effect of abolitionism upon responses to *Othello*, see Ruth Cowhig, 'Blacks in English Renaissance Drama and the Role of Shakespeare's Othello', in David Dabydeen (ed.), *The Black Presence in English Literature* (Manchester, 1985).

implicitly linking his version of the play to the slave revolt in Haiti, referred to '*le sans-culotte Othello*', while Talma's performance was hailed as an artistic expression of the republican spirit with its disdain for 'the aristocracy of colour'.[1] In such a context it is easy to see how Coleridge's notorious repudiation of 'a veritable negro' Othello as 'something monstrous' was entirely in accord with the reactionary anti-Jacobinism of his later years.[2]

Much grosser expressions of the sentiments voiced by Coleridge are to be found in the burlesque parodies of *Othello* which flourished in England between the abolition of the slave trade in 1807 and that of slavery itself in 1833, and which enjoyed further popularity across the Atlantic in the wake of United States abolition (1865). English examples include the anonymous *Othello-Travestie* (1813) and Maurice Dowling's 'Operatic Burlesque Burletta', *Othello Travestie* (1834), while the extensive American list includes George W. H. Griffin's *Othello (Ethiopian Burlesque)*, 'as performed by Griffin and Christy's Minstrels, New York' (*c.*1870), and two anonymous pieces, *Desdemonum. An Ethiopian Burlesque* (1874), and *Dar's de Money (Othello Burlesque)*, 'As originally performed at Wood's Minstrels' Hall, New York' (*c.*1880).[3] The burlesques use increasingly crude parody to neutralize the racial anxieties stirred up by Shakespeare's play (fig. 6), translating its sublime wordmusic into absurd jingles and compressing the plot so as to suggest its kinship with farce. The 1813 *Othello-Travestie* reduces Lodovico's choric conclusion to a doggerel paraphrase of Rymer:

---

[1] Hankey, p. 76.

[2] Coleridge (ed. Raysor), i. 47.

[3] Parasitic on this tradition is Alexander Do Mar's burlesque ballad (in five acts) entitled *Othello: An Interesting Drama, Rather* (n.d. [*c.*1850]). For a full listing see Henry E. Jacobs and Claudia D. Johnson, *An Annotated Bibliography of Shakespearean Burlesques, Parodies, and Travesties* (New York, 1976), pp. 55–9. So closely had *Othello* become linked with the unsavoury tradition of minstrel burlesque, that a version of French's Standard Drama edition published in the United States in the 1860s (Harvard Theatre Collection prompt-books, *Othello* 298) contained an advertisement for a series entitled 'The Ethiopian Drama', with titles including *The Mischievous Nigger*, *The Black Shoemaker*, and *Oh, Hush, or the Vurginny Cupids*. The implications of this tradition for 'the play's staging of race and racial difference' are explored by Joyce Green Macdonald, 'Acting Black: *Othello*, *Othello* Burlesques, and the Performance of Blackness', *Theatre Journal*, 46 (1994), 231–49; Macdonald, who gives extended attention to Dowling's burlesque, sees it as part of the response to Aldridge's first London appearance as Othello (1825) and the Jamaican slave rebellion of 1831, as well as to the 1833 Emancipation Act, but does not explore coincidence of the American burlesques with the period of Reconstruction.

OTHELLO.

Gains the affections of Desdemona, by the relations of his past life.

6. The burlesque tradition: the wooing of Desdemona, illustrated in Alexander Do Mar's *Othello: An Interesting Drama, Rather* (*c.* 1850).

Learn hence, ye gentlemen declined in years,
For Gretna-marriages no luck appears;–
Of *ridicules* let ladies know no lack,
Nor let the *fair* sex ever wed the *black*.[1]

The reactionary politics of burlesque are even more conspicuous in Dowling's 1834 *Travestie*: first performed in the former slaving port of Liverpool, and then transferred to London, it followed hard on the pro-slavery lobby's successful campaign against the Covent Garden production of *Othello* in 1833, starring the black American Ira Aldridge. The published text of Dowling's burlesque shows his Othello in late eighteenth-century military costume and identifies him as '*formerly an Independent Nigger, from the Republic of Hayti*',

---

[1] *Othello-Travestie* (1813), p. 57.

whilst his whisky-drinking Iago, familiarly addressed as 'Pat', is said to have been 'once a native of the Gaultee Mountains, County of Tipperary'. This district was a notorious haunt of Irish rebels; and the ancient Irish war-cry, transcribed by the English as 'Hubbaboo', forms the chorus of one of Iago's songs. Though still nominally a general, Dowling's Othello addresses even his white inferiors as 'Massa' and speaks in a ridiculous minstrel dialect, singing 'What is de cause' to the popular tune 'King of the Cannibal Islands'. Not surprisingly 'Master Blacky' proves unable to kill his white wife, who brings the action to a close with a bouncing resurrection.[1]

In England, at least, the decision by Edmund Kean and his successors to play the Moor as a relatively pale North African seems to have gradually defused the controversy over the hero's colour. But this was not the case in the United States, where the play had a potentially dangerous political charge. Thus Edwin Forrest, whose success in the lead-role brought him to fame in 1826, declared himself proud to be 'the impersonator of oppressed races'—though the savage ferocity he brought to the role may have compromised this worthy aim.[2] Not surprisingly *Othello* attracted particular hostility in the turbulent period of Reconstruction after the Civil War, when a series of travesties found their way to the American stage. One at least exploited Dowling's device of matching a minstrel Othello with an Irish Iago in order to include immigrants in its racist abuse: indeed, George Griffin's wretched *Ethiopian Burlesque* reduces the shame of Desdemona's miscegenation with the 'whitewasher' Othello[3] by extending its chauvinistic ridicule not only to Iago, but to Brabantio, whose German Jewish accent exposes his membership of another despised group. By contrast, in the latest and most degraded of these parodies, *Desdemonum* and *Dar's de Money*, the threat posed by racial intermarriage was removed altogether through the simple expedient of converting the entire cast to blackface minstrel-characters.[4]

[1] Maurice Dowling, *Othello Travestie* (1834), pp. 2, 4, 14, 34, 36.
[2] See Potter, pp. 36–7; Hankey, pp. 71–3.
[3] George W. H. Griffin, *Othello (Ethiopian Burlesque)* (Clyde, Ohio, n.d), p. 3.
[4] *Desdemonum. An Ethiopian Burlesque* (New York, 1874), and *Dar's de Money (Othello Burlesque)* (London and New York, n.d.). *Desdemonum* seems to have been conceived partly as a showcase for its publishers' other products, which (according to an advertisement in the text) included Prepared Burnt Cork and Mongolian Paste

A more orthodox means of addressing the racial anxieties stirred up by the tragedy was to play down Othello's blackness by orientalizing the Moor. Much critical ink has been wasted on the debate, initiated by Coleridge and Lamb, over the exact nature of Othello's colour.[1] It is of course true that the term 'Moor' was a remarkably flexible one in the early seventeenth century (fig. 7): not only was it indiscriminately applied to both North Africans and sub-Saharan Negroes (sometimes subdivided into 'White', 'Tawny', and 'Black' Moors), but it could also be deployed as a religious category denoting all Muslims (regardless of their ethnicity), or used as a loose descriptor of colour, embracing on occasion even the inhabitants of the New World.[2] However, the language of the play—especially the slurs of Iago, Roderigo, and Brabantio—makes it fairly plain that (as with Aaron the Moor in *Titus Andronicus*) it was a black African that Shakespeare had in mind. The stage tradition, moreover, is unequivocal: from Betterton in the late seventeenth century until Kemble at the end of the eighteenth, the hero was invariably played in blackface as a sub-Saharan 'black Moor'. Thomas Rymer was clearly used to seeing the Moor performed just as he is represented in the first known illustration of the play—an engraving commissioned for Rowe's 1709 edition—as 'a Blackmoor Captain' (fig. 4);[3] and, although the only eyewitness account from Shakespeare's lifetime is unspecific about the appearance of the Moor, there is every reason to think that this tradition simply

('for Indians, Mulattoes, etc.'): in Desdemonum's first speech, she declares: 'Since burnt-cork am de fashion, I'll not be behind— | I'll see Oteller's wisage in his highfalutin' mind' (p. 3).

[1] The nineteenth-century debate can be traced through Furness's extensive Appendix on 'Othello's Colour' (pp. 389–96), where the balance of opinion is overwhelmingly in favour of a light-skinned Moor. Particularly revealing is Knight's paradoxical insistence that '[w]hatever may have been the practice of the stage, even in Shakespeare's time,—and it is by no means improbable that Othello was represented as a Negro,—the whole context of the play is against the notion' (p. 390). By contrast, George Lewes insisted that 'Othello is black,—the very tragedy lies there: the whole force of the contrast, the whole pathos and extenuation of his doubts of Desdemona, depend on this blackness' (p. 395). Furness himself was aware that the issue was complicated by the remarkable elasticity of the term 'black' in early modern parlance (p. 395)—a point that has been elaborately documented in recent historicist criticism.

[2] See Michael Neill, ' "Mulattos," "Blacks," and "Indian Moors": *Othello* and Early Modern Constructions of Human Difference', *SQ* 49 (1998), 361–74, reprinted as chap. 10 of *Putting History to the Question*.

[3] Rymer, p. 88.

MORO DI CONDITIONE.

NOBILE DI BARBARIA.

MORO DE BARBARIA.

7. White and Black Moors (from Vecellio, *De Gli Habiti*, 1590).

carried on from the practice established by Richard Burbage, the original performer of the part. So it was probably not until Edmund Kean took over the role in 1814 that Othello was first presented as a relatively light-skinned North African (fig. 13). Indeed, Kean's contemporaries were quite clear about the radical nature of this departure, one of them complaining that 'for two hundred years, Othello was supposed to be a black man (in common parlance—a black-a-moor)'.[1] According to his first biographer, 'Kean regarded it as a gross error to make Othello either a negro or a black, and accordingly altered the conventional black to the light brown which distinguishes the Moors by virtue of their descent from the Caucasian race.'[2] Kean's ostensible motive was the desire, in the interests of greater physical expressiveness, not to obscure his features; but the extraordinary power of this performance must have had something to do with the actor's careful balancing of 'civilized' appearance and 'savage' affect, his unaccustomed pallor serving to offset his barbaric extremes of passion.[3]

The enormous success of Kean's innovation prepared the way for generations of tawny North African Moors, culminating in the dignified 'Oriental' embodied by Beerbohm Tree (fig. 8), who envisaged the Moor as 'a stately Arab of the best caste'.[4] This transformation of stage practice had the additional advantage of

---

[1] Cited from the anonymous prefatory note to an edition of the play published by Thomas Hailes Lacy (London:, n.d.) and used as a prompt-book at the Birmingham Theatre Royal in the 1860s (Birmingham Shakespeare Library, promptbook, S.l./Oth.3). The author cited details from the play itself and the evidence of Rowe's illustration—based (he claimed) on information from Betterton, who had learned it from Davenant, who himself knew Shakespeare—to argue that this was how the part had originally been conceived. This was why all actors from Quin to Kemble had 'played the part in black face'. Thus he complained that 'it was reserved for Edmund Kean to innovate and Coleridge to justify (upon expediency) the attempt to make Othello a brown moor. . . . The American commentators . . . are particularly confident upon the subject; but their opinions, however supported by able and ingenious special pleading, must fail with those who expect evidence, not eloquence to establish a point in question. Mr Kean's motive in the matter was, that his features were better seen with a light than a dark colour. The Americans have the all-powerful prejudice of education and custom to palliate their attempt to invert Shakespeare's meaning. The continental students of our great bard . . . never fell into the heresy. Everywhere, excepting in America and upon the English stage, Othello is black.'
[2] Hawkins, *Life of Edmund Kean*, i. 221, cited in Furness, p. 390.
[3] See Hankey, pp. 56–61; Rosenberg, pp. 61–9.
[4] Hankey, p. 67.

8. 'A stately Arab of the best caste': Sir Herbert Beerbohm Tree
as Othello, with Phyllis Neilson-Terry as Desdemona
(His Majesty's Theatre, 1912).

distancing the tragic Othello from his blackface counterparts in the
minstrel travesties; and for perhaps a century and a half, it was
largely effective, if not in suppressing the racial dimension of the
play, at least in reducing it to the point where it could safely be
exploited for purely sensational purposes—whether in the 'animal'
excess that so excited onlookers in performances by the Italians
Tommaso Salvini and Ernesto Rossi,[1] or in the 'thrilling'
chiaroscuro effect exploited by Macready in the murder scene,
when he thrust 'his dark, despairing face' through the virgin white

[1] Hankey, pp. 83–91; Rosenberg, pp. 102–19.

curtains of Desdemona's bed.[1] Charles Fechter's 1861 Othello may have suggested, by much agonized play with a hand-mirror, that 'It is the cause' referred to the Moor's colour;[2] but for most Victorians and their successors in the first half of the twentieth century, Othello's difference was typically understood not so much as a matter of race, as of the cultural clash implicit in Iago's contrast between 'an erring barbarian and a super-subtle Venetian' (1.3.348–9). Thus the *Athenaeum* described Salvini's Moor as a 'barbarian, whose instincts, savage and passionate, are concealed beneath a veneer of civilization so thick that he is himself scarcely conscious he can be other than he appears. . . . In the end the barbarian triumphs.'[3]

This was an approach that flattered notions of European superiority whilst conveniently damping down the racial anxieties aroused by the text's emphasis on the hero's blackness. There was, of course, a racial subtext to this story of barbaric relapse—one that typically surfaced in the recurrent metaphors of animality, unconscious echoes of Iago's slurs, with which critics signalled their approbation of the Italians' acting. Salvini was a 'splendid brute' to Clara Morris; whilst he struck Henry James (despite his reservations about Rossi's 'bestial fury') as a 'magnificent creature'—'tiger-like' in his rage and 'a wounded animal' in his remorse.[4] Others were equally impressed by this portrait of an 'angry lion', 'an incarnation of animal fury', who in the murder scene emitted 'growls as of a wild beast over his prey'; and the *Galaxy* reviewer felt 'impatient for his death, as you might be for the

---

[1] Hankey, p. 64.

[2] Hankey, p. 68; James Earl Jones conveyed the same idea in Joe Papp's 1964 production by placing Desdemona's white hand next to his own 'making the line a comment on race prejudice' (Edith Oliver, *New Yorker*, 24 Oct. 1964; cited in Potter, p. 161).

[3] *Athenaeum*, 10 Apr. 1875; *The Galaxy*, 16 (18 Dec. 1873) similarly called Salvini's Othello 'a superbly, though but physically, developed barbarian, whom the civilization of Venice has simply veneered'—both cited in Rosenberg, p. 103.

[4] Clara Morris, *Stage Confidences* (1902), p. 240, cited in Hankey, p. 88; Henry James, *The Scenic Art: notes on acting and the drama, 1872–1901*, ed. Allen Wade (1949), pp. 173–5, 189. The 'wild beast' comparison seems first to have been suggested by the later performances of Macready (who reminded Fanny Kemble, when she played Desdemona, of 'a tiger in his cage'); on the other side of the Atlantic the animal savagery of Edwin Forrest's Moor was much admired (see Potter, p. 37). Later reviewers would describe Beerbohm Tree's Othello in much the same terms (Potter, p. 90).

death of a mad dog let loose in the streets'.[1] The unspoken connection between bestial passion and African savagery becomes explicit in a handwritten note by the American actor Marcus J. Moriarty in his copy of the play (*c.*1875): 'Othello is an untamed animal, grandly majestic—with Africa's blood flowing in his veins. A man of passions so strong . . . [that] once roused, knew no bounds.'[2] Part of the thrill of the Italian Othellos clearly lay in their ability to release the racial fantasies that Victorian stage convention had only half succeeded in suppressing.

Generally speaking, however, it was only on those very rare occasions when a black actor, such as Ira Aldridge (fig. 9) or Paul Robeson (fig. 10), was cast in the leading role that race would be identified as a central issue in the play. Almost invariably this seems to have been because the casting itself was enough to collapse the distance (always vulnerable in this play) between performer and role. Promoted as 'the African Roscius' and credited with a history that uncannily mirrored Othello's own, Aldridge faced a largely patronizing response in England, but enjoyed conspicuous success in continental Europe where he was hailed as 'the real Othello', whose absolute verisimilitude was derived from his alleged origins as a genuine 'Negro from Africa's western coast';[3] he was, critics proclaimed, an artist so completely invested in his part that he utterly overwhelmed the feelings of his audience. According to a French reviewer who saw him in St Petersburg,

from the first moment of the cunning accusation against Desdemona, you see his eyes flash, you feel the tears in his voice when he questions Iago, followed by stifled sobs that almost choke him, and . . . [then] a cry of anger or rather the roaring of a wild beast escapes him, coming from the bottom of his heart. That shriek still seems to sound in my ears; it sent a thrill of horror through all the spectators. Real tears roll down his cheek, he foams at the mouth, his eyes flash fire; never have I seen an artist so completely identify himself with the person he represents. An actor told me he saw the great tragedian sob for several minutes after he came behind the scenes.

---

[1] William Winter, *Shakespeare on the Stage* (New York, 1911), p. 298; J. R. Towse, *Sixty Years of Theatre* (New York, 1916), p. 163; *Galaxy*, 16—all in Rosenberg, pp. 111, 113, 103; for other examples see Vaughan, pp. 167–8.

[2] Folger Promptbook Oth. 40.

[3] Anonymous German reviewer, cited in Hankey, p. 81.

9. 'Naturally un-white': the African-American actor Ira Aldridge
as Othello.

The public did not fail to be deeply touched, all wept, both men and women.[1]

On this same evening the actress playing Desdemona was reportedly so terrified by Aldridge's expression in the murder scene 'that she jumped out of bed, and ran away screaming with real terror' and was persuaded to return only with the greatest difficulty.[2] Aldridge's extreme identification with Othello's suffering arose directly, it was suggested, from his own past: through his

---

[1] St Petersburg correspondent of *Le Nord* (23 Nov. 1858), quoted in Errol Hill, *Shakespeare in Sable: A History of Black Shakespearean Actors* (Amherst, Mass., 1984), p. 24.
[2] Anonymous *Le Nord* correspondent (23 Nov. 1858), quoted in Hankey, p. 82.

performance, according to the Russian critic K. Zvantsev, who had seen him in St Petersburg,

> the liberation of the Negro in the United States . . . becomes something *internal*, not only for the enslaved people, but for us all. . . . From Othello is torn the deep cry 'O misery, misery, misery!' and in that misery of the African artist is heard the far-off groans of his own people, oppressed by unbelievable slavery.[1]

But so persuasive were the 'savage, and uncontrolled elements' in the passion of this 'genuine tiger' that some viewers found them unbearable—most famously a woman writing to the Slavophile newspaper *Dyen* after another of Aldridge's Russian performances in 1863. In prose whose febrile eloquence exposes the bizarre excitement that underlay her appalled response, she denounced what she saw as the performer's inadmissible assault on aesthetic distance:

> A full-blooded Negro, incarnating the profoundest creations of Shakespearean art, giving *flesh and blood* for the aesthetic judgment of Educated European society . . . how much nearer can one get to truth, to the very source of aesthetic satisfaction? But *what is truth* . . . ? As the spirit is not the body, so the truth of art is not this profoundly raw flesh. . . . Not the Moscow Maly Theater, but the African jungle should have been filled and resounded with . . . the cries of this black, powerful, howling flesh. But by the very fact that flesh is so powerful—that it is genuinely black, so naturally *un-white* does it howl—that savage flesh did its fleshly work. It murdered and crushed the spirit . . . and in place of the highest enjoyment, this blatant flesh introduced into art, this *natural* black Othello, pardon me, causes only . . . revulsion.[2]

In contrast to those in England who continued to espouse the orientalized Othello, the author of this passage was in no doubt that Othello was intended to be a black African: her objection was to the playing of the part by a black actor—an objection that a century later was to be revoiced from a very different perspective by those who had begun to see the part as a stereotypical caricature with

---

[1] K. Zvantsev, *Ira Aldridge: BiographicheskiOcherk* (St Petersburg, 1858), cited in Hankey, p. 81. The emotive power of Aldridge's Russian performances was apparently enhanced by his deliberate play on the parallels between black slavery and Russian serfdom—see Iyengar in Kolin, p. 110, and Potter, p. 116.

[2] N. S. Sodkhanskaya ('N. Kokhanovskaya'), *Dyen* (1863), quoted in Herbert Marshall and Mildred Stock, *Ira Aldridge: The Negro Tragedian* (1958), pp. 265–6.

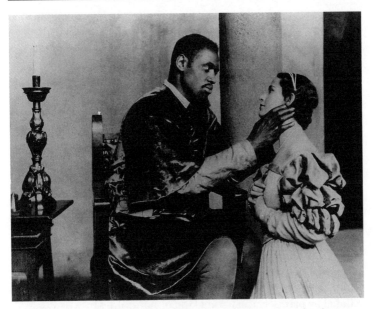

10. 'The suffering of the Negro in the role of the Moor': Paul Robeson as Othello, with Peggy Ashcroft as Desdemona (Savoy Theatre, 1930).

which no black performer could honourably be associated.[1] But first there was a battle to be fought over the right of such actors to play the part at all—especially given the overwhelming predominance of fair-skinned Moors in the performance tradition. For the German makers of the 1922 silent film of *Othello* it was not enough to cast Emil Jannings as a fair-skinned North African in a kaftan—a subtitle even had him declare a half-white lineage: 'I am [the] son of [an] Egyptian prince and [a] Spanish princess—my blood is fair like hers, my wife's.'[2] But in the same year a reviewer from the British popular press, complaining about the sallow make-up of William Stack's Othello, could aver that 'there can be no doubt that to Shakespeare Othello was not only a Moor, but a black Moor';[3] and when, eight years later, the black American singer Paul Robeson was chosen to play the part at London's Savoy Theatre (fig. 10), *The*

[1] See below, pp. 69–71.
[2] *Othello*, dir. Dmitri Buchowetski, 1922.
[3] *Morning Post*, 20 Apr. 1922.

Times praised the production for reviving the 'stage-tradition that held down to the time of Edmund Kean of a coal-black Othello'.[1] But the circulation of such views did not make the casting any less controversial.

Robeson, who reputedly took instruction in the role from Ira Aldridge's daughter,[2] offered a conspicuously restrained Othello—no doubt because this eminently political performer was conscious of how easily the role could slide into stereotypical caricature.[3] The result was that his performance did not arouse such extravagant audience reactions as Ira Aldridge had done; but once again the casting served to highlight the play's racial concerns, giving them a contemporary charge that eroded the boundary between actor and role. Robeson's acting, like Aldridge's, was described as exceptionally 'natural'; but this was not necessarily seen as an advantage. James Agate, for example, adding his voice to those critics who insisted that 'Shakespeare's Moor was not written for a coloured actor of any kind' but 'for a white man to play',[4] argued that Robeson's performance was vitiated by precisely the wrong kind of naturalness:

Coming away from the theatre on Monday evening, a lady was heard to say that the performance had seemed to her to be exceedingly natural. Precisely. But according to whose nature?—that of Shakespeare's Moor or of the player who enacted him? . . . [T]he reason that Mr Robeson failed to be Othello was that he had none of [his] highly civilized quality. . . . He was not *like* the base Indian who threw a pearl away . . . he *was* the base Indian.[5]

In this extremely negative account of a performance that he infamously dismissed as 'nigger Shakespeare',[6] Agate granted

[1] *The Times*, 20 May 1930. E. A. Baughan in the *Daily News* demurred, however: 'Shakespeare's Moor was not written for a coloured actor of any kind. I agree with Coleridge that Othello must not be conceived as a negro, but a high and chivalrous Moorish chief' (19 May 1930).

[2] Gerard Fay, *Manchester Guardian*, 6 Apr. 1959; Robeson apparently visited Amanda Aldridge at her home in Streatham whilst rehearsing for the 1930 production.

[3] A similar anxiety, resulting in a tendency to stress Othello's dignity and restraint at the expense of passion, seems to have afflicted most black actors cast in the role; see Marks, pp. 109–17.

[4] Baughan, *Daily News*, 19 May 1930; Herbert Farjeon, *The Shakespearean Scene* (n.d.), p. 165 (cited in Vaughan, p. 188).

[5] *Sunday Times*, 19 May 1930.

[6] James Agate, *Brief Chronicles: A Survey of the Plays of Shakespeare and the Elizabethans in Actual Performance* (1943), p. 287 (cited in Vaughan, p. 188).

Robeson a 'beautiful voice', but patronizingly declared that 'to ask any Negro actor, however great his qualities of mind and heart, to recite Shakespeare's blank verse would be like asking your bright English schoolboy to jump at once into the silver stride of Racine or Corneille'.[1] In a similar vein, Herbert Farjeon thought that as 'a member of a subject race, still dragging the chains of his ancestors' Robeson must necessarily be incapable of the grandeur which the part demanded.[2]

By contrast, for other reviewers, such as Ivor Brown, Robeson's blackness allowed him an instinctive understanding of the part:

Mr Robeson's ebon Othello is as sturdy as oak . . . a superb giant of the woods for the great hurricane of tragedy to whisper through, then rage upon, then break. One thinks of a tree, because *the greatness is of nature, not of art.* . . . [A]t his best in bewilderment. . . . [h]e is of a younger world, a junior as well as an alien, a child as well as a warrior-chief. . . . And when the devilry is done, you can understand the more his complete relapse to a barbaric rage.[3]

The success of Robeson's Othello, Brown implies, resulted from those stereotypical aspects of his black 'nature' (childishness, a warrior temperament, and innate barbarism) that he shared with Shakespeare's character. Whether as a political activist, or as a supremely self-conscious artist, Robeson must have had decidedly mixed feelings about this kind of praise—just as he must have had reservations about his director, Nellie Van Volkenburg, whose approach to the play was compromised, in Peggy Ashcroft's judgement, by her unmistakable racism.[4] Nevertheless he openly expressed his own identification with the part and (not surprisingly) saw the play as a mirror for the 'position [of the] coloured man in America today' and as an opportunity to 'portray the suffering of the Negro in the role of the Moor'.[5] Of the Savoy production,

---

[1] *Sunday Times*, 19 May 1930. Similar complaints were made of Aldridge's performance by the *Times* reviewer who thought that proper articulation of Shakespearian verse must be impossible 'owing to the shape of his lips', whilst the *Athenaeum* critic believed it 'impossible Mr Aldridge should fully comprehend the meaning and force or even the words he utters' (cited in Hankey, pp. 80–1).

[2] Farjeon, p. 165, cited in Rosenberg, p. 152.

[3] *The Observer*, 25 May 1930.

[4] Iyengar in Kolin, p. 112.

[5] Paul Robeson, 'My Fight for Fame. How Shakespeare Paved My Way to Stardom', *Pearson's Weekly*, 5 Apr. 1930, p. 1100, and Edwin P. Hoyt, *Paul Robeson* (Cleveland, 1967), p. 51 (both cited in Vaughan, p. 187). Cf. also Rosenberg, pp. 151–2.

the actor declared: 'Othello has taken away from me all kinds of fears, all sense of limitation, and all racial prejudice. Othello has opened to me new and wider fields; in a word, *Othello has made me free*.'[1]

It was a remarkable testament from the son of an escaped slave; and one that deserves pondering, in the light of some more recent assertions about the play's complicity in racism. For the *Express* reviewer, at least, this *Othello* was both an artistic success and a political victory that amply vindicated the courage of the company who staged it:

A wonderful audience cheered Robeson's triumph. . . . Coloured people sat dotted about the house. . . . One editor walked out after the third act, saying he did not like to be near coloured people. . . . [But] Robeson's art conquered all. Why should a black actor be allowed to kiss a white actress, I heard people say beforehand. There was no protest of that kind in the theatre.[2]

Plans for a New York season foundered, apparently through fear of American prejudice; but Robeson's London triumph ultimately prepared the way for his collaboration with Margaret Webster in a wartime performance which, after its transfer to Broadway in 1943, would become America's longest-running Shakespeare production. Webster's own comments on Othello's character suggest that the casting of Robeson was driven by the same essentialist understanding of his blackness that marked reviewers' reactions to the Savoy production:

He is more somber, profound and dangerous, primitive in simplicity, primitive also in violence, alien in blood. The gulf which divides him from Desdemona . . . is a gulf between two races, one old and soft in the ways of civilization, the other close to the jungle, and the burning, desert sands.[3]

Nevertheless, like the Savoy *Othello*, this was a political and artistic milestone, powerful enough to persuade one reviewer that 'no

---

[1] Quoted from Martin Bauml Duberman, *Paul Robeson* (1989), p. 137. For an equally positive response to the role by another prominent African-American actor, see James Earl Jones, *Othello* (2003).

[2] 'H.S.', *Express*, 20 May 1930.

[3] Margaret Webster, *Shakespeare Without Tears* (New York, 1975), p. 178 (cited in Vaughan, p. 195).

white man should ever dare play the part again'.[1] In fact, however—with the exception of the ageing Robeson's return to the part at Stratford in 1959—Othello would continue to be the virtual monopoly of white actors for another four decades. Although such major figures as Orson Welles (1951), Anthony Quayle (1952–4), and John Gielgud (1961) all turned their backs on the still dominant convention of pale-skinned Arab Othellos, it was not until 1963 that another black actor was cast in the role on the London or Stratford stages. Though predictably admired for 'sheer sincerity and passion of distress',[2] Errol John's Old Vic performance (like Robeson's before it) illustrated what was soon to emerge as a recurrent paradox of *Othello* productions: for, even as aesthetic and political pressures converged to make the casting of white actors in the lead role appear increasingly undesirable, black actors themselves were repeatedly disabled by fear of the racial stereotyping that might ensue from a full commitment to the emotional excess and extravagant theatricality of the part. The same problem was to arise to a greater or lesser degree with Joseph Marcell at the Lyric Studio Theatre, Hammersmith, with Rudolph Walker at the Young Vic (both in 1984), with Willard White at the Royal Shakespeare Company's Other Place (1989), with David Harewood at the National's Lyttelton Theatre (1997), and with Ray Fearon at the Royal Shakespeare Theatre (1999).[3] Comprehensively upstaged by the 'thunderous energy and broad comic effect' of Leo McKern's Iago,[4] John's Othello was almost immediately overshadowed by Laurence Olivier's overwhelming success in John Dexter's production at the same theatre a year later.

Conceptually speaking, Dexter's *Othello* was a strange hybrid: consciously indebted to F. R. Leavis's influential essay, which was extensively quoted in the programme, it preserved the Victorian idea of Othello as a vain and posturing barbarian whose thin

---

[1] Quoted in Potter, 'Unhaply for I am white', *TLS*, 5 Mar. 1999, p. 19.

[2] Philip Hope-Wallace, *Manchester Guardian*, 31 Jan. 1963.

[3] In fact there is evidence that even Aldridge had been handicapped by such anxieties: Théophile Gautier, expecting something 'a little barbaric and savage in the manner of Kean', was disappointed to find that 'doubtless to appear as civilized as a white, he has a quiet acting style, regulated, classic, majestic, recalling Macready . . . he smothers Desdemona with taste, and he roars properly'—*Voyage en Russie* (Paris, n.d.), pp. 154 ff., cited in Rosenberg, p. 279.

[4] *The Times*, 31 Jan. 1963. (*Times* reviews were still anonymous, as they often were in newspapers generally until around this date.)

veneer of civilization disintegrates under pressure; but at the same time it claimed 'a contemporary urgency lacking in its predecessors' by its explicit 'concern with the relations between the black and the white races'.[1] For Dexter, Othello was a 'pompous, word-spinning, arrogant black general' of a type already becoming familiar in newly independent African countries;[2] and much was made of the extraordinary pains that Olivier, anxious to avoid the pitfalls of blackface caricature, had taken to imitate the actual characteristics of black speech and body language. Olivier's own conception of the part, according to Kenneth Tynan's documentation of the production, was of 'a Negro sophisticated enough to conform to the white myth about Negroes, pretending to be simple and not above rolling his eyes, but in fact concealing (like any other aristocrat) a highly developed sense of racial superiority'. For Tynan this portrait of 'a triumphant black despot, aflame with unadmitted self-regard' was entirely persuasive: 'At the power of his voice,' the critic declared, 'the windows shook and my scalp tingled. A natural force had entered the room, stark and harsh, with vowel-sounds as subtly alien as Kwame Nkrumah's.'[3] Where Tynan had notoriously caricatured Orson Welles as 'Citizen Coon',[4] and Anthony Quayle had been mocked for his 'gollywog-style hair',[5] Olivier received widespread adulation for his 'closely studied . . . physical impersonation' of a negro[6]—even though opinions varied as to whether he had chosen his model from Harlem,[7] West Africa,[8] or the Caribbean.[9] According to Herbert Kretzmer, Olivier 'managed . . . to capture the very essence of what it must mean to be born with a dark skin . . . Sir Laurence embodies blackness',[10] whilst for Ronald Bryden '[h]e *was* the [African] continent'.[11] Once again the play's capacity to erase

---

[1] Harold Hobson, *Sunday Times*, 26 Apr. 1964.

[2] Kenneth Tynan (ed.), *'Othello': The National Theatre Production* (London, 1966; New York, 1967), pp. 4–5.

[3] Tynan, pp. 4–5.

[4] *Evening Standard*, 19 Oct. 1951.

[5] Anonymous reviewer in *The Stage*, 18 Mar. 1954.

[6] Tynan, p. 5.

[7] See B. A. Young, *Financial Times*, 23 July 1964; Richard David, *Shakespeare in the Theatre* (Cambridge, 1978), p. 466.

[8] Hankey, p. 111.

[9] Sanders, p. 47; Alan Brien, *Sunday Telegraph* (cited in Tynan, p. 104).

[10] *Daily Express*, 22 Apr. 1964.

[11] *New Statesman*, 1 May 1964.

aesthetic distance seemed to have triumphed through the mesmerizing power of an overwhelmingly 'natural' performance.

Others were less impressed, however: Alan Seymour, who generally admired Olivier's bravura playing, nevertheless admitted
that it could easily 'be dismissed as dated, tasteless, and monstrous
with artistic, social and political offensiveness. Persons hypersensi-
tive to racial prejudice could make the charge that this eye-rolling,
pink-lipped, tongue-thrusting coal-black Pappy is a demonstration
of the most rearguard white man's concept of the "primitive"
Negro.'[1] For Alan Brien, indeed, this was 'an impersonation which
might have seemed more convincing in the days when Negroes of
all shades and backgrounds were less commonly observed in London streets. Now the combination of a Louis Armstrong guttural
voice and a Stepin Fetchit sway and shuffle appears rather perfunc-
tory.'[2] Robert Kee's response was even more hostile, finding in
Olivier's coal-black face a caricature that 'could only be a figment
of a white man's imagination', so that in his 'worst moments [he
appeared] excruciatingly like something out of the *Black and White
Minstrel Show*',[3] while in the judgement of Fergus Cashin 'too often
. . . he presented us with the ludicrous picture of Al Jolson in place
of the tortured Moor'.[4]

The stereotypical exaggeration of Olivier's Moor became even
more apparent when the performance was transferred to the
screen under the direction of Stuart Burge (1966): cinematic
close-up was as unforgiving to the theatricality of his studied
'African/Caribbean' mannerisms as it was to the smudge of
black make-up that appeared on the cheek of Maggie Smith's
Desdemona; and within a decade it became difficult for student
audiences to respond to the film without embarrassment or laughter. In retrospect, then, Olivier's *Othello* begins to look like an

---

[1] 'A View from the Stalls', in Tynan, p. 13.

[2] Tynan, p. 104.

[3] Tynan, p. 106.

[4] *Daily Sketch*, 22 Apr. 1964. At the same time Harold Hobson complained that
Dexter's 'strategy demands that [Frank Finlay's] Iago should be thick-headed. The
dominating social and political fact today, as Arnold Toynbee has pointed out, is
that everywhere there is a revolt against the ideals and the faith of the white
races . . . in the light of this circumstance, *and the theatre being what it is*, it would be
unrealistic to expect that Iago, the persecutor of the blacks, should be shown as a
man of high, even if malicious intelligence' (*Sunday Times*, 26 Apr. 1964; Tynan,
p. 105).

epochal failure—one that, despite a scattered rearguard action in the 1970s and early 1980s, seriously called in question the propriety of white actors continuing to occupy the role they had played since the time of Burbage.[1] Yet, in its stage version at least, the performance was a theatrical tour de force unmatched since Salvini, or even Kean.

In what was clearly a reaction against Olivier's impersonation of negritude, most Othellos of this period reverted to variations on the orientalized Moor of the Victorians: Bruce Purchase (Mermaid, 1971) was 'no more than fashionably sunburnt',[2] Brewster Mason (RSC, 1971) played 'a traditional, pre-Olivier Moor',[3] Donald Sinden (RSC, 1979) became 'a very light brown Othello', made up (by his own account) 'to look like Nasser [the former military ruler of Egypt] . . . with a beard',[4] Paul Scofield (National Theatre, 1980) chose 'the light dusky tan of a desert ruler' and a voice marked by 'Middle Eastern inflexions',[5] while Anthony Hopkins's television Moor resembled a 'Hashemite warrior' (1981).[6] The implications were not lost on reviewers: Sinden's Othello persuaded Gareth Lloyd Evans that this was 'not a play about colour or racialism—certainly not in the modern sense. It is more of a personal tragedy than a tribal disaster';[7] while Robert Cushman recognized in Scofield's self-absorbed performance a return to 'the Eliot-Leavis view of the Moor: an egotist who deserves even more than he gets'.[8] Even the most intelligently political of these productions, John Barton's 1971 RSC *Othello*, with its nineteenth-century colonial setting, convinced Jeremy Kingston 'that the play is more about differences in rank than differences of colour', whilst to Gareth Lloyd Evans it showed that 'Othello's "blackness" is not a large issue in the play. . . . For an actor or director to worry away at

---

[1] While Olivier's mimicry of blackness is nowadays usually dismissed as irredeemably racist, it is worth recalling that the great African-American actor, James Earl Jones, who had given the first of his seven Othellos in 1956, and who profoundly disagreed with Olivier's interpretation, nevertheless thought it a performance that accurately revealed 'all the paranoia, suspicions and defensiveness of a victim of racism' (cited in Potter, p. 147).

[2] John Barber, *Daily Telegraph*, 17 Sept. 1971.

[3] Ronald Bryden, *Observer*, 12 Sept. 1971.

[4] B. A. Young, *Financial Times*, 8 Aug. 1979, 15 Aug. 1979.

[5] Irving Wardle, *Times*, 24 Mar. 1980.

[6] Pechter, p. 110.

[7] *Stratford Herald*, 10 Aug. 1979.

[8] *Punch*, 23 Mar. 1980.

Othello's colour is to confuse a detail for the whole.'[1] Ronald Bryden, agreeing that 'Shakespeare's tragedy isn't really about race', saw Barton as trying 'to free [the play] from the charge that inevitably builds up around the image of a Negro marrying a white woman'; in a production that deployed colonial images as a template for explaining the social tensions of the play, Othello emerged as 'a black Englishman, a servant of Empire, of a kind impossible before or since Victoria', but, for Bryden, Mason's 'blackness [was] not, like Olivier's, the emblem of a primitive, African violence lurking in all of us'; instead it became 'the symbol of our difference, the otherness we fear in those we love'.[2]

Some critics, however, were less than happy with this re-orientalizing of the Moor. Reviewing Scofield's Othello, Ian Stewart missed both the 'sexual and racial tensions' created by Olivier's stress on the hero's blackness and the virtuosity with which he had portrayed the heroic soldier's terrifying 'collapse into primitive chaos'.[3] Sheridan Morley was similarly dissatisfied with Sinden's over-civilized Arab, though it was not to Olivier's theatricality but to Robeson's 'natural' aptitude for the role that he nostalgically appealed:

What made Robeson [in 1959] so magical . . . was that by his very nature he caught the mix of power and utter simplicity without which Othello cannot be made plausible either as a play or as a role. Mr Sinden is simply too clever and too gentle by half. . . . Othello does not need to become the black-and-black minstrel that Olivier made of him, only a chorus away from the Swanee River. He does, however, need to be capable of falling for Iago's duplicity. . . . [Sinden] is too light of heart rather than skin, too ineffably sophisticated ever to get caught up with Bob Peck's interesting but none-too-subtle Iago.[4]

---

[1] *Punch*, 22 Sept. 1971; *Guardian*, 17 Sept. 1971.

[2] Ronald Bryden, *Observer*, 12 Sept. 1971. Despite the emphasis of most subsequent criticism, resistance to productions that stress the importance of race in the play persists: thus Patrick Marmion criticized Christopher Geelan's 2002 Cochrane Theatre production for 'hop[ing] to turn the play into a study of East–West tension, institutionalized racism, gender conflict, and even class war'; while conceding that 'there is much in the text to justify these themes, he argued that 'Geelan's modern-dress staging is still more convincing as a traditional tale of spite, gullibility, innocence and green-eyed rage' (*Evening Standard*, 7 Feb. 2002).

[3] *Country Life*, 17 Apr. 1980.

[4] *Punch*, 22 Aug. 1979. Given Robeson's formidable academic history it is difficult not to detect a racial assumption behind Morley's emphasis on the actor's natural 'simplicity' and want of sophistication.

The clear implication of Morley's criticisms was that only a black actor could fully inhabit the part; and to that extent he was prophetic, since in the two succeeding decades white Othellos would become rare enough to provoke charges of reverse racism in the British theatre. The only notable exception was Ben Kingsley's North African Moor in Terry Hands's 1985 production for the RSC. Irving Wardle praised Hands's decision to 'restore [the hero] to Islam', thereby abandoning 'the always defeated attempt to trace racial themes in this play, and root[ing] it much more profitably in a collision of culture'.[1] But even Kingsley—though he seems to have been more interested in exploring the homoerotic intensity of Othello's relationship with Iago than in the play's racial dimension[2]—was at pains to establish a special authenticity for his performance by invoking his half-Indian parentage and claiming inspiration from the Moroccans amongst whom he had been filming when asked to take the role.[3] The resulting performance, while it seemed too close to the actor's recent cinematic Gandhi for the taste of some reviewers,[4] was saluted by Michael Coveney as 'the most *genuinely ethnic* Othello since Olivier'.[5]

However questionable this judgement of Olivier's ethnic authenticity may now seem, Dexter's production was nevertheless important as an attempt to rethink the play in relation to contemporary race politics: coinciding not only with the beginning of African decolonization, but with the climactic phase of the Civil Rights struggle in America, and with the consequent spread of *négritude* and Black Power philosophies, the production spoke to the social strains as well as to the idealism generated by this period of history. Dexter's theatrical reinvestigation of Othello's blackness was matched by the work of a small group of critics—G. M. Matthews, Eldred Durosimi Jones, and G. K. Hunter—who took the first steps towards a systematic and fully historicized exploration of

---

[1] *The Times*, 25 Sept. 1985.

[2] *Observer Colour Magazine*, 22 Sept. 1985.

[3] Interview in *The Times*, 21 Sept. 1985; see also Potter, pp. 164–5.

[4] Unable to resist paraphrasing Winston Churchill's notorious sneer at the Indian leader as 'a half-naked fakir', John Barber complained of Kingsley's 'curious Fakir's choked back emotion' (*Daily Telegraph*, 26 Sept. 1985), whilst Francis King grumbled that in the last scenes he looked 'more like some sex-maddened fakir than a respected military officer' (*Sunday Telegraph*, 29 Sept. 1985).

[5] *Financial Times*, 26 Sept. 1985.

Shakespeare's treatment of race.[1] It was not, however, for another two decades that the directions charted in the mid 1960s were to be pursued by a new generation of critics and theatre practitioners.

For all the lofty dismissiveness of reviewers like Wardle, Lloyd Evans, and Bryden, who had insisted on the ultimate irrelevance of colour to the tragedy, *Othello* in the late 1980s and 1990s would become a play saturated with racial anxiety. More than anything, perhaps, it was the prominence given to racial issues by the gathering crisis in apartheid South Africa that prompted a renewed focus on the significance of Othello's blackness; and it was the deliberate political appropriation of the play by two South Africans, one a Shakespeare scholar, the other an actor and director, that marked the decisive turning-point. The 1987 publication of Martin Orkin's essay '*Othello* and the "Plain Face" of Racism' (whose activist agenda was announced by the title of the book in which it was reprinted, *Shakespeare Against Apartheid*[2]) coincided with Janet Suzman's defiantly multi-racial production at the Market Theatre in Johannesburg, with the prominent Xhosa actor John Kani in the title role. For his performance Kani was adorned with a heavy necklet, a piece of barbaric jewellery that disconcertingly resembled a slave-collar, and from which hung the small knife with which he would ultimately kill himself. The importance of *Othello*, for the makers of this production as much as for Orkin, lay in its transhistorical immediacy; thus there was no more appropriate work, Suzman and Kani believed, 'to describe the utter tragedy of our country. . . . The play addresses the notion of apartheid four hundred years before the epithet was coined—and rejects it.'[3] Introducing the television version of her production, Suzman

---

[1] Matthews, '*Othello* and the Dignity of Man', in Arnold Kettle (ed.), *Shakespeare in a Changing World* (1964), 123–45; Jones, *Othello's Countrymen: The African in English Renaissance Drama* (1965); Hunter, 'Othello and Colour Prejudice'.

[2] Martin Orkin, '*Othello* and the "Plain Face" of Racism', *SQ* 38 (1987), 166–8; in *Shakespeare Against Apartheid* (Craighall, South Africa, 1987). The only important essay to engage with the play's racial dimension in the years between Hunter's British Academy Lecture and Orkin's essay—Doris Adler's 'The Rhetoric of *Black* and *White* in *Othello*', *SQ* 25 (1974), 248–57, published in the year of the Soweto uprising in South Africa—grew out of the author's experience as a white teacher of black students at Howard University in 1969 at the height of the Black Power movement (p. 248).

[3] Janet Suzman, introducing '*Othello* in Johannesburg', Channel 4 Television, 1988.

described Iago as 'operat[ing] like your local bigot, seemingly decent on the surface, boorish and quite without compassion underneath', at which point she cut between a clip of Richard Haddon Haines's bullying, hate-filled Iago to the ranting oratory of Eugene Terreblanche, leader of the neo-fascist AWB, the extremist Afrikaner organization that rose to prominence in the last years of apartheid. Although this production was also sympathetic to the predicament of the female characters, stressing Emilia's victimization by Iago, its priorities were made clear when the dying Emilia, in a mute repudiation of her earlier racial slurs, reached out her hand for Othello—rather than for Desdemona (as she would do in Trevor Nunn's woman-centred RSC *Othello* two years later).

Suzman's *Othello* achieved a wide international currency through television and videotape; and the urgency of John Kani's performance as the Moor, together with the director's insistence on the work's contemporary relevance, contributed to the growing politicization of the play outside South Africa—especially in Britain, where the emergence of a cadre of classically trained black actors had begun to make the propriety of continuing to cast white actors in the role of Othello a matter of controversy. Starting with the appearance of Joseph Marcell and Rudolph Walker, at the Hammersmith Lyric Studio and Young Vic in 1984, a succession of black Othellos—including Clarke Peters (Greenwich, 1989), Willard White (RSC, The Other Place, 1989), Ben Thomas (Talawa Theatre Company, 1997), David Harewood (National, Lyttelton Theatre, 1997), Ray Fearon (RST, 1999), and Nicholas Monu (Cochrane Theatre, 2002)—took virtual possession of the role. Already by 1989, when Trevor Nunn cast Willard White in the lead for openly 'political reasons', Michael Billington had begun to believe that it might be impossible for the role any longer to be given to a white actor—even though he felt that 'the last truly earth-shaking Othello was Olivier a quarter of a century ago'.[1] An ironic consequence of the overwhelming pressure to cast only black Othellos was a risk-averse strategy that kept the play off the main stages for nearly a decade after Nunn's production. Significantly, when the British actor Patrick Stewart was offered the lead by the Washington Shakespeare Company in 1997, he would agree to take

---

[1] Nunn, quoted in Barbara Hodgdon, *The Shakespeare Trade: Performances and Appropriations* (Philadelphia, 1998), p. 50; Billington, *Guardian*, 26 Aug. 1989.

it only in a so-called 'photo-negative' production, in which a white Othello faced an entirely black world; and when in the same year the play at last returned to London, the National's choice of the youthful David Harewood provoked a flurry of complaint about 'political correctness'. Reviewers pointed to the convention of colour-neutral casting now operating elsewhere in the theatre, and sourly observed that no such racial sanctions appeared to operate in the casting of Verdi's opera, where Placido Domingo reigned supreme in the title role.[1] Blaming an overreaction both to the offensiveness of the minstrel tradition and to the grossness of Olivier's impersonation, Geoffrey Wheatcroft urged white actors to challenge the 'odious notion [of black-only casting] by demanding to play Othello—blacked up or *au naturel* as the theatre pleases'; if refused, they should sue under the Race Relations Act.[2]

Harewood himself responded angrily to such criticisms, insisting that 'it is now ridiculous to see a white person blacked up', and arguing (like Robeson) that the play had given him 'a grounding in black consciousness. . . . That's where Othello has helped me, I'm not playing—I'm being.'[3] As Harewood's comments imply, the politics of black casting had a number of strands: it was a reaction to the perceived offensiveness of 'blacking-up'—a convention that was seen as inextricably compromised by 'nigger-minstrel' racism; it answered to the belief, apparent from Aldridge's time onwards, that a black actor's 'natural' sympathy with the part must lend his performance an authenticity transcending mere art; and it was a natural corollary of the desire to make the play speak to contemporary racial issues. Thus the critic Richard Wilson supplied a programme note for David Thacker's 1984 Young Vic production in which he promoted *Othello* as 'Shakespeare's most topical tragedy . . . his most prophetic analysis of the psychology of colonialism and power.' The key to understanding the play, Wilson argued, lies in the fact that 'Othello is a freed slave. He prides himself on his "free condition" and his "free and open nature". Liberated from the chain-gang, he imagines that "All slaves are free". . . .

---

[1] See Alistair Macaulay, *Financial Times*, 18 Sept. 1997; John Gross, *Sunday Telegraph*, 21 Sept. 1997; Charles Spencer, *Telegraph*, 18 Sept. 1997; David Lister, 'Can it be wrong to "black up" for Othello?', *Independent*, 7 Aug. 1997.

[2] Geoffrey Wheatcroft, 'Sorry, sweetheart, but whites need not apply', *Sunday Telegraph*, 21 Sept. 1997.

[3] *Independent*, 12 May 1998.

Othello's "free and noble nature" is as oppressed in this "free" society as when he was a galley slave. . . . bound by the invisible chain of words and images. . . . *Othello* is a tragedy based on the crudest race myth, the legend of the negro's sexual danger.'

Wilson's insistence on the play's 'prophetic' character, reinforced by his anachronistic reference to the chain-gangs of segregationist America and to a Fanonian 'psychology of colonialism' with its attendant sexual fantasies, firmly relocated the play in the context of twentieth-century racial politics. Rather more oblique in its approach was Trevor Nunn's small-scale RSC production at The Other Place in 1989—subsequently televised and issued on video by the BBC. Making use of a device borrowed from John Barton's 1971 production, and later copied by both Sam Mendes (National Theatre, 1997) and Michael Attenborough (RSC, 1999), Nunn transferred the action to a setting evocative of 'the Edwardian sunset of colonial power and moral certainties'.[1] This created a context in which the racial bigotry of Iago, Roderigo, and Brabantio became readily explicable to a modern audience, whilst allowing them the comfort of a certain historical distance. By choosing the black Marsha Hunt to play Bianca, Nunn also contrived to suggest that Othello's jealous insecurities had something in common with those of this other mercenary outsider.[2] But, although Willard White was widely publicized as the first black actor to play Othello in the history of the Royal Shakespeare Company, the bravura of Ian McKellen's riveting Iago so overwhelmed the dignified restraint of White's Moor that the play became more a study of psychopathic villainy than of racial conflict. Moreover, the domestic scale of Nunn's production, which minimized the significance of the play's larger framework of Christian–Islamic conflict, tended, by its focus on 'the inner world of husbands and wives', to make gender seem more important than race.[3]

Ironically enough, in Jude Kelly's 1997 Washington Shakespeare Company *Othello*, Patrick Stewart's politically tactful insistence on

---

[1] Jack Tinker, *Daily Mail*, 26 Aug. 1989. Mendes, however, updated the colonial setting to the 1930s, suggesting an additional fascist context for Iago's racism.

[2] Nunn seems to have initiated a fashion for casting black actresses in this role, especially in the United States, thereby turning this character into 'Othello's foil, a sign of how far Othello has travelled and how far he can fall, a sign of the limits that race draws around individuals' (Iyengar in Kolin, p. 111).

[3] Vaughan, p. 218; and see below, pp. 106–9.

photo-negative casting resulted in an even more absolute neutralization of the play's racial theme. Although Kelly herself was less interested in what the play had to say about race than in its treatment of gender issues, Miranda Johnson-Haddad's programme note, invoking apartheid South Africa and the alleged murder of his white wife by the black American sporting hero O. J. Simpson, invited audiences to see the play as Shakespeare's exploration of 'the social context that enables racism . . . to develop'; and the production carefully located its white Moor in an inverted hierarchy of colour that placed olive-skinned Cypriots somewhere between the black elite and a white serving class. Helped by the barbaric tattoos on Stewart's arms and shaven head, audiences adjusted readily enough to the reversed valencies of black and white. However, Iago's repertory of racial insults necessarily lost most of its power to wound when aimed at a conspicuously white hero;[1] and significantly, the only moments in the production with a dangerous racial charge were those that ran counter to the economy of insult in the text itself—as for example when Othello's reference to 'the Cannibals that each other eat, | The Anthropophagi' (1.3.143–4) became a sardonic challenge to the (black) Venetian Senate. In this respect Stewart's 'appealing, articulate' Moor did not help: not only did he appear, when set against Ron Canada's rather stolid Iago, 'almost too intelligent' to make the plot persuasive, but his air of humorously relaxed self-confidence fitted so easily with a certain stereotype of white authority that reviewers found it 'hard to feel particularly sorry for him'.[2] Indeed, when combined with Kelly's stress on gender politics, colour reversal lent a peculiar force to the 'brothel' scene, where Stewart's physical abuse of Patrice Johnson's Desdemona, mingling fury with desire, recalled the 'primal scene' of American racial history—the violent rape of black women by white men.[3]

---

[1] See e.g. Lloyd Rose, *Washington Post*, 18 Nov. 1997; Nelson Pressley, *Washington Times*, 18 Nov. 1997; Peter Marks, *New York Times*, 21 Nov. 1997; Bob Mondello, *Washington City Paper*, 21 Nov. 1997.

[2] See Mondello and Marks, 21 Nov. 1997.

[3] See Denise Albanese, 'Black and White, and Dread All Over: The Shakespeare Theater's "Photonegative *Othello*" and the Body of Desdemona', in Dympna Callaghan (ed.), *A Feminist Companion to Shakespeare* (Oxford, 2003), 226–47 (p. 241). Albanese's detailed critique of the production attacks the implicit racial politics of its casting, which it sees as 'a parody of affirmative action' designed to neutralize the play's 'unpalatable propositions' in the interests of 'preserving an aestheticized and performatively innocuous Shakespeare' (p. 243).

By contrast, Yvonne Brewster's production for the black Talawa Theatre Company in the same year used a recent scandal in the United States to insist on the immediacy and centrality of Othello's racial predicament. The 1994 arrest of the African American football hero O. J. Simpson on suspicion of murdering his white wife had provoked numerous comparisons with Shakespeare's play[1]—to the point where, in a somewhat hyperbolic comparison, Barbara Hodgdon maintains that '[m]uch as the Holocaust . . . altered forever the meanings of Shakespeare's *Merchant of Venice*, the Simpson trial . . . made *Othello* the timeliest of Shakespeare's plays'.[2] The Talawa programme featured an essay entitled 'Orenthal and Othello', by the Barbadian novelist Austin Clark, pursuing the parallels between Simpson and Othello as black men whose success in mastering the white world, epitomized by their acquisition of white wives, exposed them to racial backlash. According to Clark, the parallels between the two cases, each of which exposed white society's 'psychosexual obsession with black men who lie in bed with white women', demonstrated that 'racism has an enduring nature, and is perennially fixed in our consciousness and in our blood':

Nothing has changed. Nothing can. [OJ's] invisibility . . . is now stripped away; the flesh of racism is added, to make him into a savage, brutish man, a black who hid his oppositeness beneath a façade of whiteness. He achieved his white destiny, but he still retained that aspect of his character. The General on the other hand, is defined even in the heyday of his municipal success, also in terms of the beast.

In the same vein, a number of reviewers responded to Oliver Parker's 1995 film of *Othello* as though it were a self-conscious meta-commentary on the scandal—a reading reinforced by the casting of Laurence Fishburne, most recently seen as the wife-beating Ike Turner in *What's Love Got To Do With It*, as Othello.[3]

---

[1] See, for instance, Hodgdon, *Shakespeare Trade*, pp. 39–41, 59–64; and James A. McPherson, 'Three Great Ones of the City and One Perfect Soul: Well Met at Cyprus', in Kaul, pp. 45–76. That the supposed parallels also impressed some more ordinary American theatregoers was indicated by an exchange of *graffiti* that appeared in the lavatories of the Folger Shakespeare Theatre at the time of the trial: 'Hey, OJ, at least Othello was sorry for what he did.' 'Yeah, and he killed himself too.'

[2] Hodgdon, *Shakespeare Trade*, p. 72.

[3] See Potter, p. 193, and Joyce Green MacDonald, 'Black Ram, White Ewe: Shakespeare, Race, and Women', in Callaghan (ed.), *Feminist Companion to Shakespeare*, 188–207 (p. 189). For a detailed analysis of Parker's film (in which Kenneth Branagh also gave particular emphasis to the violent misogyny of Iago) as 'the perfect post-O.J. *Othello*', see Hodgdon, pp. 64–73.

One danger with productions that seek such immediacy is that through their choice of familiarizing detail they can sometimes reinforce the very stereotypes they seek to combat. This seems to have happened in Michael Boyd's 1984 *Othello* at the Lyric Studio, Hammersmith: invoking the late-Victorian essentialism of Joseph Conrad, Christopher Edwards described Joseph Marcell's Sandhurst-educated African as 'retreat[ing] to the *heart of darkness*' when, succumbing to Iago's temptations, he heard 'bongo drums and jungle rhythms', and then re-entered 'with chicken feathers in his hair' as if coming from 'a voodoo sacrifice'.[1] A more successful version of essentially the same device was employed in Cathy Downes's 2001 production for the Court Theatre in Christchurch, New Zealand. Here the action was translated to the nineteenth-century land wars along the Waikato river; Othello was a missionary-adopted, British-educated general leading the British forces against his own people; while 'Cyprus' was the name of his gunboat headquarters. At the climax of his jealous disintegration, the 'careful mantle of civilisation slip[ped]' and Othello burst into the terrifying *wero* (warrior's challenge) that announced his imminent revenge.[2] But where the postcolonial politics of New Zealand allowed this to be read as a proper repudiation of the colonizer's values, the Hammersmith bongo drums merely invoked the crudest of racial stereotypes.

It was partly in order to counter the persistent 'view that Othello behaves as he does because of his race' that the 1989 Greenwich production, co-directed by Sue Dunderdale and the black actor Hugh Quarshie, matched its black Othello with a black Iago: as Quarshie's programme note explained, Cyprus with its 'olive-skinned natives' was to be seen as a 'colonial' society governed by a deeply internalized hierarchy of colour in which Iago's influence over the hero was determined partly by the relative lightness of his skin. A decade later, however, Quarshie had come to question whether the play was really amenable to the kind of reading that he and Dunderdale had attempted. Where in 1989 he had insisted that an authentic performance required that Othello be 'a black

---

[1] Christopher Edwards, *Spectator*, 29 Sept. 1984; and cf. Michael Coveney, *Financial Times*, 19 Sept. 1984.

[2] John Smythe, *National Business Review*, 15 June 2001; Faith Oxenbridge, *Listener*, 19 May 2001; Juliet Neill, *Theatre News*, June/July 2001.

man, and not someone impersonating a black man', now, in a lecture entitled 'Hesitations on *Othello*',[1] he argued that 'being a black actor gives . . . no greater insight into . . . the play, than being Danish would into *Hamlet*' (p. 3). Going further, he even speculated that since this was 'a role written for a white actor in black make-up and for a . . . white audience . . . Of all the parts in the canon, perhaps Othello is the one which should most definitely not be played by a black actor'; after all, 'if a black actor plays a role written for a white actor does he not risk making racial stereotypes seem legitimate and even true . . . does he not encourage the white way, or rather the wrong way, of looking at black men, namely that [they] are over-emotional, excitable and unstable' (p. 5).[2] With some reluctance, Quarshie conceded that in order to challenge 'the racist conventions that have persisted for so long' black actors should continue to play the part—especially since, by combining 'a radical re-reading of key passages' with 'some judicious cutting and textual emendation', it might yet be possible to produce 'a non-racist interpretation' of what he had come to think of as a fundamentally racist play.[3] In the first version of his lecture, however, Quarshie had cited the view of the African film-maker Onyekachi Wambu that 'black actors [should] renounce [their] effective monopoly of the role and encourage white actors in black make-up to . . . expose the absurdity of this grotesque fantasy';[4]

---

[1] Quarshie's lecture was first delivered as the Shakespeare Birthday Lecture in Stratford-upon-Avon, in 1998 and then (in a substantially revised form) as the first of the 1998/9 Hudson Strode Lectures at the University of Alabama. It was this latter version that formed the basis of *Second Thoughts about 'Othello'* (see above, p. 5, n. 4).

[2] Compare Marks's suggestion (pp. 116–17) that 'the tricky combination of "strangeness" and "kinship" [needed for the part] is best achieved not by a black actor, someone who is likely to imagine for Othello a subjectivity formed of the particular experiences of a black man, but an actor in what could usefully be called "racial drag". . . . A real black actor . . . has too much independent selfhood getting in the way.'

[3] *Second Thoughts*, pp. 20, 21, 3, 7. Some of Quarshie's arguments had been anticipated in a sophisticated essay by Dympna Callaghan, ' "Othello was a White Man": Properties of Race on Shakespeare's Stage', in Terence Hawkes (ed.), *Alternative Shakespeares*, vol. 2 (1996), pp. 192–215, which explores the implications of the role's having been written for a white actor.

[4] I am indebted to Robert Smallwood for supplying me with a typescript of the Stratford version. Potter (p. 175) cites a similar response from the Nigerian critic S. E. Ogude: '[a] black Othello is an obscenity. The element of the grotesque is best achieved when a white man plays the role.' However blinkered by current racial

and just such a satiric travesty, in which the play would once again become 'a minstrel show . . . played for laughs' and its protagonist a 'caricature' in blackface, has been proposed by the black American director Sheila Rose Bland as the version best calculated to expose the racist intentions of a playwright who (she wryly suggests) can never have expected his play to be taken seriously as a tragedy.[1]

Othello and Iago   When in 1623 Leonard Digges (almost as though proposing an alternative title for the tragedy) wrote of 'Honest Iago, or the Jealous Moor', he was already acknowledging the villain's propensity to compete for the dominant position in the drama.[2] Yet it is surely significant that no major tragic actor before Sir Henry Irving at the end of the nineteenth century elected to risk his reputation by choosing to play Iago in preference to Othello—though a number had essayed both roles.[3] By the beginning of the twentieth century, however, the playwright Herman Charles Merivale could confidently declare that 'rightly played' Iago must emerge as the true centre of the tragedy.[4] Merivale's claim would probably have seemed inconceivable to Henry Jackson, whose note on the 1610 Oxford performance does not even mention the villain; and for most early viewers it appears to have been the Othello of Richard Burbage, the great tragedian of Shakespeare's company, that dominated the performance. His, according to an anonymous elegiast in 1618, was 'the chiefest part, | Wherein,

politics such responses may appear to be, a disconcerting light is thrown on the play's capacity to mobilize racial fantasy by a succession of films in which the central character, a white actor cast as Othello is possessed by murderous jealousy whilst playing the role (see p. 9).

[1] Sheila Rose Bland, 'How I would Direct *Othello*', in Kaul, pp. 29–41. C. Bernard Jackson's *Iago* (see 'Reception', above, p. 13, n. 3)—a retelling of the story from the point of view of a black Emilia—concludes with the killing of an author figure named 'William'—a symbolic revenge, as Lois Potter notes (p. 171), on Shakespeare himself.

[2] See Pechter, pp. 25–6. Digges's verses appeared in the 1640 edition of Shakespeare's *Poems*, but seem to have originally been intended for the First Folio.

[3] Hankey, p. 30. Charles Macklin, known as the greatest Shylock of his time, is a partial exception; but he was physically unsuited to heroic roles—see Hankey, pp. 39–40; Rosenberg, pp. 40–1.

[4] Herman Charles Merivale, *Bar, Stage, and Platform; Autobiographic Memories* (1902), p. 149, cited in Hankey, p. 92.

beyond the rest, he moved the heart'.[1] By contrast, nothing is known of the earliest Iago, save that (according to the Restoration writer Charles Gildon) he 'was in much esteem as a comedian'.[2] Such a casting was perhaps predictable, given that Shakespeare's conception of the role (as Bernard Spivack[3] has shown) clearly owed a good deal to the Vice of medieval Morality drama—the figure whose demonic humour spawned the gleeful wickedness of Richard III and Marlowe's Barabas, as well as the more genial iniquity of Falstaff. 'Jocularity', Spivack has declared, 'is the true passion of [Iago]', whose 'emotions are simply variations on the monolithic passion of laughter. He is a creature of leaping jubilation and sardonic mirth' (pp. 17–18); and even though the role was sometimes taken by actors noted for their prowess in tragedy, including Joseph Taylor (best known as Burbage's successor in the role of Hamlet),[4] most interpretations seem to have retained a comic accent until the nineteenth century. Samuel Sandford, the most prominent Restoration Iago, was notorious for the extravagantly melodramatic style apparently encouraged by what his successor, Colley Cibber, described as his 'low and crooked person'.[5] Best known as a comic actor, Cibber offered an Iago whose ludicrously exaggerated combination of fop and villain drove one critic to complain that 'Othello must be supposed a fool, a stock if he does not see through him.'[6] Though criticized at the time, Cibber's pantomime approach seems to have set the tone for numerous

---

[1] Quoted in Furness, p. 396. The manuscript in which the elegy is preserved is possibly suspect, since it was discovered by J. P. Collier, notorious for his forgeries of Shakespearian documents.

[2] Hankey, p. 18; some scholars have suggested that the comedian may have been Armin, famous for his melancholy clowns; but a more likely possibility is John Lowin, who probably played Falstaff, as well as Sir Epicure Mammon in *The Alchemist* and Bosola in *The Duchess of Malfi*. Lowin, who was 28 in 1604, was the right age for the part—see Potter, p. 3.

[3] Spivack, esp. chaps. 1, 2, and 12. Spivack's vivid account of Iago's 'hybrid' characterization as a conventional Vice figure, wedded to malice by his diabolical nature, but disguised with a thin overlay of psychological naturalism, remains one of the best things on the play; but (as will be apparent elsewhere) I think he underestimates the extent to which Shakespeare's psychological insight succeeds in transforming the type.

[4] Hankey, pp. 18–19.

[5] Colley Cibber, *An Apology for the Life of Colley Cibber*, [1740], ed. B. R. S. Fone (Ann Arbor, 1968), p. 77, cited in Hankey, p. 30.

[6] *Gentleman's Magazine*, Nov. 1734, cited in Rosenberg, p. 47; see also John Dennis's comments, cited in Potter, pp. 71–2.

11. 'A gay, light-hearted monster': Edmund Kean as Iago (1814).

eighteenth-century Iagos, despite the moderating influence of Macklin, Garrick, and Kemble.[1] Even the great Edmund Kean (fig. 11) made of him, according to Hazlitt, 'a gay, light-hearted monster'.[2]

It comes as a shock now to find Charles Gildon in 1694 citing Iago's 'old black ram' tirade as an example of language that Shakespeare had included in the part 'to make the audience laugh'.[3] That assessment may reveal more about the notorious levity of Restoration playhouses than about the dramatist's intentions; nevertheless it remains the case that, just as part of the genius of the play's design lies in the daring with which it yokes together comic and tragic conventions, so the opposition of Othello and Iago

---

[1] See Rosenberg, pp. 49–50.
[2] *Morning Chronicle*, 9 May 1814, cited in Rosenberg, p. 122; cf. also Hankey, pp. 53–5.
[3] Cited in Hankey, p. 12.

develops much of its theatrical power from a clash of histrionic styles. Thus while the part of Othello is conceived in the lofty, magniloquent idiom of heroic tragedy,[1] it is repeatedly exposed to question by its juxtaposition with the prosaic naturalism and sardonic humour of Iago, for whom the Moor's richly ornamented language amounts to nothing more than 'a bombast circumstance | Horribly stuffed with epithets of war' (1.1.12–13). Iago's judgement is uncomfortably mirrored in the dismissive responses of such twentieth-century critics as T. S. Eliot, with his infamous assertion that Othello in his last great aria is merely 'cheering himself up', and F. R. Leavis, for whom Othello is an egotist who conceals his innate savagery with self-dramatizing bombast.[2] The danger presented by any Iago who overplays the comic opportunities of the role is that he will succeed in making his Othello appear a credulous fool unworthy of the audience's sympathy; and perhaps it was partly Rymer's experience of the Sandford Iago (even though it was matched with Betterton's mighty Othello) that persuaded him to take such a negative view of the play.

In the nineteenth century, following the lead of William Charles Macready, who stressed the 'fiendish subtlety' with which Iago makes a puppet of his victim, the part was given a more intellectual cast. Not only did this make it more attractive to leading tragedians, in many cases it also seems to have enabled a better balance between the two roles. The effect was often to turn the Othello–Iago pairing, which John Philip Kemble and George Frederick Cooke (1803–4) had already made highly competitive, into a contest of virtuosity (rather like the soprano duels of baroque opera) in which the sense of fierce rivalry between two popular actors added to the excitement of the dramatic conflict.[3] So it became common to describe the struggle between Iago and Othello in terms of a competition for acting honours.[4] Some performances, indeed, were

---

[1] On heroic character and style, see Eugene M. Waith, *Ideas of Greatness: Heroic Drama in England* (1971).

[2] T. S. Eliot, 'Shakespeare and the Stoicism of Seneca', in *Selected Essays* (1951), 126–40 (esp. pp. 129–31); F. R. Leavis, 'Diabolic Intellect and the Noble Hero', *Scrutiny*, 6 (1937), 259–83, repr. in *The Common Pursuit* (1952; repr. Harmondsworth, 1969), 136–59.

[3] See Potter, pp. 76–85.

[4] See, for example, the *Stratford Herald*'s review of Benson and Rodney, 30 Apr. 1897; the *Birmingham Post*'s review of the same pair, 16 Apr. 1902.

deliberately set up in this way: thus in 1816 Macready and Charles Young alternated the roles in a fashion that deliberately advertised their friendly rivalry. Following their lead a year later, Edmund Kean faced out an emerging competitor, Junius Brutus Booth, in what was described as a 'wrestle of talent', by inviting him to play Iago to his own powerful Othello. Kean set about 'smothering' Booth's performance and succeeded in 'beat[ing] his antagonist hollow', as *The Champion* put it—a stunt which he managed once again in the last year of his life when, despite failing health, he successfully outpointed the menacingly intellectual ensign of his bitter rival Macready (1833).[1]

The egotistical Macready himself alternated the parts in this 'terrible duel between brain and heart' with the luckless George Vandenhoff in such a fashion as to make his own Iago the supreme puppet-master of the action, whilst when the roles were reversed his partner was reduced to a mere 'stoker' of Othello's emotions.[2] Henry Irving and the American Edwin Booth (Junius Brutus's son) engaged in a more amicable exchange of the leading roles at the Lyceum in 1881. Both were reckoned stronger as Iago. Booth's 'Byronic Moor' was the more successful of the two Othellos, proving (despite his conspicuous emotional restraint[3]) a surprisingly effective match for Irving's Iago, a mischievous bullfighter[4] whose veneer of gaiety only deepened the force of his secret malice. But in the end even the dignified anguish of Booth's 'noble savage' tended to be outshone by his rival's brilliant touches of invention—as when in Act 1, for example, Irving plucked and slowly devoured a bunch of grapes, 'spitting out the seeds, as if each one represented a virtue to be put out of his mouth', or when in Act 5 he 'turn[ed] over with his foot, in indolent and mocking curiosity, the body of Roderigo, to see if life were extinct'.[5]

---

[1] Potter, pp. 77–8; Hankey, pp. 60–1; Vaughan, pp. 139–40.

[2] George Vandenhoff, *Leaves from an Actor's Notebook* (1860), pp. 208–9, cited in Potter, p. 78.

[3] See Hankey, pp. 85–6; Rosenberg, pp. 79, 82, 126–8; Potter, pp. 40–2. For Booth, Othello's character showed not the slightest trace of 'animalism' or 'bestiality': 'to my mind he is pure and noble, even in his rage' (letter of 15 Feb. 1881, cited in Hankey, p. 85).

[4] The metaphor was Irving's own: 'To me [Iago] has . . . a slight dash of the bullfighter, and during the brawl between Cassio and Montano, I used to enjoy flicking at them with a red cloak, as though they were mere bulls in the arena' (cited in Rosenberg, p. 127).

[5] *Athenaeum* (7 May 1881); Ellen Terry, *The Story of My Life* (1908), p. 32.

12. 'Glittering, hellish, self-centred strength': Edwin Booth as Iago.

By contrast, Irving's 'plaintive and lachrymose' Moor, whose attempts at heroic passion made him resemble 'an infuriated sepoy', was so comprehensively upstaged by Booth's calmly plausible Iago (fig. 12), with his cold intelligence and 'glittering, hellish, self-centred strength', that Irving ended the season vowing never to play the lead again.[1] Even if Booth's Iago was by now a little old-fashioned, there was nothing in his rival's Othello to match the famous *coup de théâtre* after the Moor's suicide, in which Iago, 'brought down the final curtain, standing over Othello, pointing triumphantly at the dead body, and gazing up at the gallery with a

---

[1] William Winter, *The Life and Art of Edwin Booth* (1893), pp. 181–2, in Hankey, p. 94; *Athenaeum* (19 Feb. 1876), in Rosenberg, pp. 77 and p. 79. Although Booth's was clearly a more sober Iago than Irving's, he too believed that a comic touch was needed for the part (Potter, p. 81).

malignant smile'.[1] 'Had the play been acted before the Borgias', wrote an American reviewer, responding to a later Booth performance of the role, 'they would have looked on Othello as a stupid brute deserving not even pity, and Iago would have appealed to them as a hero. To the aesthetic sense of today . . . Iago, when perfectly interpreted, as only Booth can do it, is the richest intellectual (as distinct from emotional) treat in the literature of the drama.'[2]

The reviewer's anxiety about the extent of Booth's power over the audience was evident in his effort to displace his own response on to the machiavellian Borgias. But the perception of Othello as a 'stupid brute', encouraged by Iago's animal metaphors, was the inevitable outcome of an interpretation shaped by the bullfighting metaphor that was Irving's key to the central relationship. It is hardly surprising that the same metaphor was to become the most well-worn cliché of reviewing in the century of Iago-dominated productions ushered in by Irving and Booth.[3] It was they whose performances helped to establish Iago as the dramatic centre of the play, surpassing a tragic hero for whom 'we really feel not much more . . . than a half-familiar, half-contemptuous pity'.[4] The Iagos they presented, however, were very different from the resentful NCO who would emerge as the standard model for Shakespeare's ensign in the class-conscious Britain of the later twentieth century. Booth's was an Italianate intellectual, described as 'the epitome of the Latin temperament . . . [exhibiting] the inborn malice of a race in its decline—a race that substitutes subtlety for wasted strength',[5] while Irving's was a more English figure, an

---

[1] Richard Dickins, *Forty Years of Shakespeare on the English Stage* (London, n.d.), p. 40, in Hankey, p. 94; while this piece of stage business was already well established (Potter, p. 83), Booth seems to have made it especially chilling.

[2] Anonymous review pasted into Folger Promptbooks Oth. 46 and 48.

[3] See Rosenberg, p. 145; and cf. Ivor Brown, *Observer*, 26 July 1942 ('There stands Mr Valk, a burly, full-voiced and singularly static Moor. Round him skips the gleaming volatile Iago of Mr Bernard Miles, half-matador, half-Machiavel, planting the darts on the great bovine shoulders. The bull lashes out, gores his dearest, and dies in the ring amid assorted carrion, as of mutilated horses in the darling sport of holy Spain'); Brown, *Observer*, 21 Mar. 1953; Kenneth Tynan, *Observer*, 15 Oct. 1956 ; Alan Brien, *Sunday Telegraph*, 15 Oct. 1956 ('The combat in the play resembles far more a stolid, half-blind ox, tormented by a tiny, blood-drunk dog'); Robert Speaight, *Tablet*, 21 Oct. 1956; Alan Dent, *Sunday Telegraph*, 26 Apr. 1964; Tynan, pp. 2, 8.

[4] *Macmillan's Magazine* (July 1881), in Hankey, pp. 92–3.

[5] See above n. 2.

upper-class dandy and adventurer, an artist in evil who (though his mannerisms occasionally hinted at a private torment beneath the cool surface) took an almost urbane pleasure in the ingenuity of his own designs.[1]

The sheer éclat of Irving's Iago is a reminder that, however mistaken the tradition of burlesque villainy epitomized by Colley Cibber's performances, the most successful interpreters of the role have always known how to exploit its comic strain. But, as we shall see, this is also the aspect of the role that can most easily tilt the delicate equilibrium at the centre of the play, tipping it fatally in the direction of Iago's corrosive cynicism. This was what happened at the Old Vic in 1938, for example, when Tyrone Guthrie cast Laurence Olivier as a 'jovial, glib, bantering . . . good companion' against Ralph Richardson's sweetly reasonable but emotionally underpowered Moor.[2] Strongly influenced by their conversations with the Freudian luminary Ernest Jones, Guthrie and Olivier found a key to Iago's character in the notion that he was driven not by hatred, but by a sublimated homosexual passion for Othello. What might have been the basis of a powerful new interpretation seems to have been vitiated, however, by Richardson's inability or refusal to understand Olivier's approach.[3] Ivor Brown in the *Observer* thought this 'a radical and profoundly interesting' Iago: '[i]t abounds in comedy, which is most useful, because this tragedy has a kind of sensual squalor which is strangely different from Shakespeare's other pictures of sensuality'.[4] But most reviewers were baffled, and, missing the dark subtext of Olivier's performance, saw only the 'gadfly' undergraduate prankster, who played so exuberantly to the crowd as to make Richardson's performance appear even more 'heavy' and bloodless than it might otherwise have done.[5] Moreover, as Brown later observed, '[I]f Iago is the patently volatile and sinister creature that Mr Laurence Olivier recently and vividly made him, nobody can believe his honesty, and so the story of Othello's credulity becomes impossible.'[6]

---

[1] Potter, pp. 83–4.

[2] Ivor Brown, *Observer*, and James Agate, *Sunday Times*, both 8 Feb. 1938.

[3] Potter, p. 92; Rosenberg, pp. 158–9.

[4] See above, n. 2.

[5] *The Times*, 9 Feb. 1938.

[6] Ivor Brown, *Observer*, 16 Apr. 1939. Reports of Sam Wanamaker's 'loud and often funny' Iago at Stratford in 1956 suggest that the success of this 'slick shyster' in gulling the other characters also tested the audience's belief (Potter, p. 130).

Similar problems beset Michael Benthall's production at the Old Vic in 1956, when John Neville and Richard Burton renewed the old Victorian device of exchanging parts on alternate nights. Neville's 'capering spiv' of an Iago, according to Kenneth Tynan, reduced the central conflict to 'a drab squabble between the Chocolate Soldier and the Vagabond King', whereas Burton's Iago, despite the inadequate scale of Neville's 'tormented sheikh' (a 'thinking Othello' who, according to Milton Shulman, 'resemble[d] some Ethiopian lawyer studying a brief'[1]), brought the production alive. 'Paradoxically,' Tynan reflected, 'the only way to play Iago is to respect the Moor. Let Iago mock the Moor with cheap laughs, and the play collapses: it becomes the farce of an idiot gull instead of the tragedy of a master-spirit. Mr Burton never underestimates Othello, nor in consequence do we. His Iago is dour and earthy enough to convince any jury in the world. He does not simulate sincerity, he embodies it. . . . the imposture is total and terrifying.'[2]

The successful Othellos of the eighteenth and nineteenth centuries had taken their cue from the great Restoration tragedian, Thomas Betterton, who was equally admired for his 'commanding mien of majesty' and for the physical intensity with which he expressed 'such a variety and vicissitude of passions as would admonish a man to be afraid of his own heart'.[3] Not every tragedian could rise to Betterton's heroic style, however: James Quin's stiffly declamatory manner fitted the dignity, but not the passion of the part; David Garrick—though he imagined the Moor as 'an African in whose veins circulated fire instead of blood . . . [whose] character could excuse all boldness of expression and all exaggerations of passion', and though he was determined to paint Othello's 'passion in all its violence'—was unable to match Betterton's majesty of stature and demeanour. This exposed him to the mockery of Quin, who claimed to have seen 'a little black boy . . . fretting and fuming about the stage; but . . . no Othello'.[4] Kemble, on the other hand, though admired for grandeur, occasional pathos,

---

[1] *Evening Standard*, 23 Feb. 1956.   [2] *Observer*, 26 Feb. 1956.
[3] Colley Cibber in Fone (ed.), *Apology*, p. 65; Richard Steele, *The Tatler*, 167 (2 May 1710)—both cited in Hankey, p. 29.
[4] Frank Hedgecock, *A Cosmopolitan Actor: David Garrick and his French Friends* (1912), p. 341 n.; William Cooke, *Memoirs of the Life of Charles Macklin* (1804), p. 113, in Rosenberg, pp. 40, 42. See also Hankey, pp. 36–8.

and the 'mantle of mysterious solemnity' in which he wrapped the character, nevertheless seemed too philosophical and restrained, too coldly 'European' to rise to the sublimity of Othello's great poetic arias.[1] In the whole eighteenth century, perhaps only Spranger Barry's Moor, with his superb physique and magnificent deportment, was able to run the gamut from 'dignified and manly forbearance' in the early scenes, through tenderness and doubt, to extravagant grief and 'an amazing wildness of rage'[2] in which '[y]ou could observe the muscles stiffening, the veins distending, and the red blood boiling through his dark skin—a mighty flood of passion accumulating for several minutes—and at length bearing down its barriers and sweeping onward in thunder, love, reason, mercy, all before it'.[3]

Equally powerful was the high-Romantic Othello of Edmund Kean (fig. 13). 'To play Othello properly,' wrote Hazlitt in his review of Kean's rival, Macready, an actor 'ought to look taller and grander than any tower'[4]—an effect that some eighteenth- and nineteenth-century actors sought to achieve with the aid of costuming. Kean, however, lacked the heroic stature of most successful Othellos—a handicap which he overcame by sheer force of personality. His fury struck G. H. Lewes as 'lion-like', and he reminded Keats of a 'wild dog [feasting on] the savage relics of an Eastern conflict'.[5] Kean's '[terrific] energy of passion', showing 'all the wild impetuosity of barbarous revenge [to be expected of] the untamed children of the sun, whose blood drinks up the radiance of fiercer skies', was ultimately sufficient to overcome even the initial scepticism of Hazlitt, who sought more brooding imagination in the role.[6] For all the emotional extravagance of his acting, how-

[1] James Boaden, *Memoirs of the Life of John Philip Kemble* (1825), pp. 292, 256, in Rosenberg, pp. 43–4. See also Hankey, pp. 48–50.
[2] John Bernard, *Retrospections of the Stage*, ii. 26, in Rosenberg, p. 45. See also Hankey, pp. 41–4.
[3] Aaron Hill, *Works*, 4 vols. (1753), i. 217–18, in Rosenberg, pp. 45–6.
[4] *The Examiner*, 13 Oct. 1816.
[5] Henry Crabb Robinson, *Diary, Reminiscences and Correspondence*, ed. Thomas Sadler, 2 vols. (1872), i. 225, in Hankey, p. 58; G. H. Lewes, *On Actors and the Art of Acting* (New York, 1956), p. 18, in Rosenberg, p. 62.
[6] William Hazlitt, *Works*, ed. P. P. Howe, 21 vols. (1930), xviii. 263, v. 216, 271, in Hankey, pp. 57–8. See also Rosenberg, pp. 61–9. However, Kean's 'violent, extravagant, and unnatural' display of passion was insufficient to convince William Robson that he was watching anything 'but a little vixenish black girl in short petticoats' (cited in Hankey, p. 59).

13. The Romantic Othello: Edmund Kean as the first in a long line of lighter-skinned, orientalized Moors.

ever, it was Kean, with his light make-up, flowing Eastern garments, and habit of preparing himself by intoning passages from the Koran,[1] who initiated the orientalization of the Moor—the process that produced the increasingly restrained, gentlemanly protagonists of the Victorian era, from the intellectual and domestic Moor introduced by Macready (fig. 14) to Beerbohm Tree's majestic Arab nobleman (fig. 8).

Macready himself seems to have attempted a more emotionally extravagant interpretation of the part in later productions;[2] but it was the Victorian domestication of the role that he initiated which made the outsized Othellos of Tommaso Salvini and Ernesto Rossi in the 1870s and 1880s appear so devastatingly effective—even though they could play the part only by the odd expedient of speaking in their native Italian, whilst the remainder of the cast usually

---

[1] Potter, p. 36.
[2] Potter, pp. 37–8.

14. The Moor domesticated—William Charles Macready's
Victorian Othello.

performed in English. At the opposite extreme from the sensitive poetic Moor offered by their contemporary Edwin Booth, these were performances that reduced the role to bare emotion, in which mere words were of incidental significance. Indeed, the fact that these Othellos spoke in a foreign tongue incomprehensible to most of the audience probably strengthened the impression of exotic barbarity and ferocious animality on which commentators invariably remarked.[1]

---

[1] Tellingly, the Czech actor, Frederick Valk, praised by Agate as 'the best Othello since Salvini' seems to have achieved his success as much *because of* as in spite of his 'inability to speak English verse like an Englishman'. Since Englishness had come to be seen as a 'handicap' in this part, a touch of foreignness was deemed helpful in bringing out the 'child and savage' in Othello—see James Agate, *The Times*, 26 July 1942; W. A. Darlington, *The Times*, 23 July 1942.

Although Salvini, a light-skinned, turbaned Othello whose robes were carefully modelled on paintings of fifteenth-century Moors, outwardly conformed to the orientalized style of Victorian protagonists, critics stressed the non-European quality of his performance, even seeing it as distinctively 'African'.[1] This, together with his interpretation of the role as involving the unsuccessful struggle of a semi-civilized barbarian to repress his innate savagery, encouraged the notion that the role was somehow of its nature beyond the reach of English actors.[2] But a more accurate lesson from Salvini's extraordinary triumph—and indeed from Olivier's a century later—might simply be that to bring Othello off successfully an actor must submit himself fully to the sheer theatricality of the part. This at least was the opinion of Godfrey Tearle, perhaps the most generally admired of twentieth-century Othellos, whose 1948 performance appeared to 'dwarf all other recent attempts at the character'.[3] Tearle's was an Othello 'in the grand manner, in which dramatic gesture and a towering presence play[ed] second fiddle only to a wonderful feeling for the music and magic of Shakespeare's words'.[4] Preparing for the role, Tearle pronounced himself 'in complete agreement with Bernard Shaw's brilliant comments on *Othello*', citing at length Shaw's description of its sublime word-music, which expressed 'exactly what I am trying to achieve in the play'.[5]

Comparing Tearle's Moor with those of recent rivals, Alan Dent likened him to 'a venerable yew surrounded by thunderbolts and all but riven by them'; rejoicing that there was 'ham enough' in this performance 'to make the very young stare, look pale, and stop chatting', Dent went on to argue that 'if you do not bring a quality of "ham" to Othello, the character just disappears'.[6] The reason, Bamber Gascoigne would later suggest when reviewing John Gielgud's disastrous Othello, is that an element of 'ham' is inscribed in the character of Othello himself:

---

[1] See e.g. James, pp. 173–5, cited in Hankey, pp. 86, 90, Rosenberg, p. 115; and cf. Vaughan, p. 165.
[2] See Rosenberg, pp. 103, 111; Vaughan, p. 167; Potter, p. 46.
[3] 'G.P.', *Manchester Guardian*, 2 Aug. 1948.
[4] Brian Harvey, *Birmingham Evening Dispatch*, 31 July 1948.
[5] Interview in the *Warwick Advertiser*, 30 July 1948.
[6] *Observer*, 1 Aug. 1948; Harold Hobson offered a similarly favourable conspectus in the *Sunday Times* a week later.

He crams his speeches with long words and learned allusions like an illiterate who has just bought an encyclopaedia. And his melodramatics are crucial to the play. How else can one believe in his stupidity, unless it is because the whole drama of jealousy mysteriously attracts him . . . This love of bombast, being itself a quality that has to do with 'performance', forces on the actor one particular style—the grand style.[1]

For Dent, however, even Tearle's performance fell somewhere short of the full extravagance demanded by the exoticism of the part: 'Mr Tearle plays Othello as well as *any pure Englishman* may hope to play him', he concluded, suggesting that it was only 'the dash of Romany in Kean that brought his Othello to its final famed perfection'.[2]

Such embarrassing appeals to racial essentialism would hardly be worth retailing if they did not relate so directly to a casting problem that has beset the play for more than a century. Responding to Anthony Quayle's performance in 1953, Harold Hobson lamented that while 'theatrical annals are full of stories about the great things done by Othellos of the past . . . no recent Othello, not even the late Sir Godfrey Tearle, has won such notices; we seem now to have lost the trick of acting this play'.[3] The trick was certainly not available to John Gielgud, arguably the greatest Shakespearian actor of the century, when he attempted the part in Franco Zeffirelli's Stratford production of 1961. Despite his physical resemblance to 'a rather prim Indian civil servant', most critics agreed that Gielgud's 'nobility [was] absolute'; and his 'vocal virtuosity [in] the recital of the Othello music'—'a torrent of operatic sound'—was widely praised;[4] but in the scenes of passion 'a querulous maniac took over and the performance deteriorated into an orgy of clawing, clutching, and ranting gestures'.[5] To Milton Shulman he resembled 'an hysterical aunt', while for Bamber

---

[1] *Spectator*, 20 Oct. 1956.

[2] *Observer*, 1 Aug. 1948.

[3] *Sunday Times*, 21 Mar. 1953. Cf. Ruth Ellis's review of the same production in the *Stratford Herald*, 28 Nov. 1952: 'The large—and, in part savage—simplicity of Othello does not lend itself to many of the endearing graces that the public expects in leading actors. There is the choice of wresting the whole play to tune with a perfect English gentleman in the name part, or risking playgoers' sympathies by trying to stick to Shakespeare.'

[4] 'W.H.W.', *Birmingham Mail*, 11 Oct. 1961; J. C. Trewin, *Birmingham Post*, 11 Oct. 1961, *Illustrated London News*, 21 Oct. 1961; *The Times*, 11 Oct. 1961.

[5] Milton Shulman, *Evening Standard*, 15 Oct. 1961.

Gascoigne, his inability to rise to the grand style reduced Othello's 'exhibitionism' to comedy: 'After Othello had reeled about the stage . . . for some time, uttering sharp cries of jealousy, I became convinced that what we were watching must be *Le Jaloux*, a long-lost comedy by Molière.'[1]

Gielgud was probably not helped by Ian Bannen's Iago: Bannen had revived Olivier's idea of a homosexually motivated tempter, but his failure to exploit the comic side of the role reduced the villain to 'a jabbering psychopath . . . in whose teeming breast nihilism and asceticism fight their deadly battle'.[2] However, to most reviewers the main weakness of the production seemed to lie in Gielgud himself—especially his failure to realize what J. C. Trewin described as 'the primitive side of the Moor. . . . [H]e is always white, clean white inside. His inflammability is not naturally racial.'[3] A great deal about Laurence Olivier's much discussed performance in the production by John Dexter at the Old Vic in 1964 can be explained in terms of his strenuous reaction to the lessons of Gielgud's failure: if Gielgud's Moor had seemed too sensitive and civilized, then the keynote of Olivier's performance would be pride and barbaric glamour; if Gielgud had been a tenor in a bass role,[4] then Olivier would lower his own voice to a rich baritone;[5] if Gielgud had seemed too 'white', Olivier, with his elaborate pastiche of African (or was it Caribbean?) speech, movement and gesture, would set out to be the 'blackest' Othello the English stage had yet seen.[6] From his celebrated first appearance, sniffing at a long-stemmed pink rose as he lolled against the set, through the famous moment in his revenge speech (3.3.460) when he tore off the crucifix that had become the symbol of his adopted Christian identity, to his final descent into 'an irrational, animal-like

---

[1] *Spectator*, 20 Oct. 1961.

[2] *Daily Mail*, 11 Oct. 1961.

[3] Trewin, *Birmingham Post*, 11 Oct. 1961.

[4] W. A. Darlington, *Daily Telegraph*, 11 Oct. 1961.

[5] See Tynan, p. 4, for Orson Welles's protests about Olivier's limitations as 'a natural tenor'; Olivier's own comments on his efforts to master the 'dark violet, velvet stuff' in this 'bass part' in Richard Meryman, 'The Great Sir Laurence', *Life*, 36:9 (18 May 1964), p. 74.

[6] While critics were significantly divided as to whether Olivier's Moor was West African or West Indian, all were struck by his self-conscious parade of blackness—see e.g. Herbert Kretzmer, *Daily Express*, 22 Apr. 1964: 'Has Othello, I wonder, ever been played by quite so black a man?'

state',[1] Olivier's Othello was the antithesis of Gielgud's noble but dangerously fragile lyricist. This was a Moor whose passionate sensuality proved to be simply the more attractive face of the unbridled savage set loose by Iago's machinations. Olivier might have delivered Othello's traveller's tales in 1.3 with an edge of irony, as though aware that this was the sort of exoticism that a white audience would expect; but it was primitive superstition as much as Christian piety that made him cross himself at Brabantio's accusations of witchcraft.[2]

As if learning a lesson from Errol John's difficulties when he played Othello in the same theatre a year earlier, Olivier was determined that there should be no contest with his Iago. 'Physically and vocally . . . too small for the part', and further handicapped by his youth, John found himself (like so many twentieth-century Othellos) paired with an Iago whose relish for the comic possibilities of his role made him a dangerously commanding theatrical presence: this was the ebullient Leo McKern, an older and more experienced performer, who had already outplayed Anthony Quayle's Othello a decade earlier.[3] Olivier was convinced that if 'no English actor in [the twentieth] century had succeeded in the part', it was mainly because '[t]he play . . . belonged to Iago, who could always make the Moor look a credulous idiot'. If he took on the challenge, he insisted, then he must not have 'a witty, Machiavellian Iago [but] a solid, honest-to-God N.C.O.'[4] This was precisely what he got from Frank Finlay (fig. 15), whose deliberately prosaic vocal style and tightly controlled underplaying contrasted as sharply with Olivier's florid histrionics as his drab costume with the latter's loose, flamboyant robes and barbaric jewellery. In the eyes of many critics, Olivier's Moor seemed to hark back to the great Othellos of the Romantic era: Alan Dent recalled G. H. Lewes's nostalgic question, 'When shall we see [again] that lion-like power and

---

[1] Tynan, pp. 6, 9; Harold Hobson, *Sunday Times*, 26 Apr. 1964 (Tynan, pp. 104–5); Richard Christiansen, *Chicago Daily News*, 23 May 1964. In a variation on Olivier's gesture that beautifully concentrated the destructive contradictions of his being, Mendes (National, 1997) had David Harewood stab himself in the neck with a blade concealed in his equally prominent crucifix, on which he and Iago had sworn their oaths at the end of the temptation scene (3.3).

[2] See Tynan, p. 6.

[3] *The Times*, 31 Jan. 1963.

[4] Tynan, p. 2.

15. 'A figment of a white man's imagination': Sir Laurence Olivier as
Othello, Frank Finlay as Iago (National Theatre, 1964).

. . . grace—that dreadful culmination of wrath, alternating with
bursts of agony, that Kean gave us?', and then announced '[t]he
answer is here and now with the Olivier Othello'.[1] Just as Kean
had seemed to Dumas *père* 'a wild beast, half-man, half tiger',[2] so
Olivier appeared to Bernard Levin 'as though a wild beast has been
sewn up inside him and is clawing to get out'.[3]

---

[1] *Financial Times*, 22 Apr. 1964 (Tynan, p. 102). By contrast, Alan Brien saw this
as 'the splendid last fling of a declining style of acting' (*Sunday Telegraph*, 26 Apr.
1964; Tynan, pp. 103–4).
[2] As cited by Dent, *Financial Times*.
[3] *Daily Mail*, 22 Apr. 1964 (Tynan, p. 103).

If Olivier's combination of aristocratic swagger and savage otherness was largely created by the very 'elements of . . . the all-stops-out "ham" acting'[1] that Gascoigne had missed in Gielgud, the restrained naturalism of Finlay's performance asked to be read as both a class and an ethnic marker. But it also helped to ensure Olivier's effortless dominance of the stage. This Iago might be the 'ring-master' of his own sadistic circus, but the peak of his psychological control was to be expressed in a watchful stillness: at the climax of the temptation scene he would remain immobile, Dexter suggested, giving the Moor only 'an occasional flick of the whip—like "Nay, that's not your way"—to keep him in order';[2] it was Olivier 'circl[ing] the stage, a caged jungle king *in extremis*' who was to be the primary focus of attention.

Ironically enough, in Stuart Burge's screen version, to which Finlay's underplaying was naturally attuned, this carefully contrived imbalance was reversed, making Olivier's theatricality seem fatally overblown; and, for those who have encountered it only through the film, the power of Olivier's stage performance has become difficult to re-imagine. Perhaps this was indeed, as Alan Brien conjectured, 'the splendid last fling of a declining style of acting';[3] for, while the years since Dexter's production have yielded a series of brilliant Iagos, they have failed to produce a single Othello to match the charismatic energy of Olivier. Thus, though it received mixed notices and was so comprehensively overshadowed by Olivier's Moor, Frank Finlay's Iago has proved in the end to be the more influential performance. Finlay's conception of the villain involved two main sources of motivation—sexual nausea and class resentment. Perhaps affected by Micheál MacLiammóir's performance in Orson Welles's film,[4] as well as by Olivier's earlier conception of the part, Finlay thought of Iago as a man whose personality was deformed by his repressed homosexuality. This sexual pathology would be more elaborately developed by later Iagos, including David Suchet (1985), Ian McKellen (1989), Simon Russell Beale (1997), and Richard McCabe (1999);[5] but in Finlay's

---

[1] Alan Seymour in Tynan, p. 14.

[2] John Dexter in Tynan, p. 10.

[3] *Sunday Telegraph*, 26 Apr. 1964.

[4] See Potter, pp. 143–4, 146.

[5] In Oliver Parker's 1995 film, Kenneth Branagh played yet another impotent, wife-beating Iago, but in his case the strongest suggestion of homosexuality came in a scene with Roderigo (Potter, p. 195).

case unacknowledged desire for Othello was conceived as part of a carefully layered set of motives and would be allowed to surface only at certain key moments—as for instance in the temptation scene, when (as Iago whispered his poisons in Othello's ear) 'the two men . . . sway[ed] together in a sickening rhythm that suggest[ed] a bond uniting them closer than marriage'.[1] Unlike some later Iagos in this tradition, including McKellen and Kenneth Branagh (1995), who found in Iago's reflections on his supposed cuckoldry a source of deep, pathological resentment, Finlay delivered his soliloquies in an almost offhand fashion—as though explanation were something offered merely to satisfy the foolish curiosity of his audience. A more conspicuous source of bitterness was supplied by the class difference insisted on by Olivier, and emphasized by Finlay's flat regional accent. If this, together with his buff-coated plainness helped to make him, in the eyes of one critic, 'the only [Iago] I have ever seen who comes near to justifying the title "honest" ',[2] it also contributed to a strong sense that class resentment fuelled the racial hatred of this 'redneck' bigot. Here Finlay was following a line of interpretation that seems to have begun with Anthony Quayle's 'Liverpudlian spiv' in Tearle's 1948 production, and which (despite its demonstrable anachronism) his own performance seems to have cemented as an orthodoxy.[3]

Thus, although John Barton's 1971 production for the RSC was conceived in conscious reaction against Dexter and Olivier, it

---

[1] Hobson, *Sunday Times*.

[2] Bamber Gascoigne, *Observer*, 26 Apr. 1964 (Tynan, pp. 107–8).

[3] Brian Harvey, *Birmingham Evening Dispatch*, 31 July 1948. However, Potter (p. 187) cites a 1929 Birmingham Repertory Theatre production for which the programme listed Iago as 'Staff Sergeant Major'. Apart from those discussed below, other Iagos in this tradition have included John Neville at the Old Vic in 1956—a 'rough-spoken, cruelly leering corner boy' (*The Times*, 22 Feb. 1956); Bob Hoskins in Jonathan Miller's 1981 production for BBC television—a 'cheerfully psychotic' cockney thug (Potter, p. 155); Philip Whitchurch's 'scouse' Iago at the Lyric, Hammersmith, in 1984; Paul Barber's Lancashire-accented corporal at the Greenwich Theatre (1989); Paul Whitworth's cockney RSM at Santa Cruz (1997); and Rupert Wickham's 'nerdish Essex-man squaddie' at the Cochrane Theatre in 2002 (Patrick Marmion, *Evening Standard*, 7 Feb. 2002). Anachronistic though its class assumptions may be, this tradition has become so entrenched in British theatre that when the English director Jude Kelly staged *Othello* in 1997 for the Shakespeare Theatre in Washington, DC, Ron Canada's Iago was presented as a burly, rather sullen Sergeant, given to vulgarly obscene gestures—even though the class suggestions of such a characterization did not map particularly well on to the American military setting of the production.

included an Iago who was indentifiably kin to Finlay's. Barton sought in a number of ways to deflect attention from the contemporary racial resonances that had been so important for Dexter's production: he relocated the action to a Victorian colonial setting, a 'Kiplingesque cantonment', 'heavy with the fantasies of men herded together in the heat';[1] while Brewster Mason's rather pale-skinned Moor deliberately eschewed any suggestion of primitive emotion. Arguably an Iago who was once again an alienated NCO, driven by bitterness over class and rank, was better suited to this conception of the play than to Dexter's.[2] But Emrys James, who exploited the comic side of the role more than Finlay had done, easily upstaged Mason's noble but rather monotonous hero. James played the ensign as 'a Figaro in puttees', '[p]ink, brisk and bristly, with the foxy smile of a regimental clown'; by turns 'frivolous', 'volatile', and ghoulishly psychopathic,[3] his was a performance that once again illustrated the dangers of allowing Iago to monopolize the play's theatricality. Barton, complained Jeremy Kingston, had made James 'the puppetmaster' and had directed Mason 'to be his creature': the result, according to Frank Marcus, more resembled the 'tragi-comedy of Iago' than the tragedy of Othello.[4]

Something similar happened in each of the three important *Othellos* that followed, beginning with Ronald Eyre's production for the RSC in 1979: transferring from Stratford to the Aldwych in 1980, it ran opposite Peter Hall's version at the National Theatre, prompting the *Evening Standard* to announce a theatrical duel between the rival principals.[5] But in each case, as with Jonathan Miller's production for the BBC Shakespeare in the following year, it was Iago who seemed to dominate. In the RSC *Othello* Sinden's

---

[1] Gareth Lloyd Evans, *Guardian*, 10 Sept. 1971. Dexter's conception of Cyprus seems to have been borrowed from the Russian director Konstantin Stanislavski, who suggested that 'Cyprus, Candia, and Mauritania [should be seen as] conquered provinces, under the heavy heel of Venice. . . . The arrogant Doges, Senators, and aristocrats do not look upon the conquered people as human beings' (*Creating a Role*, trans. Elizabeth Reynolds Hapgood (New York, 1961; repr. 1989), pp. 168–9, cited in Potter, p. 99).

[2] B. A. Young, *Financial Times*, 10 Sept. 1971; Jeremy Kingston, *Punch*, 22 Sept. 1971.

[3] Ronald Bryden, *Observer*, 12 Sept. 1971; B. A. Young, *Financial Times*, 10 Sept. 1971.

[4] *Punch*, 22 Sept. 1971; *Sunday Telegraph*, 12 Sept. 1971.

[5] '*Othello*: Scofield v. Sinden', *Evening Standard*, 16 Mar. 1980.

'handsome, immaculately uniformed Moor' aimed for something of Olivier's largeness of scale, but struck one reviewer as having 'more of the operetta than grand opera about him'; his pastiche of 'melodramatic gesture and vocal mannerisms' remaining 'too superficial to invest the part with any sense of . . . the heroic or the tragic', with the result that he was generally overshadowed by Bob Peck's 'buoyant villainy' as Iago.[1] Michael Billington thought that Sinden caught 'something of the play's vulgar excitement' in the 'high ecstasy of jealousy' that reduced him to 'rifling though his wife's laundry basket for stained sheets';[2] but for most reviewers it was Peck's 'big, tough, reliable-looking NCO' who held centre stage.[3] Playing the ensign as 'an icy upstart, with a flat, faintly Lancashire voice and an indifferent, throwaway manner', he undermined Sinden's 'romantic style' by the way in which he seemed determined to reduce the action to 'a kind of cynical farce'.[4] The effect of this comic emphasis was to expose all of the improbabilities in the plot of which Iago-critics since Rymer had complained: 'As Othello picked up each hint, he got laughs . . . these were because of the incongruous speed with which Iago's poison was working. It was like watching a mere mechanical conjuring trick. . . . I felt sorry for him as I would for a dog being baited, but I couldn't in the end get involved.'[5]

The balance between Othello and Iago was almost equally lopsided in Peter Hall's production at the National Theatre in 1980. Here Michael Bryant, 'white-haired and clownish . . . the smiling villain of melodrama playing the innocent', 'a snickering charmer with an unsatisfied sexual itch', gave what one critic described as 'a performance so staggeringly apt that you want to get up and hit him'.[6] His Iago was generally felt to overmatch Paul Scofield's mannered Othello, which—while seldom rising to 'the full "ham"

---

[1] Ian Stewart, *Country Life*, 17 Apr. 1980.

[2] *Guardian*, 15 Aug. 1980. Eric Shorter described him as 'rummag[ing] through [the] basket with real passion and appetite, sniffing like a hound at the sheets' (*Daily Telegraph*, 9 Aug. 1979).

[3] Michael Billington, *Guardian*, 8 Aug. 1979.

[4] Shorter, *Telegraph*; Alan Drury, *Listener*, 16 Aug. 1979; Gareth Lloyd Evans, *Stratford Herald*, 10 Aug. 1979.

[5] Drury, *Listener*. The critical response to David Suchet's performance in Terry Hands's 1985–6 RSC production suggests that it produced much the same result.

[6] Stewart, *Country Life*; Michael Billington, 21 Mar. 1980; Barry Took, *Punch*, 2 Apr. 1980.

of the role'—remained theatrical in a way that for most critics distracted from the characterization, rather than informing it as Olivier's had. Robert Cushman thought that the self-regarding quality of the performance signalled acceptance of 'the Eliot-Leavis view of the Moor: an egotist who deserves even more than he gets';[1] but for others it seemed gratuitous: '[w]hat set . . . Mr Scofield apart', wrote James Fenton, '[was] not his blackness, but his acting'; this Othello 'was certainly not in love with his wife, but he had deep feelings for the audience to whom he would regularly appeal with looks that seemed to say: is this face of mine not truly remarkable? this voice not utterly profound? is not the white of this eye the whitest you ever saw?'[2]

For the BBC Jonathan Miller devised a consciously small-scale domestic production, its visual style shaped by seventeenth-century Dutch interior paintings, which virtually excluded *Othello*'s larger political and social concerns to concentrate on the story of a marriage destroyed by extreme jealousy and inexplicable malice. Believing the issue of Othello's colour to be a distraction, and one that risked racial stereotyping, Miller cast Anthony Hopkins as a conspicuously pale Moor, whose racial difference from the Venetians was barely marked even by costume; and his low-key naturalistic performance, suggesting an oddly withdrawn, sometimes ironic, sometimes slightly neurotic personality, left the screen to be dominated by Bob Hoskins's gleeful cockney Iago. Strongly influenced by Miller's reading of the celebrated W. H. Auden essay, 'The Joker in the Pack', Hoskins's was a performance full of comic relish and sniggering asides, whose keynote was established in the first scene, where a panicky Roderigo was repeatedly forced to restrain Iago's boisterous improvisation outside Brabantio's window. Othello's suicide evidently struck Iago as the best joke of all. This clearly was not a production that allowed much space for heroic gesture, even had Hopkins been interested in providing it. Across the Atlantic in Stratford, Connecticut (1981), James Earl Jones, who had been Miller's first choice for Othello, was just as easily upstaged by Christopher Plummer's flamboyant Iago, who (in an exaggerated version of Edwin Booth's famous coup)

---

[1] Robert Cushman, *Observer*, 23 Mar. 1980.
[2] James Fenton, *Sunday Times*, 23 Mar. 1980.

'ended the play by rising from the floor to wave his sash in the air and laugh in triumph'.[1]

By contrast, in Ben Kingsley and David Suchet, Terry Hands's 1985/6 production for the RSC at last found what Michael Billington thought were 'an Othello and Iago of equal weight and value'.[2] Billington praised Kingsley for offering 'not the usual coffee-stained clubman, but a poised, dignified Moor with a scimitar, and white flowing robes', a man with the intelligence and confidence to win over a hostile Senate with humour; and he was equally admiring of Suchet's Iago who was 'not the calculating Audenesque practical joker, but a crafty improviser forever thinking on his feet'. 'Memorably vile . . . a profane and laughing roisterer . . . seething with a dangerous vitality', Suchet was nevertheless praised as one of those rare Iagos who 'you would swear was dead honest'.[3] Because race and class were less important than sex in Hands's conception of the play, Kingsley could suggest that 'Othello and Iago are almost two faces of the same man. They are both suffering from the same psychological disturbance.'[4] Each, Kingsley and Hands believed, was possessed by covert desire for the other; and the programme included a long excerpt from a recent psychiatric text suggesting that neurotic jealousy like Othello's might have its basis in repressed homosexuality, while (like Olivier's and Finlay's) Suchet's Iago was shown as 'secretly possessed by homosexual longing for the Moor' and driven 'to destroy what he can never possess'.[5] The ambivalence of Iago's feelings emerged most tellingly when, after Othello's fit, Suchet cradled Kingsley's head in his hands, thereby revealing 'a . . . stunning shaft of sympathetic vulnerability in his portrayal'.[6]

For some critics this was 'the best *Othello* since Olivier'.[7] For all its strengths, however, the domestic scale of the production, together with the narrowness of political focus revealed by its

[1] Scott McMillin, 'Criticism and Productions of *Othello* since 1984', in the second edition of Sanders's New Cambridge *Othello* (2003), p. 56.

[2] *Guardian*, 26 Sept. 1985.

[3] John Barber, *Daily Telegraph*, 26 Sept. 1985.

[4] *Observer Colour Magazine*, 22 Sept. 1985.

[5] Nicholas de Jongh, *Guardian*, 9 Jan. 1986; Irving Wardle, *The Times*, 25 Sept. 1985.

[6] Michael Coveney, *Financial Times*, 9 Jan. 1986.

[7] Michael Ratcliffe, *Observer*, 29 Sept. 1985; and cf. Michael Coveney, *Financial Times*, 26 Sept. 1985.

refusal to distinguish between the ordered metropolitan world of Venice and the anarchic violence of colonial Cyprus, threatened to reduce it to a 'chamber tragi-comedy';[1] and Kingsley's inability to rise to the vocal challenge of 'that pervasive Othello music which . . . gives the play its humanity', together with Suchet's tendency to play for laughs, meant that even this Iago tended to 'cut the ground from under . . . Othello' and to 'displace . . . the Moor from the forefront of attention'.[2]

When Patrick Stewart undertook Othello in 1997, he was warned by a fellow actor that 'the role is simply unactable';[3] and looking back at the history of the part on the twentieth-century stage, Charles Merivale's insistence in 1902 that Iago is the true centre of this tragedy begins to seem prophetic. In this whole period it is possible to single out no more than four outstandingly successful Othellos: of these, the triumphs of Paul Robeson and John Kani had as much to do with political context and the personal heroism of the two actors as with the intrinsic quality of their performances, whilst Godfrey Tearle's and Laurence Olivier's performances (for all the latter's ostentatious mimicry of contemporary black style) relied on personal magnetism combined with a deliberate reversion to the histrionic extravagance of Victorian heroic acting. If the naturalistic acting encouraged by film and television has made Olivier's style of heroic impersonation seem conspicuously outmoded, it has also (as both Julie Hankey and Lois Potter point out[4]) seemed to put a swagger-part like Othello beyond the reach of most contemporary actors. In so far as they have attempted to rise to the emotional theatricality of the role, they have often succeeded in arousing laughter, making the hero 'something of an embarrassment, [like] an eccentric guest, stumbling in on an intelligent conversation, out of another period, another play'.[5]

Powerful Iagos, by contrast, have been more and more the rule. The success of David Calder, as yet another 'hard-bitten N.C.O.' at the Young Vic in 1984—'a coarse, vulgar manipulator, with a

---

[1] De Jongh, *Guardian*; Ratcliffe, *Observer*.

[2] John Barber, *Daily Telegraph*, 26 Sept. 1985; Delia Couling, *Tablet*, 18 Jan. 1986; de Jongh, *Guardian*.

[3] Interview with David Richards, *Washington Post*, 12 Nov. 1997.

[4] Hankey, pp. 119–20, Potter, p. 153.

[5] Hankey, p. 119.

dirty mind and a sweaty body'—was enough to make one critic understand 'why Verdi nearly called his opera *Iago*';[1] and the drift towards full realization of Merivale's Iago-centred play probably reached its apogee in the dazzling performances of Ian McKellen (1989) and Simon Russell Beale (1997).

In Trevor Nunn's production, staged at RSC's studio theatre, The Other Place, and subsequently filmed for television, McKellen was cast opposite the Jamaican-born opera singer, Willard White. With his 'leonine' gait and appearance, and a voice 'of matchless power and resonance' White was an impressive and dignified Moor, whose performance was characterized by a certain 'old-fashioned grandeur'; but while his 'imperious rages' made a strong impression, he 'lack[ed] that tiger-like bestiality which Henry James found in the great Salvini'; and missing the 'heroic self-dramatization' of Olivier, he was reckoned even less successful at sounding 'the famous Othello music' which conveys the deep anguish of the part.[2] As a result White was inevitably overmatched by McKellen's 'devastating performance' as 'a sturdy, buttoned-down, bottled-up redneck NCO' with a Hitler moustache, a 'ramrod-straight back . . . , clipped Northern consonants', and a neurotic passion for tidiness.[3] Fixing his victims with 'the hypnotic snake-stare of true paranoia', this was a man 'with the soul of a servant and the instincts of a destroyer'.[4] In Michael Billington's judgement McKellen's was 'the most complex and fascinating Iago since that of . . . Emrys James'[5]—from which indeed much of its inspiration derived. Unlike James and many other dominant Iagos, however, McKellen—though he used his soliloquies to draw the audience into uneasy complicity—did not exploit the comic side of the character. Instead he riveted viewers' attention by means of the psychological intensity that informed the minutest details of his meticulously observed performance: his hoarding of '[a] little

---

[1] Michael Billington, *Guardian*, 11 May 1984; Brian Masters, *The Standard*, 14 May 1984; Martin Hoyle, *Financial Times*, 12 May 1984.

[2] Harry Eyres, *The Times*, 26 Aug. 1989; John Peter, *Sunday Times*, 27 Aug. 1989; Maureen Paton, *Daily Express*, 25 Aug. 1989; Michael Billington, *Guardian*, 26 Aug. 1989. Michael Coveney, however, hailed White as 'probably the first genuinely monumental black Othello . . . since Paul Robeson's in 1959' (*Financial Times*, 26 Aug.).

[3] Peter, *Sunday Times*; Coveney, *Financial Times*; Billington, *Guardian*.

[4] Jack Tinker, *Daily Mail*, 26 Aug. 1989.

[5] Billington, *Guardian*.

baccy-tin for half smoked cheroots'; 'the obsessive way he tidie[d] his barrack-room blankets' or anxiously gathered up fallen papers even as Othello was threatening to kill him; the display of false warmth with which he repeatedly embraced other characters; his careful ritualization of the mock-marriage that climaxes the temptation scene. At the end of the play, in a signature that recalled Edwin Booth's famous coup, McKellen was left to survey the carnage he had created, 'his pallid face staring down on [the] corpses [of his victims] with nothing more than blank curiosity in his dead eyes'.[1] As the *Times* reviewer observed, the problem with such a bravura display of technique is that Iago's 'victims become too easily . . . the asses he considers them to be'.[2] If White was powerful and dignified enough to fend off this danger, he still had nothing to match the sinister allure of a performance in which almost every line was decorated with some piece of beguiling business.[3]

Nunn's colonial Cyprus was a 'heat-crazed province' under military occupation, and the scenes there were full of the seamy claustrophobia of a male-dominated barrack-room world.[4] It was a remarkably similar world that Sam Mendes created for the National Theatre in 1997, except that the action was pushed forward from Edwardian times to the imperial twilight of the 1930s. This setting enabled Simon Russell Beale's 'almost too intelligent' Iago to develop the hints of fascism in McKellen's martinet, whose buttoned-up, anal-retentive characterization he had evidently studied. Better known as a comic actor, Beale made use of an impeccable sense of timing to manipulate the audience's response, without actually playing for laughs. He capitalized on his stout, rather ungainly physical appearance, coarsening his plump features with a brutal crew-cut to create an Iago whose sense of class inferiority was exacerbated by his physical unattractiveness (fig. 16), and cruelly exposed by the rogue vowels that cut through his carefully cultivated middle-class accent. Resembling a 'squat, psychotic toad', or a 'terrifyingly articulate, obscenely cunning slug', Beale was 'a Thersites pretending to be one of the boys'; '[b]rimming with aggressive geniality', he was nevertheless 'an

---

[1] Tinker, *Mail*; Potter, pp. 191–2.
[2] Eyres, *The Times*.
[3] Potter, p. 192.
[4] Tinker, *Mail*; Coveney, *Financial Times*.

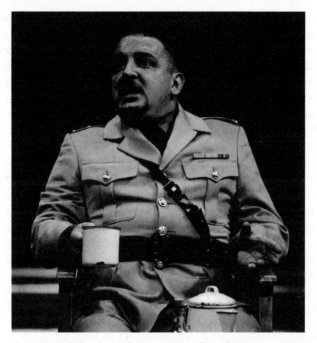

16. Drama of class hatred: Simon Russell Beale's Iago as 'tragic
bureaucrat' (Royal National Theatre, 1997).

unmistakable sadist' with a dangerously short fuse, who viciously
dashed a despatch box from a desk on 'I hate the Moor' (1.3.375),
and who contemptuously kicked Othello as he lay unconscious
after his fit in 4.1. Capable of what might even have been taken for
real tenderness in the brothel scene when he urged Desdemona 'Do
not weep' (4.2.124), he exhibited a nauseated aversion for his own
wife, which was only matched by the visceral self-disgust that had
him retching at the end of the temptation scene. Beale exploited
every psychological nuance in the text, making it plain that the
hatred and contempt seething beneath his acquiescent mask arose
from a genuinely 'gnawing conviction that Othello once bedded his
wife'.[1]

---

[1] Paul Taylor, *Independent*, 19 Sept. 1997; Charles Spencer, *Telegraph*, 18 Sept.
1997; Susannah Clapp, *Independent*, 21 Sept. 1997; John Gross, *Sunday Telegraph*,
21 Sept. 1997; Jane Edwardes, *Time Out*, 24 Sept. 1997.

Challenging the orthodox notion that Iago's express motives are simply improvised excuses, Beale made it plain that all of Iago's resentments, not least his bitterness over promotion, demanded to be taken entirely seriously, convincing John Peter that Coleridge's idea of 'motiveless malignity' had completely 'miss[ed] the point'.[1] At the dark heart of his 'sexually maimed' psyche there once again lay guilty sexual desire for the Moor: it was buried 'so deep that he hardly recognizes it in himself, but when he tenderly strokes Othello's cheek a window is thrown open on the play'.[2] Like McKellen's this was also a performance rich with telling detail:[3] as for instance at the end of 2.3, when Iago gleefully illustrated his plot with the same cards that he had just used to trick Cassio into his disastrous drinking bout, wickedly flourishing the Ace of Spades (Othello), the Queen of Hearts (Desdemona), and the Knave of Hearts (Cassio). Dubbed a 'Tragic Bureaucrat' by one American reviewer,[4] this Iago was an assiduous snapper up of unconsidered trifles, forever picking up dropped or discarded objects and stuffing them into his tight pockets for future use—so that the business with the handkerchief seemed less like a melodramatically contrived stratagem than the natural extension of a habit of politic thrift.[5]

Against '[t]his daredevil performance',[6] David Harewood's handsome but too youthful and emotionally limited Moor, with his sometimes oddly staccato or sing-song delivery, stood little chance. Mendes had planned to cast the more experienced Adrian Lester in the part, after failing to secure his original choice, the distinguished African American actor Morgan Freeman;[7] and either of these might have made for a better balanced production. Although Harewood was praised for the 'magnificent, monumental simplicity' of his conception, for the physical impressiveness of his

[1] *Sunday Times*, 21 Sept. 1997.
[2] Gross, *Sunday Telegraph*; Spencer, *Telegraph*.
[3] See also Robert Butler's perceptive review in the *Independent*, 21 Sept. 1997.
[4] Charles McNulty, *Village Voice*, 21 Apr. 1998, cited in Potter, p. 199.
[5] The handkerchief plot was more imaginatively handled in this than in any other production I know of: brilliantly exploiting the play's own propensity for blurring the boundaries of theatrical illusion, Mendes arranged that 'the fatal handkerchief gets left on the tiles throughout the interval, as if challenging one of us to pick it up and prevent a tragedy' (Butler, *Independent*).
[6] Butler, *Independent*.
[7] David Lister, *Independent*, 7 Aug. 1997.

performance, and for a moving last scene, there was a feeling that he '[did] not fully inhabit his role';[1] and the result was an entire consensus that this was Beale's play; indeed, the *Daily Mail* critic went so far as to repeat Verdi's suggestion that the tragedy 'should be retitled *Iago*'.[2]

So overwhelming was Beale's success that his performance seems to have provided an almost complete template for Richard McCabe's ensign in Michael Attenborough's RSC production (Stratford, 1999, and Barbican, 2000). Reflecting the same obsession with the imperial past that had coloured Nunn's and Mendes's productions, Attenborough once again located the main action in a Cyprus that resembled a British colonial outpost; and McCabe was yet another 'archetypal N.C.O.' '[P]allid and pudgy of face, but with neat military movements', 'poker-backed [and] pigeon-chested', McCabe was described, in language that recalls Beale, as a 'blend of slug, toad, and Fatty Arbuckle'.[3] Like Beale, he was older than his Othello (the text here was altered to make him speak of his '*five* times seven years', 1.3.304–5), and full of 'the instinctive misogyny that comes from a lifetime spent in a military environment'.[4] His pathological 'contempt for women, [and] distaste for physical contact' became particularly obvious 'when his poor wife kisse[d] him on the lips';[5] and he too took advantage of the mock-wedding at the end of the temptation scene to suggest 'a chilling . . . homoerotic current [between Iago and Othello] as they kneel almost mouth to mouth and become blood brothers'.[6] He also followed Beale's example in the way he exploited the comic conventions of his role to endow Iago with a 'disconcerting knack of turning the audience into his co-conspirators'—even as they were again made to feel that 'inside this uncannily contained fat man, there [was] a thin, violent psychopath trying to get out'.[7]

Although Ray Fearon's Moor—hailed as the first 'real black Othello' to appear on the Stratford main stage since Robeson—

[1] Peter, *Sunday Times*; Clapp, *Independent*; Alistair Macaulay, *Financial Times*, 18 Sept. 1997.
[2] *Daily Mail*, 18 Sept. 1997.
[3] Charles Spencer, *Telegraph*, 10 Jan. 2000; Michael Billington, *Guardian*, 7 Jan. 2000; Benedict Nightingale, *The Times*, 11 Jan. 2000.
[4] Potter, p. 208; Billington, *Guardian*.
[5] Nightingale, *The Times*.
[6] Nicholas de Jongh, *Evening Standard*, 22 Apr. 1999.
[7] Spencer, *Telegraph*; Paul Taylor, *Independent*, 10 Jan. 2000.

received generally more sympathetic notices than Harewood, the problem with Attenborough's production was essentially the same as with Mendes's, and with so many twentieth-century *Othellos*—that the audience's response to the hero was fatally distorted by Iago. So 'aggressively unappealing' did McCabe appear that it was hard to account for the trust reposed in him by his general, making one reviewer 'feel . . . like shouting out and telling Othello what a blind duped ass he is'.[1] By the time it reached London, Fearon's performance was enough to persuade Michael Billington that now the central action offered 'a thrilling contest of equal forces rather than a lopsided bullfight'; nevertheless most critics reckoned this Othello to be too young and vocally inexperienced to match the virtuoso performance of his opponent. Moreover the disproportionate space devoted to McCabe's Iago in nearly all reviews left little doubt that this had once again become Iago's play.[2]

Desdemona   Although the performance history of *Othello* over the last hundred years illustrates a growing difficulty in protecting the hero from his rival's tendency to usurp the central position, directors and actors have nevertheless made progress, especially in the latter part of the twentieth century, towards establishing a better balance between the competing sets of relationships around which the action revolves. If, as a result of both changed acting styles and new socio-political constraints, the part of Othello seems to have become increasingly inaccessible, then the roles of Desdemona and the other female characters have been significantly opened up by the advent of feminist approaches—in the theatre as much as in the study. At the beginning of the play's theatrical life, it was the spectacle of 'Desdemona, slain in our presence by her husband' that possessed Henry Jackson's imagination; and whatever dramatic capital Shakespeare may elsewhere have made by sophisticated reminders that his female characters were all in fact young males, for Jackson the illusion seems to have been complete, since his language implies no distinction between performer and role. Moreover, his use of the phrase *illa Desdemona* ('that Desdemona') seems to suggest that the heroine had become one of the more

---

[1] Nightingale, *The Times*; Spencer, *Telegraph*.
[2] De Jongh, *Evening Standard*; Billington, *Guardian*; Nick Curtis, *Evening Standard*, 7 Jan. 2000.

renowned characters on the early Jacobean stage.[1] At the end of the century, the murder scene could still produce open exhibitions of distress from spectators like Pepys's 'pretty lady [who] called out to see Desdemona smothered';[2] however, Thomas Rymer appeared to be in little doubt that the real heart of the action lay in the relationship between Othello and Iago. In his castigation of the tragedy, the 'poor chicken' Desdemona is mocked for her credulity and for the passivity of her response to Othello's volleys of 'scoundrel filthy language': '[w]ith us a tinker's trull would be nettled, would repartee with more spirit, and not appear so void of spleen'.[3] As a risible 'black swan' Desdemona participates in the general impossibility of the design,[4] but her function in the male-dominated drama of the Moor and his envious subordinate is conceived as a largely instrumental one.

In the eighteenth century Desdemona's role was significantly weakened by a number of cuts aimed at purging the women's speech of impropriety: the effect was to minimize her early independence of spirit, and to remove all evidence of her frank and innocent sensuality—the very things that can make her so attractive to a modern audience. For nearly two hundred years, it became customary for English stages to omit most (if not all) of Act 4, Scene 3. Since the nostalgic sentiment of the Willow Song episode might seem perfectly calculated to appeal to popular taste in the eighteenth and nineteenth centuries, the excision is at first glance puzzling.[5] It is usually attributed to anxiety about the episode's potential effect on the pace of the tragic action; but Rymer's sarcastic dismissal of what he saw as 'a filthy sort of pastoral scene, where the wedding sheets and Song of Willow . . . are not the least moving things in this entertainment',[6] suggests that decorum was the real motive: the mildly bawdy tone of the women's

---

[1] Lois Potter (p. 5) thinks it 'more likely' that the wording refers to the fame of the boy actor involved; but the whole sentence suggests Jackson's complete imaginative submission to the pathos of wife-murder.

[2] Cited in Rosenberg, p. 19.

[3] Rymer, pp. 130–1.

[4] Rymer, p. 140.

[5] Educated taste, in the Augustan period at least, was another matter: Francis Gentleman derided this as a 'trifling' scene, dismissing Desdemona's song as a 'lamentable ditty' better calculated to make the audience laugh than weep (p. 146; cited in Potter, p. 16).

[6] Rymer, pp. 135–6.

conversation, and the subversive proto-feminism of Emilia's diatribe against husbands were felt to be improper, and to compromise
the self-sacrificial saintliness attributed to the heroine.[1]

While a different tradition developed on the Continent, where a
moralizing emphasis on Desdemona's transgressive defiance of her
father made the character seem stronger and more complex—even
if less admirable—the English approach to the heroine in this
period was unremittingly sentimental.[2] Pathos was so monotonously the keynote of eighteenth-century and Victorian Desdemonas that, while an actress with the dignity and emotional
strength of Sarah Siddons could make something of it, the part was
usually felt to offer fewer opportunities than that of Emilia, which
was sometimes given higher billing. In 1770 Francis Gentleman
thought that Emilia, with her 'well-contrasted spirit', showed
'much more life than her mistress';[3] and in 1845 Charlotte Cushman's Emilia reputedly upstaged even Edwin Forrest's powerful
Othello in the play's last scene.[4] Macready went so far as to warn
Fanny Kemble that 'there is absolutely nothing to be done with [the
part of Desdemona], nothing; nobody can produce an effect in it;
and really, Emilia's last scene can be made a great deal more of. I
could understand your playing that, but not Desdemona.'[5] Unfazed
by this dismal prognosis—though she herself had scorned Eliza
O'Neill's Desdemona as 'expressly devised for a representative
victim . . . the very beau ideal of feminine weakness'[6]—Kemble
took the role, investing the heroine's death scene with new power
by eschewing both the 'wonderful equanimity' of previous English
Desdemonas and the extreme terror of their Italian counterparts in
favour of fierce resistance: 'I think I shall make a desperate fight
of it,' she had promised, 'for I feel horribly at the idea of being

---

[1] See Rosenberg, pp. 25–6, 52–3, 135–40; Potter, pp. 49–56; Hankey, pp. 50–2.
Though Irving briefly reinstated the scene in 1876, it was not until Ellen Terry's performance in 1898 that the scene came back to stay—and even then Emilia's denunciation of husbands continued to be cut for some time (Potter, pp. 53–4).

[2] See Potter, pp. 57–67.

[3] Gentleman, p. 154, cited in Potter, p. 50.

[4] Potter, p. 52.

[5] Frances Kemble, *Records of Later Life* (1882), pp. 111, 380, cited in Rosenberg,
p. 135.

[6] Frances Kemble, *Records of a Girlhood* (New York, 1882), pp. 195–6, cited in Potter, p. 50.

murdered in my bed.'[1] Macready's principal leading lady, Helen Faucit, who also fought for her life in the murder scene, was equally adamant about the heroine's moral and emotional strength: in her reflections *On Some of Shakespeare's Female Characters* (1885), she mounted a spirited defence of the character against the charge that she is 'a merely amiable, simple yielding creature', insisting that Desdemona is 'in all things worthy to be a hero's bride'.[2] Between them, Kemble and Faucit helped prepare the way for the great late-Victorian Desdemona of Ellen Terry, who played opposite Booth and Irving in 1881. Although she continued to stress the heroine's purity and the pathos of her blind adoration and undeserved suffering, Terry emphasized the resilience of her character. Scorning the mistaken notion that 'Desdemona is a ninny, a pathetic figure chiefly because she is half-baked', and rejecting the consequent habit of casting 'an actress of the dolly type, a pretty young thing with a vapid, innocent expression', Terry insisted that 'a great tragic actress, with a strong personality and a strong method is far better suited to [the part], for Desdemona is strong, not weak. . . . by nature she is unconventional'. Once this was understood, then Othello himself would seem less absurdly credulous: 'Othello's doubts that she is chaste are usually made to seem absolutely monstrous in the theatre, because Desdemona's unconventionality is ignored. She is not at all prim and demure; on the contrary, she is genially expressive, the kind of woman who being devoid of coquetry behaves as she feels.'[3]

Such interventions, however, appear to have had little effect on the habitually saccharine treatment of the heroine. 'Poor Desdemona, if she has a fault it is that she is too passive, too unsuspecting', lamented the *Stratford Herald* in 1907, praising one Evelyn Millard as perfectly suited to a role which the reviewer saw as requiring 'an actress of womanly gentleness and tenderness—a generous, romantic creature, full of kindness'.[4] This indeed was exactly how Bradley envisaged the heroine: 'Desdemona is helplessly passive. She can do nothing whatever. She cannot retaliate

---

[1] Ibid, p. 368, in Rosenberg, pp. 136–7.

[2] Cited in Rosenberg, p. 137.

[3] Ellen Terry, *Dramatic Opinions and Essays* (New York, 1906), p. 11, cited in Rosenberg, p. 139; cf. also Potter, p. 55.

[4] *Stratford Herald*, 3 May 1907.

even in speech; no, not even in silent feeling. . . . [her] suffering is like that of the most loving of dumb creatures tortured without cause by the being [s]he adores.'[1]

Although the *Birmingham Post* evidently found the pathos of Millard's 'highly lachrymose bride' a little overdone,[2] the Desdemonas of the next five decades saw few departures from the stereotype: Lily Brayton (Stratford, 1911) was a 'guileless maid, compact of simplicity and tenderness', Dorothy Green (Stratford, 1912) 'the perfection of gentleness and tenderness', and Ethel Carrington (Stratford, 1922, 1924) 'a sweet Desdemona', 'played . . . with engaging sweetness . . . and a pathetic wondering amazement'; the aptly named Joyce Bland (Stratford, 1930, 1939) 'spoke finely . . . looked beautiful, and was a pathetic figure in the latter part of the play'; while Dorothy Tutin (Stratford, 1961) was said to combine 'just the right childish simplicity and purity'.[3] Even the great Peggy Ashcroft alongside Robeson at the Savoy Theatre in 1930, despite appearing 'a little hard', seemed to the *Times* critic, 'less interesting than Desdemona ought to be'.[4] The nadir of the sentimentalist tradition, which reduced Desdemona to a doll-like creature of passive tenderness and goodness, was probably reached in Orson Welles's film of *Othello* (1952), where it was mediated by a disdainful misogyny: here Suzanne Cloutier became a figure of almost mute suffering, stripped of many of her lines, whilst a variety of other actresses dubbed her speeches, and even stood in as doubles in a number of scenes.[5] There were hints of the change to come in Moira Lister's performance at Stratford in 1945—'mercifully no puling doll'—and in Mary Ure's 'attempt at a modern, spirited woman' in the 1959 Richardson/Robeson *Othello*;[6] but it was not until the advent of Maggie Smith as Olivier's Old Vic bride in 1964 that a wholesale reinterpretation of the part, harking back to Terry's proto-feminist heroine, was attempted.

---

[1] Bradley, p. 145.
[2] *Birmingham Post*, 30 Apr. 1907.
[3] *Birmingham Daily Mail*, 25 Apr. 1911; *Stratford Herald*, 9 Aug. 1912; *Birmingham Mail*, 19 Apr. 1922; *Stratford Herald*, 15 Apr. 1924; *The Era*, 30 Apr. 1930; T. C. Worsley, *Financial Times*, 11 Oct. 1961.
[4] *The Times*, 20 May 1930.
[5] Potter, p. 142.
[6] *John O'London's Weekly*, 19 Apr. 1945; Potter, p. 130, and cf. J. C. Trewin, *Birmingham Post*, 8 Apr. 1959.

With this actress at last, Kenneth Tynan announced, '[t]he milk-sop Desdemona has been banished from this stage and a girl of real personality and substance comes into her own. Fighting back, not soppily "hurt", but damned angry, she makes the conjugal battle less one-sided and so more interesting and certainly more exciting.'[1] Smith's performance was still characterized by 'gentle graciousness and good breeding'; but when Billie Whitelaw took over the role in the following year she projected a sensuality that gave a striking physical charge to her relationship with Othello.[2] This in turn may have helped to colour several later readings of the part. Thus Sarah Stephenson (Mermaid Theatre, 1971)—unfairly notorious for her nakedness in the murder scene—convinced Michael Billington that here was 'no bloodless moppet, but a wilful, headstrong, highly sexed girl'.[3] In the RSC production that began in the same year, Lisa Harrow, for all her apparent youth and innocence, similarly struck Billington as 'transforming Desdemona from the usual spineless moppet into a headstrong sensualist, [one who], forever wandering about the camp in nothing but a Freudian slip . . . for once makes Othello's suspicions plausible'.[4] If Stephenson and Harrow stressed Desdemona's sexuality, the tough, independent side of Maggie Smith's characterization was developed by Suzanne Bertish, Donald Sinden's Desdemona in the 1979 RSC production. Here, declared Billington, was 'a Desdemona who seems worth all the fuss. . . . no mimsy moppet, but a girl of guts and courage who touchingly persists in her love for Othello, even in the agony of rejection'; she was 'a figure like Chaucer's Griselde: a woman with a limitless capacity for love and stoic fortitude'.[5] B. A. Young even found 'a touch of Joan of Arc' in a bride who wore a soldier's uniform for her arrival on besieged Cyprus.[6] At the National in 1980, Felicity Kendal was praised in much the same terms by Milton Shulman for 'convert[ing] the often wet Desdemona into a spirited, defiant creature'; while Sîan Thomas at the

---

[1] Tynan, p. 16.

[2] Alexander Anikst in *Sovetskaya Kultura*, as cited in Tynan, p. 109.

[3] *The Times*, 17 Sept. 1971.

[4] B. A. Young, *Financial Times*, 10 Sept. 1971; Billington, *Guardian*, 19 July 1972.

[5] Billington, *Guardian*, 8 Aug. 1979, 15 Aug. 1980.

[6] Young, *Financial Times*, 8 Aug. 1979. The director, Ronald Eyre, may have been influenced in this detail by Sergei Yutkevich's Russian film (1955), whose Desdemona arrived in Cyprus wearing a man's clothes.

Lyric Studio in 1984 offered 'a Desdemona who [was neither] meek victim [n]or bewildered waif, but the poised, well-bred and socially artful daughter of a noble house . . . [who died] fighting for her life like a wild cat'.[1]

Suzanne Bertish's militant rendition of the woman whom Cassio calls 'our great captain's captain' (2.1.74) remained an acknowledged influence on Emily Morgan's 'pert, spirited, rather bossy' heroine in the Dunderdale/Quarshie production at Greenwich, which cited Bertish's insistence that 'Desdemona does not have to be weak' in a programme note.[2] But subsequent productions—though still influenced by feminist responses to the play—have veered back towards more vulnerable heroines. At the RSC in 1985 Niamh Cusack used humour rather than toughness as a way of fleshing out the part, discovering in Desdemona an unexpected taste for parody.[3] In Trevor Nunn's 1989 production Imogen Stubbs 'flirt[ed] with gusto' and remained somewhat 'hoydenish' in the eyes of one reviewer; but though she 'accept[ed] Cassio's attentions as her due', she did so 'never realizing what they might mean to her husband'; and in her naivety she emerged once again as a kind of 'child-bride', for whom Willard White's ageing Othello was as much 'surrogate father' as lover or husband.[4]

Emilia and Bianca   Praised by Virginia Vaughan as charting a reorientation of the tragedy away from race towards gender, Nunn's production gave unusual prominence to its female characters.[5] Although Stubbs may not have been the most powerful of late twentieth-century Desdemonas, Nunn made sense of her vulnerability by stressing its relation to the general predicament of women in a claustrophobically male-dominated world from which they were for most practical purposes excluded. This *Othello* charted the course for a series of productions in which the roles of Emilia and Bianca were given a larger structural importance than they had hitherto enjoyed. In the case of Emilia, this was not entirely without precedent, since the character has always been

---

[1] Shulman, *Evening Standard*, 21 Mar. 1980; James Fenton, *Sunday Times*, 30 Sept. 1984.

[2] See also D. A. N. Jones, *Sunday Telegraph*, 19 Mar. 1989.

[3] Potter, p. 166.

[4] Maureen Paton, *Daily Express*, 25 Aug. 1989; Vaughan, p. 230.

[5] Vaughan, pp. 218–20, 225–31.

important as a conduit for the emotions of the audience—her denunciations of the Moor's folly in the final scene serving to articulate their own impatience and moral indignation. It was partly this which led to the role's sometimes being rated above that of Desdemona as an acting vehicle—despite the fact that eighteenth- and nineteenth-century productions typically simplified the character by cutting some of her strongest speeches, including the great diatribe against errant husbands at the end of Act 4. But contemporary directors have found in Iago's treatment of his wife a disturbing mirror for the violent misogyny into which Othello's relationship with Desdemona descends. For them, the key to understanding Emilia's marriage is to be found in Iago's contemptuous sexual banter over the purloined handkerchief in Act 3, Scene 3 (ll. 305 ff.) and in the vicious loathing exposed by the line on which he kills her: '*Filth*, thou liest' (5.2.230). In such productions Emilia's denunciation of the sexual double standards enforced by men (4.3.81–98) is transformed from a piece of wry worldly wisdom into the deeply personal complaint—the gender equivalent of Shylock's racial plea, 'Hath not a Jew eyes?' (*Merchant of Venice*, 3.1.54–68). When combined with the usual practice (for which the play offers no clear warrant) of playing Emilia as an older woman, the speech becomes an implicit testimony to years of spousal abuse. Yet, as Ronald Eyre showed in 1979, when he put Susan Tracy in the part, there are good reasons for creating a 'young and comely' Emilia, not only because it 'lends some substance to Iago's fantasies about her infidelity',[1] but also because her ''Tis not a year or two shows us a man' (3.4.99) will then point to an experience of sudden and recent disillusionment all too poignantly like Desdemona's. This was perhaps most forcefully suggested by Janet Dale's 'marvellous study in rejected sexuality' in Terry Hands's 1985 RSC production: in Act 3, Scene 3, her Emilia 'canoodl[ed] her way for a fleet moment into Iago's favour with the procured handkerchief only to find herself spun from the embrace [with] a truly shocking slap in the face';[2] it was a gesture that anticipated Othello's slapping of Desdemona two scenes later, physically enacting the Moor's contemptuous 'she can turn, and turn, and yet go on | And turn again' (4.1.245–6).

---

[1] Michael Billington, *Guardian*, 8 Aug. 1979.
[2] Michael Coveney, *Financial Times*, 26 Sept. 1985.

If the persuasions of delicacy led, in the eighteenth and nine-teenth centuries, to the mutilation of Emilia's part, they caused Bianca's to be excised from the play altogether. Although she was allowed a brief appearance by Charles Fechter when he staged the play at London's Princess's Theatre in 1861, it was only in the mid twentieth century that Bianca began to be regularly reinstated; and even then it was not until Trevor Nunn's 1989 *Othello* that the proper system of contrasts and parallels around which Shake-speare constructed the play's female world began to be properly exploited. In this production Zoë Wanamaker, as a 'tragically neglected' Emilia, 'sad, watchful, and pipe-smoking', became for some viewers 'the emotional centre of the play'; psychologically (and perhaps physically) abused by her husband, she offered a dis-concerting parallel with Desdemona's fate as 'a battered wife who is violently murdered'.[1] Significantly, in Nunn's staging it was the dying Emilia, rather than Othello, who reached out for Desde-mona's hand at the end of the play.[2] The gesture capitalized on the production's carefully crafted sense of a small community of iso-lated and maltreated women; and this was extended through the sympathetic handling of Bianca, played (in a witty inversion of the whiteness indicated by her name) by the black actress Marsha Hunt. By linking issues of race and gender, this casting helped to suggest parallels with Othello's situation—especially since McKellen managed to suggest that Iago's racial loathing of Othello was mirrored in his disdain for Bianca's colour, as if blackness were as much the visible proof of her whoredom as of the Moor's animality. Equally important was the way in which Cassio's offhand exploitation of Bianca (in sharp contrast to his courtly idealization of Desdemona) was used to expose the double standard that permeates the entire male world of the play: contemp-tuously dismissed as a 'customer' by her lover (4.1.116), Bianca is stigmatized as a whore by Iago (5.1.115), just as Desdemona and Emilia are each bewhored by their husbands. The cruellest irony (Nunn emphasized) is that Emilia herself—as revealed in her scalding dismissal of Bianca as a 'strumpet' (5.1.120)—has inter-nalized male misogyny just as effectively as, in her denunciation of

---

[1] Paton, *Daily Express*; Vaughan, pp. 219, 226, 228, 230.
[2] Potter, p. 191.

Othello's blackness, she appears to have absorbed her husband's racial bigotry (5.2.131, 155, 162, 224).

Like McKellen's homosexually driven ensign, the abused Emilias of Dale and Wanamaker seemed to mark a decisive turning point in interpretations of the role. The parallels between Desdemona and Emilia were once again important in Sam Mendes's and Jude Kelly's 1997 productions. Mendes's Desdemona, the 'dainty' Claire Skinner, was yet another 'child-bride', but nearly all traces of the hoyden had vanished in a performance that was praised as 'delicate, poised, [and] achingly generous'[1]—though it was sometimes in danger of seeming anaemically genteel. Skinner's frailty, however (unlike that of Victorian Desdemonas) seemed designed as 'a visible reproach to the military boisterousness that surrounds [the women]';[2] and her vulnerability was underlined by contrast with Maureen Beattie's drab, ageing, but forceful Emilia, whose sturdy Scots common sense barely disguised her hurt resentment and frustrated longing for Iago. Like Nunn, Mendes made use of a number of devices to capitalize on the complex ironies of the play's own system of black/white contrasts: he dressed Desdemona in black for the brothel scene (4.2), as if to render visible the way in which she (like the other women of the play) had become a creature of the corrosive misogynist fantasies fostered by Iago; and, again like Nunn, he complicated the play's treatment of race and gender by casting Bianca as the dark-skinned native of a colonial outpost. However, the point of establishing this symbolic link with both Othello and the wife whom he denounces as a 'black weed' (4.2.67) was blurred by Indira Varma's shameless vamp. This was a woman who seemed positively to invite the slurs laid on her, and who consequently proved unable to make dramatic capital out of the outraged defiance with which Bianca responds to Iago and Emilia, with its telling emphasis on the play's most obsessively repeated adjective: 'I am no strumpet, | But of life as *honest*, as you that thus | Abuse me' (5.1.120–2).

Although Jude Kelly's *Othello* for the Washington Shakespeare Theatre achieved most publicity for the 'photo-negative' casting

---

[1] Susannah Clapp, *Independent*, 21 Sept. 1997; John Peter, *Sunday Times*, 21 Sept. 1997. Skinner did, however, have one moment of moving defiance in the brothel scene, when she pounded Othello with her fists to bring him to his senses.

[2] Clapp, *Independent*.

that allowed Patrick Stewart to play a white Othello, it was more notable for its resolutely feminist reading of the text than for any new light it cast on the work's racial themes. While acknowledging that race was 'obviously critical' in the play, Kelly insisted that it was 'chiefly about male paranoia and jealousy, and the violence that comes from those things'.[1] Set in a militarized Venetian empire whose soldiers wore the combat fatigues of a contemporary American expeditionary force, the production once again emphasized the isolation of women in an overwhelmingly masculine environment. Cassio's first scene with Bianca was accompanied by a chorus of leering, mocking soldiery; and at one point a female soldier in the Cypriot ranks was nearly gang-raped by drunken Venetian troops.[2] The deep-rooted misogyny of this barrack-room world was epitomized by Ron Canada's Iago, a thick-set, middle aged NCO: as contemptuous of women as he was exaggeratedly respectful of rank, his resentful tirades were punctuated with an overplus of obscene gestures. As his wife, Franchelle Stewart-Dorn was weary from years of physical abuse and numb from the humiliating rudeness that marked even their public encounters. Visibly fearful for Desdemona, she appeared too cowed to offer practical help; and during her litany of complaint in 4.3 against the neglect and brutality of husbands 'the air was heavy with the silence of two abused wives, each too ashamed to confide in the other'.[3] So moving was her 'haggard, defensive' presence that at the end of the play Stewart (like Edwin Forrest before him) was in danger of being completely upstaged by his Emilia.[4] As Desdemona, Patrice Johnson played a confident, flirtatious and erotically intoxicated child-bride who (in a deliberate reversal of Olivier's self-pleasuring stage business with the rose) made her first appearance showering her new husband with rose petals; but, cut off from the social privilege that allowed her to behave so defiantly in Venice, this spontaneous girl had no resources for dealing with Othello's inexplicable collapse into jealous frenzy. The result, one reviewer observed, was that in the end 'the

---

[1] Interview with Nelson Pressley, *Washington Times*, 13 Nov. 1997.
[2] This piece of stage-business was perhaps suggested by Suzman's production, in which Bianca was raped and possibly killed by Iago's soldiers at the end of 5.1 (see Potter, p. 186).
[3] Potter, p. 182.
[4] Bob Mondello, *Washington City Paper*, 21 Nov. 1997.

Othello–Desdemona marriage seems so much like the Iago–Emilia relationship that you feel an ugly syndrome has been exposed and . . . the whole military culture . . . indicted'.[1]

Cassio and Roderigo The feminist reorientation of directorial approaches to the women's parts has had incidental consequences for some of the minor characters. In particular, the new prominence given to Bianca has made Cassio, conventionally played as a stylish and gallant Florentine, appear a much more ambiguous, and sometimes rather unattractive figure. Already in the Olivier *Othello*, Derek Jacobi had made Iago's resentment of this rival seem more comprehensible by stressing Cassio's class condescension and evident lack of military experience;[2] while John Barton's production turned David Calder's 'weak-chinned' Lieutenant into 'a shouting bully'.[3] More subtly, in Ronald Eyre's version, James Laurenson offered a 'gentlemanly Cassio' whose very suaveness served to make the audience 'wonder how sincere his candidness really is'.[4] Tom Mannion at the RSC in 1985 was another aristocratic carpet knight, who 'might have stepped from a Florentine *Tatler* and [seemed] suspiciously attentive to the general's wife'.[5] Subsequent productions have discovered a less socially confident figure: for Trevor Nunn, Sean Baker created a lieutenant who was 'no glamorous Florentine, but a hard-working, self-made man caught between his original social class, and that of the officers'.[6] In Mendes's production, on the other hand, Cassio's unease had less to do with class than with his callow inexperience, Colin Tierney playing him as a gawky, rather stiff young officer with an oddly mincing gait, entirely devoid of the 'daily beauty' that arouses Iago's envy (5.1.19).

The one significant character who seems to have almost entirely escaped the effects of such directorial revisionism is Roderigo. No one has apparently been willing to follow up the promising new

---

[1] Nelson Pressley, *Washington Times*, 18 Nov. 1997.

[2] Potter, pp. 149–50.

[3] Gareth Lloyd Evans, *Guardian*, 10 Sept. 1971; B. A. Young, *Financial Times*, 10 Sept. 1971.

[4] B. A. Young, *Financial Times*, 8 Aug. 1979; Gareth Lloyd Evans, *Stratford Herald*, 10 Aug. 1979.

[5] Michael Billington, *Guardian*, 26 Sept. 1985.

[6] Potter, p. 189.

direction established by Paul Scofield in Tearle's 1948 Stratford *Othello*. Modifying the 'familiar foppishness' of the role, Scofield found a Roderigo in whom 'there [was] more than a hint of the determined Elizabethan seducer, whose mouth must indeed be closed at all costs by Iago'.[1] Even the most intelligent productions appear to ignore the obvious implications of the fact that Roderigo, for all his weakness and folly, is Iago's more than willing instrument—not merely in the plot to discredit Othello and destroy his marriage, but in the conspiracy to murder Cassio. He may be Iago's 'snipe' or gull (1.3.374), but so too are most other characters in the play, including Cassio and Othello himself. The lazily observed convention—which makes its mark even on Ernst Honigmann's conjectures about the play's date in his edition (p. 346)—is that Roderigo is simply a younger version of the upper-class buffoon, Sir Andrew Aguecheek. Despite his propensity for self-pity and his ultimate ineffectuality, it might make better dramatic sense to see him as a kinsman of the aristocratic bravos who infest the streets of Verona in *Romeo and Juliet*. Such an approach might help to illuminate Roderigo's function in the play's economy of 'place'[2]—the carefully graduated, but unstable and often fiercely contested arrangements of rank, office, and service that not only give social density to its world, but become the principal motor of its plot, and a key to its murderous tangle of relationships. From an early modern perspective, as I will argue in the final section of this introduction, 'place' might well have seemed a more important dimension of Othello's tragedy than 'race'—if only because, in contrast to the period's confused attempts to articulate the latter, the former was something for which it had inherited a highly sophisticated language. However, because, for good historical reasons, race has latterly become as much the preoccupation of critics and scholars as

---

[1] 'G.P.', *Manchester Guardian*, 2 Aug. 1948.

[2] Unlike his nearest social equivalent in the play, the courtly professional soldier Cassio, Roderigo is possessed of substantial private means; as a landed gentleman (1.3.365) who has squandered a good portion of his estate in fruitless pursuit of Desdemona (1.1.1–3; 4.2.185–8), he represents those 'wealthy curlèd darlings of our nation' (3.3.68), the native aristocrats whom Desdemona has spurned in favour of the Moor—the 'wheeling stranger' whom Roderigo so despises (1.1.136). By virtue of his secure social place, Roderigo contrasts not just with the Moorish outsider, but with the man whose service they both seek to command—Iago, with his conspicuously foreign name and rankling sense of displacement (see below, pp. 147–54).

of *Othello*'s theatrical interpreters, it is to racially oriented readings of the play that I must first turn.

Interpretation

Reading Blackness

> If [*Othello*] did not begin as a play about race, then its history has made it one.
>
> Ben Okri[1]

The issue of Othello's race and what it might have meant to Shakespeare's audience first began to attract serious scholarly attention in the 1960s—significantly, at about the same time as Olivier's controversial performance. This is not to say that colour had been ignored by earlier critics: indeed, it had surfaced with insistent regularity from Rymer onwards; but it was typically treated as an embarrassing accident of the design—something to be explained away. In the theatre, Kean's decision to break with the tradition of black Othellos may have been motivated partly by the wish to make the subtleties of facial expression more visible to the audience in the large theatres of his day, but it coincided with the objections of critics like Charles Lamb, for whom the hero's colour made for 'something extremely revolting in the courtship and wedded caresses of Othello and Desdemona'.[2] The critical equivalent of Kean's orientalizing move is to be found in S. T. Coleridge's celebrated lecture on the play, which argued that the established convention of a black Othello had resulted from the 'common error' of 'mistak[ing] the epithets applied by the *dramatis personae* to each other, as truly descriptive of what the audience ought to see or know': the mere fact Othello is *called* 'black'—or even that Roderigo dubs him 'thick-lips' (1.1.66), and Iago 'old black ram', while Brabantio sneers at his 'sooty bosom' (1.2.70)—does not mean that he was ever intended to be 'a veritable negro'.[3]

---

[1] 'Leaping out of Shakespeare's Terror: Five Meditations on *Othello*', in *A Way of Being Free* (1997).

[2] Lamb, quoted in Hankey, pp. 65–6.

[3] Coleridge (ed. Raysor), i. 47. Raysor notes the possibility that this passage was a later interpolation by H. N. Coleridge; but, stamped with S. T. Coleridge's authority, the argument soon became an orthodoxy—see, for example, William Winter's remarks in his edition of Edwin Booth's prompt-book (Philadelphia, 1911): 'to make

The pre-Romantic tradition of a negroid Moor seems to have died harder in the American theatre, where (to take one notorious example) the Baltimore bluestocking Mary Preston (1869), insisted that essentially speaking 'Othello *was* a *white* man', and his apparent blackness a mere 'stage decoration, which *my* taste discards; a fault of colour from an artistic point of view. . . . one of the few erroneous strokes of the great master's brush, the *single* blemish on a faultless work'.[1] But Coleridge and Kean between them largely succeeded in suppressing the problem of the hero's blackness for the Victorians; and the new stage convention corresponded to a gathering critical prejudice in favour of a 'tawny' Othello,[2] which proved remarkably difficult to displace.

In his influential 1904 lectures on the play, A. C. Bradley repudiated the Victorian tradition, insisting that the early performance history made it quite clear that Shakespeare 'imagined Othello as a black man, and not as a light brown one';[3] while John Dover Wilson, introducing the New (Cambridge) edition in 1957, declared that Paul Robeson's performance had 'seemed to floodlight the whole drama', convincing him that 'a Negro Othello is essential to the play'.[4] For these editors, whether one approached the problem from the perspective of historical fidelity or contemporary relevance, the desirability of a black protagonist seemed indisputable. But in spite of such determined interventions, critics have continued to question the literalness of the play's language of colour, drawing attention to its historical elasticity. After all, when the villain of *Arden of Faversham* was described by Holinshed as 'a black swart man',[5] the chronicler meant only that he was dark-haired

Othello a Negro is to unpoetize the character, and to deepen whatever grossness may subsist in the subject of the tragedy. . . . expressions of opinion are not statements of fact—and may therefore be disregarded. The persons who call the Moor "thick lips" and "the black Othello" are not his friends. . . . The Moor should be painted a pale cinnamon colour, which is at once truthful and picturesque' (p. 121).

[1] Furness, p. 395.

[2] For a representative sample of opinions, see Furness, pp. 389–96.

[3] Bradley, p. 162. In a lengthy and rather tortured footnote Bradley nevertheless conceded the virtual impossibility of representing Othello 'as a black in our theatres now', suggesting that 'the aversion of our blood . . . would overpower our imagination and sink us below not Shakespeare only but the audiences of the seventeenth and eighteenth centuries' (p. 165).

[4] Walker, Introduction, p. x.

[5] Raphael Holinshed, *Chronicles of England, Scotland, and Ireland* (1587), p. 1062, in M. L. Wine (ed.), *The Tragedy of Master Arden of Faversham* (1973), p. 148.

and swarthy in complexion; and in describing foreign peoples, 'black' could refer, as occasion served, to a whole range of phenotypes, from 'tawny' North Africans, like the Prince of Morocco in *The Merchant of Venice,* to sub-Saharan Africans, like Aaron in *Titus Andronicus.* 'Moor' itself was equally flexible in its application: taken to derive from the Greek *mauros* (μαυρός, ἀμαυρός = dark, gloomy, obscure), and contaminated by association with *moros* (μωρός = dull, stupid; Latin *morus*), it could serve as a 'racial' category, but just as often it was used to mark religious or geographical affiliation—or to indicate some unstable combination of all three. Sometimes it was confined to the Arab-Berber people of the region variously called 'Mauretania' or 'Barbary'—a name that seemed to identify Moorishness with barbarity; sometimes it might extend (with or without the descriptors 'white', 'tawny', or 'black') to all the inhabitants of Africa; but, since the North African littoral continued to owe at least nominal allegiance to the Turkish sultan, Moors were not easily distinguished from Turks, and (like 'Turk') 'Moor' often came to be used as a blanket term for Muslims of any nationality. At still other times it might (like the equally promiscuous term 'Indian') be applied to any people of colour, regardless of geographical origin or religious affiliation.[1] A term so accommodating made no obvious distinction between, for example, the 'negroes and blackmoors' whose transportation from the country the Queen ordered in 1596 and 1601, and the Arab-looking Moorish ambassador who was welcomed to her court in 1600–1.[2] As a result, despite the fact that recent theatrical practice has swung decisively towards casting black actors in the central role, a number of critics have continued to make the case for a light-skinned 'Mauretanian' hero. Barbara Everett, for example, has argued

[1] See, for example, Anthony Gerard Barthelemy, *Black Face, Maligned Race: The Representation of Blacks in English Drama from Shakespeare to Southerne* (Baton Rouge, La., 1987), pp. 1–7; Emily Bartels, 'Making More of the Moor; Aaron, Othello, and Renaissance Refashionings of Race', *SQ* 41 (1990), 432–54; Daniel J. Vitkus, ' "Turning Turk" in *Othello*: The Conversion and Damnation of the Moor', *SQ* 48 (1997), 145–76; Neill, ' "Mulattos" '; Ania Loomba, ' "Delicious Traffick": Alterity and Exchange on Early Modern Stages', *SS* 52 (1999), 201–4; and Loomba, 'Othello and the Racial Question', in *Shakespeare, Race, and Colonialism* (Oxford, 2002), pp. 92–3.
[2] Jones, p. 87; Karen Newman, ' "And Wash the Ethiop White": Femininity and the Monstrous in *Othello*', in Jean E. Howard and Marion F. O'Connor (eds.), *Shakespeare Reproduced: The Text in History and Ideology* (New York, 1987), 143–62 (p. 158).

that, because English acquaintance with the Moorish world had been largely mediated through recent Spanish history, Shakespeare was most likely to have imagined his hero as one of the light-skinned North African Moors expelled from Spain after the *reconquista*—much like the historical Leo Africanus on whom he was partially modelled.[1] In his Arden edition, Ernst Honigmann advances a similar preference on the somewhat specious grounds that 'the places [Othello] names are in the Mediterranean world', and that familiarity with the recent Moorish embassage to Elizabeth's court would have predisposed the audience to expect an Arab-looking figure, like that in the well-known portrait of the ambassador.[2] In both cases, it might be argued, the effect is to diminish the tragic significance of the hero's otherness by making his marriage to Desdemona seem less transgressive. Julia Reinhard Lupton, by contrast, argues that it was not colour or 'race' but faith that marked the crucial divide for Shakespeare's contemporaries: prayers instituted by the Archbishop of Canterbury during the Turkish siege of Malta (1565) denounced Turks and other Muslim 'infidels' as 'our sworn and most deadly enemies' and referred to the prophet Mohammed as 'that wicked monster and damned soul'.[3] Thus, 'whereas for the modern reader a black Othello is more subversive, "other", or dangerous', Renaissance audiences would have been more disturbed by 'a paler Othello more closely resembling the Turks he fights'.[4]

[1] See, for example, Barbara Everett, ' "Spanish" Othello: The Making of Shakespeare's Moor', *SS* 35 (1982), 101–12, repr. in Catherine Alexander and Stanley Wells (eds.), *Shakespeare and Race* (Cambridge, 2000), 64–81. But for evidence of extensive interaction between English, Turks, and Moors in the period, see Nabil Matar, *Turks, Moors and Englishmen in the Age of Discovery* (New York, 1999).

[2] Honigmann, Introduction, pp. 14–17 and fig. 1; see also Bernard Harris, 'A Portrait of a Moor', *SS* 11 (1958), repr. in Alexander and Wells (eds.), *Shakespeare and Race*, 23–36. However, the public discontent that presumably motivated the Queen's expulsion of 'negroes and blackmoors' indicates that Londoners were probably equally familiar with black Africans.

[3] Vitkus, *Turning Turk*, p. 79.

[4] Julia Reinhard Lupton, 'Othello Circumcised: Shakespeare and the Pauline Discourse of Nations', *Representations*, 57 (1997), 73–89 (p. 74). In a riposte to Lupton, Eric Griffin maintains that Hispanic Catholicism rather than Islam was the real bugbear for Jacobean Protestants (who dreamed of an anti-papist alliance with the Turks and the Moors), that Iago and Roderigo are indicted as stereotypes of Spanish racism, and that Othello's downfall is a consequence of his conversion to Catholicism ('Un-sainting James: Or, *Othello* and the "Spanish Spirits" of Shakespeare's Globe', *Representations*, 62 (1998), 52–99).

For the Victorians, by contrast, the great advantage of an insistence upon a tawny, 'oriental', or 'Arab' hero had been that, by minimizing Othello's physical distinctiveness, it substantially diminished the scandal of miscegenation, and encouraged a culturally inflected reading of the tragedy, in which the protagonist's surrender to vindictive passion represents the disintegration of his civilized Christian identity and a return to the barbaric mores of the desert culture that spawned him. First argued by the German critic A. W. Schlegel, this approach treated Othello's colour simply as a convenient token of difference—a sign of the irreducible barbarity concealed beneath his veneer of Venetian civilization. Though dismissed by Bradley as 'hopelessly un-Shakespearean',[1] this idea of the play as a tragedy of atavistic passion proved as persistent as the orientalized image of the Moor with which it was associated, achieving its most sophisticated form in F. R. Leavis's influential essay 'Diabolic Intellect and the Noble Hero' (1937);[2] and it remained the governing idea of Laurence Lerner's 1959 essay, which discovered in the play's imagery of blackness 'the symbol . . . not only for evil but for going beyond the bounds of civilization'. For Lerner, *Othello* was 'the story of a barbarian, who (the pity of it) relapses' and yields to his 'primitive' nature;[3] and in the theatre, as we have seen, this was the reading that continued to inform the Dexter/Olivier production, whose 'portrait of a primitive man, at odds with the sophisticated society into which he has forced himself, relapsing into barbarism' could still be endorsed by the New Cambridge editor in 1984.[4] It was against this dominant reading that the Sudanese novelist Tayeb Salih protested in his

---

[1] Far from being a prey to the 'savage passions of his Moorish blood', Bradley argued, Othello is 'perfectly just' in his self-description as 'one not easily jealous'; indeed 'if anyone had told Shakespeare that no Englishman would have acted like the Moor, and had congratulated him on the accuracy of his racial psychology . . . he would have laughed' (pp. 151–2). Significantly G. K. Hunter felt compelled to elaborate Bradley's arguments against this line of criticism half a century later in 'Othello and Colour Prejudice', pp. 159–60.

[2] Leavis, *The Common Pursuit*, pp. 136–59. For Leavis the effect of Iago's insinuations is to expose the fundamental flaw of the barbaric self concealed by the hero's self-dramatizing persona: 'the stuff of which he is made begins at once to deteriorate and show itself unfit' (p. 144).

[3] Laurence Lerner, 'The Machiavel and the Moor', *Essays in Criticism*, 9 (1959), 339–60 (p. 360).

[4] Sanders, Introduction, p. 47.

reworking of the Othello story, *Season of Migration to the North* (1969), where Mustafa Sa'eed, on trial for the murder of his white mistress, refuses to be judged as a latter-day Moor: 'Othello', he declares, 'was a lie.'[1]

Despite an avoidance of explicit racial categories, the assumptions underlying the culturally based approach to Othello's difference were frequently exposed by appeals to the essentialism of 'blood';[2] and at certain points this approach becomes difficult to distinguish from the views of critics like Bradley and M. R. Ridley, with their insistence on a black Othello. Whilst Bradley maintained that 'in regard to the essentials of his character [Othello's race] is not important', his emphasis on the hero's 'simple', emotion-driven character[3] is disquietingly close to the racial stereotypes that surface more obviously in Ridley's now notorious Arden introduction (1958). Ridley concurred with Bradley's insistence on the historicity of a black Othello. He shared the latter's doubts about the acceptability of such a figure for modern audiences; but (bizarrely enough) maintained that prejudice against the idea of a Negro protagonist resulted from 'a confusion of colour with contour . . . the woolly hair, thick lips, round skull, [and] blunt features . . . of the traditional nigger minstrel'. 'That a man is black in colour', he concluded, in a painfully revealing turn of phrase, 'is no reason why he should look, even to European eyes, sub-human.'[4] But while Ridley's ideal Othello might look like a black Julius Caesar, he nevertheless conformed to the familiar colonial stereotype of the simple, child-like African, a creature governed by instinct, rather than reason:

his intellectual power is nowhere near on a par with his other qualities. Whenever he thinks he is a child, and not even a very intelligent child. . . . if I were challenged to produce a 'theme' for *Othello* I should suggest 'Reason versus instinct.' Whenever Othello trusts his instinct he is almost

---

[1] Salih, *Season of Migration*, p. 95 (see p. 13, n. 3).

[2] See, for example, the notes on the character of Othello in James H. Taylor's manuscript study book for *Othello* (Harvard Theatre Collection, *Othello* 293): 'It is only when he quits [his civilized, Venetian] character and loses all control over himself that his African blood boils over and consumes him. It is then that his passions, hitherto kept in order, rise up in rebellion against him.'

[3] Bradley, p. 152.

[4] Ridley, Introduction, p. li.

invariably right . . . whenever he thinks, or fancies himself to be thinking, he is almost invariably wrong.[1]

Faced by judgements of this kind, readers may find it difficult to separate the critic's unconscious racism from prejudices embedded in the play itself; and the effort of a great deal of recent criticism has been to resolve the issue by relocating *Othello* in the nexus of ideas about colour to which it historically belonged. If Olivier's Moor preserved the nineteenth-century conception of Othello as a relapsing savage, his exploitation of strikingly contemporary stereotypes of blackness also helped to stimulate serious debate about the significance of race in the play; and Dexter's production was quickly followed by two critical works that constituted the first systematic attempts to historicize the play's language of colour— Eldred Durosimi Jones's pioneering study of early modern representations of Africans, *Othello's Countrymen* (1965), and G. K. Hunter's influential British Academy Shakespeare Lecture on 'Othello and Colour Prejudice' (1967). Jones sought to illuminate the characterization of Othello and other stage Moors by examining the overwhelmingly pejorative accounts of black Africans in contemporary travel literature and the plays that capitalized on it. Hunter, on the other hand, was more interested in the pervasive strands of Christian symbolism that associated blackness with sin, death, animality, and sexual depravity. But they were agreed in believing that part of the power of Shakespeare's tragedy lay in its challenge to received stereotypes.

Jones saw the play as constructed on a 'double antithesis': the protagonist is visibly a black Moor, but exhibits the heroic virtues conventionally associated with North African 'white Moors'; thus the same apparent contradiction

between what Iago is supposed to be and what he is . . . also occurs in Shakespeare's portrayal of Othello. He is taken (by some of the characters) as the manifestation of a type—barbarous Moor, bondslave, pagan—and he turns out to be noble, Christian, if somewhat naïve. . . . Iago is both soldier and villain; Othello is both Moor and noble hero. (p. 108)

Hunter likewise stressed the way in which Othello's character confounds the theological associations of blackness on which Iago

---

[1] Ridley, Introduction, p. liv.

plays; he argued that Shakespeare was able to 'superimpose . . . new valuations on the audience' by drawing on a second evangelical tradition, according to which faith could transform the children of darkness into the children of light (pp. 152–3). 'It is not for us to regard the skin, but the soul', the Stuart divine Joseph Hall had written, in terms recalling both Desdemona and the Duke.

> If [the soul] be innocent, pure, holy, the blots of an outside cannot set us off from the love of him who hath said *Behold, thou art fair, my Sister, my Spouse*; if [it] be foul and black, it is not in the power of an angelical brightness of our hide, to make us other than a loathsome eye-sore to the almighty.[1]

'Foul' (1.2.62, 73; 1.3.118) is the adjective that repeatedly attaches to the man whom Emilia denounces as a 'blacker devil' (5.2.131); and 'fair devil' (3.3.478) is the oxymoron that Othello himself coins to characterize the wife whom Emilia calls an 'angel' (5.2.131); but it proves to be the 'honest' Iago whose white skin conceals the inward foulness of a 'demi-devil' (5.2.299).[2]

Martin Orkin's important essay 'Othello and the "Plain Face" of Racism' (1987) reaches a similar conclusion.[3] Orkin was concerned to expose the way in which 'racist mythology inscribes critical responses to the play', thereby supporting the institutionalized practice of regimes like that which then prevailed under the doctrine of apartheid in South Africa. He acknowledges the presence of 'racist sentiment' in the play, but argues that because it is largely confined to characters like Iago, Roderigo, and Brabantio, whom the action thoroughly discredits, Shakespeare himself is vindicated: 'in its fine scrutiny of the mechanisms underlying Iago's use of racism, and in its rejection of human pigmentation as a means of identifying human worth, the play, as it always has done, continues to oppose racism' (p. 188).

---

[1] Joseph Hall, *Occasional Meditations* (1630), cited in Hunter, p. 153.

[2] For a dazzling psychoanalytic exploration of the chiastic relation between Othello and Iago, see Janet Adelman, 'Iago's Alter Ego: Race as Projection in *Othello*', *SQ* 48 (1997), 125–44: 'in Othello's black skin Iago finds a fortuitous external sign [or] container for the internal blackness that he would project outward, the dark baby that hell and night must bring into the world's light; emptying himself out, Iago can project his faecal baby into Othello, blackening him with his own inner waste' (p. 141).

[3] See above, p. 63, n. 2.

Others have been rather less sanguine. Passionately as Orkin's case is argued, it suffers from two weaknesses: in the first place it fails to explain why so many critics, whose good faith he does not wish to impugn, should have been seduced into dangerous mis-reading; and in the second, it is (like many other contributions to this debate) founded on assumptions about the transhistorical sig-nificance of 'race' that are open to significant question. In fact even G. K. Hunter had had misgivings about the extent to which audi-ences could escape the mesmerizing influence of Iago's bigotry: because the ensign is able to exploit attitudes that are still current in 'the society to which *we* belong', Hunter argued, it is all too easy for his perspective to impose itself on the spectators, just as it does on characters in the play—not least the protagonist himself: indeed '[t]he imposition of Iago's vulgar prejudices on Othello . . . is so successful that it takes over not only Othello but almost all the critics'. Even if we partially resist Iago's seductions we will never-theless find it difficult to escape them altogether, since

> [o]ur involvement in prejudice gives us a double focus on [Othello's] real-ity. We admire him . . . but we are aware of the difficulty of sustaining that vision of the golden world of poetry; and this is so because *we* feel the disproportion and the difficulty of his social life and of his marriage (as a social act). (p. 163)

Hunter's essay thus moves, however hesitantly, beyond the liberal bardolatry that led to Jones's and Orkin's comforting conclusions about the play, edging towards an uneasy recognition of the ways in which *Othello* may be implicated (and even implicate its audi-ence) in the very prejudices we would like it to oppose.

Jack D'Amico's study of *The Moor in English Renaissance Drama* (1991) supports Orkin in arguing that Shakespeare invoked the negative stereotypes of the passion-driven, bestial, diabolic black man, only to confound them by appealing to the contrary stereo-type of the noble tawny Moor; but he nevertheless sees Othello as ultimately debasing himself by submitting to the role that Iago foists on to him: 'To those in the audience who would await a return to his barbarous self, the altered behaviour merely confirms what the black visage promised, as the seemingly noble Moor becomes . . . the incoherent savage. . . . The final paradox is that Othello is like everyone (particularly the European spectators) in his readiness to accept the negative, oversimplified stereotype of himself.'[1] For Anthony Barthelemy this 'tragic relapse to the stereotypical Moor' is tantamount to surrender on the play's part, ensuring that the audience's sympathy for Othello is only 'sympathy for his struggle to escape his fate, not sympathy for what he is fated [by his colour] to be'.[2]

In an influential essay published in the same year as Orkin's, Karen Newman discovers a similar ambivalence in the play: although Shakespeare's sympathetic treatment of a black protagonist and his transgressive spouse 'stands in a contestatory relation to the hegemonic ideologies of race and gender in early modern England', Shakespeare nevertheless presents Othello as 'both monster and hero. . . . a monster in the Renaissance sense of the word, a deformed creature like the hermaphrodites and other strange spectacles which so fascinated the early modern imagination'.[3] The African American critic Arthur Little likewise finds the play 'daring in its social critique', but insists that Othello after all 'becomes in effect the first black rapist [violating] white womanhood'.[4] In the light of these conflicted responses, it is hardly surprising that Virginia Vaughan, observing the way in which 'Shakespeare plays with us throughout *Othello*, exploiting stereotypes, arousing expectations, alternately fulfilling and frustrating our preconceptions', should conclude that the play's attitude to race is ultimately undecidable:

I think this play is racist, and I think it is not. But Othello's example shows me that if I insist on resolving the contradiction, I will forge only lies and

---

[1] Jack D'Amico, *The Moor in English Renaissance Drama* (Tampa, Fla., 1991), pp. 177, 195–6.

[2] Anthony Gerard Barthelemy, 'Ethiops Washed White: Moors of the Nonvillainous Type', in Barthelemy (ed.), *Critical Essays on Shakespeare's 'Othello'* (New York, 1994), 91–103 (pp. 102, 100)—excerpted from Barthelemy, *Black Face, Maligned Race*. A comparable position had been argued, albeit a little less forthrightly, in K. W. Evans, 'The Racial Factor in *Othello*', *Shakespeare Studies*, 5 (1969), 124–40. Vitkus, though he is interested in the Moor as an Islamic rather than a black African figure, reaches a similar conclusion: 'A baptized Moor turned Turk, Othello is "doubly damned" for his backsliding. . . . He has "traduced" the state of Venice and converted to the black Muslim Other. . . . His identity as "the noble Moor of Venice" dissolves as he reverts to the identity of the black devil, and exhibits the worst features of the stereotypical Moor or Turk—jealousy, violence, cruelty, frustrated lust, faithlessness, lawlessness, joylessness' (' "Turning Turk" ', p. 176).

[3] Newman, 'Femininity and the Monstrous', pp. 157, 152–3.

[4] Arthur L. Little Jr., *Shakespeare Jungle Fever: National-Imperial Re-visions of Race, Rape and Sacrifice* (Stanford, Calif., 2000), p. 92.

distortions. . . . the discourse of racial difference is inescapably embedded in this play just as it was embedded in Shakespeare's culture and our own.[1]

It may be, however, that Vaughan's bafflement can partly be explained by reference to her apparent belief that our own culture and Shakespeare's participate in a single 'discourse of racial difference'. This, clearly, is the supposition that underlies theatrical approaches like Suzman's which insist on the contemporary relevance of the play, as well as the politically engaged criticism of Orkin and others. But current historicist work, influenced as it has been by the sceptical methodology of Foucault, has tended to be suspicious of transhistorical continuities which, at their crudest, can appear to license the grossly simplified readings that assume the identical nature of Othello's and O. J. Simpson's predicaments in a world where 'nothing has changed'.[2]

If nothing else, it is important to recognize that the entire language of ethnic difference has been transformed in the intervening centuries: the simple fact that neither 'racism' nor any equivalent term was available to Shakespeare—while 'race' itself was a term whose connotations had more to do with lineage than with biology[3]—means that such things were apprehended differently. Where nineteenth- and twentieth-century racial thought was governed by 'scientific' principles of categorization and Darwinian hierarchy, Renaissance ideas of human difference were 'fluid, multiform and complex';[4] and this was perhaps especially true of

---

[1] Vaughan, pp. 69, 70. Vaughan's discussion of the cultural history of 'race' is usefully amplified in Alden T. Vaughan and Virginia Mason Vaughan, 'Before *Othello*: Elizabethan Representations of Sub-Saharan Africans', *William and Mary Quarterly*, 3rd ser., 54 (1997), 19–44.

[2] Journalists were quick to cite psychiatric 'experts' who detected in Simpson's crime an expression of an 'Othello syndrome'. The malign power of Shakespeare's tragedy as a mythic template for the relationship between black men and white women is variously interrogated by Tayeb Salih (*Season of Migration to the North*), Salman Rushdie (*Fury*), and in *Manawa Taua*—see above, p. 13, n. 3.

[3] Kim Hall, *Things of Darkness: Economies of Race and Gender in Early Modern England* (Ithaca, NY, 1995); Margo Hendricks, 'Civility, Barbarism, and Aphra Behn's *The Widow Ranter*', and Linda Boose, ' "The Getting of a Lawful Race": Racial Discourse in early modern England and the unrepresentable black woman', both in Hendricks and Patricia Parker (eds.), *Women, 'Race', and Writing in the Early Modern Period* (1994), 225–39, 35–54; and Hendricks, 'Surveying "race" in Shakespeare', in Alexander and Wells (eds.), *Shakespeare and Race*, 1–22 (pp. 15–20).

[4] Kim F. Hall, '*Othello* and the Problem of Blackness', in Richard Dutton and Jean F. Howard, *A Companion to Shakespeare's Works: The Tragedies* (Oxford, 2003), 357–74 (p. 364).

England, whose limited and hesitant steps towards the establishment of an overseas empire meant that there was as yet no pressing necessity to develop a coherent ideology of ethnic difference. In Spain—the country to which Iago's name appears to link him—anxieties about the loyalty of Moorish and Jewish subjects in the aftermath of the *reconquista* had led to an obsession with 'purity of blood' (*liempeza de sangre*), while the moral and economic pressures of New World exploitation had produced a serious theological debate about the boundaries of the 'human', in which the liberal inclusiveness of Las Casas was pitched against Sepulveda's neo-Aristotelian arguments for the innately slavish character of subjected peoples. But in England such issues were less urgent until, towards the end of the seventeenth century, the expansion of North American and Caribbean colonial enterprise—together with the full-scale involvement in the Atlantic slave trade with which it was associated—encouraged the development of an enabling theory of racial inferiority. By the 1680s, the Barbadian evangelist Morgan Godwyn could claim that the 'two words *Negro* and *Slave* [have] by custom grown homogeneous and convertible'[1]—articulating the assumption that would underlie Thomas Rymer's famously dismissive account of *Othello* a decade later: 'With us a blackamoor might rise to be a trumpeter, but *Shakespeare* would not have him less than a Lieutenant-General. With us a *Moor* might marry some little drab, or small-coal wench: *Shakespeare* would provide him the daughter and kin of some great lord, or privy-councillor.'[2] But for Shakespeare and his contemporaries, the relationship between ethnicity and subordination was by no means clear; and Iago's continuing hints that there is something recognizably unnatural about the vesting of authority in the Moor are seemingly annulled by the Duke's public show of respect, and by Montano's deference (' 'tis a worthy governor', 2.1.31).

For modern audiences, Othello's story of enslavement will inevitably be coloured by the horrors of that later history; but, as

---

[1] Morgan Godwyn, *The Negro's and Indians advocate* (1680), p. 3, cited in Bridget Orr, *Empire on the English Stage, 1660–1714* (Cambridge, 2001), p. 21.

[2] Rymer, pp. 91–2. Orr, however, cites the trenchant objections of Gildon (1694) and Theobald (1733) to Rymer's sneers, Gildon proclaiming that 'there is no reason in the nature of things why a Negro of equal birth and merit should not be on an equal bottom with a German, Hollander, Frenchman etc.', urging Shakespeare's 'contempt for the mere accident of their complexion' (*Miscellaneous Letters and Essays on Several Subjects*, p. 96; cited in Orr, p. 23).

the work of Nabil Matar and Daniel Vitkus has demonstrated, 'Moors' were, on balance, more likely to figure in the early seventeenth-century English imagination as enslavers than as slaves;[1] and Othello's narrative of capture, enslavement, and 'redemption thence' actually parallels the experience of many prisoners on both sides of a Muslim–Christian conflict that stretched back at least to the Crusades. As such it belongs not to the industrialized human market place of the Atlantic triangle, but to the same Mediterranean theatre of war as the Turkish invasion of Cyprus.[2] In fact, slavery bore little or no relation to discourses of 'racial' identity in early modern thought; rather, it was part of a much older construction of human difference in which the distinctions that mattered most were not those between different 'colours' or 'races', but those between master and servant, or between bond and free. This does not mean that Shakespeare's contemporaries were incapable of attitudes that we might identify as 'racist'; but it does mean that we should be wary of assuming a simple equivalence between their prejudices and our own. As Carol Neely puts it, '[t]he movement towards our own consolidated conception of "race" is emergent, but not yet completed in *Othello*'.[3] The result, for modern readers, is an uneasy paradox: that to talk about race in *Othello* is inevitably to fall into some degree of anachronism, while to ignore it is to efface something fundamental to the tragedy. *Othello* is a work that trades in ethnic constructions that are at once misleadingly *like* and confusingly *unlike* the twentieth-century ideas of 'race' to which they are, nevertheless, recognizably ancestral.

Just as the modern vocabulary of 'race' continues to be inflected by the pseudo-biological thinking of the nineteenth century, so the

---

[1] See Nabil Matar, *Turks, Moors, and Englishmen in the Age of Discovery* (New York: Columbia University Press, 1999), chap. 2, 'Soldiers, Pirates, Traders, and Captives: Britons among the Muslims', pp. 71–82; Matar, Introduction to Daniel Vitkus, *Piracy, Slavery, and Redemption: Barbary Captivity Narratives from Early Modern England* (New York, 2001), pp. 12–16; Vitkus, *Turning Turk*, pp. 78–9.

[2] There is one small hint of a New World context in Othello's reference to encounters with 'Cannibals' after his redemption from slavery (1.3.143); but, as the importation of New World material, including the anagrammatic cannibal Caliban, into the Mediterranean world of *The Tempest* shows, Shakespeare could be cavalier with such geographical niceties.

[3] Carol Thomas Neely, 'Circumscriptions and Unhousedness: *Othello* in the Borderlands', in Deborah Barker and Ivo Kamps (eds.), *Shakespeare and Gender: A History* (1995).

early modern language of colour was indelibly marked by biblical symbolism and by primitive fears that associated darkness with evil and death. Shakespeare's treatment of Aaron, the demonic Moor of his earliest tragedy, *Titus Andronicus*, capitulates almost entirely to this reading of blackness; and it is to the same understanding of colour that Emilia instinctively appeals when Othello confesses to Desdemona's murder: 'O, the more angel she, and you the blacker devil!' (5.2.131). In one of the most frequently cited scriptural passages the prophet Jeremiah had used black skin as an archetypal marker of evil: 'Can the black Moor change his skin? or the leopard his spots? *Then* may ye also do good, that are accustomed to do evil' (Jeremiah 13: 23). In this tradition blackness was not just an analogical metaphor for the ingrained and indelible nature of habitual sin, but the visible sign of sin itself. It was, moreover, strongly associated with sexual transgression, since the origins of black skin were supposed to lie in God's curse upon the adulterate offspring of Ham. So it was that the travel writer George Best, for example, explained the colour of 'all these black Moors which are in Africa' as evidence of the 'natural infection' visited on Noah's son Ham after he flouted his father's prohibition against copulation in the Ark: 'God would a son should be born [to him] whose name was Chus, who, not only [him]self, but all his posterity after him, should be so black and loathsome, that it might remain a spectacle of disobedience to all the world.'[1] The black sins which cannot be hidden from Jeremiah's God are of the same character: 'Therefore will I discover thy skirts upon thy face, that thy shame may appear. I have seen thy adulteries, thy neighings, the lewdness of thy whoredom, and thine abominations' (Jeremiah 13: 26–7). Somewhere behind Iago's obscene characterization of Othello as a rutting 'barbary horse', Shakespeare's audience will have heard these animal 'neighings', prompting them to identify Othello's blackness as the mark of an unspeakable adulteration.

[1] George Best, in Richard Hakluyt, *The Principal Navigations, Voyages, Traffiques, and Discoveries of the English Nation*, ed. Walter Raleigh, 12 vols. (Glasgow, 1903–5), vii. 263–4. See also Neill, ' "Mulattos" ', p. 272, and 'Opening the Moor: Death and Discovery in *Othello*', in *Issues of Death: Mortality and Identity in English Renaissance Tragedy* (Oxford, 1997), 141–67 (esp. pp. 145–8). On the motif of 'washing the Ethiop white', see Newman (above p. 115, n. 2) and Jean Michel Massing, 'From Greek Proverb to Soap Advert: Washing the Ethiopian', *Journal of the Warburg and Courtauld Institutes*, 58 (1995), 180–201.

Clearly this powerful strain of biblical imagery—reinforced by a habit of climatological and humoral theorizing that ascribed 'hot', passionate temperaments to the denizens of sweltering southern regions—helped to colour the frequent pseudo-ethnographic caricatures of black Africans as anarchic, passion-driven, lustful and dangerously jealous people, closer to beasts than men. Thus, for example, in Francis Bacon's *New Atlantis* the Spirit of Fornication itself is said to take the form of 'a little foul ugly Ethiope'.[1] It is on stereotypes of this kind that Iago capitalizes, not just in his images of bestial appetite, but in his stigmatization of Othello as a 'lusty' adulterer (2.1.286), an 'erring Barbarian' whose promiscuous desires can only confirm the irrational nature of a people notoriously 'changeable in their wills', i.e. sexual appetites (1.3.340–3, 348–9). But if Iago gives voice to an emerging racialism that became increasingly dominant as the seventeenth century advanced, his were by no means the only available views. Indeed, as Mary Floyd-Wilson has shown, the oldest and most authoritative geohumoral theories were fully in accord with Desdemona's belief that the torrid southern climate would burn up the hot and moist humours liable to cause jealousy, leaving the African temperament cool, dry, and melancholy: 'I think the sun where he was born | Drew all such humours from him' (3.4.28–9). Africans, according to this belief, were naturally wiser, more constant, and more restrained than Northerners whose cold environment left them a prey to the passionate influence of hot, moist humours.[2]

Moreover, the extensive travel literature of the period, while it frequently confirmed the prejudices on which Iago trades, also offered examples of more objective ethnography. According to some authorities, after all, dark skin was a phenomenon that could be explained simply as an accidental effect of the sun's burning rays.[3] Furthermore, as we have seen, there were theological traditions, founded in the Song of Songs, and bolstered by the legends of Balthasar, Prester John, and the black St Maurice, that allowed for a positive image of black people;[4] and it is upon the paradoxical

---

[1] By contrast, the Spirit of Chastity is said to have 'the likeness of a fair beautiful Cherubim': Bacon, *New Atlantis* (1659), sig. D2ᵛ.

[2] Mary Floyd-Wilson, *English Ethnicity and Race in Early Modern Drama* (Cambridge, 2003), esp. Introduction, and chap. 6, 'Othello's Jealousy'.

[3] See Neill, ' "Mulattos" ', pp. 274–7.

[4] See above, 'Sources', p. 26.

language of fair blackness fostered by these traditions that the Duke draws when he assures Brabantio that 'If virtue no delighted beauty lack, | Your son-in-law is far more fair than black' (1.3.287–8). In the secular world attitudes to black skin were also affected by a courtly fascination with exotica that we can see reflected in the bedazzled Romeo's first vision of Juliet: 'she hangs upon the cheek of night | As a rich jewel in an Ethiope's ear' (1.5.44–5). Encouraged by the tastes of Queen Anne, this fad would reach its apogee in the performance of Jonson's paired masques of *Blackness* (1605) and *Beauty* (1608), in which the Queen and her ladies appeared in blackface. Although the programme of these entertainments required that these Daughters of Niger travel to the blessed isle of Albion in order that its prince might magically perfect their beauty by turning them white, Ethiopia was nevertheless identified as a fount of ancient wisdom, while Niger himself was allowed a lyrical defence of blackness that served to validate the Queen's choice of swarthy disguise.[1]

So, although there can be no doubt that early modern culture offered plenty of purchase for the latent bigotry that Iago successfully animates among the Venetians, there was nevertheless no single explanatory template to which audiences could automatically refer in their response to a black Moor; and the play itself is at some pains to ensure the fiercely debatable significance of the protagonist's colour. Thus, while Iago's opening slurs capitalize on the vulgar stereotypes of unbridled black sensuality, they are immediately reversed when Othello and Desdemona are arraigned before the Senate: here it is she who speaks the language of sexual passion, boasting of the 'downright violence' of her feelings and openly asserting her entitlement to 'the rites for why I love him' (1.3.247, 255). Othello, by contrast, is at pains to deny that 'appetite', 'heat', or the 'light-winged toys | Of feathered Cupid' have any part in determining his behaviour (ll. 259–72), and to the end insists on his fundamentally dispassionate nature as one 'not easily jealous' (5.2.344). Far from being an example of the self-deception of which Leavis and others have accused him, this claim, as well as being consonant with mainstream geohumoral theory, is sup-

---

[1] Cf. Floyd-Wilson, chap. 5, 'Temperature and Temperance in the *Masque of Blackness*'.

ported by other characters: Lodovico, astonished by Othello's violence in 4.1, recalls the 'solid virtue' and sufficiency of a 'nature | Whom passion could not shake' (4.1.257–8); Iago himself acknowledges his 'constant, loving, noble nature' (2.1.280); while Desdemona, even after she has been subjected to his first angry outbursts against her, continues to believe that jealousy is alien to her husband's essential self. If anything, as Mary Floyd-Wilson demonstrates, it is Iago's brooding inferiority and habitual suspiciousness that identify him with the naturally jealous temperament that the English were as likely to attribute to Italians as to Moors (pp. 142–6).

Moreover, if blackness was visited upon Chus and his descendants as a 'spectacle of disobedience', a Jacobean audience would surely have noticed that obedience is actually the virtue most conspicuously associated with Othello, who takes pride in his loyal service to the Venetian state (1.2.18, 4.1.213, 5.2.338) and his willingness to 'obey the mandate' (4.1.251). By contrast, it is Iago who is cast from his first appearance in the play as the archetypal disobedient servant, whose rebellion mirrors that of Lucifer himself (1.1.42–65);[1] and if Iago's slurs work to identify Othello as a conventional 'black devil', it is the ensign himself who finally stands exposed (in the oxymoron that Othello mistakenly applies to Desdemona) as a 'fair devil'—thereby confirming the proverbial wisdom that 'the white devil is worser than the black' (Tilley D310 and cf. D231).

Nevertheless, the history of the play's critical reception is bound to act as a caution against too complacent a reading of its attitudes to colour. *Othello*, in Floyd-Wilson's words, 'stands at a crossroads in the history of ethnological ideas' (p. 140); and, given the extent to which Iago's stratagem does after all succeed in making the Moor behave exactly as hostile stereotyping would predict, a question remains as to whether *Othello* does not in some way solicit the audience's complicity in the very prejudices it appears to condemn.[2] Part of the answer to that question, I will suggest, is to be

[1] See below, pp. 164–5.

[2] Floyd-Wilson, for example, argues that 'the force of Iago's hostility' is sufficient to 'dislodg[e] the geohumoral homologies that . . . established blackness as the sign of wisdom and constancy' so that 'Desdemona's classical knowledge gives way to a racialized construction of Moors as passionate, lascivious, volatile, jealous savages' (p. 158).

found in the shocking tableau at the end of the tragedy: its display of three dead bodies—those of a black man and two white women—stretched out upon a bed.

'Othello' and Discovery

> For now is nothing hid
> Of what fear did restrain.
> No secret closely done,
> But now is uttered.
> The text is made most plain,
> That flattery glozed upon,
> The bed of sin revealed,
> And all the luxury
> That shame would have concealed.
> The scene is broken down,
> And all uncov'red lies.

Samuel Daniel, *The Tragedy of Cleopatra*, Chorus I

> The bed heightened private pleasure . . . but the bed could also be a symbol of guilt, a shadowy place, a scene of crime; the truth of what went on there could never be revealed.

Danielle Régnier Bohler[1]

If we want to understand the designs that plays have on us, endings, as Byron understood, are a good place to start: 'All tragedies', he wrote, in a wryly reductive summary of generic convention, 'are finished by a death, | All comedies are ended by a marriage' (*Don Juan*, 3.9). *Othello*, however—as befits a tragedy that makes such extensive use of comic convention[2]—ends in strange conflation of the two, as the hero transforms his suicide into a symbolic reaffirmation of the marital bond he has annihilated:

> I kissed thee ere I killed thee—no way but this:
> Killing myself, to die upon a kiss.
>
> (5.2.357–8)

With its extravagant literalization of the trope of erotic 'death', Othello's embrace does of course recall the kiss of mortal rapture

---

[1] 'Imagining the Self', in Philippe Ariès and Georges Dubuy (gen. eds.), *A History of Private Life*, 3 vols. (Cambridge, Mass., 1987), ii. 311–93 (p. 330).
[2] See above, 'Reception', pp. 5–6.

that crowns the final scene of *Romeo and Juliet*: 'Thus with a kiss I die' (5.3.120; and cf. 164–7). The recollection of *Romeo and Juliet*, however, serves as an immediate reminder of the grotesque indecorum of this ending. Shakespeare's first love-tragedy (like his last, *Antony and Cleopatra*) ends where it properly should, in a place of death—the funeral vault of the Capulets. It is only Romeo's fevered imagination that converts Juliet's tomb to the 'pallet of dim night' where Death keeps her 'to be his paramour' (*Romeo*, 5.3.103–7); by contrast, Desdemona's murder and Othello's suicide are performed on an actual marriage bed—the very property at which the endings of romantic comedy conventionally gesture.

In comedy—whether the gesture is merely implicit as in Benedick's insistence that 'the world must be peopled' (*Much Ado*, 2.3.229–30), or explicit, as in Theseus' repeated 'Lovers to bed' at the end of *A Midsummer Night's Dream* (5.1.357, 361)—the bed remains a purely imaginary property. It is the absent site of an always-deferred consummation by which the conventional 'happy-ever-after' ending proposes to keep its lovers young for ever. In *Othello*, by contrast, the bed is made shockingly present, as the locus of a marriage that appears to find its full consummation only in violent death. In this scene of butchery it is as if the 'monster ... Too hideous to be shown' that Othello detected lurking in Iago's thought (3.3.110–11) had at last taken palpable form. What results is a spectacle that Lodovico, for reasons that he cannot (will not? dare not?) articulate, finds unbearable, ordering the bed-curtains to be abruptly drawn upon it.[1] In a strange way this gesture of erasure chimes with Iago's obdurate refusal to explain his motives, reminding us that in this tragedy the compulsion to reveal is always matched by a longing for concealment. Thus in the temptation scene Iago responds to Othello's repeated demand that he 'Show' the 'horrible conceit' 'shut up in [his] brain' (3.3.117–19) by insisting upon the irrefragable privacy of the hidden self: thought, he declares, in a mocking gibe at the new science of anatomy,[2] can never be opened up to autoptic inspection: 'You

---

[1] For a more detailed analysis of the bed motif in *Othello* and its relation to the play's racial themes, see Neill, ' "Unproper Beds" '.

[2] On the operation of this motif in the play, see Neill, 'Opening the Moor'.

cannot, if my heart were in your hand' (3.3.166). His last words in the play reaffirm this contemptuous refusal to disclose the secrets of his malice, even under the threat of torture: 'Demand me nothing: what you know, you know; | From this time forth I never will speak word' (5.2.301–2).

Iago is the prime agent of the play's drive to concealment: a compulsive histrion and soliloquizer, he is like a deformed version of Hamlet, priding himself on the possession of 'that within which passeth show' (*Hamlet*, 1.2.85). But, like the Prince of Denmark, Iago is also in the business of exposure—ostensibly of Desdemona's sexual secrets ('Her honour is an essence that's not seen', 4.1.15), but in fact of Othello's psychic mysteries; and just as Hamlet's theatrical stratagem forces Claudius to confront his suppressed guilt in the anguish of the prayer soliloquy (*Hamlet*, 3.3.36–72), so Iago's performance is designed, by opening what he calls 'the door of truth' (3.3.409), to expose Othello's inner life to the gaze of fearful introspection. The Moor whom we are shown before the temptation scene is a man whose identity seems so wholly invested in his confident, slightly orotund public persona that it is almost impossible to imagine him in soliloquy. But as Iago's poisonous insinuation works upon him, Othello is progressively exposed to a psychic predation that, by the middle of this scene, drives him to agonized self-questioning (3.3.261–80). Thenceforth he is so possessed by the 'bloody thoughts' aroused in him (l. 457) that he can slide into tormented monologue even in the midst of a conversation with others (3.3.347–59; 4.2.47–64; 5.2.271–80).

What Othello discovers in the murky inner space that the ensign reveals to him is, in one sense, a fictional creation: the 'green-eyed monster' of jealousy simply replicates the 'hideous monster' that Othello was allowed to glimpse lurking in Iago's own psyche. What makes its disclosure so devastating to him, however, and so appalling to the audience, is the psychological truth enfolded in that fiction. This is something at which Iago gloatingly hints when he imagines how his poison, working with 'a little act upon the blood', will begin to 'Burn like the mines of sulphur' (3.3.327–31). 'Blood' here is usually taken to mean (jealous) passion, but by virtue of its juxtaposition with 'burn' it is also likely to suggest sexual arousal; and of course the striking thing about Othello's jealousy is the intensely erotic charge it gives to his language. As the hitherto seamless surface of 'the Moor of Venice' begins to crack, Othello descends into the first of his jealous soliloquies:

> I had rather be a toad
> And live upon the vapour of a dungeon,
> Than keep a corner in the thing I love
> For others' uses.
>
> (3.3.273–6)

Before long, however, that image will be transformed in a way that thoroughly implicates him in the scene of lechery he so abhors— the toad becoming a figure of poisonous desire, and the dungeon itself a dank 'corner' of promiscuous adultery, 'a cistern for foul toads | To knot and gender in' (4.2.61–2). From the moment that he first begins to imagine the possibility of Desdemona's betrayal, Othello's speech reveals an increasingly thirsty longing to witness the very thing he most dreads: 'be sure thou prove my love a whore . . . give me the ocular proof. . . . Make me to see't . . . Would I were satisfied' (3.3.361–2, 366, 392). The archness of Iago's dry repetition 'You would be *satisfied*? . . . How "*satisfied*"?' (ll. 395–6) highlights the way that Othello's choice of verb implicitly confesses to the same perverse appetite that is apparent in his cry 'I had been happy if the general camp, | Pioneers and all, had tasted her sweet body' (ll. 347–8). In these lines jealousy takes the form of a horrifying desire to bewhore his own wife, one that is only barely contained by the qualifying 'So I had nothing known', set off like an afterthought in the next line.

Disturbingly, this is the very desire that will seem to be gratified by the 'horrible fancy' of the brothel scene (4.2), where Othello plays the part of a customer in an exclusive bordello managed by the bawd Emilia. Referring to the privy knowledge that belongs to her professional 'mystery', he calls Emilia 'A closet, lock, and key of villainous secrets' (l. 22); but the real secret laid bare in this scene is that of Othello's own repressed desire. This is not to say that the Moor wishes to prostitute his wife in any literal sense—only that it is through the jealous fantasy of her body becoming an object of satisfaction for other men that he first discovers the terrible depth of his own need for her. That is what traps him in the sado-masochistic 'sinner's discourse' described by Harry Berger—a condition that drives him to enlist Iago's aid as 'the scourge or justicer who will help him procure the sinner's keen and bitter pleasure of hurting, punishing, destroying himself by hurting, punishing, destroying what, next to himself, he most loves'.[1]

This can happen, Berger suggests (following Stanley Cavell, p. 133), because the one thing Othello fears more than Desdemona's faithlessness is 'her faithfulness'—the extravagant abandon of a desire that invites an equal self-abandonment from him. For, in stark contrast to Roderigo's caricature of an 'extravagant and wheeling stranger' (1.1.135), Othello is a man whose high sense of himself—displayed in the cool dignity of his response to Brabantio in the second and third scenes—depends on his conviction of a self-mastery so absolute that it renders him immune to all extremes of passion and appetite. Of course the touchiness he displays in repudiating any suggestion that his wish to take Desdemona to Cyprus is meant 'To please the palate of my appetite' (1.3.259–72) might be taken to reveal an unconscious chink in this stoic armour; but even as he is about to plunge into the first frenzy of jealousy, Othello continues to take pride in the iron 'government' of his emotions (3.3.260). The terrible irony of his fate is that the very 'Chaos' he envisages as the consequence of ceasing to love Desdemona (3.3.93) comes upon him precisely as a result of abject submission to that love, in the distorted form that Iago gives to it. This psychic disintegration is what is registered in the linguistic confusion of the speech that triggers his epileptic fit:

Lie with her? Lie on her? We say 'lie on her' when they belie her. Lie with her? 'Swounds, that's fulsome! Handkerchief—confessions—handkerchief? . . . It is not words that shakes me thus. Pish! Noses, ears, and lips! Is't possible? Confess? Handkerchief? O, devil!

(4.1.33–40)

In the context of this collapse, Othello's last big speech (5.2. 337–55), with its insistence on presenting him as 'one not easily jealous', can be seen as a desperate attempt to restore the economy of emotional repression enforced by his earlier 'government' of the self. Taking the place of the funeral oration with which tragedy typically seeks to impose order on the chaotic spectacle of slaughter, Othello's apologia for his own life returns to his earlier rhetoric of

---

[1] Harry Berger Jr., 'Three's Company: The Specter of Contaminated Intimacy in *Othello*', *The Shakespearean International Yearbook* (2004), 235–63.

studied self-display. Yet, as if he were conscious of the unsustain-ability of such attitudinizing, the speech ends in the 'bloody period' of a self-undoing (the killing of his Turkish alter ego) that to the horrified onlookers seems to cancel its own significance (l. 356). Thus the final scene of the tragedy exemplifies in an extreme form the tension between secrecy and disclosure that is characteristic of its entire action. Constructed like an elaborate play on the Aris-totelian notion of *anagnorisis* (or tragic discovery), it begins by enacting a figure of simultaneous illumination and obfuscation, as Othello, standing torch in hand over the newly revealed bed, pre-pares to 'put out the light'; and it ends, just as *anagnorisis* seems to have been given grimly material form in the bed's 'tragic loading' of bodies, with a final gesture of stern erasure: 'The object poisons sight—| Let it be hid' (5.2.362–4).

The shocking force of the spectacle that Lodovico here seeks to obliterate is registered in the extraordinary wrench that he gives to the play's running metaphor of poison. Hitherto (in a figure already familiar from *Hamlet*) Iago's venomous concoctions have worked upon the ear (1.1.68; 2.3.341; 3.3.327–31); now, as if in final mocking response to the Moor's repeated demands for 'ocular proof', it is the eye that receives the poison; and Othello himself, as though the 'pestilence' that Iago poured in his ear had corrupted his whole being, has become the noxious centre-piece of a scene that threatens to infect all its lookers-on—not just the horrified Venetians, but the audience, whose gaze Lodovico directs at the corpses on the bed. The overdetermined character of this display must have been what so impressed the imagination of the play's earliest witness, who could not forget the piteous sight of the murdered Desdemona 'lying in her bed'.[1] If Johnson and Furness found the scene unendurable,[2] it nevertheless exer-cised, as we have seen, a compulsive hold on the imagination of eighteenth- and nineteenth-century illustrators: engraving after engraving, uses Desdemona's exposed body, its unconscious invitation emphasized by the parted bed-curtains, to foreground both the perverse eroticism of the spectacle and its suggestion of forbidden disclosure. In George Noble's engraving for the Boydell Gallery, the murderer himself turns away, a hand clutched over his

---

[1] See above, p. 1.
[2] See Siemon, p. 39, and Furness, p. 300.

eyes, as though blinded by Desdemona's beauty and the prospect of his crime (fig. 5).[1]

What makes this final scene so unbearable is the way in which it seems to make visible those half-occluded fantasies of sexual monstrosity with which the play has tormented its audience. It confronts us, Stanley Cavell has argued, with the very thing '*denied our sight* throughout the opening scene—the thing . . . that Iago takes Othello back to again and again, retouching it for Othello's enchafed imagination . . . the scene of murder'.[2] Beginning with the pornographic speculation aimed at Brabantio in 1.1, *Othello* works continuously to excite the scopic curiosity of its audience: if its central action turns on Othello's increasingly desperate demand for 'ocular proof' (3.3.362), his dreadful desire to become (in Iago's cruelly chosen phrase) the 'supervisor' of his wife's adultery, the play arouses a similarly ambiguous longing in the audience to 'grossly gape on' (l. 397). The repeated frustration of this need means that even a matter so apparently straightforward as the consummation of Othello's and Desdemona's marriage becomes clouded by a miasma of doubt and impertinent conjecture.

Rymer was the first to draw attention to the uncertainty surrounding the couple's sexual relations: he complained that although 'the *audience* must suppose a great many bouts, to make the plot operate', the interruption of the couple's rendezvous at the Sagittary and the tightness of the ensuing time scheme make it impossible for them to spend more than a single night together.[3] Fastening on the same apparent inconsistencies, some recent critics have questioned whether there is time for the marriage to be consummated at all. Othello's conspicuous failure to answer Iago's nudging 'Are you fast married?' (1.2.11), when combined with his later reference to the still-to-be-achieved 'fruits' and 'profit' of their love (2.3.9–10), seems to imply that their sexual union has still to be achieved when Othello and Desdemona arrive in Cyprus; and although Iago's bawdy jesting with Cassio continues to evoke a

---

[1] See Neill, ' "Unproper Beds" ', pp. 238–40 and Figs. 8–13.
[2] Cavell, p. 132; cf. also James L. Calderwood, *The Properties of Othello* (Amherst, Mass., 1989), p. 125; and Lynda E. Boose, ' "Let it be hid": The Pornographic Aesthetic of Shakespeare's *Othello*', in Lena Cowen Orlin (ed.), *Othello: Contemporary Critical Essays* (Basingstoke, 2004), 22–48.
[3] Rymer, p. 123. On the play's use of so-called 'double-time', see above, pp. 33–6.

scene of sexual pillage ('he tonight hath boarded a land-carrack', 1.2.50), his claim that Othello has 'not yet made wanton the night with' Desdemona (2.3.15–16) also suggests non-consummation— though it might mean only that they have not yet enjoyed a full night of bliss; and in any case there is no reason to believe anything that Iago says as he plays with Cassio's erotic imagination. Never-theless, when the couple's wedded bliss is interrupted for the second time—on this occasion by Cassio's drunken brawling—the audience is left with the possibility that consummation has once again been deferred. Moreover, since (given the elastic nature of stage time) we have no sure means of knowing how long a period intervenes between Othello's 'Come away to bed' (2.3.244) and Cassio's musical aubade at the beginning of 3.1, it remains possible that physical union is never accomplished.[1] That is what T. G. A. Nelson and Charles Haines have argued in a controversial essay that locates the hidden spring of the tragedy in the Moor's sexual inexperience and in the sense of impotence that is awakened in him by his failure to conquer Desdemona's virginity.[2]

The fact of the matter remains, however, that—in default of the explicit witness with which Shakespeare's theatre conventionally attested to the truth of offstage action—the question of consum-mation remains fundamentally undecidable; and that surely is the point. For it is this very uncertainty that encourages the habit of prurient speculation into which the play lures its spectators—the habit of which the Nelson and Haines's article is itself a prime ex-ample.[3] By the same token, it is the audience's frustrated appetite

---

[1] See above, 'Sources', p. 33.

[2] 'Othello's Unconsummated Marriage', *Essays in Criticism*, 33 (1983), 1–17. In *Misrepresentations* (pp. 150–1, 163–8), Graham Bradshaw, though critical of Nelson and Haines's literal-minded treatment of stage time, nevertheless concludes that Othello's tormented longing to dye the wedding-sheets with the blood of murder (5.1.37) makes sense only if they have not yet been stained with the blood of virgin-ity. But this is probably to attribute a logic to the Moor's fantasy that his jealous madness will not admit. Furthermore, as Derek Cohen has pointed out, since '[t]he wedding sheets are not presumed automatically to be on the bed in preparation for a first use[, they] must, therefore, have been previously used so that Emilia could iden-tify them as wedding sheets' (*Searching Shakespeare: Studies in Culture and Authority* (Toronto, 2003), p. 98).

[3] Ironically, the same habit is revealed in Norman Nathan's point-by-point rebuttal of Nelson and Haines, which shares their naive assumptions about the decidability of offstage actions—see 'Othello's Marriage is Consummated', *Cahiers Élisabéthains*, 34 (1988), 79–82. Oliver Parker's decision to include in his 1995 film a

for certainty, paralleling the protagonist's increasingly frantic desire to have his suspicions 'satisfied' (3.3.392–410), that enables Iago to act as a uniquely deceitful version of the *nuntius*—the normally reliable messenger-figure inherited from classical drama—one whose obscene fictions infect the imagination of the audience, even as they colonize the minds of his victims. The result is that, whatever our conscious minds may think about the causes of the tragic catastrophe, its array of corpses on a brutally violated marriage bed can feel like a confirmation of the ensign's grossest insinuations—of everything that he has suggested about the adulterate and unnatural character of the relationship for which the bed itself stands.[1]

'*Othello*' *and the Monstrous*   Meditating on the significance of the ending, G. M. Matthews describes 'a bed on which a black man and a white girl, although they are dead, are embracing', and discovers in that spectacle an icon of humanist transcendence: '[h]uman dignity, the play says, is indivisible.'[2] That may perhaps be what the play (for some viewers and readers at least) *implies*; but what it *says*, as we have already observed, is something else. Where a litany of admiration sweeps Hamlet 'like a soldier to the stage' (5.2.350), language appears simply confounded by Othello's fate—'All that's spoke is marred' (5.2.356); where the bodies of Romeo and Juliet are to be resurrected with celebratory 'statue[s] in pure gold' (5.3.298), the corpses of Othello and Desdemona, 'poison[ing] sight', must be hurriedly shut from view. Nor is Matthews's description of the scene quite accurate: for, as Emilia's request to 'lay me by my mistress' side' indicates (5.2.236), there are not two but three bodies on the bed. Together they form a kind of deathly *ménage à trois* that uneasily recalls Iago's suspicion that ''twixt my sheets | [the Moor has] done my office' (1.3.376–7). It is not, obviously, that we are meant to read the stage image as a literal confirmation of that claim, only that on the symbolic level it can

---

scene in which Othello and Desdemona are seen consummating their marriage on the first night constituted a particularly crass response to the voyeuristic curiosity aroused by Shakespeare's text.

[1] On the social symbolism of the marriage bed in early modern culture, see below, p. 173 and Neill, ' "Unproper Beds" ', pp. 266–7.

[2] Matthews, '*Othello* and the Dignity of Man', p. 145 (see above, p. 63, n. 1).

seem to taint Othello's romantic *liebestod* with the mark of adulterous impropriety.

The inarticulate horror that characterizes the Venetian response to this disturbingly improper tableau is first expressed by Montano: appalled by the sight of Desdemona 'murdered in her bed', he exclaims against what he calls this '*monstrous* act' (5.2.183, 187). To the modern ear that may sound like a cliché of outrage; but 'monstrous' and 'monster' are key terms in this play, charged with meanings that have largely dissipated in modern English:[1] derived from Latin *monere* (to warn), 'monster' originally denoted some baneful portent or prodigy, but came to refer particularly to freaks of nature, especially those hybrid creatures supposedly produced by violations of the boundaries of kind. In so far as the 'monstrous' is defined as existing beyond the proper limits of nature, it also lies in some sense beyond the limits of rational speech, in the occluded domain of the 'indescribable' or 'unspeakable'; indeed, by virtue of its horrible deformity that is where it is best kept, shut away. Yet— as the popularity of fairground freak shows, the avid collection of monstrous exhibits in Renaissance *wunderkammern,* and the playful excesses of grotesque art all illustrate—monsters were also objects of intense fascination in early modern culture; and the word, linked by false etymology to *monstrare* (to show), came to denote a creature that, by virtue of its very atrociousness, demanded to be seen—like the 'monster . . . Too hideous to be shown' that Othello detects 'shut up in [Iago's] brain' (3.3.110–19).[2]

Better than any other, then, 'monstrous' is the term that expresses *Othello*'s simultaneous drives towards revelation and concealment. Images of monstrosity crowd the play, as if spawned

[1] See Newman, 'Femininity and the Monstrous', and Neill, ' "Unproper Beds" ', pp. 259–68. For a more elaborate exploration of the trope of monstrosity in the play, see Mark Thornton Burnett, ' "As it is credibly thought": Conceiving "Monsters" in *Othello*', chap. 4 of *Constructing 'Monsters' in Shakespearean Drama and Early Modern Culture* (Basingstoke, 2002).

[2] Patricia Parker offers brilliant discussion of the motifs of hiddenness and exposure in a series of essays: 'Shakespeare and Rhetoric: "Dilation" and "Delation" in *Othello*', in Patricia Parker and Geoffrey Hartman (eds.), *Shakespeare and the Question of Theory* (New York and London, 1985), 54–174; 'Fantasies of "Race" and "Gender": Africa, Othello, and Bringing to Light', in Margo Hendricks and Patricia Parker (eds.), *Women, 'Race', and Writing in the Early Modern Period* (1994), 84–100; and '*Othello* and *Hamlet*; Spying, Discovery, Secret Faults', in Parker, *Shakespeare from the Margins: Language, Culture, Context* (Chicago, 1996), chap. 7.

by the unnatural couplings that Iago imagined taking place under the sign of the Sagittary, the man–horse hybrid that gave its name to Othello's and Desdemona's lodging in Act 1.[1] It is not for nothing that Iago will later taunt Othello with his privy knowledge of 'many a civil monster' infesting 'many a . . . populous city' (4.1.59–60); for he himself inhabits, to use his own felicitously chosen phrase, a 'monstrous world' (3.3.379), crafted in his own image. At the beginning of the play, the ensign stage-manages, for Brabantio's benefit, a kind of psychic discovery scene: drawing back the curtains of imagination he seems to expose the hidden fantasies of his society, luridly illuminating the dark Venetian street with a vision that uncannily resembles the dream from which the old man has just been awakened (1.1.142). With Roderigo's help, he compels Brabantio to envisage the very bedchamber where his daughter, 'Transported . . . To the gross clasps of a lascivious Moor' (ll. 124–5), is locked in bestial coition:

> Even now, now, very now, an old black ram
> Is tupping your white ewe.

. . . you'll have your daughter covered with a Barbary horse. . . . your daughter and the Moor are now making the beast with two backs.

(1.1.88–9, 110–16)

While targeted at the paternal outrage of Brabantio, the violent grotesquerie of the couplings envisaged here is equally calculated to excite the imagination of the audience, turning the marriage bed into a site of prurient speculation until the shocking moment of its actual discovery in Act 5. For of course it is not just in the opening scene that *Othello* goads us with the sense of something wilfully 'denied our sight': not only do the jealous anxieties rehearsed by Iago, Bianca, and Othello demonstrate their society's obsession with sexual honour as 'an essence that's not seen' (4.1.15), but the language of the play, full of allusions to beds and wedding sheets,[2] and studded with metaphors of begetting and parturition, also stimulates a growing itch of curiosity about the absent scene of

---

[1] For the centaur as a symbol of lust, barbarism, and monstrous violation of kind, see Calderwood, pp. 22–5, 36.

[2] For discussion of these details and the anxieties revealed by their systematic bowdlerization in eighteenth- and nineteenth-century productions, see ' "Unproper Beds" ', pp. 240, 251–9.

17. The Temptation Scene: Paul Robeson as Othello, José Ferrer as Iago
(Shubert Theatre, New York, 1943).

desire—a curiosity that is repeatedly gratified (though never, of course, satisfied) by Iago's bestial imaginings.

It is these obscene fictions that combine to form the 'monstrous' offspring whose birth Iago anticipates at the end of the first act (1.3.392–3). Self-engendered, like the jealous 'monster' described by Emilia ('Begot upon itself, born on itself', 3.4.156–7), this is the atrocious prodigy whose advent is foreshadowed by the 'monstrous mane' of the storm that begins Act 2, and again by the 'monstrous' brawl that Iago engineers during the first night on Cyprus (2.1.13, 2.3.208). It begins to emerge as the 'green-eyed monster' of jealousy which he conjures up in the temptation scene (3.3.169). This is the creature which Desdemona will pray heaven to keep from her husband's mind (3.4.158), but which his cry of 'monstrous!

Monstrous!' (3.3.428) shows to be already lodged amongst the 'foul toads' that 'knot and gender' in the fetid 'dungeon' of his imagination (3.3.273–4, 4.2.61–2). In Act 5 the creature at last takes physical shape in the form of the poisonous 'object' disgracing the marriage bed. Othello's hallucinated image of the planned murder as a second perverted pregnancy—'the strong *conception* | That I do groan withal' (5.2.57–8)—finally confirms that the thing so long 'denied our sight', but now about to be brought 'to the world's light' is nothing other than the 'monstrous birth' promised in Iago's annunciation (1.3.393).

Othello and Iago not only give birth to monsters, but are themselves tainted by monstrosity. Possessed by the deformed imaginings with which Iago has, as it were, impregnated his imagination, Othello begins to see himself like another deformed denizen of Iago's menagerie—'A hornèd man's a monster and a beast' (4.1.58); and Iago's suavely ambiguous reply—'There's many a beast then in a populous city, | And many a *civil monster*' (4.1.59–60)—seems to confirm that identification, his arch oxymoron implying that the Moor's 'civil' veneer, unnaturally conjoined to his bestial essence, constitutes a double violation of nature. Yet even with her last breath, Desdemona, who professes to know her husband's inward self, persists in seeing her murderer as 'my *kind* lord' (5.2.125)—the extra-stressing of that carefully insistent adjective pointing up the extreme irony of its application, even as it appeals to a realm of purified emotion where Iago-like judgements about the limits of 'kind' would appear an obscene irrelevance. For coolly regarded it is not the Moor but Iago himself—the professed Venetian rather than the 'erring stranger'—who stands disclosed to the audience as the true 'civil monster' (4.1.60)[1]—just as, in the play's colour symbolism, it is the inner blackness concealed by the white Iago's 'forms and visages of duty' (1.1.50) which serves to offset the fair 'visage in his mind' (1.3.250) that Desdemona discovers in 'the black Othello'; and we are invited to discern similarly schematic ironies in the seemingly indiscriminate application of such terms as 'honest' to Iago, Desdemona, and Bianca, or 'devil' to Desdemona, Iago, and Othello.

---

[1] This, indeed, is precisely how he is described in the ballad based on the play: 'Iago was the monster's name' (see Furness, p. 399).

In fact, however, the play never quite allows us the detachment necessary to render these schemata entirely secure. Instead it taunts the audience with the possibility that (despite Desdemona's fidelity) Iago only discovers what was always there beneath the Moor's civil manners, advertised by the blackness of his skin[1]—the barbarous and 'malignant' alien whom Othello summons as his fatal alter ego at the moment of suicide (5.2.352). The very fact that the play's opening scene grants Iago the structural position of a prologue, introducing us to Othello and Desdemona, well before they are allowed to represent themselves, gives him an inestimable advantage in this regard: because the most lurid of his erotic fantasies are placed so early in the action, the lovers can never entirely escape their vile taint. In his evocation of their love-making, the gathering imputation of something obscenely deviant in the conjunction of black ram and white ewe, of stallion and girl, is rhetorically confirmed by the monstrous deformity of the creature it produces—a 'beast with two backs'. It is as if the hidden coupling had already spawned the 'monstrous birth' of Iago's fantasy; and this is what works (at the irrational level of suggestion) to underwrite Brabantio's insistence that his daughter's marriage constitutes a profound violation of the natural order:

> For *nature* so preposterously to err—
> Being not deficient, blind, or lame of sense—
> Sans witchcraft could not. . . .
>   and she—in spite of *nature*,
> Of years, of country, credit, everything—
> To fall in love with what she feared to look on?
> It is a judgement maimed and most imperfect
> That will confess perfection so could err
> Against all rules of *nature* . . .
>
>   (1.3.63–5, 97–102)

The rhetorical power of this denunciation is given dramatic emphasis by the way in which Othello himself is made to echo it, as

---

[1] Kenneth Burke beautifully conveys the power of inarticulate suggestion that Iago exploits in the play: 'there is whispering. There is something vaguely feared and hated. In itself it is hard to locate, being woven into the very nature of "consciousness": but by the artifice of Iago it is made local. The tinge of malice vaguely diffused through the texture of events can here be condensed into a single principle, a devil, giving the audience as it were flesh to sink their claw-thoughts in': '*Othello*: An Essay to Illustrate a Method', in Susan Snyder (ed.), *'Othello': Critical Essays* (New York, 1988), 127–68 (p. 131).

(under Iago's tutelage) he begins to internalize the libels of his enemies. At a fatal moment in the temptation scene, prompted by
Othello's insistence on the infallibility of ocular judgement ('she
had *eyes* and chose me. . . . I'll *see* before I doubt' (3.3.192–3), Iago
reminds the Moor of Brabantio's charges:

> She did deceive her father, marrying you;
> And when she seemed to shake and fear your looks,
> She loved them most. . . .
> She that so young could give out such a seeming
> To seel her father's eyes up, close as oak—
> He thought 'twas witchcraft!
>
> (ll. 209–14)

Iago's well-timed paraphrase cunningly transfers the charge of
'witchcraft' from Othello to Desdemona, just as it reassigns the
imputation of blindness from the bewitched daughter to the gulled
patriarch—and therefore by implication to the deceived husband;
but it is otherwise close enough to Brabantio's speech to remind
Othello of the paradoxical notion of 'perfection . . . err[ing] |
Against all rules of *nature*', as he begins to contemplate the possibility of Desdemona's infidelity: 'And yet how *nature*, erring from
itself—' (l. 231). Othello's conscious meaning is only that his wife
may have erred sufficiently from her 'honest' character to have
been tempted by Cassio; but the predatory swiftness of Iago's
response, with its continuing paraphrase of Brabantio's diatribe,
shows how carefully the rhetorical trap has been sprung: if Desdemona's liaison with Othello was itself 'unnatural' in the first place,
how much more probable (indeed 'natural') must her 'unnatural'
adultery now appear:

> Ay, there's the point! As—to be bold with you—
> Not to affect many proposèd matches
> Of her own clime, complexion, and degree,
> Whereto we see in all things *nature* tends—
> Foh! One may smell in such a will most rank,
> Foul disproportions, thoughts *unnatural* . . .
>
> (ll. 232–7)

The success with which this speech appears to demonstrate a compelling symmetry between Desdemona's marriage and her necessary betrayal of that marriage depends on a rhetorical sleight of
hand; but, for seventeenth-century audiences, it was underpinned

by deep-laid cultural assumptions about the unnaturalness of certain kinds of transgressive liaison—assumptions that remain part of the dangerous substrata of racist discourse in our own time.

In early modern thought adultery was conceived (as the etymology of the two words indicates) quite literally as a form of adulteration: involving both pollution of a divinely sanctioned bond, and an assault on the 'natural' genealogical boundaries of the family, its monstrous character was mirrored in its bastard offspring.[1] Conveniently for Iago, medieval theology had enlarged the concept of adultery to include marriage with non-Christians—Jews, Muslims, and pagans—under the rubric of 'interpretive adultery'. In this connection the ambiguity of 'Moor' as both a religious and an ethnic category is doubly useful to the villain, since he can also exploit the popular prejudice—still reflected in such locutions as 'bastard race'—that regarded any form of miscegenation unnatural and adulterate. Thus in Ben Jonson's *Volpone*, the deformed brood of bastards who make up the protagonist's 'true family' are seen as doubly monstrous by virtue of their being illegitimately 'begot on . . . Gypsies, Jews, and black-moors' (*Volpone*, 1.1.506–7). Iago's language insidiously capitalizes on these widely diffused notions, as well as on the biblical texts that linked blackness with sexual transgression;[2] but it is also energized by ancient beliefs (going back at least to Pliny) that associated Africa with monsters like those 'Anthropophagi, and men whose heads | Do grow beneath their shoulders' whom Othello describes in his 'travailous history' (1.3.139, 144–5)—creatures whose deformity, according to the sixteenth-century writer Jean Bodin, was to be explained by 'promiscuous coition of men and animals'.[3] It is the special triumph of the villain's insinuations to plant the suggestion that the Moor's colour is the mark of such monstrosity: thus it becomes proof of the 'unnatural' character of his marriage, making Desdemona's elopement seem like a breach of the most

---

[1] In the drama bastard characters are conventionally credited with a moral monstrosity, that is sometimes (as in the case of Thersites, in *Troilus and Cressida*, for example) mirrored in physical deformity—see Michael Neill, ' "In Everything Illegitimate": Imagining the Bastard in English Renaissance Drama', in *Putting History to the Question*, 128–47 (esp. pp. 139–47).

[2] See above, p. 126.

[3] Jean Bodin, *Method for the Easy Comprehension of History* (1565), trans. Beatrice Reynolds (New York, 1966). See App. F(iv).

fundamental laws of kind; and because her marriage constitutes an act of generic adulteration, it must inevitably spawn further adultery, since 'very nature will instruct her . . . to some second choice' (2.1.228–9).

The disconcerting capacity of such passages to possess the imagination of an audience is indicated by the way in which Iago's language has so frequently insinuated itself into criticism of the play, especially when it addresses issues of race. Thus Rymer, whose irritation at the play's generic and structural irregularities is often hard to disentangle from his moral disgust with its fable, denounces *Othello* as a 'monstrous' work, the 'foul disproportion' of whose design is only matched by the 'thoughts unnatural' on which it is founded.[1] Coleridge's notorious critique pins its sense of the play's deformity even more explicitly to the idea of racial *mésalliance*, discovering something 'monstrous' in Desdemona's love for Othello, 'a *disproportionateness*, a want of balance'; and this response finds an unexpected echo even in G. K. Hunter's enlightened essay, when he admits to feeling 'the *disproportion* . . . of Othello's . . . marriage (as a social act)'.[2] But for Iago, of course, 'the point' is not at all what it is for Coleridge: eloquent as his instinctive resentment of foreigners may make him in the coining of racial slurs, these are only a means to what he calls his 'peculiar end' (1.1.60). Indeed, one of the frightening things about *Othello* is the almost casual, improvisational way in which Iago sets about coining his disturbingly modern language of racial hatred: it is frightening because once such a language has been invented, it cannot readily be dis-invented. That is why the play's involvement in the history of racial thought has seemed such a profoundly ambiguous matter; and it is why it is possible to imagine, with Ben Okri, that *Othello*'s history may have made it into something it was never intended to be—'a play about race'.

However, while modern audiences are likely to feel a particular poignancy in the Moor's capitulation to the idea that revulsion at his blackness has driven Desdemona to infidelity, seventeenth-century playgoers are unlikely to have reacted so keenly; and it is significant that the motive crosses Othello's mind only as a fleeting possibility—something on a par with the disparity in their ages, or

---

[1] See Rymer, pp. 111, 121, 127, 145.
[2] Coleridge (ed. Raysor), i. 47; Hunter, p. 163.

his own want of courtly sophistication (3.3.266–9). Therefore, although it is probably impossible—and ultimately undesirable—to set aside our awareness of the play's implication in the history of 'race', there may nevertheless be some advantage in trying to imagine how different *Othello* might have felt in its own time. The murderous resentments by which its hero is destroyed were, after all, keyed to a world in which matters of rank, deference, and subordination were all-important, whereas nascent ideas of racial difference were of more incidental significance.

Place, Office, and Occupation   In order to understand the social discourse operating in *Othello*, it may be helpful to put more pressure on the language that Iago deploys to demonstrate the 'foul disproportions' of Desdemona's match. When he cites her unnatural rejection of suitors belonging to her own 'clime, complexion, and degree', it is tempting to give his words a straightforwardly racial construction, forgetting that 'clime' meant no more than 'region', and that 'complexion', though it could refer to the appearance of the skin or face, did so only as these things were thought to reflect the temperament shaped by the balance of humours in a given person's constitution. Of course, in so far as this balance was liable to be affected by the climate of a particular region, such notions necessarily contributed to contemporary understandings of racial difference—black skin being explained by some authorities as resulting from changes in the humoral constitution of the body produced by the excessive heat of the sun.[1] So colour is not exactly irrelevant here (indeed, the use of 'foul' to mean 'dirty-coloured' maintains a current of racial innuendo to the end of the speech); but Iago's primary emphasis is on the 'disproportions' of condition between husband and wife—the incompatibilities of origin and temperament that render Othello a stranger to Venice, and the alleged disparity of rank that makes Desdemona's match what contemporaries would have called a 'marriage of disparagement'.

'Disproportions', in Iago's mouth, is a marvellously resonant word: for this is a man who prides himself on the exactness of the moral calculations for which he 'stand[s] accountant' (2.1.284), and a man who understands all human qualities as belonging to a

---

[1] See above, p. 127, and Commentary, 2.3.197, App. F(iv).

zero-sum game of comparison in which another's 'beauty' serves only to make him ugly (5.1.18–20). It is proportion, after all—deriving from the Latin *pro portione* ('in respect of his share')—that the 'double knavery' of his revenge seeks to restore—whether it involves the proprieties of military rank, or the rights of marital 'office'. Tellingly, it is the aggrieved sense of disproportion resulting from the supposed usurpation of his rightful share that supplies the theme of Iago's first great tirade in the play, his denunciation of Cassio's promotion (1.1.7–32). Harping on his own 'price' and 'worth', and bridling at his general's indifference to the advocacy of 'three great ones of the city', he denounces the wilful neglect of both proven merit and 'old gradation' in the preposterous decision that, by cheating him of the lieutenancy that was his due, has reduced him to 'his Moorship's Ensign'. The key word in this outburst—the one on which Iago's sense of violated proportion fixes, and which provides an indispensable clue to the social tensions that animate the play, is 'place'.[1]

Location in the geographical sense is obviously important in a work whose action moves so decisively from Venice to Cyprus. In Venice Othello the Moor and Cassio the Florentine are marked as outsiders; in Cyprus no one is at home. Venice, admired for its wealth, its cosmopolitan society, and its stable republican constitution, embodies the civilized order of the *polis*—the idealized city of classical theory—a place where the turbulence of individual emotion is subjected to the rational calm of authority. Cyprus, which Shakespeare's audience knew as the Venetian colony briefly rescued from Turkish invasion by the celebrated Battle of Lepanto (1571), is an embattled military outpost where no such predictable sanctions obtain. The island belongs to the stormy domain of the passions; and its distance from Venice is symbolically marked by the ferocious tempest that opens the second act. Famous for its mythic association with the love-goddess, Aphrodite, Cyprus is linked in the play to the figure of Desdemona herself, subject as she is to a kind of erotic siege that proves more dangerous than the Turkish assault on the island to which Brabantio compares it (1.3.209–10). Yet as a Venetian and a woman Desdemona is as much a stranger in this male-dominated fortress as Othello

---

[1] See 'Places'; and cf. also Julia Genster, 'Lieutenancy' (see above, p. 32, n. 1).

feels himself among the suave 'chamberers' of the metropolis (3.3.268); and her connection with Venice allows Iago to taint her with a different kind of eroticism altogether—one associated with the promiscuous 'country disposition' of the city's notorious courtesans (3.3.204–7).

The primary significance of Venice, however, is that, as the metropolitan centre of Othello's world, it supplies (or pretends to supply) each individual with a clearly defined 'place' within an established social order—this indeed is what distinguishes it from the barbarous world beyond its boundaries, the vaguely imagined wilderness of Othello's past travails; and, if matters of geographical place and displacement figure so prominently in the play's metaphoric structure, the further sense of 'place', as a term embracing 'rank', 'status', and 'office', provides an even more important key to its social preoccupations. This application of the word reveals a great deal about the peculiarly spatialized terms in which early modern social and political relations were imagined.

Fiercely committed to fictions of stability, yet haunted by exaggerated fears of the anarchy threatened by social-climbing 'upstarts', this was a society that (in official ideology at least) still liked to see itself mirrored in the fixed order of the Ptolemaic heavens, where every body had its appointed place, and could move only within its appointed 'sphere'. Just as disorder in the macrocosm—when 'certain stars [meteors or comets] shot madly from their spheres' (*Dream*, 2.1.153)—threatened catastrophe, so in the social microcosm, the refusal to be confined to one's proper place threatened social chaos.[1] Thus, for example, in Middleton and Rowley's *The Changeling* (1622), it is the ungoverned ambition of the discontented servant De Flores—a decayed gentleman, conspicuously 'out of his place' (1.1.136) and described by his principal victim as 'yon meteor' (5.3.154)—that reduces the world of the play to ruin. Disobedient servants and disappointed place-getters of

---

[1] Even someone as committed to climbing 'the winding stair' that leads to 'great place' as Francis Bacon tends to characterize ambition as a kind of violence, and to idealize proper place as a kind of rest, 'merit and good works' being in a double sense 'the end of motion', the path to 'rest': 'as in nature things move violently to their place, and calmly in their place; so virtue in ambition is violent, in authority settled and calm' ('Of Great Place', in Bacon, *Essays*, intro. Oliphant Smeaton (1906), pp. 32–3).

this sort infest the drama of the period;[1] typically, like De Flores, the gentleman-born whose 'hard fate has thrust [him] out to servitude' (*Changeling*, 2.1.48), or like Bosola, the frustrated ex-scholar in Webster's *Duchess of Malfi*, they are men who inhabit the shadowy borderlands that marked the all-important boundary between the gentry and the great mass of people without 'name or note' who can claim no place in the annals of society. Full of an aggrieved sense of social entitlement, they are humiliatingly dependent on servile employment increasingly governed by the cash nexus. As a result they can seem strikingly modern figures, whose frustrations prefigure the gnawing condition of 'status anxiety' that some commentators have diagnosed as the defining malaise of capitalist society.[2]

It was surely Iago, the arch-exemplar of such subversive underlings, who did most to establish the type. Though he is a senior officer in Othello's entourage, he is never (unlike Cassio and Roderigo) clearly identified as a gentleman; and he speaks of his relation to his general as though it were no more than a kind of degrading domestic service (1.1.41–60). Maddened by Cassio's courtly manners, he must nevertheless play the role of his loyal subordinate, while (as the carefully distributed pronouns of his opening exchange with Roderigo remind us[3]) the necessities of his purse force him to defer even to his most gullible victim, whose hired instrument he must pretend to be. Better even than Bosola or De Flores, Iago articulates the bitter dissatisfactions of service and the obsession with place to which they can lead. As Barbara Everett long ago pointed out, at the heart of Shakespeare's reworking of Cinthio lies 'the corruption and inversion of the master–servant relationship' that is most shockingly displayed in the temptation scene (p. 74). But in Iago's case the rankling sense of injustice produced by his failure to gain the lieutenancy fuels a deep suspicion

[1] The sheer familiarity of the ambitious servant figure allows for a striking metatheatrical irony in *Othello*: when Emilia learns of Othello's extreme jealousy, her immediate conclusion is that he must have been slandered by 'Some cogging, cozening slave, *to get some office*' (4.2.133). Some actors, especially in the nineteenth century, have chosen to play this speech as if Emilia already suspected her husband, but the play offers no evidence for this: it is theatrical convention alone that warrants her conjecture.

[2] See Alain de Botton, *Status Anxiety* (2004); Vance Packard, *The Status Seekers* (1960).

[3] See Commentary, 1.1.2.

about other kinds of displacement, involving both his chauvinist resentment of outsiders and paranoid fears of sexual usurpation; and the fact that, with his oddly Spanish name and ambiguous social status, Iago is himself so uncertainly located in the Venetian world, only deepens the sense of his insecurity.

It is not enough that the ensign has been cheated of his 'place' by a desk-soldier, a 'bookish . . . counter-caster' (1.1.23–30), but this 'great arithmetician' is also an outsider, 'a Florentine' (ll. 18–19), a fellow out of his place; it is not enough that Iago finds himself 'beleed' by his general's neglect, but this general (as the sarcastic coined honorific 'his Moorship' stresses[1]) is even more of a foreigner—a 'wheeling stranger | Of here and everywhere', as Roderigo calls him, describing a man so alien to Venetian civility that he has no proper place at all (1.1.135–6). To make matters worse, the titles at issue in Iago's striving for place punningly compound the insult: to be 'his Moorship's ensign', or standard-bearer, is to be reduced (in Iago's own phrase) to a mere 'flag and sign' (l. 155), a symbol of his master's anomalous presence. A lieutenant, by contrast, is his superior's 'second' or substitute—one who (as the etymology of the word indicates) can literally take his place.[2] This oddly recursive piece of word-play is important because it initiates a whole chain of puns and quibbles that not only expose the working of Iago's fantasies, but will play a crucial part in arousing Othello's own panic of erotic displacement. Puns—those notorious adulterators of meaning that surreptitiously enable illegitimate suggestions to take the place of legitimate meanings—are peculiarly fitting vehicles for the irrational suspicion that feeds emotions like jealousy and envy, with their dreams of improper substitution. From Iago's point of view it is the very fact that Othello and Cassio have colluded to displace him in one kind of office that makes it probable that they have cheated him of another:

> I hate the Moor,
> And it is thought abroad that 'twixt my sheets
> He's done my *office*.
>
> (1.3.376–8)

---

[1] So pronounced is the shadow of the conventional honorific here that it produced a memorial slip in Q, which prints 'his Worships'.

[2] See above, 'Sources', p. 32.

> I do suspect the lusty Moor
> Hath leapt into my *seat*. . . .
> I fear Cassio with my *nightcap* too . . .
> (2.1.286–7, 298)[1]

Tormented as he is by such images of obscene displacement, it will
be Iago's special pleasure to poison the man he holds responsible
with similar fantasies of usurpation in a world where cuckolded
'millions . . . nightly lie in those unproper beds, | Which they dare
swear peculiar' (4.1.63–5).

Iago's quibble on 'office' is enough to make the link between the
two kinds of displacement that so enrage him. Critics who follow
Coleridge in regarding Iago as a diabolic incarnation of 'motiveless
malignancy', make a mistake in dismissing the Ensign's suspicions
of adultery and his resentment at the lost lieutenancy as excuses
designed to conceal the unfathomable nature of his malice. They
overlook the meticulous ingenuity of Iago's counter-schemes of
adulterous replacement, just as they ignore the self-lacerating
punctilio with which he continues to stress the treacherous word
'Lieutenant' even after Cassio is formally stripped of his rank.[2] It is,
moreover, the fatal word that, at the triumphant conclusion of the
temptation scene, he will force Othello to pronounce: 'Now art
thou my lieutenant' (3.3.478). The juxtaposition of this declara-
tion with Othello's resolve to 'furnish . . . some swift means of
death' for Desdemona, points to the double displacement that Iago
has achieved; for the place properly ascribed to a wife in early modern discourses of domestic government was precisely that of her
husband's deputy or second—in effect, his lieutenant.[3]

Othello's conferment of the lieutenancy upon Iago—coming as
it does after the kneeling exchange of 'sacred vow[s]' in which the
two men enact a grim parody of wedding ritual (3.3.460–70)—
marks the point at which the ensign not only reclaims the office of
which Cassio bilked him, but simultaneously insinuates himself
into the place that belongs to Desdemona. This is the very displacement so weirdly literalized in the 'monstrous' oneiric fantasy that

---

[1] See Commentary for the word-play involved in 'seat' and 'nightcap'.
[2] See above, 'Sources', p. 32.
[3] The analogy between military and domestic chains of command is pointed up
by Cassio's playful description of Desdemona as 'our great captain's captain'
(2.1.75) and by Iago's more cynical claim that 'our general's wife is now the
general' (2.3.301–2).

Iago concocts earlier in the scene, in which he himself takes the place of Desdemona in Cassio's adulterous embrace:

> In sleep I heard him say 'Sweet Desdemona,
> Let us be wary, let us hide our loves';
> And then, sir, would he gripe and wring my hand,
> Cry 'O, sweet creature!', and then kiss me hard,
> As if he plucked up kisses by the roots
> That grew upon my lips, then laid his leg
> Over my thigh, and sighed, and kissed, and then
> Cried 'Cursèd fate that gave thee to the Moor!'
>
> (3.3.420–27)

Iago's usurpation of Desdemona's place is an ingenious variation on the more commonplace symmetry of revenge, through which, by himself replacing Othello in Desdemona's bed, he once planned to be 'evened with him, wife for wife' (2.1.290). But the Ensign's vanity cannot in the end be satisfied by such a simple calculus of adulterous exchange: his sense of proportion requires a more elaborately ironic scheme, according to which Cassio, the man whom Othello has allowed to cheat Iago of his military promotion, will not merely suffer the loss of his own 'place' (2.3.291), but be punished as the imagined usurper of Othello's matrimonial office. Moreover, the instruments of this preposterous displacement are to be the very same qualities by which Iago feels himself slighted, judged, and shunted aside—Cassio's 'proper . . . person' (1.3.382–7), Othello's 'free and open nature' (1.3.388), and the 'goodness' of Desdemona's disposition, 'so free, so kind, so apt, so blessed' (2.3.307–8):

> So will I turn her virtue into pitch,
> And out of her own goodness make the net
> That shall enmesh them all.
>
> (2.3.345–7)

The more effectually Desdemona is persuaded to help 'put [Cassio] in [his] place again' (2.3.306–7), the more Othello will be made to misconstrue the nature of that 'place' and her role as 'solicitor' for it (3.3.27). So in the temptation scene Iago's most innocent-seeming speeches are peppered with lewd *doubles entendres* that heat Othello's suspicions even as the tempter professes to soothe them with reassurances of Cassio's merit and Desdemona's generosity:

> Although 'tis fit that Cassio have his *place*—
> For sure he *fills it up* with great *ability*—
> Yet, if you please to *hold him off* a while,
> You shall by that perceive him and his means:
> Note if your lady *strain* his *entertainment*
> With any strong or vehement importunity;
> Much will be seen in that. In the meantime,
> Let me be thought too busy in my fears
> (As worthy cause I have to fear I am)
> And hold her *free*, I do beseech your *honour*.
>   (3.3.250–9)[1]

As Iago progressively colonizes Othello's mind, the Moor's gathering sense of displacement is registered in similar passages of word-play—though in his case the double meanings are beyond his own control, erupting through the rational surface of his language, as if mimicking the release of hidden, deeply repressed knowledge. Thus, when he grasps Desdemona's hand in 3.4, as if reaching for reassurance, the ambiguous tenor of his speech, as it plays on recollections of her 'free' and generous nature, matches the ambiguous signs he reads on her palm itself—an effect magnified for the audience by the uncanny echo of Iago's insinuating 'She's framed as fruitful | As the free elements' (2.3.326–7):

> This hand is moist, my lady. . . .
> This argues *fruitfulness* and *liberal* heart:
> Hot, hot and moist! This hand of yours requires
> A sequester from *liberty*—fasting and prayer,
> Much castigation, exercise devout—
> For here's a young and sweating devil here
> That commonly rebels. 'Tis a good hand,
> A *frank* one. . . .
> A *liberal* hand. The hearts of old gave hands,
> But our new heraldry is hands, not hearts.
>   (3.4.34–45)

Somewhere just beneath the surface of this speech, its presence signalled by the rhetorical stress on 'hands' as well as by the heraldry of hearts, is a maddened recollection of the fatal handkerchief. As

---

[1] For 'hold off' as a term for sexual resistance, see *Troilus and Cressida*, 1.2.282; the bawdy significance of the other italicized words is glossed in Gordon Williams, *A Glossary of Shakespeare's Sexual Language* (1997).

a devious substitute for 'ocular proof', the handkerchief itself constitutes a complex visual pun. Imbued with a dye 'Conserved of maidens' hearts' (3.4.74), it stands in for the bloodstained sheets whose public display was so important to the symbology of early modern nuptials; but the strawberries with which it is embroidered are capable of a remarkably contradictory set of meanings. No doubt by virtue of its heart-like shape and colour, the strawberry became a badge of Venus, and could stand for love, but also for sensuality and voluptuousness—as it does in Hieronymus Bosch's painting *The Garden of Earthly Delights*; in Christian iconography, by contrast, the plant's habit of simultaneous flowering and fruiting had made it an emblem for the chastity and fertility of the Virgin Mary; while in Renaissance emblem books it frequently appeared with a serpent concealed in its leaves as a figure for deceit.[1] It is the recollection of this ambiguously decorated handkerchief—charged as it is with an excess of meanings that lie beyond any rational scrutiny—that seems to set off Othello's fit in 4.1 and that turns his own heart to stone as he envisages it once again, clasped in Cassio's hand, just before the murder (5.2.64–5).

If the visual pun of the handkerchief can trigger violence in this way, other kinds of amphibology, like the command delivered to Othello in 4.1 '[d]eputing Cassio in his government' (l. 229), can prove equally volatile. Resonating unluckily with Iago's vicious equivocations on lieutenancy and the 'place' that Cassio 'fills' with such ability, the order precipitates Othello's sudden violence against his wife (l. 231), as we can tell from the incoherent fury of his exit: 'Cassio shall have my place. . . . Goats and monkeys!' (ll. 253–5). Again and again the word-play returns to this theme—most conspicuously perhaps in the notorious conclusion of the Moor's farewell to military honour and renown (3.3.349–59). Here Othello struggles to efface the fantasy of Desdemona's body surrendered to the filthy appetites of 'the general camp', by invoking the glamour of 'plumèd troops . . . the neighing steed and the shrill trump . . . The royal banner, and all quality, | Pride, pomp, and

---

[1] See Geoffrey Whitney, *A Choice of Emblemes* (1586), no. 24; Lawrence J. Ross, 'The Meaning of Strawberries in Shakespeare', *Studies in the Renaissance*, 7 (1960), 225–40; Lynda E. Boose, 'Othello's Handkerchief: "The Recognizance and Pledge of Love"', *ELR* 5 (1975), 360–74; Edward A. Snow, 'Sexual Anxiety and the Male Order of Things in *Othello*', *ELR* 10 (1980), 384–412; Nelson and Haines, 'Unconsummated Marriage', 8–10.

circumstance of glorious war'—only for the fantasy to erupt again in an obscene quibble, 'Farewell! Othello's *occupation*'s gone'. Here 'occupation' as 'profession' shades into 'occupation' as possession of place (Othello's command of occupied Cyprus), which in turn suggests possession of Desdemona's body. This association is partly enabled by an ironic echo (ll. 344–5) of the Duke's consolatory platitudes to Brabantio in the council scene. In that exchange the old man (drawing on the familiar tropes of erotic siege) identified the contested island with his stolen daughter:

> So let the Turk of Cyprus us beguile—
> We lose it not, so long as we can smile . . .
> (1.3.209–10)

Just as the storm at the beginning of Act 2 drove the Turks from their intended occupation of Cyprus, so the Moor (himself destined to 'turn Turk' in the murder that 'traduce[s]' the state he served) now feels himself driven from possession of his marital territory—the sexual 'place' at which he gestures in Act 4:

> But *there*, where I have garnered up my heart,
> Where either I must live or bear no life,
> The fountain from the which my current runs
> Or else dries up—to be discarded *thence*,
> Or keep it as a cistern for foul toads
> To knot and gender in! Turn thy complexion *there*,
> Patience, thou young and rose-lipped cherubin,
> Ay there, look grim as hell.
> (4.2.57–64)

The obsessively indicated 'there' of Othello's speech is both the marriage bed (that locus of matrimonial office) and the beloved's breast (that Petrarchan lodging of the surrendered heart); but, as the imagery gathers force, it becomes something else, the equivalent of *King Lear*'s 'forfended place', the 'dark and vicious place' of begetting (*Trag. Lear*, 5.1.11, 5.3.163)—the female wellspring of life itself, imagined as a reptilian mating pond. For Othello at this moment, and again in the brothel scene, the female genitalia become, as they do for Lear (*Trag. Lear*, 4.5.124), a kind of 'hell' (l. 93); yet 'to be discarded thence', to be expelled, as he still feels it, from the very source of his own being is to be consigned to a radical placelessness—a condition that only the monstrous consummation counselled by Iago seems able to assuage: 'Do it not with poison; strangle her in her bed, even the bed she hath contaminated' (4.1.200–1). The place of love will be transmuted into the place of punishment; and the ironic 'justice' of the suggestion 'pleases' the Moor because it converts his murder into a species of abstract ritual—not so much the killing of a woman as the ceremonial cleansing of a polluted place: 'Thy bed, lust-stained, shall with lust's blood be spotted' (5.1.37). It is this that accounts for the curiously impersonal grammar of his soliloquy over the sleeping Desdemona—'this sorrow's heavenly, | It strikes *where* it doth love' (5.2.21–2)—as if Desdemona were merely his 'place', the place Cassio has taken, which must somehow be restored to his ownership. Yet ironically the effect of the murder is only to betray the Moor to a state of dispossession and hellish dislocation more absolute than any he has so far experienced:

> Where should Othello go? . . .
> Whip me, ye devils,
> From the possession of this heavenly sight,
> Blow me about in winds, roast me in sulphur,
> Wash me in steep-down gulfs of liquid fire . . .
> (5.2.270–9)

Othello's last great speech in the play, the apology for his life with which he ushers in his suicide, constitutes a desperate effort to relocate himself in both political and erotic terms. In a fleeting recapitulation of the exotic traveller's tales with which he once beguiled Desdemona, Othello returns to the scene of a former triumph in the very heart of enemy territory, the Ottoman city of Aleppo: symbolically annihilating, in the 'malignant' figure of the 'turbaned Turk', the savage infidel that Iago has made of him, this Moor-turned-Christian-turned-Turk[1] reasserts his Venetian identity with a gesture that allows him to reclaim his place beside Desdemona on the violated marriage bed:

> I kissed thee ere I killed thee—no way but this:
> Killing myself, to die upon a kiss.
> (ll. 357–8)

The chiastic balance of Othello's rhyming couplet rhetorically perfects an ending whose symmetries are designed to replace those of

---

[1] On Othello's enactment of this motif, see Vitkus, *Turning Turk*, pp. 103–6.

Iago's vindictive design. At the same time, the reasserted contrast between the hero and his antagonist is intensified by the way in which the Moor defines his suicide as a last act of 'service' to the Venetian state; for it is upon their deeply conflicting attitudes towards the institution of service that the opposition between Othello and Iago largely depends; and ultimately the whole action of the tragedy can be seen to turn upon it.[1]

Love, Service, and Identity   The theme of service is among Shakespeare's more conspicuous additions to the material he found in *Hecatommithi*. While, as we shall see, it answered to anxieties that were widespread in the dramatist's own society, its appearance in the play was almost certainly mediated by a passage in Lewis Lewkenor's translation of Cardinal Contarini's *The Commonwealth of Venice* (1599): there the dramatist would have read how certain 'foreign men and strangers' were 'adopted into [the] number of citizens, either in regard of their great *nobility*, or that they had been *dutiful towards the state*, or else had done unto them *some notable service*'.[2] This passage would have helped to explain the peculiar standing of Giraldi's Moorish captain, a foreigner whose prudence, courage, and martial energy had rendered him 'very dear to the Signoria'; and in *Othello* it is the Moor's nobility and exceptional service to the state that warrants his oxymoronic claim to be 'of Venice', enabling him to defy the scorn of those who see him as the 'extravagant and wheeling stranger' of Roderigo's sneer (1.1.136).

Among the Venetians themselves faithful service is imagined as the very ground of social being: Montano, the governor of Cyprus who yields his office to Othello as a master whom he is proud to have 'served' (2.1.36–7), is defined by his role as the 'trusty and most valiant servitor' of the city (1.3.41). Cassio's self-image is similarly inseparable from the 'place' secured by 'love and service' to his general (3.3.17–18); and his hopes of reinstatement after his disgrace rest on an appeal to the value of this 'service past'

---

[1] With a witty gesture common in such prolegomenary material, Thomas Walkley's prefatory epistle, 'The Stationer to the Reader', plays on the importance of this motif in the play. Likening '*a book without an epistle*' to 'a blue coat without a badge' (i.e. a token of service to the reader), he takes this '*piece of work*' upon himself as a substitute for the dead author.

[2] Gasparo Contarini, *The Commonwealth of Venice*, trans. Lewis Lewkenor (1599), p. 18.

(3.4.112), as well as (more ambiguously) upon his courtly preten-
sions as Desdemona's 'true servant' (3.3.9). But more than anyone
it is Othello whose place and identity are invested in the ideology of
obedience to those he serves as 'My very noble and approved good
masters' (1.3.78). Acknowledged as 'the *noble* Moor, whom our full
Senate | Call all in all sufficient' (4.1.256–7), he not only attracts
the admiration of fellow servants of the state, like Lodovico, Cassio,
and Montano, but compels a grudging praise even from the scornful Iago ('Another of his fathom they have none', 1.1.151). It is
from this that the Moor derives the confidence and sense of high
desert which characterize the two great arias of self that begin
and end his part in the play (1.2.18–28; 5.2.337–55). On his first
appearance, Othello's disdain for Brabantio's malice rests on a
proud awareness of 'My *services* which I have done the Signiory'
(1.2.18); later, as he descends into the chaos of jealousy, he tries to
shore himself against the rage precipitated by the order 'Deputing
Cassio in his government' (4.1.229), by reaffirming his faithful obedience to the 'mandate' of Venice (l. 251); and at the very end,
when his Venetian self seems to have disintegrated into the unbe-
ing of 'he that *was* Othello' (5.2.282), he seeks to restore it with the
reminder that 'I have done the state some *service*, and they know't',
(l. 338), before tendering a final act of service in his suicidal re-
execution of the malignant Turk who 'Beat a Venetian and traduced the state' (l. 353).

If Othello is sustained by his commitment to the ideals of service,
they turn out to be an equally urgent preoccupation for Iago. In his
case, too, they are deeply bound up with questions of identity: but
the contrast between his attitude and Othello's could hardly be
more extreme. Where his role as servant of the state is what gives
Othello his firm sense of place, for Iago the servile deference implicit in his sour recognition that 'We cannot all be masters' (1.1.43)
amounts to a radical displacement—an affront to the integral selfhood that he locates in the unfettered 'power and corrigible
authority' of his individual will (1.3.321). That indeed is among
the several meanings enfolded in the famously enigmatic conclusion of the speech on service which concludes his resentful tirade
in 1.1, 'I am not what I am' (l. 65). Iago is and is not the Moor's
servant. To be 'his Moorship's ensign' is to be identified as what, in
his own estimate, Iago essentially is not—a man defined only in
relation to his master; on the other hand, to limit his allegiance to

mere 'shows of service' (l. 52)—thereby covertly refusing to be what society publicly pretends he is—allows the ensign to turn this shameful obedience to his own advantage, converting (in the quibble he so relishes) the obligation to serve a master into an opportunity to 'serve [his own] turn upon him' (l. 42).

In this preoccupation with being and seeming, Iago, I have suggested, is partly Hamlet's heir; and even his vindictive determination to undo the perceived 'disproportions' of his society can seem to mirror the Prince's need to set right a world that the usurpation of his appointed place has rendered radically 'out of joint' (*Hamlet*, 1.5.189). But whereas Hamlet believes himself committed to the restoration of true hierarchical order, Iago's consuming indignation at what he calls 'the curse of service' (1.1.34) exposes him as an envious leveller for whom any kind of subordination is insufferable:

> You shall mark
> Many a duteous and knee-crooking knave
> That, doting on his own obsequious bondage,
> Wears out his time, much like his master's ass,
> For naught but provender, and when he's old—cashiered.
> Whip me such honest knaves! Others there are
> Who, trimmed in forms and visages of duty,
> Keep yet their hearts attending on themselves,
> And, throwing but shows of service on their lords,
> Do well thrive by them, and when they have lined their coats
> Do themselves homage. These fellows have some soul,
> And such a one do I profess myself—for, sir,
> It is as sure as you are Roderigo,
> Were I the Moor, I would not be Iago:
> In following him, I follow but myself—
> Heaven is my judge, not I for love and duty,
> But seeming so for my peculiar end.
>
> (1.1.44–60)

The key word in this tirade is 'honest', an adjective which the other characters in the play will turn into an approving sobriquet for the ensign himself—'honest Iago'—but which in his mouth is loaded with scorn. Often used to describe female chastity (as it is in the case of Desdemona, 4.2.12, 17, 38, 65), the word could still carry its old meaning of 'honourable' (as it does when Iago ironically applies it to the courtly Cassio, 3.3.128–33); but its reference was increasingly confined to the plain bourgeois virtues of decency, truthfulness and sincerity. Moreover, because it was also used to define 'honest' trades and occupations, including those humbler forms of domestic service which, though respectable, were seen as being 'for a gentleman utterly unmeet', it typically conveyed as much social condescension as approval.[1] Consequently, from Iago's point of view, to submit to its one-sided moral imperatives is to surrender to the ideological fraud that governs the entire institution of service, thereby debasing oneself to the 'bondage' of a mere knave, the lowest form of menial. Modern readers, encountering this speech in the mouth of a disappointed military officer, may be surprised by its domestic-sounding language of masters and servants; but this makes complete sense in terms of the ideology and practice of early modern service.

This institution, considered in its broadest application, embraced virtually all conventional forms of social relationship in the world Shakespeare knew. When the theorist of household government, William Gouge, wrote in his treatise *Of Domesticall Duties* (1622) that 'servant' was 'a general title . . . applied to all such as by any outward civil bond, or right, owe their service to another',[2] he was describing a world that still imagined itself in quasi-feudal terms; in it the social 'place' of every individual was substantially determined by their relation to a more powerful master, forming an unbroken chain that stretched from the lowliest peasant to the monarch (who himself owed service to God). Power itself (as a play like *King Lear* reminds us) was typically expressed in the ability to command service; so that Jacobean society, lacking a clear distinction between the public and private spheres, saw the humblest forms of domestic labour as existing in an absolute continuum with service to the state. Moreover, because the functions of both civil and military service were still managed by networks of individual patronage and influence,[3] its bonds and obligations were habitually understood in the same personal, affective terms that

---

[1] See *The English Courtier, and the Countrey-gentleman* (1586), in *Inedited Tracts: Illustrating the manners, opinions, and occupations of Englishmen during the sixteenth and seventeenth centuries* (Roxburghe Library, 1868), p. 25; and cf. Cassio's address to the Clown as 'mine honest friend' (4.1.18).

[2] William Gouge, *Of Domesticall Duties Eight Treatises* (1622), p. 160.

[3] See Linda Levy Peck, *Court Patronage and Corruption in Early Stuart England* (Boston, 1990), pp. 30–74.

governed the patriarchal household, where (as Peter Laslett has written) 'every relationship could be seen as a love-relation-ship'.[1] That Iago's hopes of promotion were staked as much on the 'personal suit' of 'three great ones of the city' as on his own military prowess is not a sign of graft but a proof of his standing in the regime of service.

By the same token, it is the personal nature of servantly obliga-tion that governs the performance of the ensign's military duties. Thus, while both he and Cassio are professional soldiers, their rela-tionship to their general is of fundamentally the same order as that of domestic retainers to their lord: when Othello dismisses Cassio with 'never more be *officer of mine*' (2.3.240), his use of the posses-sive is a reminder of the extent to which a commander's officers belonged to him in the same way as the higher servants or 'officers' of a great house belonged to their master. That is why Iago's resentments over promotion are cast in the language of mastery and service; and it is why his dedication of 'hands [and] heart' to Othello's service in the temptation scene mimics the language of love (3.3.465–7)—just as it is why the disgraced Cassio dreams only of reinstating himself as 'a member of [Othello's] love' by perform-ing 'the office of [his] heart' (3.4.108–9). The organic nature of Cassio's metaphor, which figures him as a mere limb of Othello's household body, a creature who can fully 'exist' only as an aspect of his master's presence, illustrates how it was almost impossible to conceive of a properly human existence outside the hierarchy of masters and servants that made up the early modern 'society of orders'. '[T]o be no part of any body, is to be nothing', wrote John Donne, in a letter lamenting the failure of his ambitions in the 'service' to which he had 'submitted [him]self'.[2] In effect a well-trained and loyal servant became simply a 'part of his master',[3] obeying him, in the words of one popular manual, 'not as a water-spaniel, but as the hand is stirred to obey the mind'.[4] Behind such

---

[1] Peter Laslett, *The World We Have Lost—Further Explored*, 3rd edn. (1983), p. 5.
[2] John Donne, *Letters to Severall Persons of Honour* (1651), intro. M. Thomas Hester (New York, 1977), p. 51.
[3] Steffano Guazzo, *La civile conversatione* (1574), cited in Dennis Romano, *House-craft and Statecraft: Domestic Service in Renaissance Venice 1400–1600* (Baltimore, 1996), p. 20.
[4] John Dod and Robert Cleaver, *A Godly Forme of Household Government* (1630), sig. Aa3.

thinking it is possible to glimpse the symbolic meaning of the servant's 'livery', a word that originally comprehended not just the
coat and heraldic badge in which a master dressed his servants,
but the food he supplied to them: the liveried man was not merely
clothed in his master's identity, but absorbed into his social body,
to be fed as his own body was fed.

In Iago's case, however, the naturalized rhetoric of hand
and heart disguises a brutally material understanding of the
master–servant relationship—in which livery is reduced to the
supply of animal 'provender' and the wearing of 'coats' whose
sole function is to conceal their 'lining' of pecuniary self-interest.
Professing to be one of those who know how to '[d]o themselves
homage', Iago identifies himself as a kind of 'masterless man', part
of that reprobate community of social exiles who haunted the
early modern imagination—creatures whose very being constituted something of a paradox, since service was presented as a condition so universal that to be a man at all was necessarily to be
somebody else's 'man'. In this respect, however, the ensign's resistance to the obligations of service is by no means unusual, given
his membership in a whole gallery of disaffected and rebellious servants, whose prominence in the drama of the period bears eloquent testimony to the increasing stresses affecting the ideology of
universal service—stresses that can also be documented from
numerous contemporary sources, including the very manuals
of domestic government that set out to reinforce the ideology.
Thus William Gouge repeatedly inveighs against servants who,
forgetting 'their present place and condition' and 'wilfully pre-
sum[ing] above it', think 'their master's house a prison to them,
muttering and murmuring against their strait keeping in, as they
deem it' (pp. 599, 611).

If, for such malcontents, the obligations of their calling constituted a form of 'obsequious bondage', a humiliating infringement
of individual dignity and a denial of the longing to be 'one's own
man', that was because servants (especially those below a certain
rung in the hierarchy) were understood to have voluntarily surren-
dered any claim to authority over their own lives: 'while the term
of their service lasteth', wrote Gouge, '. . . they are not their
own. . . . both their persons and their actions are their master's'
(p. 604). So literally was this the case that to many such hirelings
their lot must often have felt little different from slavery. In the

Latin word *servus* the conditions of 'servant' and 'slave' had indeed
been indistinguishable; but the official doctrine of Shakespeare's
time, insisting as it did upon the sublime virtue of willing obedience, stressed the absolute distinction between 'servile' and
'liberal' servants—between bondslaves and those whose service
was undertaken 'by voluntary contract' (p. 160). Since actual slavery had no significant place in English experience at this time
(except for those, like Othello, taken in war), the force of this distinction was largely rhetorical: the importance of slavery lay in the
idea of an utterly abject bondage which served to define all that the
free servant was *not*, thereby sustaining the ideal of service as a
system of voluntary engagement maintained by profoundly naturalized 'bonds' of mutual duty and affection. This is the distinction
on which Iago insists in defining the limits of his bounden duty to
Othello (3.3.138–40); and it helps to explain why 'slave'—the epithet repeatedly hurled at Iago in the last act of the play—was
among the most potent terms of abuse in the extensive early modern lexicon of status-based insult.

Underpinning the idealization of free service was a theological
insistence on the Christian subject's duty to God as the pattern of
all servant–master relationships. Supported by a number of para-
bles in which God's relationship with humanity was analogized to
that of a master with his servants, this doctrine required a quasi-
religious 'duty of reverence' towards masters: not only had Christ
himself, by freely '[taking] upon him the form of a servant', offered
the perfect model of willing service, he was also the pattern of all
masters.[1] Thus servants were doubly 'bound to obedience' since
(as Gouge put it)

masters, by virtue of their office and place, bear Christ's image and stand
in his stead . . . it followeth that servants in performing duty to their master perform duty to Christ, and in rebelling against their master, they rebel
against Christ. (p. 641)

Non serviam ('I will not serve') was notoriously the watchword of
Lucifer and his rebellious cohorts; for if the faithful servant's office
was to be understood as an expression of Christian duty and humility, Lucifer's sin of pride was imagined precisely as a refusal of ser-

---

[1] Gouge, pp. 603, 618, 641.

vice: 'in heav'n they scorned to serve, so now in hell they reign', wrote Phineas Fletcher of the rebel angels (*Purple Island*, 6.10), anticipating the famous defiance of Milton's Satan: 'Better to reign in hell, than serve in heaven' (*Paradise Lost*, 1.263).[1]

Thus, if the Venetians seek to contain the threat posed by Iago's subversive determination to 'follow but [him]self' by rhetorically consigning him to the outcast condition of 'slave' (5.2.242, 275, 290, 331), the extremity of that threat is registered in Othello's identification of him as a 'devil' (5.2.285, 299). From an orthodox perspective, Iago's repudiation of service is recognizably part of the profane 'Divinity of hell' (2.3.335) preached by a 'demi-devil' whose 'I am not what I am' constitutes a blasphemous unspeaking of the biblical name of God ('I am that I am', Exodus 3: 14). The diabolical nature of the ensign's disobedience is predictably compounded by his delight in the 'heavenly shows' that make up his 'flag and sign of love' to his master (2.3.337; 1.1.155). It was just such 'forms and visages of duty' that the handbooks of domestic government taught their readers to expect in practitioners of what Gouge (following Ephesians 6: 6) called 'eye-service' (p. 165). Comparing them to Judas, the archetype of those who betray their masters, Gouge describes these servile dissemblers, in words that echo Iago's refusal to wear his 'heart upon [his] sleeve' (1.1.64), as having 'a heart, and a heart, making show of one heart outwardly, and have another, even a clean contrary heart within them'.[2] So 'possessed with a devil' are these inhuman creatures that 'they will seek all the revenge they can, if they be corrected, [and] secretly endeavour to take away the life of their masters' (p. 614).

This, then, is the social and moral framework within which the play's conflicting attitudes to service are judged. But, if that were all, it would be difficult to explain the seductive power that Iago, though he may lack the charismatic grandeur of Milton's Satan, has exercised over the imagination of audiences and readers alike. The dangerous energy of drama always depends on its ability to animate attitudes that its own official voice deplores; and Iago's dissidence has the capacity to engage the sympathy of anyone who

---

[1] Compare faithful Abdiel's wish only to '*serve* | In heaven God ever blest, and his divine | Behests *obey*' (vi. 183–5).

[2] Gouge, p. 617; the Judas comparison is also made in 'I.M.', *A Health to the Gentlemanly Profession of Servingmen* (1598), p. 148.

has felt the arrogance of authority. It can do so because of the skill with which his rhetoric exploits antipathies and resentments which ran deep in early modern society. The ideal universal service was confronted by challenges from radical thinkers on one side and from disillusioned conservatives on the other. Iago, with a characteristic disdain for consistency, draws on both kinds of critique. His repudiation of 'obsequious bondage' and insistence upon the freedom and integrity of the individual will echoes the defiance of the turbulent radicals denounced by Gouge—those who cited St Paul's 'be not ye the servants of men' (I Corinthians 7: 23) to argue that it was 'against nature for one to be a servant, especially a bond-servant to another, [since] it is the prerogative of Christians to be all one; [and] subjection of servants to masters is against that prerogative, [because it] is against the liberty that Christ hath purchased for us . . . wherewith he hath made us free' (pp. 591–4). At the same time, Iago's nostalgic appeal to 'the old gradation' and his denunciation of the habitual ingratitude of masters, recalls the complaints of conservative social critics, who saw the institution of service as corrupted by the new commercial dispensation of wage-labour; and his scorn for the servant who 'Wears out his time, much like his master's ass, | For naught but provender', only to be 'cashiered' in his old age, mirrors the invective of men like Richard Brathwait who deplored 'the unthankfulness or disrespect of masters towards their servants, when they have spent their strength and wasted them in their service'.[1]

The menace of such ingratitude lay in its capacity to expose the empty pretence of mutual affection and reciprocal obligation that underpinned the ideals of service; and the emotional force of Iago's complaint depends partly on the brutally material relationship that his subdued pun in 'cashiered' helps to discover beneath the chivalric rhetoric of military 'office'—one in which the degrading possibility of cashierment is understood as a permanent condition of 'soldiership'.[2] Othello himself, though the play tactfully suppresses the fact, is a species of mercenary; and Iago makes clear

---

[1] Richard Brathwait, *The English Gentleman* (1630), pp. 158–9.
[2] It is symptomatic of the absence of real distinction between military and other forms of service that the verb *cashier* (a newly coined term-of-art imported by soldiers returning from the Low Countries in 1585) was almost immediately extended to the domestic realm—so in *Histrio-mastix* (1599) the young lords are described as having 'cashiered their trains' of servants (3.370).

to Roderigo that the prime consideration governing all human relations is cold cash ('Put money in thy purse', 1.3.333–71). In the
Venetian world where, he claims, 'the old gradation' founded upon
natural ties of 'love' and 'duty' has been displaced by engines of
improper influence ('letter and affection'), service is best treated as
a commercial contract—a system of pecuniary reward governed
by legally enforceable 'just term[s]' (1.1.35–9). To imagine otherwise is to submit to an 'obsequious bondage' that mockingly disguises itself in the language of natural 'bonds' and offices of the
heart. Thus Iago presents his 'forms and visages of duty' (l. 50) as
demonstrations of the necessary hypocrisy to which any honest
serving-man will be driven if he is to resist the ideological cheat
through which his profession is controlled.

The extent to which Iago's discontent could capitalize on a more
general shift in social attitudes is nicely indicated by the changed
meaning of 'obsequious'—a word that (deriving from the Latin for
'follow') could still mean merely 'dutiful', but had very recently
taken on the contemptuous sense of 'sycophantic' which it has for
the ensign. Even Gouge, whose idea of true service involved a kind
of self-surrender, subsuming one's individual identity in the larger
social 'countenance' of one's master, cautioned against the excessive servility that he dubbed 'obsequious' (pp. 593–4). But Iago
allows for no such nice distinctions: his determination to 'follow
but myself' is a conscious renunciation of the whole doctrine of
service, and one that looks forward to the Leveller Richard Overton's claims for the 'self-propriety' of the individual. In his loathing
of servitude Iago voices the same bitterness as historical malcontents like the musician and tutor Thomas Whythorne, who, determined to be '[his] own man' and insisting that a tutor's role was 'to
be free and not bound, much less to be made slave-like', declared
that 'to be a serving-creature or servingman . . . was so like the life
of a water-spaniel, that must be at commandment to fetch or bring
here, or carry there, with all kind of drudgery, that I could not like
of that life'.[1]

The power of Iago's rhetoric to compel a reluctant assent from
the audience depends upon its eloquent mimicry of such *ressenti-
ment*; and once we are alert to the social context of his grievance,

---

[1] James M. Osborn (ed.), *The Autobiography of Thomas Whythorne* (1962), pp. 10,
28, 46.

the smallest details of his relationship with Othello—like the moment when the General, with a patronizing 'good Iago', orders his subordinate to 'disembark [his] coffers' from the ship (2.1.202–3)—can appear charged with murderous feeling: for what else but the humiliating labour of 'his master's ass', or the menial 'fetching' of a water spaniel is the ensign being asked to perform? Indeed 'fetch', with its edge of contempt, is the very verb that Iago uses to describe his task ('I must *fetch* his necessaries', 2.1.275).[1] In this context, the language of the temptation scene, with its elaborate parade of the loyalty, 'duty', and 'love' that servants were supposed to owe their masters, will acquire a dangerous new edge—as, for example, when Iago responds to Othello's demand to know his thoughts:

> Good my lord, pardon me:
> Though I am *bound* to every act of *duty*,
> I am not *bound* to that all *slaves* are *free* to . . .
> (3.3.137–9)

Equally loaded are the terms of his response to Othello's insistence upon proof:

> now I shall have reason
> To show the *love and duty* that I bear you
> With franker spirit. Therefore—as I am *bound*—
> Receive it from me.
> (3.3.196–9)

The rhetoric of this speech is calculated to persuade Othello of the maddening contrast between the frankness (freedom and honesty) of Iago's servantly 'love and duty' and the deviousness of Desdemona's supposed betrayal of wifely fidelity.[2] But, for the audience, the heavy metrical stress on 'bound' will act as a reminder of social bonds of a more degrading kind, underlining the covert sarcasm in Iago's recollection of the 'obsequious bondage' that he despises.

---

[1] Shakespeare himself makes the satiric link between domestic service and the fetching of water-spaniels in *Two Gentlemen of Verona*, 3.1.268–72.

[2] It is part of Iago's strategy to promote himself from the subordinate role of servant to the equality of 'friend' (3.3.380). Plutarch's widely quoted and imitated essay in the *Moralia*, 'How to Tell a Flatterer from a Friend', explores the problem of false friendship to which the great are especially vulnerable. Cf. Robert C. Evans, 'Flattery in Shakespeare's *Othello*: The Relevance of Plutarch and Sir Thomas Elyot', *Comparative Drama*, 35 (2001), 1–41.

With its elaborate profession of servile self-surrender, it prepares the way for the climax of the scene and Iago's yielding of hands and heart to Othello's service: 'Let him *command*, | And to *obey* shall be in me remorse, | What bloody business ever' (3.3.467–9).

If Iago's language identifies their kneeling exchange of vows as a blasphemous troth-plighting, a parody of the wedding rite whose knot he has patiently untied, he means Othello to accept it as a formal reaffirmation of his 'office'—an act of absolute self-surrender to the master's will ('I am your own for ever', 3.3.479), and an exhibition of the 'duty', 'service', and 'homage' that we have seen him privately reserving for himself (1.1.49–54). With proper magnanimity, Othello duly welcomes this enactment of the reciprocal bonds between master and servant: 'I greet thy love, | Not with vain thanks, but with acceptance bounteous' (3.3.469–70). But the bitter irony of Iago's Judas-like ritual of submission is that his eye-service has precisely reversed its ostensible meaning; for it is actually Othello who (like Marlowe's Faustus when he binds Mephostophilis to be 'his servant') has indentured his soul to his own subordinate—as his unwitting confession earlier in the scene suggests: 'I am *bound* to thee for ever' (l. 216). Try then, as both the Venetians and Othello may, to reaffirm the proprieties of 'service' and 'place' (5.2.338, 368), it is difficult to avoid the levelling implications of a plot that shows the master 'Fallen', as Lodovico puts it, 'in the practice of a damnèd slave' (5.2.290), rhetorically bound to his subordinate by their shared abjection. Not only that, but as we shall now see, the play's whole take on duty and submission is complicated by its treatment of the female characters for whom obedience proves to be a profoundly equivocal virtue.

The Place of Women   If the main action of *Othello* is bracketed by the protagonist's two great demonstrations of obedience to Venice—his departure to confront 'the general enemy Ottoman' (1.3.50) and his killing of the 'malignant . . . Turk'—it is likewise framed by two conspicuous acts of female disobedience—Desdemona's defiance of her father's will, and Emilia's refusal of her husband's commands. The place of women in the economy of service was in some respects an anomalous one: while the manuals of household government typically imagined the social order in terms of a male hierarchy of masters and servants, there was of course a parallel female hierarchy. In a strictly patriarchal society, however, the ranking of women was complicated by their general duty of obedience to men—a duty not only enjoined on them in scripture, official homilies, and domestic treatises, but (in the case of husbands) sanctified by the order of matrimony itself. Of course wives might sometimes command, but only as substitutes or lieutenants, taking the place of their husbands for highly specific purposes; otherwise their role was a subordinate one. When Desdemona demands of Emilia 'Who is thy lord?' (4.2.101), the waiting-woman's reply, 'He that is yours, sweet lady', draws attention to a close symmetry between the roles of wife and servant—one that is also emphasized by the way in which Desdemona is made to vie with Iago in the claim to 'honesty' (3.3.229, 386, 434; 4.2.12, 17, 38, 65) much as he competes with her in protestations of 'love' to the Moor.

The subordination of women, as the ambiguous reference of Emilia's 'lord' indicates, was a complex affair that involved potentially conflicting obligations to masters, fathers, and husbands; and this exposure to the contradictions of what Desdemona calls 'divided duty' (1.3.180) in turn had the capacity to reveal uncomfortable splits in the notionally seamless structure of authority. It is not surprising therefore that the two tragedies in which Shakespeare most conspicuously tests the limits of obedience, *Othello* and *King Lear*, should both accord particular structural prominence to episodes in which women find themselves compelled to resist patriarchal authority.

When Desdemona is summoned before the Senate to account for her elopement, Brabantio, like Lear after him, is confounded by his daughter's behaviour. Unable to reconcile his daughter's revolt with his notion of her as a female paragon, incapable of either self-will or appetite—'A maiden never bold, | Of spirit so still and quiet that her motion | Blushed at herself' (1.3.95–7)—Brabantio can only ascribe her behaviour to 'witchcraft' on the part of her seducer (1.3.65); but the whole tenor of Desdemona's defence makes it clear that she has acted as a free agent, asserting the right to fulfilment of her own desire. Her courageous frankness anticipates Cordelia's sturdy resistance to Lear's emotional absolutism. When her father demands to know '[w]here most you owe obedience' (l. 179), Desdemona acknowledges the familial bonds of 'life and education' that define her place as daughter, only to insist that her primary obligation is now defined by her chosen place as wife:

And so much duty as my mother showed
To you, preferring you before her father,
So much I challenge that I may profess
Due to the Moor my lord.

(ll. 185–8)

Desdemona's emphasis on feminine submission in 'duty', 'bound', and 'due' is balanced by the strikingly masculine independence of 'challenge', just as her wish to accompany Othello to war is justified not in terms of wifely duty, but of sexual entitlement and a disdain for feminine 'quiet' ('if I be left behind | A moth of peace . . . The rites for why I love him are bereft me', ll. 253–5).

After the bold self-determination of this beginning, modern readers and audiences are liable to be disconcerted (as Bradley was) by Desdemona's apparently helpless passivity in the face of her husband's jealous rage. The saint-like quietism with which she embraces death can appear especially shocking: commending herself to Othello with her last breath as 'my kind lord' (5.2.125), she answers Emilia's question about who has killed her with a rhetorical cancellation of her own identity: 'Nobody—I myself' (l. 124). It is a mistake, however, to read this as evidence of weakness. Desdemona, as the best actors of the part have always known, is strong in the way that Cordelia is strong; but for both women independence is ultimately constrained by certain socially prescribed limits: for them, as for the rebellious 'servant-monster' Caliban, whose vaunted 'freedom' consists only of the claim to choose 'a new master' (*Tempest*, 2.2.183–6), liberty is conceivable only as the willing transfer of allegiance to a new 'lord'. If Brabantio was once his daughter's 'lord of duty', the name of 'husband' usurps that lordship (1.3.183–4).

Shakespeare is hardly oblivious to the irony of this situation; but the play also demands respect for a resolve which matches Othello's faithful submission to the demands of the state, and which the play's language invests with an almost religious value. If Othello's self-image is defined by his office as servant of the state, Desdemona's is invested in her place as 'true and loyal wife' (4.2.34). Each is committed to a kind of service that is imagined (in imitation of a familiar Christian paradox) as perfect freedom. Just as the Christian subject's love for God expresses itself in the language of unconditional obedience, so Desdemona constantly speaks of her love as a form of glad subordination: 'My heart's *sub-dued* | Even to the very quality of my lord' (1.3.248–9); 'Be as your fancies teach you: | Whate'er you be, I am *obedient*' (3.3.89–90). Being freely chosen, Desdemona's allegiance to her husband is as different from her subjection to paternal tyranny as Othello's 'free condition' (1.2.26) is from the bondage into which he was once sold; and if his deliverance from slavery constituted one form of 'redemption' (1.3.138), the love that Desdemona 'consecrates' to her husband's honour is another (1.3.252). In Othello's mind it is only Desdemona who stands between him and the 'Chaos' or 'perdition' that he associates with his former state (3.3.91–3). Thus it is not simply Cassio's habit of courtly hyperbole that licenses the lieutenant to dress her in the poetry of Marian adoration:

> O, behold,
> The riches of the ship is come on shore!
> You men of Cyprus, let her have your knees.
> Hail to thee, lady; and the grace of heaven,
> Before, behind thee, and on every hand,
> Enwheel thee round!
>
> (2.1.82–7)

There is something saint-like about Desdemona's endurance under the lash of Othello's jealousy; and it is the resolute maintenance of her submission in the face of private abuse and public humiliation, even after her husband has struck her in public, that prompts Lodovico's wonder: 'Truly, an obedient lady' (4.1.239). Whilst such apparent passivity may not be to the liking of modern audiences, from the play's perspective, Desdemona's patient fidelity in the face of Othello's jealous madness is not a betrayal of her earlier spirit, but a confirmation of it.

Yet Shakespeare remains fully awake to the fact that it is just the qualities associated with Desdemona's generous spirit that render her vulnerable to Iago's insinuations. The 'free . . . disposition' which licenses the 'violence' of her love to Othello (2.3.307–8; 1.3.247) is what Iago can punningly interpret as the promiscuous 'country disposition' supposedly characteristic of Venetian women (3.3.204); and, under his tutelage, Othello will learn to read his wife's steadfast compliance as a proof of her erotic pliancy: 'And she's obedient, as you say, obedient, | Very obedient'

(4.1.247–8)—obedient, he means, to any man's will.[1] Brabantio's embittered warning ('She has deceived her father, and may thee', 1.3.291), which Iago is so careful to repeat ('She did deceive her father, marrying you', 3.3.209), spells out the patriarchal logic of this conclusion—a logic that Othello will prove unable to resist: for a woman to betray one man, it insists, is to reveal her lascivious propensity to 'betray more men' (5.2.6).

The material sign of the tragic contradictions that destroy Desdemona is the very theatrical property whose discovery ushers in the final scene—the bed, which is at once the symbol of Desdemona's matrimonial bond and her designated 'death-bed' (5.2.53). In early modern culture the marriage bed was much more than a necessary piece of furniture: almost oppressively over-determined in its public and private meanings, it was the site of crucially significant rituals governing both the beginning and the end of life, just as it was the locus for the most important of all domestic duties, nuptial consummation and perpetuation of the lineage—the matrimonial 'office' (1.3.377) over whose usurpation Iago broods. The almost totemic significance accorded to the marriage bed is perhaps best suggested by those ornate tester tombs, canopied beds of gilded marble, on which the figures of Elizabethan magnates and their wives lie pillowed for eternity, proclaiming the triumph of wedded love over death. Mesmerized by his own fantasy, in which murder becomes a priestly sacrifice sanctified by heavenly sorrow (5.2.21, 67), Othello envisions the sleeping Desdemona, with her white skin 'smooth as monumental alabaster' (l. 5), as just such a serene piece of funeral sculpture. But the final spectacle of three corpses lying side by side on the same bed, revisits that resemblance in the form of atrocious parody, capitalizing on the morbid fantasies that invade Desdemona's imagination after the brothel scene, and on the intimate association of sexuality and death so characteristic of the period's erotic imagination.

Denounced by her husband as 'that cunning whore of Venice | That married with Othello' (4.2.90–1), Desdemona has attempted a symbolic reaffirmation of their marriage bond by calling on Emilia to 'Lay on my bed my wedding sheets' (l. 105). The social

---

[1] For the word-play on the second syllable of 'obedient' that helps to license this misreading, see Commentary, 4.1.247–8.

symbolism of wedding sheets was as powerful as that with which the marriage bed itself was invested: marked with the blood that announced the death of a virgin and her rebirth as a wife, and customarily displayed to prove the consummation of a marriage, they became the fetishized tokens of the physical and emotional transformation that rendered husband and wife 'one flesh'. In *Othello* their significance is further complicated by an iconic link with the purloined handkerchief, itself imbrued with a dye 'Conserved of maidens' hearts', whose fatal witness her sheets are meant to contradict. But their meaning, as Desdemona's uncanny premonition in the next scene reminds us, proves to be dangerously unstable: 'If I do die before thee, prithee shroud me | In one of these same sheets' (4.3.22–3). Her sentimental desire appeals to a well-documented contemporary fashion amongst aristocratic women whose wills required that they be wound for burial in their own wedding sheets. In this way their funeral obsequies might be transformed into a ceremonious re-enactment of nuptials, perpetuating the marital bond beyond the gates of the grave.[1] In Desdemona's case, however, it is as though the conversion of sheet to shroud traps her into unconscious collusion with Iago, who has already nominated her bed as a place of death, where the blood of murder will cancel out the blood of adulterous desire: 'Do it not with poison; strangle her in her bed, even the bed she hath contaminated' (4.1.200–1).[2] In this way the most intimate token of Desdemona's fidelity to her 'office' becomes the sign of her impending murder in a grotesque literalization of the sex–death metaphor so characteristic of Renaissance erotics.

Sharply contrasted with Desdemona is the play's other wife, Emilia, who follows an almost opposite trajectory through the play. In her relationship with Iago, Emilia exhibits for most of the time a cowed compliance that makes her so much an accessory to his plotting that she not only steals the handkerchief for him, but (in spite

---

[1] The will of Lady Frances Stuart, for example, included the instruction to 'wind me up again in those sheets . . . wherein my Lord and I first slept that night we were married', cited in Clare Gittings, *Death, Burial and the Individual in Early Modern England* (1984), p. 193; see also pp. 111–12.

[2] The deeply symbolic choice of the violated marriage bed as the site of revenge, where Othello imagines chopping Desdemona 'into messes' (l. 176) was perhaps influenced by *Arden of Faversham*, where the jealous Arden vows that his wife's lover 'Shall on the bed which he thinks to defile | See his dissevered joints and sinews torn' (1.40–1).

of her deep sympathy for Desdemona) conceals her knowledge of it until too late. However, just as Desdemona's domestic obedience matches Othello's fidelity to public duty, so Emilia's slavish deference to her husband's will conceals a bridling rebelliousness that parallels his own secret resentment of service. Shakespeare orchestrates the contrast with Desdemona to brilliant theatrical effect in the women's last scene alone together, where the plangent romanticism of Desdemona's Willow Song is set against the indignant common sense of Emilia's tirade against the selfish tyranny of husbands:

> But I do think it is their husbands' faults
> If wives do fall: say that they slack their duties,
> And pour our treasures into foreign laps,
> Or else break out in peevish jealousies,
> Throwing restraint upon us; or say they strike us,
> Or scant our former having in despite—
> Why, we have galls; and though we have some grace,
> Yet have we some revenge. Let husbands know,
> Their wives have sense like them; they see, and smell,
> And have their palates both for sweet and sour
> As husbands have. What is it that they do,
> When they change us for others? Is it sport?
> I think it is. And doth affection breed it?
> I think it doth. Is't frailty that thus errs?
> It is so too. And have not we affections,
> Desires for sport, and frailty, as men have?
> Then let them use us well: else let them know,
> The ills we do, their ills instruct us so.

(4.3.81–98)

It is sometimes thought that the heat with which Emilia defends the idea of female adultery as payback may help to explain Iago's jealous suspicion of his wife; but the real significance of Emilia's proto-feminism lies in its appropriation of the idea of revenge as an instrument of social redress. For revenge, of course, is Iago's strong suit; and Emilia's denunciation of husbandly oppression is in many ways the equivalent of Iago's denunciation of the iniquity of masters and the humiliations of service. Driven by the same desire to be 'evened', it exploits the same claim to equality that is implicit in Iago's vindictive accountancy against Othello and Cassio; and it is just this explosion of outrage against the 'despite' governing the male order of things that prepares for Emilia's open revolt in the final scene, when she three times publicly defies her husband:

> IAGO
> What, are you mad? I charge you get you home.
> EMILIA
> Good gentlemen, let me have leave to speak:
> 'Tis proper I obey him, but not now.
> Perchance, Iago, I will ne'er go home. . . .
> IAGO 'Swounds, hold your peace.
> EMILIA 'Twill out, 'twill out! I peace?
> No, I will speak as liberal as the north;
> Let heaven and men and devils, let them all,
> All, all, cry shame against me, yet I'll speak.
> IAGO
> Be wise, and get you home.
> EMILIA
> I will not.
>
> (5.2.192–5, 217–23)

If Emilia's refusal of obedience forms a kind of structural rhyme with Desdemona's defiance of Brabantio at the beginning of the play, her shift from 'not now' to the absolute defiance of 'never' makes it much the more radical gesture of the two; and in her domestic rebellion Richard Strier has discovered the starting point for Shakespeare's celebration of 'virtuous disobedience' in *King Lear*.[1] As she herself implies, Emilia's insubordination reneges against the misogynistic prescriptions of orthodox social doctrine: her repeated refusal to return home to her 'proper' domestic sphere, like her fierce insistence on speaking her mind—in spite of the silence enjoined on women by 'heaven and men'—renders her in Iago's eyes a 'villainous whore', a shamefully indisciplined public woman. In the same way, of course, Desdemona's supposed adultery degraded her from the 'still and quiet' maiden of Brabantio's description to the 'public commoner' denounced by Othello in the brothel scene (4.2.73). By virtue of her disgracefully public character, a whore is in some ways the female equivalent of a masterless man, an errant creature 'of here and everywhere', owing

---

[1] Richard Strier, 'Faithful Servants: Shakespeare's Praise of Disobedience', in Heather Dubrow and Richard Strier (eds.), *The Historical Renaissance: New Essays on Tudor and Stuart Literature and Culture* (Chicago, 1988), 104–33 (p. 111).

obedience to no one; and both Emilia and Desdemona are seen by their husbands as women out of their place, creatures whose rebellious extravagance consigns them to what this society (in spite of its official pretences) actually imagines as the default position for women—that of whore. In Venice, Iago warned Othello (trading on the city's reputation as the capital of European prostitution) 'wife' is simply another guise for a courtesan: 'their best conscience | Is not to leave't undone, but keep't unknown' (3.3.206–7).

The predictable answer to this scandalous collapsing of opposites might have been to use the play's third woman, Bianca, as a straightforward foil to set off the virtues of Desdemona. Bianca is, after all, dismissed as a 'strumpet' not only by Iago, but by a self-righteous Emilia, and even by her own lover, Cassio. Yet, if the absurd misidentification orchestrated by Iago in 4.1 stresses the difference between the two, the 'whiteness' denoted by Bianca's name associates her with the 'fair' Desdemona in a way that is not simply ironical. The evident genuineness of her love for Cassio makes his sneer at her as a mere 'customer' seem cheap and cold-hearted (4.1.116); and, in her indignant reaction to the slurs cast on her transgressive independence by Iago and Emilia, she is allowed to speak for all the abused women of the play—Desdemona above all: 'I am no strumpet, | But of life as honest, as you that thus | Abuse me' (5.1.120–2). The marvellously adroit stressing of 'honest' (which here connotes candour and integrity rather than sexual purity) exposes that slippery adjective to one last test: for not only does Bianca's use of the word offer the play's first open challenge to the much vaunted 'honesty' of Iago, it also calls in question the value of the purely technical chastity by which the male world sets such frantic store. In that sense it chimes with Emilia's defiant proclamation of the rights of wives and allows Bianca to claim a kind of kinship with the two more conventionally honest women of the play, Desdemona and Emilia—the martyred wives who themselves become rhetorically indistinguishable in Othello's question 'why should Honour outlive Honesty?' (5.2.244).

Conclusion Like the improvised motto with which the Earl of Kent endeavours to fix the meaning of Lear's opening scene ('To plainness honour's bound, | When majesty falls to folly', 1.1.148–9), the Moor's rhetorical question is an attempt to reduce the meaning of the play to the comfortable certainties of moral allegory: Honour cannot outlive Honesty, he means us to think, because properly understood they are one thing—rather as (honourable) man and (honest) wife are one flesh. 'Honourable' is, after all, one of the meanings of 'honest'. But the ambiguities and ambivalences that Shakespeare progressively exposes in the latter term serve to remind us of the play's resistance to schematization of any kind. This introduction has traversed a range of historical concerns that were, I believe, of crucial significance in shaping the course of *Othello's* action. Awareness of these matters can help us to understand the particularity of the murderous social tensions that animate the tragedy: they include the early modern politics of gender, the ideology of rank and service, ideas of place and displacement, fantasies of monstrosity and discovery, and (perhaps most significantly for modern readers of the play) the emergent discourse of 'race'. But the play will not submit to the thematic tyranny of any one of these, any more than it would yield to those old-fashioned analyses that sought to neutralize its social engagement by presenting it as a 'universal' tragedy of jealousy, or as a drama of superficial civilization overcome by innate barbarity. That, no doubt, is why scholars interested in what Othello may have to reveal about the evolution of racial thought have found it so difficult to arrive at any consensus about the play's own attitude towards the hero's colour—leaving a critic as scrupulous as Virginia Vaughan trapped in irreducible contradiction: 'I think this play is racist; and I think it is not' (p. 70).

In the end it may be vain to expect a conclusive resolution of such moral issues. Although Renaissance dramatists consistently defended themselves against the enemies of the stage by maintaining the impeccably didactic virtues of their work, their real concern lay in exploiting the theatrical potential of social conflict, rather than in seeking ways to reform human imperfection. Shakespeare was no exception; and even if his penetrating social and psychological intelligence made him an exceptionally acute observer of historical process, his intentions were scarcely of a documentary character either. To confront a play like *Othello* in performance is to be reminded that the turbulent social currents by which its characters—white and black, male and female, master and servant, hero and villain—are swept along, mattered to Shakespeare above all as sources of dramatic and poetic energy:

they are what enabled him to transform Giraldi's squalid bourgeois narrative of adultery and murder into a tragedy of exceptional power, ensuring that the superficial absurdities of plot, which so preoccupied Rymer and Shaw, would be overwhelmed in the theatre by the great brass music that erupts from Othello's passion and despair.

EDITORIAL PROCEDURES

FOR reasons explained in Appendix B, the text of this edition is based on that of the 1623 First Folio, using the version prepared by Charlton Hinman for the Norton Facsimile,[1] which I have collated with the copy held in the Public Library in Auckland, New Zealand. The F text has been carefully compared with those of the First Quarto of 1622 and the Second Quarto of 1630, using the facsimile prepared by Charlton Hinman for Q1 and the electronic version of the Huntington Library copy for Q2.[2] In some cases I have incorporated words and short passages from Q that do not appear in F— this applies particularly to the oaths and profanities that seem to have been purged from the F text; all are recorded in the collation. The text has been thoroughly modernized in accordance with the principles adumbrated by the General Editor.[3] Modernization is generally silent, except where it may be contentious or where significant word-play is involved—as with Iago's rank of ensign ('ancient' in both Q and F); in such cases the alteration is collated and (if necessary) discussed in the commentary. F and Q are alike in the inconsistency of their abbreviations: each often fails to indicate elision when the metre clearly requires it, and each equally often marks it when the effect is metrically disruptive. Accordingly such variants are treated in this edition as no different from other accidents of spelling and punctuation.

Act and scene divisions are those of the Folio, which have been followed by all subsequent editions. However, it needs to be remembered that such divisions (which do not appear in the 1622 Quarto)

---

[1] Charlton Hinman (ed.), *The First Folio of Shakespeare: The Norton Facsimile* (New York, 1968). This is not a reproduction of a single copy of the Folio, but a composite of pages from thirty copies owned by the Folger Shakespeare Library.

[2] Charlton Hinman, *Othello 1622*, Shakespeare Quarto Facsimiles (Oxford, 1975); *The Tragœdy of Othello* (1630), *Early English Books Online* (Ann Arbor, Mich., 1999).

[3] See Stanley Wells, 'Modernizing Shakespeare's Spelling', in Wells and Gary Taylor, *Modernizing Shakespeare's Spelling, with Three Studies in the Text of Henry V* (Oxford, 1979); and Wells, *Re-Editing Shakespeare for the Modern Reader* (Oxford, 1984). Editorial procedures for the entire series are laid out in Gary Taylor's edition of *Henry V* (Oxford, 1982), pp. 75–81.

are editorial rather than authorial, and bear little relation to the continuous staging practised in the theatre for which Shakespeare originally wrote the play: there even act divisions remained for the most part a classical fossil, until the so-called 'private' theatres (where candles had to be regularly trimmed and replaced) instituted the custom of playing music between the acts; and scene divisions were a literary, rather than theatrical convention, which did not necessarily involve any changes of scenic effect. Indeed, Shakespeare and his contemporaries made use of a largely bare stage, where (with the exception of a limited number of stage properties, like the bed in *Othello*, 5.2) location was for the most part left to the audience's imagination. Accordingly in this edition both act and scene divisions are rendered as inconspicuous as possible, and matters of location (where they are of any relevance) are addressed only in the commentary.

All significant alterations to F's stage directions are collated, and any that may be debatable are distinguished in the text by the use of half-brackets and usually discussed in the commentary. Directions for characters to speak 'aside' or to address another character are entirely editorial and therefore not normally collated. Where necessary the end of an aside will be indicated by a dash. Speech prefixes are silently normalized and given in full.

The collation employs the format described in Taylor's *Henry V*:

303–4 Why . . . gentleman?] F ('Why thou silly Gentleman?'); Why, thou silly Gentleman. Q1; Why thou silly Gentleman. Q2; Why, thou silly gentleman! ROWE

The lemma, representing the chosen reading, is followed by the source of the reading, then by the rejected Folio and/or Quarto reading(s), and finally by the proposals of other editors, if any. The latter are recorded only when they seem particularly plausible or interesting. Early editions are cited *literatim*, ignoring only 'long s' and ligatures. In addition to collating emendations, contentious modernizations, and significant changes in punctuation, this edition also records realignments of verse and prose; since these have a bearing on sometimes controversial issues of versification, they are best studied as a group and are therefore consigned to a separate appendix.

The commentary employs *OED*'s abbreviations for different parts of speech and its numbering system for definitions and usages, which are often paraphrased without acknowledgement. Proverbs and proverbial expressions have been checked against both Tilley and Dent. References to other works of Shakespeare are keyed to the Oxford edition of *The Complete Works*, ed. Stanley Wells and Gary Taylor (Oxford, 1986). This edition was prepared independently of that in the Oxford *Complete Works*; but I have of course consulted that edition and made use of it at several points. Biblical citations are to the Geneva Bible (1560).

Because Shakespeare's use of his major source, Giraldi Cinthio's *Gli Hecatommithi*, is so extensive, it has seemed useful to print a full text of the original novella, rather than clog up the commentary with long quotations. The commentary does, however, alert the reader to the more significant borrowings, and Giraldi's text is annotated with act, scene, and line numbers to make cross-referencing as efficient as possible. Further appendices are devoted to the dating of the play, to its complicated and much-debated textual history, and to its important use of music.

Place of publication, unless otherwise specified, is London. Uncorrected and stop-press corrected states of early texts are indicated by (*uncorr.*) and (*corr.*).

Abbreviations and References

EDITIONS OF SHAKESPEARE

F, F1	The First Folio (1623)
F2	The Second Folio (1632)
Q, Q1	The First Quarto (1622)
Q2	The Second Quarto (1630)
Alexander	Peter Alexander, *Complete Works* (1951)
Andrews	John F. Andrews, *Othello*, Everyman (1995)
Bevington	David Bevington, *Complete Works* (New York, 1997)
Cambridge	W. G. Clark, J. Glover, and W. A. Wright, *Works*, The Cambridge Shakespeare, 9 vols. (1863–6)
Cambridge 1891	W. G. Clark, J. Glover, and W. A. Wright (revised W. A. Wright) *Works*, The Cambridge Shakespeare, 9 vols. (1891–3)
Capell	Edward Capell, *Comedies, Histories, Tragedies, and Poems*, 10 vols. (1767–8)
Collier	John Payne Collier, *Works*, 8 vols. (1842–4)

Delius	Nicolaus Delius, *Werke*, 7 vols. (Elberfeld, 1854–60)
Dyce	Alexander Dyce, *Works*, 6 vols. (1857)
Dyce 1864	Alexander Dyce, *Works*, 2nd edn., 9 vols. (1864–7)
Dyce 1875	Alexander Dyce, *Works*, 3rd edn., 10 vols. (1875–6)
Furness	Horace Howard Furness, *Othello*, New Variorum (Philadelphia, 1907)
Hanmer	Thomas Hanmer, *Works*, 6 vols. (Oxford, 1743–4)
Hart	H. C. Hart, *Othello*, Arden, 1st ser. (1928)
Hinman, *F*	Charlton Hinman, *The First Folio of Shakespeare: The Norton Facsimile* (New York, 1968)
Hinman, *Q*	Charlton Hinman, *Othello 1622*, Shakespeare Quarto Facsimiles (Oxford, 1975)
Honigmann	E. A. J. Honigmann, *Othello*, Arden, 3rd ser. (1997)
Jennens	Charles Jennens, *Othello, the Moor of Venice* (1773)
Johnson	Samuel Johnson, *Plays*, 8 vols. (1765)
Keightley	Thomas Keightley, *Plays*, 6 vols. (1864)
Knight	Charles Knight, *Comedies, Histories, Tragedies, and Poems*, Pictorial Edition, 7 vols. (1838–43)
McMillin, *Q*	Scott McMillin, *The First Quarto of Othello* (Cambridge, 2001)
Malone	Edmond Malone, *Plays and Poems*, 10 vols. (1790)
Mowat–Werstine	Barbara A. Mowat and Paul Werstine, *Othello*, New Folger (New York, 1993)
Muir	Kenneth Muir, *Othello*, New Penguin (Harmondsworth, 1968)
Murphy	Andrew Murphy, *The Tragedie of Othello, The More of Venice*, Shakespearean Originals; First Editions (1995)
Oxford	Stanley Wells and Gary Taylor (general editors), *Complete Works* (Oxford, 1986)
Pope	Alexander Pope, *Works*, 6 vols. (1725)
Ridley	M. R. Ridley, *Othello*, Arden, 2nd ser. (1962)
Riverside	G. Blakemore Evans (textual editor), *The Riverside Shakespeare* (Boston, Mass., 1974)
Rowe	Nicholas Rowe, *Works*, 6 vols. (1709)
Sanders	Norman Sanders, *Othello* (Cambridge, 1984; rev. edn. 2003)
Steevens	Samuel Johnson and George Steevens, *Plays*, 10 vols. (1773)

Steevens 1785	Samuel Johnson and George Steevens, *Plays*, 10 vols. (1785)
Steevens–Reed	George Steevens and Isaac Reed, *Plays*, 15 vols. (1793)
Theobald	Lewis Theobald *Works*, 7 vols. (1733)
Theobald 1740	Lewis Theobald *Works*, 8 vols. (1740)
Walker	Alice Walker and John Dover Wilson, *Othello* (Cambridge, 1957)
Warburton	William Warburton, *Works*, 8 vols. (1747)
White	Richard Grant White, *Works*, 12 vols. (Boston, Mass., 1857–66)

OTHER WORKS AND ABBREVIATIONS

Adelman	Janet Adelman, 'Iago's Alter Ego: Race as Projection in *Othello*', *SQ* 48 (1997), 125–44
Berger	Thomas L. Berger, 'The Second Quarto of *Othello* and the Question of Textual "Authority"', in Virginia Vaughan and Kent Cartwright (eds.), *Othello: New Perspectives* (Madison, Wis., 1991), 26–47
Bible	*The Geneva Bible: A Facsimile of the 1560 Edition*, intro. Lloyd E. Berry (Madison, Wis., 1969)
Bodin	Jean Bodin, *Method for the Easy Comprehension of History* (1565), trans. Beatrice Reynolds (New York, 1966)
Bowers	Fredson Bowers, *Bibliography and Textual Criticism* (Oxford, 1964)
Bradley	A. C. Bradley, *Shakespearean Tragedy* (1904; repr. 1961)
Bradshaw	Graham Bradshaw, *Misrepresentations: Shakespeare and the Materialists* (Ithaca, NY, 1993)
Bristol	Michael Bristol, 'Charivari and the Comedy of Abjection in *Othello*', *Renaissance Drama*, NS 21 (1990), 3–21; repr. in Linda Woodbridge and Edward Berry (eds.), *True Rites and Maimed Rites: Ritual and Anti-Ritual in Shakespeare and His Age* (Urbana, Ill., 1992), 75–97
Bullough	Geoffrey Bullough, *Narrative and Dramatic Sources of Shakespeare*, 8 vols. (1957–75), vol. vii
Burton	Robert Burton, *The Anatomy of Melancholy*, ed. Floyd Dell and Paul Jordan-Smith (New York, 1927)

Calderwood	James L. Calderwood, *The Properties of Othello* (Amherst, Mass., 1989)
Cavell	Stanley Cavell, *Disowning Knowledge in Six Plays of Shakespeare* (Cambridge, 1987)
Chambers	E. K. Chambers, *William Shakespeare: A Study of Facts and Problems*, 2 vols. (Oxford, 1930)
Coghill	Nevill Coghill, *Shakespeare's Professional Skills* (Cambridge, 1964)
Coleridge	S. T. Coleridge, *Coleridge's Shakespeare Criticism*, ed. T. M. Raysor, 2 vols. (Cambridge, Mass., 1930)
Collier MS	Manuscript emendations in J. P. Collier's copy of F2 (the 'Perkins Folio'), generally assumed to be in Collier's hand
Davies	Edward Davies, *The Art of War and Englands Traynings* (1620)
Dent	R. W. Dent, *Shakespeare's Proverbial Language: An Index* (Berkeley, Calif., 1981)
Dobson	E. J. Dobson, *English Pronunciation 1500–1700*, 2nd edn., 2 vols. (Oxford, 1968)
ELR	*English Literary Renaissance*
Everett	Barbara Everett, ' "Spanish" Othello: The Making of Shakespeare's Moor', in Catherine Alexander and Stanley Wells (eds.), *Shakespeare and Race* (Cambridge, 2000), 64–81 (repr. from *SS* 35 (1982), 101–12)
Faustus	Christopher Marlowe, *Dr Faustus and Other Plays*, ed. David Bevington and Eric Rasmussen (Oxford, 1995)
Florio	John Florio, *Queen Anna's New World of Words* (1611)
Floyd-Wilson	Mary Floyd-Wilson, *English Ethnicity and Race in Early Modern Drama* (Cambridge, 2003)
Giraldi	Giovanbattista [Giambattista, Giovanni Battista] Giraldi Cinthio, *Gli Hecatommithi* (1565). Appendix C reprints Third Decade, Story 7; other extracts are reprinted in Bullough.
Greg	W. W. Greg, *The Shakespeare First Folio* (Oxford, 1955)
Gurr	Andrew Gurr, 'Maximal and Minimal Texts: Shakespeare v. the Globe', *SS* 52 (1999), 68–87

Hankey	Julie Hankey, *Othello*, Plays in Performance (Bristol, 1987)
Hinman, *Printing*	Charlton Hinman, *The Printing and Proof-Reading of the First Folio of Shakespeare*, 2 vols. (Oxford, 1963)
Honigmann, 'Revised Plays'	E. A. J. Honigmann, 'Shakespeare's Revised Plays: *King Lear* and *Othello*', *The Library*, 6th ser., 4 (1982), 142–73
Honigmann, *Texts*	E. A. J. Honigmann, *The Texts of 'Othello' and Shakespearian Revision* (1996)
Hunter	G. K. Hunter, 'Othello and Colour Prejudice', *Proceedings of the British Academy*, 53 (1967), 139–63
Jackson, 'Copy'	MacD. P. Jackson, 'Printer's Copy for the First Folio Text of *Othello*: the Evidence of Misreadings', *The Library*, 6th ser., 9 (1987), 262–7
Jackson, '*Texts* review'	MacD. P. Jackson, review of Honigmann, *The Texts of 'Othello' and Shakespearian Revision*, *Shakespeare Studies*, 26 (1998), 364–72
JEMCS	*Journal for Early Modern Cultural Studies*
Jones	John Jones, *Shakespeare at Work* (Oxford, 1995)
Jonson	Ben Jonson, *Works*, ed. C. H. Herford and P. and E. Simpson, 11 vols. (Oxford, 1925–52)
Jorgenson	Paul A. Jorgenson, *Shakespeare's Military World* (Berkeley, Calif., 1956)
Kaul	Mythili Kaul (ed.), *Othello: New Essays by Black Writers* (Washington, DC, 1997)
Kellner	Leon Kellner, *Restoring Shakespeare* (1925)
Knolles	Richard Knolles, *Generall Historie of the Turkes* (1603); repr. in Bullough
Kökeritz	Helge Kökeritz, *Shakespeare's Pronunciation* (New Haven and London, 1953)
Kolin	Philip C. Kolin (ed.), *Othello: New Critical Essays* (New York, 2002)
Leavis	F. R. Leavis, 'Diabolic Intellect and the Noble Hero', in *The Common Pursuit* (1952; repr. Harmondsworth, 1969), 136–59 (repr. from *Scrutiny*, 6 (1937), 259–83)

Lewkenor	Lewis Lewkenor, *The Commonwealth and Government of Venice* (1599); translation of Gasparo Contarini, *De Magistratibus et Republica Venetorum* (1543)
McMillin, 'Hypothesis'	Scott McMillin, 'The *Othello* Quarto and the "Foul-Paper" Hypothesis', *SQ* 51 (2000), 67–85
McMillin, 'Mystery'	Scott McMillin, 'The Mystery of the Early *Othello* Texts', in Kolin, 401–24
Marks	Elise Marks, ' "Othello/me": Racial Drag and the Pleasures of Boundary-Crossing with *Othello*', *Comparative Drama*, 35 (2001), 101–23
Muir, *Sources*	Kenneth Muir, *The Sources of Shakespeare's Plays* (1977)
Neill, ' "Mulattos" '	Michael Neill, ' "Mulattos," "Blacks," and "Indian Moors": *Othello* and Early Modern Constructions of Human Difference', in *Putting History to the Question: Power, Politics and Society in English Renaissance Drama* (New York, 2000); repr. from *SQ* 49 (1998), 361–74
Neill, 'Opening'	Michael Neill, 'Opening the Moor: Death and Discovery in *Othello*', in *Issues of Death: Mortality and Identity in English Renaissance Tragedy* (Oxford, 1997), 141–67
Neill, 'Places'	Michael Neill, 'Changing Places in *Othello*', in *Putting History to the Question*, 207–36 (repr. from *SS* 37 (1984), 115–31)
Neill, ' "Unproper Beds" '	Michael Neill, ' "Unproper Beds": Race, Adultery and the Hideous in *Othello*', in *Putting History to the Question*, 237–68 (repr. from *SQ* 40 (1989), 383–412)
N&Q	*Notes and Queries*
OED	*Oxford English Dictionary*, online version <http://www.oed.com/>
Onions	C. T. Onions, *A Shakespeare Glossary* (Oxford, 1911; rev. edn., Oxford, 1977)
Parker, 'Dilation'	Patricia Parker, 'Shakespeare and Rhetoric: "Dilation" and "Delation" ', in Patricia Parker and Geoffrey Hartman (eds.), *Shakespeare and the Question of Theory* (New York and London, 1985), 54–174
Parker, *Margins*	Patricia Parker, *Shakespeare from the Margins: Language, Culture, Context* (Chicago, 1996)

Partridge	Eric Partridge, *Shakespeare's Bawdy* (1947)
Paster	Gail Kern Paster, *Humoring the Body: Affects, Materialism and the Early Modern Stage* (Chicago, 2004)
Pechter	Edward Pechter, *Othello and Interpretive Traditions* (Iowa City, 1999)
Pliny	Philemon Holland, *The Historie Of The World. Commonly called, The Naturall Historie Of C. Plinius Secundus* (1601); translation of Gaius Plinius Secundus, *Naturalis Historia*
Potter	Lois Potter, *Othello*, Shakespeare in Performance (Manchester, 2002)
RES	*Review of English Studies*
Rizvi	Pervez Rizvi, 'Evidence of Revision in *Othello*', *N&Q* NS 45 (1998), 338–43
Rosenberg	Marvin Rosenberg, *The Masks of Othello* (Berkeley, Calif., 1961; repr. Newark, Del., n.d.)
Rubinstein	Frankie Rubinstein, *A Dictionary of Shakespeare's Sexual Puns and their Significance* (1984)
Rymer	Thomas Rymer, *A Short View of Tragedy* (1693)
Schäfer	Jürgen Schäfer, *Documentation in the O.E.D.: Shakespeare and Nashe as Test Cases* (Oxford, 1980)
Siemon	James R. Siemon, ' "Nay, that's not next": *Othello*, V.ii in Performance, 1760–1900', *SQ* 37 (1986), 38–51
Sisson	C. J. Sisson, *New Readings in Shakespeare*, 2 vols. (Cambridge, 1956)
Snow	Edward A. Snow, 'Sexual Anxiety and the Male Order of Things in *Othello*', *ELR* 10 (1980), 384–412
SQ	*Shakespeare Quarterly*
SS	*Shakespeare Survey*
Stratioticos	Leonard and Thomas Digges, *An arithemetical warlike treatise named Stratioticos* (1579; 2nd edn. 1590)
subs.	substantively
Taylor	Gary Taylor, 'The Folio Copy for *Hamlet*, *King Lear*, and *Othello*', *SQ* 34 (1983), 44–61
Taylor and Jowett	Gary Taylor and John Jowett, *Shakespeare Reshaped, 1606–23* (Oxford, 1993)

TC	Stanley Wells and Gary Taylor with John Jowett and William Montgomery, *William Shakespeare: A Textual Companion* (Oxford, 1987)
Tilley	Maurice Palmer Tilley, *A Dictionary of Proverbs in England in the Sixteenth and Seventeenth Centuries* (Ann Arbor, Mich., 1950)
TLS	*Times Literary Supplement*
Tynan	Kenneth Tynan (ed.), *'Othello': The National Theatre Production* (London, 1966; New York, 1967)
Upton	John Upton, *Critical Observations on Shakespeare* (1746)
Vaughan	Virginia Mason Vaughan, *Othello: a contextual history* (Cambridge, 1994)
Vitkus, '"Turning Turk"'	Daniel J. Vitkus, '"Turning Turk" in *Othello*: The Conversion and Damnation of the Moor', *SQ* 48 (1997), 145–76
Vitkus, *Turning Turk*	Daniel Vitkus, *Turning Turk: English Theater and the Multicultural Mediterranean, 1570–1630* (Basingstoke, 2003)
Walker, 'Texts'	Alice Walker, 'The 1622 Quarto and the First Folio Texts of *Othello*', *SS* 5 (1952), 16–24
Walker, *Problems*	Alice Walker, *Textual Problems of the First Folio* (Cambridge, 1953)
Walton	J. K. Walton, *The Quarto Copy for the First Folio of Shakespeare* (Dublin, 1971)
Warner	Richard Warner, *A letter to David Garrick . . . concerning a glossary to the plays of Shakespeare* (1768)
Wells	Stanley Wells, *Re-Editing Shakespeare for the Modern Reader* (Oxford, 1984)
Wells, *All Time*	Stanley Wells, *Shakespeare: For All Time* (2002)
Whitney	Lois Whitney, 'Did Shakespeare know Leo Africanus?', *PMLA* 37 (1922), 470–88
Williams, *Dictionary*	Gordon Williams, *A Dictionary of Sexual Language and Imagery in Shakespearean and Stuart Literature*, 3 vols. (1994)
Williams, *Glossary*	Gordon Williams, *A Glossary of Shakespeare's Sexual Language* (1997)
Wright	George T. Wright, *Shakespeare's Metrical Art* (Berkeley, Calif., 1988)

Othello, the Moor of Venice

THE PERSONS OF THE PLAY

OTHELLO, 'the Moor', general of the Venetian forces

BRABANTIO, 'father to Desdemona', a Venetian Senator
Michael CASSIO, 'an honourable lieutenant', Othello's second-in-command
IAGO, 'a Villain', Othello's ensign
RODERIGO, 'a gulled gentleman', suitor to Desdemona
DUKE of Venice

MONTANO, 'Governor of Cyprus'
LODOVICO
GRATIANO, brother to Brabantio } 'two noble Venetians'
CLOWN

DESDEMONA, 'wife to Othello', and daughter of Brabantio
EMILIA, 'wife to Iago', and waiting-woman to Desdemona
BIANCA, 'a courtesan', mistress of Cassio

SENATORS

SAILOR

MESSENGER

HERALD

OFFICERS

GENTLEMEN 'of Cyprus'

MUSICIANS

Attendants and servants

THE PERSONS OF THE PLAY] *after* F (*following the text*: 'The Names of the Actors'); *not in* Q
RODERIGO] Q (*throughout*); Rodorigo F (*throughout*)   EMILIA] Q ('Emillia' *throughout*); Æmilia F
(*throughout*)

THE PERSONS OF THE PLAY The order of characters broadly follows the list of 'The Names of the Actors' printed at the end of F, from which the descriptions in quotation marks also derive. This is one of seven such lists printed at the end of plays in F. All seem to have been included to fill up large areas of blank page, suggesting that they were added in the printing house, although Honigmann (*Texts*, pp. 70–2; Arden edn., p. 333) has linked five of them to the editorial practice of the scribe Ralph Crane (see App. B, pp. 421–3, 431). However, the identification of Montano as 'Governor of Cyprus' may indi-

cate an authorial origin for the list, since his office cannot easily be deduced from the text itself (see below).
OTHELLO In Giraldi Cinthio the central character is identified simply as 'a Moor' (*un Moro*). The exact origin of his name in the play is obscure. The name 'Otello', although rare, did exist in Italian; and Shakespeare may have been influenced in his choice by 'Thorello', the name of the jealous husband in the first version of *Every Man In His Humour* (printed 1601) in which Shakespeare had performed a few years earlier: see Robert S. Miola's introduction to his edition of Jonson's

193

comedy (Manchester, 2000), p. 65. However, the resemblance of 'Othello' to 'Othman'—the founder of the Ottoman (or 'Othoman') Turkish empire—is unlikely to be accidental and it lends additional irony to Othello's final self-identification with the 'malignant and . . . turbaned Turk' (5.2.351) whose killing is re-enacted in his own suicide. Some critics observe a curious chime between the 'hell' contained in O*thell*o and the 'demon' in Des*demon*a.

general A relatively novel military term. See App. F(i).

Cassio The name Michael Cassio appears to be Shakespeare's invention, though it may have been suggested by that of Lucas Michael, a commander sent into Crete by the Venetians in Knolles's *Generall Historie of the Turkes* (1603), a probable source for the play. In view of Cassio's disgrace in Act 2, it must involve a play on the verb 'cass' = cashier (*OED v.* 2). Shakespeare may also have known the Italian adjective *casso*, glossed by Florio (*Queen Anna's New World of Words*, p. 87) as 'deprived, frustrated, crossed, cashiered'. See also 1.1.48.

lieutenant See App. F(i) for a note on this military term.

IAGO, RODERIGO Shakespeare's choice of Spanish names for two Venetians full of chauvinist resentment against 'strangers' (whether they be Florentines or Moors) is surely a deliberate irony. Jacobean audiences, aware of the Venetian practice of employing mercenary officers, might easily have identified Iago as a Spaniard, particularly because his name was likely to have recalled that of Spain's patron saint, known (fittingly enough for this play) as *Sant'Iago Matamoros* (St James, Hammer of the Moors): see Everett, pp. 67–8. Moreover, Iago is identified as 'a false Spaniard' in the ballad *Tragedie of Othello the Moore* (Furness, pp. 398–402), usually supposed to be a forgery by J. P. Collier. Significantly Giraldi appears to identify Iago's prototype, the *alfieri*, as a foreigner when, at the end of the tale, he has him 'return . . . to his own country'.

ensign See App. F(i).

MONTANO, 'Governor of Cyprus' Like the Q stage direction at 2.1.0.1 ('*Enter Montanio, Governor of* Cypres'), from which it may derive, this description presumably reflects either some unfulfilled authorial intention or a detail of early staging and costuming, since in the text itself Montano is never described as Governor, but simply as the 'trusty and most valiant servitor' of Venice (1.3.40–1); nor is he treated with any special deference by the arriving Venetians in 2.1.

GRATIANO, brother to Brabantio See 5.2.200.

DESDEMONA The name derives from Giraldi, where the murdered heroine's father is blamed for having given her 'a name of unlucky augury', *Disdemona* being a version of the Greek *dusdaimon* = unfortunate. It is possible that Shakespeare also heard a punning reference to the demonic in the name of Othello's 'fair devil'.

BIANCA 'white'. Another name chosen for its ironic suggestiveness—one that complicates the contrast between her and the chaste heroine whose husband denounces her in the same language ('whore', 'strumpet') that Iago and Emilia direct against Bianca. She is an amalgam of two anonymous characters in Giraldi, a serving-woman who copies the embroidery on Disdemona's purloined handkerchief, and the courtesan with whom the *capo di squadra* 'used to amuse himself'. However, while Bianca is described as 'courtesan' in F's list, there is little in the play to confirm this description: although her anomalous position as a young woman living alone and willing to entertain a man to 'supper' will clearly have seemed suspicious, her love for Cassio appears entirely genuine. The Venetian institution of courtesans was well known from the reports of travellers like Thomas Coryat: as distinct from common prostitutes, courtesans were often cultured women of relatively high status, who frequently hired themselves for extended periods to a single lover.

The Tragedy of Othello, the Moor of Venice

1.1   *Enter Roderigo and Iago*

RODERIGO

Tush, never tell me! I take it much unkindly
That thou, Iago, who hast had my purse
As if the strings were thine, shouldst know of this.

IAGO

'Sblood, but you'll not hear me! If ever I

1.1] F (*Actus Primus. Scæna Prima.*); *not in* Q   0.1 *Roderigo and Iago*] F; *Iago and Roderigo* Q   1 Tush] Q; *not in* F   2 thou . . . hast] F; you . . . has Q1; thou who hast Q2   4 'Sblood] Q1; *not in* F, Q2   you'll] F, Q2; you will Q1

1.1.0–1 Enter . . . Iago F typically prefers to arrange the characters in order of conventional precedence, while Q (which has Iago enter first here) may sometimes register the dramatic suggestiveness of having the ensign precede his natural superiors (see e.g. 1.3.48, 4.1.0). However, in this case the ensuing dialogue suggests that Roderigo is walking impatiently away, while Iago, following behind, begs him to listen.

1 **Tush** Mild expletive expressing impatience; seemingly cut here as part of F's often over-cautious suppression of oaths and profanities (see App. B, pp. 420–1, 430–1). Cf. also *'Sblood* (l. 4). McMillin, noting their extra-metricality, suggests that both expletives were actors' interpolations (Q, p. 30). However, such exclamations are often extra-metrical, and in any case elision will readily smooth out the irregularity of this line ('take't').

2 **thou** Since *th* could be written in a form that closely resembled *y*, Q's 'you' is almost certainly based on a misreading; the Q2 editor, spotting the error, restored not simply the grammar of the original, but the aggressive condescension of the singular pronoun. Iago soothingly adopts

the more respectful plural form (see *Anthony and Cleopatra*, ed. M. Neill (Oxford, 1994), App. C, 'A Note on Pronoun Usage').

3 **this** Roderigo presumably rebukes Iago for having been party to Othello's courtship of Desdemona even while he was supposedly hired to act in Roderigo's interest; but Shakespeare plays on the audience's curiosity by leaving the event unspecified.

4–7 **'Sblood . . . city** The lineation here is problematic. Neither Q nor F (whose expurgation of Iago's oath may have forced some realignment) seems satisfactory; but no obvious solution presents itself. With the notable exception of Honigmann, who follows F, most editions have accepted Steevens's solution, partially regularizing Q by transferring 'abhor me' to a line by itself. However, this renders both 4 and 6 as incomplete lines; and although a pause at the end of l. 4, after Iago's outburst of irritation and before the more conciliatory 'If ever I did dream . . . ', might be dramatically appropriate, it is harder to justify a second lengthy pause after 'Abhor me'. The present arrangement, whilst regularizing

---

Did dream of such a matter, abhor me.   5

RODERIGO

Thou told'st me thou didst hold him in thy hate.

IAGO

Despise me if I do not. Three great ones of the city,
In personal suit to make me his lieutenant,
Off-capped to him; and, by the faith of man,
I know my price, I am worth no worse a place.   10
But he—as loving his own pride and purposes—
Evades them with a bombast circumstance,
Horribly stuffed with epithets of war;
And in conclusion
Non-suits my mediators. For 'Certes,' says he,   15
'I have already chose my officer.'
And what was he?

---

9 Off-capped] F; Oft capt Q   14 And in conclusion] Q1; *not in* F, Q2   16 chose] F, Q2; chosen
Q1

ll. 4–6, preserves Q's overcrowded l. 7;
this might, however, be smoothed over in
performance by rapid delivery.

4 **'Sblood** God's blood. A strong oath
expurgated from F.

5 **abhor** Stress on first syllable.

6–39 **him . . . his Moorship . . . the Moor**
For more than thirty lines the object
of Iago's and Roderigo's outrage remains completely anonymous, a dismissive stratagem that also serves to arouse
further curiosity in the audience. When at
last he is identified it is only in contemptuously generic terms: not until his entry in
1.3, when the Duke needs to exploit his
good will, is Othello dignified with his personal name. Cf. 5.2.289, 365.

9 **Off-capped** removed their hats (as a
gesture of deference). First citation in
OED.

10 **I know . . . place** Iago's telling alteration of the usual deferential expression,
'I know my place' (cf. *Twelfth Night*,
2.5.51–2) is emphasized by the subdued
word-play in the second half of this line,
where 'price' is explained as the 'place' of
which he has been deprived (see Introduction, pp. 150–4).
price personal worth, excellency (*OED n.*
7b); but also 'prize' (*OED n.* 14); and 'the

amount of money or other consideration
by which a man's support . . . may be
purchased' (*OED n.* 4).
place position, office, rank

12 **Evades** avoids giving a direct answer to
(*OED v.* 3b; earliest citation)
bombast rhetorically inflated or grandil-
oquent. 'Bombast' was a form of cotton
wool used to pad doublets, breeches, cod-
pieces, etc.; hence *stuffed* (l. 13).
circumstance circumlocution

13 **stuffed** Earliest instance of the
metaphorical application of this *ppl. a.* in
OED.
epithets of war specialized military
terminology

14 **And in conclusion** A Q-only line that
Rizvi suggests may represent a linking
phrase inserted by the scribe to replace an
illegible passage. Something is certainly
missing from F at this point, however, and
Q2's decision to drop the Q1 line is difficult
to account for.

15 **Non-suits my mediators** causes my
petitioners to withdraw their suit
Certes assuredly, or 'to tell the truth';
sometimes (as here) monosyllabic.

16 **officer** office-holder (here close to 'lieutenant', in the sense that it denotes someone capable of deputizing in Othello's
'office')

Forsooth, a great arithmetician,
One Michael Cassio, a Florentine—
A fellow almost damned in a fair wife—   20
That never set a squadron in the field,
Nor the division of a battle knows
More than a spinster—unless the bookish theoric,
Wherein the toga'd consuls can propose
As masterly as he! Mere prattle without practice   25
Is all his soldiership. But he, sir, had th'election;

---

20 damned] F (damn'd); dambd Q   24 toga'd] Q1 (toged); Tongued F, Q2

---

18 **arithmetician** As the full title of Digges's *An arithemetical warlike treatise named Stratioticos* indicates, the study of mathematics was actually recommended by most theorists of military art. In his epistle 'To the Reader', Thomas Digges set out to counter the resentful arguments of those like Iago who, having 'been in a few skirmishes, or taken any degree in field . . . thought it . . . a disgrace that anything should be desired in a soldier that wanted in themselves' (sig. B2). See also Jorgenson, pp. 113–15.

19 **Florentine** i.e. a foreigner (Florence and Venice being independent city-states). Iago's contempt is conveyed by the extra stress placed on the first syllable by the preceding succession of three unstressed syllables. Honigmann may be right in supposing that the familiar association of Florence with the craft of Machiavelli is relevant in the context of Iago's disdain for 'bookish theoric', especially in view of the irony that Iago himself is the true machiavel of the play.

20 **damned in a fair wife** Apparently based on the Italian proverb '*L'hai tolta bella? Tuo danno*' ('Have you a fair wife? Then you're damned'), this clearly expresses both Iago's misogyny and his sexual envy of Cassio; but its precise reference, which provokes five pages of commentary in Furness, remains obscure. It may represent a change of intention on Shakespeare's part, since there is no evidence in the play that Cassio is married; it may mean that Cassio is on the brink of marriage to a beautiful woman, and will soon suffer the consequences (cuckoldry in Iago's opinion); or perhaps (as Ridley suggested) Iago is speaking loosely, and means simply that Cassio is a ladies' man. Alternatively it might be taken to imply that Cassio is already engaged in an adulterous affair—something that accords with Iago's later suspicions of the lieutenant's relations with both Desdemona and Bianca. Bradshaw (pp. 156–9) argues that this is a proleptic reference to Bianca who is to be understood as a Venetian courtesan accompanying him to Cyprus (see 4.1.116).

21 **squadron** body of troops drawn up in a defensive square

22 **division of a battle** organization of an army into battle array

23 **unless . . . theoric** except as a matter of academic theorizing

24 **toga'd consuls** A contemptuously anachronistic description of the civilian authorities in Venice; the toga (a garment worn in peacetime by the citizens of ancient Rome) sarcastically alludes to their lack of military expertise. Q1's reading has been generally accepted; but the fact that the editor of Q2 preferred F's 'tongued' should give pause for thought (see App. B, pp. 407–8), especially since *OED* records no earlier instance of either word. 'Tongued' (= loquacious) would certainly make acceptable sense here, forming a chain of association with 'spinster' (loquacity being regarded as a typically feminine characteristic) and 'prattle'.
propose discourse; put forward a scheme

25 **prattle without practice** Cf. Dent P550.1, 'More prattle than practice' (1611).

26 **had th'election** was chosen

And I—of whom his eyes had seen the proof
At Rhodes, at Cyprus, and on other grounds,
Christened and heathen—must be beleed and calmed
By debitor and creditor. This counter-caster,   30
He, in good time, must his lieutenant be,
And I—God bless the mark!—his Moorship's ensign.

RODERIGO
By heaven, I rather would have been his hangman!

IAGO
Why, there's no remedy, 'tis the curse of service:
Preferment goes by letter and affection,   35

---

28 Cyprus] F (Ciprus); *Cipres* Q (*throughout*)   other] Q; others F   29 Christened] F
(Christen'd), Q2; Christian Q1   be beleed] F (be-leed), Q2; be led Q1; be leed HEATH *conj.*
32 God bless the mark] Q1; (blesse the marke) F; Sir (blesse the marke) Q2   Moorship's] F
(Mooreships), Q2; Worships Q1   ensign] F (Auntient), Q (Ancient); *so throughout, various
spellings*   34 Why] F; But Q

27 **eyes . . . proof** A casual anticipation of the play's obsession with 'ocular proof'.

28 **Rhodes . . . Cyprus** Important island strongholds in the struggle between Venice and Turkey for control of the Eastern Mediterranean. After a failed attack in 1480, Rhodes was finally captured by the Turks in 1522; the Venetians retained control of Cyprus until 1571 when the principal city of Famagusta fell to a year-long siege.

29 **Christened** Here again Q2 prefers the F reading which there seems no particular reason to change, since 'christened' could be applied to land as well as people (cf. Drayton (1596), 'As well in Christened as in heathen land', cited in *OED*).
beleed cut off from the wind and becalmed (as a ship is by another vessel's standing in the way). Many editors are persuaded by Heath's emendation ('be leed'), which can be justified as lying behind Q1's 'be led', as well as being metrically more regular; but 'heathen' (like 'heaven') can be treated as monosyllabic, and Q2 once again opts for the F reading. *OED* cites no examples of 'lee' used as a verb in this way, and gives this passage as its only instance of 'belee'.

30 **debitor . . . creditor . . . counter-caster** Iago dismisses Cassio as a mere pen pusher or accountant; ironically it is he himself who typically employs the language and calculus of accounting (cf. 'price . . . worth', l. 15).

30 **counter-caster** Apparently Shakespeare's coinage (*OED*).

31 **in good time** opportunely (sarcastic)

32 **God . . . mark** 'An apologetic or impatient exclamation when something horrible or disgusting has been said' (*OED, mark, n.*[1] 18).
his Moorship Sarcastically coined mock honorific (cf. 'his worship').
ensign standard-bearer (see 'Persons of the Play', above)

34 **service** military service; serving a master. The two meanings were closer in the 17th century when captains appointed their own officers, who were thus effectively in the individual service of their commanders; but it is typical of Iago's social resentment that he more than once equivocates on the military and domestic connotations of the word (see e.g. 1.1.41–54), as though his military rank were a mark of servile inferiority.

35–6 **Preferment . . . gradation** promotion is decided by patronage, by letters of recommendation and by favouritism, not by the old system of seniority (a frequent complaint in early modern military circles). Henry Knyvett, for example, advocates returning to 'the ancient custom . . . to rise from place to place even from private soldiers to every degree in the field not above a colonel, as the fortune of the wars may afford their worthy actions; and not to be chopped and changed and misplaced for favour, as

And not by old gradation, where each second
Stood heir to th' first. Now sir, be judge yourself
Whether I in any just term am assigned
To love the Moor?
RODERIGO I would not follow him then.   40
IAGO O sir, content you.
I follow him to serve my turn upon him.
We cannot all be masters, nor all masters
Cannot be truly followed. You shall mark
Many a duteous and knee-crooking knave   45
That, doting on his own obsequious bondage,
Wears out his time, much like his master's ass,

36 And not by] F; Not by the Q   38 assigned] Q1; Affin'd F, Q2   43 all be] F, Q2; be all Q1

nowadays to the great discouragement
of forward spirits is so much used'
(*The Defence of the Realme*, 1596 (Oxford,
1906), pp. 60–1). Iago's complaint is of
course completely inconsistent with his
assertion that Othello ignored the pressure brought to bear by his own influential friends, and indeed with his claim that
he ought to have been promoted as the
better soldier; but his inconsistencies do
not necessarily mean that his expressed
motives are merely concocted (see Introduction, pp. 31–2).

38 **in . . . term** under any fair and reasonable conditions of service (usually plural)
assigned designated, directed, required
(*OED v.* 6–7). Despite Q2's endorsement
of F, Q seems to offer the better reading
here, since the word has specifically military resonances and is consistent with the
bitter quibbling on Iago's rank that continues with 'flag and *sign* of love' (l. 156).
Affined would be an easy misreading for
'assi[g]ned' when written with the long
's'. It is usually defended as = 'bound by
any tie', though this is the only instance
of this meaning cited in *OED*.

40 **I . . . then** The line is metrically amphibious: i.e. it can be treated as completing
both lines 39 and 41. The scansion requires
a slurring together of 'Follow *him*'.

40, 42, 44 **follow** serve

41–65 **O sir . . . I am** For discussion of this
speech in the context of the play's treatment of service, see Introduction, pp.
150–1, 160–1; and Michael Neill, ' "His
Master's Ass:" Slavery, Service, and Subordination in *Othello*', in Tom Clayton et

al. (eds.), *Shakespeare in the Mediterranean*
(Newark, Del., 2004), 215–92. *Stratioticos*
urges that the ensign should be 'a man of
good account, honest and virtuous, that
the captain may repose affiance in, and
not as some captains fondly do commit
the same to some of his inferior servants'
(sig. O4ᵛ).

42 **serve . . . upon him** exploit him in pursuit of my own interests (Dent TT25).
Iago's quibble on 'serve' (see above, l. 34)
also has an edge of menace, by association with *serve* = deal blows; play a trick;
do a bad turn (*OED v.* 45).

44 **You shall mark** you may readily observe

45 **knee-crooking** abjectly bowing
knave (a) servant, menial; (b) one of low
degree; (c) rogue

46 **obsequious** compliant; sycophantic
(with a quibble on its derivation from the
Latin *sequor* = follow). *OED*'s earliest citation for this derogatory use of a word
that had originally meant merely 'dutiful'
is from Marston's *Antonio and Mellida*
(1602); the older, complimentary meaning is still preserved in *Hamlet* (1.2.92)
dating from the same year. The shift in
meaning is symptomatic of changing attitudes to service (see Introduction, pp.
149–50).

47 **his master's ass** In scripture the ass
(which carried Christ into Jerusalem) is a
type of servantly compliance: 'The ox
knoweth his owner, and the ass his master's crib' (Isaiah 1: 3); but Iago probably
intends a sly reference to Balaam's ass,
an exemplar of justified disobedience.
Balaam's ass defied the punishments of
its master for refusing to carry him past

For naught but provender, and when he's old—
    cashiered.
Whip me such honest knaves! Others there are
Who, trimmed in forms and visages of duty,   50
Keep yet their hearts attending on themselves,
And, throwing but shows of service on their lords,
Do well thrive by them, and when they have lined their
    coats
Do themselves homage. These fellows have some soul,
And such a one do I profess myself—for, sir,   55
It is as sure as you are Roderigo,
Were I the Moor, I would not be Iago:

48 naught] F; noughe Q   53 them] F; em Q   54 These] F; those Q   57 Moor] F, Q (Moore);
Moor's KELLNER *conj.*

the angel of the Lord, by reminding him of
its lifetime of service: 'Am not I thine ass,
upon which thou hast ridden ever since I
was thine own?' (Numbers 22: 30).

48 **provender** food (esp. dry food for horses,
etc.)
cashiered Though it can be metrically
accommodated by treating this line as a
hexameter, this word should perhaps be
treated as a part-line on its own, since a
pause after *old* would be dramatically
appropriate. The verb to *cashier* was a
newly coined term-of-art, apparently
imported by soldiers returning from the
Low Countries in 1585, and Iago should
probably produce it with something of a
flourish—especially since it plays on
Cassio's name (which could itself mean
'cashiered'; see 'Persons') and on his
alleged mercenary credentials as a
'counter-caster' (l. 30).
49 **Whip me . . . knaves** for my part I'd like
to see all such honest menials whipped.
Me is a so-called 'ethic [or ethical] dative',
a relatively common construction in
Shakespearian English, implying that a
person other than the subject or object of
the sentence has an indirect interest in
the stated facts.
honest knaves An oxymoronic quibble
on *knave* = villain; whipping was the usual
punishment for one judged to be a dishon-
est knave.
50 **trimmed in forms and visages** decked
in the conventional appearances
51 **attending on** serving

52 **throwing** directing towards, offering;
usually with a suggestion of hostility or
contempt (*OED, throw, v.*[1] 15a).
53 **Do . . . coats** Can be scanned as a hexameter; but Q's *by 'em* suggests that elision
was intended, and with the easy further
elision of *they have* this will produce a
pentameter.
lined their coats A servant wore a liv-
ery-coat (or 'blue-coat'); Iago's alteration
of the more usual 'lined their *pockets*'
reflects his bitter obsession with the
marks of servile status.
54 **Do themselves homage** become their
own masters. *Homage* was the formal
action by which a vassal declared himself
the 'man' of a feudal lord or master and
bound himself to his service.
soul i.e. spirit
56 **Roderigo** As sometimes happens with
proper names in Shakespeare (e.g.
Coriolanus), the pronunciation of this
name appears to vary: here the metre
requires the sounding of all four syllables,
with a stress on the third ('Roderígo').
More commonly, it is trisyllabic; either, as
at l. 172, with the stress on the penulti-
mate syllable ('Rod'rígo'), or, as at l. 95,
with the stress on the first syllable
('Ród'rigo').
57 **Were . . . Iago** The first of a number of
oddly gnomic formulations that characterize Iago's devious way of speaking. It
seems to mean something like 'If I were
able to rise to the position of mastery now
occupied by Othello, I would have no wish
to return to my present servile status.'

In following him, I follow but myself—
Heaven is my judge, not I for love and duty,
But seeming so for my peculiar end;   60
For when my outward action doth demonstrate
The native act and figure of my heart
In compliment extern, 'tis not long after
But I will wear my heart upon my sleeve
For daws to peck at: I am not what I am.   65

RODERIGO
What a full fortune does the thick-lips owe
If he can carry't thus?

IAGO   Call up her father:
Rouse him, make after him, poison his delight,

61 doth] F, Q2; does Q1   65 daws] F (Dawes), Q2; Doues Q1   66 full] Q; fall F   thick-lips] Q
(thicklips); Thicks-lips F1; Thicke-lips F2   67 carry't] F, Q2; carry'et Q1   father:] F; ~, Q

But, in the context of Iago's bitter obsession with the humiliations of service,
Kellner's conjecture (p. 132) that QF
'Moore' is a mistake for 'Moors' or
'Moores' (i.e. Moor's) is worth consideration: in which case Iago would mean 'If I
really belonged to the Moor (were the
Moor's true servant) then I would not be
the man I am.'

59 **not I for** I don't do this out of
60 **peculiar end** private purposes
61 **demonstrate** exhibit. Placing the accent
on the second syllable, as required by the
metre, will make the word resonate with
the play's obsessive anxiety about the
'monstrous'—to which it was in any case
linked by the false etymology which
derived 'monster' from the Latin *monstro*
(show).
62 **native** innate, natural
act and figure activity and form. Perhaps, since Iago is contrasting '*visages* of
duty' with his inner truth, a play on
French *figure* (face) is involved.
63 **compliment extern** outward exhibitions of courtesy. But as 'complement'
and 'compliment' were not distinct in
early 17th-century usage, it may also suggest outward behaviour that comple-
ments and completes the feelings of the
heart.
64 **wear . . . sleeve** expose my feelings to
everyone (the earliest example of this
proverbial phrase in *OED*; see *heart, n.*
15f). Servants wore their badge of household allegiance upon their sleeve.

65 **daws** The proverbial foolishness of jack-
daws was expressed in their appetite for
gawdy trifles. Q's 'doves', though an easy
misreading for 'dawes', is defensible since
doves are associated with love, and so
might be sarcastically linked to the tender
heart that Iago despises.
I . . . am Another of Iago's teasingly
obscure formulations; parodying the
scriptural name of God, 'I am that I am'
(Exodus 3: 14), which Shakespeare also
plays with in Sonnet 121 and in *Richard
III*, it seems to mean something like 'I am
playing a role that does not correspond to
my true nature'. For a similarly gestic use
of 'I am', see *Antony*, 1.3.13, 'I am sick
and sullen' (= 'Watch me do my sick and
sullen act').
66 **full fortune** abundant or perfect good
luck (perhaps with a glance at Desdemona's dowry)
thick-lips A strong indication that
Shakespeare conceived his Moor as a
black African. A Shakespearian coinage
(*OED*). See Introduction, fig. 7.
owe own
67 **carry't thus** succeed in this way; get
away with this
68–9 **Rouse . . . Proclaim him** Editors are
divided as to whether the pronouns refer
to Othello (as F's punctuation might suggest), or to Brabantio (as Q appears to
indicate). Though 'rouse' might seem to
anticipate the noisy waking of Brabantio
which follows, the other injunctions seem
more appropriate to Othello.
68 **make after** pursue

Proclaim him in the streets. Incense her kinsmen,
And, though he in a fertile climate dwell,   70
Plague him with flies: though that his joy be joy,
Yet throw such chances of vexation on't
As it may lose some colour.

RODERIGO

Here is her father's house, I'll call aloud.

IAGO

Do, with like timorous accent and dire yell   75
As when, by night and negligence, the fire
Is spied in populous cities.

RODERIGO

What ho! Brabantio, Signor Brabantio, ho!

IAGO

Awake! What ho, Brabantio! Thieves, thieves, thieves!
Look to your house, your daughter, and your bags!   80
Thieves, thieves!

Enter Brabantio at a window above

BRABANTIO

What is the reason of this terrible summons?
What is the matter there?

RODERIGO

Signor, is all your family within?

---

69 streets] F; streete Q   72 chances] F; changes Q; charges WALKER *conj.*   on't] F; out Q
78 Signor] Q ('Seignior' *throughout*); Siginor F (*elsewhere* 'Signior')   79 Thieves, thieves,
thieves] Q (theeues); Theeues, Theeues F   80 your daughter] F, Q2; you ~ Q1   81.1 *Enter Brabantio . . . above*] This edition;   *Bra. Aboue.* F (*as speech prefix*);   Brabantio *at a window* Q

69 **Proclaim** denounce as a traitor or
outlaw
70–1 **though . . . flies** though he is in
a state of apparent good fortune
and happiness, torment him with
miseries
71–3 **though . . . As** Paraphrases the previous metaphor: 'no matter how real his
happiness may be, taint it with such in-
furiating possibilities that'.
73 **colour** ground or reason for its
existence
75 **timorous** fearful, terrifying
76 **by night . . . fire** a nocturnal fire caused
by negligence. In Stratford, hundreds of

buildings were destroyed by fires in 1594
and 1596 (Wells, *All Time*, p. 28).
80 **house . . . bags** Desdemona is regarded
simply as an item in Brabantio's catalogue of property. Cf. Shylock's reported
reaction to his daughter's abduction in
Merchant, 2.8.15–22.
81.1 **window above** Most Elizabethan playhouses had a balcony or 'tarras' that
could serve either as a playing space for
action 'above', or to accommodate spectators when not so required; in some
cases it seems to have been flanked by
windows, placed above the entry doors on
the main stage.

IAGO

Are your doors locked?

BRABANTIO   Why? Wherefore ask you this?   85

IAGO

'Swounds, sir, you're robbed; for shame, put on your
        gown!
Your heart is burst, you have lost half your soul:
Even now, now, very now, an old black ram
Is tupping your white ewe. Arise, arise!
Awake the snorting citizens with the bell,   90
Or else the devil will make a grandsire of you.
Arise, I say!

BRABANTIO   What, have you lost your wits?

RODERIGO

Most reverend signor, do you know my voice?

BRABANTIO Not I; what are you?

RODERIGO My name is Roderigo.   95

BRABANTIO The worser welcome:

I have charged thee not to haunt about my doors:
In honest plainness thou hast heard me say
My daughter is not for thee; and now in madness,
Being full of supper, and distempering draughts,   100
Upon malicious bravery, dost thou come

---

85 Are . . . locked] F, Q2; Are all doore lockts? Q1   86 'Swounds] Q1 (Zounds); *not in* F, Q2
you're] F (y'are); you are Q   88 now, now, very] F; now, very Q   96 worser] F (worsser);
worse Q   101 bravery] Q; knauerie F

---

86 **'Swounds** by Christ's wounds (a strong
      oath)
   gown i.e. the 'nightgown' in which Bra-
      bantio appears at l. 158.1.
88 **black ram** Apart from the ram's associa-
      tion with lust and sexual potency, its
      blackness (like its horns) suggests that it is
      an incarnation of the devil (cf. l. 91). The
      animal imagery here and elsewhere in the
      play presents miscegenation as a violation
      of the natural order: something literally
      monstrous, in the sense that monsters
      were supposed to be the offspring of
      unnatural coupling between different
      kinds of creatures. Devils too were
      often represented as having monstrous
      shapes.
89 **tupping** copulating with (from the
      northern dialect *tup* = ram; first use of the
      verb cited in *OED*)
   white ewe For the subdued pun

(*ewe/you*) that makes Brabantio the victim of Othello's violation by identifying
the daughter as a mere extension of the
patriarchal body, see Neill, 'Places',
pp. 208–36.
90 **snorting** snoring (perhaps with a further
      suggestion of animality)
93 **reverend** worthy of respect
95 **My . . . Roderigo** An amphibious line:
      Roderigo is trisyllabic (see l. 56 n.).
96 **worser** Double comparative; common in
      Shakespeare.
100 **distempering draughts** intoxicating
      drinks
101 **bravery** defiance, bravado. F's 'knav-
      ery', though it makes reasonable sense, is
      an easy misreading and misses the point
      of Brabantio's indignation, which is that
      Roderigo, despite having been sent pack-
      ing, has stubbornly persisted in returning
      to the house.

To start my quiet.

RODERIGO   Sir, sir, sir—

BRABANTIO   But thou must needs be sure
My spirit and my place have in their power
To make this bitter to thee.

RODERIGO   Patience, good sir!

BRABANTIO
What tell'st thou me of robbing? This is Venice: 105
My house is not a grange.

RODERIGO   Most grave Brabantio,
In simple and pure soul, I come to you.

IAGO 'Swounds, sir, you are one of those that will not serve
God if the devil bid you. Because we come to do you
service, and you think we are ruffians, you'll have your   110
daughter covered with a Barbary horse, you'll have your
nephews neigh to you, you'll have coursers for cousins
and jennets for germans.

BRABANTIO
What profane wretch art thou?

IAGO I am one, sir, that comes to tell you your daughter and   115
the Moor are now making the beast with two backs.

---

103 spirit] Q; spirits F   their] F; them Q   105 What tell'st] F; What, tell'st Q   108
'Swounds] Q1 (Zouns); *not in* F, Q2   110 and] F; *not in* Q   115 comes] F; come Q   116 now]
Q; *not in* F

102 **start my quiet** disturb my peace
    Sir, sir, sir— An extra-metrical interruption. The fact that Brabantio completes his own verse line may indicate that he speaks over the top of Roderigo's interruption.
103 **spirit** character; mettle, willingness to assert myself
    place rank, office
106 **grange** country house (isolated and vulnerable)
107 **simple** honest, straightforward
111 **covered with** mated by
    Barbary horse Arab stallion (with a quibble on 'barbarian'); i.e. the Moor, Othello. 'Barbary' was strictly the home of the Barbary Moors (Berbers), west of Egypt, but sometimes referred more loosely to the larger North African littoral.
112 **nephews** grandsons (*OED* 3)
    neigh Cf. Jeremiah 5: 8: 'They rose up in the morning like fed horses: for every

man neighed after his neighbour's wife';
and 13: 27: 'I have seen thine adulteries,
and thy neighings, the filthiness of thy
whoredom . . . and thine abominations'
(Geneva Bible, 1560). The second passage
closely follows that in which the prophet
identifies blackness as the mark of
ingrained sin: 'Can the black Moor
change his skin . . .?' (13: 23).
    coursers chargers, war-horses; stallions
(with a pun on 'corsair' = Barbary
pirate)
    cousins Punning on 'cozen' = deceive,
beguile. For Shakespeare's habitual wordplay on *cousin* and *german* (l. 113), see
Parker, *Margins*, pp. 127–36, 154–5,
177–8.
113 **jennet** small Spanish horse
    germans close relatives (with a quibble
on Germans)
114 **profane** foul-mouthed
116 **making . . . backs** copulating. Italian

BRABANTIO

Thou art a villain.

IAGO   You are a senator.

BRABANTIO

This thou shalt answer. I know thee, Roderigo.

RODERIGO

Sir, I will answer anything. But I beseech you,
If't be your pleasure and most wise consent—   120
As partly I find it is—that your fair daughter,
At this odd-even and dull watch o'th' night,
Transported with no worse nor better guard
But with a knave of common hire, a gondolier,
To the gross clasps of a lascivious Moor—   125
If this be known to you and your allowance,
We then have done you bold and saucy wrongs.
But if you know not this, my manners tell me
We have your wrong rebuke. Do not believe
That from the sense of all civility   130
I thus would play and trifle with your reverence.
Your daughter—if you have not given her leave—
I say again hath made a gross revolt,
Tying her duty, beauty, wit, and fortunes
In an extravagant and wheeling stranger,   135

120–36 If . . . yourself] F, Q2; *not in* Q1   122 odd-even] MALONE; odde Euen F

and French proverb (Dent B151): *Far la bestia a due dossi*; *faire la beste a deux dos.* See e.g. Rabelais, 1.3; 5.30 (Honigmann).

117 **Thou . . . You** Iago responds to Brabantio's contemptuous 'thou' with sarcastic mock-politeness.
 villain Not merely 'scoundrel' but also 'low-born peasant'.

118 **answer** answer for

120–36 **If't . . . yourself** The incomplete syntax of the sentence begun by 'I beseech you' might suggest, as Honigmann once argued, that these lines were added to F ('Revised Plays', pp. 161–2); but Shakespeare sometimes uses such incompletion to register the speaker's emotional excitement; and Honigmann himself (*Texts*, p. 12) now argues that, because Brabantio's questioning at ll. 162–7 seems to refer back to this passage, a cut must have been involved.

121 **As . . . is** as [given your response to our news] I half think it must be

122 **odd-even** Usually explained by reference to *Macbeth*, 3.4.125–6: 'What is the night? | Almost at odds with morning, which is which.' Johnson suggested that 'the *even* of *night* is *midnight*, the time when night is divided into *even* parts'; thus *odd* might indicate a time on either side of the midnight hour.
 dull gloomy, dark; drowsy

126 **and . . . allowance** and has your approval

127 **saucy** insolent

130 **from** contrary to

133 **gross** flagrant; disgusting

135 **extravagant** wandering, vagrant (a characteristic attributed to barbarians generally: cf. *erring barbarian*, 1.3.348–9)
 wheeling giddy, restless, wandering (see *OED ppl. a.* d, citing this as the earliest example)

Of here and everywhere. Straight satisfy yourself:
If she be in her chamber or your house,
Let loose on me the justice of the state
For thus deluding you.
BRABANTIO   Strike on the tinder, ho!
Give me a taper. Call up all my people.   140
This accident is not unlike my dream;
Belief of it oppresses me already.
Light, I say, light!   *Exit Brabantio*
IAGO   Farewell, for I must leave you.
It seems not meet, nor wholesome to my place
To be produced—as, if I stay, I shall—   145
Against the Moor; for I do know the state—
However this may gall him with some check—
Cannot with safety cast him. For he's embarked
With such loud reason to the Cyprus wars
(Which even now stands in act) that, for their souls,   150
Another of his fathom they have none,
To lead their business; in which regard,
Though I do hate him as I do hell pains,
Yet, for necessity of present life,

139 For . . . you] F, Q2; For this delusion Q1   143 *Exit*] F; *not in* Q   144 place] F, Q2; pate Q1
145 produced] Q (produc'd); producted F   147 However] F, Q (*corr.*) (How euer); Now euer Q
(*uncorr.*)   148 cast him] Q; cast-him F   151 none] F, Q2; not Q1   153 hell pains] DYCE (hell-
paines); hells paines Q; hell apines F

stranger The usual term for 'foreigner' or 'alien'.

136 **Of here and everywhere** of no fixed abode

139 **Strike . . . tinder** strike up a light. A reminder that the scene (though played in daylight on the Globe stage) is imagined as taking place in the dark. Like *Macbeth*, *Othello* contains an unusually high number of night scenes (1.1–3; 2.3; 5.1–2) which help to set the mood of the play and resonate with its black–white, light–dark symbolism.

140 **taper** wax candle

141 **accident** misfortune

142 **oppresses me** weighs heavily on my spirits

144 **meet** fitting
place position (as Othello's ensign)

145 **produced** i.e. as a witness. F's 'product-ed' is a possible reading, since 'product' sometimes occurs as an alternative verbal form; but, since there are no other instances in Shakespeare and it disrupts the metre without altering the meaning, F probably reflects a simple misreading.

147 **gall . . . check** bring the trouble of a reproof upon him. Sanders suggests a subdued equestrian metaphor: 'slightly hurt a horse by pulling back the rein'.

148 **cast** cast off, discharge
embarked involved (in), committed (to)

149 **With . . . reason** for such clamorously urgent reasons

150 **stands in act** are under way (a singular verb with a plural noun is not uncommon in Shakespeare, especially when, as in the case of *wars*, the noun can be thought of as a collective).
for their souls to save their souls

151 **fathom** depth of understanding, grasp; ability (*OED n.* 2b; first example of this usage)

154 **life** livelihood

I must show out a flag and sign of love—   155
Which is indeed but sign. That you shall surely find him,
Lead to the Sagittary the raised search,
And there will I be with him. So farewell.   *Exit*
    Enter Brabantio in his nightgown, and servants with
    torches

BRABANTIO

It is too true an evil. Gone she is;
And what's to come of my despisèd time   160
Is naught but bitterness. Now Roderigo,
Where didst thou see her?—O, unhappy girl!—
With the Moor sayst thou?—Who would be a father?—
How didst thou know 'twas she?—O, she deceives me
Past thought!—What said she to you?—Get more
    tapers;   165
Raise all my kindred.—Are they married, think you?

RODERIGO

Truly, I think they are.

BRABANTIO

O heaven, how got she out? O treason of the blood!
Fathers, from hence trust not your daughters' minds
By what you see them act. Is there not charms   170

---

157 Sagittary] F (Sagitary); Sagittar Q   158.1–2 *Enter . . . torches*] Q; *Enter Brabantio, with Seruants and Torches.* F   161 bitterness. Now] F; ~∧ now Q   164 she deceives] F, Q2; thou deceiuest Q1

155 **flag and sign** Playing ironically on Iago's 'place' as Othello's *ensign* or standard-bearer.

156 **sign** show, pretence (punning on *sign* = standard)

157 **Sagittary** an inn with the sign of Sagittarius (one of the twelve signs of the Zodiac, depicting a centaur with a bow and arrow). The Centaur was a monster with the body of a horse and torso of a man: the inn-sign thus becomes another perverted 'sign of love' with an ironic appropriateness to the union of Othello and Desdemona which Iago has already depicted as a monstrous coupling of horse and woman (ll. 110–13); see above, pp. 140–1. Calderwood notes the monster's ancient significance as a symbol of lust, barbarism, and (through the Centaurs' assault on Lapith women) the violation of kind (pp. 22–5, 36).

158.1 **nightgown** 'an ankle-length gown with long sleeves and collar . . . worn for warmth both indoors and out' (M. C. Linthicum, *Costume in the Drama of Shakespeare and his Contemporaries* (Oxford, 1936), p. 184).

160 **what's . . . time** the rest of my despicable life

165 **Past thought** beyond belief

168 **treason of the blood** Brabantio's exclamation plays on several senses of *blood*: Desdemona's elopement is a violation of her noble nature and lineage (blood); a betrayal of duty to her family (blood) and especially to her father (whose authority, in patriarchal theory, was directly analogous to that of a monarch); and an instance of treacherous rebellion against the sovereign reason by rebellious passion (blood).

170 **charms** magical devices, spells

By which the property of youth and maidhood
May be abused? Have you not read, Roderigo,
Of some such thing?

RODERIGO   Yes sir, I have indeed.

BRABANTIO

Call up my brother!—O, would you had had her!—
Some one way, some another!—Do you know   175
Where we may apprehend her and the Moor?

RODERIGO

I think I can discover him, if you please
To get good guard and go along with me.

BRABANTIO

Pray you lead on. At every house I'll call—
I may command at most. Get weapons, ho!   180
And raise some special officers of night:
On, good Roderigo; I will deserve your pains.   *Exeunt*

I.2   *Enter Othello, Iago, and attendants with torches*

IAGO

Though in the trade of war I have slain men,
Yet do I hold it very stuff o'th' conscience
To do no contrived murder: I lack iniquity
Sometime to do me service. Nine, or ten times

---

171 maidhood] F; manhood Q   173 Yes . . . indeed] F, Q2; I haue sir Q1   174 would] F, Q2;
that Q1   179 Pray . . . on] F, Q2; Pray leade me on Q1   181 night] Q1; might F, Q2   183 I
will] F; Ile Q

I.2] F (*Scena Secunda*); *not in* Q   0.1 *and*] Q; F *omits*   2 stuff o'th'] F (stuffe), Q2; stuft of Q1
4 Sometime] F; Sometimes Q

---

171 **property** nature (what is *proper* to
something)
172 **abused** deceived, taken advantage of;
perverted (from its natural condition);
violated, ravished
174 **brother** Presumably Gratiano (see
5.2.199).
177 **discover** Literally 'uncover', 'reveal'; a
term with specific theatrical resonances,
appropriate to a play obsessed with the
hidden scene of erotic consummation
that is finally revealed when Desdemona's
bed is 'discovered' in the last scene (see
5.2.0.1).
181 **officers of night** The role of these officials (one elected from each of the city's
six 'tribes') is described in Lewkenor in a
passage marginally annotated 'Officers of

night' (pp. 96–8). Charged with ensuring
'that there be not any disorder done in
the darkness of the night, which always
emboldeneth men ill-disposed to naughti-
ness, and that there be not any houses
broken up, nor thieves, nor rogues lurking in corners with intent to do violence'
(p. 98), these officials had authority to
punish minor offences with summary
imprisonment or whipping.
182 **deserve your pains** recompense you
for your trouble
I.2.2 very stuff essential substance
3 **contrived** premeditated
4 **do me service** serve my turn (a
subdued allegory, in which the vice
Iniquity is imagined as Iago's potential
servant)

I had thought t'have yerked him here, under the ribs.   5
OTHELLO
'Tis better as it is.
IAGO   Nay, but he prated,
And spoke such scurvy and provoking terms
Against your honour
That, with the little godliness I have,
I did full hard forbear him. But I pray, sir,   10
Are you fast married? Be assured of this,
That the *magnifico* is much beloved,
And hath in his effect a voice potential
As double as the Duke's: he will divorce you,
Or put upon you what restraint and grievance   15
The law, with all his might to enforce it on,
Will give him cable.
OTHELLO   Let him do his spite:
My services which I have done the Signory
Shall out-tongue his complaints. 'Tis yet to know—
Which, when I know that boasting is an honour,   20
I shall provulgate—I fetch my life and being

5 yerked] F; ierk'd Q   10 pray] Q; pray you F   11 Be assured] F; For be sure Q   15 and] Q; or F   16 The] F, Q2; That Q1   17 Will] F; Weele Q   20 Which ... know] F, Q2; *not in* Q1   21 provulgate—] Q1 (~,); promulgate. F, Q2

5 **yerked** struck (usually with a rod or whip, but here with a dagger). Q's *ierked* (jerked) probably means the same thing, since the two words have a common derivation and were not wholly distinct at this time.
7 **scurvy** insulting, contemptible
10 **I ... him** it was difficult to resist attacking him
11 **fast** firmly. Perhaps implying sexual consummation, since non-consummation could be cited as grounds for dissolution of a marriage (cf. 2.3.15–17).
12 *magnifico* The *magnifici* were the magnates or nobility of Venice (cf. *Merchant*, 3.2.278).
13–14 **hath ... Duke's** has a voice potentially as influential as the Duke's, which is worth twice that of any other senator. Need not imply that the Duke had a casting vote—a widespread misconception according to William Thomas's *History of*

England (1549); but Lewkenor would have informed Shakespeare otherwise.
15 **grievance** suffering, punishment
16 **his** its
17 **give him cable** give him rope (or scope)
18 **Signory** *Signoria* (the governing body of Venice)
19 **out-tongue** speak louder than (first use cited in *OED*)
'**Tis ... know** it is not yet generally known that
21 **provulgate** publish abroad, make widely known (in this context with a mildly derogatory suggestion, deriving from its etymological connection with the Latin *vulgus* = crowd, mob, common people). By implication the true aristocrat should disdain such self-advertisement. As the more common word, F's *promulgate* (meaning much the same thing, but without the derogatory nuance) is likely to be a simple misreading.

From men of royal siege; and my demerits
May speak unbonneted to as proud a fortune
As this that I have reached. For know, Iago,
But that I love the gentle Desdemona,   25
I would not my unhousèd free condition
Put into circumscription and confine
For the seas' worth.
            Enter Cassio and Officers with lights and torches
                    But look, what lights come yond?

IAGO
Those are the raisèd father and his friends:
You were best go in.

OTHELLO   Not I—I must be found: 30
My parts, my title, and my perfect soul
Shall manifest me rightly. Is it they?

22 siege] F (Seige); height Q   28 *Enter . . . torches*] Q (*Enter* Cassio *with lights,* Officers, *and torches.*); *Enter Cassio, with Torches.* F (*after l.* 28)   yond] F; yonder Q   29 Those] F; These Q
32 Is it they?] F, Q2; it is they. Q1

22 **royal siege** throne, or seat of empire: a synecdoche for royal rank or blood. The physically impressive David Harewood (National Theatre, 1997) was among the few Othellos to prefer Q's 'royal height', which looks to be the result of misreading.
   demerits merits
23 **unbonneted** Editors are divided as to whether this means 'with my hat removed (as a sign of respect)', i.e. 'with all due modesty', or 'keeping my hat defiantly on my head', i.e. without any false modesty. Although the latter reading is in many ways the more attractive, *OED* (which cites this as the first appearance of the word) offers no warrant for it. However, the general sense of the passage is clear enough: Othello's merits make him more than worthy of marriage to Desdemona (his 'proud . . . fortune').
   proud lofty, grand (but with a glance at the aristocratic arrogance of Brabantio)
25 **gentle** well-born; soft natured
26 **unhousèd** without a house, household, or family; hence 'unconfined'. Implicitly contrasts Othello's condition as an unattached field-soldier with that of Brabantio as the self-conscious householder (1.1.105–6); but the 'free' and houseless condition that Othello so values is merely the other face of the 'extravagant', 'erring' barbarity denounced by Iago and

Brabantio. The dangerous (though often enviable) 'liberty' enjoyed by barbarians is a recurrent theme of both Renaissance and classical writers.
27 **confine** confinement
28 **seas' worth** the worth of all the treasures lying scattered over the sea-bed (cf. *Henry V*, 1.2.163–5; *Richard III*, 1.4.24–33; *Tempest*, 1.2.400–4. But ello may also have in mind the extraordinary riches fetched from ocean voyaging in this period.
   lights and torches Q's direction calls for both 'lights' and 'torches'; this may be mere redundancy, but since 'lights' (candles) and 'torches' (flaming brands) are properly distinct, this massed entry may involve both. For Shakespeare's audience, the context will have activated the iconographic association of torches with the classical gods of marriage and erotic love (Hymen and Cupid).
29 **raisèd** roused from sleep; roused to anger
31 **parts** talents. Calderwood notes, however, that 'the word . . . turns false and takes on a theatrical cast', hinting at the histrionic side of Othello's character (p. 104).
   title legal rights (as a husband; and perhaps also as a high-ranking soldier in the service of the state)
   perfect soul blameless character; clear conscience

IAGO

   By Janus, I think no.

OTHELLO

   The servants of the Duke? And my lieutenant?

   The goodness of the night upon you, friends.   35

   What is the news?

CASSIO   The Duke does greet you, general;

   And he requires your haste-post-haste appearance,

   Even on the instant.

OTHELLO   What is the matter, think you?

CASSIO

   Something from Cyprus, as I may divine—

   It is a business of some heat: the galleys   40

   Have sent a dozen sequent messengers

   This very night at one another's heels;

   And many of the consuls, raised and met,

   Are at the Duke's already. You have been hotly called

      for,

   When, being not at your lodging to be found,   45

   The Senate hath sent about three several quests

   To search you out.

OTHELLO   'Tis well I am found by you:

   I will but spend a word here in the house,

   And go with you.   ⌜*Exit*⌝

CASSIO   Ensign, what makes he here?

34 Duke?] Q (~,); Dukes? F   lieutenant?] F, Q2; Leiutenant, Q1   35 you, friends] F, Q2;
your∧ ~ Q1   41 sequent] F, Q2; frequent Q1   46 hath sent about] F; sent aboue Q   48 I will
but] F; Ile Q   49 *Exit*] ROWE; *not in* F, Q

33 **Janus** Roman god of doors, gateways,
and beginnings, the gatekeeper of
Elysium. Traditionally represented as
two-faced, he is an appropriate deity for
the shifty Iago to invoke.
34 **The . . . lieutenant** Here, as at ll. 93–4
and elsewhere, F's question marks can
equally be interpreted as exclamation
marks, since the two were not always distinguished in early modern orthography.
38 **matter** business
39 **divine** guess
40 **heat** urgency
41 **sequent** successive
43 **consuls** Shakespeare could have read in
Lewkenor about 'certain peculiar Judges,
called properly Judges or Consuls of the

merchants [*Consoli di Marcantanti*]' (p.
107), but he seems to use the term to refer
to members of the Great Council, the
principal governing body of the Venetian
Republic.
43 **raised** roused from their beds; stirred to
common action
44 **hotly** urgently
46 **several** separate; distinct
49–53 ***Exit . . . Enter*** Although editors traditionally supply these directions, the
action (as Honigmann points out) need
only require that Othello hold a conversation at the tiring-house door (the imagined entrance to the Sagittary) whilst
Iago and Cassio converse downstage.
49 **makes** does

IAGO

Faith, he tonight hath boarded a land-carrack;   50
If it prove lawful prize, he's made for ever.

CASSIO

I do not understand.

IAGO   He's married.

CASSIO   To who?

IAGO

Marry to—
⌈*Enter Othello*⌉
                    Come, captain, will you go?

OTHELLO   Have with you.

Enter Brabantio, Roderigo, and Officers with torches,
lights, and weapons

CASSIO

Here comes another troop to seek for you.

IAGO

It is Brabantio—general, be advised,   55
He comes to bad intent.

OTHELLO   Holla, stand there.

---

50 land-carrack] *after* Q1 (land Carrick); Land Carract F; land Carriact Q2   52 who?] F, Q1;
whom? Q2   53 *Enter Othello*] ROWE (*after* 'go'); *not in* F, Q   Have with you] F, Q2 (Ha' with
you); Ha, with who? Q1   53.1–2 *Enter . . . weapons*] This edition; *Enter Brabantio, Rodorigo,*
with Officers, and Torches. F (*after l.* 54); *Enters* Brabantio, Roderigo, *and others with lights and*
weapons. Q (*after* 'To who?', *l.* 53)   54 comes another] F (*corr.*) (come sanother), Q; come
another F (*uncorr.*)

---

50 **boarded** A common metaphor for sexual
conquest (perhaps with an additional pun
on 'bawd': cf. *Romeo*, 3.2.21).
carrack large galleon (of the sort frequently used to transport treasure from
the New World)

51 **made** Perhaps with a sexual innuendo
(*make* = seduce).

52 **I . . . who?** In the light of what is later
revealed about his role in Othello's wooing, Cassio is presumably (as many editors
suppose) feigning ignorance here, as well
as refusing to comprehend Iago's bawdy
innuendo.

53 **Marry to—**Unlike the words that follow
Iago's aposiopesis, which produce an
extremely rough hexameter, 'Desdemona' would fit the metre here: the effect
is like that of witholding an expected
rhyme at the end of a couplet. *Marry* =
'[by the Virgin] Mary', by this time a
rather mild exclamation.
Have with you let's go together. Q2's
'Ha' with you' suggests the likely reason
for Q1's misreading.

56 **to** with

RODERIGO

Signor, it is the Moor.

BRABANTIO   Down with him, thief.

Both sides draw their swords

IAGO

You, Roderigo? Come, sir, I am for you.

OTHELLO

Keep up your bright swords, for the dew will rust them.

Good signor, you shall more command with years   60

Than with your weapons.

BRABANTIO

O thou foul thief, where hast thou stowed my daughter?

Damned as thou art, thou hast enchanted her;

For I'll refer me to all things of sense,

If she in chains of magic were not bound,   65

Whether a maid, so tender, fair, and happy,

So opposite to marriage that she shunned

The wealthy curlèd darlings of our nation,

Would ever have, t'incur a general mock,

Run from her guardage to the sooty bosom   70

Of such a thing as thou—to fear, not to delight?

---

57 BRABANTIO] F (*Bra.*), Q2; *Cra.* Q1   Both . . . swords] ROWE (*subs.*); *not in* Q, F   58 You, Roderigo? Come] F (*corr.*) (You, *Rodorigo*c? Cme); You *Roderigo*, Come Q, F (*uncorr.*) (*Rodorigo*) 59 them] F; em Q   64 things] F, Q2; thing Q1   65 If . . . bound] F, Q2; *not in* Q1   68 darlings] Q; Deareling F

57, 62 **thief** Cf. 1.3.207, 3.3.161, 340–5, etc. The play's recurrent references to theft are in no sense metaphorical, but express the way in which patriarchal ideology constructed women as, quite literally, a species of masculine property.

58 **You, Roderigo?** Iago singles out Roderigo in order to conceal the true nature of their relationship.

59 **Keep . . . swords** Honigmann cites John 18: 1–11, where Christ, betrayed by Judas (as Othello has been by Iago), is arrested by officers 'with lanterns and torches and weapons' (18: 3; cf. l. 53.1) and orders Peter 'Put up thy sword into thy sheath' (18: 11).

60–2 **you . . . thou** Cf. 1.1.117–118.

62, 73 **foul** loathsome; wicked; ugly; dirty; discoloured. As the opposite of 'fair', *foul* can sometimes mean 'dark' or 'black' as well as 'ugly', as in Linschoten's description of the 'Moors of *Guinea*, that are foul

and deformed' (*Discours of Voyages*, 1598, p. 202) or Bacon's representation of the Spirit of Fornication as 'a little foul ugly Ethiope' (see Introduction, p. 127).

63 **Damned** For blackness as a sign of damnability, see Introduction, p. 1.
enchanted i.e. taken possession of her through the forbidden 'black arts' (cf. 1.1.170–2)

64 **refer . . . sense** appeal to the judgement of all reasonable creatures

66 **fair** beautiful; unblemished; unstained, of spotless reputation; but also 'fair-skinned' in contrast to Othello's 'foul' blackness (cf. 1.3.288).
happy Not merely 'contented' but also 'fortunate'.

67 **opposite** opposed, hostile

70 **her guardage** the guardianship of her father (first use cited in *OED*)

71 **to fear . . . delight** (one calculated) to cause fear rather than delight

Judge me the world, if 'tis not gross in sense,
That thou hast practised on her with foul charms,
Abused her delicate youth with drugs or minerals
That weakens motion. I'll have't disputed on—   75
'Tis probable, and palpable to thinking.
I therefore apprehend and do attach thee
For an abuser of the world, a practiser
Of arts inhibited and out of warrant.
Lay hold upon him! If he do resist,   80
Subdue him at his peril.

OTHELLO   Hold your hands,
Both you of my inclining and the rest!
Were it my cue to fight, I should have known it
Without a prompter. Whither will you that I go
To answer this your charge?

BRABANTIO   To prison, till fit time   85
Of law and course of direct session
Call thee to answer.

OTHELLO   What if I do obey?
How may the Duke be therewith satisfied,
Whose messengers are here about my side
Upon some present business of the state,   90
To bring me to him.

OFFICER   'Tis true, most worthy signor:
The Duke's in council, and your noble self
I am sure is sent for.

72–7 Judge . . . attach thee] F, Q2 ("Tis portable', *l.* 76); *not in* Q1   78 For] F, Q2; Such Q1
84 Whither] F (Whether); where Q   85 To answer] F, Q2; And ~ Q1   87 I] Q; *not in* F
91 bring] F; beare Q

72–7 **Judge . . . thee** Almost certainly a cut
from Q (along with l. 65), as Ridley notes:
the substitution of 'Such an abuser'
covers the join only roughly, since it is
not Othello's supposed dabbling in 'arts
inhibited' but his 'sooty bosom' that is
supposed to make him repugnant to
Desdemona.

72 **Judge . . . world** may the world judge
me
  gross in sense obvious to any
observer

73 **practised on** plotted against

74 **minerals** medicines or poisons

75 **weakens motion** render the emotions
and desires more vulnerable
  disputed on debated, investigated

77 **attach** arrest

78 **abuser** deceiver, corrupter

78–9 **practiser . . . warrant** practitioner of
forbidden and illegal arts

82 **inclining** party, faction

83 **cue** Q's *Qu* is identified by Honigmann
(*Texts*, p. 160) among its characteristically Shakespearian spellings.

86 **course of direct session** due process of
an immediate court sitting

90 **present** immediate, urgent

BRABANTIO　　　　　　How? The Duke in council?
In this time of the night? Bring him away!
Mine's not an idle cause: the Duke himself,　　　　95
Or any of my brothers of the state,
Cannot but feel this wrong as 'twere their own;
For if such actions may have passage free,
Bondslaves and pagans shall our statesmen be.　　*Exeunt*

1.3　*Enter Duke and Senators, seated at a table, with lights,*
　　　Officers, and attendants

DUKE
There is no composition in these news
That gives them credit.

FIRST SENATOR　　　　　　Indeed, they are disproportioned:
My letters say, a hundred and seven galleys.

DUKE
And mine a hundred forty.

SECOND SENATOR　　　　　　And mine two hundred.
But though they jump not on a just account—　　　5
As, in these cases where the aim reports,
'Tis oft with difference—yet do they all confirm
A Turkish fleet, and bearing up to Cyprus.

1.3] F (*Scæna Tertia*); *not in* Q　0.1–2 *Enter . . . attendants*] *after* Q (*set at a Table with lights and*); *Enter Duke, Senators, and Officers.* F　1 There is] Q; There's F　these] Q; this F　4 forty] F; and forty Q　6 the aim] F; they aym'd Q1; they ayme Q2

95 **idle cause** trivial case
96 **brothers . . . state** fellow potentates
98 **have . . . free** be freely allowed
99 **Bondslaves and pagans** i.e. men who are *both* slaves and heathen. On Othello's past enslavement, see 1.3.138. Although the Atlantic slave-trade was well established by the early 17th century, slavery at this time was by no means confined to African, or even to pagan peoples (see above, pp. 124–5). Othello, moreover, often speaks as though he were a Christian. Nevertheless underlying Brabantio's contemptuous phrase seems to be the assumption of a 'natural' connection between colour, paganism, and enslavement.
1.3.0.1 *seated* The Q direction is ambiguous: the Duke and senators may be discovered

seated around a table, placed either in a 'discovery space' in the tiring-house façade, or perhaps in the same curtained booth that may have been used for the 'bulk' in 5.1 and the bed in 5.2 (see 5.1.1 and 5.2.0.1); but since 'sit' and 'set' are often alternative spellings of the same word, it could be equally that they are meant to enter and seat themselves.

1 **composition** consistency, congruity (the only example of this usage in *OED*)
2 **credit** credibility
　disproportioned numerically inconsistent
5 **jump** precisely agree, tally
　just account exact estimate
6 **aim** conjecture (cf. *Hamlet*, 4.5.9: 'They aim at it')

DUKE
Nay, it is possible enough to judgement:
I do not so secure me in the error,   10
But the main article I do approve
In fearful sense.
SAILOR (*within*)   What ho, what ho, what ho!
        Enter Sailor

OFFICER
A messenger from the galleys.
DUKE   Now, the business?

SAILOR
The Turkish preparation makes for Rhodes—
So was I bid report here to the state   15
By Signor Angelo.
DUKE How say you by this change?
FIRST SENATOR This cannot be,
By no assay of reason. 'Tis a pageant
To keep us in false gaze: when we consider   20
Th'importancy of Cyprus to the Turk,
And let ourselves again but understand
That, as it more concerns the Turk than Rhodes,
So may he with more facile question bear it,
For that it stands not in such warlike brace,   25

10 in] F; to Q   11 article] F, Q2; Articles Q1   12 SAILOR] F; *One* Q   12.1 *Enter Sailor*] F;
Enter a Messenger. Q (*after* 'sense', *l.* 12)   13 OFFICER] F, Q2; *Sailor* Q1   galleys] F, Q2; Galley
Q1   Now,] Q; ~? What's, F   16 By . . . Angelo] F, Q2; *not in* Q1   25–31 For . . . profitless] F,
Q2; *not in* Q1

9 **to judgement** in the light of careful
consideration
10–12 **I . . . sense** the confusion about the
details does not make me so over-
confident that I fail to recognize the fearful implications in the main thrust of this
news
13 **Now** F's 'Now? What' creates an extra-
metrical syllable; but since 'now' and
'what' are more or less interchangeable in
a question of this kind, it may be that
'what', which chimes rather awkwardly
with the sailor's repeated 'what ho', was
meant to be cancelled in the manuscript
from which F derives.
14 **preparation** a force or fleet fitted out for
attack or defence (*OED n.* 3a)
16 **Angelo** Presumably the commander of
the Venetian fleet (rather than the Gover-

nor of Cyprus, as Honigmann suggests).
The name seemingly derives from that
of the naval captain Angelus Sorianus
(Angelo Soriano) who in Knolles carries
the Turkish ultimatum regarding Cyprus
to the Venetians (Bullough, p. 213).
17 **How . . . change** A metrically amphibious line.
    How . . . by what is your opinion of
19 **assay** weighing up, test; endeavour
    pageant mere show
20 **in false gaze** looking in the wrong
direction
24 **more . . . it** capture it with an easier
struggle
25–31 **For . . . profitless** Another almost
certain cut from Q: not only is it difficult
to see why any reviser would feel the need
to pad out the Senator's part by adding

But altogether lacks th'abilities
That Rhodes is dressed in. If we make thought of this,
We must not think the Turk is so unskilful
To leave that latest which concerns him first,
Neglecting an attempt of ease and gain   30
To wake and wage a danger profitless.

DUKE
Nay, in all confidence he's not for Rhodes.

OFFICER Here is more news.

Enter a Messenger

MESSENGER
The Ottomites, reverend and gracious,
Steering with due course toward the isle of Rhodes,   35
Have there injointed with an after fleet.

FIRST SENATOR
Ay, so I thought: how many, as you guess?

MESSENGER
Of thirty sail; and now they do re-stem
Their backward course, bearing with frank appearance
Their purposes toward Cyprus. Signor Montano,   40
Your trusty and most valiant servitor,

32 Nay] F, Q2; And Q1 33.1 M*essenger*] F; 2. *Messenger* Q 36 injointed] Q1; inioynted
them F, Q2; injoin'd ROWE 37 FIRST . . . guess?] F (1 *Sen.*), Q2; *not in* Q1 38 re-stem] F;
resterine Q1; resterne Q2 40 toward] F; towards Q

such strictly unnecessary information,
but the removal of these lines damages
the logic of the speech by removing the
explanation for Cyprus's vulnerability.
25 **For that** because
   brace state of defence (*OED n.*[2] 1c, citing
   only this example); presumably adapted
   from *brace* = armour (esp. for the arms), or
   from *brace, v.*[1] 5, = summon up resolution
   for a task, brace oneself.

26 **abilities** power, capacity
27 **dressed in** equipped with
31 **wage** contend with
32 **Nay** Q's 'And' is exactly the kind of
   small alteration we should expect if the
   previous lines had been cut, making
   the Duke's dismissive 'Nay' no longer
   appropriate: but the effect is to turn the
   Duke into a somewhat improbable secon-
   der of the Senator; so we can be fairly
   confident that the lines are not an addition in F.

34 **Ottomites** Ottoman Turks (earliest citation in *OED*)
   reverend and gracious Addressed to
   the Duke (or perhaps to the senators
   generally).
36 **injointed** linked up. Since this is the only
   use of *injoint* recorded in *OED*, and since
   F's 'them' is extra-metrical (though
   a judicious slurring of the line might
   accommodate it), Rowe may have been
   right to suppose that Shakespeare originally wrote 'injoined them': a common
   form of the verb *enjoin* (= join together),
   which was frequently reflexive.
36 **after** following
38–9 **re-stem . . . course** turn their course
   back again, once again turn their prows
   on course (for)
39–40 **bearing . . . purposes** steering with
   apparently quite open intentions

With his free duty, recommends you thus
And prays you to believe him.

DUKE

'Tis certain then for Cyprus.
Marcus Luccicos, is not he in town?   45

FIRST SENATOR He's now in Florence.

DUKE

Write from us to him—post-post-haste, dispatch.

FIRST SENATOR

Here comes Brabantio and the valiant Moor.

> *Enter Brabantio, Othello, Cassio, Iago, Roderigo and*
> *Officers*

DUKE

Valiant Othello, we must straight employ you
Against the general enemy Ottoman.   50
(*To Brabantio*) I did not see you: welcome, gentle
    signor—
We lacked your counsel, and your help tonight.

BRABANTIO

So did I yours. Good your grace pardon me:

---

43 believe] F, Q (beleeue); relieve JOHNSON (*conj.* T. Clark)   45 he] F, Q2; here Q1   47 us to
him—post] F (vs, | To him, Post), Q2; vs, wish him post Q1   48.1 *Cassio, Iago, Roderigo*] F;
Roderigo, Iago, Cassio, Desdemona Q; *Iago, Roderigo* CAPELL   52 lacked] F (lack't), Q2; lacke
Q1

---

42 **free duty** unstinting service
   recommends you informs you (*OED v.*[1]
   1e, citing only this example); but perhaps
   it means only 'commends himself to you'.

43 **believe** Clark's conjectural emendation
   'relieve' has won some favour on the
   grounds that, as the subsequent dialogue
   suggests, it is not Montano's credibility
   that is at stake but his urgent need for
   reinforcement; and both Walker and
   Honigmann treat it as one of the 'common errors' that suggest 'contamination'
   of F by Q (see below, Appendix B pp. 413,
   416, 422–3). But the Duke and Senators
   are sifting the reliability of different
   reports and conjectures concerning
   Turkish intentions, and Montano's
   despatch conflicts with Angelo's.

45 **Marcus Luccicos** Presumably intended
   as a Greek name, though (following
   Capell's 'Lucchese') a number of attempts
   have been made to substitute a more
   Italianate version.

48.1–2 **Enter . . . Officers** Q's inclusion of
   Desdemona may be a survival from an
   earlier plan for the scene in which Desdemona was present from the beginning.
   Capell and a number of later editors
   assume that the same is true of Cassio,
   who is given nothing to say in this scene;
   but since he was sent to fetch Othello to
   the Duke (1.2.36–8) his presence here
   seems natural. Q's suggestion that Iago
   should enter before the newly promoted
   Cassio may be worth preserving (cf.
   1.1.0.1).

49 **Othello** In this respectful address by the
   Duke, the hero (hitherto referred to only
   as 'the Moor') is called by name for the
   first time.
   straight immediately

50 **general** i.e. the enemy of all
   Christendom

51 **gentle** i.e. of gentle birth

Neither my place nor aught I heard of business
Hath raised me from my bed; nor doth the general care   55
Take hold on me. For my particular grief
Is of so flood-gate and o'er-bearing nature
That it engluts and swallows other sorrows,
And it is still itself.

DUKE   Why? What's the matter?

BRABANTIO
My daughter; O, my daughter!

SENATORS   Dead?

BRABANTIO   Ay, to me: 60
She is abused, stolen from me, and corrupted
By spells and medicines bought of mountebanks.
For nature so preposterously to err—
Being not deficient, blind, or lame of sense—
Sans witchcraft could not.   65

DUKE
Whoe'er he be that in this foul proceeding
Hath thus beguiled your daughter of her self,
And you of her, the bloody book of law
You shall yourself read in the bitter letter
After your own sense—yea, though our proper son   70

54 nor] Q; hor F   56 hold on] F; any hold of Q1; hold of Q2   grief] F (griefe), Q2; griefes Q1
59 Why?] F; ~, Q   60 SENATORS] F (*Sen.*); *All.* Q; HONIGMANN *reads* 1 SENATOR
64 Being . . . sense] F, Q2; *not in* Q1   65 Sans] F, Q1 (*corr.*) (Saunce), Q2; Since Q1 (*uncorr.*)
70 your] F; its Q   yea] F, Q2; *not in* Q1

54 **place** official position (as a senator)
55 **general care** concern for the public interest
56 **particular** personal
57 **flood-gate** torrential (i.e. like the water suddenly released from sluice-gates)
58 **engluts** devours
61 **abused** Cf 1.1.172.
   corrupted The word had a much more strongly physical sense, suggesting that Desdemona's body is literally tainted, poisoned, or putrefied by the Moor's 'spells and medicines'.
62 **mountebanks** charlatans. As Jonson's *Volpone* (2.2) suggests, Italy (especially Venice) was seen as being the particular home of such quackery.
63 **preposterously** monstrously, perversely, contrary to the order of nature. The

literal sense of the word is arsy-versy: on the preposterous in *Othello*, see Parker, *Margins*, pp. 48–52.
   err Desdemona's supposed errancy links her with the 'extravagant' and 'erring' Othello (1.1.135, 1.3.348).
65 **Sans** without
   could not ('be' is understood)
67 **beguiled** cheated, stolen by fraud
68 **bloody . . . law** i.e. that part of the law which prescribed capital punishment for witchcraft
69–70 **You . . . sense** you shall pass sentence according to the harshest letter of the law as you yourself interpret it. F's Duke offers Brabantio much more arbitrary licence than Q's.
70 **our proper son** my very own son (the Duke employs the royal 'we')

Stood in your action.

BRABANTIO   Humbly I thank your grace.
Here is the man: this Moor, whom now it seems
Your special mandate for the state affairs
Hath hither brought.

ALL   We are very sorry for't.

DUKE (*to Othello*)
What, in your own part, can you say to this?   75

BRABANTIO
Nothing, but this is so.

OTHELLO
Most potent, grave, and reverend signors,
My very noble and approved good masters;
That I have ta'en away this old man's daughter,
It is most true; true I have married her—   80
The very head and front of my offending
Hath this extent, no more. Rude am I in my speech,
And little blessed with the soft phrase of peace;
For, since these arms of mine had seven years' pith,
Till now some nine moons wasted, they have used   85
Their dearest action in the tented field:
And little of this great world can I speak

---

82 extent, no] Q2; extent; no F; extent no Q1   83 soft] F; set Q

71 **Stood . . . action** were the object of your legal suit
75 **in . . . part** on your own behalf
78 **approved** proved; esteemed
  masters Othello's deferential language picks up the emphasis on servants and masters in I.I.
81 **head and front** summit, highest extent (*OED*, *head*, *n.* 42, citing this as the earliest example of the phrase). There is subdued word-play on *front* = 'forehead' and probably on *front* = 'affront', or 'effrontery' (though *OED* does not record the latter sense before 1653).
82 **Rude** rough, unrefined. The self-deprecation may indicate something of Othello's sense of himself both as a 'barbarian' outsider (see l. 349) and as a soldier untrained in the civilian arts; but in the context of his characteristically eloquent (and even slightly orotund) public manner it is clearly hyperbolical. In fact Othello's ensuing speeches are themselves syntactically elegant and larded with choice terms: *portance* (l. 139), *antres* (l. 140), *incline* (l. 146), *discourse* (l. 150), *dilate* (l. 153), and *distressful* (l. 157), which *OED* describes as 'literary and chiefly poetical'.
83 **soft** pleasing, relaxed, melodious; ingratiating; effeminate. Q's 'set' (= conventional) is, however, a genuine (if less complex) alternative, since 'soft' might have resulted from a misreading of manuscript 'sett'.
84 **since . . . pith** i.e. since I was seven years old ('pith' = strength)
85 **Till . . . wasted** until nine months ago
85-6 **used . . . action** whose most glorious deeds have been confined to the world of military encampments and battlefields (with a quibble on the erotic sense of 'dearest')
86 **tented** covered with tents (*OED a.* 1a; earliest citation)

More than pertains to feats of broil and battle;
And therefore little shall I grace my cause
In speaking for myself. Yet, by your gracious patience,   90
I will a round, unvarnished tale deliver
Of my whole course of love: what drugs, what charms,
What conjuration, and what mighty magic—
For such proceeding I am charged withal—
I won his daughter.
BRABANTIO   A maiden never bold,   95
Of spirit so still and quiet that her motion
Blushed at herself, and she—in spite of nature,
Of years, of country, credit, everything—
To fall in love with what she feared to look on?
It is a judgement maimed and most imperfect   100
That will confess perfection so could err
Against all rules of nature, and must be driven
To find out practices of cunning hell
Why this should be. I therefore vouch again
That with some mixtures powerful o'er the blood,   105
Or with some dram conjured to this effect,
He wrought upon her.

88 feats of broil] CAPELL; Feats of Broiles F, Q2; feate of broyle Q1   91 unvarnished] Q; vn-
varnish'd u F   94 proceeding] F; proceedings Q   I am] F; am I Q   95–6 bold . . . so] Q2;
bold: | Of spirit so F; bold of spirit, | So Q1   99 on?] Q; ~; F   100 maimed] Q (maimd);
main'd F   imperfect∧] Q (~,); imperfect. F   101 could] F; would Q   107 wrought upon] Q;
~ vp on F

91 **round** blunt, plain
   unvarnished plain, unadorned (earliest
   citation in *OED*)
92–5 **what . . . daughter** The syntax
   appears to require 'with what', but as Furness notes (p. 51) the omission of the
   preposition in such adverbial constructions is not uncommon in Shakespearian
   English.
96 **motion** emotion, desire. The play on 'still'
   (= motionless) is enabled by the fact that
   early modern physiology described the
   activity of the emotions in kinetic terms.
97, 102 **nature** Brabantio's reiteration of
   this term emphasizes what he (like Iago)
   sees as the monstrous unnaturalness of
   miscegenation (see 1.1.88–9).
98 **years** The disparity in years between
   Othello and Desdemona is often seen (not
   least by Othello himself; cf. 3.3.268–9) as
   another ground of incompatibility. The

yoking of an elderly man to a young wife
was a stock ingredient of comic plotting;
and part of the shock-effect of this
'domestic' drama depends on the way
in which it turns traditionally comic
material to tragic ends (see Introduction,
pp. 4–6).
   credit reputation
100 **maimed** F's 'main'd' represents variant
   spellings (mained, mayned) still common
   in Shakespeare's time.
101 **err** Cf. l. 63.
103 **practices** evil trickery, machinations,
   plots
105 **blood** sexual desire
106 **dram** small medicinal draught
   conjured . . . effect produced for this
   purpose (with a hint of magic). *Conjured* is
   accented on the second syllable.
107 **wrought upon her** worked up her
   feelings

DUKE   To vouch this is no proof
Without more wider and more overt test
Than these thin habits and poor likelihoods
Of modern seeming do prefer against him.   110

FIRST SENATOR
But, Othello, speak:
Did you by indirect and forcèd courses
Subdue and poison this young maid's affections?
Or came it by request and such fair question
As soul to soul affordeth?

OTHELLO   I do beseech you,   115
Send for the lady to the Sagittary,
And let her speak of me before her father:
If you do find me foul in her report,
The trust, the office I do hold of you
Not only take away, but let your sentence   120
Even fall upon my life.

DUKE   Fetch Desdemona hither.
                    Exeunt two or three attendants

OTHELLO
Ensign, conduct them—you best know the place.
                    ⌈*Exit Iago after them*⌉
And till she come, as truly as to heaven
I do confess the vices of my blood,
So justly to your grave ears I'll present   125

DUKE] Q; *not in* F   vouch] F, Q2; youth Q1   108 wider] F; certaine Q   overt] Q (ouert); ouer
F   109 Than these] F (Then these); These are Q   110 seeming do] F; seemings, you Q   111
FIRST SENATOR] Q (1 *Sena.*); *Sen.* F   116 Sagittary] F (Sagitary), Q2; Sagittar Q1   119 The
trust . . . you] F, Q2; *not in* Q1   121.1 *Exeunt . . . attendants*] Q (*Exit two or three.*); *not in* F
122.1 *Exit . . . them*] ROWE (*subs.*); *not in* F, Q   123 till] Q; tell F   truly] F, Q2; faithfull Q1
124 I . . . blood] F, Q2; *not in* Q1

107 **vouch . . . proof** Cf. Dent S1019, 'Suspicion (accusation) is no proof'.

108 **wider** more ample or extensive, fuller
overt apparent, manifest; from which
criminal intent can be inferred (*OED a.* 2)
test evidence (*OED n.*³ 2)
109 **thin habits** insubstantial appearances
109–10 **poor . . . seeming** feeble conjectures based on observation of superficial
commonplaces
112 **indirect . . . courses** crooked and
forcible means
114–15 **such . . . affordeth** such candid
and unblemished conversation as two

souls will allow one another (*OED, fair, a.*
9–10; *question, n.* 2a). However, in this
play the term 'fair' (like 'foul') is probably
never without a racial loading (whether
or not the speaker is assumed to be conscious of it); see 1.2.66, and cf. l. 126
below.
118 **foul** wicked, guilty; and see above, ll.
114–15 and 1.2.62.
124 **blood** fleshly nature; sexual desire. In
this context, however, the term is also
likely to carry the suggestion of 'race' (i.e.
'the vices peculiar to my nature as a
Moor').
125 **justly** faithfully

How I did thrive in this fair lady's love,
And she in mine.

DUKE   Say it, Othello.

OTHELLO
Her father loved me, oft invited me,
Still questioned me the story of my life
From year to year: the battles, sieges, fortunes   130
That I have passed.
I ran it through, even from my boyish days
To th' very moment that he bade me tell it—
Wherein I spoke of most disastrous chances:
Of moving accidents by flood and field,   135
Of hair-breadth scapes i'th' imminent deadly breach,
Of being taken by the insolent foe
And sold to slavery; of my redemption thence,
And portance in my travailous history,
Wherein of antres vast and deserts idle,   140
Rough quarries, rocks, and hills whose heads touch
      heaven,

130 battles] Q; Battaile F   fortunes] Q; Fortune F   134 spoke] F; spake Q   135 accidents
by] F, Q2; accident of QI   138 slavery; of] F (slauery. Of), Q2; slauery, and QI   139 portance in my travailous] HONIGMANN (*conj.* Proudfoot); portance in my Trauellours F; with it all
my trauells QI; portance in my trauells Q2   140 antres] THEOBALD; Antars F, Q2; Antrees QI
141 and hills] Q; Hills F   heads] Q; head F

present A legal term, meaning 'to lay
before a court' (*OED v.* 8).

129–45 story . . . shoulders   Othello's
account of his 'travailous history' seems
to draw on John Pory's description of Leo
Africanus in the epistle 'To the Reader'
which prefaces his translation of Leo's
Geographical Historie of Africa (1600). See
above, pp. 18–19.
129 Still continually
135 by . . . field by sea and land. But in
Othello's case 'field' will inevitably
suggest 'battlefield'; so perhaps the
phrase is really shorthand for 'in sea and
land battles'.
136 scapes escapes
    imminent . . . breach gap (in the wall
of a besieged town or castle) which may
prove deadly at any moment
139 portance bearing; conduct
    travailous history Proudfoot's sugges-
tion that F 'Trauellours' resulted from a
misreading of 'Travellous' seems plausible, since 'travailous history', with its

quibble on 'travel' and 'travail', is exactly
the kind of slightly pompous, recherché
phrase that Othello favours. Given the
exotic nature of Othello's tales, it may be
worth recalling the proverb 'A traveller
may lie with authority' (Dent T476).
140 antres caverns (apparently Shakespeare's coinage from Latin *antrum* =
cave: *OED*). On caves as a conspicuous
feature of Leo's African landscape, see
Whitney, p. 479; Pory's addendum detail-
ing 'places undescribed by John Leo'
includes a section on *Africa Troglodytica*,
'in old times inhabited by the Troglodytae,
a people so called because of their dwelling
in caves under the ground' (p. 10).
vast From Latin *vastus*, whose meanings
include 'empty' as well as 'immense'.
idle useless (and therefore encouraging
the idleness attributed to the nomadic
denizens of such places). The original
sense of the word was 'empty', which is
probably also present here, as Honigmann suggests, though *OED* offers no
examples later than 1450.

223

It was my hint to speak—such was my process—
And of the Cannibals that each other eat,
The Anthropophagi, and men whose heads
Do grow beneath their shoulders. This to hear   145
Would Desdemona seriously incline;
But still the house affairs would draw her thence,
Which ever as she could with haste dispatch
She'd come again, and with a greedy ear
Devour up my discourse; which I observing   150
Took once a pliant hour, and found good means
To draw from her a prayer of earnest heart
That I would all my pilgrimage dilate,
Whereof by parcels she had something heard,
But not intentively. I did consent,   155
And often did beguile her of her tears
When I did speak of some distressful stroke
That my youth suffered. My story being done,
She gave me for my pains a world of sighs:

142 hint] F, Q2; hent Q1   my process] F, Q2; the ~ Q1   143 other] Q; others F   144
Anthropophagi] Q (*Anthropophagie*); *Antropophague* F   145 Do grow] Q; Grew F   this] Q1;
These things F; these Q2   147 thence] Q; hence F   148 Which] F, Q2; And Q1   154
parcels] F; parcell Q   155 intentively] Q; instinctiuely F   157 distressful] F, Q2; distressed Q1
159 sighs] Q; kisses F

142 **hint** occasion, opportunity; implication
(*OED n.* 1a, 2a; earliest example of either
use)
   process story; drift of (my) narrative
143 **Cannibals . . . eat** The description is
not redundant, since *Cannibal* (a variant
of Carib, originally coined by Columbus)
was still a proper name referring to
warlike (and supposedly cannibalistic)
Caribbean peoples. See App. F(ii) for notes
on the sources of Othello's exotic ethnography in ll. 143–5.
144 **Anthropophagi** (literally) man-eaters
145 **This to hear** in order to hear this
146 **seriously** earnestly, keenly
   incline Probably suggests physical as
well as mental *inclination*; Desdemona
would lean close to hear him.
151 **pliant hour** opportune moment; but
pliant may also be a transferred reference
to Desdemona's susceptible and yielding
disposition at that moment.
153 **my . . . dilate** relate (or enlarge upon)
the whole story of my journeying.
Othello's life-journey is perhaps imagined

as a 'pilgrimage' because it brought him
finally to Christian Venice (and to the
'divine' Desdemona?).
154 **by parcels** piecemeal
155 **intentively** with full attention
156 **beguile her of** charm her out of.
Othello plays ironically with the same
word (with its connotations of fraud and
magical deceit) that the angry Duke used
at l. 67.
159 **pains** Equivocates between 'my sufferings' and 'my trouble' (in telling the
story).
   sighs Not only does the Q reading seem
appropriate to the delicacy of Desdemona's situation and the elliptical 'hint'
with which she conveys her feelings (l.
166), it neatly introduces the following
four lines, which become amplifications of
her sighing protestations. *Kisses*, however, is scarcely a plausible misreading for
sighs, and its presence in F is, in Ridley's
words, 'almost as difficult to account for
as it is to accept'. Whether the variants
reflect systematic revision by Shakespeare

She swore 'in faith 'twas strange, 'twas passing strange,   160
'Twas pitiful, 'twas wondrous pitiful!'
She wished she had not heard it, yet she wished
That heaven had made her such a man; she thanked
    me,
And bade me, if I had a friend that loved her,
I should but teach him how to tell my story   165
And that would woo her. Upon this hint I spake.
She loved me for the dangers I had passed,
And I loved her that she did pity them.
This only is the witchcraft I have used.
Here comes the lady: let her witness it.   170
    Enter Desdemona, Iago, and attendants

---

160 in faith] F; Ifaith Q   166 hint] F; heate Q   170.1 *attendants*] F; *and the rest* Q; *after* 'pity them' (*l.* 168) OXFORD; *after* 'used' HONIGMANN

or a change made (with or without his endorsement) in the theatre, there is no means of knowing. With the exception of Oxford (which suggests that 'Desdemona may be thought of as impulsively affectionate': *TC*, p. 479), almost all editions, regardless of the general preference for F as a copy-text, print *sighs*. It was Pope who first questioned the propriety of F: '[t]he lady had been forward indeed, to give him a world of *kisses* upon the bare recital of his story.' However, as Furness points out, noting the openness with which Cassio kisses Emilia in 2.1, 'kissing in Elizabeth's time was not as significant as it is now'. Moreover, because of their prominence amongst the expressive conventions of Petrarchan love-poetry, sighs could sometimes be as erotically charged as kisses. Olivier, evidently thinking even 'a world of sighs' suggestive enough, delivered 'upon this hint' with an ironic chuckle.

160 **passing** extremely
163 **That . . . man** Usually glossed 'that she had been born a man like that'; but the alternative sense ('that heaven had destined such a man for her') seems more likely in view of her subsequent lines. Again editors are offended by what they see as the inappropriate forwardness suggested by the more obvious sense.
166 **hint** Muir is almost certainly right to insist that 'hint' must have its original

meaning of 'opportunity' or 'occasion' here (as at l. 142), rather than 'covert suggestion' (*OED n.* 2, citing this as the first example), since Desdemona's behaviour (even if we read *sighs* rather than *kisses* at 159) seems to go well beyond hinting. But the modern meaning was certainly available by 1609 and (as Honigmann recognizes) is difficult to exclude, with the result that audiences easily laugh at this line. Q's *heat* has been universally rejected, even by editors like Ridley and Honigmann, who argue for Q as a copy-text. If the Q1's copy read 'hent' (a variant spelling of 'hint') as it presumably did at l. 142, then 'heat' would of course be an easy misreading. But the misreading could be in either direction, and the Q reading is defensible as a genuine alternative: *Upon this heat* = 'at this [display of] ardour or feeling'. In the context of Q's 'sighs' it may be worth noting that lovers' sighs were conventionally hot (*Twelfth Night*, 1.5.245; *Romeo*, 1.1.196; *Cymbeline*, 1.6.67–8, etc.).
169 **This . . . used** Probably echoing, as E. H. W. Meyerstein suggested, the response of a former bondslave in Pliny, who, when accused of acquiring wealth by corrupt means, pointed to his agricultural implements and declared 'these are the sorceries, charms, and all the enchantments that I use' (letter in *TLS*, 1940, p. 72; cited in Bullough, p. 211).

DUKE

I think this tale would win my daughter too—
Good Brabantio, take up this mangled matter at the best:
Men do their broken weapons rather use,
Than their bare hands.

BRABANTIO   I pray you hear her speak!
If she confess that she was half the wooer,   175
Destruction on my head if my bad blame
Light on the man! Come hither, gentle mistress,
Do you perceive in all this noble company
Where most you owe obedience?

DESDEMONA   My noble father,
I do perceive here a divided duty.   180
To you I am bound for life and education;
My life and education both do learn me
How to respect you: you are the lord of duty,
I am hitherto your daughter. But here's my husband;
And so much duty as my mother showed   185
To you, preferring you before her father,
So much I challenge that I may profess
Due to the Moor my lord.

BRABANTIO   Goodbye, I've done!
Please it your grace, on to the state affairs.
I had rather to adopt a child than get it.   190

---

176 on my head] F; lite on me Q   183 the lord of] F, Q2; Lord of all my Q1   188 Goodbye]
This edition *after* Q (God bu'y); God be with you F   I've] *after* Q (I ha); I haue F

172 **take . . . best** Cf. Dent B326, 'Make the
best of a bad bargain'.
177 **gentle mistress** From a father to a
daughter this honorific will sound
sardonic.
180–8 **duty . . . bound . . . lord**   Desdemona, as befits a child of the patriarchal
family, conceives of her relationship to
both father and husband in the language
of service and deference to a master or
'lord'.
181 **education** upbringing
182 **learn** teach (survives in expressions
such as 'that'll learn you')
186 **preferring . . . before** elevating you
above
187 **challenge** lay claim to, demand as a
right
188 **Goodbye** Q's 'God bu'y' (like 'God by

you', 3.3.377) is simply a contracted form
of F's 'God be with you', the style of dismissal or farewell which by the early 18th
century came to be rendered 'Goodbye'. It
appears elsewhere in Shakespeare as 'God
be wy you' (*LLL*, 3.1.146), 'God b'uy' (*1
Henry VI*, 3.5.32), 'God buy'ye' (*Hamlet*,
2.2.551), the degree of contraction being
largely determined by metrical consid-
erations. Here it will have been phonetically almost indistinguishable from the
modern form; however, it is possible
(given the play's preoccupation with
damnation and redemption) that the
meaning may be coloured by the false etymology implicit in the Q contraction
('God buy you' = God redeem you).
189 **Please it** if it pleases
190 **get** beget

Come hither, Moor:
I here do give thee that with all my heart
Which, but thou hast already, with all my heart
I would keep from thee. For your sake, jewel,
I am glad at soul I have no other child;   195
For thy escape would teach me tyranny
To hang clogs on them. I have done, my lord.

DUKE
Let me speak like yourself, and lay a sentence,
Which as a grece or step may help these lovers
Into your favour.   200
When remedies are past, the griefs are ended
By seeing the worst, which late on hopes depended.
To mourn a mischief that is past and gone
Is the next way to draw new mischief on.
What cannot be preserved when Fortune takes,   205
Patience her injury a mockery makes.
The robbed that smiles steals something from the thief;
He robs himself that spends a bootless grief.

BRABANTIO
So let the Turk of Cyprus us beguile—
We lose it not so long as we can smile: 210

---

193 Which . . . heart] F, Q2; *not in* Q1   197 them] F; em Q   200 Into . . . favour] Q; *not in* F
204 new] F; more Q   205 preserved] Q (preseru'd); presern'd F

---

193 **Which . . . heart** Probably omitted
from Q as a result of compositorial eye-
skip, since both 192 and 193 end in
'heart'.
but . . . hast if you did not already possess it
194 **For your sake** thanks to you
197 **hang clogs** shackle them to heavy
logs of wood to prevent their escape
(as practised with slaves as well as
animals)
198 **sentence** maxim, aphorism
199 **grece** stairway, step. This more usual
form of the archaic noun better represents its pronunciation than F *grise* (cf. Q
greese).
200 **Into . . . favour** Q's half-line marks a
convenient pause before the Duke launch-
es into the formal advice whose senten-
tious apothegms are pointed up by the use
of rhyming couplets.
201 **When . . . ended** Cf. Dent R71, 'Where

there is no remedy it is folly to chide';
C921, 'Past cure, past care'; C922, 'What
cannot be cured must be endured'.
202 **By . . . depended** by our actually expe-
riencing the worst eventualities, which
were hitherto dependent on the outcome
of our hopes
203 **mischief** misfortune
204 **next** most immediate
205–6 **What . . . makes** when chance robs
us of what we cannot in any case hope to
keep, the exercise of patience will enable
us to make light of the blows. The Duke's
figure imagines a familiar allegorical contest between Patience and Fortune.
208 **spends** wastes
bootless pointless, beyond remedy
210 **lose** The F spelling 'loose' suggests a
bawdy quibble from animal husbandry no
longer available in modern English (*loose*
= release the female to the male; cf. 'loose
her to an African', *Tempest*, 2.1.131).

He bears the sentence well that nothing bears
But the free comfort which from thence he hears;
But he bears both the sentence and the sorrow
That, to pay Grief, must of poor Patience borrow.
These sentences, to sugar or to gall,   215
Being strong on both sides, are equivocal.
But words are words: I never yet did hear
That the bruised heart was piercèd through the ear.
I humbly beseech you proceed to th'affairs of state.

DUKE The Turk with a most mighty preparation makes for   220
Cyprus. Othello, the fortitude of the place is best known
to you; and though we have there a substitute of most
allowed sufficiency, yet opinion, a more sovereign mistress of effects, throws a more safer voice on you. You
must therefore be content to slubber the gloss of your   225
new fortunes with this more stubborn and boisterous
expedition.

---

218 piercèd] Q (pierced); pierc'd F; pieced THEOBALD (*after* WARBURTON)   ear] Q; eares F   219
I . . . state] F; Beseech you now, to the affaires of the state Q   220 a most] F; most Q   223
more sovereign] F; soueraigne Q

211–12 **He . . . hears** anyone can respond
well to such maxims who doesn't have to
put up with anything more than the
cheap consolation which is all he can
derive from them (with quibbles on *sentence* = moral maxim; judicial punishment; and *free* = generous, lavish;
without cost).
214 **That . . . borrow** that to deal with his
grief must seek support from no richer
resource than patience. Brabantio plays
sardonically with the Duke's allegory (ll.
205–6).
215 **gall** bile; poison; bitterness
216 **equivocal** equally appropriate
217 **words are words** Dent W832 (and cf.
W833, W840.1).
218 **bruised** crushed, mangled, smashed
piercèd penetrated, touched, affected;
lanced, and so cured (Sanders). Some editors prefer Theobald's 'pieced' = mended,
restored. Brabantio's figure ironically
anticipates Iago's strategy of poison
through the ear (see e.g. 2.3.341).
219 **I . . . state** Q (allowing for the normal
elision, 'th'affairs') preserves the metre

here. But in F Brabantio seems to initiate
the switch to prose continued in the
Duke's speech. As Honigmann notes, the
abrupt switch from stylized couplets to
prose, as the discussion turns from philo-
sophic generalizations to the hard reality
of public affairs, is a deliberate stylistic
effect; though whether it makes Othello's
return to verse rhythms (ll. 228 ff.) 'sound
self-indulgent' is open to question.
220 **preparation** Cf. l. 15.
221 **fortitude of the place** strength of the
citadel (*OED, place, n.* 5c)
222 **substitute** deputy; i.e. the Governor,
(presumably) Montano
223 **allowed sufficiency** approved or recognized competency
opinion public opinion
223–4 **a more . . . effects** a more powerful
determinant of what happens
224 **more safer** Cf. 1.1.96.
225 **slubber** soil; darken
226 **stubborn and boisterous** fierce and
rough
227 **expedition** The context suggests 'haste'
or 'speed' as well as 'military enterprise'.

OTHELLO

The tyrant custom, most grave senators,
Hath made the flinty and steel couch of war
My thrice-driven bed of down. I do agnize   230
A natural and prompt alacrity
I find in hardness, and do undertake
This present wars against the Ottomites.
Most humbly therefore bending to your state,
I crave fit disposition for my wife,   235
Due reference of place and exhibition,
With such accommodation and besort
As levels with her breeding.

DUKE

Why, at her father's!

BRABANTIO   I'll not have it so.

OTHELLO

Nor I.

DESDEMONA Nor would I there reside   240
To put my father in impatient thoughts

228 grave] F (graue), Q2; great Q1   229 couch] Q (Cooch); Coach F   231 alacrity] Q;
Alacartie F   232 do] F, Q2; would Q1   233 This ... wars] F (This ... Warres), Q1;
This ... warre Q2; These ... wars MALONE   236 reference] F, Q2; reuerence Q1   237 With
such accommodation] F, Q2; Which ~ Accomodation? Q1   239 Why ... father's] F (Why at
her Fathers?); If you please, bee't at her fathers Q   I'll] Q (Ile); I will F   240 Nor would I] F;
Nor I, I would not Q

229 **flinty and steel couch** 'The allusion is
to sleeping on the ground in armour'
(Sanders).
230 **thrice-driven** i.e. the very softest
down, from which the heaviest feathers
have been separated by three winnow-
ings.
agnize acknowledge, confess
231–2 **A ... hardness** that I find myself
naturally eager to undertake hardship
233 **This ... wars** For the use of *wars* as a
singular collective noun, see *OED*, *war*,
n.[1] 1c; cf. *Troilus*, 5.3.51, and *All's Well*,
2.3.288.
234 **bending ... state** deferring to your
authority. But since *bend* can also mean
'bow' and *state* 'throne', Othello may bow
to the enthroned Duke as he speaks the
words.
235 **fit disposition** suitable arrangements
236 **Due ... place** proper respect for her
rank (*OED, reference, n.* 3)

236 **exhibition** maintenance, support
237 **accommodation** lodgings (*OED* 7; earliest recorded use here or *Measure*, 3.1.14)
besort suitable retinue. The word seems
to be a Shakespearian coinage and exists
elsewhere only in *Lear*, where it is a verb:
'such men as may besort your age' (*Trag.
Lear*, 1.4.229).
238 **As ... breeding** as befits her station
239–40 **Why ... reside** The Q version of
this passage is metrically complete, which
suggests the possibility of corruption in F.
On the other hand, the incomplete lines
could be used to signal tense pauses after
breeding and *Nor I*.
240 **Nor ... reside** In Q Desdemona echoes
Othello's defiant refusal of the Duke's
suggestion: 'Nor I, I would not there
reside ... '; the F version seems to soften
the vehemence of her response.

By being in his eye. Most gracious Duke,
To my unfolding lend your prosperous ear,
And let me find a charter in your voice
T'assist my simpleness—

DUKE   What would you, Desdemona?   245

DESDEMONA

That I did love the Moor to live with him,
My downright violence and scorn of fortunes
May trumpet to the world. My heart's subdued
Even to the very quality of my lord:
I saw Othello's visage in his mind,   250
And to his honours and his valiant parts
Did I my soul and fortunes consecrate;
So that, dear lords, if I be left behind
A moth of peace, and he go to the war,

---

243 your prosperous] F; a gracious Q   245 T'assist my simpleness—] Q2 (simplenesse.—);
~ ~ simplenesse. F; And if my simplenesse.—Q1   F, Q2; you—speake.
Q1   246 did] Q; *not in* F   247 scorn] Q1 (scorne); storme F, Q2   fortunes] F, Q; fortune
KEIGHTLEY   249 very quality] F, Q2; vtmost pleasure Q1

243 **unfolding** disclosure, revelation
    prosperous favourable
244 **charter** grant of privilege or pardon
245 **simpleness** innocence, naivety
247 **violence** vehemence of personal feeling
    or action; extreme ardour or fervour
    (*OED n.* 5). Sanders suggests 'violation of
    the norm', and Honigmann 'violent rup-
    ture with conventional behaviour'.
    scorn of fortunes disdain for any conse-
    quences. Many editors follow Q2 in pre-
    ferring F's *storm*: the two words could
    easily be confused, since *c* and *t* were diffi-
    cult to distinguish in Elizabethan hands
    (cf. *Troilus*, 1.1.37, 'sun doth light a
    scorn', where Rowe's emendation of QF
    'scorn' to 'storm' has been widely accept-
    ed); and 'storm of fortune' was a phrase
    with almost proverbial currency, which
    the compositor might be encouraged to
    recall by the juxtaposition with *violence*.
    But *scorn* makes better sense here, since,
    while Desdemona has clearly defied For-
    tune, she can scarcely be said to have suf-
    fered its storms yet.
248 **subdued** reduced to obedience,
    brought into spiritual subjection (*OED v.*
    1e, 2a–b)
249 **very quality** true character, nature.
    The suggestion of sexual desire in Q's

'utmost pleasure' is absent from F, a
difference consistent with its slightly
softened and more passive presentation
of Desdemona in Act I. For a vigorous
defence of the F reading's 'rich fusion of
submission and self-assertion', see Snow,
pp. 407–8. The greater iambic regularity
of the Q version suggests a possible actor's
substitution (cf. App. B, pp. 430–1).
250 **visage** Often has the sense of 'countenance', i.e. the face as 'expressive of feeling or temperament' (*OED n.* 3); but it can
also mean 'assumed appearance . . . a
pretence or semblance'. Both senses are
probably in play here: Desdemona implies
that the blackness of Othello's face is
merely a deceptive outward show, and
that his true countenance is to be discovered in his mind. Cavell suggests,
however, that the line 'more naturally
says . . . that she saw his visage as he sees
it' (p. 129).
251 **valiant parts** military virtues
253–8 **So . . . voice** Closely based on Giraldi,
where, however, it is the Moor who first
expresses his reluctance to part from Disdemona (see App. C, p. 437).
254 **moth** Usually glossed 'an idle, useless
creature'; but 'moth' normally denotes
'clothes-moth' and its connotations are

The rites for why I love him are bereft me,   255
And I a heavy interim shall support
By his dear absence. Let me go with him.

OTHELLO

Let her have your voice.
Vouch with me, heaven, I therefore beg it not
To please the palate of my appetite,   260
Nor to comply with heat the young affects

---

255 rites] F, Q; rights WARBURTON   why] F; which Q   258–9 Let . . . heaven] F; Your voyces
Lords: beseech you let her will, | Haue a free way Q1; Your voyces Lords: beseech you let her
will | Haue a free way: | Vouch with me heauen Q2   260 my] F, Q; me CAPELL (*conj.* Upton)

---

more destructive; cf. 'moth to honour'
(*Revenger's Tragedy*, 1.4.31).

255 **rites** Since 'rites' and 'rights' were
interchangeable spellings as well as
homonyms, it is difficult to be completely
certain which is meant here; and though
Warburton's emendation to 'rights' provoked Styan Thirlby to exclaim 'Why,
thou goose', an audience will probably
hear both meanings. *Rites* picks up the
sacramental suggestion of *consecrate* (l.
252); but 'rites of love' is also a stock term
for both sexual fulfilment and the affectionate indulgences of friendship (cf.
Romeo, 3.2.8; *1 Henry VI*, 1.3.92; *Richard
III*, 5.5.54 ['rights of love', Oxford]; *Much
Ado*, 2.1.335; *All's Well*, 2.4.41). 'Rights'
in the sense of the 'privileges (due to a
wife)' is arguably less probable in the
mouth of a woman who boasts of her
'downright violence', though it is perhaps
better fitted to F's slightly more decorous
treatment of Desdemona's character.
256 **heavy** weary; full of grief
    support 'endure (with a quibble on prop-
    ping up something heavy)' (Honigmann).
257 **dear absence** (a) the absence of him
    who is so dear to me; (b) his costly, griev-
    ous absence
258–9 **Let . . . heaven** The omission of any
    reference to Desdemona's *will* (whose
    meanings include 'sexual desire') leaves
    only Othello's *appetite* at issue; this is con-
    sistent with F's generally more conser-
    vative treatment of her character. The
    metrically incomplete l. 258 suggests
    some tampering with the text, which, in
    light of the slightly awkward repetition of
    Let from l. 257, may not be authorial (see
    App. B, pp. 431–2).

258 **voice** approval
259 **Vouch with me** bear witness
259–63 **I therefore . . . mind** The general
    sense of what Othello is saying is clear
    enough: he is not asking that Desdemona
    be allowed to accompany him simply to
    gratify his appetite or because he is driven
    by his desires in a way that would be inap-
    propriate to a man of his age, but because
    he responds generously to her mental
    qualities. However, the detail of his
    speech is harder to explicate, and editors
    generally suspect corruption in ll. 261–2.
    Numerous attempts have been made to
    emend the passage, the debate running to
    nearly four pages in Furness: the most
    widely accepted solution is Upton's, sub-
    stituting 'me' for 'my' and assuming a
    parenthetic construction: 'nor to indulge
    the heat of desire—my youthful passions
    being now dead—and the allowable [or
    "personal"] physical satisfactions (of
    marriage)'; but this is syntactically awk-
    ward, and a well-favoured alternative is to
    treat 'defunct' as a misreading, usually
    (as Theobald proposed) for 'distinct' (=
    individual). If, however, *defunct* is under-
    stood as a Latinism, no emendation is
    necessary.
259 **I . . . not** I don't beg it in order to
261 **comply with** Several alternatives are
    possible: (a) 'fill with' (*OED*, *comply*, *v.*[1]
    from Latin *complere* = fill up); (b) 'enfold
    in' (*OED*, *comply*, *v.*[2] from Latin *complicare*
    = enfold, embrace); (c) 'urge on with' (cf.
    OED, *apply*, *v.* 17; *ply*, *v.*[2] 4b).
    heat erotic excitement, appetite
261–2 **young . . . satisfaction** the youthful
    passions [expressed] in the natural
    performance and satisfaction of marital
    desires

In my defunct and proper satisfaction,
But to be free and bounteous to her mind;
And heaven defend your good souls that you think
I will your serious and great business scant   265
For she is with me—no, when light-winged toys
Of feathered Cupid seel with wanton dullness
My speculative and officed instruments,
That my disports corrupt and taint my business,
Let housewives make a skillet of my helm,   270
And all indign and base adversities
Make head against my estimation!

DUKE

Be it as you shall privately determine,
Either for her stay or going: th'affair cries haste,
And speed must answer it.

A SENATOR   You must away tonight.   275

DESDEMONA

Tonight, my lord?

262 defunct] F, Q; distinct THEOBALD; disjunct MALONE   263 to her] F, Q2; of her Q1   265 great] F; good Q   266 For] Q; When F   267 Of] F; And Q   seel] F; foyles Q   268 officed] F (offic'd); actiue Q   instruments] Q; Instrument F   272 estimation] F; reputation Q   274 her] F, Q2; *not in* Q1   th'affair cries] F (th'Affaire), Q2 (*subs.*); the affaires cry Q1   275 answer it.] F; answer, you must hence to night, Q   A SENATOR . . . tonight] F (*Sen.*); *not in* Q   276 DESDEMONA . . . night] Q; *not in* F

262 **defunct** Usually taken to mean 'extinct, dead'; but more easily understood as a Latinism based on the original meaning of *defunctus* ('discharged, performed').
263 **free** generous
264 **defend** forbid
266 **For** because
266-7 **light-winged . . . Cupid** i.e. Cupid's arrows (the frivolous business of love)
267 **seel** sew up (as the eyes of young hawks were stitched during training)
wanton dullness drowsiness resulting from sexual indulgence
268 **speculative . . . instruments** eyes ('organs whose special function it is to see'). One of Othello's characteristically orotund locutions.
269 **That** to the point at which
disports (erotic) diversions
business official duties
270 **housewives** The Q spelling, 'huswiues', is a reminder of the usual pronunciation, 'hussif', from which 'hussy' derives; the two terms often overlap in 17th-century usage. Cf. 2.1.112, 4.1.90.

270 **skillet** small cooking pot
271 **indign** unworthy; shameful
272 **Make head against** rise up against, attack
estimation Q's *reputation* gets the sense. Noting that 'reputation' is an important theme in the play, Rizvi argues that Shakespeare, when revising the text for the theatre, substituted *reputation* 'in order to strengthen the use of the keyword' (p. 340). However, the F reading accords better with Othello's somewhat inflated style, and Q would be an obvious actor's substitution.
274 **cries** demands
275 **answer** deal with (playing on 'cries')
276 **Tonight . . . This night** F's omission of Desdemona's interjection and the Duke's reply may simply be (as Oxford suggests) the result of eye-skip, but is again consistent with a treatment of her character that generally makes her appear more restrained and passive than in the Q version.

DUKE   This night.
OTHELLO   With all my heart.
DUKE
At nine i'th' morning here we'll meet again.
Othello, leave some officer behind
And he shall our commission bring to you,
With such things else of quality and respect   280
As doth import you.
OTHELLO   So please your grace, my ensign—
A man he is of honesty and trust—
To his conveyance I assign my wife,
With what else needful your good grace shall think
To be sent after me.
DUKE   Let it be so.   285
Goodnight to everyone—and, noble signor,
If virtue no delighted beauty lack,
Your son-in-law is far more fair than black.
A SENATOR
Adieu, brave Moor, use Desdemona well.
BRABANTIO
Look to her, Moor, if thou hast eyes to see: 290
She has deceived her father, and may thee.
              Exeunt Duke, Brabantio, Senators, Officers,
                                      and attendants

OTHELLO
My life upon her faith! Honest Iago,

277 nine i'th'] F, Q2; ten i'the QI   280 With] Q; And F   and] F, Q2; or QI   281 import] F,
Q2; concerne QI   So please] F; Please Q   290 if . . . see] F, Q2; haue a quicke eye to see QI
291 and may] F, Q2; may doe QI   291.1–2 *Exeunt . . . attendants*] *after* Q (*Exeunt.*); *Exit.* F;
after 'faith' (*l.* 292) SANDERS

280–1 **such . . . you** such other matters
whose nature and importance make them
of concern to you
282 **honesty** The first reference to Iago's
'honesty', the quality which characters in
the play repeatedly identify as the distin-
guishing mark of his character. Contemporary meanings of the word included
'honour', 'honourable character', and
'generosity', as well the modern 'upright-
ness', 'integrity', and 'truthfulness'.
283 **conveyance** escorting
287 **virtue** Not merely 'moral excellence',

but also 'manly strength and courage';
the sense of 'inherent quality' (used e.g.
of medicines, herbs, etc.) is probably also
present.
delighted delightful
288 **fair** (a) fair-skinned; (b) beautiful; (c)
free from moral blemish
black (a) dark-skinned; (b) baneful,
malignant, sinister; (c) foul, wicked
292 **Honest** honourable; upright, straightforward; but also 'a vague epithet of
appreciation or praise, esp. as used in a
patronizing way to an inferior' (*OED* 1c).

My Desdemona must I leave to thee:
I prithee let thy wife attend on her,
And bring them after in the best advantage.   295
Come Desdemona, I have but an hour
Of love, of worldly matter and direction
To spend with thee. We must obey the time.

       Exeunt Othello and Desdemona, ⌈attended by Cassio⌉

RODERIGO

  Iago.

IAGO   What sayst thou, noble heart?

RODERIGO

  What will I do, think'st thou?

IAGO   Why, go to bed and sleep.   300

RODERIGO

  I will incontinently drown myself.

IAGO If thou dost, I shall never love thee after. Why, thou
  silly gentleman?

RODERIGO It is silliness to live, when to live is torment; and
  then have we a prescription to die, when death is our   305
  physician.

IAGO O villainous! I have looked upon the world for four
  times seven years, and, since I could distinguish betwixt a

---

295 them] F; her Q   297 worldly] Q; wordly F   matter] F; matters Q   298 the] Q; the the F
298.1 *Exeunt . . . Cassio*] This edition; *Exit Moore and* Desdemona. (*after* 'Iago', l. 299) Q; *Exit.*
F   302 If] F; Well, if Q   after] F; after it Q   302–3 Why . . . gentleman?] F (Why thou silly
Gentleman?); Why, thou silly Gentleman. Q1; Why thou silly Gentleman. Q2; Why, thou silly
gentleman! ROWE   304 torment] F; a torment Q   305 have we] F; we haue Q   307 O vil-
lainous] F, Q2; *not in* Q1   have] F; ha Q   308 betwixt] F; betweene Q

---

295 **in . . . advantage** at the most convenient juncture
297 **direction** instructions
298 **obey the time** comply with present
necessity (Dent T340.2)
298.1 **attended . . . Cassio** If Cassio's
entry with Othello at 48.1 is not a 'ghost'
direction, then he should exit either
with the Duke (as Sanders, following
Capell, assumes) or with Othello and
Desdemona; as the Duke has said farewell to Othello's party, it seems more
likely that Cassio would accompany his
commander.
299–301 **Iago . . . myself** It is not clear
from either F or Q whether these lines are
meant to be in verse. Editors generally
print them as prose, but if l. 300 is treated
as a hexameter, they conform to the

metre, and a dramatic point can be made
by Iago's shifting to prose in his burst of
sardonic irritation beginning at l. 302.
297 **thou** Iago's shift to the singular pronoun marks a subtle alteration in his relationship with Roderigo (cf. 1.1.2, 118).
301 **incontinently** immediately
303 **silly** A number of meanings are probably in play: (a) deserving of pity; (b)
weak, feeble; (c) ignorant, foolish, simple-
minded.
304 **silliness** First example cited in *OED*.
305 **prescription** (a) ancient right; (b)
doctor's order
307 **O villainous!** what a shameful,
detestable idea
307–8 **I . . . years** Iago is significantly
younger than Othello; though, given
the much shorter life expectancy of

benefit and an injury, I never found man that knew how
to love himself. Ere I would say I would drown myself for   310
the love of a guinea-hen, I would change my humanity
with a baboon.

RODERIGO What should I do? I confess it is my shame to be
so fond; but it is not in my virtue to amend it.

IAGO Virtue? A fig! 'Tis in ourselves that we are thus, or   315
thus. Our bodies are our gardens to the which our wills
are gardeners; so that if we will plant nettles or sow
lettuce, set hyssop and weed up thyme, supply it with one
gender of herbs or distract it with many—either to have it
sterile with idleness or manured with industry—why, the   320
power and corrigible authority of this lies in our wills.
If the beam of our lives had not one scale of reason to
poise another of sensuality, the blood and baseness of
our natures would conduct us to most preposterous
conclusions; but we have reason to cool our raging   325

---

309 man] F; a man Q   316 are our] F; are Q   322 beam] THEOBALD; braine F; ballance Q

Jacobeans, he is hardly in the prime of
youth; hence his condescending attitude
towards the 'young quat' Roderigo
(5.1.11).

311 **guinea-hen** (female) turkey or
guinea-fowl; (in slang) a prostitute
(*OED* 2b, citing this as the earliest
example). In context, the connection
with Guinea (West Africa) seems
significant, especially when linked with
'baboon'.

312 **baboon** Sometimes used (like *ape*) as a
synonym for fool or buffoon. Honigmann,
citing *Kinsmen*, 3.5.134 ('the babion with
long tail and eke long tool'), notes that
baboons were thought to be especially
lecherous.

314 **fond** foolish; besotted

315 **virtue** power, strength of character
fig On the sexual significance of *figs* see
Williams, *Dictionary*, pp. 480–1; Florio
glosses *fica* ('fig'): 'Also used for a
woman's quaint, and women in Italy use
it as an oath to swear by.' The oath was
usually accompanied by an obscene gesture (sometimes known as the 'Spanish
fig') in which the thumb was thrust
between the fingers of a clenched fist, or
into the mouth.

316 **bodies . . . gardens** As Honigmann
notes, this is a theological commonplace,
appropriate to a speech that is constructed as a kind of mock-sermon. On Iago's
fetishization of individual will as a
characteristic of corrupt Italianate
inwardness, see Floyd-Wilson, pp. 143–4,
151–2.

317–18 **nettles . . . thyme** These plants
were complementary opposites, nettles
and hyssop being 'dry', and lettuce and
thyme 'wet'; for this reason they were
thought, when planted together, to aid
one another's growth.

318 **set** plant

319 **gender** kind
distract it with divide it between

321 **corrigible . . . this** power to correct
this

322 **beam** bar from which the two scales are
suspended, or (by extension) the instrument itself. In the light of Q's *balance*,
Theobald's suggestion that F's 'braine' is
resulted from a misreading of 'beame' is
entirely plausible.
poise counterbalance

323 **blood** passion

324 **preposterous** See l. 63.

325 **conclusions** results

motions, our carnal stings, our unbitted lusts—whereof
I take this that you call 'love' to be a sect or scion.

RODERIGO It cannot be.

IAGO It is merely a lust of the blood and a permission of the
will. Come, be a man! Drown thyself? Drown cats and   330
blind puppies! I have professed me thy friend, and I
confess me knit to thy deserving with cables of perdurable
toughness. I could never better stead thee than now. Put
money in thy purse; follow thou the wars; defeat thy
favour with an usurped beard. I say, put money in thy   335
purse. It cannot be long that Desdemona should continue
her love to the Moor—put money in thy purse—nor he
his to her. It was a violent commencement in her, and
thou shalt see an answerable sequestration—put but
money in thy purse. These Moors are changeable in their   340

---

326 our unbitted] Q; or vnbitted F   329 permission] F, Q; perversion KELLNER *conj.*
331 have professed] F; professe Q   333 than] F (then), Q (then)   334 thou the] F; these Q
336 It . . . continue] F; It cannot be, that *Desdemona* should long continue Q   337 to] F; vnto
Q   338 his] F, Q2; *not in* Q1   in her] F; *not in* Q

---

326 **motions** emotions, impulses
  unbitted unbridled. The horse was a
  stock emblem of desire.
327 **sect or scion** cutting (Latin *sectum*) or
  slip (for grafting)
329–30 **permission of the will** Something
  licensed by either (a) the rational will of
  which Iago has just been speaking (ll.
  316–27) or (b) sexual desire. An unusual
  phrase whose unsatisfactoriness is perhaps indicated by Honigmann's slightly
  desperate conjecture: 'perhaps alluding to God's "permissive will", which
  tolerates the existence of evil (see *Paradise
  Lost*, 3.685)'. Given the easy misreading
  of *m* for *u/v*, it is tempting to accede to
  Kellner's 'perversion'.
330 **be a man** This injunction, with its
  implicit challenge to the masculinity of
  Iago's victim, illustrates what will emerge
  as one of his most characteristic tools of
  manipulation; see 3.3.376, 4.1.57, 61,
  73, 85; and cf. his drinking song, 2.3.65.
332 **knit . . . deserving** committed to
  achieving what you deserve
  perdurable indestructible
333 **stead** help
333–4 **Put . . . purse** sell everything you
  can to raise cash. The story of the feckless
  heir who mortgages his estates to pursue

his amours is a standard theme of 17th-
century satire.
334–5 **defeat . . . beard** spoil your looks
  with a false beard (or perhaps, by growing
  a beard which would suit a soldier, but
  not a refined young gentleman like
  yourself)
339 **answerable sequestration** corre-
  spondingly violent separation. There may
  be a quibble on *commencement* = taking a
  degree (in divinity) and *sequestration* =
  excommunication.
340–1 **These Moors . . . wills** Iago's use of
  the demonstrative *these* implies that he
  possesses a comprehensive knowledge of
  African *mores*; but, whilst his claims
  could be supported by reference to the
  writings of travellers such as Leo
  Africanus, the stereotype of the irrational
  and sexually insatiable black man was
  by no means so well established in
  Shakespeare's time as it would become
  in the 19th century. Indeed, Galenic
  humoral theory maintained that the cool,
  dry constitution of southern peoples, and
  the predominance of black bile in their
  temperament, inclined them to constancy; see, for example, Bodin, p. 124;
  and cf. Floyd-Wilson, chap. 6. See also
  below, 3.4.28–9, and App. F(iv).

wills: fill thy purse with money. The food that to him now
is as luscious as locusts shall be to him shortly as acerb as
coloquintida. She must change for youth: when she is
sated with his body she will find the errors of her choice.
She must have change, she must. Therefore, put money   345
in thy purse. If thou wilt needs damn thyself, do it a more
delicate way than drowning: make all the money thou
canst. If sanctimony and a frail vow betwixt an erring
barbarian and a super-subtle Venetian be not too hard for
my wits and all the tribe of hell, thou shalt enjoy her—   350
therefore make money. A pox of drowning thyself! It is
clean out of the way. Seek thou rather to be hanged in

342 acerb] Q1; bitter F, Q2   as] F, Q2; as the Q1   343 She . . . youth] F, Q2; *not in* Q1   344
errors] F; error Q   345 She . . . must] Q; *not in* F   349 a super-subtle] Q (a super subtle);
super-subtle F   350 of] F; a Q   351 thyself] F; *not in* Q   It is] F; tis Q

341 **wills** Iago again equivocates on the
meanings of 'rational intention' and
'sexual desire'.
342 **luscious as locusts** Cf. the description
of John the Baptist's desert sojourn in
Matthew 3: 4: 'his meat was also locusts
and wild honey'. Ridley cites Gerard's
Herball (1597): 'The carob groweth in
Apulia and other countries eastward,
where the cods are so full of sweet
juice that it is used to preserve
ginger. . . . Moreover both young and old
feed thereon with pleasure. This is of
some called St. John's bread, and thought
to be that which is translated *locusts*.' Cf.
also Revelation 10: 10: 'It was then in my
mouth as sweet as honey: but when I had
eaten it, my belly was bitter.'
acerb bitter. Despite Q2's preference for
F *bitter*, Q *acerb* is clearly preferable.
Not only is it a characteristically
Shakespearian coinage, but one that
derives directly from the play's Italian
source where the Moor's love for
Disdemona is transformed to '*acerbissimo
odio* [bitterest hate]' (Honigmann, p.
374). It is not easy to see why the dramatist would have substituted the more commonplace word; unless, perhaps, he had
come to think of *acerb* as too exotic for the
generally plain-spoken, 'honest' Iago.
Thus the F reading probably indicates
some editorial sophistication of Shakespeare's text, or even an unconscious substitution (perhaps prompted by the echo

of Revelation in the phrasing of the sentence: see above) on the part of a scribe
or compositor who found the original
difficult.
343 **coloquintida** colocynth, bitter apple.
Native to the southern Mediterranean
and Sinai regions and valued for its
purgative properties (Gerard's *Herball*,
1597).
for youth for someone younger
347 **delicate** pleasant
348 **sanctimony** holiness of life, perhaps
with a suggestion of hypocrisy (*OED* 1, 3).
erring (a) wandering; (b) sinning. Cf.
1.1.136, 1.2.26, 1.3.63, 341.
349 **barbarian** (a) foreigner; savage; (b)
inhabitant of Barbary, a 'Barbary Moor'
or Berber. Cf. Leo Africanus: 'The tawny
people of the said region were called by
the name of *Barbar*, being derived of the
verb *Barbara*, which in their tongue signifieth to murmur: because the African
tongue soundeth in the ears of the
Arabian, no otherwise than the voice of
beasts, which utter their sounds without
any accents. Others will have *Barbar* to be
one word twice repeated, forsomuch as
Bar in the Arabian tongue signifieth a
desert' (1.5–6).
subtle (a) delicate, refined; (b) cunning.
350 **and . . . hell** Perhaps an aside
(Honigmann).
352 **clean . . . way** completely out of the
question

compassing thy joy than to be drowned, and go without
her.

RODERIGO Wilt thou be fast to my hopes, if I depend on the   355
issue?

IAGO Thou art sure of me—go, make money!—I have
told thee often, and I re-tell thee again and again, I
hate the Moor. My cause is hearted; thine hath no
less reason: let us be conjunctive in our revenge against   360
him. If thou canst cuckold him, thou dost thyself a
pleasure, me a sport. There are many events in the
womb of Time which will be delivered. Traverse! Go!
Provide thy money! We will have more of this tomorrow.
Adieu.   365

RODERIGO
Where shall we meet i'th' morning?

IAGO   At my lodging.

RODERIGO
I'll be with thee betimes.

IAGO   Go to, farewell.

355-6 if . . . issue] F, Q2; *not in* Q1   358 re-tell] F; tell Q   359 hath] F; has Q   360 conjunctive] F (coniunctiue), Q2; communicatiue Q1   362 me] F, Q2; and me Q1

353 **compassing** (a) achieving; possessing; (b) embracing

355 **be fast to** support steadfastly

359 **hearted** fixed in the heart

360 **conjunctive** united, mutually supportive

362-3 **events . . . delivered** Iago plays with the proverb 'Truth is child (or daughter) of time' (Tilley T580).

363 **Traverse** A military command (cf. *2 Henry IV*, 3.2.268; *Merry Wives*, 2.3.23) whose exact significance has been debated by editors; it seems, however, to involve a dodging movement from side to side (*OED v.* 5, 15).

367 **betimes** early

367-71 **Go . . . your purse** Neither Q nor F seems entirely satisfactory here. F's omission of Iago's teasing references to Roderigo's threats of drowning leaves 'Do you hear?' (l. 368) a little unmotivated, so that some scribal or compositorial error

seems a more likely explanation than revision—though that cannot be excluded. Alternatively, since the passage occurs near the bottom of the page in F, poor casting off may be to blame (Honigmann, *Texts*, p. 47). The omission of l. 371 might result from eye-skip caused by the repetition of *purse* in l. 372, if that repetition did not in any case make 371 sit rather awkwardly in Q, where it may have been meant for cancellation; at the same time, the opening of Iago's soliloquy in Q seems less than adequately prepared for, at least in the absence of some reassurance like 'I'll sell all my land'. Honigmann conjectures that the Q compositor, having reached the end of his page and run out of text, may even have interpolated padding of his own to fill up the space (*Texts*, p. 47).

367 **Go to** Exclamation of humorous impatience.

Do you hear, Roderigo?

RODERIGO   What say you?

IAGO

No more of drowning, do you hear?

RODERIGO   I am changed:

I'll go sell all my land.   370

IAGO

Go to, farewell, put money enough in your purse.

Exit Roderigo

Thus do I ever make my fool my purse:

For I mine own gained knowledge should profane

If I would time expend with such a snipe,

But for my sport and profit. I hate the Moor,   375

And it is thought abroad that 'twixt my sheets

He's done my office. I know not if't be true,

But I, for mere suspicion in that kind,

Will do as if for surety. He holds me well:

The better shall my purpose work on him.   380

Cassio's a proper man—let me see now:

To get his place, and to plume up my will

In double knavery. How? How? Let's see—

368–9 What . . . changed] Q; *not in* F   370 I'll . . . land] Q2; *not in* Q1; Ile sell all my Land F
371 Go . . . your purse] Q1; *not in* F, Q2   371.1 *Exit Roderigo*] This edition; *after* 'Land' *in* F
(*Exit.*), Q2; *after* 'changed' Q1   374 a snipe] Q; Snpe F   377 He's] F2; She ha's F1; H'as Q
378 But] F; Yet Q   382 his] F; this Q   plume] F, Q2; make Q1   383 In] F; A Q   Let's] F; let
me Q

373 **gained** hard won
profane abuse. The religious sense ('desecrate') is also present, resonating ironically with the financial connotations of 'gained'.
374 **snipe** worthless creature, fool; the first example of this term of abuse in *OED*.
376 **abroad** widely
377 **done my office** i.e. made love to Emilia. The use of this expression, as well as locating marriage inside a discourse of domestic authority rather than love, links Iago's resentment over the supposed usurpation of his bed with the usurpation of the military 'office' or 'place' to which he believes himself entitled (1.1.8–32; 1.3.382); see Introduction, pp. 151–4. Although some critics have been sceptical of what Coleridge called 'the motive hunting of motiveless malignity' (i. 49), Iago's sexual jealousy, which surfaces again at

2.1.285–90, is independently confirmed by Emilia (4.2.145–7).
378 **in that kind** in that regard
379 **do . . . surety** act as if it were certain fact
well in high esteem
381 **proper** ideal, admirable, excellent; of good character; handsome; perhaps also implying 'a man ideally suited to my purposes'.
382 **place** Cf. l. 377.
plume up The exact sense is a little uncertain, but the phrase seems to mean something like 'preen' or 'adorn with feathers' (*OED v.* 5); Honigmann suggests 'ruffle the feathers' (as e.g. in a breeding display).
383 **double** (a) doubly wicked; (b) duplicitous
383–5 **How . . . wife** Cf. Giraldi, App. C, p. 438.

After some time to abuse Othello's ears
That he is too familiar with his wife;   385
He hath a person and a smooth dispose
To be suspected, framed to make women false.
The Moor is of a free and open nature
That thinks men honest that but seem to be so,
And will as tenderly be led by th' nose   390
As asses are.
I have't! It is engendered: Hell and Night
Must bring this monstrous birth to the world's light.

                                                Exit

2.1   *Enter Montano, Governor of Cyprus, with two*
        other Gentlemen

MONTANO
  What from the cape can you discern at sea?
FIRST GENTLEMAN
  Nothing at all: it is a high-wrought flood;
  I cannot 'twixt the heaven and the main

---

384 ears] F; eare Q   386 hath] F; has Q   388 The . . . nature] F, Q2; The Moore a free and open nature too Q1   389 seem] F (seeme); seemes Q   393.1 *Exit*] Q; F *omits*
    2.1] F (*Actus Secundus. Scena Prima.*), Q (*Actus 2. Scæna 1.*)   0.1–2 *Enter . . . gentlemen*] Q (Montanio); *Enter Montano, and two Gentlemen.* F   3 heaven] F, Q2; hauen Q1

385–6 **he** i.e. Cassio
386 **person** 'body with its clothing and adornment as presented to the sight of others' (*OED n.* 4a (*b*)).
    dispose external manner
388 **free** generous, frank, spontaneous
390–1 **And . . . are** Q prints this as one line but with three dashes after *nose*, suggesting that F's lineation is meant to signal a similar pause before Iago completes his simile.
390 **tenderly** gently, easily
    led . . . nose Proverbial (Dent N233, and cf. Tilley T221).
392–3 **engendered . . . birth** Iago gives a diabolical twist to the proverb he alluded to at ll. 362–3. Cf. also the related 'Time brings the truth to light' (Dent T324).
2.1.0.1 *Enter . . . Gentlemen* Q's stage direction gives the clearest indication of Montano's rank in the play, and this will affect the way his (and subsequent scenes involving this character) are to be played. However, because neither Cassio nor Othello appears to treat him as though he

were the outgoing Governor, Sanders (p. 197) speculates that 'first and second authorial thoughts' may have been involved. Honigmann (*Texts*, p. 37) also takes the direction as evidence of authorial first intentions; but, as McMillin points out, it is just as likely to have a theatrical origin, related to the requirements for Montano's costuming (Q, p. 13).
2 **high-wrought** furiously agitated (earliest citation in *OED*). Like the Turkish threat to Cyprus, the storm, with all its symbolic suggestiveness, involves a significant alteration to Giraldi's story, in which the Moor and Disdemona cross to Cyprus 'with a sea of utmost tranquillity'.
    flood sea
3 **heaven . . . main** i.e. the Gentleman vainly scans the sea for sails outlined against the sky. Honigmann (following Malone) prefers Q's *haven*; but in Shakespeare's time the two words (often linked by associative word-play) were easily confused by both spelling and pronunciation.

Descry a sail.

MONTANO

Methinks the wind hath spoke aloud at land—   5
A fuller blast ne'er shook our battlements;
If it hath ruffianed so upon the sea,
What ribs of oak, when mountains melt on them,
Can hold the mortise? What shall we hear of this?

SECOND GENTLEMAN

A segregation of the Turkish fleet: 10
For do but stand upon the foaming shore,
The chidden billow seems to pelt the clouds,
The wind-shaked surge with high and monstrous mane
Seems to cast water on the burning Bear
And quench the guards of th'ever-fixèd Pole.   15
I never did like molestation view
On the enchafèd flood.

MONTANO   If that the Turkish fleet

---

5 hath spoke] F; does speake Q   8 mountains . . . them] F (Mountaines), Q2 (mountaine);
the huge mountaine mes lt Q1   11 foaming] F, Q2; banning Q1   12 chidden] F; chiding Q
13 mane] KNIGHT; Maine F; mayne Q   15 ever-fixèd] F; euer fired Q

7 **ruffianed** raged, blustered (with a quibble on 'roughen')
8 **ribs of oak** framing timbers of a ship
  mountains mountainous waves
9 **mortise** The joint(s) holding the ship's timbers together.
10 **segregation** dispersal, splitting up (earliest citation in *OED*)
11 **foaming** Though Honigmann dismisses it as 'an easy misreading, improbable here', Sanders prefers Q *banning* (= chiding, cursing), which is arguably the stronger alternative, extending as it does the metaphor in the following line ('chidden billow'); oddly enough, however, as Delius pointed out, 'banning' makes better sense with F's 'chidden' than with Q's 'chiding'.
13 **wind-shaked** First example cited in *OED*.
  mane The wave-crests are imagined as the flying mane of some monstrous creature (cf. the modern 'white horses'); 17th-century orthography did not distinguish between 'main' and 'mane' (either of which could be spelt 'maine', as in F, or

'mayne', as in Q). Here a pun on *main* is inevitable.
14 **cast water** throw water; but perhaps also 'urinate', 'vomit' or 'spew' (cf. *OED, cast, v.* 20c, 25a).
  Bear 'probably the Little Bear [*Ursa Minor*], since the *guards* are the two stars in that constellation next in brightness to the Pole Star. They are frequently mentioned, along with the Pole Star, as guides to navigation' (Ridley).
15 **ever-fixèd** The Pole Star's usefulness to navigators seeking to take their bearings was that it was one of the so-called 'fixed stars'. Honigmann justifies Q's *euer fired* by appealing to Iago's 'ever-burning lights above' (3.3.463), but the expression seems slightly wrenched and a misreading would be easy.
16 **like molestation** such turbulence. *Molestation* (from Latin *molestare* = to trouble) is not found elsewhere in Shakespeare and seems to be adapted from Giraldi Cinthio's *estrema molestia* (Honigmann, p. 372).
17 **enchafèd** furious (literally 'heated'; earliest citation in *OED*)

Be not ensheltered and embayed, they are drowned:
It is impossible to bear it out.

Enter a third Gentleman

THIRD GENTLEMAN

News, lads! Our wars are done: 20
The desperate tempest hath so banged the Turks
That their designment halts. A noble ship of Venice
Hath seen a grievous wrack and sufferance
On most part of their fleet.

MONTANO How? Is this true?   25

THIRD GENTLEMAN The ship is here put in,
A Veronese; Michael Cassio,
Lieutenant to the warlike Moor Othello,
Is come on shore; the Moor himself at sea,
And is in full commission here for Cyprus.   30

MONTANO

I am glad on't; 'tis a worthy governor.

THIRD GENTLEMAN

But this same Cassio, though he speak of comfort
Touching the Turkish loss, yet he looks sadly
And prays the Moor be safe; for they were parted

19 to] F, Q2; they Q1   19.1 Enter ... gentleman] Q; *Enter a Gentleman.* F   20 THIRD GENTLE-
MAN] Q ('3 *Gent.*' *throughout*); 3 F   lads] F, Q2; Lords Q1   Our] F; your Q   21 Turks] F
(Turkes); *Turke* Q   22 A noble] F, Q2; Another Q1   24 their] F, Q2; the Q1   26–7 in, | A
Veronese; Michael Cassio] *This edition after* THEOBALD (in, a Veronessa); *in:* A *Verennessa,
Michael Cassio* F, Q (in: | A Veronessa,)   29 on shore] F; ashore Q   34 prays] Q (prayes);
praye F

18 **embayed** protected by a bay
19 **bear it out** weather the storm
21 **desperate** extremely dangerous (literally
   'leaving no room for hope; inducing
   despair')
22 **designment** enterprise, undertaking
   halts wavers
23 **wrack** destruction; shipwreck
   sufferance damage (earliest use cited in
   OED); suffering
25 A metrically amphibious line.
27 **Veronese** Four syllables (as in Italian).
   F and Q are unanimous in treating the
   word as referring to Cassio, rather than
   (as editors since Theobald have assumed)
   the ship. Both readings are problematic:
   the ship has just been identified as 'A
   noble ship of Venice', whilst Cassio has
   been denounced by Iago in the first scene
   as 'a Florentine', an identification
   apparently confirmed by Cassio himself at

3.1.40. Neither of these contradictions is
insuperable. Sanders suggests that 'there
may lie behind F's spelling . . . some particular type of ship, perhaps a cutter
whose name was derived from the Italian
nautical term *verrinare* (= to cut
through)'; more plausibly Honigmann
points out that Verona was at this time a
Venetian dependency and, though an
inland city, supplied ships of its own at
the Battle of Lepanto. But if the F and Q
punctuation is correct, then the seeming
confusion probably represents a minor
change of intention on Shakespeare's
part regarding Cassio's origins. Cf.
4.1.115.
30 **is ... Cyprus** has been sent to Cyprus
   with complete authority
33 **Touching** concerning
   sadly grave

With foul and violent tempest.

MONTANO   Pray heavens he be!   35
For I have served him, and the man commands
Like a full soldier. Let's to the seaside, ho!—
As well to see the vessel that's come in
As to throw out our eyes for brave Othello,
Even till we make the main and th'aerial blue   40
An indistinct regard.

THIRD GENTLEMAN   Come, let's do so:
For every minute is expectancy
Of more arrivance.

    Enter Cassio

CASSIO
Thanks, you the valiant of this warlike isle
That so approve the Moor. O, let the heavens   45
Give him defence against the elements,
For I have lost him on a dangerous sea.

MONTANO Is he well shipped?

CASSIO
His barque is stoutly timbered, and his pilot
Of very expert and approved allowance;   50
Therefore my hopes, not surfeited to death,
Stand in bold cure.

VOICES (*shouting within*) A sail, a sail, a sail!

CASSIO What noise?

---

35 heavens] F; Heauen Q   39 throw out] Q; throw-out F   40–1 Even . . . regard] F, Q2; *not in* Q1   40 aerial] F (Eriall); Ayre all Q2   41 THIRD GENTLEMAN] Q; *Gent.* F   43 arrivance] Q; Arriuancie F   44 Thanks, you the] KNIGHT; Thankes you, the F; Thankes to the Q   this] Q; the F   warlike isle] F; worthy Isle Q1; Isle Q2   45 O, let] F (Oh let); and let Q   46 the] F; their Q   51 hopes, not . . . death,] *after* F3; hope's (not . . . death) F1, Q2; hope's not . . . death Q1   52 Stand . . . cure]   F; Stand . . . cure. *Enter a Messenger.* Q; Stand . . . cure. *Enter another Gentleman.* CAPELL   53 VOICES . . . within] F (*subs.*: 'Within'); *Mess.* Q

---

37 **full soldier** one possessing all the qualities of a true soldier

40–1 **Even . . . regard** until (by dint of staring so hard) we make the ocean and blue sky indistinguishable. The omission of this passage from Q leaves the first line of the Third Gentleman's speech metrically incomplete, suggesting that a cut was involved.

40 **aerial** First recorded use in *OED*.

42 **is expectancy** gives expectation

43 **arrivance** arrivals (earliest citation in *OED*)

45 **approve** commend, demonstrate the worth of

50 **Of . . . allowance** acknowledged to be a man of demonstrated expertise.

51–2 **not . . . cure** though not dangerously indulged, are confident of a successful outcome (*cure* continues the medical conceit in *surfeited*)

243

SECOND GENTLEMAN
  The town is empty; on the brow o'th' sea
  Stand ranks of people, and they cry 'A sail!'   55
CASSIO
  My hopes do shape him for the governor.
           A shot is heard
SECOND GENTLEMAN
  They do discharge their shot of courtesy:
  Our friends, at least.
CASSIO   I pray you, sir, go forth,
  And give us truth who 'tis that is arrived.
SECOND GENTLEMAN   I shall.   *Exit*
MONTANO
  But, good lieutenant, is your general wived?   60
CASSIO
  Most fortunately: he hath achieved a maid
  That paragons description and wild fame,
  One that excels the quirks of blazoning pens,
  And in th'essential vesture of creation,
  Does tire the ingener.
           Enter Second Gentleman
                          How now? Who has put in?   65

54 SECOND GENTLEMAN] HONIGMANN *after* F (*Gent.*); *Mess.* Q   56 the governor] F (Gouernor);
guernement Q1; gouernement Q2   56.1 *A shot is heard*] Q ('*A shot.*' *after* 'least', *l*. 58); *not in* F
57, 59, 66, 94 SECOND GENTLEMAN] Q (2 *Gen.*); *Gent.* F   57 their] F; the Q   58 friends] F;
friend Q   63 quirks of] F, Q2; *not in* Q1   65 tire the ingener] F (Ingeniuer); beare all excellency Q1; beare an excellency Q2   *Second Gentleman*] Q ('2. *Gentleman*' *after* 'in?'); *Gentleman* F
(*after* 'ingener')   How now?] F; —now, Q

56 **shape him for** imagine it is
57 **shot of courtesy** salute (with cannon or
   musketry)
61 **achieved** won (chivalric term for accom-
   plishing a quest)
62 **paragons** excels (earliest use cited in
   OED). In Renaissance aesthetic discourse
   paragone was the mode of emulous imitation through which an artist strove to
   outreach his predecessors.
   wild fame the most extravagant rumour
63 **quirks** fantastic conceits
   blazoning Originally heraldic ('describing or depicting according to the rules of
   heraldry'), but often more loosely used to
   refer to either honourable or boastful
   description. In love poetry a 'blazon' was
   an elaborate figurative cataloguing of the

parts of a woman's body. Schäfer cites as
earliest known use.
64 **essential . . . creation** An obscure passage which has been variously explained:
   'the *etherially pure*, or *celestial* garb of her
   nature' (Hart); 'the quintessence of loveliness' (Walker); 'as God made her'
   (Ridley); 'absolute beauty of the human
   form' (Sanders); 'in the essential clothing
   in which she was born' or 'in her inner-
   most nature (*essential vesture* = soul, not
   body)' (Honigmann). It is possible, however, that 'creation' refers to the creativi-
   ty of the artist, and 'vesture' to the
   rhetorical 'dress' in which the poet seeks
   to capture the essential nature of female
   beauty.
65 **tire** (a) exhaust; (b) attire

SECOND GENTLEMAN
  'Tis one Iago, ensign to the general.
CASSIO
  He's had most favourable and happy speed:
  Tempests themselves, high seas and howling winds,
  The guttered rocks and congregated sands
  (Traitors ensteeped to clog the guiltless keel)   70
  As having sense of beauty, do omit
  Their mortal natures, letting go safely by
  The divine Desdemona.
MONTANO   What is she?
CASSIO
  She that I spake of: our great captain's captain,
  Left in the conduct of the bold Iago,   75
  Whose footing near anticipates our thoughts
  A sennight's speed. Great Jove, Othello guard
  And swell his sail with thine own powerful breath
  That he may bless this bay with his tall ship,
  Make love's quick pants in Desdemona's arms,   80
  Give renewed fire to our extincted spirits
       Enter Desdemona, Iago, Roderigo, and Emilia
  And bring all Cyprus comfort—O, behold,
  The riches of the ship is come on shore!
  You men of Cyprus, let her have your knees.

67 CASSIO] F; *not in* Q   He's] *after* F (Ha's); He has Q   68 high] F, Q2; by Q1   70 ensteeped]
F (ensteep'd), Q2; enscerped Q1   clog] Q; enclogge F   72 mortal] F; common Q   74 spake]
F, Q2; spoke Q1   80 Make . . . in] F; And swiftly come to Q   81.1 *Enter . . . Emilia*] F; *after*
'arms' (*l.* 80) Q   82 And . . . comfort] Q; *not in* F   83 on shore] F, Q2; ashore Q1   84 You]
F; Ye Q

ingener An old form of 'engineer' = one
who contrives, designs, or invents; an
author (*OED, engineer, n.* I); cf. also
ingener, v. (from Latin *ingenerare* = engender). Both because the metre requires a
stress on the first syllable, and because
there is a subdued quibble on 'ingenious',
it seems best to preserve the old spelling.

69 **guttered** furrowed, gullied; hence
'jagged' (Sanders).
  congregated sands sandbanks
(Honigmann)
70 **ensteeped** submerged; apparently
coined from *steep, v.*[1] (*OED*, citing only
this example). As White (following
Steevens) suggested, Q's 'enscerped'

might be a version of *enscarped* or *escarped*
(= steep), but this does not fit the image
of treacherous sandbanks; in any case, of
these alternatives, only the latter is listed
in *OED*, and not before 1728. *C/t* and *e/r*
misreadings are, however, quite possible.
  clog The Q reading fits the metre better;
elision is possible, but F's *enclog* is probably contaminated by *ensteeped*.

71-2 **omit . . . natures** refrain from
indulging their deadly natures
75 **in the conduct of** to be escorted by
76 **footing** landing
77 **sennight** week
79 **tall** handsome; doughty; tall-masted
80 **quick** (a) lively; (b) rapid
81 **extincted** extinguished

245

Hail to thee, lady; and the grace of heaven,   85
Before, behind thee, and on every hand,
Enwheel thee round!

DESDEMONA   I thank you, valiant Cassio.
What tidings can you tell me of my lord?

CASSIO
He is not yet arrived; nor know I aught
But that he's well and will be shortly here.   90

DESDEMONA
O, but I fear—how lost you company?

CASSIO
The great contention of sea and skies
Parted our fellowship.
            Voices shout within: 'A sail, a sail!'
                    But hark—a sail!

        ⌈*A shot is heard*⌉

SECOND GENTLEMAN
They give their greeting to the citadel:
This likewise is a friend.

CASSIO   See for the news.   95
                    Exit Second Gentleman
Good ensign, you are welcome. Welcome, mistress!
    He kisses Emilia

88 me] Q; *not in* F   92 sea] F; the sea Q   93 *Voices . . . sail*] COLLIER; *Within* A Saile, a Saile.
F, *after* 'Hearke, a Saile' (*l.* 93); [*within.*] *A saile, a saile.* Q, *after* 'company' (*l.* 91)   93.1
A . . . heard] CAPELL (*subs.*); *not in* F, Q   94 their] Q; this F   95 See . . . news] F, Q2; So
speakes this voyce Q1   95.1 *Exit . . . Gentleman*] CAPELL; *not in* F, Q   96.1 *He kisses Emilia*]
JOHNSON (*subs.*); *not in* F, Q

85 **Hail . . . heaven** Honigmann suggests a
    possible echo of the 'Hail Mary' at this
    point.
85–7 **thee** Honigmann notes Cassio's use of
    the intimate form in this moment of
    excitement; later he reverts to the more
    decorous *you*.
87 **Enwheel** encircle, surround; with a play
    on the *wheeling* movement of the heavens
    (earliest use recorded in *OED* and almost
    certainly a coinage).
92 **The . . . skies** For metrical reasons,
    most editors prefer the Q reading 'the sea'
    here; but F scans perfectly well if 'con-
    tention' is treated as four syllables with a
    stress on the first and fourth syllables.
93 **fellowship** company; i.e. the group of
    ships (*OED n.* 6).

Voices . . . sail Unlike the previous cry
    'within' which completes a line (l. 52),
    this one is extra-metrical; so it should
    probably be treated as a background
    noise, rather than as part of the dialogue.
96–9 **Good . . . courtesy** Honigmann de-
    tects 'a touch of condescension' in the
    repetition of 'good', a term of approba-
    tion often used to greet social inferiors
    (pp. 85, 168). Cassio's flowery explana-
    tion of his 'courtesy' and 'breeding' is, of
    course, even more insulting, implying as
    it does that the kiss which he gives Iago's
    wife is a refinement of courtly manners
    which a rough soldier like Iago could not
    possibly understand. An actor will have to
    decide whether the insult, like the kiss
    itself, is simply a sign of Cassio's poor

Let it not gall your patience, good Iago,
That I extend my manners. 'Tis my breeding
That gives me this bold show of courtesy.

IAGO

Sir, would she give you so much of her lips   100
As of her tongue she oft bestows on me,
You'd have enough.

DESDEMONA Alas, she has no speech!

IAGO In faith, too much!
I find it still when I have leave to sleep.   105
Marry, before your ladyship, I grant,
She puts her tongue a little in her heart,
And chides with thinking.

EMILIA   You have little cause to say so.

IAGO

Come on, come on! You are pictures out of doors;
Bells in your parlours; wild-cats in your kitchens;   110

---

100 Sir] F, Q2; For Q1   101 oft bestows] F; has bestowed Q   102 You'd] Q; You would F
104 In faith] F, Q2; I know Q1   105 it still] F, Q2; it, I Q1   when] F; for when Q   have leave]
F, Q2 (ha' leaue); ha' list Q1   109 of doors] Q2; of doore F; adores Q1

judgement, or whether it is a calculated
affront, responding to a tension that
already exists between them. Though
kissing (in England, if not in Italy) was a
normal method of greeting and need not
have implied any flirtation, Cassio seems
somewhat self-conscious about the 'boldness' of his gesture. Cf. also Commentary
1.3.159.

98 **extend my manners** take such unusual
freedoms in my behaviour
breeding Whilst *breeding* could sometimes refer to 'birth' or 'lineage', it more
usually denoted 'upbringing', 'education', or the results of such training.

99 **courtesy** elegant manners; in this period
a term still largely confined to the world of
courtiers, and therefore containing an
implicit claim to social superiority on
Cassio's part.

101 **tongue** 'Iago coarsely hints at kissing,
as well as scolding, with the tongue'
(Honigmann).

103 **Alas . . . speech** Amphibious. Before
Cassio can respond, Desdemona intervenes playfully, as if to defuse the growing hostility registered in Iago's sarcastic

reply; she means either that Emilia has
been struck dumb with embarrassment,
or that she is far from being the garrulous
nagger that Iago describes; or perhaps
that the first proves the second.

105 **still** always
leave permission (frequently, as here,
used ironically)

106 **before . . . ladyship** in your ladyship's
presence

107-8 **She . . . thinking** i.e. she keeps her
shrewish speeches to herself. The heart is
often imaged as a cabinet of secrets.

109-13 **You . . . beds** Cf. Dent W702,
'Women are in church saints, abroad
angels, at home devils'.

109 **You are** The metre requires elision here
('you're').
pictures The contrast with clanging *bells*
seems to require something like Sanders's
'silent appearances (of virtue)'. A *picture*
could be a sculpture as well as a painting;
but Kittredge was probably right to sense
'a suggestion that they owe their beauty
to painting'.

110 **parlours** Playing on the original meaning of a 'room set aside for conversation'
(Honigmann).

Saints in your injuries; devils being offended;
Players in your housewifery; and housewives
In your beds.

DESDEMONA   O fie upon thee, slanderer!

IAGO

Nay, it is true, or else I am a Turk:
You rise to play, and go to bed to work.   115

EMILIA

You shall not write my praise.

IAGO   No, let me not.

DESDEMONA

What wouldst thou write of me, if thou shouldst praise
       me?

IAGO

O gentle lady, do not put me to't,
For I am nothing if not critical.

DESDEMONA

Come on, assay—there's one gone to the harbour?   120

IAGO Ay, madam.

DESDEMONA

I am not merry; but I do beguile
The thing I am by seeming otherwise.
Come, how wouldst thou praise me?

---

113 DESDEMONA] F, Q2; *not in* Q1   117 wouldst thou] Q; wouldst F

112 **Players** actors, triflers; with a bawdy
quibble on sexual 'play' (cf. l. 116).
housewives Cf. 1.3.270; 4.1.89.
Oxford's 'hussies' gets the meaning but
obscures the word-play, which an actor
might still be able to activate, however,
by pronouncing 'hussifry . . . hussifs'.
Murphy suggests a double word-play on
the two senses of 'housewife': ' "you
take your [domestic] duties lightly and
are promiscuous" . . . or "you manage
your households economically and are
equally parsimonious with your sexual
favours" '.

114 **I . . . Turk** A hybrid of Dent J49.1 ('I am
a Jew . . . else') and T609 ('To turn Turk',
i.e. convert to Islam); particularly appropriate to a play in which a Moor turned
Christian ends by symbolically 'turning
Turk' (5.2.351–5). Since the extended
meanings of *Turk* included 'a cruel,
rigorous, or tyrannical man; anyone

behaving as a barbarian or savage; one
who treats his wife hardly' (*OED n.* 4),
Iago too may be regarded as a Christian
'turned Turk'.

115 **rise . . . play . . . work** All three words
contain sexual innuendo: the implication
is that fornication is women's only pas-
time and business.

116 **praise** i.e. verses in my praise

117–18 **What . . . me** Desdemona again
intervenes to deflect an argument, this
time between Iago and Emilia. Q (which
assumes a feminine ending) seems
metrically preferable here since the sense
requires that Desdemona's first *me* be
stressed and the second unstressed.

118 **put me to't** put me to the test

120 **assay** In early modern English *essay* (=
attempt) and *assay* (= make trial of) were
not distinct, and both meanings are probably involved here.

122 **beguile** divert attention from (*OED v.* 5)

IAGO

I am about it; but indeed my invention　　　　125
Comes from my pate as birdlime does from frieze—
It plucks out brains and all. But my Muse labours,
And thus she is delivered:
If she be fair and wise: fairness and wit,
The one's for use, the other useth it.　　　　130

DESDEMONA

Well praised! How if she be black and witty?

IAGO

If she be black and thereto have a wit,

---

127 brains] F (Braines); braine Q　129–30, 132–3, 135–6, 140–1, 146–58] *as here* Q1; *in italic* F, Q2　130 useth] F, Q2; vsing Q1

---

126 **birdlime** A glutinous substance spread on trees and bushes to entrap birds.

frieze Usually a kind of coarse woollen cloth with a nap (to which birdlime would easily stick); but *frieze* could also be used to describe the nap on plants, and this may be what is meant here.

127–8 **labours . . . delivered** Iago's quibbling picks up the metaphors of pregnancy and giving birth that conclude his soliloquy at the end of Act 1.

129–58 **If . . . beer** F's use of italics for Iago's rhyming verses highlights the element of self-conscious quotation in what Desdemona mockingly calls his 'old fond paradoxes' (l. 137).

129–47 **If . . . loud** Honigmann notes the play with proverbial formulations: 'Fair and foolish, black and proud, long and lazy, little and loud' (Dent F28).

129 **fair** (a) beautiful; (b) fair-haired
wit intelligence

130 **use . . . useth** The obscene innuendo is clear enough: Iago is suggesting that an intelligent woman will know how to employ her beauty by making her body available for *use*, i.e. sexual 'use' for a usurious return (prostitution). Cf. *Revenger's Tragedy*, 2.2.97: 'Her tongue has turned my sister into use.'

131 **black** Depending on its context this could mean either 'dark-skinned' or 'dark-haired'. The latter is the primary meaning here, but the play's preoccupation with 'colour' makes the other meaning impossible to exclude, and Iago's reply immediately activates it.

witty wise, intelligent, endowed with

good judgement; but in the context of the clever verbal play between Iago and Desdemona (reminiscent of the conventional banter between Lady and Fool in the comedies) the hint of cleverness and intellectual sparkle is also appropriate.

132–3 **black . . . white** A complex piece of word-play: in addition to the pun on *wight* (= man), there is also a quibble on *wit* (= man of wit), possibly because the diphthongization of the *i* in *white* was not complete in Shakespearian English (see Dobson, ii, section 12.1). *Blackness* here is a typical piece of Iago bawdy: like *black* itself, it could refer (via the pubic hair) to the female sex organs (Williams, *Dictionary*, pp. 110–11, *Glossary*, p. 43). Moreover, the couplet that Williams cites from the pseudo-Donne lyric 'On Black Hayre and Eyes' ('if I might direct my shaft aright, | The black mark would I hit and not the white') and another from Brome's *The English Moor* (*c*.1637: 'This is the worthy man whose wealth and wit, | To make a white one must the black mark hit', 4.4.59–60) suggest that a further play on *white* = centre of an archery target (nowadays the 'gold') is involved. Thus Q's *hit* seems likely to be the correct reading here, a conclusion supported by a similar passage of bawdy in *LLL* (4.1.107–38). F's *fit*, while equally obscene, misses the point of the conceit, and in some Elizabethan hands could have been a possible misreading for *hit*.

132 **wit** To the meanings already in play Iago adds a suggestion of 'ingenuity' or 'cunning'.

She'll find a white that shall her blackness hit.

DESDEMONA

Worse and worse.

EMILIA   How if fair and foolish?

IAGO

She never yet was foolish that was fair,   135

For even her folly helped her to an heir.

DESDEMONA These are old fond paradoxes to make fools
laugh i'th' alehouse. What miserable praise hast thou for
her that's foul and foolish?

IAGO

There's none so foul and foolish thereunto,   140

But does foul pranks which fair and wise ones do.

DESDEMONA O heavy ignorance! Thou praisest the worst
best. But what praise couldst thou bestow on a deserving
woman indeed? One that, in the authority of her merit,
did justly put on the vouch of very malice itself.   145

IAGO

She that was ever fair and never proud,

Had tongue at will and yet was never loud,

Never lacked gold and yet went never gay,

Fled from her wish and yet said 'Now I may';

She that being angered, her revenge being nigh,   150

Bade her wrong stay and her displeasure fly;

She that in wisdom never was so frail

---

133 hit] Q1; *fit* F, Q2   136 an heir] F, Q2; a haire Q1   137 fond] F; *not in* Q   142 Thou prais-
est] F (thou); that praises Q   144 merit] F; merrits Q

---

134 **Worse and worse** 'Said admiringly
in wit-combats' (Honigmann); cf. the
admiring use of 'bad', 'mean', 'wicked' in
modern idiomatic usage.

134–5 **foolish** Desdemona's 'foul and
foolish' (l. 138) suggests that, in the context of jokes about fairness and blackness
a *fool/foul* (= black) pun may be involved
here (see Kökeritz, p. 75; cf. 1.2.62,
5.2.232, 322).

136 **folly** (a) foolishness; (b) unchastity
helped . . . heir (a) helped her to marry
a rich heir; (b) helped her to produce a
bastard son (Honigmann)

137 **fond** foolish

139–40 **foul** (a) ugly; (b) dirty; (c) black; (d)
wicked; (e) obscene, revolting

141 **pranks** sexual tricks

142 **heavy** intense

143–4 **deserving . . . indeed**   genuinely
deserving woman

144–5 **One . . . itself** one whose virtue had
such confident authority that she could
reasonably encourage malice itself to testify against her (*OED, put, v.* 47h)

147 **Had . . . will** could always speak as elo-
quently as occasion demanded

148 **gay** showily dressed

149 **Fled . . . may** turned her back on her
desires even when she knew she was in a
position to fulfil them

151 **Bade . . . stay** restrained her sense of
injustice

152 **frail** morally weak

To change the cod's head for the salmon's tail;
She that could think and ne'er disclose her mind,
See suitors following and not look behind: 155
She was a wight—if ever such wights were—

DESDEMONA To do what?

IAGO
To suckle fools and chronicle small beer.

DESDEMONA O most lame and impotent conclusion! Do
not learn of him, Emilia, though he be thy husband.   160
How say you, Cassio, is he not a most profane and liberal
counsellor?

CASSIO He speaks home, madam: you may relish him more
in the soldier than in the scholar.

IAGO (*aside*) He takes her by the palm—ay, well said, whis-   165
per!—with as little a web as this will I ensnare as great a
fly as Cassio.—Ay, smile upon her, do! I will gyve thee in
thine own courtship.—You say true, 'tis so indeed.—If
such tricks as these strip you out of your lieutenantry, it

---

155 See . . . behind] F, Q2; *not in* Q1   156 wights] F; wight Q   166 with] F, Q2; *not in* Q1   I]
F, Q2; *not in* Q1   167 fly] F, Q2 (Flie); Flee Q1   gyve] F2; giue F1; catch Q   167–8 thee in
thine own courtship] F; you in your owne courtesies Q1; you in your own courtship Q2

---

153 **change . . . tail** Honigmann cites Pliny
on fish tails as a delicacy to suggest
that the first meaning is 'to exchange
something worthless for something of
greater value'; although Balz Engler suggests that the proper contrast is between
the worthy head and the ignoble tail,
the general meaning remains the same
('*Othello*, II.i.155: "To Change the Cod's
Head for the Salmon's Tail"', *SQ* 35
(1984), 202–3). But, as critics since
Partridge have recognized, the familiar
bawdy senses of *cod* (testicles), *head*
(penis), *tail* (female or, sometimes, male
sex organs), together with the sexual
associations of fish, make an obscene
construction inevitable. Despite the
heavy weather made of this, the meaning
seems clear enough: Iago (habitually
thinking of all women as whores) imagines sexual congress between the male
and female members as a form of commercial exchange.

156 **wight** person

158 **small beer** Literally 'weak or inferior

beer', but here 'trivial matters' (first
recorded use in *OED*).

159 **impotent conclusion** In the context of
Iago's bawdy jokes it is difficult to avoid
the bawdy sense of *conclusion* (= 'but-
tocks' or 'coitus'): see Rubinstein, pp. 54,
92, 143, and cf. l. 254 and 3.3.429.

161 **profane** irreverent, wicked, ribald
liberal licentious (*OED a.* 3a)

163 **home** to the point, directly; so as to
penetrate effectually (cf. 'thrust home')

163–4 **relish . . . in** appreciate him more in
the role of

165 **well said** As Ridley and others note, this
can simply mean 'well done'; but cf. 'You
say true' (l. 170).

167 **gyve** fetter

168 **courtship** courtly behaviour (with a
sardonic play on 'wooing')
You . . . indeed Since their conversation
is inaudible to the audience, it is probably
meant to be so to Iago also; but he may
emphasize his sarcasm by an elaborate
show of eavesdropping.

169 **lieutenantry** First recorded use in *OED*.

had been better you had not kissed your three fingers so   170
oft, which now again you are most apt to play the sir in.—
Very good, well kissed, and excellent courtesy! 'Tis so
indeed.—Yet again, your fingers to your lips? Would they
were clyster-pipes for your sake.
        Trumpets within
(*Aloud*) The Moor! I know his trumpet.

CASSIO   'Tis truly so.   175
DESDEMONA
Let's meet him and receive him.
CASSIO   Lo, where he comes!
        Enter Othello and attendants
OTHELLO
O, my fair warrior!
DESDEMONA   My dear Othello!
OTHELLO
It gives me wonder great as my content
To see you here before me. O my soul's joy,
If after every tempest come such calms,   180
May the winds blow till they have wakened death,
And let the labouring barque climb hills of seas
Olympus-high, and duck again as low
As hell's from heaven. If it were now to die,
'Twere now to be most happy; for I fear   185
My soul hath her content so absolute

---

170 kissed] F; rist Q   172 Very] F, Q2; *not in* Q1   and] F, Q2; an Q1   173 to] F; at Q   174
clyster-pipes] Q (Clisterpipes); Cluster-pipes F   174.1 *Trumpets within*] Q (*after* 'Trumpet',
l. 175); *not in* F   175 *Aloud*] OXFORD; *not in* F, Q   176.1 *Enter . . . attendants*] F; *after* 'Trumpets within*' (l. 175) Q   180 calms] F (Calmes); calmnesse Q

170 **kissed . . . fingers** A courtly gesture of
    flirtation similarly mocked for its foppish
    extravagance in *LLL* (4.1.145) and *Twelfth
    Night* (3.4.30–1).
171 **play the sir** play the gallant
172 **and . . . courtesy** F's *and* suggests that
    courtesy = bow (cf. modern *curtsy*), while
    Q's *an* seems to make it descriptive of the
    hand-kissing (= courtly behaviour). If
    McMillin's theories are correct, Q may
    reflect a scribal mishearing.
174 **clyster-pipes** enema tubes (first citation
    in *OED*). For perceptive psychoanalytical
    accounts of Iago's preoccupation with
    purging and evacuation, see Adelman,

pp. 125–44, and Ben Saunders, 'Iago's
Clyster: Purgation, Anality, and the
Civilizing Process', *SQ* 55 (2004), 148–76.
175 **his trumpet** See App. D (i). Each com-
    mander had his own distinctive trumpet
    call; here, as at *Troilus*, 4.6.65 ('The
    Trojans' trumpet'), a play on 'strumpet' is
    probably involved.
180 **If . . . calms** Dent S908, 'After a storm
    comes calm'.
181 **wakened death** An apocalyptic image
    (cf. the more usual 'wakened the dead').
183 **Olympus** The mountain on which the
    Greek gods were supposed to dwell; here
    standing for *heaven* (l. 180).

That not another comfort like to this
Succeeds in unknown fate.
DESDEMONA   The heavens forbid
But that our loves and comforts should increase
Even as our days do grow.
OTHELLO   Amen to that, sweet powers!   190
I cannot speak enough of this content:
It stops me here, it is too much of joy.
        They kiss
And this, and this the greatest discords be
That e'er our hearts shall make.
IAGO (*aside*)   O, you are well tuned now!
But I'll set down the pegs that make this music,   195
As honest as I am.
OTHELLO (*to Desdemona*) Come, let us to the castle.
(*To the rest*) News, friends: our wars are done, the Turks
        are drowned.
How does my old acquaintance of this isle?—
Honey, you shall be well desired in Cyprus;
I have found great love amongst them. O my sweet,   200
I prattle out of fashion, and I dote
In mine own comforts!—I prithee, good Iago,

190 powers] F, Q2; power Q1   192.1 *They kiss*] Q (*after* 'be', l. 193); *not in* F   193 discords] F;
discord Q   198 does my] F (do's), Q2; doe our Q1   this] F, Q2; the Q1

188 **Succeeds . . . fate** can possibly ensue
in our unknowable, but predetermined
future
190 **as . . . grow** as we grow older
192 **stops me here** Sanders suggests 'pre-
vents me in my heart'; but Othello probably means that his emotions choke his
organs of speech. In either case *here* can
be gestural, referring to his heart, or may
simply mean 'here and now; at this
point'. For the physiological basis of
Othello's emotion, see Paster, pp. 64–6.
193–4 **discords . . . hearts** As so often in
the period, the musical metaphor (which
Iago develops, ll. 191–2) is complicated by
a recollection of the Latin root of *discord*
and *concord* (*cor* = heart).
195 **set . . . pegs** i.e. untune the instrument
by loosening its strings; Iago probably
quibbles on the bawdy use of *music* as a

term for intercourse and of *peg* as a
word for penis (see Williams, *Dictionary*,
pp. 922–4, 1006–7), thereby threatening
Othello with emasculation.
196 **As . . . am** An ironic backward glance at
'I am not what I am' (1.1.65); several
meanings of *honest* are in play:
'honourable'; 'upright, of good character'; 'frank, truthful, straightforward'.
198 **acquaintance** friends
199 **well desired** much sought after
200 **great love** Perhaps a reminder of the
traditional associations of Cyprus as the
birthplace of the love-goddess, Aphrodite,
and a centre of her cult (see Neill,
'Places', p. 117).
201 **out of fashion** clumsily; inappro-
priately
201–2 **dote . . . comforts** am besotted with
sheer happiness

Go to the bay and disembark my coffers.
Bring thou the master to the citadel;
He is a good one, and his worthiness   205
Does challenge much respect.—Come, Desdemona,
Once more well met at Cyprus!

> *Exeunt Othello and Desdemona followed by all but*
> *Iago and Roderigo*

IAGO (*to a departing attendant*) Do thou meet me presently at
the harbour. (*To Roderigo*) Come hither, if thou be'st
valiant—as they say base men being in love have then a   210
nobility in their natures more than is native to them—list
me: the lieutenant tonight watches on the court of
guard. First, I must tell thee this: Desdemona is directly in
love with him.

RODERIGO With him? Why, 'tis not possible.   215

IAGO Lay thy finger thus, and let thy soul be instructed:
mark me with what violence she first loved the Moor but
for bragging, and telling her fantastical lies. To love him

207.1–2 *Exeunt . . . Roderigo*] *after* F (*Exit Othello and Desdemona.*); *Exit* Q   209 hither] Q;
thither F   213 must . . . this: Desdemona] F; will tell thee, this *Desdemona* Q1; will tell thee
this, *Desdemona* Q2   218 To] F; and will she Q

203 **disembark my coffers** unload my
chests and trunks. Honigmann notes that
Othello 'treats Iago almost as a personal
servant', which perhaps accounts for the
alacrity with which the ensign starts issu-
ing his own orders as soon as Othello is
offstage.
204 **master** ship's captain
206 **challenge** claim, invite (i.e. deserve)
207 **well met at** welcome to
208–9 **thou . . . thou** Since Roderigo is
later instructed to meet Iago at the
citadel (l. 274), Delius is surely right to
suppose that the first *thou* is addressed to a
servant: a context that will make Iago's
switch to the condescending singular
pronoun seem especially insulting to
Roderigo.
210 **base** low-born. Either Iago now feels
confident enough of his power over
Roderigo (who appears to be Iago's social
superior, and is described as a 'gentleman' in F's 'Names of the Actors') to
insult him openly, or this parenthesis may
be (as Honigmann conjectures) an aside.
212 **watches** is on watch-duty
    court of guard A corruption of French

corps de garde, meaning either the 'body of
soldiers on guard', or the guard-house
itself (*OED n.* 1, 2).
213 **directly** completely, unambiguously.
216–61 **Lay . . . minister** In Iago's speeches
here there is an exceptional amount of
variation between F and Q, including a
large number of words and phrases found
only in the former. This may indicate
detailed revision of the passage or (if
memorial contamination is involved)
the slightly greater difficulty involved in
accurately mastering long passages of
prose.
216 **Lay . . . thus** i.e. on his lips. Listed by
Tilley and Dent as a proverb (F239); but in
reality this is the standard gesture for
silence prescribed by classical rhetori-
cians, described by Jonson in *Bartholomew
Fair* (5.6.20) and *Timber* (p. 15) in the
phrase *digito compesce labellum*, and illustrated in John Bulwer's *Chirologia: or
the Natural Language of the Hand and Chi-
ronomia: or, The Art of Manual Rhetoric*
(1644) over the inscription *Tacite* (be
quiet).
217 **violence** excessive ardour (*OED n.* 5)

still for prating? Let not thy discreet heart think it! Her
eye must be fed. And what delight shall she have to look   220
on the devil? When the blood is made dull with the act of
sport, there should be a game to inflame it, and (to give
satiety a fresh appetite) loveliness in favour, sympathy in
years, manners, and beauties—all which the Moor is
defective in. Now, for want of these required conve-   225
niences, her delicate tenderness will find itself abused,
begin to heave the gorge, disrelish and abhor the Moor;
very nature will instruct her in it, and compel her to some
second choice. Now sir, this granted (as it is a most pregnant and unforced position), who stands so eminent in   230
the degree of this fortune, as Cassio does—a knave very
voluble, no further conscionable than in putting on the
mere form of civil and humane seeming for the better
compass of his salt and most hidden loose affection? Why

219 thy] F; the Q   219 it] F; Q2; so QI   222 a game] F, Q2; againe QI   222 and (to give]
after F (and to giue);   and giue Q   223 appetite) loveliness] This edition *after* THEOBALD (appetite,
lovelines);   appetite. Louelinesse F; appetite. Loue lines QI; appetite. Louelines Q2   228 in]
F; to Q   230 eminent] F; eminently Q   fortune] F (Forune), Q]   232 further] F; farder Q
233 humane seeming] F, Q2; hand-seeming QU   234 compass] F; compassing Q   234
most . . . affection] F, Q2;   hidden affections QI   234–5 Why none, why none] F;   *not in* Q

219 **still for prating** for his continual
boasting
discreet judicious
221 **devil** Cf 1.1.87–92.
dull sluggish. The juxtaposition with
inflame is a reminder of the subdued quibble on Greek *moros* (μωρόζ) = 'dull, stupid' and Med. Latin *morus* = 'Moor',
which makes of the union between the
fair Desdemona and the dark Othello a
kind of punningly embodied oxymoron
(= 'bright-dull'). See also 5.2.224, and
cf. 4.3.37.
222 **sport** copulation
a game amorous sport or play (*OED n.*
3b). Q2's preference for the more suggestive F reading is significant; Q's *againe*
(though preferred by most editors) is
weaker and could easily result from either
misreading or aural confusion.
223 **satiety** surfeit, satiation
favour appearance; face
sympathy affinity, similarity
225–6 **required conveniences** necessary
advantages
226 **delicate** fragile, vulnerable.
tenderness youthfulness; soft-hearted-
ness, impressionability; love

abused cheated, deceived
227 **heave the gorge** retch
disrelish find disgusting
227 **very nature** nature itself
229–30 **pregnant** convincing (from OF
preindre = 'to press' and therefore etymologically unrelated to female *pregnancy*,
though the two homonyms were frequently confused).
230 **unforced position** plausible
hypothesis
230–1 **who . . . fortune** who is better
placed to benefit from this turn of events
(so *eminent in the degree* = on so high a
rung of the ladder)
231 **knave** (a) crafty rogue; (b) man of low
birth. Iago's obsessive harping on the
word (ll. 235, 238, 240) reveals his social
resentment against Cassio.
232 **voluble** (a) full of glib eloquence; (b)
inconstant
no . . . than whose conscience does not
extend beyond
233 **humane** courteous
234 **compass** compassing, achieving
salt lecherous
affection passion, lust

none, why none—a slipper and subtle knave, a finder   235
of occasion, that has an eye can stamp and counterfeit
advantages (though true advantage never present itself),
a devilish knave! Besides, the knave is handsome, young,
and hath all those requisites in him that folly and green
minds look after—a pestilent complete knave, and the   240
woman hath found him already.

RODERIGO I cannot believe that in her: she's full of most
blest condition.

IAGO Blest fig's end! The wine she drinks is made of grapes.
If she had been blest, she would never have loved the   245
Moor. Blest pudding! Didst thou not see her paddle with
the palm of his hand? Didst not mark that?

RODERIGO Yes, that I did—but that was but courtesy.

IAGO Lechery, by this hand!—an index and obscure
prologue to the history of lust and foul thoughts. They   250
met so near with their lips that their breaths embraced
together. Villainous thoughts, Roderigo! When these
mutualities so marshal the way, hard at hand comes the
master and main exercise, th'incorporate conclusion.
Pish! But sir, be you ruled by me—I have brought you   255

235 slipper and subtle] F (slipper, and subtle); subtle slippery Q 236 of occasion] F; out of occasions Q has] Q; he's F 237 advantages . . . itself] F, Q2; the true aduantages neuer present themselues Q1 238 a devilish knave] F (A); *not in* Q 239 hath] F; has Q 246 Blest pudding] F; *not in* Q 247 Didst not mark that] F, Q2; *not in* Q1 248 that I did] F; *not in* Q 252 Villainous . . . Roderigo] F; *not in* Q1; villanous thoughts Q2 253 mutualities] Q; mutabilities F hard at hand] F; hand at hand Q 254 master and] F; *not in* Q1; master and the Q2 255 Pish] F; *not in* Q

235 **slipper** shifty, deceitful, insincere (*OED a*. 3)
 subtle crafty (the adjective applied to the serpent who tempts Eve in Genesis)
236 **occasion** opportunity
 stamp coin
240 **complete** consummate; but also a sneer at Cassio's courtliness: 'accomplished'.
241 **found him** found him out, discovered what he's up to (by implication, with pleasure); Honigmann suggests a possible bawdy meaning
244 **fig's end** For *fig* see 1.3.315; *end* = genitalia.
246 **pudding** sausage; slang for 'penis' (see Williams, *Dictionary*, pp. 1106–7).
 paddle toy, play idly

249 **index** table of contents; preface, prologue. Since Iago is explicating a manual gesture, and has just sworn by his own hand, some sort of gestural word-play must also be indicated, punning on the pointing *index*[-*finger*] often used to draw attention to significant passages in early modern books.
253 **mutualities** exchanges of intimacy
254 **main** Probably punning on French *main* to continue (with *hard at hand* and *incorporate*) the word-play on *hand*.
 incorporate (a) bodily; (b) united in one body (like the 'beast with two backs' as Honigmann suggests)
 conclusion See l. 159, and 3.3.429.
255–7 **be . . . upon you** Although Iago has returned to the polite plural form of

from Venice. Watch you tonight. For the command, I'll
lay't upon you: Cassio knows you not; I'll not be far from
you; do you find some occasion to anger Cassio, either by
speaking too loud, or tainting his discipline, or from what
other course you please which the time shall more   260
favourably minister.

RODERIGO Well.

IAGO Sir, he's rash and very sudden in choler, and haply
with his truncheon may strike at you—provoke him that
he may; for even out of that will I cause these of Cyprus   265
to mutiny, whose qualification shall come into no true
taste again but by the displanting of Cassio. So shall you
have a shorter journey to your desires by the means I
shall then have to prefer them; and the impediment most
profitably removed, without the which there were no   270
expectation of our prosperity.

RODERIGO I will do this, if you can bring it to any
opportunity.

IAGO I warrant thee. Meet me by and by at the citadel. I
must fetch his necessaries ashore. Farewell.   275

RODERIGO Adieu.   *Exit*

IAGO

That Cassio loves her, I do well believe't;

256 the command] F; your command Q1; command Q2   260 course] F, Q2; cause Q1
263–4 haply] Q; happely F   with his truncheon] Q; *not in* F   267 taste] F, Q2; trust Q1
again] F (againe); again't Q   270 the which] F; which Q   272 if you] F; if I Q

address, and although *be ruled* need only
mean 'take my advice', a sly irony in
his speech highlights the transformation
in their power-relations that bringing
Roderigo to Cyprus has brought about.

256–7 **For . . . you** This could mean either
'As for taking the lead (in our joint
action), I'll leave it to you' (Honigmann);
or 'I'll arrange for you to be appointed,
given orders' (Bevington); or 'I'll give you
the orders'. The ambiguity is no doubt
calculated.

259 **tainting** impugning; sullying
discipline military skill and experience
261 **minister** furnish, provide
263 **sudden in choler** Either 'impetuous
when roused to anger', or 'quick to
anger'.
haply perhaps

264 **truncheon** officer's baton
266–7 **whose . . . taste** who will only be
properly appeased
267 **displanting** uprooting, supplanting
269 **prefer** advance
271 **prosperity** success; but (as with 'profitably', l. 270) in the context of Iago's
financial exploitation of Roderigo an
ironic play on the commercial sense of the
word is probably present.
272–3 **bring . . . opportunity** create an
opportunity (for me)
274 **I warrant thee** I assure you; you can
depend on it (a colloquial phrase, equivalent to 'you bet' or 'sure thing')
by and by The original meaning of
'immediately' was still current, but the
present-day sense of 'in due course, after
a while' was also well established
275 **his necessaries** i.e. Othello's luggage

That she loves him, 'tis apt and of great credit.
The Moor (howbeit that I endure him not)
Is of a constant, loving, noble nature;   280
And I dare think he'll prove to Desdemona
A most dear husband. Now I do love her too,
Not out of absolute lust (though peradventure
I stand accountant for as great a sin)
But partly led to diet my revenge,   285
For that I do suspect the lusty Moor
Hath leapt into my seat—the thought whereof
Doth, like a poisonous mineral, gnaw my inwards;
And nothing can or shall content my soul
Till I am evened with him, wife for wife;   290
Or, failing so, yet that I put the Moor
At least into a jealousy so strong
That judgement cannot cure—which thing to do,
If this poor trash of Venice, whom I trace
For his quick hunting, stand the putting on,   295

280 loving, noble] F; noble, louing Q   284 accountant] F (accomptant), Q]   285 led] F, Q
(lead)   286 lusty] F; lustfull Q   289 or] F; nor Q   290 evened] F (eeuen'd), Q2; euen
Q1   for wife] Q; for wift F   294 trace] F, Q2; crush Q1; trash STEEVENS, HONIGMANN *and many
editors*

278 **apt ... credit** fitted to the facts and
   entirely credible
279–82 **The   Moor ... husband**   Cf.
   Giraldi, App. C, p. 438.
282 **dear** (a) beloved, cherished; (b) expensive (i.e. she'll pay dearly for her choice)
   Now ... love her Cf. Giraldi, App. C,
   p. 438.
283 **peradventure** Either 'as it happens' or
   'it may be the case that'.
284 **accountant** accountable. Iago probably has in mind the final 'account' of the
   Last Judgement (*OED, account, n.* 8b), but
   the word inevitably resonates with Iago's
   commercial language, and cf. his description of Cassio as a 'counter-caster'
   (1.1.30).
285 **diet** feed
286 **lusty** (a) lustful; (b) vigorous, (sexually)
   energetic
287 **leapt** mounted sexually (Williams,
   Glossary, p. 184, *Dictionary*, pp. 791–3:
   'used originally of farm quadrupeds')
   seat (a) chair set apart for someone in
   authority (standing for here Iago's
   domestic place as master of his own
   household); (b) by extension, a man's

residence or 'place'; (c) saddle (suggesting, with 'leapt', the common equestrian
   metaphor for sex); (d) vulva. Adelman
   suggests that the bawdy meaning is capable (like some other passages in the play)
   of a homosexual construction, so that it is
   as if Iago's own body is violated by the
   Moor's adultery (p. 129).
288 **mineral** Cf. 1.2.74.
290 **wife for wife** Honigmann compares
   Exodus 21: 23–4, the so-called *lex talionis*
   (law of revenge): 'and if any mischief follow, then thou shalt give life for life, eye
   for eye, tooth for tooth'.
294 **trash** worthless person
294–5 **trace ... hunting** track, in order to
   profit from his energetic pursuit (of Desdemona); Steevens may have been right
   to conjecture that the original reading
   was the punning 'trash' (= control with a
   leash) which seems to fit the hunting
   metaphor more neatly. Misreading would
   then readily account for Q's *crush*, and
   perhaps also for *trace* (often spelt 'trase').
295 **putting on** Perhaps combining 'laying
   on the scent' (*OED, put, v.*[1] 47 l (*a*)) with
   'urging on' (*OED, put, v.*[1] 47 h).

I'll have our Michael Cassio on the hip,
Abuse him to the Moor in the rank garb
(For I fear Cassio with my nightcap too),
Make the Moor thank me, love me, and reward me
For making him egregiously an ass   300
And practising upon his peace and quiet
Even to madness. 'Tis here, but yet confused:
Knavery's plain face is never seen till used.   *Exit*

2.2   *Enter Othello's herald with a proclamation*

HERALD (*reads*) 'It is Othello's pleasure, our noble and
valiant general, that, upon certain tidings now arrived,
importing the mere perdition of the Turkish fleet, every
man put himself into triumph: some to dance, some to
make bonfires, each man to what sport and revels his   5
addiction leads him; for, besides these beneficial news,
it is the celebration of his nuptial.'—So much was his
pleasure should be proclaimed. All offices are open and
there is full liberty of feasting from this present hour of

---

297 rank] Q; right F   298 nightcap] Q; Night-Cape F
    2.2] F (*Scena Secunda*); *not in* Q   0.1 *Othello's herald with*] F; *a Gentleman reading* Q   1 HER-
ALD] F; *not in* Q   *reads*] *after* Q ('*reading*', l. 0.1); *not in* F   3 every] F; that euery Q   4–5 to
make] F; make Q   6 addiction] Q2; addition F; minde Q1   7 nuptial] F; Nuptialls Q   9 of
feasting] F; *not in* Q

---

296 **on the hip** ready to give him a
decisive fall (a wrestling term). Cf. Dent
H474.
297 **rank**   gross, offensive; corrupt;
lascivious.
    garb manner
298 **nightcap** Bawdy metonym for 'wife'. It
is difficult to know if F's *Night-Cape* represents a genuine variant or not, since *cape*
could be a variant spelling for *cap* (which
in any case has the same etymological origin). *OED* gives *night-cape* as an expression for 'wife' (*night, n.* 14) but without
citing any examples. It is easy to see how a
wife might be described as a 'night-cape'
in which a man wraps himself for
warmth; on the other hand, as Williams
shows (*Dictionary*, pp. 201–2), the vaginal
associations of *caps* and *hats* were well
established. Since *cap* can also be a 'cap of
maintenance' or 'cap of office' (*OED n.*
4g) the Q reading fits more neatly with the

social resentments of the speech (cf. *seat*,
l. 287).
301 **practising upon** plotting against
302 **here** i.e. in his head. An implied stage
direction.
303 **plain** Iago equivocates ironically between 'frank, candid' and 'undisguised,
true'.
2.2.2 **upon** because of, in response to
    certain sure, reliable
3 **importing** concerning
    mere perdition absolute destruction
4 **put . . . triumph** prepare himself for
public celebration
6 **addiction** inclination. While F's 'addition' (= rank) is possible, Q's 'mind'
(= wish), makes it likely that the Q2 emendation was well founded.
8 **offices** rooms in a house, castle, or palace
devoted to domestic services: e.g. kitchens, pantries, butteries, cellars, etc.
(*OED n.* 9a).

five till the bell have told eleven. Heaven bless the isle of　　10
Cyprus and our noble general, Othello!　　　　　　　*Exit*

2.3　　*Enter Othello, Desdemona, Cassio, and attendants*

OTHELLO
Good Michael, look you to the guard tonight.
Let's teach ourselves that honourable stop
Not to out-sport discretion.

CASSIO
Iago hath direction what to do;
But notwithstanding, with my personal eye　　　　　　5
Will I look to't.

OTHELLO　　　　　　Iago is most honest.
Michael, goodnight. Tomorrow with your earliest,
Let me have speech with you.—Come, my dear love,
The purchase made, the fruits are to ensue:
That profit's yet to come 'tween me and you.　　　　10
Good night.　　　　　　　　　*Exeunt all but Cassio*
　　　　Enter Iago

CASSIO
Welcome, Iago. We must to the watch.

IAGO　Not this hour, lieutenant: 'tis not yet ten o'th' clock.
Our general cast us thus early for the love of his
Desdemona—who let us not therefore blame: he hath　　15
not yet made wanton the night with her, and she is sport
for Jove.

CASSIO　She's a most exquisite lady.

10 have] F; hath Q　Heaven bless] Q; Blesse F　11 *Exit*] F; *not in* Q
　　2.3] CAPELL (*after* THEOBALD, 'The Castle'); *not marked in* F, Q　0.1 *Enter . . . attendants*] F;
Enter Othello, Cassio, and Desdemona. Q　2 that] F, Q2; the Q1　4 direction] F, Q2; directed
Q1　10 That] F, Q2; The Q1　'tween] F; twixt Q　11 *Exeunt . . . Cassio*] This edition (*after* Q,
'*Exit* Othello *and* Desdemona.'); *Exit.* F　13 o'th' clock] F; aclock Q

10 **told** Presumably = 'counted', but also a
　　possible spelling for 'tolled'.
2.3.2 stop restraint
　3 **out-sport** carry revelry beyond the
　　bounds of. The only use of this apparent
　　coinage cited in *OED*.
　7 **with your earliest** at your earliest
　　convenience
　9 **purchase . . . ensue** Usually taken to
　　indicate that the marriage has not yet
　　been consummated (cf. l. 16); but it might
　　refer more generally to the fulfilment of
　　their love.

13 **Not this hour** not for an hour yet
14 **cast** dismissed (*OED v.* 27)
16 **made . . . night** Usually understood to
　　mean 'taken her virginity', but Iago
　　might mean only that Othello and
　　Desdemona have not yet shared a whole
　　night of pleasure.
　　sport Cf. 2.1.222.
17 **Jove** Classical mythology is full of stories
　　of Jupiter's amours with mortal
　　women.
18 **exquisite** of consummate excellence and
　　beauty. The suavely accomplished Cassio

IAGO And, I'll warrant her, full of game.

CASSIO Indeed she's a most fresh and delicate creature.   20

IAGO What an eye she has! Methinks it sounds a parley to provocation.

CASSIO An inviting eye—and yet methinks right modest.

IAGO And when she speaks, is't not an alarum to love?

CASSIO She is indeed perfection.   25

IAGO Well, happiness to their sheets! Come, lieutenant, I have a stoup of wine, and near without are a brace of Cyprus gallants that would fain have a measure to the health of black Othello.

CASSIO Not tonight, good Iago: I have very poor and un-   30
happy brains for drinking. I could well wish courtesy would invent some other custom of entertainment.

IAGO O, they are our friends! But one cup—I'll drink for you.

CASSIO I have drunk but one cup tonight—and that was   35
craftily qualified too—and behold what innovation it makes here. I am infortunate in the infirmity, and dare not task my weakness with any more.

IAGO What, man? 'Tis a night of revels; the gallants desire it.   40

CASSIO Where are they?

IAGO

Here at the door. I pray you call them in.

CASSIO I'll do't, but it dislikes me.   *Exit*

---

21 to] F; of Q   24 is't not an alarum] F (Is it); tis an alarme Q   25 She] F, Q2; It QI
27 near] F (neere); heere Q   29 black] F; the blacke Q   35 have] F; ha Q   37 infortunate]
F; vnfortunate Q

tries to deflect the bawdy suggestiveness of Iago's praise.

19 **game** amorous sport. Cf. also 'daughters of the game' = prostitutes (*Troilus*, 4.6.64).

21–2 **sounds . . . provocation**   Like 'alarum' (l. 22) this metaphor draws on the familiar erotic vocabulary of warfare: Desdemona's eye is like a trumpet summoning sexual excitement (*provocation*) to discuss terms for surrender.

24 **alarum** call to arms

27 **stoup** tankard or flagon

brace pair

28–9 **would . . . health** want a measure [of wine] to toast the health

30–1 **I . . . drinking** I have a bad head for liquor (*unhappy* = unfortunate)

32 **entertainment** amusement, recreation; hospitality

36 **qualified** diluted
innovation revolution, topsy-turveydom

37 **here** Cf. 2.1.302.

38 **task** test

43 **dislikes me** makes me unhappy

IAGO

If I can fasten but one cup upon him,
With that which he hath drunk tonight already,   45
He'll be as full of quarrel and offence
As my young mistress' dog. Now my sick fool Roderigo,
Whom love hath turned almost the wrong side out,
To Desdemona hath tonight caroused
Potations pottle-deep; and he's to watch.   50
Three else of Cyprus—noble, swelling spirits
That hold their honours in a wary distance,
The very elements of this warlike isle—
Have I tonight flustered with flowing cups,
And they watch too. Now 'mongst this flock of
    drunkards   55
Am I to put our Cassio in some action
That may offend the isle. But here they come.
    Enter Cassio, Montano, and Gentlemen
If consequence do but approve my dream,
My boat sails freely, both with wind and stream.

CASSIO

Fore God, they have given me a rouse already.   60

MONTANO

Good faith, a little one—not past a pint,
As I am a soldier!

IAGO   Some wine, ho!
    (*Sings*)   And let me the cannikin clink, clink,
                     And let me the cannikin clink.

48 hath] F; has Q   out] F; outward Q   50 watch. | Three] F; watch∧ | ~ Q1; watch: | ~ Q2
51 else] F; lads Q   52 honours] F; honour Q   55 they watch] F; the watch Q   56 Am I] F; I
am Q   to put] Q; put to F   57.1 *Enter . . . Gentlemen*] F; *Enter* Montanio, Cassio, *and others.* Q
(*after* 'isle', *l.* 57)   60 God] Q; heauen F   63 *Sings*] ROWE; *not in* F, Q   63–7 And . . . drink]
in italic F, Q   64 clink] F; *clinke, clinke* Q

44 **fasten . . . upon** force . . . upon
46 **full . . . offence** ready to quarrel or take
    offence
50 **pottle** half-gallon (2.25 litre) container
51 **Three else** three other men
    swelling proud, haughty, arrogant
52 **hold . . . distance** are careful to keep
    their honour out of reach (of potential
    slanderers), i.e. would be quick to take
    offence
53 **elements** essential components; i.e.
    'exactly the sort of characters who make
    this island the warlike place it is'.

56 **put . . . action** push our friend Cassio
    into some fight
58 **If . . . dream** if the outcome only proves
    my hopes true
59 **My . . . stream** Cf. Dent W429, 'Sail
    with the wind and tide'.
60 **rouse** full draught of liquor
63–7 **And . . . drink** Probably a popular
    drinking song: Hart cites fragments of a
    number of similar ditties. For possible
    musical settings, see App. D (ii).
63 **cannikin** a drinking vessel (diminutive of
    can)

A soldier's a man;   65
O, man's life's but a span—
Why then let a soldier drink.
Some wine, boys!
CASSIO   Fore God, an excellent song!
IAGO I learned it in England, where indeed they are most
potent in potting. Your Dane, your German, and your   70
swag-bellied Hollander—drink, ho!—are nothing to
your English.
CASSIO Is your Englishman so exquisite in his drinking?
IAGO Why, he drinks you with facility your Dane dead
drunk; he sweats not to overthrow your Almain; he   75
gives your Hollander a vomit ere the next pottle can be
filled.
CASSIO To the health of our general!
MONTANO I am for it, lieutenant; and I'll do you justice.
IAGO O sweet England!   80
(*Sings*)   King Stephen was and a worthy peer,
His breeches cost him but a crown,

---

66 O, man's] F; *a* Q   68 God] Q1; Heauen F, Q2   73 Englishman] Q; Englishmen F   exquisite] F, Q2; expert Q1   81 *Sings*] ROWE; *not in* F, Q   81–8 King . . . thee] *in italic* F, Q1 (*except l. 81*), Q2   81 and a] F, Q2; *a* Q1

---

66 **man's . . . span** Proverbial (Dent L251) from Psalms 39: 6, 'thou hast made my days as it were a span long'. *Span* = very short time (lit. the span of a hand).

69–76 **England . . . Hollander** A nudging in-joke directed at the audience. For the stereotype of Danish drunkenness, see *Hamlet* Add. Pass. B.1–6 (1.4.19–24). Germans and Dutch were also proverbially heavy drinkers, as were the English ('The Dutchman drinks his buttons off, the English doublet and all away', Tilley D655; G86, 'The German drinks away his sorrow . . .'; and cf. D656); though, as Sanders points out, English drunkenness was often blamed on 'the bad habits brought back by soldiers returning from the wars in the Netherlands'.

70 **potting** drinking

71 **swag-bellied** having a great swaying paunch

73 **exquisite** accomplished; but probably also with the additional ironic sense of 'dainty' or 'refined'

74 **drinks you** Ethic dative (see 1.1.49), here equivalent to 'let me tell you'.

75 **Almain** German

81–8 **King . . . thee** Adapted from stanza 7 of the ballad variously called 'Bell my wife' or 'Take thy old cloak about thee', first printed in Percy's *Reliques of Old English Poetry* (1765), ii. 7, but already paraphrased in Robert Greene's attack on courtly ambition and extravagance, *A quip for an upstart courtier* (1592), sig. C3ᵛ. The ballad consists of an argument between a yeoman, who wants to abandon his farm to become a courtier, and his wife (the speaker of this stanza), who mocks his pride. The extravagant cost of ambitious dressing above one's station (which the sumptuary laws passed by successive Tudor monarchs vainly sought to curb) is a recurrent theme of 16th- and 17th-century satire; here it may be used to reflect Iago's resentment of the courtly Cassio. See App. D (ii) for possible settings and sources.

81 **and** Sometimes introduced as a meaningless extra syllable to fill out the metre; cf. *Twelfth Night*, 5.1.385, 'When that I was and a little tiny boy'.

He held them sixpence all too dear,
    With that he called the tailor lown.
He was a wight of high renown,   85
    And thou art but of low degree:
'Tis pride that pulls the country down,
    Then take thy old cloak about thee.
Some wine, ho!

CASSIO 'Fore God, this is a more exquisite song than the   90
other!

IAGO Will you hear't again?

CASSIO No, for I hold him to be unworthy of his place
that does those things. Well, God's above all, and there
be souls must be saved, and there be souls must not be   95
saved.

IAGO It's true, good lieutenant.

CASSIO For mine own part—no offence to the general, nor
any man of quality—I hope to be saved.

IAGO And so do I too, lieutenant.   100

CASSIO Ay; but, by your leave, not before me: the lieutenant
is to be saved before the ensign. Let's have no more of
this: let's to our affairs. God forgive us our sins!
Gentlemen, let's look to our business. Do not think,
gentlemen, I am drunk: this is my ensign; this is my right   105
hand, and this is my left. I am not drunk now: I can
stand well enough, and I speak well enough.

GENTLEMEN Excellent well.

---

88 Then] Q; *And* F   thy] F; *thine* Q   old] Q2 (*auld*); *awl'd* F; *owd* Q1   90 'Fore God] Q1;
Why F, Q2   93 to be] F; *not in* Q   94 God's] Q1; heau'ns F, Q2 (*Heauen's*)   95 must] F; *that
must* Q   95–6 and . . . not be saved] F; *not in* Q   100 too] F; *not in* Q   103 God] Q1; *not in* F,
Q2   106 left] F; left hand Q   107 I speak] F; speake Q   108 GENTLEMEN] F (*Gent.*); *All.* Q

84 **lown** Alternative spelling of the more
common *loon* = idler, rogue, base fellow;
since both forms are now obsolete, there
seems no point in disturbing the rhyme
for a confusing semi-modernization.

90 **exquisite** Cassio's drunkenness is reflected in his clumsily obsessive repetition of
this adjective.

93–7 **place . . . lieutenant** Ironically
Cassio hits precisely on the motive of
Iago's plot to prove him unworthy of his
place (rank), so Iago's 'good lieutenant'
will be heavily loaded.

94 **does those things** Cassio may be referring to the vices of conspicuous consumption satirized in the song, or to the
unseemliness of drunken singing whilst
on watch; but he is probably too drunk to
know quite what he means.
God's above all Proverbial (Dent H348).

101 **not before me** Arguments about precedence were frequent causes of duelling in
this period. Cassio becomes irrationally
heated and aggressive at this point, before
checking himself on 'Let's have no more
of this.'

CASSIO Why, very well then—you must not think, then,
that I am drunk. *Exit* 110
MONTANO
To th' platform, masters, come; let's set the watch.
IAGO
You see this fellow that is gone before?
He's a soldier fit to stand by Caesar
And give direction; and do but see his vice—
'Tis to his virtue a just equinox, 115
The one as long as th'other. 'Tis pity of him:
I fear the trust Othello puts him in,
On some odd time of his infirmity,
Will shake this island.
MONTANO But is he often thus?
IAGO
'Tis evermore the prologue to his sleep: 120
He'll watch the horologe a double set
If drink rock not his cradle.
MONTANO It were well
The general were put in mind of it.
Perhaps he sees it not, or his good nature
Prizes the virtue that appears in Cassio, 125
And looks not on his evils: is not this true?
Enter Roderigo
IAGO (*aside to Roderigo*)
How now, Roderigo?
I pray you, after the lieutenant go. *Exit Roderigo*

109 Why] F, Q2; *not in* Q1   think, then] F, Q2; thinke Q1   117 puts] F; put Q   120 the] Q; his F   125 Prizes the virtue] F; Praises the vertues Q1; Praises the vertue Q2   126 looks] F (lookes), Q2; looke Q1   126.1 *Enter Roderigo*] F; *after* 'How now Roderigo' (l. 127) Q   128 *Exit Roderigo*] Q; *not in* F

111 **platform** i.e. gun-platform
set the watch mount guard
113 **fit . . . Caesar** worthy to be ranked with Caesar; or, to stand alongside him as his second-in-command
115 **just equinox** exact and equal counterpart
117 **trust . . . puts** The Q reading (*put*) is attractive here, since it appears to make Iago refer specifically to the disputed lieutenancy (*trust* = office, position of trust; *OED n.* 5d), rather than to a more general confidence in his subordinate.

118 **On . . . infirmity** at some unpredictable moment when he is overcome by his weakness
121 **He'll . . . set** stay awake for two complete revolutions of the clock
127 *aside to Roderigo* Capell's suggested direction is almost certainly correct, since the success of Iago's explanation of the brawl to Othello (ll. 216–37) depends on Montano's being ignorant of the ensign's manipulation of Roderigo.

MONTANO

    And 'tis great pity that the noble Moor

    Should hazard such a place as his own second   130

    With one of an ingraft infirmity:

    It were an honest action to say so

    To the Moor.

IAGO   Not I, for this fair island!

    I do love Cassio well, and would do much

    To cure him of this evil—

        Voices within cry 'Help! Help!'

                    But hark, what noise?   135

      Enter Cassio driving in Roderigo

CASSIO 'Swounds, you rogue, you rascal!

MONTANO What's the matter, lieutenant?

CASSIO A knave teach me my duty? I'll beat the knave into a

    twiggen bottle!

RODERIGO Beat me?   140

CASSIO Dost thou prate, rogue?

MONTANO Nay, good lieutenant! I pray you, sir, hold your

    hand.

CASSIO Let me go, sir, or I'll knock you o'er the mazard.

MONTANO Come, come, you're drunk.   145

CASSIO Drunk?

---

133 Not] F, Q2; Nor Q1   135 *Voices . . . Help!*] Q ('*Helpe, helpe, within.*' *after* 'doe much'); *not in* F   135.1 *driving in*] Q; *pursuing* F   136 'Swounds] Q1 (Zouns); *not in* F, Q2   138 duty? I'll] F; duty: but I'le Q   139 twiggen] F; wicker Q   142 Nay] F; *not in* Q I pray you] F; pray Q

130 **such . . . second** such an (important) office as that of his own deputy. Underlying Montano's concern is the fact that military manuals of the time identified the lieutenant as a 'friendly mediator to the captain for the inferior officers' and laid particular stress on his duty of 'pacification of discords and difference among the soldiers' (*Stratioticos*, sig. P1^v; Davies, *Art of War*, sig. N4).

131 **ingraft** engrafted, ingrained

132 **honest** commendable. Iago's shocked response implies his allegiance to a higher kind of 'honesty'.

135.1 **driving in** Honigmann argues that the unusual wording of the Q direction indicates its authorial provenance: cf. *1 Henry VI*, 1.7.0.1–2 ('*Enter Joan . . . driving Englishmen before her*') and *Tem-*

pest 5.1.258.1 ('*Enter Ariel, driving in Caliban*'); but the formula occurs outside Shakespeare, as McMillin points out (Q, p. 13).

138 **beat the knave** Honigmann notes that such beatings, administered to servants and other social inferiors (cf. *knave*), were a stock comic routine.

139 **twiggen bottle** bundle of twigs or wicker (*OED*, *bottle*, n.^{3}), i.e. Cassio will smash him to pieces; or perhaps (as Ridley et al. suggest) a wicker-covered flask, like a chianti bottle, in reference to the stripes on his back.

144 **mazard** mazer or drinking-bowl; but jocularly applied (as in *Hamlet*, 5.1.87) to the head (perhaps in reference to the pagan custom of using skulls for this purpose).

They fight
IAGO (*aside to Roderigo*)
  Away, I say! Go out and cry 'a mutiny!'   *Exit Roderigo*
  Nay, good lieutenant! God's will, gentlemen!
  Help, ho! Lieutenant! Sir Montano! Sir!
    Montano is wounded
  Help, masters! Here's a goodly watch indeed!   150
    A bell rings
  Who's that which rings the bell? Diablo!—Ho!
  The town will rise. God's will, lieutenant, hold!
  You'll be ashamed for ever!
    Enter Othello, and attendants with weapons
OTHELLO What is the matter here?
MONTANO 'Swounds, I bleed still!   155
  I am hurt to th' death.
  (*Lunging at Cassio*)   He dies!
OTHELLO   Hold, for your lives!
IAGO
  Hold, ho! Lieutenant! Sir Montano! Gentlemen!

146.1 *They fight*] Q; *not in* F   147 *Exit Roderigo*] Q2; *not in* F, Q1   148 God's will] Q; Alas F
149 Lieutenant! Sir Montano! Sir!] Q1 (Leiutenant: Sir *Montanio*, sir,); Lieutenant. Sir *Montano*: F; Leiutenant: Sir, Montanio, sir, Q2; Lieutenant, sir! Montano, sir! SANDERS; Lieu-tenant! sir—Montano—sir—HONIGMANN   149.1 *Montano is wounded*] This edition; *not in* F, Q
150.1 *A bell rings*] Q2; '*A bell rung.*' *after* 'mutiny' Q1; *not in* F   151 which] F; that Q   152 God's . . . hold] Q1; Fie, fie, Lieutenant F; fie, fie, Leiutenant, hold Q2   153 You'll be ashamed] F; You will be sham'd Q   153.1 *Enter . . . attendants*] F; *Enter . . . Gentlemen.* Q   *with weapons*] Q; *not in* F   155 'Swounds] Q1 (Zouns); *not in* F, Q2   156 *Lunging at Cassio*] CAPELL (*subs.*); *not in* F, Q   He dies] F; *not in* Q1; *he faints.* Q2 (*as stage direction*)

---

147 **mutiny** riot; revolt against authority
150.1 **bell** Church bells were customarily rung as a public alarm.
151 **Diablo** devil (Spanish). It is interesting that Iago, with his Spanish name, is the only character in Shakespeare to use this oath.
152 **rise** i.e. in rebellion; riot
153–6 **You'll . . . lives** This edition assumes that *He dies* was inadvertently omitted from 154 in Q (which would explain its ending in a colon). It may be, of course, that Malone was correct in supposing that these words were simply added to F in order to compensate metrically for the removal of Q's *Zouns*; and they seem to have puzzled the editor of Q2, who having apparently interpreted them as a stage direction, but observing that Montano does not in fact die, substituted the direc-

tion *he faints*. Rizvi argues that the words are indeed a stage direction, but that they represent a false start which Shakespeare intended to cancel (p. 339). However (as Honigmann points out), the words can be made to fit the metre even if the Q oath is restored, and if they are taken to signal a fresh attack on Cassio, they motivate Othello's and Iago's hasty interventions in the following lines in a way that Q fails to do. This edition treats l. 154 as amphibious, rather than as completing 153 (as Malone's conjecture would suggest).

153 **ashamed** Here, evidently, meaning 'exposed to shame' as well as 'filled with shame'.

157 **Sir Montano** The F and Q punctuation suggests Iago uses 'Sir Montano' as a respectful mode of address, equivalent to Italian '*Ser* Montano'.

Have you forgot all sense of place and duty?
Hold! The general speaks to you: hold, for shame!

OTHELLO

Why, how now! Ho! From whence ariseth this?   160
Are we turned Turks, and to ourselves do that
Which Heaven hath forbid the Ottomites?
For Christian shame, put by this barbarous brawl!
He that stirs next to carve for his own rage
Holds his soul light: he dies upon his motion.   165
Silence that dreadful bell; it frights the isle
From her propriety. What is the matter, masters?
Honest Iago, that looks dead with grieving,
Speak: who began this?—On thy love I charge thee!

IAGO

I do not know. Friends all, but now, even now,   170
In quarter and in terms like bride and groom
Divesting them for bed; and then but now,

---

158 sense of place] HANMER; place of sense F, Q   159 hold, for] F (hold for); hold, hold, for Q
160 ariseth] F; arises Q   162 hath] F; has Q   163 For] F, Q2; forth Q1   164 for] F; to Q

---

158 **sense of place** The F and Q reading
'place of sense' can be justified as meaning either 'dignity derived from office'
(Sanders), or 'position of common sense
and respect' (Oxford), or as approximating to 'the ordinary decencies'
(Riverside). However, the construction
(though it seems to have presented no difficulty to the Q2 editor) seems strained;
and since (as Sanders concedes) inversion
errors of this kind are not uncommon,
Hanmer's emendation is persuasive (cf.
4.2.54, *scorn of time*). Errors of this sort
give support to the notion that a common
manuscript lies somewhere behind Q and
F (see App. B, pp. 413–14, 416 n. 3,
422–3).

161–3 **turned   Turks . . . barbarous**
Strictly speaking to *turn Turk* meant to
convert to Islam; but in common
idiomatic usage (Dent T609) it could
mean simply 'betray', 'renege' or (as
here) exhibit the barbarous behaviour
attributed to Turks. In the mouth of a
Moor-turned-Christian who will himself
metaphorically 'turn Turk' at the end of
the play (5.2.351–5) the phrase is clearly

ironic. A similar irony invests *barbarous*
with its echo of Iago's 'Barbary horse'
(1.1.111) and 'erring barbarian'
(1.3.348–9).

161–2 **that . . . Ottomites** i.e. killing each
other in the way that the heaven-sent
storm has prevented the Turks from
killing them. Lawrence Danson, however,
suggests a reference to the 'widely
known' injunction in the Koran 'against
internecine strife amongst the faithful';
see his 'England, Islam, and the
Mediterranean World', *JEMCS* 2 (2002),
1–25 (pp. 11–12).

164 **carve . . . rage** Othello literalizes the
proverbial expression 'To carve for
oneself', meaning 'to please (or help)
oneself'; he means 'satisfy his personal
outrage by stabbing as he pleases'.

165 **light** of little account
    upon his motion the instant he moves

166 **dreadful** terrifying, filling with dread

167 **propriety** proper or natural condition
    (of peace)

171 **quarter** relations with, or conduct
    towards another (*OED n.* 17a)

172 **Divesting them** undressing

As if some planet had unwitted men,
Swords out, and tilting one at other's breasts
In opposition bloody. I cannot speak   175
Any beginning to this peevish odds;
And would in action glorious I had lost
Those legs that brought me to a part of it!

OTHELLO
How comes it, Michael, you are thus forgot?

CASSIO
I pray you pardon me, I cannot speak.   180

OTHELLO
Worthy Montano, you were wont be civil;
The gravity and stillness of your youth
The world hath noted; and your name is great
In mouths of wisest censure. What's the matter,
That you unlace your reputation thus,   185
And spend your rich opinion for the name
Of a night-brawler? Give me answer to it.

MONTANO
Worthy Othello, I am hurt to danger:
Your officer Iago can inform you—
While I spare speech, which something now offends
        me—   190
Of all that I do know; nor know I aught
By me that's said or done amiss this night—
Unless self-charity be sometimes a vice,
And to defend ourselves it be a sin

---

174 breasts] F; breast Q   178 Those] F, Q2; These Q1   179 comes . . . are] F; came . . . were Q   181 wont be] Q; wont to be F   184 mouths] F, Q2; men Q1   193 sometimes] F; sometime Q

---

173 **unwitted** driven mad (only use cited in OED). According to astrological doctrine not only the moon but other planets were capable of an influence that could unhinge the mind.
175 **opposition** combat
176 **peevish** foolish, mad; malignant; headstrong
    odds strife
178 **to . . . it** to take part in it
181 **were wont be** have always been
    civil well-behaved, civilized; i.e. exhibiting those qualities proper to citizens of a well-ordered state. Since the *civil* is con-

strued as the opposite of the *barbarous* there is a calculated irony in making the man whom Iago has dismissed as an 'erring barbarian' (1.3.348–9) the mouthpiece of civility (cf. ll. 161–3, and 4.1.59–60).
182 **stillness** quietness of temper
184 **censure** judgement
185 **unlace** open the purse strings of
186 **spend . . . opinion** squander the high esteem in which you are held
190 **something . . . me** causes me some pain at the moment
193 **self-charity** care for oneself

When violence assails us.

OTHELLO　　　　　　　　　　Now, by heaven,　　　　195
My blood begins my safer guides to rule,
And passion, having my best judgement collied,
Assays to lead the way. 'Swounds, if I stir,
Or do but lift this arm, the best of you
Shall sink in my rebuke. Give me to know　　　200
How this foul rout began, who set it on,
And he that is approved in this offence—
Though he had twinned with me, both at a birth—
Shall lose me. What, in a town of war
Yet wild, the people's hearts brim-full of fear,　　　205
To manage private and domestic quarrel?
In night, and on the court and guard of safety?
'Tis monstrous! Iago, who began't?

MONTANO

If, partially affined or leagued in office,
Thou dost deliver more or less than truth,　　　210

---

197 collied] F; coold Q　198 'Swounds . . . stir] Q1 (Zouns); If I once stir F, Q2　206 quarrel]
F; quarrels Q　207 court and guard of] F, Q; court of guard and THEOBALD　208 began't] F;
began Q　209 partially] F; partiality Q　leagued] POPE; league F, Q

196 **blood** temper
197 **collied** darkened, blackened (cf. 'collied
night', *Dream*, 1.1.145); but punning on
'choler' (anger; or, one of the four
humours of the body thought to produce
feelings of anger). An early instance of a
train of images whose cumulative effect
is to 'racialize' Othello's impassioned
behaviour. For the physiological basis of
such blackening from the fiery heat of
'choler', see Paster, and Floyd-Wilson,
pp. 36–41, 69–70, 78–86.
200 **sink** fall
　　rebuke violent blow (given in
reproof)
201 **rout** riot
202 **approved in** proved guilty of
204 **town of war** garrison town (cf. *Henry
V*, 2.4.7)
205 **wild** violently excited, out of control,
chaotic. A kind of oxymoron is involved,
since *wildness* was a property of the
uncivil world, the barbarous 'wilderness',
beyond the margins of the urban *polis*.
206 **manage** conduct. A neat subdued quibble is involved, since one could 'manage'
(= wield) weapons as well as domestic

matters (the word is etymologically
related to French *ménage* = household).
　　domestic internal
207 **on . . . safety** *Court* is presumably short
for 'court of guard', and the whole phrase
means 'here in the guard-house and during the very watch meant to secure the
safety of the city'. Editors understandably
find Theobald's transposition to 'court of
guard and safety' tempting in the light of
2.1.212; it assumes a common error in
the copy for F and Q, but a similar transposition occurs in both texts at l. 158.
However, 'and safety' seems an unsatis-
factorily vague construction.
208 **monstrous** The trisyllabic pronunciation (*monsterous*) required by the metre
will help to alert a modern audience to the
stronger sense of the word, which means
not merely 'outrageous' but 'unnatural',
i.e. what one might expect of monsters,
like those creatures who populate the
wilderness of Othello's travel narrative
(1.3.143–5).
209 **partially . . . office** made partial [to
Cassio] by any ties of affinity or allied by
your military positions

Thou art no soldier.

IAGO   Touch me not so near—
I had rather have this tongue cut from my mouth
Than it should do offence to Michael Cassio;
Yet I persuade myself to speak the truth
Shall nothing wrong him. This it is, general: 215
Montano and myself being in speech,
There comes a fellow crying out for help,
And Cassio following with determined sword
To execute upon him. Sir, this gentleman
Steps in to Cassio and entreats his pause;   220
Myself the crying fellow did pursue,
Lest by his clamour (as it so fell out)
The town might fall in fright. He, swift of foot,
Outran my purpose; and I returned then, rather
For that I heard the clink and fall of swords   225
And Cassio high in oath, which till tonight
I ne'er might say before. When I came back—
For this was brief—I found them close together
At blow and thrust, even as again they were
When you yourself did part them.   230
More of this matter cannot I report.
But men are men: the best sometimes forget.
Though Cassio did some little wrong to him,
As men in rage strike those that wish them best,
Yet surely Cassio, I believe, received   235
From him that fled some strange indignity,

212 cut from] F; out from Q1; out of Q2   215 This] F; Thus Q   218 following with] POPE;
following him with F, Q   224 then, rather] F (then rather); the rather Q   226 oath] F, Q2;
oaths Q1   227 say] F, Q2; see Q1   231 cannot I] F; can I not Q

211 **Touch . . . near** be careful not to
     wound my honour so intimately
218 **following with** F's and Q's *him* is both
     redundant and extra-metrical, so Pope
     was almost certainly right to assume it
     had been accidentally imported from the
     following line.
219 **execute** use
220 **entreats his pause** begs him to stop
222 **as . . . out** as did indeed happen
224–5 **rather . . . that** all the sooner
     because

226 **high** loud
230 **When . . . them** The short line marks a
     dramatic pause for breath at the end of
     Iago's narrative.
232 **men . . . forget** Proverbial: see Dent
     M541, and B316.1 ('The best go astray').
233 **him** Montano
234 **As . . . best** Apparently not an actual
     proverb, but characteristic of the senten-
     tious way of speaking by which 'honest'
     Iago mimics the voice of common
     wisdom.

Which patience could not pass.
OTHELLO   I know, Iago,
Thy honesty and love doth mince this matter,
Making it light to Cassio.—Cassio, I love thee;
But never more be officer of mine.   240

Enter Desdemona attended

Look if my gentle love be not raised up!
I'll make thee an example.
DESDEMONA
What is the matter, dear?
OTHELLO   All's well now, sweeting:
Come away to bed. (*To Montano*) Sir, for your hurts
Myself will be your surgeon. Lead him off.   245

Montano is led off

Iago, look with care about the town,
And silence those whom this vile brawl distracted.
Come, Desdemona: 'tis the soldier's life
To have their balmy slumbers waked with strife.

Exeunt all but Iago and Cassio

IAGO What, are you hurt, lieutenant?   250
CASSIO Ay, past all surgery.
IAGO Marry, God forbid!
CASSIO Reputation, reputation, reputation! O, I have lost
my reputation. I have lost the immortal part of myself,
and what remains is bestial. My reputation, Iago, my   255
reputation!

240.1 *Enter . . . attended*] F; *Enter* Desdemona, *with others.* Q   243 dear] F; *not in* Q   now]
Q; *not in* F   245 Lead him off] F, Q; *as stage direction* MALONE *conj.*   245.1 *Montano . . . off*]
CAPELL; *not in* F, Q   249.1 *Exeunt . . . Cassio*] *after* Q ('*Exit Moore,* Desdemona, *and attendants.*'
after 'Lieutenant', *l.* 250); *Exit.* F   252 Marry, God] Q1 (Mary); Marry Heauen F, Q2 (Mary)
253 reputation! O] F (Reputation: Oh); *not in* Q   254 part] F; part sir Q

---

237 **pass** overlook
238 **mince** make light of. The phrase is
    proverbial (Dent M755).
239 **Making . . . to Cassio** making it
    appear of less importance so far as Cassio
    is concerned
240 **But . . . mine** Cf. Giraldi, App. C,
    p. 439.
254–5 **immortal . . . bestial** The *immortal
    part* would normally refer to the soul, the
    possession of which was supposed to dis-
    tinguish human beings from beasts:
    Cassio's hyperbolic conceit plays with the
    ancient idea of fame as immortal in order

to suggest that reputation *is* his soul. Cf.
also Dent C817, 'He that hath lost his
credit is dead to the world'. *Stratioticos*
places particular stress on the ideal lieutenant's 'credit' and 'reputation' (sig.
P1), and, like the *Art of War*, emphasizes
his role as conciliator: since (as Davies
puts it) 'particularly the pacification of
discords and difference among the soldiers . . . appertains unto him, which
must be done without choler or passion';
he must 'have special care that by his
means no quarrels do grow . . . for fear of
banding and mutinies' (Davies, sig. O1).

IAGO As I am an honest man, I thought you had received
some bodily wound; there is more of sense in that than
in 'reputation'. 'Reputation' is an idle and most false
imposition, oft got without merit, and lost without   260
deserving. You have lost no reputation at all, unless you
repute yourself such a loser. What, man! there are more
ways to recover the general again. You are but now cast in
his mood—a punishment more in policy than in malice,
even so as one would beat his offenceless dog to affright an   265
imperious lion. Sue to him again and he's yours.

CASSIO I will rather sue to be despised than to deceive so
good a commander with so slight, so drunken, and so
indiscreet an officer. Drunk, and speak parrot, and
squabble? Swagger, swear, and discourse fustian with   270
one's own shadow? O, thou invisible spirit of wine, if
thou hast no name to be known by, let us call thee devil!

IAGO What was he that you followed with your sword?
What had he done to you?

CASSIO I know not.   275

257 thought] Q; had thought F   258 of   sense] CAMBRIDGE 1891; sense F; offence
Q 262–3 more ways] F; wayes Q   268 slight] F; light Q   and so] F; and Q
269–71 Drunk . . . shadow] F, Q2; *not in* Q1   271 invisible] F, Q; enticeable KELLNER *conj.*;
invincible THEOBALD 1740

258 **sense** feeling, physical sensation.
Sanders may be right to suggest that the
Q's *offence* represents a misreading of
manuscript 'of sense' with a long initial
s; but it could also be accounted for as a
mishearing. In any case, F's *sense* is perfectly comprehensible on its own, and
there is no need to substitute the conjectural reading.

260 **imposition** Perhaps, as editors
generally assume, 'something imposed
by others'; but the sense seems to be closer to 'imposture' or 'cheat', significantly
predating the earliest recorded examples
of this usage (*OED n.* 6).

261–2 **You . . . loser** A quasi-proverbial
piece of consolation: cf. 1.3.207–10, and
Dent M254.

263 **recover** reconcile, win back to friendship (*OED n.* 3b)
   cast discarded; cashiered

263–4 **in his mood** because of his (temporary) burst of anger

264 **in policy** in a spirit of prudence or
expediency

265–6 **beat . . . lion** Cf. Dent D443: 'Beat

the dog before the lion'; under normal
circumstances Cassio would find the
analogy profoundly insulting. 'Imperious
lion' may recall the fact that a winged lion
was the heraldic badge of the Venetian
empire.

265 **offenceless** Earliest citation in *OED*.

269–71 **Drunk . . . shadow** Probably
omitted by the Q compositor in order to
make space at the bottom of the page,
when setting by formes. Cf. also
4.1.169–71.

269 **parrot** gibberish. Cf. Dent P60, 'To
speak like a parrot'.
   squabble First example cited in *OED*.

270 **fustian** inflated nonsense. Another
term, like *bombast* (see 1.1.12), borrowed
from the vocabulary of clothing: *fustian*
was originally a kind of coarse, heavy
cloth made from cotton and linen.

271 **invisible** The adjective seems oddly
redundant, spirits normally being invisible by definition. Perhaps the manuscript
read 'intisable' (i.e. 'enticeable' = en-
ticing, seductive) as Kellner suggests, or
'invincible', as Theobald proposed.

IAGO Is't possible?

CASSIO I remember a mass of things, but nothing distinctly
—a quarrel, but nothing wherefore. O God, that men
should put an enemy in their mouths to steal away their
brains; that we should, with joy, pleasance, revel, and   280
applause, transform ourselves into beasts!

IAGO Why, but you are now well enough: how came you
thus recovered?

CASSIO It hath pleased the devil drunkenness to give place
to the devil wrath; one unperfectness shows me another   285
to make me frankly despise myself.

IAGO Come, you are too severe a moraller. As the time, the
place, and the condition of this country stands, I could
heartily wish this had not so befallen; but since it is as it
is, mend it for your own good.   290

CASSIO I will ask him for my place again, he shall tell me I
am a drunkard. Had I as many mouths as Hydra, such an
answer would stop them all. To be now a sensible man, by
and by a fool, and presently a beast—O strange! Every
inordinate cup is unblessed, and the ingredient is a   295
devil.

---

278 God] Q1; *not in* F, Q2   280 pleasance, revel] F; Reuell, pleasure Q   282 Why,] Q; ~? F
288 and] F; *not in* Q   289 not so] Q; not F   294 O strange] F; *not in* Q   295 inordinate] F,
Q2; vnordinate Q1   ingredient] F; ingredience Q

276 **Is't possible** This question will become
a recurrent motif in the next two acts, as
though the play (in the sardonic voice
it sometimes shares with Iago) were
confessing its own improbabilities and
thereby pre-empting the audience's
incredulity. Cf. 3.3.360, 3.4.67, 4.1.40,
4.2.87.

279 **enemy** A standard euphemism for
'devil', the literal meaning of Satan being
'adversary' (cf. l. 272).

280–1 **that . . . beasts** As Honigmann suggests, the metamorphosis recalls the bestial transformations of Circe's island. This
episode from the *Odyssey* was reworked in
numerous Renaissance texts, including
the Bower of Bliss episode in Spenser's
Faerie Queene (2.12.39–40, 84–7). Compare the bestial metamorphosis that

Othello himself will undergo as a result of
his jealousy.

280 **pleasance** pleasure

284–5 **It . . . wrath** Echoes Ephesians 4:
26–7, 'let not the sun go down upon your
wrath, Neither give place to the devil'.

286 **frankly** unreservedly, abundantly

287 **moraller** moralizer (*OED*, citing only
this example)

291–2 **I will . . . drunkard** A conditional
construction ('If I ask . . . he'll tell
me . . .').

292 **Hydra** A many-headed monster in
Greek mythology (cf. Dent H278, 'As
many heads as Hydra').

293 **stop** close, silence

295 **inordinate** intemperate (perhaps with
a quibble on the religious meaning of
'ordain')

IAGO Come, come, good wine is a good familiar creature
if it be well used: exclaim no more against it. And, good
lieutenant, I think you think I love you.

CASSIO I have well approved it, sir—I drunk?   300

IAGO You, or any man living, may be drunk at a time, man.
I tell you what you shall do: our general's wife is now the
general. I may say so in this respect, for that he hath
devoted and given up himself to the contemplation,
mark, and denotement of her parts and graces. Confess   305
yourself freely to her; importune her help to put you in
your place again. She is of so free, so kind, so apt, so
blessed a disposition, she holds it a vice in her goodness
not to do more than she is requested. This broken joint
between you and her husband entreat her to splinter.   310

301 a time, man] F; some time Q1; some time, man Q2   302 I] F; I'll Q   303 hath] F; has Q
305 denotement] Q2; deuotement F, Q1   306 her help to] F; her she'll Q1; her, she'll help to
Q2   307 of so] F; so Q   308 she holds] F; that she holds Q   309 broken joint] F, Q2; braule
Q1

297 **familiar** friendly, sociable; but with a
sardonic quibble on the 'familiars' or
'familiar creatures' supposedly kept by
witches, animals in which diabolic spirits
were lodged.
   creature created thing, invention; but
creature could be used to describe any kind
of human sustenance, and was often
humorously applied to alcohol (*OED n.*
1c–d); the sense of 'puppet, slave, toady'
may also be present.
300 **approved** proved
301 **at a time** at some time, once in a
while
302–3 **our . . . general** A quibbling suggestion that Desdemona has become 'general' property may underlie the gibe at
Othello's uxoriousness.
303 **for that** because
305 **mark** observation (*OED n.*[1] 20)
   denotement noting (earliest citation in
OED). One of Q2's rare independent
emendations: the editor appears to
have noticed the infelicitous 'deuoted
. . . deuotement' and assumed a misprint
based either on misreading (*n* and *u* being
almost indistinguishable in many early
modern hands) or a turned letter (as
Theobald later argued); the guess is
probably correct, since *denotement* is
suitably close in meaning to *contemplation*
and *mark*; Q and F *deuotement* (= devotion)
makes satisfactory sense, however, and

would fit with the religious sense of
contemplation, though less easily with
mark.
   parts and graces accomplishments and
physical charms
306–7 **put . . . place** reinstate you in your
office; but 'place' will develop an obscene
suggestiveness as the play goes on, and
the first hint of it may come here (see
Williams, *Dictionary*, p. 1048, *Glossary*,
p. 237; and Neill, 'Places', pp. 222–6).
307 **free** Cf. 1.3.261. It is significant that this
is a word that has been several times
applied to Othello: twice by himself (see
also 1.2.26) and once by Iago (1.3.388).
Here, in conjunction with 'place . . .
kind . . . apt . . . vice . . . do', it probably
has a bawdy sense (= sexually available;
Williams, *Dictionary*, p. 542) to which
Cassio is deaf.
   kind Perhaps quibbling on the sense
'sexually complaisant' (Williams, *Dictionary*, p. 760).
   apt susceptible, easily persuaded; but
also 'apt for love; nubile and desirous'
(Partridge, p. 59)
309 **do** For the bawdy sense of this word, see
Williams, *Dictionary*, pp. 395–8, *Glossary*,
pp. 101–2.
309–12 **This . . . before** Cf. Dent B515, 'A
broken bone is the stronger when it is well
set'.
310 **splinter** apply a splint to

And—my fortunes against any lay worth naming!—this
crack of your love shall grow stronger than it was before.
CASSIO You advise me well.
IAGO I protest, in the sincerity of love and honest kindness.
CASSIO I think it freely; and betimes in the morning I will   315
 beseech the virtuous Desdemona to undertake for me. I
 am desperate of my fortunes if they check me here.
IAGO You are in the right. Good night, lieutenant: I must to
 the watch.
CASSIO Good night, honest Iago.   *Exit*   320
IAGO
 And what's he then that says I play the villain,
 When this advice is free I give, and honest,
 Probal to thinking, and indeed the course
 To win the Moor again? For 'tis most easy
 Th'inclining Desdemona to subdue   325
 In any honest suit. She's framed as fruitful
 As the free elements; and then for her
 To win the Moor—were't to renounce his baptism,
 All seals and symbols of redeemèd sin—
 His soul is so enfettered to her love   330
 That she may make, unmake, do what she list,
 Even as her appetite shall play the god,

---

315 I will] F; will I Q   317 here] Q; *not in* F   328 were't] Q (wer't); were F

---

311 **lay** bet, wager
311–12 **this crack . . . stronger** this frac-
 ture in your love will knit and make it
 stronger
315 **freely** unreservedly
316 **undertake for me** take up my cause
316–17 **I . . . check me** I shall think my fortunes are quite hopeless if I am rebuffed.
321 **play the villain** Iago's metatheatrical
 jokiness recalls Richard III (cf. also l. 332).
322 **free . . . and honest** Iago continues to
 play with various meanings of these key
 words: here *free* can mean either 'free of
 charge; generous, frank, spontaneous;
 innocent, unbiased', or any combination
 of these; *honest*, similarly, can mean
 'honourable; truthful, frank; or chaste'.
 Like most of what Iago tells his other
 gulls, Roderigo and Othello, Iago's advice
 is in one sense perfectly truthful, though
 its motives are scarcely honourable.

323 **Probal** probable (first use cited in *OED*)
325 **inclining** compliant; already predisposed
326 **honest** (sexually) honourable
326–7 **framed . . . elements** created as
 generous and productive as the unfettered
 natural order itself. The heavy alliteration
 on 'framed . . . fruitful . . . free' will make
 it easy for an actor to bring out a bawdy
 innuendo.
329 **seals** tokens, signs, or symbols authen-
 ticating a covenant
330 **enfettered** Earliest citation in *OED*.
331 **list** wishes
332 **her appetite** his desire for her; but
 perhaps equivocating on Desdemona's
 imputed desire for power over Othello.
 play the god The phrase suggests a
 disconcerting analogy with Iago's
 own propensity to 'play the villain' (l.
 321).

With his weak function. How am I then a villain
To counsel Cassio to this parallel course
Directly to his good? Divinity of hell!   335
When devils will the blackest sins put on,
They do suggest at first with heavenly shows,
As I do now. For, whiles this honest fool
Plies Desdemona to repair his fortune,
And she for him pleads strongly to the Moor,   340
I'll pour this pestilence into his ear:
That she repeals him for her body's lust;
And by how much she strives to do him good
She shall undo her credit with the Moor.
So will I turn her virtue into pitch,   345
And out of her own goodness make the net
That shall enmesh them all.
          Enter Roderigo
                    How now, Roderigo?
RODERIGO I do follow here in the chase, not like a hound
    that hunts, but one that fills up the cry. My money
    is almost spent; I have been tonight exceedingly   350
    well cudgelled; and I think the issue will be, I shall
    have so much experience for my pains, and so, with

---

336 the] F; their Q   338 whiles] F; while Q1; whilst Q2   339 fortune] F; fortunes Q
347 enmesh] Q; en-mash F   347.1 *Enter Roderigo*] Q; *after* 'now Roderigo' F   351 and] F;
not in Q   352 and so, with] F; as that comes to, and Q1; and so no Q2

no money at all and a little more wit, return again to
Venice.

IAGO

How poor are they that have not patience!   355
What wound did ever heal but by degrees?
Thou know'st we work by wit and not by witchcraft,
And wit depends on dilatory time.
Does't not go well? Cassio hath beaten thee,
And thou by that small hurt hast cashiered Cassio.   360
Though other things grow fair against the sun,
Yet fruits that blossom first will first be ripe.
Content thyself awhile. By th' mass, 'tis morning:
Pleasure and action make the hours seem short!
Retire thee, go where thou art billeted.   365
Away, I say! thou shalt know more hereafter—
Nay, get thee gone!   *Exit Roderigo*
              Two things are to be done:
My wife must move for Cassio to her mistress—
I'll set her on—
Myself a while to draw the Moor apart   370
And bring him jump when he may Cassio find
Soliciting his wife. Ay, that's the way:
Dull not device by coldness and delay.   *Exit*

---

353 a little more] F; with that Q1; with a little more Q2   356 again] F; *not in* Q   359 Does't]
Dos't F; Dos't Q   hath] F; has Q   360 hast] Q; hath F   362 Yet] F, Q2; But Q1   363 By th'
mass] Q; Introth F   367 *Exit Roderigo*] F; *not in* Q   Two] F; Some Q   369–70 on. . . . to] Q
(on. | My selfe awhile, to); on my selfe, a while, to F   373 *Exit*] F; *Exeunt.* Q

353 **wit** common sense
355 **How . . . patience** Cf. Dent P103, 'He
    that has no patience has nothing'.
356 **What . . . degrees** Although Tilley
    cites no exact equivalent, this apothegm
    sounds proverbial too. Cf. W929,
    'Though the wound be healed yet the
    scar remains'.
358 **dilatory** (a) tardy, prone to delay; (b)
    expanding; (c) involving accusations or
    the laying of information against some-
    one. For a suggestive discussion of the
    range of meanings in this word, see
    Parker, ' "Dilation" '. See also 3.1.127.
360 **cashiered Cassio** The juxtaposition
    points up the latent pun in Cassio's name
    (see 'Persons').
361 **against** when fully exposed to

362 **Yet . . . ripe** Another piece of
    apparently pseudo-proverbial wisdom;
    as Honigmann points out, the claim is not
    even always true. The logic of Iago's
    'Though . . . yet' is perhaps deliberately
    obscure, since he is bamboozling the
    slow-witted Roderigo into believing,
    despite his recent cudgelling, that every-
    thing is going well.
364 **Pleasure . . . short** Proverbial; Dent
    H747, 'Hours of pleasure are short'.
368 **move** plead
369 **I'll . . . on** The short line indicates a
    meditative pause.
371 **jump** exactly
373 **Dull . . . coldness** don't let my plots
    lose their impetus through lack of
    enthusiasm

3.1 *Enter Cassio with Musicians*

CASSIO

Masters, play here—I will content your pains—
Something that's brief; and bid 'Good morrow, general!'
They play. Enter Clown

CLOWN Why, masters, have your instruments been in
Naples that they speak i'th' nose thus?

BOY MUSICIAN How, sir? how? 5

CLOWN Are these, I pray you, wind instruments?

BOY MUSICIAN Ay, marry are they, sir.

CLOWN O, thereby hangs a tail.

BOY MUSICIAN Whereby hangs a tale, sir?

CLOWN Marry, sir, by many a wind instrument that I know. 10

3.1] F (*Actus Tertius. Scena Prima.*), Q2 (*Actus 3. Scœna I.*); *not in* Q1 0.1 *Enter . . . musicians*]
Q2 (*subs.*); *Enter Cassio, Musitians, and Clowne.* F; *Enter* Cassio, *with Musitians and the Clowne.*
Q1 2.1 *They . . . Clown*] Q2 (*subs.*); *not in* F, Q1 5, 7, 9, 14, 18 BOY MUSICIAN] This edition;
Mus. F; *Boy.* Q 6 pray you,] F; pray, cald Q

3.1 Shakespeare seems to have been obliged
to include a part for the company's resident clown in every play; but the two
scenes in *Othello* are unusually perfunc-
tory and are often omitted in performance
(cf. 3.4.1–20). The function of this
episode, with its obscene badinage, is to
taint Cassio's serenade with something
of the quality of the 'rough music' with
which early modern communities
expressed their disapprobation of inappropriate weddings. See Bristol,
'Charivari'.

1 **content** reward
2 **Good morrow** After the wedding night,
songs and music were customarily performed outside the bridal chamber to
greet the dawn. Donne's lyric 'The Good-
Morrow' is a sophisticated imitation of
this folk-ritual. See App. D (iii).
2.1 ***They . . . Clown*** It is so unusual for Q2
to make any changes to Q not based on F
that this interpolated direction probably
preserves the editor's recollection of what
he had seen on the stage; though he
might have deduced from the subsequent
dialogue that the Clown, rather than
being Cassio's companion, is a member of
Othello's household who enters in
response to the noise of the serenade.
3 **Naples . . . nose** 'The Clown may mean
that the music has an ugly nasal twang
like the Neapolitan accent, but there is

probably also a reference to venereal disease [syphilis, known as 'the Neapolitan
disease'] which attacked the bridge of the
nose' (Sanders). According to Parr (cited
in Furness) 'every Clown knew that
Pulcinella [in *commedia dell'arte* and puppet shows] is the Neapolitan mask, and
that Pulcinella speaks through the nose'.
It is possible that a bilingual pun may also
be involved ('*nez* pulls') illustrated by the
clown's pulling his own nose (to make his
speech sound comically nasal), or possibly tweaking the nose of his interlocutor. Shylock's complaints about the
bagpipe that 'sings i'th' nose' and 'the vile
squealing of the wry-necked fife' (*Merchant*, 4.1.48, 2.5.30) offer a possible clue
as to the instruments envisaged here.
5, 7, 9, 14, 18 BOY MUSICIAN Since the Q2
editor was at such pains to correct both
Q and F on the Clown's entry, we can
perhaps assume that he saw Q's *Boy*
as correct. The Clown's crude bawdy
will perhaps have sounded funnier
when delivered to a naive (or *faux naïf*)
child.
8 **thereby . . . tail** The clown teases the
musician by punning on a proverbial
phrase (Dent T48, 'Thereby hangs a
tale'); the 'tail' he has in mind is a penis.
10 **wind instrument** anus (sometimes
referred to as the *ars musica*, according to
Partridge, pp. 219–20)

But, masters, here's money for you; and the general so
likes your music that he desires you, for love's sake, to
make no more noise with it.

BOY MUSICIAN Well, sir, we will not.

CLOWN If you have any music that may not be heard, to't   15
again—but (as they say) to hear music the general does
not greatly care.

BOY MUSICIAN We have none such, sir.

CLOWN Then put up your pipes in your bag, for I'll away.
Go, vanish into air, away!   20

                                        Exeunt Musicians

CASSIO Dost thou hear, mine honest friend?

CLOWN No, I hear not your honest friend—I hear you.

CASSIO Prithee, keep up thy quillets—there's a poor piece
of gold for thee: if the gentlewoman that attends
the general's wife be stirring, tell her there's one   25
Cassio entreats her a little favour of speech. Wilt thou do
this?

CLOWN She is stirring, sir: if she will stir hither, I shall seem
to notify unto her.

CASSIO

Do, my good friend.   *Exit Clown*
     Enter Iago

                In happy time, Iago.   30

---

12 for love's sake] F, Q2; *of all loues* Q1   19 up] F; *not in* Q   20 into air] F, Q2; *not in* Q1
20.1 *Exeunt Musicians*] F (*Exit Mu.*); *not in* Q   21 hear, mine] THEOBALD; *heare me, mine* F;
heare my Q   25 general's wife] Q; Generall F   30 CASSIO . . . friend] Q; *not in* F   *Exit Clown*]
Q2 (*after* 'Iago'); *after* 'vnto her' (*l.* 29) F; *not in* Q1

---

12 **for love's sake** 'for the sake of any affection you may have for him—with a pun
on "for the sake of his erotic concentration" ' (Sanders)

13 **noise** Sanders suggests a pun on 'nose'.

16–17 **but . . . care** '[A]s they say' suggests
a punning reference to the artistic indifference of the general public (cf. 'caviare
to the general', *Hamlet*, 2.2.439–40).

18 **none such** ' "Nonesuch" was the name
of a popular tune' (Honigmann).

19 **put . . . pipes** put away your pipes. The
clown playfully restores its literal meaning to a proverbial phrase meaning 'make
an end'.

    in your bag Presumably the bag in which

they carry their instruments; but punning on 'bagpipe', and perhaps with a
quibble on 'pipe' = penis, and 'bag' =
vagina (or scrotum).

21 **honest friend** Perhaps a glance at
'honest Iago'.

23 **quillets** quibbles

24 **attends** serves

28–9 **She . . . her** The Clown mocks
Cassio with a parody of courtly
circumlocution.

28 **stirring** sexually arousing (cf. *Measure*,
2.2.190; *Revenger's Tragedy*, 1.2.179,
2.1.196; and Williams, *Glossary*, p. 290)

30 **In . . . time** you have arrived at a lucky
moment

IAGO
  You haven't been a-bed then?
CASSIO   Why, no: the day had broke
  Before we parted. I've made bold, Iago,
  To send in to your wife. My suit to her
  Is that she will to virtuous Desdemona
  Procure me some access.   35
IAGO   I'll send her to you presently:
  And I'll devise a mean to draw the Moor
  Out of the way, that your converse and business
  May be more free.   *Exit*
CASSIO   I humbly thank you for't.
  I never knew a Florentine more kind and honest!   40
    Enter Emilia

EMILIA
  Good morrow, good lieutenant. I am sorry
  For your displeasure, but all will sure be well.
  The general and his wife are talking of it,
  And she speaks for you stoutly. The Moor replies
  That he you hurt is of great fame in Cyprus   45
  And great affinity; and that in wholesome wisdom
  He might not but refuse you. But he protests he loves you
  And needs no other suitor but his likings
  To take the safest occasion by the front
  To bring you in again.

---

31 haven't] *after* Q (ha not); haue not F   32 I've] *after* Q (I ha); I haue F   40.1 Emilia] F (*Æmilia*); Emilla Q   42 sure] F; soone Q   49 To . . . front] Q; *not in* F

31–6 **Why . . . presently** The lineation here is difficult to reconstruct with any certainty; but Sanders's solution has the merit of allowing for some slightly awkward pausing around the question of Cassio's access to Emilia.
36 **presently** forthwith
37 **mean** means
40 **a Florentine** even a Florentine (i.e. one of his own countrymen, hence the intensified sense of *kind*)
42 **your displeasure** the disfavour into which you have fallen
44 **stoutly** resolutely, vigorously
46 **great affinity** he has powerful family connections

wholesome wisdom prudent common sense
47 **might not but** had no option but to
49 **To . . . front** In Renaissance iconography Occasion or Opportunity was represented as a bald-headed woman with a single lock of hair hanging over her forehead (*front*); it was necessary to seize her by the forelock before she passed out of reach. Cf. Dent T311, 'Take time (occasion) by the forelock, for she is bald behind'. The line was probably omitted from F as a result of eye-skip to the second *To*.

CASSIO.   Yet I beseech you,   50
　If you think fit, or that it may be done,
　Give me advantage of some brief discourse
　With Desdemon alone.
EMILIA   Pray you, come in:
　I will bestow you where you shall have time
　To speak your bosom freely.
CASSIO   I am much bound to you.   55
                                                   Exeunt

3.2   *Enter Othello, Iago, and Gentlemen*
OTHELLO
　These letters give, Iago, to the pilot,
　And by him do my duties to the Senate;
　That done, I will be walking on the works:
　Repair there to me.
IAGO   Well, my good lord, I'll do't.
OTHELLO
　This fortification, gentlemen, shall we see't?   5
GENTLEMEN
　We'll wait upon your lordship.   *Exeunt*

3.3   *Enter Desdemona, Cassio, and Emilia*
DESDEMONA
　Be thou assured, good Cassio, I will do
　All my abilities in thy behalf.
EMILIA
　Good madam, do: I warrant it grieves my husband,
　As if the cause were his.
DESDEMONA
　O, that's an honest fellow. Do not doubt, Cassio,   5

---

53 Desdemon] F; *Desdemona* Q   55 CASSIO . . . you] F, Q2; *not in* Q1   55.1 *Exeunt*] Q; *not in* F
3.2] F (*Scœna Secunda.*); *not in* Q   0.1 *and Gentlemen*] F; *and other Gentlemen* Q   1 pilot] F;
Pilate Q   2 Senate] F; State Q   6 We'll] F (Well); We Q
3.3] F (*Scœna Tertia.*); *not in* Q   3 warrant] F; know Q   4 cause] F; case Q

---

50 **To . . . again** to reinstate you in your
　office (*OED v.* 18d)
55 **speak your bosom** utter your most inti-
　mate thoughts
　bound to you Part of the play's rhetoric
　of service, equivalent to 'your servant'.
3.2.2 do my duties offer my dutiful service

3 **works** fortifications
6 **wait upon** attend (as servants 'attend' or
　'wait upon' their masters)
3.3 The temptation scene is elaborated from
　a number of discrete episodes in Giraldi;
　see App. C, pp. 439–43.
1 **do** apply, use (*OED n.* 3, 9)

But I will have my lord and you again
As friendly as you were.
CASSIO   Bounteous madam,
  Whatever shall become of Michael Cassio,
  He's never anything but your true servant.
DESDEMONA
  I know't. I thank you. You do love my lord;   10
  You have known him long; and be you well assured
  He shall in strangeness stand no farther off
  Than in a politic distance.
CASSIO   Ay; but, lady,
  That policy may either last so long,
  Or feed upon such nice and waterish diet,   15
  Or breed itself so out of circumstances,
  That, I being absent and my place supplied,
  My general will forget my love and service.
DESDEMONA
  Do not doubt that: before Emilia here,
  I give thee warrant of thy place. Assure thee,   20
  If I do vow a friendship I'll perform it
  To the last article. My lord shall never rest,

10 I know't] F; O sir Q   12 strangeness] F; strangest Q   14 That] F, Q2; The Q1   16 circumstances] F; circumstance Q

9 **servant** The nuances of Cassio's language here will be difficult for a modern audience to catch: *true servant* is essentially a routine courtesy, but one complicated by awareness of Cassio's subordinate role as an officer in the *service* (l. 18) of a general whose wife (as Iago's hyperbole has it) 'is now the general' (2.3.302–3); moreover, *servant* can also mean 'lover' (a usage deriving from the conventions of chivalric love, which typically involved a knight's offer of 'service' to the wife of his lord). While Cassio (in the conventional way of Renaissance courtiers) does no more than glance playfully at this latter meaning, for the audience it is inevitably given a more dangerous charge by Iago's insinuations. It is thus a further reminder of the way in which Cassio's relations with women are tinged with an urbanely eroticized gallantry that can easily be turned against him. Desdemona's switch in the following line from the intimate *thou*, usual in her conversations with Cassio, to the more formal *you*, may indicate that she herself is sensitive to the implications of his language, and feels the need to re-establish a proper distance between them.

12–13 **He ... distance** the estranged distance he puts between you will be no greater than practical wisdom requires

15 **nice and waterish** Usually interpreted as 'thin and dilute'; but in this context a more appropriate sense would seem to be 'luxurious and succulent' (*OED*, *nice, a.* 4d, 14; *waterish, a.* 11).

16 **breed ... circumstances** generate itself (or develop) as a result of casual circumstances

18 **love and service** Cf. l. 9. The innocent conjunction of 'love and service' may again be tinged with unfortunate suggestions.

19 **doubt** fear

20 **warrant** guarantee

22 **article** clause in a contract or treaty

283

I'll watch him tame and talk him out of patience;
His bed shall seem a school, his board a shrift;
I'll intermingle everything he does   25
With Cassio's suit. Therefore be merry, Cassio,
For thy solicitor shall rather die
Than give thy cause away.

       Enter Othello and Iago

EMILIA   Madam, here comes my lord.

CASSIO

  Madam, I'll take my leave.

DESDEMONA   Why stay, and hear me speak.

CASSIO

  Madam, not now: I am very ill at ease,   30
  Unfit for mine own purposes.

DESDEMONA Well, do your discretion.   *Exit Cassio*

IAGO Ha? I like not that.

OTHELLO What dost thou say?

---

28 thy cause away] F, Q2; thee cause: away Q1   28.1 *Enter . . . Iago*] F; *Enter* Othello, Iago,
and Gentlemen. Q   31 purposes] F; purpose Q

---

23 **watch him tame** tame him by keeping
him awake; a metaphor from the practice
of falconry, more usually applied to the
domestication of wives by husbands (cf.
Shrew, 4.1.176–97; *Troilus*, 3.2.41–2).

24 **bed . . . board** Alluding to the legal definition of marriage as an agreement to
share 'bed and board'; the usual form of
marital separation, for example, was
known as *divortium a mensa et thoro* (=
divorce from table and bed); and at least
one medieval version of the marriage rite
contained the phrase 'to hold and to have
at bed and at board' (*OED n.* 1c); cf. also
Hymen's song in *AYLI*, 5.4.140: 'O
blessèd bond of board and bed').

   school In *Shrew* Shakespeare had made
extensive comic capital from the idea of
the household as a kind of school
designed to discipline an unruly spouse,
especially through Petruccio's 'taming-
school' (4.2.55). Desdemona's schooling
of Othello will reverse the conventional
gender roles.

   board table

   shrift place of confession or penance

27 **solicitor** Literally 'one who petitions
or entreats'; but in the context of

Desdemona's legal language ('warrant
. . . article . . . suit . . . cause') a play on
the relatively novel technical sense of the
word ('one practising in a court of equity,
as distinguished from an *attorney*', *OED n.*
3a) seems likely.

28 **give . . . away** abandon your case. The
sense of moral 'cause' is also present.

32–4 **Well . . . say** Most editors treat 32–3 as
a single line and 34 as a half-line, but 33
may combine amphibiously with ll. 32
and 34, creating lines that are respectively
one syllable long and one syllable short.
Despite these irregularities, the rhythmic
quality of the lines suggests that they are
intended as verse; and it would be equally
possible to treat them as three incomplete
lines, indicating awkward pausing rather
than quick, nervous cueing.

32 **do your discretion** behave as you think
wise

33 **Ha?** In Shakespeare's time a question
mark was often used where we would
expect an exclamation mark; and editors
normally assume that this is the case
here. But Iago's *ha* may indeed be a
rhetorical interrogative, equivalent to
'eh?' or 'what's that?'

IAGO

  Nothing, my lord; or if—I know not what.   35

OTHELLO

  Was not that Cassio parted from my wife?

IAGO

  Cassio, my lord?—No, sure, I cannot think it

  That he would steal away so guilty-like,

  Seeing you coming.

OTHELLO I do believe 'twas he.   40

DESDEMONA How now, my lord?

  I have been talking with a suitor here,

  A man that languishes in your displeasure.

OTHELLO Who is't you mean?

DESDEMONA

  Why, your lieutenant, Cassio—good my lord,   45

  If I have any grace or power to move you,

  His present reconciliation take;

  For if he be not one that truly loves you,

  That errs in ignorance and not in cunning,

  I have no judgement in an honest face.   50

  I prithee call him back.

OTHELLO Went he hence now?

DESDEMONA Yes, faith: so humbled

  That he hath left part of his grief with me

  To suffer with him. Good love, call him back.   55

OTHELLO

  Not now, sweet Desdemon—some other time.

DESDEMONA

  But shall't be shortly?

---

38 steal] F, Q2; sneake Q1   39 you] Q; your F   53 Yes, faith] Q; I sooth F   54 hath] F; has
Q   grief] F; griefes Q   55 To] F, Q2; I Q1   56 Desdemon] F, Q2; *Desdemona* Q1

---

40 **I . . . he** Metrically amphibious.
42–75 **I have . . . do much** Cf. Giraldi, App.
   C, p. 439.
43 **languishes** Stronger than today: it suggests that Cassio's health is broken by his
   remorse.
46 **grace** pleasing quality, beauty; favour
   (in your eyes)
47 **His . . . take** Either 'restore him to
   immediate favour' (Sanders; *OED, reconciliation, n.* 1c); or 'accept the reconciliation he now sues for'.

49 **in cunning** knowingly; because of his
   crafty nature (as opposed to his 'honest
   face')
51–3 **I . . . humbled** Here again the versification is uncertain. Most editors treat
   51–2 as forming a single line; but, since
   quick cueing seems desirable here, 52
   is probably amphibious, and *humbled*
   trisyllabic.

OTHELLO   The sooner, sweet, for you.

DESDEMONA
  Shall't be tonight, at supper?

OTHELLO   No, not tonight.

DESDEMONA
  Tomorrow dinner, then?

OTHELLO   I shall not dine at home:
  I meet the captains at the citadel.   60

DESDEMONA
  Why then tomorrow night, or Tuesday morn,
  On Tuesday noon, or night, on Wednesday morn—
  I prithee name the time, but let it not
  Exceed three days. I'faith he's penitent;
  And yet his trespass, in our common reason—   65
  Save that they say the wars must make example
  Out of her best—is not almost a fault
  T'incur a private check. When shall he come?
  Tell me, Othello! I wonder in my soul
  What you would ask me, that I should deny   70
  Or stand so mamm'ring on? What? Michael Cassio,
  That came a-wooing with you, and so many a time,
  When I have spoke of you dispraisingly,
  Hath ta'en your part—to have so much to do
  To bring him in? By'r Lady, I could do much—   75

OTHELLO
  Prithee no more: let him come when he will—
  I will deny thee nothing.

DESDEMONA   Why, this is not a boon:

61 or] Q; on F   62 noon] F; morne Q   on Wednesday] F; or Wensday Q   64 I'faith]
Q (Ifaith); Infaith F   66 example] F; examples Q   67 her best] F, Q; their best ROWE
70 would] F; could Q   71 mamm'ring] F, Q2; muttering Q1   75 By'r Lady] Q1; Trust me F,
Q2

59 **dinner** The meal was eaten about noon.
65 **trespass** offence
   in . . . reason in the general opinion; or,
   from a common-sense point of view
67 **her best** the most distinguished, or high-
   est-ranking soldiers. Honigmann follows
   Rowe in emending to 'their best'; but *wars*
   is treated as a singular noun elsewhere;
   see e.g. 1.1.149–50, 1.3.233, 3.3.351–2.
67–8 **is . . . check** is scarcely a serious
   enough fault to deserve even a private
   rebuke (let alone public humiliation)

71 **mamm'ring** stammering with indecision
74 **to do** This may be the substantival
   to-do (= ado, fuss, business: *OED*, *do*, *v.*
   33b), a slightly stronger usage which
   would fit the playful impatience of the
   speech.
75 **To . . . in** Cf. 3.1.50.
77–84 **Why . . . granted** Desdemona contrasts the cosily domestic entreaties
   proper to a dutiful wife with the extravagant trials conventionally imposed on
   chivalric lovers by their mistresses.

'Tis as I should entreat you wear your gloves,
Or feed on nourishing dishes, or keep you warm,
Or sue to you to do a peculiar profit   80
To your own person. Nay, when I have a suit
Wherein I mean to touch your love indeed,
It shall be full of poise and difficult weight,
And fearful to be granted.
OTHELLO   I will deny thee nothing.
Whereon, I do beseech thee, grant me this: 85
To leave me but a little to myself.

DESDEMONA
Shall I deny you? No! Farewell, my lord.

OTHELLO
Farewell, my Desdemona, I'll come to thee straight.

DESDEMONA
Emilia, come. (*To Othello*) Be as your fancies teach you:
Whate'er you be, I am obedient.   90

                    Exeunt Desdemona and Emilia

OTHELLO
Excellent wretch, perdition catch my soul
But I do love thee! and when I love thee not,
Chaos is come again.

83 difficult weight] F, Q2; difficulty Q1   89 Be] F; be it Q   90.1 *Exeunt . . . Emilia*] Q (*subs.*);
Exit. F

80–1 **do . . . person** do yourself a special favour
82 **touch** put to the test (*OED v.* 8a)
83 **poise** weight, gravity, importance
85 **Whereon** for which reason; or, 'so, for the moment'
88 **straight** at once
89 **fancies** moods, whims
90 **obedient** Obedience was the first quality required of a good wife under the patriarchal rules of domestic government. The word will become the object of Othello's obsessive attention in Act 4, Scene 1 (ll. 239–48), with its violent replay of Desdemona's submissive departure here.
91 **wretch** Mock-denigration commonly used as endearment.
91–2 **perdition . . . do love thee** A significant ambiguity: either (a) may I be damned if I do not love you; or (b) I love you even at the risk of incurring damnation.

93 **Chaos . . . again** This line is often taken as a reference to the barbaric confusion of Othello's pre-Venetian past: Patrick Stewart, for example, spoke it with a heavy stress on *again*. But for contemporaries it will have had a larger, more philosophic resonance, since it invokes the classical myth according to which only the power of Love (the first of the immortals to emerge from primal Chaos) prevents the created universe from falling back into its original confusion, a Chaos imagined as primordial blackness. So in *Venus*, Venus imagines the death of her beloved in language strikingly close to Othello's: 'For he being dead, with him is beauty slain, | And beauty dead, black chaos comes again' (ll. 1019–20). Cf. also Spenser, *An Hymne of Love* (ll. 57–91); Jonson, *Masque of Beautie*, ll. 282–4, 325–6, and *Love Freed from Ignorance and Folly*, 36–7.

IAGO My noble lord—

OTHELLO What dost thou say, Iago? 95

IAGO
Did Michael Cassio, when you wooed my lady,
Know of your love?

OTHELLO He did, from first to last—
Why dost thou ask?

IAGO
But for a satisfaction of my thought,
No further harm.

OTHELLO Why of thy thought, Iago? 100

IAGO
I did not think he had been acquainted with her.

OTHELLO
O yes, and went between us very oft.

IAGO Indeed?

OTHELLO
Indeed? Ay, indeed. Discern'st thou aught in that?
Is he not honest?

IAGO Honest, my lord? 105

OTHELLO Honest? Ay, honest.

IAGO
My lord, for aught I know.

OTHELLO What dost thou think?

IAGO Think, my lord?

OTHELLO
'Think, my lord'? By heaven, thou echo'st me,
As if there were some monster in thy thought 110

96 you] Q; he F 99 thought] F, Q2; thoughts Q1 102 oft] F, Q2; often Q1 103 Ay] F (I),
Q2; *not in* Q1 109 By heaven, thou echo'st] POPE (*subs.*); Alas, thou ecchos't F; By heauen he
ecchoes Q1; why dost thou ecchoe Q2 110 thy] F, Q2; his Q1

94 **My . . . lord** This part-line is treated as amphibious, but the verse scheme is uncertain here.

104–6 **Is . . . Ay, honest** The versification is again uncertain: these may (as here) be treated as three separate half-lines, requiring heavy pausing; or as two incomplete (nine-syllable) lines linked by an amphibious l. 105; or the speakers may simply lapse into prose. Any decision will have a significant effect on the pacing of the scene. Pregnant pauses, however,

seem justified by the stress on the key term 'honest'.

104, 105, 106 **honest** (a) frank, straightforward and dependable; (b) honourable; (c) chaste. Iago's repetition of the word has the effect of opening up its dangerous ambiguities to Othello.

110 **monster** deformed, unnatural creature, prodigy. Othello's metaphor ironically echoes Iago's vision of his plot as a 'monstrous birth' (1.3.393).

Too hideous to be shown. Thou dost mean something:
I heard thee say even now thou likedst not that,
When Cassio left my wife. What didst not like?
And when I told thee he was of my counsel
In my whole course of wooing, thou criedst 'Indeed?'   115
And didst contract and purse thy brow together,
As if thou then hadst shut up in thy brain
Some horrible conceit. If thou dost love me,
Show me thy thought.
IAGO My lord, you know I love you.   120
OTHELLO I think thou dost;
And, for I know thou'rt full of love and honesty,
And weigh'st thy words before thou giv'st them breath,
Therefore these stops of thine fright me the more—
For such things in a false, disloyal knave   125
Are tricks of custom, but in a man that's just,
They're close dilations, working from the heart,

---

111 dost] F, Q2; didst Q1   112 even] F; but Q   115 In] Q; Of F   118 conceit] F, Q2; counsell
Q1   123 giv'st them] F; giue em Q1; giu'st 'em Q2   124 fright] F, Q2; affright Q1   127 dila-
tions] F, Q2; denotements Q1; delations STEEVENS (*conj.* Johnson)

---

111 **Too . . . shown** Othello's hyperbole
picks up on the false etymology that
derived *monster* from Latin *monstro*
(= show) rather than *moneo* (= warn); a
play on *hide/hideous* also seems to be
involved: see Introduction, pp. 139–42.
114 **of my counsel** in my confidence
118 **conceit** notion, fancy; with a subdued
play on 'conception' that again links it
to Iago's obscenely 'engendered' plot
(1.3.392–3).
119 **Show . . . thought** The idea of
thoughts as substantial objects, capable of
discovery in a body that can be opened to
the view, may owe something to the new
science of anatomy. See Neill, 'Opening',
pp. 142–5, and cf. l. 166.
120 **My . . . love you** Ridley detects 'a horrible reminiscence' of St Peter's 'Lord,
thou knowest that I love thee' (John 21:
15–17). Metrically amphibious.
124 **stops** abrupt breakings off
126 **tricks of custom** customary habits
(*OED*, *trick, n.* 7); i.e. predictable and
purely external behaviour, as opposed to
the intimate signs of inward emotion
characteristic of 'a man that's just'.

Inevitably too, in this context, *tricks* will
have the additional suggestion of 'under-
hand stratagems'.
127 **close** secret; intimate
dilations (a) delays, evasions; (b) amplifications or enlargements, either of
meaning or (as Kittredge suggested) of
the overcharged heart; (c) delations,
denunciations: equivalent to Q's *denotements*. If Q2's emendation at 2.3.305 is
correct, then *denotement* was certainly a
word in the dramatist's mind during the
composition of the play. But the F reading
here, as at l. 128 (*be sworn* for Q *presume*),
is not only stronger, but sufficiently different to suggest revision on the dramatist's
part. The rarity of *denotement* makes it
unlikely that it was simply an actor's substitution (as *presume* might otherwise
easily be), unless it were imported from
2.3.305. For detailed analysis of the complex play of suggestions in this passage,
see Parker, 'Dilation'. As Parker points
out, Steevens's *delations*, while apposite, is
not really a true emendation, since the
words were not at this time orthographic-
ally distinct.

That passion cannot rule.

IAGO   For Michael Cassio,
I dare be sworn, I think, that he is honest.

OTHELLO
I think so too.

IAGO   Men should be what they seem—   130
Or those that be not, would they might seem none.

OTHELLO
Certain, men should be what they seem.

IAGO
Why, then I think Cassio's an honest man.

OTHELLO
Nay, yet there's more in this!
I prithee speak to me as to thy thinkings,   135
As thou dost ruminate, and give thy worst of thoughts
The worst of words.

IAGO   Good my lord, pardon me:
Though I am bound to every act of duty,
I am not bound to that all slaves are free to—
Utter my thoughts? Why, say they are vile and false—   140
As where's that palace whereinto foul things
Sometimes intrude not?—who has that breast so pure
Where no uncleanly apprehensions
Keep leets and law-days, and in sessions sit
With meditations lawful?   145

---

129 be sworn . . . that] HONIGMANN; be sworne, I thinke that F, Q2; presume, I thinke that
Q1; *most editors read* 'be sworn I think that'   130 what] F, Q2; that Q1   134 Nay, yet] F,
Q2; ~∧ ~ Q1   135 as to] F, Q2; to Q1   136 thy . . . thoughts] F, Q2; the worst of thought Q1
137 words] F, Q2; word Q1   139 I . . . free to] Q; I . . . that: All Slaues are free: F   142 that]
F; a Q   143 Where no] This edition (*conj.* Furness); Wherein F; But some Q   144 sessions]
F; Session Q

---

128 **That . . . rule** that passion is unable to
control; i.e. Iago's 'stops' are signs of an
emotion that inevitably betrays itself.

130 **Men . . . seem** Dent S214, 'Be what
thou would seem to be'.

131 **none** nothing of the sort. One of Iago's
typically oblique constructions.

139 **that . . . to** that which even slaves are
free to do [or not to do]. Behind his apparently genial philosophizing, Iago is mak-

ing a loaded point about the limits of
'service'; cf. 1.1.43–60.

143 **uncleanly apprehensions** foul ideas

144 **leets** manorial courts of record; here =
the sessions of such courts.
    law-days days assigned for the sessions of
leets and other courts. Cf. Stubbes, *Anatomy of Abuses*, 1583 (cited in *OED, law-day,
n.* 1), 'In every shire or county be courts,
law days, and leets . . . every month'.

OTHELLO

Thou dost conspire against thy friend, Iago,
If thou but think'st him wronged, and mak'st his ear
A stranger to thy thoughts.

IAGO   I do beseech you—
Though I perchance am vicious in my guess
(As I confess it is my nature's plague   150
To spy into abuses), and oft my jealousy
Shapes faults that are not—that your wisdom yet,
From one that so imperfectly conjects,
Would take no notice, nor build yourself a trouble
Out of his scattering and unsure observance.   155
It were not for your quiet, nor your good,
Nor for my manhood, honesty, and wisdom,
To let you know my thoughts.

151–2 oft . . . Shapes] Q; of . . . Shapes F; of . . . Shape KNIGHT   152 that your wisdom yet]
Q2; that your wisedome F; I intreate you then Q1; that your wisdom then WALKER   153 con-
jects] Q1 (coniects); conceits F, Q2   154 Would] F, Q2; You'd Q1   155 his] F; my Q
157 and] F; or Q

146 **thy friend** An important moment:
responding to Iago's protestation of 'love'
(l. 120), Othello elevates him from the
servantly role defined by his rank
(1.1.41–60) to the intimate status of
'friend'. The intimacy of his gesture is
stressed by the singular pronoun. Renaissance texts on friendship stress the equal
and disinterested nature of friendship,
and the consequent impossibility of a subordinate's acting as a true friend, uncon-
taminated by self-interest.

148–55 **I . . . observance** This convoluted
sentence, in which parenthesis is enfolded
within parenthesis and clause piled on
clause, is a beautiful example of Iago's
technique of syntactical mystification.

151 **oft my jealousy** F's *of my jealousy* makes
sense if combined with Knight's emendation of *shapes* to *shape*; but the fact that
both F and Q print *shapes* makes it more
likely that a t has dropped from F, either
through misreading or compositorial
carelessness.

jealousy (excessive) zeal, vigilance; mis-
trustfulness. However, for the audience
the word will inevitably recall Iago's jealous suspicions of Othello and Cassio, and
the 'jealousy so strong' into which
he vengefully plans to drive the Moor
(2.1.285–302).

152 **that your wisdom** Q's *I intreate you
then*, which simplifies Iago's contorted
syntax while diluting the meaning,
looks like the sort of convenient substitution that an actor, wrestling with the
sense of the line, might well be tempted to
make.

153 **conjects** conjectures. F's *conceits*
(= imagines) is also possible, but looks like
a very easy misreading for Q's much rarer
coniects.

155 **scattering . . . observance** erratic and
unreliable observation (*OED*, *scattering*,
ppl. a. 1a)

156, 157 **for** good for

158 **What . . . mean** Honigmann's attempt
to incorporate Q's *Zouns* (on the
assumption that it was purged from
F: see App. B, pp. 420–1) produces an
awkward extra-metrical lurch in the
middle of the line. Unlike Q, F is metrically complete here and (it can be argued)
dramatically stronger. Given that Q may
contain elements of memorialization, it
is easy to see how an actor might have
imported *Zouns* from l. 168, where it
would have been replaced by F's *Ha?*
when the text was purged of oaths;
certainly Q's incomplete version of that
line suggests the possibility of textual
corruption.

OTHELLO   What dost thou mean?

IAGO

Good name in man—and woman—dear my lord,

Is the immediate jewel of their souls;   160

Who steals my purse, steals trash: 'tis something
   nothing;

'Twas mine, 'tis his, and has been slave to thousands.

But he that filches from me my good name

Robs me of that which not enriches him,

And makes me poor indeed.

OTHELLO   By heaven, I'll know thy thoughts!   165

IAGO

You cannot, if my heart were in your hand;

Nor shall not, whilst 'tis in my custody.

OTHELLO

'Swounds!

IAGO   O beware, my lord, of jealousy!

It is the green-eyed monster which doth mock

The meat it feeds on. That cuckold lives in bliss   170

Who, certain of his fate, loves not his wronger;

158 What . . . mean] F, Q2; Zouns Q1; Zounds! . . . mean HONIGMANN   159 woman—dear]
F, Q2 (woman,); woman's deere Q1   160 their] F; our Q   161 something nothing] HONIG-
MANN (something-nothing); ~, ~ F, Q   165 By heaven] Q1; *not in* F, Q2   thoughts] F, Q2;
thought Q1   168 'Swounds!] This edition (*after* Q 'Zouns', l. 158); Ha? F; *not in* Q   my lord, of
] F, Q2; *not in* Q1   170 The] F, Q2; That Q1

159–60 **Good . . . souls** Cf. Dent N22, 'A
good name is better than riches'. Elabora-
tions of this theme are commonplace in
the period.

161 **trash** dross (often contemptuously applied to money; see e.g. *Caesar*, 4.3.26)
  something nothing a something made
of nothing. Despite the agreement of F
and Q in punctuating *something, nothing*,
Iago's paradox seems to be a stock formulation: see Dent S620.1.

166 **if . . . hand** Honigmann cites Dent
H331.2, 'To have someone's heart in
one's hand', a hyperbolic metonym for
murder which occurs in a number of
plays, and which perhaps drew on the
symbolic language of public executions in
which the hearts of traitors were displayed to the crowd by the executioner;
but Iago's figure seems more closely
related to the investigative delving of anatomy, in which the interior spaces of
the body were opened to the curiosity of
an audience (see above, l. 119). The two

figures come together in the ripping out of
Annabella's heart at the end of John
Ford's tragedy, *'Tis Pity She's a Whore*.

168 **'Swounds** See above, l. 158

169 **green-eyed** Cf. *Merchant*, 3.2.110,
'green-eyed jealousy'. According to the
doctrine of the humours, jealousy was a
bilious condition that was supposed to
impart a greenish hue to the complexion;
it is green-*eyed* because of the exaggerated
watchfulness that in this play translates
itself into Othello's compulsive desire for
'ocular proof' (l. 362).
  mock deride, render ridiculous; deceive,
delude, befool; tantalize.

170 **meat . . . on** i.e. its victim. The figure
suggests something of the strangely self-
generating, self-devouring quality of this
emotion: cf. Emilia's 'It is a monster |
Begot upon itself, born on itself'
(3.4.156–7).

171 **his wronger** his adulterous wife. But
the phrase may also recall Othello's much
emphasized 'love' for Cassio.

But O, what damnèd minutes tells he o'er,
Who dotes yet doubts, suspects yet soundly loves!

OTHELLO O misery!

IAGO

Poor and content is rich, and rich enough, 175
But riches fineless, is as poor as winter,
To him that ever fears he shall be poor:
Good God the souls of all my tribe defend
From jealousy!

OTHELLO   Why? Why is this?
Think'st thou I'd make a life of jealousy, 180
To follow still the changes of the moon
With fresh suspicions? No: to be once in doubt
Is once to be resolved. Exchange me for a goat
When I shall turn the business of my soul
To such exsuffilate and blown surmises, 185

---

173 soundly] F; strongly Q; fondly KNIGHT   178 God] Q1; Heauen F, Q2   183 once] Q; *not in* F   185 exsuffilate] This edition (*after* HANMER, 'exsuffolate'); exufflicate F, Q   blown] Q; blow'd F

---

172 **tells** counts

173 **soundly** to the full (with perhaps a paradoxical suggestion of undisturbed possession, as if the doting lover were consumed by doubts at one moment and absurdly complacent the next; cf. 'sleeping soundly'). Many editors accept Knight's emendation, *fondly*, which is graphically possible; but the alliterative balance of this antithetical line requires either *soundly* or Q's *strongly*, which looks like an alternative (or perhaps a substitution) rather than a misreading.

174 **O misery** Some actors (including Kean and Macready) have made this the point at which Othello first glimpses his jealous destiny; but it can be played simply as a general comment on the torment Iago has described.

175 **Poor ... enough** Cf. Dent C629, 'Contentment is great riches', and Tilley W194, 'The greatest wealth is contentment with a little'.

176–7 **riches ... poor** Cf Tilley R109, 'Riches bring care and fears'. 'Poor as winter', though not listed in Dent or Tilley, also has the proverbial ring characteristic of Iago's common-sensical idiom (see 2.3.234).

176 **fineless** limitless (first use cited in *OED*)

178–9 **Good ... jealousy** Cf. Dent J38.1, 'From jealousy the good Lord deliver us' (not recorded before *Othello*).

178 **tribe** kindred. The division of the population of Venice into six 'tribes', no doubt modelled on those of republican Rome, is described in Lewkenor, pp. 44, 97.

181 **To ... moon** by always responding to each new phase of the moon (as a madman would do)

182–3 **to ... resolved** to feel the slightest suspicion demands that one make up one's mind to free oneself immediately and permanently from doubt; *once* = both 'at once' and 'once and for all'; *resolved* = both 'determined' and 'freed from uncertainty'; *doubt* = both 'uncertainty' and 'suspicion'.

  goat A type of bestial lust; its horns associate it with cuckoldry.

185 **exsuffilate** A much debated crux; the reading proposed here would mean 'hissed, whispered'. See App. F(iii) for a note on the textual reasoning.

  blown Either (a) whispered (*OED, blown, ppl. a.*[1] 4); or (b) bandied about, rumoured (*blow, v.*[1] 13); or (c) stale, tainted (*blown, ppl. a.*[1] 3); or (d) fly-blown (*blow, v.*[1], 28); or (e) inflated, exaggerated (*blown, ppl. a.*[1] 5b). In support of (b) Sanders suggestively

Matching thy inference. 'Tis not to make me jealous
To say my wife is fair, feeds well, loves company,
Is free of speech, sings, plays, and dances well—
Where virtue is, these are more virtuous—
Nor from mine own weak merits will I draw   190
The smallest fear or doubt of her revolt,
For she had eyes and chose me. No, Iago,
I'll see before I doubt; when I doubt, prove;
And, on the proof, there is no more but this:
Away at once with love or jealousy!   195

IAGO

I am glad of this; for now I shall have reason
To show the love and duty that I bear you
With franker spirit. Therefore—as I am bound—
Receive it from me. I speak not yet of proof:
Look to your wife, observe her well with Cassio;   200
Wear your eyes thus: not jealous, nor secure—
I would not have your free and noble nature
Out of self-bounty be abused—look to't.
I know our country disposition well:
In Venice they do let God see the pranks   205
They dare not show their husbands; their best
    conscience

---

188 well] Q; *not in* F   196 this] F; it Q   201 eyes] F; eie Q   205 God] Q1; Heauen F, Q2

cites *2 Henry IV*, Ind.15–16 'Rumour is a
pipe | Blown by surmises, Jealousy's con-
jectures'. F's *blow'd*, though it exists as an
occasional alternative to *blown*, is a plausible misreading for *blown* (especially if the
copy read *blow'n*).

186 **inference** conclusion; implication (the
conclusion one is entitled to draw)
186–8 **'Tis . . . well** In the dialogue that
introduces Giraldi's *Hecatommithi*, Fabio
warns his interlocutors against the
deceitful attractions of women who 'with
beauty of body and under semblance of
virtue, for instance in singing, playing,
dancing lightly and speaking sweetly,
hide an ugly and abominable soul'
(Bullough, vii. 240).
188 **free** unreserved (can also have the negative sense of 'over-familiar', 'sexually
bold').

191 **doubt** suspicion
    revolt betrayal, infidelity
193 **doubt** Cf. ll. 182–3.
    prove (a) put my suspicions to the test;
    (b) prove my suspicions true.
196–200 **now . . . Cassio** Cf. Giraldi, App.
    C, p. 440.
201 **Wear** use (*OED v.*[1] 2b)
    secure free from mistrust, over-confident
202 **free** noble; ingenuous, free from
    suspicion
203 **self-bounty** innate generosity and
    goodness
    abused deceived, taken advantage of,
    wronged
204 **I . . . country** Iago is the privileged
    insider, Othello the ignorant 'stranger';
    for the obscene play on 'country' see
    Pechter, p. 88, and cf. *Hamlet*, 3.2.111
    ('country matters').
205 **pranks** Cf. 2.1.141

Is not to leave't undone, but keep't unknown.
OTHELLO Dost thou say so?
IAGO
  She did deceive her father, marrying you;
  And when she seemed to shake and fear your looks,   210
  She loved them most.
OTHELLO   And so she did.
IAGO   Why, go to, then!
  She that so young could give out such a seeming
  To seel her father's eyes up, close as oak—
  He thought 'twas witchcraft!—But I am much to blame;
  I humbly do beseech you of your pardon   215
  For too much loving you.
OTHELLO   I am bound to thee for ever.
IAGO
I see this hath a little dashed your spirits.
OTHELLO
  Not a jot, not a jot.
IAGO   I'faith, I fear it has.
  I hope you will consider what is spoke
  Comes from your love. But I do see you're moved.   220
  I am to pray you not to strain my speech
  To grosser issues, nor to larger reach
  Than to suspicion.

207 leave't] F, Q2; leaue Q1   keep't] Q2; kept F; keepe Q1   213 seel] F (seele); seale Q
218 I'faith] Q1; Trust me F, Q2   220 your] F; my Q

209–11 **She . . . most** A sly reminder of Brabantio's threat, 'She has deceived her father and may thee' (1.3.291).
213 **seel** See 1.3.267. Q's *seal* is probably not a genuine variant, since the spelling of the two words did not become completely distinct until the early 19th century. However, it usefully draws attention to the word-play indicated by 'close as oak'.
  close as oak i.e. as the tight grain of this timber. Proverbial: Dent O1, citing this as the earliest example.
214 **He . . . witchcraft** Again remembering Brabantio's denunciations (cf. 1.3.65, 103, 169).
216 **bound to thee** Usually glossed as 'indebted to you'; but it also carries the sense of 'tied or bonded to you', hyperbolically inverting the terms of service to make Othello Iago's indentured 'bond-man'. Like Iago's 'I am your own for ever' (l. 479), which closes the scene, Othello's line seems to announce (however unconsciously) a kind of diabolical pact like that between Faustus and his diabolic 'servant' Mephostophilis in Marlowe's *Dr Faustus*.
220 **your love** i.e. my love of you. This construction (the so-called 'objective genitive') is found elsewhere in Shakespeare, see e.g. *Winter's Tale*, 4.4.500–1: 'most opportune to her need, I have | A vessel rides fast by', where *her need* is equivalent to 'our need of her [the ship]'. Cf. also l. 254; 4.1.90.
221 **am to pray** must beg
  strain force the meaning of (*OED v.*[1] 11a)
222 **grosser** (a) larger; (b) more indecent
  issues conclusions
  reach scope

OTHELLO I will not.
IAGO Should you do so, my lord,   225
    My speech should fall into such vile success
    Which my thoughts aimed not at: Cassio's my worthy
        friend—
    My lord, I see you're moved.
OTHELLO   No, not much moved:
    I do not think but Desdemona's honest.
IAGO
    Long live she so!—And long live you to think so!   230
OTHELLO
    And yet how nature, erring from itself—
IAGO
    Ay, there's the point! As—to be bold with you—
    Not to affect many proposèd matches
    Of her own clime, complexion, and degree,
    Whereto we see in all things nature tends—   235
    Foh! One may smell in such a will most rank,
    Foul disproportions, thoughts unnatural—
    But pardon me: I do not in position
    Distinctly speak of her—though I may fear
    Her will, recoiling to her better judgement,   240
    May fall to match you with her country forms,

---

227 Which] F; As Q   aimed] F (aym'd); aime Q   at] Q; *not in* F   worthy] F, Q2; trusty Q1
236 Foh! One] F (Foh, one); Fie we Q   237 disproportions] F; disproportion Q

---

224 **I will not** Cf. ll. 32–4. Probably amphibious, although it creates two nine-syllable lines.
226 **fall . . . success** produce such a despicable outcome.
229 **honest** chaste
233–7 **Not . . . unnatural** Again remembering Brabantio's slurs (1.3.97–102); and cf. Giraldi, App. C, p. 442.
234 **clime** region; latitude
    complexion temperament, nature; skin-colour (thought to be a marker of temperament because it expressed the humoral constitution of the body)
    degree rank
236 **will** (a) disposition; (b) wilfulness; (c) sexual appetite; (d) genitals.
    rank (a) rebellious, impetuous; (b) over-

grown, overfed; (c) lustful; (d) corrupt, festering, foul-smelling
237 **disproportions** deformities, monstrosities. Iago is hinting at the kinds of unnatural coupling he described to Brabantio (1.1.88–9, 110–16). 'Foul' (= 'dirty-coloured' (i.e. black), as well as 'ugly, filthy, diseased, abominable', *OED adj.* 1c, 2, 4b,7, 11a) links them once again to Othello himself.
238 **in position** in this assertion
239 **Distinctly** particularly
240 **recoiling** returning
241 **fall to match** start comparing
    her country forms the style of beauty recognized in her own country
    country A bawdy pun is probably intended (see l. 204 n.).

And happily repent.

OTHELLO   Farewell, farewell.

If more thou dost perceive, let me know more:

Set on thy wife to observe. Leave me, Iago.

IAGO (*going*)

My lord, I take my leave.   245

OTHELLO

Why did I marry? This honest creature doubtless

Sees and knows more, much more than he unfolds.

IAGO (*returning*)

My lord, I would I might entreat your honour

To scan this thing no farther: leave it to time.

Although 'tis fit that Cassio have his place—   250

For sure he fills it up with great ability—

Yet, if you please to hold him off a while,

You shall by that perceive him and his means:

Note if your lady strain his entertainment

With any strong or vehement importunity;   255

Much will be seen in that. In the meantime,

Let me be thought too busy in my fears

(As worthy cause I have to fear I am)

And hold her free, I do beseech your honour.

OTHELLO

Fear not my government.

IAGO   I once more take my leave.   260

Exit

242 Farewell, farewell] F; Farewell Q   245 *going*] CAPELL; *not in* F, Q   248 IAGO] F, Q2; *before* 'To scan' (*l.* 249) Q1 (*corr.*); *not in* Q1 (*uncorr.*)   *returning*] CAPELL; *not in* F, Q   249 farther] F; further Q   250 Although 'tis] F; Tho it be Q1; And though 'tis Q2   252 hold] Q; *not in* F1; put F2   254 his] F; her Q   260.1 *Exit*] F, Q1 (*corr.*), Q2; *not in* Q1 (*uncorr.*)

242 **happily** perhaps
247 **unfolds** reveals
250–1 **place . . . fills it up** An obscene innuendo. Cf. Marlowe, *Massacre at Paris*, Scene xviii, 1–5 (Folger MS version): 'Now sir, to you that dares to make a duke cuckold . . . and fill up his room that he should occupy.'
253 **means** Usually glossed as 'methods', but perhaps rather 'meaning, intention' (i.e. what he's up to): *OED, means, n.*

254 **strain his entertainment** (over-)insist upon his reinstatement. Another objective genitive (see l. 220).
257 **busy** prying, officious
259 **free** A treacherous equivocation: (a) innocent; (b) licentious, sexually available (Williams, *Dictionary*, p. 542; *Glossary*, p. 134).
260 **government** self-control

OTHELLO

This fellow's of exceeding honesty,
And knows all qualities, with a learnèd spirit
Of human dealings. If I do prove her haggard,
Though that her jesses were my dear heart-strings,
I'd whistle her off and let her down the wind   265
To prey at fortune. Haply, for I am black
And have not those soft parts of conversation
That chamberers have, or for I am declined
Into the vale of years—yet that's not much—
She's gone, I am abused, and my relief   270
Must be to loathe her. O curse of marriage,
That we can call these delicate creatures ours,
And not their appetites! I had rather be a toad
And live upon the vapour of a dungeon,

262 qualities] Q1; quantities F, Q2   learnèd] Q (learned); learn'd F   263 dealings] F, Q2;
dealing Q1   266 Haply] F; Happily Q   268 chamberers] F, Q (*corr.*); Chamlerers Q (*uncorr.*)
269 vale] F, Q2; valt Q1   274 of] F; in Q

262 **qualities** characteristics, natures of
people. Q2's decision to emend to F's
quantities is a strange one, perhaps
prompted by a misunderstanding of deal-
ing(s) as 'commercial intercourse'.
262–3 **with . . . dealings** with a mind well-
versed in all aspects of human conduct
263 **haggard** A term from falconry: 'caught
after having assumed adult plumage',
hence 'wild, untamed'.
264 **jesses** Straps tied to the legs of a hawk,
used to attach it to the leash.
   heart-strings nerves or tendons supposed (in early modern anatomy) to brace
the heart. The snapping of these strings,
under the pressure of great grief, would
produce a 'broken heart'.
265 **I'd . . . wind** Falconers would launch
hawks from their wrist with a whistle: up
wind when in search of prey, and down
wind when they were being turned loose.
266 **at fortune** at random (i.e. look after
herself)
   Haply, for perhaps, because
267 **soft** Contradictory meanings are probably involved, registering the soldier's
ambiguous attitude towards the courtly
world: 'pleasing, gentle, refined', but also
'idle, effeminate, foolish'.
   conversation social behaviour; also
(though this is probably not part of

Othello's conscious meaning) a standard
euphemism for sexual intercourse.
268 **chamberers** frequenters of ladies'
chambers, carpet-knights; also a term for
valet or chamberlain.
269 **vale of years** *OED's* first recorded use of
this quasi-proverbial expression. Perhaps
coined by collapsing 'vale of tears' (current since at least 1554) with 'the valley of
the shadow of death' (Psalms 23: 4); Q's
valt ('vault'), though an easy misreading,
would also make sense as a hyperbolic reference to the tomb.
270 **gone** lost, undone
272 **delicate** A number of meanings are
probably in play: charming; voluptuous;
tender, tenderly reared; fastidious; exquisite (*OED adj.* 1, 2a, 4, 5, 6b, 8).
273 **toad** Othello's imagination (as critics
often observe) is beginning to be tainted
with the bestial imagery hitherto characteristic of Iago. For the quasi-proverbial
hatefulness of toads, see *Troilus*,
2.3.157–8: 'I do hate a proud man as I
hate the engendering of toads' (and cf.
Richard III, 4.4.81).
274 **vapour of a dungeon** Castle dungeons
were notoriously filthy: Marlowe's
Edward II, for example, is confined to 'a
vault up to the knees in water, | To which
the channels [sewers] of the castle run, |

Than keep a corner in the thing I love   275
For others' uses. Yet 'tis the plague to great ones:
Prerogatived are they less than the base.
'Tis destiny unshunnable, like death:
Even then this forkèd plague is fated to us
When we do quicken. Look where she comes—   280
    Enter Desdemona and Emilia
If she be false, O then heaven mocks itself:
I'll not believe't.

DESDEMONA   How now, my dear Othello?
Your dinner, and the generous islanders
By you invited, do attend your presence.

OTHELLO
I am to blame.

DESDEMONA   Why do you speak so faintly?   285
Are you not well?

OTHELLO
I have a pain upon my forehead, here.

DESDEMONA
Faith, that's with watching: 'twill away again.
Let me but bind it hard, within this hour
It will be well.

OTHELLO   Your napkin is too little.   290

---

275 keep] F, Q (*corr.*) (keepe); leepe Q (*uncorr.*)   the thing] F; a thing Q   276 to] F; of Q
280 Look where she] F; *Desdemona* Q   280.1 *Enter . . . Emilia*] F; *after* 'beleeue it.' Q   281 O
then heaven mocks] Q; Heauen mock'd F   283 islanders] F; Ilander Q   285 do . . . faintly]
F; is your speech so faint Q   288 Faith] Q1; Why F, Q2   289 it hard] F, Q2; your head Q1
290 well] F, Q2; well againe Q1

From whence a damp continually ariseth | That were enough to poison any man' (*Edward II*, 5.5.2–5).

275 **keep a corner** reserve a small space. 'Corner' was a slang term for vagina (Williams, *Dictionary*, p. 310; *Glossary*, p. 82), and the bawdy senses of *keep* (= keep a whore or mistress) and *use* (= sexual use) are also present.

277 **Prerogatived** privileged

278–9 **'Tis . . . fated** Cf. Dent C889, 'Cuckolds come by destiny'.

278 **unshunnable** First use cited in *OED*.

279 **forkèd** i.e. marked with the horns of cuckoldry

280 **quicken** receive life (at conception or birth)

281 **heaven mocks** i.e. when creating someone so innocent-seeming

283–4 **dinner . . . presence** Honigmann suggests this may be a cue for sounds of offstage revelry.

283 **generous** noble, high-ranking; gallant, courageous

287 **pain . . . forehead** Deliberately ambiguous; the presence of a cuckold's horns was supposedly betrayed by an aching brow; but, if what Iago says at 4.1.46 is to be trusted, this might be the first symptom of an epileptic fit.

288 **watching** keeping vigilantly awake

She drops her handkerchief
Let it alone. Come, I'll go in with you.

DESDEMONA

I am very sorry that you are not well.

Exeunt Othello and Desdemona

EMILIA

I am glad I have found this napkin:
This was her first remembrance from the Moor;
My wayward husband hath a hundred times   295
Wooed me to steal it; but she so loves the token—
For he conjured her she should ever keep it—
That she reserves it evermore about her
To kiss and talk to. I'll have the work ta'en out,
And give't Iago: what he will do with it   300
Heaven knows, not I—
I nothing, but to please his fantasy.

Enter Iago

IAGO

How now? What do you here alone?

EMILIA

Do not you chide: I have a thing for you.

IAGO

You have a thing for me? It is a common thing—   305

EMILIA Hah?

IAGO To have a foolish wife.

EMILIA

O, is that all? What will you give me now
For that same handkerchief?

290.1 *She . . . handkerchief*] ROWE; *not in* F, Q   292.1 *Exeunt . . . Desdemona*] ROWE *after* Q ('Ex. Oth. *and* Desd.' *after* 'napkin', *l.* 293); *Exit.* F (*after* 'you', *l.* 291)   302 but to please] F, Q2; know, but for Q1   302.1 *Enter Iago*] F; *after* 'not I' (*l.* 301) Q   305 You have] F; *not in* Q   307 wife] F, Q2; thing Q1

293–324 **I am glad . . . find it** Cf. Giraldi, App. C, p. 441. In Giraldi, however, Iago steals the handkerchief from Disdemona's girdle.

293 **napkin** handkerchief (*OED n.* 2a). For the medicinal powers associated with the dyeing of this handkerchief in 'mummy', see below, 3.4.73–4 nn.

294 **remembrance** keepsake. In Shakespeare's time handkerchiefs were luxury items, often (like this one) elaborately and expensively embroidered.

295 **wayward** wilful, capricious.

297 **conjured** made her swear. The accent falls on the second syllable.

299 **work ta'en out** embroidery copied (*OED, work, n.* 16; *take, v.* 87e).

301 **Heaven . . . I** Cf. Dent G189.1.

302 **I . . . but** I know nothing except **fantasy** capricious desires

305 **common thing** Iago plays on the contemptuously bawdy sense of both words: 'a cunt available to anyone'.

IAGO   What handkerchief?

EMILIA What handkerchief?   310

  Why that the Moor first gave to Desdemona,

  That which so often you did bid me steal.

IAGO

  Hast stolen it from her?

EMILIA

  No, faith, she let it drop by negligence,

  And, to th'advantage, I being here took't up: 315

  Look, here it is.

IAGO   A good wench! Give it me.

     ⌈*He snatches it*⌉

EMILIA

  What will you do with it, that you have been

  So earnest to have me filch it?

IAGO   Why, what's that to you?

EMILIA

  If it be not for some purpose of import,

  Give't me again. Poor lady, she'll run mad   320

  When she shall lack it.

IAGO   Be not acknown on't:

  I have use for it. Go, leave me.   *Exit Emilia*

  I will in Cassio's lodging lose this napkin,

  And let him find it. Trifles light as air

---

310 handkerchief] F (*throughout*), Q2; handkercher Q1 (*throughout, except sometimes* 'han-
kercher')   313 stolen] F (stolne); stole Q   314 No, faith,] Q; No: but∧ F   316 it is] Q; 'tis F
316.1 *He snatches it*] This edition *after* ROWE (*before* 'Why . . .', l. 318); *not in* F, Q   317 with it]
Q; with't F   318 what's] Q; what is F   320 Give't me] F; Giue mee't Q   321 acknown] F
(acknowne); you knowne Q1; you acknowne Q2   323 lose] Q; loose F

312 **so often** Frequently cited as an example
of the play's so-called 'double-time
scheme' (see Introduction, pp. 33–6).
Emilia's role as Desdemona's waiting-
woman presumably dates only from Othello's request at 1.3.294. Perhaps we are
meant to assign Iago's importunity to the
voyage; but audiences seldom notice such
details.

315 **to th'advantage** by good fortune; taking advantage of the opportunity

316 **A good wench** Playful semi-bawdy:
actors often play up the cynical eroticism
of this encounter, which Iago brings to an
abrupt end at ll. 321–2.

318 **So . . . you** A hexameter line that
requires some elision ('t'have').

319 **of import** important

321 **lack** miss

    Be . . . on't Do not acknowledge you
know anything about it. Unique in
Shakespeare and already a somewhat
antiquated form, which may explain
Q's substitution of 'Be not you known
on't'.

323 **lose** Early modern orthography did not
distinguish between *lose* and *loose* (F's
spelling); thus the senses 'let loose' and
'shoot' or 'let fly' (as in *loose an arrow*) are
also appropriate here, given the dangerous thing that Iago has made of the
handkerchief.

Are to the jealous confirmations strong   325
As proofs of holy writ. This may do something.
The Moor already changes with my poison:
Dangerous conceits are in their natures poisons,
Which at the first are scarce found to distaste,
But, with a little act upon the blood,   330
Burn like the mines of sulphur. I did say so.
      Enter Othello
Look where he comes. Not poppy, nor mandragora,
Nor all the drowsy syrups of the world
Shall ever medicine thee to that sweet sleep
Which thou owedst yesterday.
OTHELLO   Ha, ha, false to me?   335
IAGO
Why, how now, general? No more of that!
OTHELLO
Avaunt, be gone! Thou hast set me on the rack:
I swear 'tis better to be much abused
Than but to know't a little.
IAGO   How now, my lord?

---

327 The . . . poison] F, Q2; *not in* Q1   330 act upon] F, Q2; art, vpon Q1   331 mines] F, Q2;
mindes Q1   331.1 *Enter Othello*] F; *after* 'blood' (*l.* 330) Q   335 to me] F; to mee, to mee Q
339 know't] F, Q2; know Q1

326 **of holy writ** culled from the Bible
327 **The . . . poison** Omission of this line
      from Q may represent a deliberate cut, or
      an actor's omission; but it might equally
      be the result of eye-skip to 'poisons' at l.
      328. Rizvi (see 2.3.153–6), finding the
      repetition of 'poison' awkward, suggests
      that the line represents a false start
      intended for cancellation; he may be cor-
      rect, but the Q2 editor clearly thought the
      line worth restoring.
328 **conceits** ideas, imaginings
329 **distaste** offend the taste, nauseate
330 **act** action
      blood Both literal and metaphorical:
      Iago's poisonous insinuations act upon
      Othello's passions ('blood') as poison acts
      upon the life fluid itself.
331 **Burn . . . sulphur** Hart cites Pliny,
      35.15: 'Sulphur . . . is engendered within
      the Islands Aeoliae, which lie between
      Italy and Sicily . . . which . . . do always
      burn by reason thereof' (sig. Bbb2ᵛ); and

Greene, *Orlando Furioso* (ed. 1874, p.
107b): 'Naught can serve to quench the
aspiring flames | That burn as do the fires
of Sicily'. In Iago's mouth, however,
the words are bound to suggest the
'sulph'rous . . . flames' of hell (*Hamlet*,
1.5.3), and (in the context of Othello's
jealousy) perhaps also the 'sulphurous
pit' that Lear locates in the 'hell' of female
genitalia (*Trag. Lear*, 4.5.124–5).
332–5 **Not . . . yesterday** A 'chillingly
effortless, mocking parody of sustained
Othello-like sonorities' (Bradshaw, p.
271).
332 **poppy** opium (used as a painkiller and
sedative)
      mandragora The mandrake plant, from
      which a narcotic, valued for its analgesic
      properties, was extracted. Cf. *Antony*,
      1.5.3–5.
335 **owedst** owned (*OED v.* 1a)
337 **Avaunt** away with you
338 **abused** Cf. l. 203.

OTHELLO

What sense had I in her stolen hours of lust? 340
I saw't not, thought it not—it harm'd not me;
I slept the next night well, fed well, was free, and merry;
I found not Cassio's kisses on her lips.
He that is robbed, not wanting what is stolen,
Let him not know't, and he's not robbed at all. 345

IAGO

I am sorry to hear this.

OTHELLO

I had been happy if the general camp,
Pioneers and all, had tasted her sweet body,
So I had nothing known. O, now for ever
Farewell the tranquil mind; farewell content; 350
Farewell the plumèd troops, and the big wars
That makes ambition virtue—O, farewell!
Farewell the neighing steed and the shrill trump,
The spirit-stirring drum, the ear-piercing fife,
The royal banner, and all quality, 355
Pride, pomp, and circumstance of glorious war;
And O you mortal engines, whose rude throats

---

340 in] F; of Q   342 fed well] F; *not in* Q   345 know't] F, Q2; know'r Q1   351 troops] F
(Troopes); troope Q   357 you] F; ye Q   rude] F; wide Q

340 **What sense** how much awareness (i.e.
Othello implies that his senses were
asleep)
in during
341 **I . . . me** Cf. Dent K179.1 ('What one
does not know does not hurt') and L461
('He that is not sensible of his loss has lost
nothing').
342 **free** carefree
344–5 **He . . . all** Cf. l. 341. Othello's language ironically echoes the paradoxes of
Brabantio's argument with the Duke
(1.3.207–10).
344 **wanting** feeling the lack of
347 **general camp** whole army
348 **Pioneers** troops employed to dig roads,
trenches, fortifications, mines, etc. (often
the equivalent of punishment battalions).
Dirty and ill-paid, they were generally the
lowest and least honourable type of soldiery. The F and Q spelling ('pyoners')
indicates a slightly different accenting of
the word with a stress on the first syllable
only.

349 **So** provided that
350 **tranquil** First recorded use in *OED*.
351 **big** mighty, violent (*OED a*. 1, 2)
351–2 **wars . . . makes** Cf. l. 67.
352 **virtue** (a) moral virtue; (b) manly
excellence, courage: cf. Latin *virtus* (*OED
n*. 7)
354 **spirit-stirring** courage-rousing (first
example cited in *OED*)
355 **royal** magnificent, splendid
quality excellence (*OED n*. 1c)
356 **Pride** (a) self-esteem; (b) arrogance; (c)
splendid ostentation; (d) honour, glory
(*OED n*.[1] 1, 2, 6a, 8b).
circumstance ceremony (*OED n*. 7a)
glorious proud, vaunting; eager for
glory; illustrious; conferring glory; full of
magnificent display; splendid (*OED a*.
1–5)
357 **mortal engines** deadly instruments
(i.e. cannon)
rude harsh, violent; discordant (*OED a*.
5, 7)

Th'immortal Jove's dread clamours counterfeit,
Farewell! Othello's occupation's gone.

IAGO
Is't possible, my lord?   360

OTHELLO
Villain, be sure thou prove my love a whore!
Be sure of it; give me the ocular proof;
⌈*He seizes Iago by the throat*⌉
Or, by the worth of mine eternal soul,
Thou hadst been better have been born a dog
Than answer my waked wrath!

IAGO   Is't come to this?   365

OTHELLO
Make me to see't; or, at the least, so prove it
That the probation bear no hinge nor loop
To hang a doubt on—or woe upon thy life!

IAGO My noble lord—

OTHELLO
If thou dost slander her and torture me,   370
Never pray more! Abandon all remorse,
On horror's head horrors accumulate,
Do deeds to make heaven weep, all earth amazed!
For nothing canst thou to damnation add
Greater than that.

IAGO   O grace! O heaven forgive me!   375

358 dread clamours] F; great clamor Q1; great clamors Q2   361 thou] F, Q (*corr.*); you Q
(*uncorr.*)   362.1 *He seizes . . . throat*] *after* ROWE; *not in* F, Q   363 mine] F; mans Q1; my Q2
375 forgive] F; defend Q

358 **Jove's dread clamours** i.e. thunder
359 **occupation** (a) career; (b) sexual pos-
     session (of Desdemona); cf. ll. 250–1.
360 **Is't possible** Cf. 2.3.276.
361–5 **Villain . . . wrath** Closely modelled,
     as Honigmann points out (pp. 232, 377),
     on Giraldi (see App. C, pp. 440, 443).
     Ocular was perhaps suggested by Giraldi's
     occhi; but Honigmann cites also Jonson,
     Cynthia's Revels (1600), 2.3.11 ('ocular
     . . . witness') and *Poetaster* (1601), 4.5.75
     ('ocular temptation')
362.1 **He . . . throat** Rowe's direction prob-
     ably recorded late 17th- and early 18th-
     century stage business, which may in
     turn have derived from practice in Shake-
     speare's time. This piece of business
     became standard in what was often

referred to as the 'collaring scene', and is
often preserved in modern productions:
Olivier, for example, 'lock[ed] Finlay by
the throat and hurl[ed] him to the
ground' (Tynan, p. 8).
367 **probation** proof
     hinge 'that on which something is con-
     ceived to hang' (*OED n.* 4a, citing this as
     the first example); *hinge* derives originally
     from 'hang', and (since the *probation*) will
     serve as a weapon of sorts, Shakespeare
     perhaps had in mind the 'frogs' and *loops*
     from which a sword (or 'hanger') was sus-
     pended from the belt.
372 **accumulate** pile up (imperative)
373 **amazed** Stronger than now: 'stupefied,
     terrified, crazy'.

Are you a man? Have you a soul or sense?
God by you, take mine office—O wretched fool
That lov'st to make thine honesty a vice!
O monstrous world! Take note, take note, O world,
To be direct and honest is not safe!—   380
I thank you for this profit, and from hence
I'll love no friend, sith love breeds such offence.

OTHELLO

Nay, stay. Thou shouldst be honest.

IAGO

I should be wise; for honesty's a fool,
And loses that it works for.

OTHELLO   By the world,   385
I think my wife be honest, and think she is not;
I think that thou art just, and think thou art not:
I'll have some proof. Her name, that was as fresh

---

377 God by you, take mine] F (buy), Q1 (*corr.*); God buy, you take thine Q1 (*uncorr.*);
God buy you, take my Q2   378 lov'st] F; liuest Q   thine] F, Q1 (*corr.*), Q2; mine Q1 (*uncorr.*)
382 sith] F; since Q   385–92 By . . . satisified] F, Q2; *not in* Q1   388 Her] Q2; My F

---

377 **God by you** Goodbye (i.e. 'I wash my
hands of you'). Cf. 1.3.188.
   take mine office cashier me
378 **lov'st . . . vice** Iago accuses himself of
habitually following the promptings of his
innate honesty to such extremes that it
becomes a vice.
381 **profit** 'that which is to the advantage of
some one', useful lesson (*OED n.* 1b, citing
only this example and *Measure*, 1.4.60)
382 **I'll . . . offence** A characteristically
ambiguous line: Iago is ostensibly talking
about the affront his honesty has caused
to his 'friend' Othello (l. 146); but
since 'friend' can also mean 'mistress' or
'lover' he can also seem to be glancing
at the hurt caused by Othello's love for
Desdemona, and Desdemona's love for
Cassio.
   sith since
383 **shouldst be** seem as if you should be
384 **should be** ought to be (if I had any
sense)
   honesty's a fool Cf. Dent H539.1 (citing
this as the first example). Perhaps another
of Iago's pseudo-proverbs.
385 **loses . . . works for** Possibly with an
ironic glance at Desdemona's advocacy of
Cassio's cause.
385–92 **By . . . satisfied** This passage can
hardly be an addition to F, since its

absence removes the cue for Iago's goad-
ing play with 'satisfy' (ll. 395, 396, 403,
410), together with part of the justification for 'eaten up with passion' (l. 393);
moreover, l. 385 in the Q version is metrically incomplete; presumably, therefore,
its omission from Q was a result of inexpert theatrical cutting.
386 **honest** Iago's remorseless iteration of
the word reminds Othello of its sexual
meaning.
388 **Her** A famous crux: Q2's emendation of
My to *her* has no independent authority,
and the error (if it is one) is hard to
account for. Ridley, following Knight,
argued strongly for the superiority of F's
reading on the grounds that Othello is
characteristically obsessed with the stain
on his own honour. Dyce, on the other
hand, thought this argument invalidated
by the *own* in 'mine own face' which F
makes superfluous; and to this Honigmann adds that 'the comparison with
Diana (the moon goddess, patron of
chastity) points to a woman and *her*
chastity, not to a man'. The contrast
between the unstained purity of 'Dian's
visage' and his own 'begrimed . . . face'
also suggests that it is Desdemona's name
that Othello has in mind.
   fresh unsullied

As Dian's visage, is now begrimed and black
As mine own face. If there be cords, or knives,   390
Poison, or fire, or suffocating streams,
I'll not endure it. Would I were satisfied!

IAGO

I see, sir, you are eaten up with passion:
I do repent me that I put it to you.
You would be satisfied?

OTHELLO   Would? Nay, and I will!   395

IAGO

And may—but how? How 'satisfied', my lord?
Would you the supervisor grossly gape on?
Behold her tupped?

OTHELLO   Death and damnation! O!

IAGO

It were a tedious difficulty, I think,

---

393 sir] Q; *not in* F   395 and] F; *not in* Q   397 supervisor] Q1; super-vision F, Q2 (superui-sion)   398 tupped] POPE 1728; top'd F; topt Q

389 **begrimed** A metatheatrical conceit: the actor's face will have been literally *begrimed* (covered with soot) to darken his skin.

390–1 **cords . . . streams**   Traditional instruments of suicidal despair (cf. Spenser, *Faerie Queene*, 1.9.50–1, where Despair offers the Redcrosse Knight a dagger, 'swords, ropes, poison, fire, | And all that might him to perdition draw'; and Kyd, *The Spanish Tragedy*, 3.12.0, '*Enter Hieronimo with a poniard in one hand and a rope in the other*'). However, as Honigmann points out, Othello may equally be brooding on murder.

391 **suffocating** First example cited in *OED*.

392, 395, 396, 403, 410 **satisfied . . . satisfaction** Othello means 'freed from doubt', but Iago equivocates on two other meanings, involving the achievement of 'satisfaction' or atonement through a duel or revenge killing (*OED n.* 4), and sexual 'satisfaction' (Williams, *Glossary*, pp. 267–8). The same quibble torments the jealous Leontes in *Winter's Tale* (1.2.234–6).

393 **eaten up** A glance at Iago's earlier description of jealousy as a monster 'which doth mock The meat it feeds on' (ll. 169–70).

394 **put it to** raised it with

397 **supervisor** spectator, looker-on (*OED's* first instance of this usage, a literal translation of the Latin original); but perhaps also with a hint of the more usual sense, 'one who supervises the activity of others', implying that Othello will become a pimp to his own wife. Q seems almost certainly correct here; but the normally careful Q2 editor's choice of the F reading is disconcerting, especially since *OED* records no earlier use of *supervision*, which must therefore have been an unusual word: here it could be the object of *gape on*, and mean something like 'the spectacle you are gazing down upon'.

398 **tupped** Far from representing a 'softening' of 'topped' (as Rosenberg suggests, p. 36), Pope's emendation restores the proper connection with 1.1.89. *OED* lists *top* = 'copulate with, cover' (*v.*[1] 11), citing this as the earliest example; but it seems likely, as Williams suggests (*Dictionary*, p. 1405) that it is simply a variant of *tup*. The word, with its powerfully animalistic suggestions, is clearly a favourite of Iago's, and it seems important to preserve the echo of 1.1. Cf. also 5.2.136.

399–410 **It . . . have't** Cf. Giraldi, App. C, p. 440.

To bring them to that prospect. Damn them, then,   400
If ever mortal eyes do see them bolster
More than their own. What then? How then?
What shall I say? Where's satisfaction?
It is impossible you should see this,
Were they as prime as goats, as hot as monkeys,   405
As salt as wolves in pride, and fools as gross
As ignorance made drunk. But yet, I say,
If imputation and strong circumstances,
Which lead directly to the door of truth,
Will give you satisfaction, you might have't.   410

OTHELLO
Give me a living reason she's disloyal.

IAGO
I do not like the office;
But sith I am entered in this cause so far,
Pricked to't by foolish honesty and love,
I will go on: I lay with Cassio lately;   415

401 do] F; did Q   bolster] F (boulster), Q; balter HONIGMANN *conj.*   405 prime] F, Q; primed
HONIGMANN *conj.*   410 might] F; may Q   411 reason she's] F; reason, that shee's Q   413 in]
F; into Q

400 **to that prospect** into a position from
which they can be viewed in that way
(*OED, prospect, n.* 2b)
401 **bolster** lie with. *OED* lists no other
examples of this usage (*v.* 6) which seems
to be Iago's characteristically vulgar
coinage. Reducing human bodies to inan-
imate bed-furnishing, its meaning is probably coloured by the more common sense
'to stuff' (*OED v.* 4).
402 **More** other
405–6 **prime . . . hot . . . salt** ruttish, sexually aroused, lecherous. This is the only
example in *OED* of *prime* used in this
sense; it is presumably connected to *prime*
(*n.*[1] 7–9) = 'spring', 'prime of life/youth',
i.e the period of greatest (sexual) vigour.
Cf. also Sonnet 97.7, 'the wanton burden
of the prime', and *AYLI*, 5.3.35, 'Love is
crownèd with the prime'.
405 **goats . . . monkeys** Types of lecherous
desire. Cf. Dent G167, 'As lecherous as a
goat', and *Hist. Lear* 7.194–5, 'monkeys
[are tied] by the loins'. A marginal
illustration in the fourteenth-century
Macclesfield Psalter (Fitzwilliam Museum

MSI-2005 f. 155r) shows a monkey and a
goat in a passionate embrace.
406 **wolves** cf. Dent W601.1, 'As lecherous
as a she-wolf'.
in pride on heat
gross big, monstrous; stupid, ignorant
408 **imputation** accusation
circumstances circumstantial evidence
409 **door of truth** Iago's figure makes brutally concrete the play's obsession with
discovering the hidden: 'Othello is led in
imagination to stand outside the closed
bedroom door' (Ridley).
412 **office** duty, job; but the word also
recalls Iago's offer to surrender his commission (l. 377), thus implying reluctant
acceptance of a new 'office' as Othello's
intelligencer or domestic spy.
413 **cause** (a) affair; (b) controversy; (c)
legal case; (d) Othello's cause. Cf. 5.2.1.
414 **Pricked** spurred on
415 **lay with** Beds being expensive items,
they were commonly shared by same-sex
friends and by members of the family.
However, the erotic dream conjured up
in Iago's fiction produces a kind of

And, being troubled with a raging tooth,
I could not sleep. There are a kind of men
So loose of soul that in their sleeps will mutter
Their affairs—one of this kind is Cassio:
In sleep I heard him say 'Sweet Desdemona,   420
Let us be wary, let us hide our loves';
And then, sir, would he gripe and wring my hand,
Cry 'O, sweet creature!', and then kiss me hard,
As if he plucked up kisses by the roots
That grew upon my lips, then laid his leg   425
Over my thigh, and sighed, and kissed, and then
Cried 'Cursèd fate that gave thee to the Moor!'

OTHELLO

O monstrous! Monstrous!

IAGO   Nay, this was but his dream.

OTHELLO

But this denoted a foregone conclusion.

IAGO

'Tis a shrewd doubt, though it be but a dream;   430
And this may help to thicken other proofs,
That do demonstrate thinly.

421 wary] F, Q2; merry Q1   423 Cry 'O] F (Cry, Oh); Cry out Q   and] Q; *not in* F   425 then laid] Q; laid F; lay ROWE; then lay POPE; and lay STEEVENS 1785   426 Over] Q; ore F   426–7 sighed . . . kissed . . . Cried] Q; sigh . . . kisse . . . cry F   429 denoted] F, Q2; deuoted Q1   430 IAGO 'Tis . . . dream] Q1; *continued to Othello* F, Q2   431 And] Q1; *Iago.* And F; *Iag.* And Q2

homosexual displacement that, by associ-ation, further taints Desdemona's sup-posed adultery with the 'monstrous' and 'unnatural'. Iago's reluctant role as 'Des-demona' in the dream (apart from its metatheatrical glance at the fact that all females on Shakespeare's stage were really males) prepares for his active usurpation of her 'place' in the mock-marriage that concludes this scene (see 'Places', pp. 123, 128–30).

418 **loose of soul** careless about their most inward secrets; but the additional sugges-tion of 'dissolute' is borne out by the rest of Iago's narrative.

422 **gripe** clutch, squeeze. At this point Edwin Booth would grasp the Moor's hand, which Othello would then with-draw in disgust (Furness, p. 207).

425–7 **That . . . Moor** The awkwardness of F's metre here, combined with the syntac-tical confusion of *laid . . . sigh . . . kiss . . . cry* suggests that more was involved than a simple misreading of 'lay'd' for 'lay' (as editors who favour the F reading assume). F's copy seems to have been cor-rupt at this point, perhaps because the scribe was faced with a partly illegible passage in the manuscript he was transcribing.

429 **foregone conclusion** previous copula-tion. For the bawdy meaning of 'conclu-sion' see 2.1.159, 254.

430 **shrewd** (a) vile; (b) vexatious, piercing; (c) ominous, damaging; (d) strongly indicative, coming dangerously near the truth
doubt suspicion

431 **thicken** strengthen, make more substantial
proofs evidence

432 **demonstrate thinly** prove less convincingly

OTHELLO   I'll tear her all to pieces!

IAGO

Nay, yet be wise: yet we see nothing done—
She may be honest yet. Tell me but this,
Have you not sometimes seen a handkerchief   435
Spotted with strawberries in your wife's hand?

OTHELLO

I gave her such a one—'twas my first gift.

IAGO

I know not that; but such a handkerchief—
I am sure it was your wife's—did I today
See Cassio wipe his beard with.

OTHELLO   If it be that—   440

IAGO

If it be that, or any, it was hers.
It speaks against her with the other proofs.

OTHELLO

O, that the slave had forty thousand lives—
One is too poor, too weak for my revenge!
Now do I see 'tis true. Look here, Iago: 445
All my fond love thus do I blow to heaven—'tis gone!

---

433 yet be] F; but be Q   441 any, it was hers.] F; any, it was hers, Q; any that was hers,
MALONE (*conjecturing MS 'yt' as abbreviation for* 'that')   445 true] F, Q2; time Q1

433–4 **yet . . . yet . . . yet** In a way that
makes the precise meaning of his reassurance hard to pin down, Iago equivocates
across several meanings of this word:
(a) still; (b) so far, for the time being; (c)
but, however; (d) nevertheless, despite
everything.

433, 435, 440 **See . . . seen . . . See** The
repetition of the verb contrives to hint
that the handkerchief itself is a kind of
'ocular proof' that renders the unseen
visible.

433 **done** Iago quibbles on *do* = copulate
(Honigmann) and *nothing* = vagina
(Williams, p. 219).

434 **honest yet. Tell** As Honigmann indicates, this line could be significantly
repunctuated: 'honest—yet. Tell'; or even
'honest—yet . . . Tell'.

434–6 **Tell . . . hand** Cf. Giraldi, App. C,
p. 442.

436 **Spotted** (a) marked, decorated; (b)
stained, blemished

strawberries For their ambiguous symbolism, see Introduction, p. 155.

442 **proofs** As at l. 431 this means only 'evidence', but through sheer repetition the
word begins to acquire the confident certainty of its other meaning.

446 **fond** affectionate; foolishly doting;
imbecile, mad

thus . . . gone An implicit stage direction, though whether the gesture involves
Othello's puffing his love to heaven (as
most actors assume), or something
more violent, depends on one's interpretation of *blow* which might mean
'blast': see *Hamlet*, Add. Pass. H.7–8
(3.4.209–10): 'I will delve one yard below
their mines | And blow them at the
moon'. Othello's gesture is repeated in
Fletcher's *The Woman's Prize*: 'the plea-
sure I take in her, | Thus I blow off'
(4.5.115–16).

Arise, black Vengeance from thy hollow hell,
Yield up, O Love, thy crown and hearted throne
To tyrannous Hate. Swell, bosom, with thy fraught,
For 'tis of aspics' tongues.

IAGO   Yet be content.   450

   Othello kneels

OTHELLO   O, blood, blood, blood!

IAGO

Patience, I say: your mind perhaps may change.

OTHELLO

Never, Iago. Like to the Pontic Sea,

---

447 thy] Q; the F   hell] F; Cell Q   450 Yet] F; Pray Q   450.1 *Othello kneels*] Q1 (*he kneeles*);
not in F; *after* 'aspics' tongues' (*l.* 450) Q2; *after* 'Swallow them up' (*l.* 459) OXFORD   451 blood,
blood, blood] F; blood, *Iago*, blood Q   452 perhaps] Q; *not in* F   453–60 Iago . . . heaven] F,
Q2; *not in* Q1

447–9 **Arise . . . Hate** Othello imagines
his transformation in terms of a *psychomachia* of the kind found in morality
drama, in which allegorized virtues and
vices do battle for the soul of Mankind.

447 **black Vengeance** Revenge is traditionally clad in black, the colour of death and
sin; see for instance the 'sad [i.e. dark]
habiliment' of Tamora in her guise as
Revenge in *Titus* (5.2.1). In the context of
the racial anxieties that Iago has worked
up in Othello, however, it is inevitably
associated with the Moor's own
blackness.

hell A notorious crux, in which equally
forceful arguments have been advanced
for F's *hell* and Q's *cell*. Hell (as Knight
observed) seems to balance *heaven* in l.
446. In *Titus* Tamora appears as Revenge
and claims to come from 'th'infernal
kingdom' which Titus calls 'hell' (5.2.30,
86); and in *Caesar* the Fury Ate (or
Revenge) is said to 'come hot from hell'
(3.1.274); Hart cites 'hollow hell' from
Jasper Heywood's *Thyestes* (1560), Scene
4, but against this notes an apparent reminiscence of *Othello* in Armin's *Two Maids
of More-Clacke* (1609): 'Rouse thee black
Mischief from thy ebon cell'; Sanders
notes that *Titus* refers to 'Revenge's cave'
(3.1.269); while Honigmann notes the
resemblance to death's 'eternal cell' in
Hamlet, 5.2.319.

449 **fraught** freight, burden

450 **aspics** asps. Venomous North African
snakes, variously identified with the
Egyptian sacred cobra and several species

of viper, and famously used in Cleopatra's
suicide; a recollection of Othello's African
past. Cf. also 4.2.16, 5.2.283, 363.
content calm

450.1 *Othello kneels* The ritual of kneeling
whilst pronouncing an oath gave it an
additional sacred force.

451–78 **O blood . . . fair devil** 'Blood'
refers not just to Othello's longing for
blood revenge, but also to the passion of
jealousy that drives him, and to the
'blood' of sexual desire (Desdemona's and
his own).

453–60 **Iago . . . heaven** While it is conceivable that this passage was added to
the F text, Q's isolated 'Never' is metrically suspicious; and this speech, for all its
emotional power, would have been an
easy one to cut, since it amounts to a
rhetorical elaboration of 'never'.

453–6 **Like . . . Hellespont** As Muir shows
(*Sources*, pp. 188–90), this passage contains recollections of several passages in
Pliny describing the Pontic Sea; notably
'And the sea Pontus evermore floweth
and runneth out into Propontis, but the
sea never retireth back again within Pontus' (2.97; sig. E4), and 'out of Pontus the
sea always floweth, and never ebbeth
again' (4.13; sig. I1). 'Icy' (l. 454) and
'wide' (l. 459) both occur in the immediate context of the latter passage, whose
emphasis on the power of the Pontic tide
may also have suggested 'compulsive
course' and 'violent pace'; whilst 'Swallow them up' seems to derive from a third
passage at the beginning of Book 6.

Whose icy current and compulsive course,
Ne'er feels retiring ebb, but keeps due on   455
To the Propontic and the Hellespont,
Even so my bloody thoughts, with violent pace,
Shall ne'er look back, ne'er ebb to humble love,
Till that a capable and wide revenge
Swallow them up. Now, by yon marble heaven,   460
In the due reverence of a sacred vow,
I here engage my words.
IAGO   Do not rise yet.
        Iago kneels
Witness, you ever-burning lights above,
You elements that clip us round about,
Witness that here Iago doth give up   465
The execution of his wit, hands, heart,
To wronged Othello's service. Let him command,

---

455 feels] Q2; keeps F; knows WHITE (*conj.* Southern)   462.1 *Iago kneels*] Q2; *not in* F; *after* 'about' (*l.* 464) Q1   463 you] F, Q1; the Q2   466 execution] F, Q2; excellency Q1   hands] F; hand Q

Shakespeare's simile may have been suggested by the title of the chapter in which the first passage occurs: 'What is the reason of the reciprocal ebb and flow of the seas: and where it is that *they keep no order, and are without reason*' (p. 42; emphasis added).

453 **Pontic Sea** Black Sea

454 **compulsive** onward-driving
456 **Propontic** Sea of Marmora
    Hellespont Dardanelles
459 **capable** capacious, i.e. comprehensive (*OED* 2a-b)
460 **Now . . . heaven** At this point Olivier, in a sensational gesture that impressed nearly all reviewers, tore off his crucifix in order to declare 'Othello's a Moor again', and then (as Harold Hobson saw it) 'bowed his head to the ancient gods of magic, barbarism, and human sacrifice' (Tynan, pp. 9, 105).
    marble An epithet found elsewhere (e.g in Marston's *Antonio and Mellida* (*c.*1600), 2.1.230; *Timon*, 4.3.192, and *Cymbeline*, 5.5.181) presumably referring to the variegated patterns of sky and clouds, but perhaps also suggesting the cold indifference of the heavens. Hart (citing Upton and Hazlitt) suggests a classical deriva-

tion, imitating such collocations as Virgil's *aequor marmoreum* ('the sea shining or resplendent like marble').

462 **engage** pledge
462.1 ***Iago kneels*** Iago's response to Othello's gesture, when combined with the language of his speech ('hands, heart . . . service . . . obey') and Othello's response ('I greet thy love') turns the ritual into a grotesque troth-plighting in which Iago usurps not merely Cassio's but also Desdemona's 'place'.
464 **elements** atmospheric agencies or powers (*OED n.* 11); cf. *Trag. Lear*, 3.2.16: 'I tax not you, you elements, with unkindness'.
    clip embrace, encompass
466 **execution** performance, operation
    wit intelligence
    hands, heart 'Hand and heart' is a standard formula for surrender to married love.
467 **Othello's service** The first time that Iago, who elsewhere addresses Othello as 'my lord' or 'general', is confident enough to use Othello's name to his face; but even now it falls short of direct address (cf. 4.1.44), and its implicit claim to intimacy and equality is balanced by the offer of *service*. Iago takes ironic satis-

And to obey shall be in me remorse,
What bloody business ever.

OTHELLO   I greet thy love,

⌜*They rise*⌝

Not with vain thanks, but with acceptance bounteous;   470
And will upon the instant put thee to't.
Within these three days let me hear thee say
That Cassio's not alive.

IAGO   My friend is dead:
'Tis done at your request. But let her live.

OTHELLO

Damn her, lewd minx! O, damn her, damn her!   475
Come, go with me apart; I will withdraw
To furnish me with some swift means of death
For the fair devil. Now art thou my lieutenant.

IAGO

I am your own for ever.   *Exeunt*

---

468 in me] F, Q2; *not in* Q1   469 business] F; worke so Q   474 at your] F; as you Q
475 damn her, damn her] F; dam her Q

faction, of course, in invoking the very concept that caused him such bilious indignation in the first scene (1.1.41–65), here colouring it with the chivalric idealism embodied in the *service* that medieval knights rendered to their lord. In keeping with the erotically charged ambiguities of Iago's ritual, *service*, in the language of courtly love, was also what the lover offered to his lady.

467–8 **command . . . obey** While these words are appropriate to the military relation between Iago and Othello, they are equally appropriate to the relation between husband and wife; cf. l. 90.

468 **remorse** (a manifestation of) pity or tender feeling. Honigmann is almost certainly right in rejecting *OED's* gloss 'a solemn obligation' (*n.* 4c, citing only this example), which seems a long way from any recognized use of the word.

470 **vain** empty
    bounteous Hinting at generous reward.
471 **put thee to't** put you to the test

474 **But . . . live** Othello has not yet mentioned killing Desdemona; it is Iago who is planting the suggestion.

475 **minx** whore

478 **fair devil** *Fair* = fair-skinned (as well as 'beautiful'). This oxymoronic formula had a proverbial currency: see Tilley D310, 'The white devil is worse than the black', and cf. Webster's *The White Devil* (1612).
    Now . . . lieutenant Cf. l. 216. This speech announces the completion of Iago's usurping project: not only has he taken the places of Cassio and Desdemona, but, through his progressive inversion of the proper power relation between ensign and general, Iago has become Othello's place-taker too. See 'Places', pp. 128–9.

479 **your own for ever** Replete with irony: 'your own' appeals to a language of service in which the man is said to 'belong' to the master, but 'for ever' hints at the Mephistophelian bargain by which Iago has ensnared Othello's soul.

3.4   *Enter Desdemona, Emilia, and Clown*

DESDEMONA Do you know, sirrah, where Lieutenant Cassio lies?

CLOWN I dare not say he lies anywhere.

DESDEMONA Why, man?

CLOWN He's a soldier, and for me to say a soldier lies—'tis   5
stabbing.

DESDEMONA Go to! Where lodges he?

CLOWN To tell you where he lodges, is to tell you where I lie.

DESDEMONA Can anything be made of this?

CLOWN I know not where he lodges; and for me to devise a   10
lodging, and say he lies here, or he lies there, were to lie in
mine own throat.

DESDEMONA Can you enquire him out, and be edified by
report?

CLOWN I will catechize the world for him—that is, make   15
questions, and by them answer.

DESDEMONA Seek him, bid him come hither: tell him I have
moved my lord on his behalf, and hope all will be well.

CLOWN To do this is within the compass of man's wit, and
therefore I will attempt the doing it.   *Exit*   20

3.4] F (*Scæna Quarta.*); *not in* Q   0.1 *Enter . . . Clown*] F; *Enter* Desdemonia Emilla *and the
Clowne.* Q   1 Lieutenant] F; the Leiutenant Q   5 CLOWN] F, Q2; *not in* Q1   He's] F; He is Q
me] F; one Q   'tis] F; is Q   8–9 CLOWN . . . this] F, Q2; *not in* Q1   11 he lies here, or] F; *not in*
Q   12 mine own] F, Q2; my Q1   16 by] F, Q; bid THEOBALD   18 on] F; in Q   19 man's wit]
F, Q2; a man Q1   20 it] F; of it Q

3.4.1–20 Like the Clown's earlier scene with
  Cassio (3.1.2.1–30), this episode is frequently omitted in performance. The sudden change of mood after the temptation
  can, however, work to powerfully ironic
  effect.
 1 **sirrah** term of address to social
  inferiors
 1–11 **lies . . . his** The Clown's frivolous quibbling on three senses of *lie* ('goes to bed';
  'dwells'; 'tells falsehoods') anticipates
  the tormented word-play of 4.1.32–4.
 5–6 **He's . . . stabbing** Apparently proverbial. Hart cites Dekker, *Seven Deadly
  Sinnes of London* (1606; Arber reprint, p.
  22), 'he that gives a soldier the lie, looks to
  receive the stab'; and Jonson, *Every Man
  In His Humour* (1616), 4.4.12–14 : '*Cob.*
  How, the lie! . . . do you long to be
  stabbed, ha? *Tib.* Why, you are no soldier,

I hope.' To accuse a man publicly of lying
  (to 'give the lie') was tantamount to challenging him to a duel.
 8 **is . . . lie** to confess myself a liar (because
  I don't know where he lodges)
 13 **edified** instructed. A mock-pompous
  locution whose religious sense ('gain spiritual benefit') is picked up in the clown's
  'catechize'.
 15 **catechize** interrogate (in the question-
  and-answer fashion of the Christian
  catechism)
 16 **by them answer** 'by them be enabled to
  answer, or get the information to use in
  my answer' (Rolfe in Furness); i.e. 'be edified by report'.
 18 **moved** solicited (*OED v.* 12b); but with
  the unwitting, ironic sense of 'roused to
  anger' (9b).
 19 **compass** reach

DESDEMONA

Where should I lose the handkerchief, Emilia?

EMILIA I know not, madam.

DESDEMONA

Believe me, I had rather have lost my purse
Full of crusadoes; and but my noble Moor
Is true of mind, and made of no such baseness   25
As jealous creatures are, it were enough
To put him to ill thinking.

EMILIA   Is he not jealous?

DESDEMONA

Who, he? I think the sun where he was born
Drew all such humours from him.

EMILIA   Look where he comes.

         Enter Othello

DESDEMONA

I will not leave him now till Cassio   30
Be called to him. How is't with you, my lord?

OTHELLO

Well, my good lady. (*Aside*) O hardness to dissemble!—
How do you, Desdemona?

DESDEMONA   Well, my good lord.

OTHELLO

Give me your hand. This hand is moist, my lady.

DESDEMONA

It yet hath felt no age, nor known no sorrow.   35

---

21 the] F; that Q   23 have lost] F; loose Q   29.1 *Enter Othello*] F; *after* 'him' (*l.* 29) Q
30 till] F, Q2; 'Tis Q1 (*uncorr.*); Let Q1 (*corr.*)   35 yet] Q; *not in* F   hath] F; has Q

---

21 **should I lose** could I have lost
24 **crusadoes** Portuguese gold coins
stamped with an image of the Cross.
but were it not that
28–9 **sun . . . him** Cf. Othello's description
of himself as 'one not easily jealous'
(5.2.344). Giraldi's Disdemona, however,
claims that Moors are naturally volatile.
See App. F(iv) for further discussion.
29 **humours** moods, dispositions. More literally, the four principal bodily fluids
(blood, phlegm, choler or yellow bile, and
melancholy or black bile) whose balance
was supposed to determine one's
temperament.

32 **hardness** how hard it is
34–6 **This . . . heart** Cf. Tilley H86, 'A
moist hand argues an amorous
nature (fruitfulness)'; *Antony*, 1.2.46–7,
'if an oily palm be not a fruitful prognosti-
cation'; and *Venus*, ll. 25–6, 'his sweating
palm, | The precedent of pith and liveli-
hood'. On the intrinsic bond supposed to
exist between *hand* and *heart*, see Michael
Neill, 'Amphitheaters in the Body: Playing with Hands on the Shakespearian
Stage', in *Putting History to the Question*,
pp. 167–203 (pp. 184–5).

OTHELLO

This argues fruitfulness and liberal heart:
Hot, hot and moist! This hand of yours requires
A sequester from liberty—fasting and prayer,
Much castigation, exercise devout—
For here's a young and sweating devil here   40
That commonly rebels. 'Tis a good hand,
A frank one.

DESDEMONA   You may indeed say so;
For 'twas that hand that gave away my heart.

OTHELLO

A liberal hand. The hearts of old gave hands,
But our new heraldry is hands, not hearts.   45

DESDEMONA

I cannot speak of this. Come now, your promise.

---

37 Hot, hot] F, Q2; Not ~ Q1   38 prayer] F; praying Q   44 hearts . . . hands] F, Q;
hands . . . hearts HANMER   46 Come now] F, Q2; come, come Q1

---

36 **argues** indicates
36, 44 **liberal** (a) free; (b) generous; (c)
lascivious
37 **hot** By implication a sign of lustfulness;
or simply 'lustful'
38 **sequester** shutting away (as in a prison
or nunnery). Accent on first syllable.
39 **castigation** chastisement
exercise disciplinary suffering; spiritual
exercise, religious observance (*OED n.* 6c,
10a).
40 **sweating** (a) labouring; (b) cf. *hot and
moist*
41 **commonly** generally; but with a play
on the sexual sense of 'common' (see
3.3.305).
42 **frank** Cf. *liberal*, l. 31.
44–5 **The hearts . . . not hearts** Cf.
William Cornwallis's *Essays* (1601): 'They
[our forefathers] had wont to give their
hands and their hearts together; but we
think it a finer grace to look asquint,
our hand looking one way and our heart
another' (Essay 28). Although Hanmer's
emendation, which gives Othello's lines
an attractive chiastic balance, has been
widely accepted, the F and Q reading
(which the Q2 editor saw no reason to
change) makes good contextual sense: at
l. 38 Desdemona seeks to counter Othel-

lo's sneer at the promiscuity of her 'frank'
hand by reminding him that this was the
hand that gave him her heart. Othello
then responds with further sarcasm:
where at l. 31, he had taken her hand as
the sign of her *liberal heart*, he now suggests that it's the *hand*, since it allegedly
gave away her heart, that deserves to be
called *liberal*; but where once lovers
indeed gave each other their hands as a
sign of their loving hearts, the new mode
is to give the hand alone with no commitment from the heart. The figure recalls
Iago's sardonic references to wearing his
heart upon his sleeve (1.1.64) and to
Othello's holding it in his hand (3.3.166).
Warburton detected an allusion to the
Red Hand of Ulster, the heraldic badge
awarded by James I to members of his
newly instituted order of baronets in
1612; but this would require an unlikely
later insertion into both the F and Q
manuscripts.
45 **heraldry . . . hearts** Alliteration points
up the quibble on *heart* (in which *r* was
still sounded) and *heraldry* (whose pronunciation is indicated by contemporary
spellings of 'herald', which included
'heraud', 'harald', and Ben Jonson's
'harrot').

OTHELLO What promise, chuck?

DESDEMONA
  I have sent to bid Cassio come speak with you.

OTHELLO
  I have a salt and sorry rheum offends me:
  Lend me thy handkerchief.

DESDEMONA   Here, my lord.   50

OTHELLO
  That which I gave you.

DESDEMONA   I have it not about me.

OTHELLO Not?

DESDEMONA No, faith, my lord.

OTHELLO
  That's a fault: that handkerchief
  Did an Egyptian to my mother give;   55
  She was a charmer and could almost read
  The thoughts of people; she told her, while she kept it
  'Twould make her amiable and subdue my father
  Entirely to her love—but if she lost it,
  Or made a gift of it, my father's eye   60
  Should hold her loathèd, and his spirits should hunt
  After new fancies. She dying gave it me
  And bid me, when my fate would have me wived,
  To give it her. I did so; and, take heed on't,

---

49 sorry] F; sullen Q   53 faith] Q1; indeed F, Q2   59 Entirely . . . it] *Repeated in* Q, *at foot of H4^v and top of I1.*   61 loathèd] F, Q2; lothely Q1   63 wived] F (wiu'd); wiue Q

---

47 **chuck** Term of endearment, probably deriving from northern dialect *chuck* = chicken.

49–95 **I have a salt . . . 'Swounds** Cf. Giraldi, App. C, p. 442.

49 **salt . . . rheum** running cold
  sorry grievous; Q *sullen* = stubborn (but cf. also 'sick-of-the-sullens' = ill from bad humour). Like *bitter* at 1.3.342, the more commonplace *sorry* seems an unlikely revision, but might represent a scribal sophistication. On the other hand, Q's *sullen* is the kind of substitution that might easily be encouraged by the double alliteration with *salt*.

50–4 **Lend . . . that handkerchief** One of a number of dialogue passages where lineation is extremely problematic: it may be that the whole passage is best treated as prose.

54–64 **that . . . her** The veracity of this story may be called in question by 5.2.214–15, where Othello gives a different account of the origin of the handkerchief, making it an instrument of his father's power over his mother.

55 **Egyptian** Perhaps = 'gypsy', since gypsies were supposed to come from Egypt (cf. the description of Cleopatra as a 'gypsy', *Antony*, 1.1.10); but Egypt was famously associated with magic.

56 **charmer** enchanter

58 **amiable** desirable

61 **spirits** vital power; can mean 'semen'.

62 **fancies** amorous inclinations, loves

63 **wived** The suggestion of passivity (in the context of 'fate') makes F seem superior to Q's 'wive'.

Make it a darling like your precious eye: 65
To lose't or give't away were such perdition
As nothing else could match.

DESDEMONA   Is't possible?

OTHELLO

'Tis true; there's magic in the web of it:
A sybil, that had numbered in the world
The sun to course two hundred compasses,   70
In her prophetic fury sewed the work;
The worms were hallowed that did breed the silk,
And it was dyed in mummy, which the skilful
Conserved of maidens' hearts.

DESDEMONA   I'faith, is't true?

OTHELLO

Most veritable; therefore look to't well.   75

DESDEMONA

Then would to God that I had never seen't!

OTHELLO Ha? Wherefore?

---

66 lose't] F (loose't); loose Q   70 course] F, Q2; make Q1   73 which] F, Q2; with Q1
74 Conserved] F; Conserues Q   I'faith,] Q1 (I'faith); Indeed? F; Indeed, Q2   76 God] Q;
Heauen F

---

65 **Make ... eye** Cf. Dent E249.1: 'To love
as one's own eye'.
66 **perdition** (a) loss; (b) ruin, damnation
67 **Is't possible** Cf. 2.3.275.
68–74 **there's ... hearts** Ironically the
story of the handkerchief seems to recall
just those 'drugs', 'charms', 'spells and
medicines bought of mountebanks' of
which Brabantio spoke in his accusations
of 'witchcraft' (1.1.170–2, 1.2.73–9,
1.3.61–5).
68 **magic** The magical qualities of the handkerchief are part of Shakespeare's additions to the story; in Giraldi it is simply
'a handkerchief–a gift from the Moor—
which was must delicately embroidered in
the Moorish fashion and much treasured
by the Lady and the Moor alike' (App. C,
p. 441).
web warp; hence 'weaving'.
69 **sibyl** prophetess
69–70 **that ... compasses** Usually interpreted to mean she was two hundred
years old, extreme age being a frequent
attribute of prophets (cf. the Cumaean

sibyl in Virgil's *Aeneid*). Honigmann,
however, following Johnson's gloss, 'she
numbered the sun to *course*, to run . . . two
hundred annual circuits', understands
Othello to say that the sibyl had prophe-
sied that the world would end in two hundred years.
71 **prophetic fury** Hunter traced the phrase
to Sylvester 'where it is frequent', but
Muir (*Sources*) plausibly suggests that the
whole passage imitates the description of
the pavilion magically woven by the
prophetess Cassandra in Ariosto's *Orlando
Furioso*, 46.77–80; stanza 80 contains
the phrase *il furor profetico*.
work See 3.3.299.
73 **mummy** 'an unctuous liquid or gum used
medicinally' (*OED n.*[1] 1a). See App. F(iv)
for a fuller note on the substance and its
use.
74 **maidens' hearts** Mummy prepared
from the remains of virgins was
thought especially effective, including
as a charm against jealousy. See App.
F(iv).

317

DESDEMONA

Why do you speak so startingly and rash?

OTHELLO

Is't lost? Is't gone? Speak, is it out o'th' way?

DESDEMONA Heaven bless us!   80

OTHELLO Say you?

DESDEMONA

It is not lost; but what an if it were?

OTHELLO How?

DESDEMONA

I say it is not lost.

OTHELLO   Fetch't, let me see't.

DESDEMONA

Why, so I can, sir; but I will not now: 85

This is a trick to put me from my suit—

Pray you, let Cassio be received again.

OTHELLO

Fetch me the handkerchief; my mind misgives.

DESDEMONA

Come, come: you'll never meet a more sufficient man—

OTHELLO

The handkerchief!

DESDEMONA   I pray talk me of Cassio—   90

OTHELLO

The handkerchief!

DESDEMONA   —a man that all his time

Hath founded his good fortunes on your love,

---

78 rash] F, Q2; rashly Q1   80 Heaven] Q1; *not in* F, Q2   83 How?] F; Ha. Q   85 sir] Q; *not in* F   87 Pray you] F; I pray Q   88 the] F; that Q   89–90 DESDEMONA ... handkerchief] Q1; *not in* F, Q2

---

78 **startingly** with a start, by starts; impetuously (*OED adv.*, citing this as the earliest example)

rash rashly, impetuously (*OED, rash, adv.* 1)

79 **out o'th' way** misplaced, missing

85 **sir** 'This word creates a distance between them' (Honigmann), but it might also be used playfully, and the rest of Desdemona's speech certainly attempts to lighten the tone.

88 **misgives** is suspicious (full of misgivings)

89–91 **Come ... time** The repetition of *handkerchief* makes it likely that F's omission of 'I pray ... handkerchief' (ll. 90–1) was due to eye-skip. However, since either of Desdemona's speeches at ll. 89–90 can be construed as the first part of a sentence that continues in ll. 91–3, it is possible that a deliberate cut was involved, or even that Q preserves a cancelled alternative. Honigmann again speculates on the possibility of interpolation by the Q compositor (cf. 1.3.367–71).

89 **sufficient** capable

Shared dangers with you—
OTHELLO
The handkerchief!
DESDEMONA   I'faith, you are to blame.
OTHELLO 'Swounds!   *Exit*   95
EMILIA
Is not this man jealous?
DESDEMONA   I ne'er saw this before.
Sure, there's some wonder in this handkerchief;
I am most unhappy in the loss of it.
EMILIA
'Tis not a year or two shows us a man:
They are all but stomachs, and we all but food;   100
They eat us hungerly, and when they are full
They belch us.
            Enter Iago and Cassio
                Look you, Cassio and my husband.
IAGO
There is no other way: 'tis she must do't—
And lo, the happiness! Go, and importune her.

94 I'faith] Q1; Insooth F, Q2 (In sooth)   95 'Swounds] Q1 (Zouns); Away F, Q2   96 ne'er] Q (ne're), F (neu'r)   98 the] F, Q (*corr.*); this Q (*uncorr.*)   of it] F, Q2; *not in* Q1   102 *Enter . . . Cassio*] F; *after* 'loss of it' (*l.* 93) Q

96–102 **I ne'er . . . belch us** Cf. Giraldi, App. C, p. 442.
97 **wonder** supernatural property
98 **unhappy** (a) unlucky; (b) wretched
99–102 **'Tis . . . us** The defiant feminism of Emilia's speech is usually seen as an implicit comment on Iago's treatment of her; but it is not simply an expression of solidarity with Desdemona, since Emilia is covering up here: she has stood silently by during Othello's increasingly frantic questioning and has elected not to reveal what she knows about the handkerchief.
99 **a year or two** Johnson thought this an indication that 'the author intended the action of this play to be considered as longer than is marked by any note of time', though he was unable to 'see any vacuity into which *a year or two*, or even a month or two, could be put'; see Introduction, pp. 33–6.
100 **are . . . stomachs** consist only of appetite

101 **hungerly** Shakespeare's usual equivalent of 'hungrily'; an adverb derived from 'hunger' rather than 'hungry'.
102 **belch** vomit up
    Enter . . . Cassio Q's placing of this entry has its attractions, since for Emilia to make her denunciation of husbands while Iago is on the stage would create an effective dramatic irony while emphasizing the parallel between his attitude towards Emilia and Cassio's dismissive treatment of Bianca at the end of this scene. Emilia's 'look you' would then register anxiety that she might have been overheard. On the other hand, Q's early entry may simply reflect the kind of anticipation that is common in copies used by the playhouse book-holder, so-called 'prompt-books' (cf. 4.2.89.1).
104 **lo, the happiness!** look, what good luck! Luck of course doesn't come into it, since Iago has clearly stage-managed the encounter.
    importune Accent on second syllable.

DESDEMONA

How now, good Cassio, what's the news with you?   105

CASSIO

Madam, my former suit: I do beseech you
That, by your virtuous means, I may again
Exist and be a member of his love,
Whom I, with all the office of my heart,
Entirely honour. I would not be delayed: 110
If my offence be of such mortal kind
That nor my service past, nor present sorrows,
Nor purposed merit in futurity
Can ransom me into his love again—
But to know so must be my benefit;   115
So shall I clothe me in a forced content,
And shut myself up in some other course
To fortune's alms.

DESDEMONA   Alas, thrice-gentle Cassio,
My advocation is not now in tune:
My lord is not my lord; nor should I know him,   120
Were he in favour as in humour altered.
So help me every spirit sanctified,
As I have spoken for you all my best,
And stood within the blank of his displeasure
For my free speech! You must awhile be patient: 125

109 office] F, Q2; duty Q1   112 nor my] F; neither Q1; not my Q2   117 shut] F, Q2; shoote Q1

108 **Exist . . . love** i.e. as Christians experienced their true being only through Christ's love and as members of his body; a piece of typically gallant hyperbole on Cassio's part.

109 **office . . . heart** devoted service. Cassio's elegant word-play tactfully suggests that the exhibition of one kind of *office* will restore him to another. But there is a sense in which, for him, the two kinds of *service* (l. 112) are genuinely inseparable.

110 **would not** do not wish to be

111 **mortal** fatal; but with the hyperbolic suggestion that his *offence* against Othello constitutes a mortal sin.

113 **purposed . . . futurity** the merit I mean to demonstrate in the future. **futurity** Earliest citation in *OED*.

115 **to . . . benefit** simply knowing the worst must be my only reward

117–18 **shut . . . alms** confine myself to some other way of winning fortune's charity

119 **My advocation . . . tune** this is not an appropriate moment for my advocacy

121 **favour** appearance, countenance **humour** mood; but with a literal reference to the balance of physical 'humours' thought to determine the temper of an individual (see 3.4.29 n.).

124 **the blank** Probably 'point blank range' (see J. R. Hale, 'The True Shakespearean Blank', *SQ* 19 (1968), 33–40); but 'blank' could also refer to the 'white' at the centre of the target (*OED n.* 2a; and cf. 2.1.132–3).

What I can do, I will; and more I will
Than for myself I dare. Let that suffice you.

IAGO

Is my lord angry?

EMILIA   He went hence but now,
And certainly in strange unquietness.

IAGO

Can he be angry? I have seen the cannon   130
When it hath blown his ranks into the air
And, like the devil, from his very arm
Puffed his own brother—and is he angry?
Something of moment then: I will go meet him,
There's matter in't indeed, if he be angry.   135

DESDEMONA

I prithee do so.   *Exit Iago*
                  Something sure of state—
Either from Venice, or some unhatched practice
Made demonstrable here in Cyprus to him—
Hath puddled his clear spirit; and in such cases
Men's natures wrangle with inferior things,   140
Though great ones are their object. 'Tis even so;
For let our finger ache and it endues
Our other, healthful members even to a sense
Of pain. Nay, we must think men are not gods,
Nor of them look for such observancy   145

133 is he] F; can he be Q   136 *Exit Iago*] F ('*Exit*', *after l.* 130); *not in* Q   141 their] F; the
Q   142 endues] F, Q; subdues JOHNSON *conj.*; induces KEIGHTLEY   143 a sense] F; that ~ Q
145 observancy] F (obseruancie); obseruances Q

129 **unquietness** agitation
133 **Puffed** (a) blown; (b) extinguished
134 **moment** importance
136 **Something . . . state** it must surely be
some matter of public affairs
137 **unhatched practice** still concealed
plot. Desdemona's metaphor resonates
ironically with Iago's birth metaphors
(see 1.3.392–3; 2.1.127–8; and cf.
ll.156–7 below).
138 **Made demonstrable** made evident,
exposed
139 **puddled** muddied. As Paster points out
(see 2.1.192 n.), Desdemona's language is
not merely figurative: 'spirit' includes the
so-called 'animal spirits', thought to be
'concocted out of blood and inspired air',

which Galenic medicine identified as the
source of all activity in the body. Imagined as a pure fluid, these spirits might
become fouled as a result of humoral
disturbance: as Thomas Walkington
expressed it, 'where there is a fulness &
repletion of infected and malignant
humours . . . the subtle spirits be not only
tainted but even corrupted with *puddle*
humours' (*The Opticke Glasse of Humors*,
1631 (repr. Delmar, NY, 1981), p. 103;
emphasis added).

142 **endues** instructs, inducts; brings (into
a certain state) (*OED v.* 3).
145 **observancy** respectful and ceremoni-
ous attention

As fits the bridal. Beshrew me much, Emilia,
I was—unhandsome warrior as I am—
Arraigning his unkindness with my soul;
But now I find I had suborned the witness,
And he's indicted falsely.

EMILIA   Pray heaven it be   150
State matters, as you think, and no conception
Nor no jealous toy concerning you.

DESDEMONA
Alas the day! I never gave him cause.

EMILIA
But jealous souls will not be answered so;
They are not ever jealous for the cause,   155
But jealous for they're jealous. It is a monster
Begot upon itself, born on itself.

DESDEMONA
Heaven keep the monster from Othello's mind.

EMILIA Lady, amen!

DESDEMONA
I will go seek him. Cassio, walk here about: 160
If I do find him fit, I'll move your suit
And seek to effect it to my uttermost.

CASSIO
I humbly thank your ladyship.
                              Exeunt Desdemona and Emilia
            Enter Bianca

---

147 unhandsome warrior] F, Q1 (*uncorr.*), Q2; vnhandsome, ~ Q1 (*corr.*)   158 the] F; that Q
163.1 *Exeunt . . . Emilia*] Q (*opposite ll. 161–2*); *Exit* F (*after l. 162*)   163.2 *Enter Bianca*] F; *after*
'Cassio' (*l. 164*) Q

---

146 **As . . . bridal** as befits the wedding day itself
Beshrew me may evil befall me (a mild oath, often playfully used)
147 **unhandsome** unskilful (*OED a.* 3, citing only this example; but the sense is easily derived from *a.* 2, 'ill-adapted').
148 **unkindness** unnatural cruelty
149 **suborned** corrupted
150–2 **Pray . . . you** Emilia's anxiety about her deceit shows through these lines.
151 **conception** Cf. ll. 156–7.

152 **jealous** In this case F's 'jealious' indicates the trisyllabic pronunciation required by the metre.
toy foolish notion; trifle (*OED a.* 4–5)
155–6 **They . . . they're jealous** On the self-motivating nature of jealousy and envy, see Neill, 'Places', p. 218.
156–7 **monster . . . born on itself** Cf. the 'monstrous birth' of Iago's imagination (1.3.392–3) and his description of the self-devouring nature of jealousy, 'the green-eyed monster' (3.3.169).

BIANCA

'Save you, friend Cassio.

CASSIO   What make you from home?

How is't with you, my most fair Bianca?   165

I'faith, sweet love, I was coming to your house.

BIANCA

And I was going to your lodging, Cassio.

What, keep a week away? Seven days and nights?

Eight-score eight hours? And lovers' absent hours

More tedious than the dial eight-score times!   170

O weary reckoning!

CASSIO   Pardon me, Bianca:

I have this while with leaden thoughts been pressed;

But I shall in a more continuate time

Strike off this score of absence. Sweet Bianca,

Take me this work out.

⌈*He gives her Desdemona's handkerchief*⌉

BIANCA   O Cassio, whence came this?   175

This is some token from a newer friend.

To the felt absence now I feel a cause.

Is't come to this? Well, well.

CASSIO   Go to, woman!

Throw your vile guesses in the devil's teeth,

From whence you have them. You are jealous now   180

---

166 I'faith] Q1; Indeed F, Q2   171 O] F (Oh), Q2; No Q1   172 leaden] F, Q2; laden Q1
173 continuate] F, Q2; conuenient Q1   175 *He gives . . . handkerchief*] ROWE (*subs.*); *not in* F, Q
176–7 friend. | To . . . absence now] *after* Q1 (friend, | To . . . absence, now); Friend, |
To . . . Absence: now F; friend | To . . . absence, now Q2   178 Well, well] F, Q2; *not in* Q1

168–9 **What . . . eight hours** An important passage for those concerned with
the play's 'double-time scheme', since
Othello and his party seem to have
spent no more than a single night in
Cyprus. See Introduction, pp. 33–6.

170 **dial** clock

171 **reckoning** (a) counting; (b) account;
(c) settling of accounts, judgement, punishment, revenge

172 **leaden** as heavy as lead, burdensome,
depressing
pressed oppressed. But, as Sanders
points out, there is also a play on the

idea of pressing with heavy weights,
a form of torture commonly used to
extract confessions from recalcitrant
prisoners.

173 **continuate** uninterrupted.

174 **Strike . . . score** discharge this debt
(picking up the second sense of Bianca's
reckoning)

175 **Take me . . . out** Ethic dative: 'copy
this embroidery for me'. The eagerness of
both Cassio and Emilia to copy its design
indicates the rare and luxurious quality of
the handkerchief.

176 **friend** mistress

That this is from some mistress, some remembrance—
No, by my faith, Bianca.

BIANCA   Why, whose is it?

CASSIO

I know not neither: I found it in my chamber.
I like the work well: ere it be demanded—
As like enough it will—I would have it copied.   185
Take it and do't, and leave me for this time.

BIANCA Leave you? Wherefore?

CASSIO

I do attend here on the general,
And think it no addition nor my wish
To have him see me womaned.

BIANCA   Why, I pray you?   190

CASSIO

Not that I love you not.

BIANCA   But that you do not love me.

I pray you bring me on the way a little,
And say if I shall see you soon at night.

CASSIO

'Tis but a little way that I can bring you,
For I attend here; but I'll see you soon.   195

BIANCA

'Tis very good—I must be circumstanced!   *Exeunt*

---

182 by my faith] Q1; in good troth F, Q2   183 neither] F; sweete Q   190–1 Why . . . not] F,
Q2; *not in* Q1   196 *Exeunt*] Q; *Exeunt omnes.* F

181 **remembrance** keepsake, love-token (cf.
   Hamlet, 3.1.95, 'I have remembrances of
   yours')
183 **not neither** Double negatives were
   commonly used as intensifiers in 17th-
   century English as they still are in some
   modern dialects.
188 **attend here on** wait for (but with an
   additional hint of 'am in attendance on'
   that flatters Cassio's masculine self-
   importance)
189 **addition** A heraldic term, meaning
   something added to a coat of arms as a
   badge of honour (*OED n.* 5); here used

metaphorically to mean 'advantage to my
   honour'.
190 **womaned** accompanied by a woman,
   and thereby effeminated. The misogyny
   revealed in Cassio's turn of phrase, which
   contrasts so extremely with his courtly
   compliments to Desdemona ('The riches
   of the ship is come on shore', 2.1.83), is
   disquietingly like Iago's.
194 **bring** accompany
196 **circumstanced** A unique usage (*OED*).
   It seems to mean something like 'forced to
   submit to circumstances' or even 'fobbed
   off with circumstances'.

4.1   *Enter Iago and Othello*

IAGO

Will you think so?

OTHELLO   Think so, Iago?

IAGO   What,

To kiss in private?

OTHELLO   An unauthorized kiss!

IAGO

Or to be naked with her friend in bed

An hour or more, not meaning any harm?

OTHELLO

Naked in bed, Iago, and not mean harm?   5

It is hypocrisy against the devil.

They that mean virtuously and yet do so,

The devil their virtue tempts, and they tempt heaven.

IAGO

If they do nothing, 'tis a venial slip;

But if I give my wife a handkerchief—

OTHELLO   What then?   10

4.1] F (*Actus Quartus. Scena Prima.*), Q2 (*Actus 4. Scoena 1.*); *Actus 4.* Q1   0.1 *Enter . . . Othello*]
Q; *Enter Othello, and Iago.* F   3, 5 in bed] F; abed Q   9 If] F; So Q

4.1 The prompt-books of Edmund Kean
(London, 1831) and J. W. Wallack (New
York, 1837) indicate that this scene was
frequently cut in the 19th century, presumably because it was felt to compromise Othello's heroic stature (Folger
Othello Promptbooks 17 and 7). The opening of the scene mirrors that of 1.1: Iago
once again enters in the middle of an
agitated conversation with a gull whom
he is leading by the nose. In each case
the Q direction implies that Iago
should enter first: this seems especially
appropriate here, where the reversal of
the normal order of social precedence
would make a strong dramatic point, acting out the role-reversal foreshadowed
at 1.1.42–4 ('I follow him to serve my
turn upon him. | We cannot all be
masters, nor all masters | Cannot be truly
followed').

1 **Think so, Iago?** Mirroring the role-
reversal referred to above, Othello seems
to have picked up Iago's habit of interrogative echoing from 3.3.

3–4 **naked . . . harm** Honigmann notes the
romance convention according to which

lovers sometimes contrived to share a
bed whilst remaining sexually innocent.
In the Arthurian cycle, for example,
Lancelot and Guinevere temporarily preserve their chastity by sleeping with a
naked sword between them.

6 **hypocrisy . . . devil** 'as common hypo-
crites cheat men by seeming good, and yet
living wickedly, these men would cheat
the devil, by giving him flattering hopes,
and at last avoiding the crime which he
thinks them ready to commit' (Johnson).
Against also implies that their actions constitute   a   challenge   to   the
devil: it is as unwise to tempt him as it is to
'tempt heaven'.

8 **The devil . . . heaven** The injunction
against tempting God is a biblical commonplace; see esp. Matthew 4: 7, where
Jesus rebukes the temptations of the
devil: 'It is written again, Thou shalt not
tempt the Lord thy God.'

9 **venial slip** pardonable error.

10 **What then** This can be treated as completing a hexameter with the last line
of Iago's speech (in which case quick,
nervous cueing is involved) or as an

IAGO

    Why then 'tis hers, my lord; and, being hers,

    She may, I think, bestow't on any man.

OTHELLO

    She is protectress of her honour too:

    May she give that?

IAGO

    Her honour is an essence that's not seen,   15

    They have it very oft that have it not.

    But, for the handkerchief—

OTHELLO

    By heaven, I would most gladly have forgot it!

    Thou saidst—O, it comes o'er my memory

    As doth the raven o'er the infectious house: 20

    Boding to all—he had my handkerchief.

IAGO

    Ay—what of that?

OTHELLO   That's not so good now.

IAGO   What

    If I had said I had seen him do you wrong?

    Or heard him say—as knaves be such abroad

    Who, having by their own importunate suit   25

    Or voluntary dotage of some mistress

    Convincèd or supplied them, cannot choose

    But they must blab—

OTHELLO   Hath he said anything?

---

20 infectious] F; infected Q   26 Or] F, Q2; Or by the Q1   27 Convincèd] F (Conuinced), Q1 (*corr.*), Q2; Coniured Q1 (*uncorr.*)

---

incomplete line on its own, requiring significant pausing. Either would be dramatically effective.

20–1 **raven . . . Boding** The raven was a bird of ill-omen (Dent R33, 'The croaking raven bodes misfortune'), and sometimes associated with the spread of diseases like the plague. In Marlowe's *The Jew of Malta*, for example, Barabas compares himself to 'the sad presaging raven that tolls | The sick man's passport . . . And . . . Doth shake contagion from her sable wings'; cf. also *Macbeth*, 1.5.37–9, and *Hamlet*, 3.2.241–2.

20 **infectious** full of infection

22 **Ay . . . What** Like ll. 1 and 32, a virtuoso example of the dramatic effect that can be created by the quick cueing required by a shared line. Particularly riveting here is the 'What' with which Iago pounces on the end of Othello's line, followed by the briefest of teasing pauses, before he goes on to explain what he has in mind.

24 **as . . . abroad** as there *are* villains around

26 **voluntary dotage** willing infatuation

27 **Convincèd or supplied** conquered (*OED, convince, v.* 1) or satisfied sexually (Rubinstein, p. 264). The verbs refer back to *importunate suit* and *voluntary dotage* respectively.

IAGO

He hath, my lord, but be you well assured,
No more than he'll unswear.

OTHELLO   What hath he said?   30

IAGO

Faith, that he did—I know not what he did.

OTHELLO

What? What?

IAGO   Lie.

OTHELLO   With her?

IAGO   With her, on her—what you will.

OTHELLO Lie with her? Lie on her? We say 'lie on her' when
they belie her. Lie with her? 'Swounds, that's fulsome!
Handkerchief—confessions—handkerchief? To confess,   35
and be hanged for his labour? First to be hanged and then
to confess! I tremble at it. Nature would not invest herself
in such shadowing passion without some instruction. It
is not words that shakes me thus. Pish! Noses, ears, and
lips! Is't possible? Confess? Handkerchief? O, devil!   40
        He falls down in a trance

31 Faith,] Q1; Why F, Q2   what he did] Q, F; what. He did—HONIGMANN   32 What? What?]
F; But what? Q1; What? Q2   34 'Swounds] Q1 (Zouns); *not in* F, Q2   35–40 To . . . devil] F,
Q2; *not in* Q1   40.1 He . . . trance] F (*Falls in a Traunce.*), Q2; *He fals downe.* Q1 (*corr.*); *not in* Q1
(*uncorr.*)

32 **what you will** An offhand colloquial
phrase (Dent W280.5) that supplied the
subtitle for Shakespeare's *Twelfth Night*
and the title for one of Marston's plays.
Iago may give it an additional cruel twist,
however, by quibbling on *will* (= sexual
desire), thus returning Othello to the tor-
menting voyeurism of the temptation
scene (3.3.396–410).

33–40 **Lie . . . devil** Othello's emotional
breakdown is signalled both by his collapse into prose, and by the disintegration
of his syntax. 'At this late stage in the
play, Othello is the only character who
has never been heard speaking in prose:
in poetic-dramatic terms that *measures*
the catastrophic descent' (Bradshaw, p.
224).

33 **We . . . her** Othello tries to salvage some
comfort from the habitual ambiguities of
Iago's speech: *lie on her* can mean 'tell lies
about (*belie*) her'.

34 **fulsome** lustful; obscene, disgusting,
morally repugnant (*OED a.* 2c, 6)

35–6 **confess . . . hanged** Proverbial (Dent
C587; *OED, confess, v.* 10), an offensive
way of 'giving the lie' (see 3.4.1); here
meant more literally, but triggered by
association with the puns on 'lie'.

36–7 **First . . . confess** Cf. Dent L590, 'First
hang and draw, and then hear the cause',
referring to so-called 'Lydford Law',
named after a small village in Devon notorious for lynchings.

38 **shadowing** prefiguring, ominous (*OED
ppl. a.* 2).
passion violent attack or fit of a disease
(*OED n.* 4b), referring to *tremble*.
instruction solid information

39–40 **Noses . . . lips** 'surrogate genital
images' (Honigmann); but perhaps also
frantic images of dismemberment, as
Steevens suggested. Cf. ll.137–8, 193.

40 **Is't possible** Repeats Iago's question at
2.3.276. Coming at the very moment of
the collapse that confirms Othello's transformation into the instrument of Iago's
plot, the echo creates a terrible irony.

IAGO

Work on, my medicine, work! Thus credulous fools are
   caught,
And many worthy and chaste dames even thus,
All guiltless, meet reproach. What ho, my lord!
My lord, I say! Othello!
         Enter Cassio
                              How now, Cassio!

CASSIO What's the matter?   45

IAGO

My lord is fallen into an epilepsy—
This is his second fit; he had one yesterday.

CASSIO

Rub him about the temples.

IAGO   No, forbear:
The lethargy must have his quiet course;
If not, he foams at mouth, and by and by   50
Breaks out to savage madness. Look, he stirs.
Do you withdraw yourself a little while:
He will recover straight; when he is gone,
I would on great occasion speak with you.
                                        Exit Cassio
How is it, general? Have you not hurt your head?   55

OTHELLO

Dost thou mock me?

---

41 medicine, work] Q (worke); Medicine workes F   44.1 *Enter Cassio*] F; *after* 'Cassio!' Q   48
No, forbear] Q; *not in* F   54.1 *Exit Cassio*] ROWE; *not in* F, Q1; *after* 'mock me' (l. 56) Q2

---

43 **my lord** At this point Simon Russell
   Beale's Iago registered his triumph over
   his prostrate commander with a contemptuous kick.
44 **Othello** The first and only time that Iago
   directly addresses his general by name, an
   impertinence he can risk only because
   Othello is unconscious (cf. 3.3.467).
44–177 **How now ... hurts my hand**
   This section of the scene was cut by
   Salvini on the grounds that Othello's role
   as passive eavesdropper is incompatible
   'with a man of the Moor's violent and
   haughty temper. Would you not suppose
   that he would spring like a tiger on Cassio
   and tear him to pieces?' (cited in Furness,
   p. 237).

47 **This ... yesterday** Iago is presumably
   lying to cover his tracks: there is no other
   reference to a previous fit, nor is there any
   evidence that Othello is epileptic, unless
   we take his violent headache in 3.3 to be a
   symptom. Cf. 3.3.287.
48 **No, forbear** Iago's words were almost
   certainly omitted from F by a careless
   compositor or scribe, since they complete
   Cassio's line, which is three syllables
   short.
49 **lethargy** morbid drowsiness
54 **great occasion** matter of great
   importance
55 **hurt your head** Deliberately ambiguous,
   since it may refer to the headache caused
   by the cuckold's horns (cf. 3.3.287)

IAGO   I mock you not, by heaven!
Would you would bear your fortune like a man.

OTHELLO
A hornèd man's a monster and a beast.

IAGO
There's many a beast then in a populous city,
And many a civil monster.   60

OTHELLO
Did he confess it?

IAGO   Good sir, be a man:
Think every bearded fellow that's but yoked
May draw with you. There's millions now alive
That nightly lie in those unproper beds,
Which they dare swear peculiar. Your case is better.   65
O, 'tis the spite of hell, the fiend's arch-mock,
To lip a wanton in a secure couch,
And to suppose her chaste. No, let me know;
And, knowing what I am, I know what she shall be.

OTHELLO
O, thou art wise; 'tis certain.

IAGO   Stand you a while apart;   70

---

56 you . . . heaven!] F; you? no by Heauen, Q   57 fortune] F; fortunes Q   61 confess it] F;
confesse Q   Good] F, Q1 (*corr.*); God Q1 (*uncorr.*)   64 lie] F (lye), Q2; lyes Q1   67 couch] F
(Cowch), Q2; Coach Q1   69 what she shall] F, Q; what shall STEEVENS *conj.*

---

58 **A hornèd . . . beast** Cf. Dent C876.2, 'A
    cuckold is a beast'; Othello's alteration of
    the proverb links the cuckold's horns to
    the motif of unnatural deformity.

60 **civil monster** Apart from its recollection
    of Iago's insinuations about the sexual
    mores of Venetian wives (3.3.205–7), this
    phrase is an oxymoronic gloss on what it
    means to be a 'Moor of Venice'. Civil = (a)
    city-dwelling; (b) civilized. Monsters, of
    course, belong to the uncivil wilderness
    beyond the bounds of the city (*polis*).

61 **be a man** Honigmann compares Iago's
    patronizing reproofs to Roderigo: 'the
    phrase helps to *unman* Othello'.

62 **bearded fellow** mature man

62–3 **yoked . . . draw** i.e. as an ox is yoked
    to draw the plough. An insulting quibble
    on the 'yoke' of matrimony.

64 **unproper** not exclusively theirs; com-
    mon (*OED a.* 4; citing only this example)

65 **peculiar** their own private property

67 **lip** kiss (first recorded use in *OED*)
    secure free from anxiety, doubt, or
    suspicion

68–9 **let . . . be** Another of Iago's obscurely
    portentous remarks, whose obliquity
    prompted Steevens to propose that *she*
    was corrupt and redundant. It seems to
    mean something like: 'Let me know for
    certain, and then, recognizing my own
    frailty, I shall understand her true nature
    well enough.' But the heavy rhetorical
    emphasis on *know* matters more than
    the precise meaning; indeed, the ob-
    scurity is surely part of Iago's strategy of
    mystification.

70 **'tis certain** May refer either to Iago's
    wisdom, or to Desdemona's infidelity.
    Stand . . . apart Honigmann notes the
    use of a stock 'comedy routine [in which]
    a victim is tricked into overhearing what
    others want him to overhear'; cf. *Much
    Ado*, 2.3 and 3.1.

Confine yourself but in a patient list:
Whilst you were here, o'erwhelmèd with your grief—
A passion most unsuiting such a man—
Cassio came hither. I shifted him away,
And laid good 'scuse upon your ecstasy;   75
Bade him anon return and here speak with me—
The which he promised. Do but encave yourself,
And mark the fleers, the gibes, and notable scorns
That dwell in every region of his face.

For I will make him tell the tale anew: 80
Where, how, how oft, how long ago, and when
He hath, and is again to cope your wife.
I say, but mark his gesture—marry, patience!
Or I shall say you're all in all in spleen,
And nothing of a man.

OTHELLO   Dost thou hear, Iago?   85
I will be found most cunning in my patience,
But—dost thou hear?—most bloody.

IAGO   That's not amiss;
But yet keep time in all. Will you withdraw?
          Othello withdraws
Now will I question Cassio of Bianca,
A hussy that by selling her desires   90

72 o'erwhelmèd] F, Q2; ere while, mad Q1   73 unsuiting] Q1 (*corr.*) (vnsuting); resulting F;
vnfitting Q1 (*uncorr.*), Q2   75 'scuse] Q; scuses F   76 Bade] F (Bad), Q2; Bid Q1   return] F;
retire Q   77 Do but] F; but Q   78 fleers, the gibes] F; Ieeres, the Iibes Q1 (*corr.*); geeres,
the gibes Q1 (*uncorr.*), Q2   82 hath] F; has Q   88.1 *Othello withdraws*] ROWE; *not in* F, Q
90 hussy] OXFORD; Huswife F, Q

71 **in . . . list** Usually glossed 'within the
bounds of self-control' (*OED, list, n.*³,
8a); but *list* = 'listening' (*n.*¹) and *list*
= 'desire' (*n.*⁴ 2) may also be involved.
74 **shifted him away** got him out of the way
(*OED v.* 16; citing this as earliest example). In this context *shift* = 'practise
shifts, evasions, or fraud' may also be relevant (*v.* 6).
75 **ecstasy** condition of being outside or
beside oneself (*OED n.* 1), i.e. Othello's fit.
76 **anon** presently
77 **encave** hide, as in a cave or cellar. There
is perhaps a distant echo of the savage
landscape of Othello's travel narrative
('antres vast', 1.3.140). For further comment on this apparent coinage (*OED*), see
Neill, 'Opening', pp. 155-9.

78 **fleers** sneers, gibes (earliest use in *OED*)
82 **cope** encounter; with a strong sexual
innuendo, perhaps influenced by *cope* =
cover. See Williams, *Glossary*, p. 81.
83 **gesture** behaviour, manner
84 **all in spleen** completely overwhelmed by
violent rage
85 **nothing . . . man** Cf. l. 61.
86 **patience** Othello (in Iago's own fashion)
twists the meaning of Iago's word from
'long-suffering' to 'willingness to wait
[for my revenge]'.
88 **keep time in all** control yourself. A stock
musical metaphor: Dent T308.1.
89-163 **Now will . . . no more** Cf. Giraldi,
App. C, p. 441.
90 **hussy** As at 1.3.270 and 2.1.112 (see
notes), it is almost impossible for an editor

Buys herself bread and clothes. It is a creature
That dotes on Cassio—as 'tis the strumpet's plague
To beguile many, and be beguiled by one.
He, when he hears of her, cannot restrain
From the excess of laughter. Here he comes.   95
      Enter Cassio
As he shall smile, Othello shall go mad;
And his unbookish jealousy must construe
Poor Cassio's smiles, gestures, and light behaviours
Quite in the wrong.—How do you now, lieutenant?

CASSIO
The worser that you give me the addition   100
Whose want even kills me.

IAGO
Ply Desdemona well, and you are sure on't:
(*Speaking lower*) Now, if this suit lay in Bianca's power,
How quickly should you speed!

CASSIO Alas, poor caitiff!   105

OTHELLO (*aside*) Look how he laughs already.

IAGO
I never knew a woman love man so.

91 clothes] Q (cloathes); Cloath F   94 restrain] F; refraine Q   95.1 *Enter Cassio*] F; *after*
'one' (l. 93) Q   97 construe] *after* Q (conster); conserue F   98 behaviours] F; behauiour Q
99 now] Q; *not in* F   103 *Speaking lower*] ROWE; *not in* F, Q   power] Q; dowre F   107 a] Q;
not in F

to decide whether to print *hussy* or *house-*
wife here, since both meanings of F and Q
huswife are involved, even though the
insulting *hussy* (= prostitute) is Iago's primary sense.
 her desires Probably an objective genitive (see 3.3.220): = others' desire of her.

93 **To beguile . . . one** Cf. Dent D179, 'He
that deceives (beguiles) another is oft
deceived (beguiled) himself'.

97 **unbookish** First recorded use (*OED*). Cf.
Iago's sneer at Cassio for being 'bookish'
(1.1.23).
 construe interpret; with a play on the
technical application of the term to Greek
and Latin translation, suggested by
unbookish. F's *conserue* suggests that the
copy may have read *construe*, though Q's
conster conforms to what seems to have
been Shakespeare's preferred spelling of
the verb.

98 **light** frivolous. But, because it can
also mean 'unchaste', the word itself
wittily epitomizes Othello's problem of
'construing'.

100 **addition** title. The malicious pleasure
which Iago takes in persistently addressing Cassio by the rank of which he has
deprived him gives the lie to those critics
who, arguing that Iago's complaints in
1.1 are soon forgotten, like Coleridge
attribute them to 'the motive-hunting of
motiveless malignity' (see Introduction,
p. 31).

102 **Ply** importune, work away at
 sure on't sure to be reinstated

104 **speed** attain your desire

105 **Alas . . . caitiff** Metrically amphibious.
 caitiff wretch. Expressing affection, like
rogue (l. 108), but with an edge of patronizing disdain.

CASSIO

   Alas, poor rogue! I think i'faith she loves me.

OTHELLO (*aside*)

   Now he denies it faintly, and laughs it out.

IAGO

   Do you hear, Cassio?

OTHELLO (*aside*)   Now he importunes him   110
   To tell it o'er. Go to, well said, well said!

IAGO

   She gives it out that you shall marry her.
   Do you intend it?

CASSIO Ha, ha, ha!

OTHELLO (*aside*)

   Do you triumph, Roman, do you triumph?   115

CASSIO I marry—what, a customer? Prithee bear some
   charity to my wit; do not think it so unwholesome. Ha,
   ha, ha!

OTHELLO (*aside*) So, so, so, so: they laugh that wins.

IAGO Faith, the cry goes that you marry her.   120

CASSIO Prithee say true.

108 i'faith] Q1; indeed F, Q2 111 o'er] F; on Q   well said, well said] F; well said Q
115 you . . . Roman] Q; ye . . . Romaine F; you . . . rogue WARBURTON *conj.*; you . . . o'er me
COLLIER MS *conj.* 116 I . . . Prithee] F; I marry her? I prethee Q1; I marry her? what? a
Customer; I prethee Q2 119 they] F, Q2; *not in* Q1 120 Faith,] Q1; Why ∧ F; Why, Q2
that you] F; you shall Q1; that you shall Q2

109 **faintly** feebly, without conviction
    out off
111 **well said** well done (need not imply that
    Othello actually overhears)
112 **marry her** Bianca's boasts may account
    for Iago's description of Cassio as 'almost
    damned in a fair wife' (1.1.20), if we
    assume that Bianca, as Bradshaw argues
    (pp. 154–6), has accompanied her lover
    from Venice.
115 **Roman** It is not easy to see the reason for
    this epithet: perhaps it has been suggested
    to Othello's increasingly fevered imagina-
    tion by an odd linkage between the Roman
    associations of 'triumph' (the triumphal
    procession through the streets of Rome
    allowed to a victorious general) with the
    contemporary notion of Rome as 'a city
    notorious for sexual vice' (Williams, *Dic-
    tionary*, p. 1167). But Warburton and
    Collier may have been right in supposing
    corruption at this point, and the associa-
    tions of *triumph* may simply have sug-

gested 'Roman' to a puzzled scribe at some
point in the transmission of the text (see
Honigmann, *Texts*, chap. 9). It is also possible that 'Roman', like *Veronese* (2.1.27),
represents an unresolved confusion in
Shakespeare's mind about the exact
nature of Cassio's foreignness.
116 **customer** prostitute (a much more contemptuous term than *courtesan*, the
description given of Bianca in F's 'The
Names of the Actors'); perhaps a nonce
or regional usage, since *OED*'s only other
example is also Shakespearian, and
comes from a play written fairly soon after
Othello, All's Well (5.3.288).
116–17 **bear . . . wit** give some credit to my
judgement.
117 **unwholesome** morally tainted; but in
the context of *customer* there is inevitably
a play on the literal sense, 'diseased'.
119 **wins** The singular verb was probably in
fluenced by the wording of the proverb
'He laughs that wins' (Dent L 93).

IAGO I am a very villain else.

OTHELLO (*aside*) Have you scored me? Well.

CASSIO This is the monkey's own giving out: she is
persuaded I will marry her, out of her own love and   125
flattery, not out of my promise.

OTHELLO (*aside*) Iago beckons me: now he begins the story.

CASSIO She was here even now; she haunts me in every
place. I was the other day talking on the sea-bank with
certain Venetians, and thither comes the bauble: by this   130
hand, she falls thus about my neck—

⌈*Cassio embraces Iago*⌉

OTHELLO (*aside*) Crying 'O dear Cassio!' as it were: his
gesture imports it.

CASSIO So hangs, and lolls, and weeps upon me; so shakes,
and pulls me—ha, ha, ha!   135

---

123 Have . . . Well] F, Q2; Ha you stor'd me well Q1   127 beckons] Q; becomes F   129 the
other] F; tother Q   130 the bauble] F; this ~ Q   130–1 by . . . falls] Q1; and falls me F; fals
me Q2   131.1 *Cassio . . . Iago*] This edition; *not in* F, Q   134 shakes] F; hales Q

122–204 **I am . . . midnight** In accordance
with the comic decorum of its cuckold-
gulling convention (see above, l. 70 n.)
this section of the scene lapses into a
prose idiom that includes even the habitual verse-speaker, Othello.

123 **scored** wounded, branded. *Score* could
also mean 'achieve sexual conquest'
(Williams, *Glossary*, p. 269), and if it is
read this way, then *me* should perhaps be
taken as an ethic dative; or perhaps, since
'husband and wife is one flesh', Othello
merely thinks of Desdemona's conquered
body as an extension of his own. Honigmann defends Q's *stored* on the grounds
that *store* 'could mean to provide for the
continuance of a stock or breed', in which
case Othello would mean 'Have you
begotten children for me?'; but Q2 evidently found the word puzzling, and a
simple misreading seems more likely.

124 **monkey** A term of playful contempt
(*OED n.* 2b) used especially of children
and young women (cf. *Macbeth*, 4.2.60;
Jonson, *Devil is an Ass*, 2.8.83). In this
context the use of monkeys as an emblem
of lust must also be relevant (cf. 3.3.405).

127 **Iago beckons** It may be, as the Oxford
direction indicates, that Othello should
draw closer at this point; but *beckon* could
refer to signalling of any kind and Iago
may simply be gesturing for him to pay
close attention. As Honigmann points out
F's *becomes* is an easy misreading for such
variant spellings as 'becons'.

129 **sea-bank** sea-shore

130 **bauble** plaything, trinket; contemptuously applied to women (see Williams,
Dictionary, p. 79); foolish or childish
person (*OED n.* 5b).

130–1 **by this hand** Innocuous asservera-
tion, but purged from F and Q2 along with
more serious oaths; for details linking this
with the practice of Ralph Crane, see
Honigmann, *Texts*, p. 166.

131–131.1 **thus . . . *embraces Iago*** What
Othello sees at this point will resemble a
mimed re-enactment of Cassio's dream
(3.3.415–27), its confusing displacements
further complicated by the fact that
Cassio will seem to play the part of
Desdemona, while Iago takes the place
of Cassio.

133 **imports** betokens

OTHELLO (*aside*) Now he tells how she plucked him to my
  chamber. O, I see that nose of yours, but not that dog I
  shall throw it to.

CASSIO Well, I must leave her company.

IAGO Before me, look where she comes!   140
  Enter Bianca

CASSIO 'Tis such another fitchew—marry, a perfumed one!
  What do you mean by this haunting of me?

BIANCA Let the devil and his dam haunt you! What did you
  mean by that same handkerchief you gave me even now?
  I was a fine fool to take it! I must take out the work?—A   145
  likely piece of work, that you should find it in your
  chamber and know not who left it there! This is some
  minx's token—and I must take out the work? There, give
  it your hobby-horse!
  ⌈*She throws down the handkerchief*⌉
  Wheresoever you had it, I'll take out no work on't.   150

CASSIO How now, my sweet Bianca? How now? How
  now?

OTHELLO (*aside*) By heaven, that should be my handkerchief.

BIANCA If you'll come to supper tonight, you may; if you
  will not, come when you are next prepared for.   *Exit*   155

---

137 O] F; *not in* Q   140 IAGO] F, Q1; *not in* Q2   140.1 *Enter Bianca*] F; *after* 'company' (l. 139)
Q   141 CASSIO] F; *not in* Q   fitchew] F, Q2; ficho Q1   marry, a perfumed one!] HART; marry
a perfum'd one? F; marry a perfum'd one, Q   145 work] F, Q2; whole worke Q1   147 know
not] F; not know Q   149 your] F; the Q   149.1 *She . . . handkerchief*] This edition; *not in* F, Q
154 If . . . if] F; An . . . an Q

---

137 **nose** For the nose as penis-surrogate,
see Partridge, p. 154, Williams, *Dictionary*, pp. 954–6, *Glossary*, pp. 218–19.
The Elizabethan Homily 'Against
Whoredom and Adultery' cites amputa-
tion of the nose as a form of punishment for adultery among the ancient Egyp-
tians, a penalty still extant in some
Islamic codes.

140 **Before me** Mild asseveration, 'perhaps
formed on the analogy of "before God"'
(Honigmann).

141 **such another** 'like all the rest of them'
(Ridley). A mocking but often playfully
affectionate phrase; cf. *Troilus*, 1.2.254,
267.
  fitchew polecat (notorious for lechery),

i.e. whore (*OED*, *polecat*, *n.* 2; Williams,
Glossary, pp. 127, 241–2)
  perfumed Cf. Tilley P461, 'To stink like a
polecat'.

143 **devil and his dam** Cf. Dent D225.
  dam mother. Usually contemptuous and
typically used of animals; see *OED n.*[2] 2,
3.

145 **I must . . . work** See 3.3.299.

146 **likely . . . work** likely business (improbable story).

148 **minx** See 3.3.475.

149 **hobby-horse** whore. See Williams, *Dictionary*, pp. 669–70, *Glossary*, pp. 158–9;
Partridge, p. 121.

155 **when . . . for** when I next prepare supper for you (i.e. never)

IAGO After her, after her!

CASSIO Faith, I must; she'll rail in the streets else.

IAGO Will you sup there?

CASSIO Faith, I intend so.

IAGO Well, I may chance to see you, for I would very fain   160
speak with you.

CASSIO Prithee come—will you?

IAGO Go to, say no more.   *Exit Cassio*

OTHELLO (*coming forward*) How shall I murder him, Iago?

IAGO Did you perceive how he laughed at his vice?   165

OTHELLO O, Iago!

IAGO And did you see the handkerchief?

OTHELLO Was that mine?

IAGO Yours, by this hand! And to see how he prizes the
foolish woman your wife: she gave it him, and he hath   170
given it his whore.

OTHELLO I would have him nine years a-killing. A fine
woman, a fair woman, a sweet woman!

IAGO Nay, you must forget that.

OTHELLO Ay, let her rot and perish and be damned tonight,   175
for she shall not live! No, my heart is turned to stone:
⌈*He beats his breast*⌉
I strike it, and it hurts my hand. O, the world hath not a
sweeter creature: she might lie by an emperor's side, and
command him tasks.

IAGO Nay, that's not your way.   180

OTHELLO Hang her, I do but say what she is: so delicate with
her needle, an admirable musician—O, she will sing the

---

157 Faith] Q1; *not in* F, Q2   streets] F; streete Q 159 Faith] Q1; Yes F, Q2 163 *Exit Cassio*] Q; *not in* F 164 *coming forward*] This edition (*after* CAPELL); *not in* F, Q 169–71 Yours . . . whore] F; *not in* Q (*which prints only prefix, as catchword*) 174 that] F, Q2; *not in* Q1 175 Ay] F (I); And Q 176.1 *He beats his breast*] This edition; *not in* F, Q 177 hath] F; has Q

---

160 **I . . . fain** I very much desire to

163 **Go to** come, come

164–206 **How . . . Excellent good** Cf. Giraldi, App. C, p. 443.

169–71 **Yours . . . whore** This speech is omitted from the quartos, but Q1 includes the prefix as a catchword at the bottom of sig. K1, indicating that it was inadvertently dropped by the compositor. Cf. 2.3.269–71.

169 **by this hand** Sanders notes 'the quibble by means of which Iago makes the common oath the literal truth'.

176 **heart . . . stone** Cf. Dent H311, 'A heart of stone', and SS24, 'To stone one's heart'; echoed at 5.2.65.

180 **not your way** no way to think

savageness out of a bear—of so high and plenteous wit
and invention!

IAGO She's the worse for all this.　　　　　　　　　　　　　185

OTHELLO O, a thousand thousand times! And then of so
gentle a condition—

IAGO Ay, too gentle.

OTHELLO Nay, that's certain—but yet the pity of it, Iago; O
Iago, the pity of it, Iago!　　　　　　　　　　　　　　190

IAGO If you are so fond over her iniquity, give her patent to
offend; for if it touch not you, it comes near nobody.

OTHELLO I will chop her into messes—cuckold me?

IAGO O, 'tis foul in her.

OTHELLO With mine officer!　　　　　　　　　　　　　　195

IAGO That's fouler.

OTHELLO Get me some poison, Iago, this night. I'll not
expostulate with her, lest her body and beauty unprovide
my mind again. This night, Iago.

IAGO Do it not with poison; strangle her in her bed, even the　　200
bed she hath contaminated.

OTHELLO Good, good, the justice of it pleases, very good.

IAGO And for Cassio, let me be his undertaker: you shall
hear more by midnight.

OTHELLO

Excellent good.

　　　　Trumpet sounds within

---

186 O] F; *not in* Q　a . . . times] Q; a thousand, a thousand times F　189 Nay] F, Q2; I
Q1　189–90 O . . . Iago] F; the pitty Q1; oh the pitty Q2　191 are] F; be Q　192 touch] F;
touches Q　198 night. I'll] F (Ile); night I'le Q　205.1 *Trumpet . . . within*] DYCE; '*A Trumpet.*'
after 'midnight' (*l.* 204) Q; *not in* F

183 **high** exalted, lofty
187, 188 **gentle** Othello probably has both
　　Desdemona's noble birth and her soft dis-
　　position in mind (since *condition* can
　　mean either 'rank' or 'temperament');
　　but Iago characteristically twists the word
　　to mean 'tame, easily managed' (used of
　　animals, esp. horses).
191 **fond** foolish, doting
　　patent licence
　　touch affect, injure
193–202 **I will . . . very good** Cf. Giraldi,
　　App. C, p. 443.
193 **messes** portions of meat; pulpy or semi-

liquid food. A disturbing echo of the cannibal monsters in Othello's traveller's
tales (1.3.143–4).
198 **expostulate** complain, remonstrate;
debate
　　unprovide disequip, disarm
203 **be his undertaker** undertake to deal
with him. An *undertaker* was one who
'undertook' a task on another's behalf,
an entrepreneur or contractor, hence
'funeral undertaker'; but this profession
did not come into being before the end of
the 17th century.
205 *Trumpet* See App. D (i).

What trumpet is that same?   205

IAGO I warrant something from Venice.

>*Enter Lodovico,* ⌜*Gratiano,*⌝ *Desdemona, and*
>*attendants*

'Tis Lodovico, this, comes from the Duke.

See, your wife's with him.

LODOVICO God save you, worthy general!

OTHELLO With all my heart, sir.   210

LODOVICO (*giving Othello a letter*)

The Duke and senators of Venice greet you.

OTHELLO (*putting the letter to his lips*)

I kiss the instrument of their pleasures.

>*Othello opens the letter and reads*

DESDEMONA

And what's the news, good cousin Lodovico?

IAGO

I am very glad to see you, signor—

Welcome to Cyprus.   215

LODOVICO

I thank you—how does Lieutenant Cassio?

IAGO Lives, sir.

DESDEMONA

Cousin, there's fallen between him and my lord

An unkind breach; but you shall make all well.

OTHELLO

Are you sure of that?

206–8 I . . . him] F; Something from *Venice* sure, tis *Lodouico,* | Come from the Duke, and see your wife is with him Q; I . . . Lodovico—this comes . . . him SISSON; I warrant, something from Venice . . . 'Tis Lodovico! | This comes from the Duke; and see your wife is with him WALKER 206.1–2 *Enter . . . attendants*] HANMER; *after 'A Trumpet'* (l. 205) F, Q *Gratiano*] This edition (*conj.* HONIGMANN); *not in* F, Q 209 God save] QI; Saue F, Q2 you] F, Q2; the QI 211 *giving . . . letter*] ROWE (*subs.*); *not in* F, Q and] Q; and the F 212 *putting . . . lips*] This edition; *not in* F, Q 212.1 *Othello . . . reads*] CAPELL (*subs.*); *not in* F, Q

206.1 **Gratiano** Honigmann is almost certainly right in suggesting that Gratiano, as Desdemona's uncle and an important member of the Venetian delegation, should enter here.

209 **God . . . general** Metrically amphibious.

214–16 **I . . . Lives, sir** Honigmann notes how Iago butts in here; Lodovico's response seems pointedly cool, especially in the way he appears more interested in

Cassio's absence than in Iago's welcome; Iago's reply is either negligent or sullen, and he then remains silent for nearly fifty lines.

219 **unkind** (a) unnatural; (b) cruel, hurtful

220 **Are . . . that** Othello's line may be a reaction to something in the letter, as Lodovico imagines (l. 223), or it may be aimed at Desdemona, as she supposes.

DESDEMONA   My lord?   220
OTHELLO (*reads*)
'This fail you not to do, as you will'—
LODOVICO
He did not call; he's busy in the paper.
Is there division 'twixt my lord and Cassio?
DESDEMONA
A most unhappy one: I would do much
T'atone them, for the love I bear to Cassio.   225
OTHELLO
Fire and brimstone!
DESDEMONA   My lord?
OTHELLO   Are you wise?
DESDEMONA
What, is he angry?
LODOVICO   Maybe the letter moved him;
For, as I think, they do command him home,
Deputing Cassio in his government.
DESDEMONA
By my troth, I am glad on't.
OTHELLO   Indeed?
DESDEMONA   My lord?   230
OTHELLO
I am glad to see you mad.

---

221 *reads*] THEOBALD; *not in* F, Q   223 'twixt my] F, Q2; betweene thy Q1   230 By my troth]
Q1; Trust me F, Q2

---

224 **unhappy** unlucky
225 **atone** reconcile (literally 'set *at one*')
226 **Fire and brimstone** The instruments by which God punished the reputed sexual profligacy of Sodom and Gomorrah (Genesis 19: 24); but also among the torments of hell nominated in Revelation, where a lake of fire and brimstone is reserved for (amongst others) 'whoremongers . . . and all liars' (see Revelation 21: 8; and cf. 9: 17, 14: 10, 19: 20), a text that Othello will remember again when he sees Desdemona as 'like a liar gone to burning hell' (5.2.129).
Fire Probably disyllabic here (as often elsewhere).
brimstone sulphur
229 **Deputing** As Honigmann points out,

the original sense of the word is simply 'appointing'; but in Othello's mind, at least, the idea of 'substitute', maddeningly associated with lieutenancy and place-taking, must also be involved (see Introduction, pp. 155–6; cf. also l. 253, 4.2.221).
government office as governor (*OED n.* 3)
231 **I . . . mad** Othello's sarcastic response to Desdemona's 'I am glad on't' has caused editors more trouble than it need: *mad* = crazy [enough to reveal your love for Cassio]. However, as Ridley noted, Mary Cowden Clarke's emendation 'mad to see you glad' has some plausibility, especially in view of the fact that such transposition errors are not uncommon (see e.g. 2.3.158).

DESDEMONA   Why, sweet Othello!

OTHELLO (*striking her*)   Devil!

DESDEMONA

I have not deserved this.

LODOVICO

My lord, this would not be believed in Venice,
Though I should swear I saw't. 'Tis very much—
Make her amends: she weeps.

OTHELLO   O devil, devil!   235

If that the earth could teem with woman's tears,
Each drop she falls would prove a crocodile—
Out of my sight!

DESDEMONA   I will not stay to offend you.

LODOVICO

Truly, an obedient lady.
I do beseech your lordship call her back.   240

OTHELLO Mistress!

DESDEMONA   My lord?

OTHELLO What would you with her, sir?

LODOVICO Who I, my lord?

OTHELLO

Ay, you did wish that I would make her turn:
Sir, she can turn, and turn, and yet go on   245
And turn again; and she can weep, sir, weep;
And she's obedient, as you say, obedient,

---

231 Why . . . Othello!] This edition *after* F ('Why . . . *Othello?*'); How . . . *Othello?* Q
231.1 *striking her*] THEOBALD; *not in* Q, F   236 woman's] F; womens Q   240 an] Q; *not in* F

234 **very much** an extremely grave matter
236 **teem with** (a) swarm with; (b) be impregnated by
237 **Each . . . crocodile** A complex conceit, referring simultaneously to the belief that crocodiles were generated spontaneously from the Nile mud by the action of the sun (*Antony*, 1.3.68–9, 2.7.26–7) and to the proverbial hypocrisy of 'crocodile tears' (Dent C831).
242 **What . . . sir** Metrically amphibious, making complete pentameters with both ll. 241 and 243. The bawdy innuendo in this line ('What do you want her for? | What would you like to do with her?') leads into the open obscenity of the brothel scene (4.2) where Othello treats his wife as though she were a prostitute.
244, 245, 246 **turn** A complex piece of

word-play is involved: (a) return (*OED v.* 21); (b) be converted, change faith (*v.* 30b); (c) revolt, desert (*v.* 30c); be inconstant (*v.* 36); (c) have intercourse (Williams, *Dictionary*, pp. 1440–2, *Glossary*, p. 316; Partridge, p. 207). The archaic sense 'mislead, beguile, cheat' (*OED* 14b) may also be involved. Since *turn* is the usual colloquial word for 'apostatize' (cf. 2.3.159), the idea of Othello himself as a Moor 'turned' Christian may provide an ironic context for the passage.

247–8, 251 **obedient . . . obey** Othello implicitly contrasts his own obedience as an officer of Venice with Desdemona's betrayal of her domestic office. *Obedient* could also mean 'yielding to desires, compliant' (*OED a.* 3), while the 17th-century

---

339

Very obedient.—Proceed you in your tears?—
Concerning this, sir—O well-painted passion!—
I am commanded home.—Get you away;   250
I'll send for you anon.—Sir, I obey the mandate,
And will return to Venice.—Hence, avaunt!—

Exit Desdemona

Cassio shall have my place. And sir, tonight
I do entreat that we may sup together.
You are welcome, sir, to Cyprus.—Goats and monkeys!   255

Exit

LODOVICO

Is this the noble Moor, whom our full Senate
Call all in all sufficient? Is this the nature
Whom passion could not shake? Whose solid virtue
The shot of accident nor dart of chance
Could neither graze nor pierce?

IAGO   He is much changed.   260

LODOVICO

Are his wits safe? Is he not light of brain?

IAGO

He's that he is: I may not breathe my censure

---

248 tears?] This edition (*conj.* Warner); teares. F; teares, Q 250 home] F, Q2; here Q1
252.1 *Exit Desdemona*] ROWE; *not in* F, Q 255.1 *Exit*] F, Q (*corr.*); *not in* Q (*uncorr.*) 256–
7 Is . . . nature] F; This the noble nature Q 262 censure | What] JENNENS; censure. | What
F; censure, | What Q

pronunciation of *obedient* would allow an
actor to disclose the word *bed* mockingly
concealed in its second syllable.

249 **this** i.e. the letter from Venice
painted depicted, represented; acted,
feigned. The metaphor is taken from the
language of criticism, but in this context
is inevitably tainted by association with
the *painting* of cosmetics (a stock object of
contemporary misogynistic satire).
passion (a) emotion; (b) the sufferings of
a martyr. *Passion* also seems to have been
used as a technical term in the theatre to
describe a passionate speech or mimed
display of emotion (cf. *Hamlet*, 3.2.10).

252 **avaunt** be gone

253 **place** The bawdy sense of the word
is now irresistible (cf. 2.3.306–7,
3.3.250–1). According to Tynan, 'Olivier
turned this line into an ironic double

entendre—hasn't Cassio already usurped
his place in bed?' (p. 10).

255 **Goats and monkeys** Echoing Iago at
3.3.405.

256 **full** complete, whole

257 **sufficient** competent

258 **virtue** manly courage

260 **graze** Earliest use cited in *OED*.

262 **He's . . . is** Cf. 'I am not what I am'
(1.1.64).

262–4 **I . . . were** Iago at his most teasingly
opaque. The reference of *might* appears to
shift in a confusing way: 'it's not for me to
conjecture about his sanity; if indeed he is
not everything that he might be, then I
only wish he were'. But it is possible (as
Sanders suggests) that he means: 'if he is
not out of his mind, I wish to God he were
(for only that could serve to excuse his
actions)'.

262 **censure** opinion

What he might be; if what he might, he is not,
I would to heaven he were.

LODOVICO   What? Strike his wife?

IAGO

Faith that was not so well; yet would I knew   265
That stroke would prove the worst!

LODOVICO   Is it his use?
Or did the letters work upon his blood
And new-create his fault?

IAGO   Alas, alas!
It is not honesty in me to speak
What I have seen and known. You shall observe him,   270
And his own courses will denote him so
That I may save my speech: do but go after
And mark how he continues.

LODOVICO

I am sorry that I am deceived in him.   *Exeunt*

4.2   *Enter Othello and Emilia*

OTHELLO

You have seen nothing then?

EMILIA

Nor ever heard, nor ever did suspect.

OTHELLO

Yes, you have seen Cassio and she together.

EMILIA

But then I saw no harm; and then I heard
Each syllable that breath made up between them.   5

OTHELLO   What? Did they never whisper?

EMILIA   Never, my lord.

263 if what] F, Q2; if as Q1   264 his] F; this Q   271 denote] Q; deuote F (*uncorr.*; 'u' *is turned* 'n'); deonte F (*corr.*)
    4.2] F (*Scena Secunda.*); *not in* Q   3 you] F; and you Q

266 **use** normal way of behaving
267 **blood** passion
268 **new-create** Earliest citation in *OED*.
271 **courses** conduct, esp. of a reprehensible kind (*OED n.* 23b)
    denote reveal the truth about
4.2.1–4 **seen . . . heard** Where Othello emphasizes seeing, Emilia assumes that hearing supplies the most persuasive form of evidence, a contrast that reflects ironic-

ally on Othello's folly in the eavesdropping episode at the beginning of 4.1, where his reliance upon 'ocular proof' entirely deceived him.
2 **nor . . . suspect** As Honigmann suggests, 'suspect' may be transitive; in which case Emilia's speech remains incomplete, Othello interrupting her before she can complete the sentence.
7 **Never . . . lord** Metrically amphibious.

OTHELLO Nor send you out o' the way?

EMILIA Never.

OTHELLO

To fetch her fan, her gloves, her mask, nor nothing?   10

EMILIA

Never, my lord.

OTHELLO   That's strange.

EMILIA

I durst, my lord, to wager she is honest,
Lay down my soul at stake: if you think other,
Remove your thought; it doth abuse your bosom.
If any wretch have put this in your head,   15
Let heaven requite it with the serpent's curse;
For if she be not honest, chaste, and true,
There's no man happy: the purest of their wives
Is foul as slander.

OTHELLO   Bid her come hither—go.

                                                Exit Emilia

She says enough; yet she's a simple bawd   20
That cannot say as much. This is a subtle whore,

---

10 her gloves, her mask] F; her mask, her gloues Q   16 heaven] F, Q2; heauens Q1   18 their
wives] F, Q2; her Sex Q1   19.1 *Exit Emilia*] F; *after* 'slander' (*l.* 20) Q

---

10 **mask** Worn as a disguise during the
Venetian carnival, but also used to protect
ladies' complexions from the sun.

13 **Lay . . . stake** stake my soul as a wager;
but *lay down* suggests 'lay down my life'
and hence a martyr's burning at the
stake.

15 **If any wretch** Of course she already has
Iago in mind: this is as close as Emilia dare
come to acknowledging her own part in
what has happened.

16 **serpent's curse** 'Then the Lord God
said to the serpent, Because thou hast
done this, thou art cursed above all
cattle, and above every beast of the
field: upon thy belly shalt thou go, and
dust shalt thou eat all the days of thy
life. I will also put enmity between
thee and the woman, and between thy
seed and her seed. He shall break thine
head, and thou shalt bruise his heel'
(Genesis 3 : 14–15). The recollection of the
Genesis story (which was often interpret-

ed as making death the punishment for
sexual knowledge) is appropriate in a
number of ways: not only has Iago
(whom the language of the play repeatedly identifies as a kind of 'demi-devil'
(5.2.299) tempted Emilia to steal the
handkerchief as the satanic serpent
tempts Eve to pluck the forbidden fruit,
but the curse of murderous enmity
between them will be acted out in the final
scene. Cf. also 3.3.449, 5.2.363.

20 **bawd** procuress.

21–3 **This . . . do't** Many editors take the
'whore' to be Desdemona, but it is Emilia
who is cast in Othello's imagination as
the guardian of 'villainous secrets' (ll.
27–30). Acknowledging this, Honigmann sentimentally suggests that *kneel
and pray* must refer to Desdemona, but
there is no reason why such routine piety
should be attributed to her alone; Othello
is emphasizing the hypocrisy of Emilia's
discretion.

A closet, lock, and key of villainous secrets;
And yet she'll kneel and pray—I have seen her do't.
Enter Desdemona and Emilia

DESDEMONA
My lord, what is your will?

OTHELLO   Pray you, chuck, come hither.

DESDEMONA
What is your pleasure?

OTHELLO   Let me see your eyes—   25
Look in my face.

DESDEMONA   What horrible fancy's this?

OTHELLO (*to Emilia*)
Some of your function, mistress:
Leave procreants alone and shut the door,
Cough or cry 'Hem!' if anybody come.
Your mystery, your mystery—nay, dispatch!   30

Exit Emilia

DESDEMONA (*kneeling*)
Upon my knee, what doth your speech import?

22 closet, lock, and key] This edition; A Closset Lockeand Key F; closet, locke and key, Q; closset-locke and key ROWE   24 Pray you] F; Pray Q   27 mistress:] F (Mistris); mistrisse, Q   30 nay] Q; May F   31 *kneeling*] This edition; *not in* F, Q   kneel] F; knees Q   doth] F; does Q

22 **closet, lock, and key** The *closet* (normally a small inner chamber) was a place of enhanced importance in early modern households, a site of exceptional privacy, and one of the few spaces in the house that were liable to be locked: cf. Angel Day, *The English Secretary* (1586), ii. 103 (cited in *OED*): 'We do call the most secret place in the house appropriate unto our own private studies . . . a Closet.' In allegorized descriptions of the human body, the heart (or bosom) is often imaged as a closet of emotional secrets.

24–5 **will . . . pleasure** For Othello, the sexual *doubles entendres* in these innocently meant words can easily be interpreted as proof of Desdemona's vicious secrets.

25–6 **Let . . . face** Cf. Dent E231, 'The eye is the window of the heart'. This will be 'ocular proof' in a double sense.

26 **fancy** fantasy

27–9 **Some . . . come** It is unclear whether (as is usually assumed, and as the F punctuation suggests) the first part of the speech consists of a series of commands,

amplifying an initial insistence that Emilia should perform the proper role of a bawd (*Some of your function* = 'show us some of the behaviour proper to your trade'; *OED, function, n.* 3), or whether (as the Q punctuation might suggest) Othello begins with a description of what others in the trade do (*Some of your function* = 'some people in your profession'), and then orders Emilia to play the part.

28 **procreants** procreators (first recorded use of *procreant* as a noun in *OED*). Here an ironic euphemism for 'fornicators'.

31–40 **kneeling . . . rising** Desdemona's words indicate that she should kneel at l. 31, but it is not entirely clear where she ought to rise; however, the talk of swearing, damnation, and heaven in ll. 35–9 seems appropriate to the kneeling gesture, while Desdemona's indignant questions at l. 40 provide a natural cue for her to rise. The repeated kneelings of this scene, with their echo of the Iago–Othello oath-taking in 3.3, produce a powerful visual *leitmotif* (cf. l. 151).

31 **import** mean

I understand a fury in your words,
But not the words.

OTHELLO   Why, what art thou?

DESDEMONA
Your wife, my lord, your true and loyal wife.

OTHELLO
Come swear it: damn thyself,   35
Lest, being like one of heaven, the devils themselves
Should fear to seize thee. Therefore be double-damned:
Swear thou art honest.

DESDEMONA   Heaven doth truly know it.

OTHELLO
Heaven truly knows that thou art false as hell.

DESDEMONA ⌈*rising*⌉
To whom, my lord? With whom? How am I false?   40

OTHELLO
Ah, Desdemon, away, away, away!

DESDEMONA
Alas the heavy day, why do you weep?
Am I the motive of these tears, my lord?
If haply you my father do suspect
An instrument of this your calling back,   45
Lay not your blame on me: if you have lost him,
I have lost him too.

OTHELLO   Had it pleased heavens

---

33 But . . . words] Q; *not in* F   37 seize] F (ceaze); cease Q   40 *rising*] This edition; *not in* F, Q
41 Ah, Desdemon] F; O *Desdemona* Q   43 motive] F; occasion Q   these] F; those Q   44
haply] Q; happely F   46–7 lost . . . lost] F, Q2; left . . . left Q1   47 I] F; Why I Q   heavens]
JOHNSON; Heauen F; heauen Q; God OXFORD

33 **But . . . words** Q's line completes the
sense; perhaps omitted from F through a
confusion resulting from the repetition of
words.
38 **truly know it** Both 'really know it' and
'know it to be true'.
39 **false as hell** Proverbial: Dent H398.
41 **Desdemon** Patrick   Stewart
(Washington, 1997) used the abbreviation to bring out the latent pun in the
name: 'Des-*demon*'.
    away '*Either* she clings to him and he
pushes her away, *or* he wants to get away,
or he means "let's get away from all this
pointless talk"' (Honigmann); an actor

should perhaps be conscious of all three
meanings.
42 **why . . . weep** Cf. 5.2.38 n.
44–5 **If . . . back** The   suddenness   of
Othello's recall is sometimes cited as evidence of the play's 'double time scheme',
since it is impossible for the Venetian
Senate to have heard of the dispersal
of the Turkish fleet; but Desdemona's
response suggests that Othello may simply be the victim of her father's political
lobbying.
47–53 **Had . . . patience** Othello imagines
himself as Job, the type of suffering
patience (see Job 2: 3–7).

To try me with affliction, had they rained
All kind of sores and shames on my bare head,
Steeped me in poverty to the very lips,   50
Given to captivity me and my utmost hopes,
I should have found in some place of my soul
A drop of patience; but, alas, to make me
The fixèd figure for the scorn of time,
To point his slow and moving finger at!   55
⌈*He groans*⌉
Yet could I bear that too, well, very well:
But there, where I have garnered up my heart,
Where either I must live or bear no life,
The fountain from the which my current runs
Or else dries up—to be discarded thence,   60
Or keep it as a cistern for foul toads

48 they rained] F, Q2; he ram'd Q1; he rained OXFORD   49 kind] F; kindes Q   51 utmost] F; *not in* Q   52 place] F; part Q   54 The] F; A Q   scorn of time] This edition (*conj.* MALONE); time of Scorne F, Q (scorne)   55 and moving finger] F; vnmouing fingers Q1; vnmouing finger Q2   55.1 *He groans*] *after* Q (– oh, oh); *not in* F

47–8 **heavens . . . they** It is conceivable that F's *heaven* is a collective noun (= the heavenly powers), but it seems more likely that a final *s* was dropped at some point in the transmission. Some editors conjecture, on the basis of Q's *heaven . . . he*, that the original read *God*; but such substitutions are not characteristic of Q, and *he* is more probably a mistaken attempt to resolve the confusion of number.

51 **utmost** (a) greatest; (b) last

54–5 **The fixèd . . . finger** The metaphor is that of a clock, whose slow-moving hand points, as if in contempt, at the *fixèd figure* of Othello.

54 **scorn of time** F's and Q's '*time of scorn*' could = 'this scornful time', or it may be (as Honigmann suggests) that the line should be repunctuated to read 'The fixèd figure, for the time, of scorn' (i.e. the fixed target of scorn for this whole age); but, in the light of *Hamlet*'s 'scorns of time' (3.1.72) the phrase seems more likely to represent a not uncommon kind of accidental transposition, presumably occurring in a manuscript which lies somewhere behind both printed texts. Cf. 2.3.158, *sense of place*.

55 **slow and moving** Though both readings have their defenders, Q's *unmoving* is con-tradictory and could easily have resulted from aural confusion.

57–62 **But . . . there** Sanders and Honigmann note the echo of Proverbs 5: 15–18 (whose chapter title, in the Geneva version, is 'Whoredom forbidden'): 'Drink the water of thy cistern, and of the rivers out of the mids[t] of thine own well. Let thy fountains flow forth . . . let thy fountain be blessed, and rejoice with the wife of thy youth.' Honigmann further cites *Homilies*, 114, where whoredom is described as 'that most filthy lake, foul puddle, and stinking sink, whereunto all kinds of sins and evils flow'. The sexual suggestiveness of the lines was brought out by Bruce Purchase (Mermaid, 1971) who delivered them staring hard at Desdemona's crotch.

59 **fountain** spring. For early modern conceptions of the heart as both 'receptacle [and] fountain' of emotion see Paster, pp. 69–70.

61 **cistern** water-tank, reservoir. The meaning 'cesspool', favoured by Sanders and Mowat–Werstine, is not warranted by *OED*; but cf. *Antony*, 2.5.96, 'A cistern for scaled snakes'.

toads Paster cites Nashe, *Terrors of the Night*: 'And even as slime and dirt in a

345

To knot and gender in! Turn thy complexion there,
Patience, thou young and rose-lipped cherubin,
Ay there, look grim as hell.

DESDEMONA

I hope my noble lord esteems me honest. 65

OTHELLO

O ay, as summer flies are in the shambles,
That quicken even with blowing. O thou black weed,
Who art so lovely fair, and smell'st so sweet
That the sense aches at thee, would thou hadst ne'er
   been born!

DESDEMONA

Alas, what ignorant sin have I committed? 70

OTHELLO

Was this fair paper, this most goodly book
Made to write 'whore' upon?—What committed?

63 thou] F; thy Q   64 Ay] THEOBALD; I F, Q   there, look] CAPELL, *after* THEOBALD (there look); heere looke F, Q   66 as] F (*corr.*), Q; as a F (*uncorr.*)   summer] F; summers Q   67 black] Q; *not in* F   68 Who] F; why Q   fair, and] F; faire? | Thou Q   69 ne'er] Q (ne're); neuer F   72 upon] F, Q2; on Q1

standing puddle, engender toads and frogs . . . so this slimy melancholy humour still thickening as it stands still, engendreth many misshapen objects in our imaginations' (*The Unfortunate Traveller and Other Works*, ed. J. B. Steane (Harmondsworth, 1972)). Cf. also 3.3.273–6.

62 **knot** couple
   gender procreate
   Turn thy complexion Either 'turn and look' (*complexion* = face; *OED* n. 4b, citing only this example); or 'change your temperament' (as revealed in the appearance of your face, i.e. from 'rose-lipped' to 'grim as hell', i.e. black).
63 **rose-lipped** Earliest citation in *OED*.
64 **Ay, there . . . hell** For a subtle analysis of this line in the context of the syntactical and semantic complexities of the speech, including the possible word-play on 'Ay/I' suggested by the F and Q spelling, see Pechter, pp. 89–90. Like Honigmann (Commentary and *Texts*, p. 90), Pechter defends F and Q 'here look'; but the gestural emphasis of the speech from l. 57 makes 'there' more rhetorically effective.

66 **shambles** slaughterhouse
67 **quicken** (a) come alive; (b) become pregnant
   even with blowing (a) as soon as they are laid; (b) as soon as they deposit their eggs. In this highly condensed image it is as though the very maggots are impregnated at the moment of their birth.
   black McMillin (Q, p. 41) suggests that this is an actor's (or possibly a scribe's) interpolation to fill out the metrical deficiency created by Q's confused lineation. On the other hand, the antithesis with *lovely fair* is characteristic of the play's imagery, and Shakespeare may have written a hexameter line.
70, 72, 73, 76, 80 **committed** Othello sniffs out another unwitting *double entendre*: commit = commit adultery (*OED* v. 6c).
71–2 **Was . . . upon** A very early instance of the (now commonplace) image of woman as a *tabula rasa* awaiting male inscription. The figure of a lover as a book occurs elsewhere, however: e.g. *Romeo*, 1.3.83–94, 3.2.83–4, *King John*, 2.1.486, *Dream*, 2.2.127–8.

'Committed'! O thou public commoner,
I should make very forges of my cheeks
That would to cinders burn up modesty   75
Did I but speak thy deeds. What committed?
Heaven stops the nose at it, and the moon winks;
The bawdy wind that kisses all it meets
Is hushed within the hollow mine of earth
And will not hear't.—What committed?   80
Impudent strumpet!

DESDEMONA   By heaven you do me wrong.

OTHELLO
Are not you a strumpet?

DESDEMONA   No, as I am a Christian.
If to preserve this vessel for my lord
From any other foul unlawful touch
Be not to be a strumpet, I am none.   85

OTHELLO
What, not a whore?

DESDEMONA   No, as I shall be saved.

OTHELLO Is't possible?

73–6 Committed . . . committed] F, Q2; *not in* Q1   79 hollow] F, Q2; hallow Q1   80 hear't] F,
Q; hear it STEEVENS   81 Impudent strumpet] Q; *not in* F   84 other] F, Q2; hated Q1

73–6 **Committed . . . committed** Probably
omitted from Q as a result of eye-skip
to the second *What committed?*, but a
possible cut; less likely to be an addition
to F.
73 **public commoner** common prostitute
74–5 **I . . . modesty** Othello imagines his
inflamed cheeks as a blacksmith's forge
heated by the fires of shame. While perhaps strengthened (as Honigmann suggests) by an implicit comparison between
cheeks and the bellows that heat the
forge, the blushing image is inconsistent
with Othello's supposed blackness;
though it might be argued that this
reflects his unconscious internalization of
the white Venetian norm.
77 **stops** blocks
    moon symbol of chastity
    winks shuts her eye
78 **The . . . meets** Playing on the proverbial
'As free as the wind' (Dent A88) by inter-
preting 'free' as 'licentious'. Cf. *Merchant*,
2.6.19: 'the strumpet wind'.
79 **hollow mine** i.e. the Cave of the Winds
(see Virgil, *Aeneid*, 1.52)

80 **hear't** Steevens's emendation to 'hear
it' regularizes the metre but still leaves
the line a syllable short. However, a
brief silence after *not hear't* before the
final explosive *What committed!* seems
appropriate.
81 **Impudent** Both 'insolent' and 'shameless' (from Latin *pudere* = feel shame).
83 **vessel** Used in scripture as a metaphor for
the body: 'every one of you should know
how to possess his vessel in holiness and
honour, and not in the lust of concupis-
cences' (Thessalonians 4: 4–5); but often
given a bawdy sense, because of the reference in 1 Peter 3: 47 to 'woman as . . . the
weaker vessel' (see Williams, *Glossary*,
pp. 324–5, *Dictionary*, pp. 1479–80).
87 **Is't possible?** The last repetition of this
question can be used to taunt the audience with the suggestion that even now,
just before he instructs Emilia (in a
symbolically loaded phrase) to 'turn the
key', Othello glimpses the truth of his
terrible mistake. In Sam Mendes's 1997
production the line provided the cue for
a despairingly tender and lingering

347

DESDEMONA O heaven forgive us!

OTHELLO I cry you mercy then.

     Enter Emilia

    I took you for that cunning whore of Venice   90

    That married with Othello. (*To Emilia*) You, mistress,

    That have the office opposite to Saint Peter

    And keeps the gate of hell, you, you!—Ay, you:

    We've done our course; there's money for your pains;

    I pray you turn the key, and keep our counsel.   *Exit*   95

EMILIA

    Alas, what does this gentleman conceive?

    How do you, madam? How do you, my good lady?

DESDEMONA Faith, half asleep.

EMILIA

    Good madam, what's the matter with my lord?

DESDEMONA

    With who?

EMILIA   Why, with my lord, madam.   100

DESDEMONA

    Who is thy lord?

88 forgive us] F, Q2; forgiuenesse Q1   89 then] F, Q2; *not in* Q1   89.1 *Enter Emilia*] This edition; *after* 'Mistris' (*l.* 91) F; *after* 'saued' (*l.* 86) Q1; *after* 'Venice' (*l.* 90) Q2   93 gate of] F;
gates in Q   you, you!—ay, you] F (You, you: I you), Q2 (you, you, I, You); I, you, you, you Q1
94 We've] *after* Q (We ha)   101 Who . . . lady] F, Q2; *not in* Q1

embrace, broken violently on 'I cry you
mercy then'. Cf. 2.3.276.

88 **O . . . us** Metrically amphibious.
89 **I . . . mercy** I beg your pardon
89.1 **Enter Emilia** It is clear from Emilia's
words at ll. 115 and 120 that Emilia is
meant to overhear Othello calling his wife
'whore', so F's placing of the direction
must be wrong. However, it is not uncommon for playhouse scripts (such as Q
appears to be) to anticipate entries, so
that actors could be alerted by the book-
holder. Moreover, the dialogue provides
no very plausible cue for Emilia's re-entry
at l. 86, as the Q2 editor seems to have
noticed when he made the unusual decision to reject both F and Q, and have
Emilia re-enter on 'I took you for that cunning whore of Venice', an entry perfectly
cued by Desdemona's terrified cry 'O
heaven forgive us!' (l. 88).
92–3 **That . . . hell** For *hell* as the vagina see
Williams, *Glossary*, p. 156, *Dictionary*,

p. 660; and cf. *Trag. Lear*, 4.5.124–6;
office picks up Iago's bawdy innuendo at
1.3.377. For the use of singular verbs
with plural subjects, see 1.1.150.
94 **done our course** finished our sexual
bout; *course* is a common sexual pun,
combining metaphors of food, the chase,
riding, racing, and jousting (*OED n.* 26, 7,
1, 3, 5).
95 **counsel** secret
96 **conceive** imagine; but also echoing the
imagery of unnatural conception from
1.3.392–3, 3.4.151–2.
98 **half asleep** half-dead, stunned (*OED n.* 3,
4). Emilia's anxiously repeated 'How do
you?' suggests that Desdemona may have
collapsed.
101 **thy lord . . . yours** The play on two
slightly different senses of *lord* ('master'
and 'husband') is a reminder of the similar way in which patriarchal ideas of
household government constructed the
roles of wife and servant. See Introduction, p. 110.

EMILIA   He that is yours, sweet lady.
DESDEMONA
I have none: do not talk to me, Emilia—
I cannot weep, nor answers have I none
But what should go by water. Prithee tonight
Lay on my bed my wedding sheets, remember,   105
And call thy husband hither.
EMILIA   Here's a change indeed.

                                                        Exit

DESDEMONA
'Tis meet I should be used so, very meet.
How have I been behaved that he might stick
The small'st opinion on my least misuse?
        Enter Iago and Emilia
IAGO
What is your pleasure, madam? How is't with you?   110
DESDEMONA
I cannot tell—those that do teach young babes
Do it with gentle means and easy tasks:
He might have chid me so, for in good faith
I am a child to chiding.
IAGO   What is the matter, lady?
EMILIA
Alas, Iago, my lord hath so bewhored her,   115
Thrown such despite and heavy terms upon her
That true hearts cannot bear it.

---

103 answers] F; answer Q   105 my wedding] F, Q2; our wedding Q1   107 very meet] F, Q2;
very well Q1   109 least misuse] F, Q2; greatest abuse Q1   109.1 *Enter . . . Emilia*] F, Q2; *after*
'Madam' (*l.* 110) Q1   114 to] F, Q2; at Q1   117 That] F; As Q   hearts] F (*corr.*), Q; heart F
(*uncorr.*)   it] F; *not in* Q

---

102 **I have none** Cf. Othello at 5.2.99: 'I
  have no wife.'
104 **go by water** travel by water (i.e. be conveyed by tears); perhaps, in the context of
  the wedding sheets, tinged with nostalgic
  recollection of Desdemona's elopement
  by gondola (1.1.124).
105 **wedding sheets** For the considerable
  significance with which wedding sheets
  were invested in early modern culture, see
  Introduction, pp. 173–4.
108–9 **stick . . . opinion** fasten the least
  hint of (unfavourable) conjecture. In con-

temporary moral discourse *opinion* was
  typically opposed to rational judgement.
109 **misuse** ill conduct
112 **tasks** Honigmann suggests that this
  may = reproofs (from *task, v.* 5 = take to
  task, reprove).
114 **I . . . chiding** I am as unaccustomed as
  any child to reproof
115 **bewhored** called her a whore (first
  example in *OED*)
116 **despite** scorn, abuse
  heavy angry, violent; hard to bear,
  grievous (*OED a.* 22, 23)

DESDEMONA

Am I that name, Iago?

IAGO   What name, fair lady?

DESDEMONA

Such as she said my lord did say I was.

EMILIA

He called her 'whore': a beggar in his drink   120
Could not have laid such terms upon his callet.

IAGO Why did he so?

DESDEMONA

I do not know: I am sure I am none such.

IAGO

Do not weep, do not weep—alas the day!

EMILIA

Hath she forsook so many noble matches,   125
Her father, and her country, and her friends,
To be called whore? Would it not make one weep?

DESDEMONA

It is my wretched fortune.

IAGO   Beshrew him for't!
How comes this trick upon him?

DESDEMONA   Nay, heaven doth know.

EMILIA

I will be hanged if some eternal villain,   130
Some busy and insinuating rogue,
Some cogging, cozening slave, to get some office,
Have not devised this slander; I'll be hanged else.

---

119 said] F; sayes Q   125 Hath] F; Has Q   126 and her friends] F, Q2; all her friends Q1

---

121 **callet** slut, whore
128 **Beshrew him** Cf. 3.4.146.
129 **How ... him** how has this delusion
overcome him? (But 'trick' can also suggest 'hoax'.)
130–44 **I ... west** Some actors have
assumed that Emilia's tirade is directed at
Iago (as his angry replies might be taken
to recognize); and she could not, of
course, accuse him directly without dis-
closing her own betrayal of Desdemona.
But there is no other evidence for such
distrust. Charles Fechter's acting edition
(1861) included a direction indicating

that Emilia 'suspiciously eye[s] Iago'; however, Edwin Booth's acting edition (1875)
vigorously challenged this suggestion in
favour of a more subtle dramatic irony
(see Potter, p. 51). For the metatheatrical
basis of Emilia's conjecture, see Introduction, p. 160, n. 1.
130 **eternal** inveterate (and, by implication,
damned)
131 **busy** prying, meddlesome
insinuating artfully ingratiating
132 **cogging** fraudulent
cozening cheating

IAGO

Fie, there is no such man! It is impossible.

DESDEMONA

If any such there be, heaven pardon him.   135

EMILIA

A halter pardon him, and hell gnaw his bones!
Why should he call her whore? Who keeps her
    company?
What place? What time? What form? What likelihood?
The Moor's abused by some most villainous knave,
Some base, notorious knave, some scurvy fellow.   140
O heaven, that such companions thou'dst unfold,
And put in every honest hand a whip
To lash the rascals naked through the world,
Even from the east to th' west!

IAGO   Speak within door.

EMILIA

O, fie upon them! Some such squire he was   145
That turned your wit the seamy side without
And made you to suspect me with the Moor.

IAGO

You are a fool—go to!

DESDEMONA   O God, Iago,
What shall I do to win my lord again?
Good friend, go to him; for, by this light of heaven,   150
I know not how I lost him.

---

139 most villainous] F, Q2; outragious Q1   141 heaven] Q; Heauens F   143 rascals] F; ras-
call Q   144 door] F (doore); dores Q   145 them] F; him Q   148 O God] ALEXANDER (*after* Q,
'O good'); Alas F   151–64 Here . . . me] F, Q2; *not in* Q1   151 *She kneels*] ROWE (*subs.*); *not
in* F

---

136 **halter** hangman's noose
137 **keeps her company** Perhaps playing
    on the colloquial sense, 'courts her'.
138 **form** manner
139 **abused** Cf. 2.1.226.
140 **knave** (a) villain; (b) man of low rank
    fellow Like *knave* (b), a term of social
    disdain.
141 **companions** low fellows (*OED n.*[1] 4)
    unfold expose
142 **honest** The pointedness of Emilia's
    attack is emphasized by the way she turns
    Iago's own sobriquet against him.

143 **To . . . world** Lashing through the
    streets was a standard punishment.
144 **Even . . . west** Cf. Dent E43.1.
    within door more quietly, more
    discreetly
145 **squire** Contemptuous; equivalent to
    fellow (*OED n.* 1d).
146 **turned your wit** turned your wits
    inside out
    seamy worst or roughest (side of a gar-
    ment). Earliest citation in *OED*.
147 **suspect me** Cf. 1.3.375–7, 2.1.286–90.
148 **go to** Exclamation of impatience, here
    equivalent to 'shut up!'

She kneels

Here I kneel:
If e'er my will did trespass 'gainst his love,
Either in discourse, or thought, or actual deed,
Or that mine eyes, mine ears, or any sense
Delighted them in any other form,   155
Or that I do not yet—and ever did,
And ever will, though he do shake me off
To beggarly divorcement—love him dearly,
Comfort forswear me! Unkindness may do much,
And his unkindness may defeat my life,   160
But never taint my love. I cannot say 'whore':
It does abhor me now I speak the word,
To do the act that might th'addition earn
Not the world's mass of vanity could make me.

IAGO ⌈*helping her to rise*⌉

I pray you be content: 'tis but his humour;   165
The business of the state does him offence,
And he does chide with you.

DESDEMONA If 'twere no other—

153 discourse, or] Q2; discourse of F   155 them in] Q2; them: or F   165 *helping her to rise*]
BOOTH *in* Furness; '*She rises*' *after* 'love' (*l.* 161) OXFORD; *not in* F, Q   167 And . . . you] Q; *not
in* F

151–64 **Here . . . make me** Almost certainly a cut in Q, as the metrical incom-
pleteness of l. 151 in that text suggests.
151 **She kneels** The visual echo of Iago's and
Othello's sinister troth-plighting at the
end of 3.3 is especially significant here,
since Desdemona is not only reasserting
her marital vows of love and obedience,
but kneeling before her persecutor just as
Othello has done.
152 **trespass** sin (as in e.g. the Lord's Prayer)
153 **discourse . . . deed** Cf. the liturgical
formula from the general confession
'thought, word, and deed' (1559 *Book
of Common Prayer*, service of Holy
Communion).
154, 156 **that** if
155 **Delighted them** took pleasure (ethic
dative)
form body, outward appearance; beauty
(*OED n.* 3, 1e)
156 **yet** still
159 **Comfort forswear me** may I lose all
hope of comfort
159, 160 **Unkindness** (a) cruelty; (b) unnat-

ural behaviour. A play on the racial sense
of 'kind' may also be involved.
161 **I . . . 'whore'** Cf. ll. 120–7.
162 **abhor me** (a) cause me abhorrence; (b)
render me abhorrent; with a familiar
pun on *whore*. Honigmann cites *Homilies*,
109: 'whoredom . . . ought to be ab-
horred'.
163 **addition** title, badge of honour (*OED n.*
4, 5)
164 **world's . . . vanity** all the empty pride
and worthless treasures of the world
165 **humour** mood, whim
166 **does** causes
167 **And . . . you** An inessential amplification, whose disappearance from F is consistent with revision, since Desdemona's
reply follows a little more naturally from
the previous line.
168 **If . . . other**—Metrically amphibious.
Oxford may be right in treating this as an
exclamation (= 'If only that were all!'),
rather than (as most editors assume) an
incomplete or interrupted speech.

IAGO It is but so, I warrant.

    ⌜*Trumpets sound within*⌝

  Hark how these instruments summon to supper: 170
  The messengers of Venice stays the meat.
  Go in, and weep not: all things shall be well.

                           Exeunt Desdemona and Emilia

    Enter Roderigo

  How now, Roderigo?

RODERIGO I do not find that thou deal'st justly with me.

IAGO What in the contrary?   175

RODERIGO Every day thou doffest me with some device,
  Iago, and rather, as it seems to me now, keepest from
  me all conveniency than suppliest me with the least
  advantage of hope. I will indeed no longer endure it,
  nor am I yet persuaded to put up in peace what already I   180
  have foolishly suffered.

IAGO Will you hear me, Roderigo?

RODERIGO Faith, I have heard too much, for your words and
  performances are no kin together.

IAGO You charge me most unjustly.   185

RODERIGO With naught but truth: I have wasted myself out
  of my means; the jewels you have had from me to deliver
  Desdemona would half have corrupted a votarist; you
  have told me she hath received them, and returned me
  expectations and comforts of sudden respect and   190
  acquaintance, but I find none.

---

169 It is . . . warrant] F; Tis . . . warrant you Q   *Trumpets . . . within*] ROWE (*subs.*, *after l.*
170); *not in* F, Q   170 summon] F; summon you Q   171 The messengers] F; And the
great Messengers Q1; The meate, great Messengers Q2   stays the meat] F; stay Q   172.1
Exeunt . . . Emilia] F; *Exit women.* Q   172.2 *Enter Roderigo*] F; *after* 'Roderigo' (*l.* 173) Q
176 doffest] Q; dafts F   177 now, keepest] F, Q2; thou keepest Q1   183 Faith] Q1; *not in* F,
Q2   I . . . and] Q; I haue heard too much: and your words and F (*corr.*); And hell gnaw his
bones F (*uncorr.*)   184 performances] F; performance Q   186 With . . . truth] F, Q2; *not in*
Q1   187 my] F; *not in* Q   deliver] F; deliuer to Q   189 hath] F; has Q   190 expectations] F;
expectation Q   191 acquaintance] F, Q2; acquittance Q1

169.1 **Trumpets** See App. D (i).
171 **stays the meat** await their meal
172 **all . . . well** Proverbial: Dent A164
176 **doffest me** put me off
    device contrivance, trick
178 **conveniency** convenient opportunity
    (*OED n.* 4c; earliest example *c.*1645)
179 **advantage of** occasion for
180 **put up** put up with
188 **votarist** nun

190 **comforts** encouragement (*OED n.* 1a)
    sudden immediate
    respect esteem; favour, partiality (*OED n.*
    16, 13b). Stronger than it sounds to us: in
    Trag. Lear the King of France's 'love . . .
    kindle[s] to inflamed respect' (1.1.255).
191 **acquaintance** familiarity; perhaps with
    a bawdy quibble on 'quaint' (= vagina; see
    Williams, *Glossary*, p. 252). Q's 'acquit-
    tance' (= recompense) is also possible.

IAGO Well, go to, very well!

RODERIGO 'Very well', 'go to'? I cannot 'go to', man, nor 'tis
not 'very well'; by this hand, I say 'tis very scurvy, and
begin to find myself fopped in it.   195

IAGO Very well.

RODERIGO I tell you, 'tis not very well! I will make myself
known to Desdemona: if she will return me my jewels,
I will give over my suit and repent my unlawful solicita-
tion; if not, assure yourself I will seek satisfaction of you.   200

IAGO You have said now.

RODERIGO Ay, and said nothing but what I protest
intendment of doing.

IAGO Why, now I see there's mettle in thee, and even from
this instant do build on thee a better opinion than ever   205
before. Give me thy hand, Roderigo: thou hast taken
against me a most just exception; but yet I protest I have
dealt most directly in thy affair.

RODERIGO It hath not appeared.

IAGO I grant indeed it hath not appeared; and your   210
suspicion is not without wit and judgement. But,
Roderigo, if thou hast that in thee indeed which I have
greater reason to believe now than ever—I mean
purpose, courage, and valour—this night show it. If
thou the next night following enjoy not Desdemona, take   215

192 well] F, Q2; good Q1   193 nor 'tis] F, Q2; it is Q1   194 by . . . very] Q1; Nay I think
it is F; I say t'is very Q2   197 I tell you, 'tis] F; I say it is Q   202 said] F, Q2; I haue said Q1
205 instant] F, Q2; time Q1   207 exception] F; conception Q   208 affair] F (Affaire), Q2;
affaires Q1   212 in] F; within Q   215 enjoy] F; enioyest Q

193 **go to** Roderigo quibbles on the bawdy
sense of the phrase: cf. *Trag. Lear*,
4.5.111–12: 'the wren goes to't. . . . let
copulation thrive' (and see Williams,
Glossary, p. 144, *Dictionary*, pp. 605–6;
Partridge, pp. 121–2).

195 **fopped** made a fool of, duped

200 **seek satisfaction** seek repayment;
demand atonement (perhaps with the
implication 'challenge to a duel')

201 **You have said** 'You have had your say'
(Honigmann); 'What you now say is true'
(Onions). But perhaps in the light of the
next two speeches it should be taken as a

response to Roderigo's ambiguous hint of
a challenge, meaning 'I heard that (and
don't expect to back out of it)'.

202–3 **protest intendment of** insist that I
have every intention of

204 **mettle** courage, spirit

206–7 **taken . . . exception** taken under-
standable offence, justifiably found fault
with me

208 **directly** straightforwardly

209–10 **It . . . appeared** Iago slightly turns
the meaning of Roderigo's phrase from
'there's been no evidence of it' to 'that is
how it may have *seemed*'.

me from this world with treachery, and devise engines for my life.

RODERIGO Well, what is it? Is it within reason and compass?

IAGO Sir, there is especial commission come from Venice to depute Cassio in Othello's place.   220

RODERIGO Is that true? Why, then Othello and Desdemona return again to Venice.

IAGO O no, he goes into Mauretania and taketh away with him the fair Desdemona, unless his abode be lingered here by some accident—wherein none can be so   225 determinate as the removing of Cassio.

RODERIGO How do you mean 'removing' him?

IAGO Why, by making him uncapable of Othello's place— knocking out his brains.   230

RODERIGO And that you would have me to do?

IAGO Ay, if you dare do yourself a profit and a right. He sups tonight with a harlotry, and thither will I go to him. He knows not yet of his honourable fortune: if you will watch his going thence—which I will fashion to fall out   235 between twelve and one—you may take him at your pleasure; I will be near to second your attempt, and he shall fall between us. Come, stand not amazed at it, but go along with me: I will show you such a necessity in his death that you shall think yourself bound to put it on   240 him. It is now high supper time, and the night grows to waste: about it!

---

218 what is it] F; *not in* Q   220 commission] F, Q2; command Q1   224 taketh] F; takes Q
228 removing] F; remouing of Q   232 if] F; and if Q   a right] F; right Q   233 harlotry] F,
Q2; harlot Q1

---

216 **engines** snares, plots
219 **compass** bounds (of what's possible)
224 **Mauretania** i.e. the land of the Moors in North Africa. There is no other evidence that this is Othello's intention, and it may simply be Iago's fiction designed to goad Roderigo into action.
225 **abode be lingered** stay be prolonged
227 **determinate** decisive
229 **uncapable . . . place** In the context of the bawdy meaning acquired by 'place' (see 2.3.306–7 3.3.250–1, 4.1.253) this may seem to hint at castration.
233 **harlotry** harlot

234 **He . . . fortune** The implication seems to be: 'and therefore will not be protected by a train of followers (as the governor would normally be)'.
235 **fall out** occur
238 **amazed** bewildered
240 **put** inflict
241 **high supper time** high [fully] time for supper; Andrews suggests *high supper* = feast (by analogy with 'high tea'), but *OED* provides no warrant for this.
241–2 **grows to waste** is wasting away (and we are wasting our time)

RODERIGO I will hear further reason for this.

IAGO And you shall be satisfied.   *Exeunt*

4.3   *Enter Othello, Lodovico, Desdemona, Emilia,*
           and attendants

LODOVICO

  I do beseech you, sir, trouble yourself no further.

OTHELLO

  O, pardon me, 'twill do me good to walk.

LODOVICO

  Madam, good night; I humbly thank your ladyship.

DESDEMONA

  Your honour is most welcome.

OTHELLO   Will you walk, sir?—

  O Desdemona!

DESDEMONA   My lord?

OTHELLO   Get you to bed   5

  On th'instant; I will be returned forthwith:

  Dismiss your attendant there—look't be done.   *Exit*

DESDEMONA I will, my lord.

EMILIA

  How goes it now? He looks gentler than he did.

DESDEMONA

  He says he will return incontinent,   10

  And hath commanded me to go to bed,

  And bid me to dismiss you.

EMILIA   Dismiss me?

DESDEMONA

  It was his bidding; therefore, good Emilia,

  Give me my nightly wearing, and adieu:

244 *Exeunt*] F, Q2; *Ex. Iag. and* Rod. Q1
    4.3] F (*Scena Tertia*); *not in* Q   0.1–2 *Enter . . . attendants*] F; Enter *Othello, Desdemona,
Lodouico . . . and Attendants.* Q1 (*after* 'about it', 4.2.242), Q2 (*at this point*)   2 'twill] F; it
shall Q   7 Dismiss] F; dispatch Q   11 And] F; He Q   12 bid] F; bad Q

244 **satisfied** Sardonically picking up
    Roderigo's demand for 'satisfaction' (l.
    200), but perhaps with a sexual innuendo
    (cf. 3.3.392 ff.).
4.3.0.1 **Enter . . . attendants** Q's placing of
    this entry after l. 242 of the previous
    scene is a reminder of the artificiality of
    F's scene divisions in the continuous stag-
    ing of Shakespeare's theatre.

10 **incontinent** immediately. Although
    Desdemona cannot intend it, the adjecti-
    val meaning 'wanting in sexual restraint'
    is difficult to exclude in the context of the
    brothel scene and Desdemona's prepara-
    tions for bed.
14 **nightly wearing** nightclothes

We must not now displease him.   15

EMILIA

I would you had never seen him.

DESDEMONA

So would not I: my love doth so approve him
That even his stubbornness, his checks, his frowns—
Prithee unpin me—have grace and favour in them.

EMILIA

I have laid those sheets you bade me on the bed.   20

DESDEMONA

All's one, good faith, how foolish are our minds!
If I do die before thee, prithee shroud me
In one of these same sheets.

EMILIA   Come, come, you talk!

DESDEMONA

My mother had a maid called Barbary;

16 I would] Q1; I, would F; Would Q2; Ay, would KNIGHT   18 his frowns] F; and frownes Q
19 in them] Q; *not in* F   20 those] F, Q2; these Q1   21 All . . . how] This edition; All's one:
good Father, how F; All's one good faith: how Q1; All's one, goodfather; how Q2   22 before
thee] Q; before F   23 these] F; those Q

17 **approve** commend (*OED v.* 6). The more
usual senses of the verb at this time are
probably also present: 'prove to be true',
'put to the text of experience' (*OED v.* 1,
8).

18 **checks** reproofs, rebuffs

19, 32 **unpin** Usually played (since the time of
Ellen Terry at least) as a direction to *unpin*
Desdemona's hair; but *OED* entries (*v.*
3–4) suggest that from the 16th century to
the 18th it referred to the unpinning of a
lady's dress. Fashionable clothes at this
time were assembled from discrete bodices,
sleeves, etc., held together by pins.

19 **grace and favour** A standard colloca-
tion, normally referring to the good will
and generosity of a monarch (see e.g.
Richard III, 3.4.91; *Trag. Lear*, 1.1.229);
here both words = 'attractiveness, charm,
beauty', but are also coloured by the more
usual meaning of the phrase.

20 **sheets . . . bed** Honigmann suggests
that '[p]erhaps the bed is already visible';
but this is to miss an important aspect of
the play's technique in which the marriage bed is made constantly present to
the minds of the audience from the opening scene, but is withheld from view until
the climactic 'discovery' of 5.2 (see
Introduction, pp. 134–6).

23 **you talk** how you prattle!

24–9 **My mother . . . mind** It is difficult to
account for the presence of these lines in
Q, unless the singing of the Willow Song
was always intended to have been part of
this scene, rather than being added (as
Coghill and others supposed) in the revision that supposedly lay behind F. The
parallel excision of the dying Emilia's
echo of this scene at 5.2.245–7 makes it
virtually certain that a deliberate cut was
involved. Cf. also l. 100 n.

24 **Barbary** Alternative form of Barbara.
The name is strangely evocative in this
play, however, since it recalls the 'Barbary Moors' of North Africa, and Iago's
description of Othello as a 'Barbary
horse' (1.1.111) and an 'erring barbarian'
(1.3.348–9). Black body-servants were
becoming fashionable in this period, and
perhaps we should think of Barbary as a
black maid, like Zanche in Webster's
White Devil. Interestingly enough this was
the assumption made by Le Tourneur
whose French translation (1776) adds the
words '*C'étoit une Moresse, une pauvre
Moresse*' ('She was a Moorish woman, a
poor Moorish woman') to Desdemona's
speech (Furness, p. 389).

She was in love, and he she loved proved mad,   25
And did forsake her. She had a 'Song of Willow'—
An old thing 'twas, but it expressed her fortune,
And she died singing it. That song tonight
Will not go from my mind. I have much to do
But to go hang my head all at one side   30
And sing it like poor Barbary: prithee dispatch.

EMILIA
Shall I go fetch your nightgown?
DESDEMONA   No, unpin me here.
This Lodovico is a proper man.
EMILIA
A very handsome man.
DESDEMONA   He speaks well.
EMILIA I know a lady in Venice would have walked
barefoot to Palestine for a touch of his nether lip.   35
DESDEMONA (*sings*)
The poor soul sat sighing by a sycamore tree,

---

26 had] F, Q2; has Q1   29–48 I . . . next] F, Q2; *not in* Q1   33 This . . . proper man] F, Q2;
assigned to Emilia HONIGMANN (*conj.* Ridley)   35 barefoot] F; barefooted Q2   37 *sings*] Q2; *not
in* F   37–52 The . . . men] *lyrics in italic* F, Q2   37 sighing] Q2; *singing* F (*corr.*); *sining* F
(*uncorr.*)

---

25 **mad** Probably 'wild' or 'extravagantly
imprudent' (*OED a.* 7, 2) rather than
'lunatic'.
26–7 **Willow . . . fortune** The willow was
a traditional emblem for the grief of lost
or unrequited love (cf. *Twelfth Night*,
1.5.257–60; *Hamlet*, 4.7.138–47).
29–48, 50–2, 55–8 For the probability that
these lines, including the entire Willow
Song, were cut from the Q text, see ll.
24–9 n., and App. B, pp. 418–19.
29–30 **I . . . hang** I can hardly restrain
myself from hanging
30 **hang . . . side** i.e. in the traditional pos-
ture of love melancholy
32 **nightgown** See 1.1.158.1 n.
33 **This . . . proper man** Honigmann (following Ridley's conjecture) reassigns
these words (which appear only in F) to
Emilia on the grounds that '[f]or Desdemona to praise Lodovico at this point
seems out of character'. In this case Desdemona's 'He speaks well' would become
a polite deflection, like Cassio's replies to
Iago's nudging remarks about Desde-

mona in 2.3. But there is no reason why
Desdemona's mood of pained nostalgia
should not carry her into a half-conscious
regret for the 'many noble matches'
which, as Emilia has reminded her, she
rejected in order to marry Othello
(4.2.125).
proper A quibble is involved: while Desdemona probably means 'excellent; of
good character, honest, respectable, worthy' (*OED a.* 8a-b), Emilia chooses to
understand her as meaning 'fine-looking,
handsome, elegant' (*OED a.* 9).
35–6 **walked . . . Palestine** i.e. like a peni-
tential pilgrim
37–52 **The poor . . . men** Adapted, like
many of Shakespeare's best-known
songs, from a traditional ballad. See App.
D (iv).
37 **sycamore** Originally the *Syco-morus*
(fig-mulberry), by this time also used
of the maple species to which it now
usually refers. Both were prized as shade
trees, thus either might provide the
shadows sought by the melancholy;

Sing all a green willow.
Her hand on her bosom, her head on her knee;
　Sing willow, willow, willow.   40
The fresh streams ran by her and murmured her moans;
　Sing willow, willow, willow.
Her salt tears fell from her, and softened the stones.
　Sing willow—
(*Speaks*)　　　　Lay by these—
　　　　　　　　　　(*sings*) willow, willow.
(*Speaks*) Prithee, hie thee: he'll come anon.   45
　(*Sings*) Sing all a green willow must be my garland.
Let nobody blame him, his scorn I approve—
(*Speaks*) Nay, that's not next.—Hark, who is't that
　　　　knocks?

EMILIA It's the wind.

DESDEMONA (*sings*)
I called my love 'false love'; but what said he then?   50
　Sing willow, willow, willow.
If I court more women, you'll couch with more men.
(*Speaks*) So get thee gone, goodnight. Mine eyes do itch:
Doth that bode weeping?

EMILIA　　　　　　　　　　　'Tis neither here nor there.

DESDEMONA
I have heard it said so. O, these men, these men!   55

40, 51 Sing . . . willow] Q2; *Sing Willough, &c.* F   44 Sing willow] OXFORD; *Sing Willough, &c.*
F, Q2   44, 45, 46, 53 Speaks] *not in* F, Q2   44, 46, 50 *sings*] *not in* F, Q2   48 who is't] F; who's
Q   49 It's] F; It is Q1; T'is Q2   50–2 I . . . men] F, Q2; *not in* Q1   50 'false love'] F (*False
Loue*); *false* Q2   53 So] F, Q2; Now Q1   54 Doth] F; does Q   55–8 DESDEMONA I . . . ques-
tion] F, Q2; *not in* Q1

neither has any established connection
with love-melancholy, except via the
quibble (sick-*amour*) suggested by F's
spelling, 'sicamour', which apparently
licenses the same association in *Romeo*
(1.1.118). The pun may be complicated
here by a false etymology linking *morus* =
mulberry (Latin) with *morus* = Moor
(Med. Latin); see Patricia Parker, 'What's
in a Name: and More', *Revista de la
Sociedad Española de Estudios Renacentistas
Ingleses*, ed. Pilar Cuder Domínguez et al.,
SEDERI 11 (2002), 101–50. Cf. 2.1.221,
5.2.224.

38 **a** Common abbreviation for *of*.

43 **Her . . . stones** Cf. Dent D618, 'Constant
dropping will wear the stone'; an implicit
allusion to H311, 'A heart as hard as
stone' is also involved.
44 **Lay by these** put these away
45 **hie thee** hurry up
　anon any minute
47–8 **Let . . . next** Honigmann draws attention to Desdemona's 'Freudian slip': the
misplaced line significantly looks forward
to her self-abnegating absolution of
Othello at 5.2.124–5.
52 **couch** lie, copulate (from French
coucher)
54 **'Tis . . . there** Proverbial phrase: Dent
H438.

Dost thou in conscience think—tell me Emilia—
That there be women do abuse their husbands
In such gross kind?

EMILIA   There be some such, no question.

DESDEMONA
Wouldst thou do such a deed for all the world?

EMILIA
Why, would not you?

DESDEMONA   No, by this heavenly light.   60

EMILIA
Nor I neither, by this heavenly light:
I might do't as well i'th' dark.

DESDEMONA
Wouldst thou do such a thing for all the world?

EMILIA
The world's a huge thing: it is a great price
For a small vice.

DESDEMONA   God's troth, I think thou wouldst not.   65

EMILIA By my troth, I think I should, and undo't when I
had done. Marry, I would not do such a thing for a

---

58 kind] F; kindes Q2   59 deed] F, Q2; thing Q1   62 do't as well] F, Q1 (doe it as well); as well doe it Q2   63 thing] Q1; deed F, Q2   65 God's troth] This edition; Introth F, Q2 (In troth); Good troth Q1   66 By my troth] Q1; Introth F, Q2 (In troth)   67 done] F; done it Q

60–2 **Why . . . dark** Hongimann argues that the (admittedly suspicious) repetition of l. 59 at l. 63 indicates a passage of cancelled text which F copied from Q (*Texts*, pp. 34–5). He may be correct but his argument that '[a]fter what has happened not even someone as slow-witted as Emilia could make a joke of Desdemona's marital fidelity' (*Texts*, p. 35) makes insufficient allowance for the half-playful tone with which Desdemona covers her own anguish, and seems (like his reassignment of l. 33) to depend on a sentimentalization of Desdemona's chastity. For a rebuttal of Honigmann, emphasizing that 'performers have been playing these lines as written for centuries', see McMillin, Q, p. 12.

63 **thing** Q's *thing* seems justified by the way Emilia picks it up in the following line, creating an odd echo of her exchange

with Iago at 3.3.304–5; F's *deed* can then be explained as a careless repetition of the phrasing remembered from l. 61. Q2's transposition of the two words presumably results from compositorial carelessness (cf. Kellner, pp. 151–2).

64–5 **The . . . vice** Q's lineation makes a doggerel couplet appropriate to Emilia's mock-smugness.

64 **price** 'Price' and 'prize' were originally variant spellings of the same word; either sense will fit here.

65 **God's** The fact that F prints 'In' here while Q prints 'Good' suggests that (as at 4.2.148) the editor was expurgating blasphemy, and that Q resulted from a misreading.

66 **By my troth** Evidently altered as a profanity in F and Q2.

67 **done** finished. The bawdy sense of *do* is also involved.

joint-ring, nor for measures of lawn, nor for gowns, petticoats, nor caps, nor any petty exhibition. But for all the whole world? 'Ud's pity, who would not make her husband a cuckold to make him a monarch? I should venture purgatory for't. 70

DESDEMONA
Beshrew me, if I would do such a wrong
For the whole world!

EMILIA Why, the wrong is but a wrong i'th' world; and having the world for your labour, 'tis a wrong in your own world, and you might quickly make it right. 75

DESDEMONA
I do not think there is any such woman.

EMILIA
Yes, a dozen—and as many to th' vantage,
As would store the world they played for. 80
But I do think it is their husbands' faults

68 joint-ring, nor] F (ioynt Ring); ioynt ring; or Q 69 petticoats] F, Q2; or Petticotes Q1 petty] F, Q2; such Q1 all] F; *not in* Q 70 'Ud's pity] Q1; why F, Q2 81–98 But . . . so] F, Q2; *not in* Q1

68 **joint-ring** Or 'gimmal ring'; made in two parts, often decorated with two clasped hands holding a heart and used to symbolize the union of lovers (first recorded use in *OED*). Cf. Dryden, *Don Sebastian*, 5.1: 'Those rings . . . a curious artist wrought them | With joints so close as not to be perceived: | Yet are they both each other's counterpart; | Her part had Juan inscribed, and his had Zaida | . . . and in the midst | A heart divided in two parts was placed.'
lawn A fine and costly white linen.
69 **caps** Associated with the vanity of fashion and conspicuous consumption in e.g. *Shrew*, 4.3.63–85.
petty exhibition trivial reward or gift (*OED n.* 2); perhaps coloured by the sense of 'display' (not before 1663 in *OED*, but available from the verb *exhibit*).
69–70 **all . . . world** The wording recalls Matthew 16: 26: 'what doth it profit man if he win *all the whole world* and lose his own soul' (Bishops' Bible); but the situation, together with Emilia's talk of making her husband 'a monarch', recalls Satan's temptation of Christ, when 'the devil . . . showed him all the kingdoms of the world. . . . And . . . said, All this

power will I give thee, and the glory of those kingdoms' (Luke 4: 5–6; Geneva version).
70 **'Ud's** God's
72 **venture purgatory** risk being condemned to the punishments of purgatory. Ironic, not just because of Emilia's allusions to satanic temptation, but because of what she has already risked to make her husband a mere lieutenant.
73 **Beshrew me** Cf. 3.4.146.
79–80 **Yes . . . for** Treated as prose in F, Q and most editions; but, as Honigmann notes, a prose beginning to a verse speech is unusual, and if *world* is treated as disyllabic (a pronunciation encouraged by the rolled Elizabethan *r*) two passable pentameter lines result. Alternatively, a brief reflective pause before the next part of the speech would be dramatically appropriate.
79 **to th' vantage** in addition
80 **store** stock, populate
played (a) gambled; (b) copulated
81–98 **But . . . so** Of all the long passages missing from Q, this one seems most plausible as a possible addition; especially because Emilia's previous two speeches are in prose and ll. 79–80 are printed as

If wives do fall: say that they slack their duties,
And pour our treasures into foreign laps,
Or else break out in peevish jealousies,
Throwing restraint upon us; or say they strike us,   85
Or scant our former having in despite—
Why, we have galls; and though we have some grace,
Yet have we some revenge. Let husbands know,
Their wives have sense like them; they see, and smell,
And have their palates both for sweet and sour   90
As husbands have. What is it that they do,
When they change us for others? Is it sport?
I think it is. And doth affection breed it?
I think it doth. Is't frailty that thus errs?
It is so too. And have not we affections,   95
Desires for sport, and frailty, as men have?
Then let them use us well: else let them know,
The ills we do, their ills instruct us so.

DESDEMONA

Good night, good night. God me such uses send,
Not to pick bad from bad, but by bad mend.   *Exeunt*   100

99 God] Q1; Heauen F, Q2   uses] F, Q2; vsage Q1

prose in both F and Q, so that her lengthy
verse meditation on the shortcomings of
husbands might easily be a later insertion, designed to make Emilia's role more
sympathetic. On the other hand, Desdemona's final couplet seems to follow more
naturally from Emilia's own closing couplet than from ll. 79–80: not only do her
'uses' (99) echo Emilia's 'use' (97), but
the antithetical structure of l. 100, with
its repeated 'bad', seems designed to balance l. 98, with its repeated 'ills'.

82 **fall** succumb sexually. Continues the
motif of sin and temptation, since the Fall
of Eve was often construed in sexual
terms; Emilia wittily reverses the usual
attribution of blame.
duties marital (including sexual)
obligations
83 **pour . . . laps** A bourgeois version of the
classical myth in which Danaë is impregnated by the adulterous Jove in the form
of a shower of gold; for the vaginal sense
of *lap* see *Hamlet*, 3.2.107–15 (and cf.
Williams, *Dictionary*, pp. 784–5, *Glossary*,
p. 182).

84 **peevish** Cf. 2.3.176.
86 **scant . . . having** reduce what was previously allowed us
87–98 **Why . . . so** Often compared to
Shylock's 'Hath not a Jew eyes?' speech
(*M. of V.* 3.1.54–68), another appeal to
common humanity which is also a
justification of revenge.
87 **galls** spirit to resent injury
grace (a) physical charm; (b) mercy
89 **sense** (a) physical senses; (b) sensual
desires; (c) feelings; (d) reason
92, 96 **sport** (a) fun; (b) sexual indulgence
93 **affection** passion, lust
94, 96 **frailty** (a) sexual susceptibility; (b)
moral or physical weakness. A joke about
the stereotype of women as 'the weaker
sex'.
97 **use** treat. With a play on sexual *use*; cf.
duties, l. 81.
99 **uses** custom, habit, behaviour (*OED n.* 7,
8)
100 **Not . . . mend** Not to imitate the bad
behaviour of others, but to learn from it
how to mend my own vices. Desdemona
appears to respond directly to Emilia's
scenario of sexual tit-for-tat, thus render-

5.1   *Enter Iago and Roderigo*

IAGO

Here, stand behind this balk; straight will he come.
Wear thy good rapier bare, and put it home—
Quick, quick, fear nothing, I'll be at thy elbow.
It makes us or it mars us: think on that,
And fix most firm thy resolution.   5

RODERIGO

Be near at hand, I may miscarry in't.

IAGO

Here, at thy hand: be bold and take thy stand.
                    He retires

RODERIGO (*aside*)

I have no great devotion to the deed,
And yet he hath given me satisfying reasons—
⌐Aloud⌐ 'Tis but a man gone: forth my sword, he dies!   10

5.1] F (*Actus Quintus. Scene Prima.*), Q2 (*Actus 5. Scoena 1.*); *Actus. 5.* Q1   1 balk] This edition;
Barke F; Bulke Q   4 on] F; of Q   5 most] F, Q1; more Q2   7 stand] F, Q2; sword Q1   71 *He*
retires] CAPELL (*subs.*); *not in* F, Q   8 deed] F, Q2; dead Q1   9 hath] F; has Q

ing it unlikely that ll. 81–98 were a later
addition, and making a cut in Q once
again more probable than F revision. Cf.
also ll. 24–9.

5.1 This is one of three scenes (including
1.1 and 2.3) in which an exhilarated
Iago orchestrates an explosion of public
violence, and the second in which he
has Othello play the role of eavesdrop-
ing spectator (ll. 28–37). But this is his
masterpiece: here he manipulates, in
the fashion of a busy puppeteer, a whole
succession of characters (Roderigo,
Cassio, Lodovico and Gratiano, Bianca,
and Emilia), coolly murdering one and
probably wounding another in the
process. His apparently complete success
makes the unmasking of 5.2 appear
even more sudden and catastrophic.
Shakespeare's technique here somewhat
resembles that of Marlowe and Jonson
in the startling denouements of plays
like *The Jew of Malta, Volpone,* and *The*
Alchemist.

1 **balk** timber beam; here presumably
referring to one of the two large pillars
that supported the 'heavens' over the

stage in Elizabethan public playhouses.
Not only could 'u' and 'a' be quite easily
confused in a manuscript, but the variant
spellings of *balk* recorded in *OED* include
'balke', 'bulk', and 'bauk', so the same
word is likely to lie behind both F and Q
readings. Most editors, however, prefer
'bulk' = stall or framework projecting
from a shop-front; in which case Iago and
Roderigo may have hidden in the small
corner where the tiring-house projected
beyond the line of the playhouse
galleries. For the alternative suggestion
that the 'bulk' was a curtained booth
used in 5.2 to contain Desdemona's bed,
see 5.2.0.1.

2 **put** thrust

3 **I'll . . . elbow** Dent EE5, 'To be at one's
elbow'; and cf. D243.1, 'The devil is at
one's elbow'.

4 **makes . . . mars us** Proverbial phrase:
Dent M48.

9 **satisfying** Earliest citation of this adjecti-
val participle in *OED*.

10 **Aloud** The whole of Roderigo's speech is
usually treated as an aside, but Iago's 'he
grows angry' suggests that he is meant to
hear this line.

IAGO (*aside*)

    I have rubbed this young quat almost to the sense,
    And he grows angry. Now, whether he kill Cassio,
    Or Cassio him, or each do kill the other,
    Every way makes my gain. Live Roderigo,
    He calls me to a restitution large   15
    Of gold, and jewels, that I bobbed from him,
    As gifts to Desdemona—
    It must not be. If Cassio do remain,
    He hath a daily beauty in his life
    That makes me ugly; and besides, the Moor   20
    May unfold me to him: there stand I in much peril—
    No, he must die. But so: I hear him coming.
        Enter Cassio

RODERIGO

    I know his gait, 'tis he. (*Attacking Cassio*) Villain, thou
    diest!

CASSIO

    That thrust had been mine enemy indeed,
    But that my coat is better than thou know'st—   25
    I will make proof of thine.
        He wounds Roderigo

---

11 quat] F, Q2; gnat Q1   12 angry. Now whether] F; angry now: whether Q1; angry, now, whether Q2   14 gain] F (gaine); game Q   16 Of] F; For Q   19 hath] F; has Q   21 much] F, Q2; *not in* Q1   22 But so] F; be't so Q; But soft DYCE 1875 *conj.*   hear] Q (heare); heard F   23 *Attacking Cassio*] ROWE (*subs.*); *not in* F, Q   24 mine] F; my Q   25 know'st] F, Q2; think'st Q1   26 He . . . Roderigo] CAPELL (*subs.*); *not in* F, Q

---

11 **quat** pimple, small boil (*OED n.*[1] 1); contemptuous term for young man (*OED n.*[1] 2; earliest example cited). Johnson identified this as a Midlands dialect word.
    to the sense to the quick
14 **makes my gain** will profit me
    Live Roderigo if Roderigo lives
16 **bobbed** filched
17 **As** i.e. under the pretence that they were
19 **daily** constant; i.e. manifest in everything he does
21 **unfold** expose
22 **so** so be it (*OED* 5e). Q's *Be't so* makes equally good sense and would be an easy actor's substitution, but it seems more likely that a misreading lies behind either Q or F.

25 **coat . . . knowest** Presumably Cassio is wearing beneath his doublet a protective coat of mail (or 'privy coat'), like that worn by the honest captain Aquinus in Shirley's *The Politician* (4.6), though he may be referring simply to the thickness of his padded doublet.
26 **make proof of** test
26.1 **Iago . . . exit** Theobald's direction has been accepted by virtually all editors and has become part of the standard stage-business in this scene; but, although it sharpens the irony of Iago's behaviour later in the scene, it has no clear warrant in the text.

RODERIGO   O, I am slain!

⌈*Iago wounds Cassio in the leg from behind, and exit*⌉

CASSIO

  I am maimed for ever. Help, ho! Murder, murder!

    Enter Othello

OTHELLO (*aside*)

  The voice of Cassio: Iago keeps his word.

RODERIGO O, villain that I am.

OTHELLO (*aside*) It is even so.   30

CASSIO O help, ho! Light! A surgeon!

OTHELLO (*aside*)

  'Tis he: O brave Iago, honest and just,

  That hast such noble sense of thy friend's wrong,

  Thou teachest me!—Minion, your dear lies dead,

  And your unblest fate hies: strumpet, I come!   35

  Forth of my heart those charms, thine eyes, are blotted;

  Thy bed, lust-stained, shall with lust's blood be spotted.

                                          Exit

    Enter Lodovico and Gratiano

CASSIO

  What ho! No watch? No passage? Murder, murder!

GRATIANO

  'Tis some mischance; the voice is very direful.

CASSIO O, help!   40

LODOVICO Hark!

26.1 *Iago . . . exit*] THEOBALD (*subs.*); *not in* F, Q   27 maimed] F (maym'd), Q2; maind Q1
Help] F; light Q   30 It is] F; Harke tis Q   35 unblest] F, Q2; *not in* Q1   hies] F, Q2; hies apace
Q1   36 Forth] Q; For F   39 voice] F; cry Q

28 **Iago . . . word** Iago has clearly arranged
for Othello to be present at this scene: cf.
4.1.203–4.

30 **It . . . so** Metrically amphibious. The
metre requires that *even* be treated as one
syllable ('e'en' or 'ev'n').

32 **brave** worthy

34 **Minion** mistress, paramour (addressed to
Desdemona)

35 **unblest** i.e. damned
  hies hurries on (to meet you)

36 **Forth** out
  charms Not simply 'charming things',
but also 'magical tokens'; picking up
the theme of witchcraft from 1.1.170–2,
1.2.72–9, 1.3.61–107, and 3.4.68–74.
  blotted effaced (*OED v.* 4). The sense is

probably also coloured by the common
meaning 'stigmatize, calumniate' (*v.*
3b).

37 **Thy . . . spotted** Since *blood* can mean
not only 'desire', but also 'semen'
(because of the Pythagorean notion that
male seed was a concoction of the blood:
Williams, *Dictionary* pp. 113–16, *Glossary*,
pp. 44–5), Othello's presentation of the
murder, as both a properly symmetrical
punishment for Desdemona's adultery
and as a perverse nuptial consummation,
is also a vicious tautology.
  spotted Echoes Othello's description of
the handkerchief at 3.3.436 (see note).

38 **passage** passers by (*OED n.* 1b); cf.
Errors, 3.1.100.

RODERIGO O wretched villain!
LODOVICO
　Two or three groan. It is a heavy night;
　These may be counterfeits: let's think't unsafe
　To come in to the cry without more help.   45
RODERIGO
　Nobody come? Then shall I bleed to death.
　　　Enter Iago with a light and his sword drawn
LODOVICO Hark!
GRATIANO
　Here's one comes in his shirt, with light and weapons.
IAGO
　Who's there? Whose noise is this that cries on murder?
LODOVICO
　We do not know.
IAGO　　　　　　　Do not you hear a cry?   50
CASSIO
　Here, here! For heaven sake help me!
IAGO　　　　　　　　　　　　　　　What's the matter?
GRATIANO
　This is Othello's ensign, as I take it.
LODOVICO
　The same indeed, a very valiant fellow.
IAGO
　What are you here that cry so grievously?
CASSIO
　Iago? O, I am spoiled, undone by villains—   55
　Give me some help!

---

43 groan] F (groane); grones Q It is a] Q; 'Tis F 46.1 *Enter . . . drawn*] This edition (*after* Q, '*Enter* Iago *with a light*'); *Enter* Iago. F 48 light] F; lights Q 50 We] F; I Q Do] F; Did Q 51 heaven] F; heauens Q

---

43 **It . . . night** F leaves the line two syllables short, unlike Q's perfectly iambic 'It is a heavy night'. But the verse in this scene of confusion is often disturbed, and a pause after 'groan' as Lodovico strains to listen might be dramatically appropriate.
　heavy (a) dark, gloomy; (b) distressful, unfortunate
45, 60 **come in** approach. Honigmann takes *come in* at l. 60 to mean 'enter' and to refer

to the 'bulk' or booth in which Cassio is lying.
45 **cry** clamour, outcry
48 **in his shirt** i.e. night attire
49 **cries on** cries out against
51 **heaven sake** The apostrophe s is often dropped before another s; but, as Honigmann points out, this could also be an old genitive form.
55 **spoiled** destroyed, badly injured (*OED v.*[1] 10)

366

IAGO

O me, lieutenant! What villains have done this?

CASSIO

I think that one of them is hereabout

And cannot make away.

IAGO   O treacherous villains!

⌈*To Lodovico and Gratiano*⌉

What are you there? Come in and give some help.   60

RODERIGO

O, help me there!

CASSIO   That's one of them.

IAGO   O murd'rous slave!

O villain!

He stabs Roderigo

RODERIGO O damned Iago! O inhuman dog!

⌈*Roderigo groans*⌉

IAGO

Kill men i'th' dark? Where be these bloody thieves?

How silent is this town! Ho, murder, murder!

(*To Lodovico and Gratiano*)

What may you be? Are you of good or evil?   65

LODOVICO

As you shall prove us, praise us.

IAGO   Signor Lodovico?

LODOVICO He, sir.

IAGO

I cry you mercy—here's Cassio hurt by villains.

---

57 me, lieutenant] F, Q2; my Leiutenant Q1   58 that] F; the Q   60, 64 *To . . . Gratiano*]
THEOBALD; *not in* F, Q   61 there] F; here Q   62 *He stabs Roderigo*] ROWE (*after* Q2, '*Thrusts him
in.*'); *not in* F, Q1   dog!] F; dog,– o,o,o. Q   62.1 *Roderigo groans*] This edition (*after* Q, 'o,o,o');
not in F   63 men] F, Q2; him Q1   these] F; those Q

57 **O   me** 'A "genteel" exclamation'   considered part of the line, but rather
(Honigmann).   as a form of direction, indicating that
lieutenant Cf. 4.1.100.   Roderigo's groans should continue as
59 **make away** escape   Iago speaks. On this form of 'crypto-
60 **What . . . there** The form of Iago's   direction' see Honigmann, 'Re-enter the
demand seems to parallel his challenge to   Stage Direction: Shakespeare and Some
Cassio (l. 54), and to anticipate his later   Contemporaries', *SS* 29 (1976), 117–25.
challenge to Lodovico and Gratiano (l.   McMillin (*Q*, pp. 29–31) regards exclama-
65); but, as Honigmann points out, it   tions of this kind as likely theatrical
might also be punctuated 'What, are you   interpolations.
there?' and understood as addressed to   66 **prove** find by trial
the 'villains'.   **praise** appraise, value. Cf. Dent P614.2.
62.1 **Roderigo groans** Q's 'o, o, o' is extra- 68 **I . . . mercy** I beg your pardon; 'a "gen-
metrical and should probably not be   teel" phrase' (Honigmann).

GRATIANO Cassio?

IAGO How is't, brother?   70

CASSIO My leg is cut in two.

IAGO Marry, heaven forbid!

Light, gentlemen: I'll bind it with my shirt.

Enter Bianca

BIANCA

What is the matter, ho? Who is't that cried?

IAGO

Who is't that cried?

BIANCA   O my dear Cassio,   75

My sweet Cassio, O Cassio, Cassio, Cassio.

IAGO

O notable strumpet! Cassio, may you suspect

Who they should be, that have thus mangled you?

CASSIO No.

GRATIANO

I am sorry to find you thus; I have been to seek you.   80

IAGO

Lend me a garter. So.

He binds Cassio's leg

O for a chair to bear him easily hence!

BIANCA

Alas, he faints! O Cassio, Cassio, Cassio!

IAGO

Gentlemen all, I do suspect this trash

To be a party in this injury.   85

---

76 My sweet Cassio, O Cassio] F; O my sweet *Cassio* Q   78 have thus] F; thus haue Q   81–2
Lend . . . hence] F, Q2; *not in* Q1   81.1 *He . . . leg*] This edition; *not in* F, Q   85 be . . . injury]
F; beare a part in this Q1; beare a part in this iniurie Q2

---

70 **brother** Cf. Giraldi, App. C, p. 443.

71 **My . . . two** Metrically amphibious. Cf.
Giraldi, App. C, p. 443.

78 **mangled** mutilated

80 **I am . . . seek you** The metre requires
elision of both *I am* and *I have*.

82, 96–7 **chair** Some sort of sedan chair
(carried on poles) must be intended,
though *OED* does not list this meaning
before 1634.

82 **easily** comfortably, carefully; without
difficulty

83 **Alas . . . Cassio** If *Cassio* is treated as
disyllabic then Bianca's speech will
form a single pentameter line with a
feminine ending (as in F and Q);
however, treating it as trisyllabic (as it is
in ll. 75, 86 for example) enables Bianca to
complete Iago's half-line, while her cry
'O . . . Cassio' becomes a complete line on
its own.

84 **trash** Cf. 2.1.294.

Patience a while, good Cassio! (*To Lodovico and Gratiano*)
    Come, come,
Lend me a light: (*Going to Roderigo*) know we this face, or
    no?
Alas, my friend and my dear countryman,
Roderigo! No?—Yes, sure!—O heaven, Roderigo!

GRATIANO What, of Venice?   90

IAGO Even he, sir—did you know him?

GRATIANO Know him? Ay.

IAGO

Signor Gratiano? I cry your gentle pardon:
These bloody accidents must excuse my manners
That so neglected you.

GRATIANO   I am glad to see you.   95

IAGO

How do you, Cassio? ⌈*Calling*⌉ O, a chair, a chair!

GRATIANO   Roderigo?

IAGO

He, he, 'tis he.
        Enter attendants with a chair
                    O, that's well said—the chair!
Some good man bear him carefully from hence,
I'll fetch the general's surgeon. (*To Bianca*) For you,
    mistress,
Save you your labour.—He that lies slain here, Cassio,   100
Was my dear friend. What malice was between you?

CASSIO

None in the world; nor do I know the man.

IAGO (*to Bianca*)

What? Look you pale? (*To attendants*) O, bear him out
    o'th' air!

---

86 Come, come] F, Q2; *not in* Q1   87 *Going . . . Roderigo*] OXFORD; *not in* F, Q   89 O heaven]
Q1; Yes, 'tis F, Q2   93 your] F; you Q   97 He, he] F; He Q   *Enter . . . chair*] CAPELL (*subs.*);
not in F, Q   the] F; a Q   101 between] F; betwixt Q   103 out] Q; *not in* F

---

91 **Even . . . him** Metrically amphibious.

93–5 **Signor . . . you** Iago at his most
    courtly and deferential.

94 **accidents** unlucky events, disasters

97 **well said** well done

99–100 **For . . . labour** as for you, madam,

don't trouble yourself (by trying to help
Cassio any more)

103 **bear . . . air** Fresh air was supposed to
    be dangerous for the sick and wounded
    (cf. Tilley A93).

(*To Lodovico and Gratiano*)
Stay you, good gentlemen.

                   Exeunt attendants with Cassio in the chair
                ⌈*and the body of Roderigo*⌉
        (*To Bianca*) Look you pale, mistress?
(*To Lodovico and Gratiano*) Do you perceive the gastness of
    her eye?   105
(*To Bianca*) Nay, if you stare we shall hear more anon.
(*To Lodovico and Gratiano*) Behold her well, I pray you,
    look upon her:
Do you see, gentlemen? Nay, guiltiness
Will speak though tongues were out of use.
    Enter Emilia

EMILIA

'Las, what's the matter? What's the matter, husband?   110

IAGO

Cassio hath here been set on in the dark
By Roderigo and fellows that are scaped:
He's almost slain, and Roderigo quite dead.

EMILIA

Alas, good gentleman! Alas, good Cassio!

IAGO

This is the fruits of whoring. Prithee, Emilia,   115
Go know of Cassio where he supped tonight.
(*To Bianca*) What, do you shake at that?

---

104 gentlemen] F; Gentlewoman Q   *Exeunt . . . Roderigo*] WALKER (*subs.*); *not in* F, Q   105 gastness] F (gastnesse); ieastures Q   106 if you stare] F; an you stirre Q   hear] F (heare); haue Q   107 well, I pray you, look] HONIGMANN; well: I pray you looke F; well I pray you, looke Q   109.1 *Enter Emilia*] Q; *not in* F   110 'Las, what's] Q; Alas, what is F   What's] Q; What is F   111 hath] F; has Q   113 quite dead] F; dead Q   115 fruits] F; fruite Q   Prithee] F, Q2; pray Q1

---

104 **Stay you** don't leave. In the Q version Bianca attempts to slip away with Cassio, but is prevented by Iago.

105 **gastness** terrified appearance

106 **if . . . anon** Presumably Iago means that Bianca's wildly staring eyes are an indication of guilt and that they can expect her to confess shortly. If Q's 'stirre' (an easy aural mistake) is correct, then Bianca is struggling to escape, and Iago suggests that if she succeeds they can expect to hear of more outrage before long.

109 **though . . . use** even if human beings were to lose the power of speech

113 **He's . . . dead** Most editors follow Q in omitting *quite*, but the line has a nice rhetorical balance if extra stress is given to '*almost*' and '*quite*'; as in the previous line, *Roderigo* is scanned as trisyllabic, with a stress on the first, and the second elided.

115 **This is the fruits** The F reading is made more probable by *Richard III*, 2.1.136: 'This is the fruits of rashness'.

116 **know of** learn from

BIANCA

He supped at my house, but I therefore shake not.

IAGO

O did he so? I charge you go with me.

EMILIA

O, fie upon thee, strumpet!

BIANCA   I am no strumpet,   120
But of life as honest as you that thus
Abuse me.

EMILIA   As I? Foh! Fie upon thee!

IAGO

Kind gentlemen, let's go see poor Cassio dressed.
(*To Bianca*) Come, mistress, you must tell's another
   tale.—
Emilia, run you to the citadel   125
And tell my lord and lady what hath happed.

                                        Exit Emilia

(*To Lodovico and Gratiano*)
Will you go on afore? (*Aside*) This is the night

---

120 O, fie] F; Fie, fie Q1; Fie Q2   122 Foh] Q1; *not in* F; now Q2   126 hath] F; has Q   126.1
Exit Emilia] OXFORD (*after* 'afore', *l.* 127); *not in* F, Q   127 afore] F; I pray Q

---

119 **charge** command

120, 122 **thee** The venom of Emilia's sudden attack on Bianca is emphasized by her use of the contemptuous second person pronoun.

120–2 **I . . . Abuse me** Though Bianca's liaison with Cassio opens her to the charge of whoredom in the broad sense, the question of whether she is or is not technically a prostitute has been extensively debated (see 'Persons'). This is finally less important, however, than her structural position as part of a trio of women, all of whom are denounced as whores by the men. Her claim to be *as honest* (= chaste) as Emilia, who in the previous scene argued that any woman would prostitute herself if the price were high enough, draws attention to the relative nature of that absolutist concept; and this simple irony is complicated by the suggestion that Emilia is merely displacing on to an even more vulnerable woman the insults that Iago (who regards

all women as whores) visits on herself. Bianca's insistence on her own dignity, like her apparently genuine love for Cassio, makes her claim to 'honesty' seem (in at least one sense of this by now complicated word) entirely justified.

122 **Abuse** (a) malign; (b) mistreat. The word has gathered ironic resonances through its insistent use to describe both Othello's alleged seduction of Desdemona (1.1.172; 1.2.74, 78; 1.3.61), Iago's deception of Othello (1.3.384; 4.2.14, 142) and libelling of Cassio (2.1.297), Othello's predicted failings as a husband (2.1.226), Desdemona's alleged infidelity and deception of Othello (3.3.151, 203, 270, 338), female infidelity generally (4.3.57), and the self-corruption of Othello's jealousy (4.2.14).

123 **Cassio dressed** i.e. his wounds

124 **tell's . . . tale** make a true confession to us. Ironic use of a proverbial expression (Dent T49) meaning something like 'sing another song' or 'change your tune'.

That either makes me, or fordoes me quite.
  Exeunt Lodovico and Gratiano, followed by Iago

5.2   *Enter Othello with a light, and Desdemona in her bed
          asleep*

OTHELLO

It is the cause, it is the cause, my soul—
Let me not name it to you, you chaste stars:
It is the cause. Yet I'll not shed her blood,
Nor scar that whiter skin of hers than snow
And smooth as monumental alabaster—   5
Yet she must die, else she'll betray more men.
Put out the light, and then put out the light—

---

128 makes] F, Q2; markes Q1   128.1 *Exeunt . . . Iago*] This edition; *Exeunt* F, Q

  5.2] F (*Scæna Secunda.*); *not in* Q   0.1–2 *Enter . . . bed*] *after* F (*Enter Othello, and Desdemona
in her bed.*) *and* Q (*Enter* Othello *with a light.*)   0.2 *asleep*] ROWE; *not in* F, Q

128 **fordoes** ruins; kills
  quite utterly
128.1 **followed by Iago** The order of departure is clearly indicated by the implied
  stage direction in Iago's 'Will you go on
  afore?'; Iago's aside will be spoken as the
  others make their exit.
5.2 The lineation of the dialogue in this
  scene varies significantly between F and
  Q; neither seems wholly satisfactory, but
  most editorial attempts at rearrangement
  have only created new irregularities of
  their own. This edition, therefore, whilst
  making free use of both F and Q, generally avoids the relineation of later editors.
  In fact it is not uncommon in later
  Shakespeare for versification to become
  highly irregular in episodes of emotional
  stress, lines of apparent prose being
  mixed with lines of fairly regular verse.
  Moreover, a writer accustomed to iambic
  rhythms will often write a highly
  cadenced prose, making the verse–prose
  distinction an even more uncertain one.
0.1 **in her bed** See App. F(iv) for a discussion
  of the staging here, and also Introduction, pp. 173–4.
1–2 **It . . . stars** Othello implies that to
  name the *cause* would affront the chastity
  of the stars; but there is a strong suggestion that it is something he cannot bring
  himself to name, either because he fears
  to confront it, or because the true 'cause'
  of his actions remains in some deep sense
  obscure to him. Fechter's acting edition

(1861) required the use of a mirror to indicate that the cause lay in the colour of his
skin.
1, 3 **cause** (a) reason, motive; (b) end or purpose; legal case or suit, matter of dispute;
charge, accusation (*OED n.* 1, 3, 4, 7–8,
9). Cf. 3.3.413.
4 **whiter . . . snow** Cf. Dent S591, 'As
white as the driven snow'. The proverb
also exists in the form 'As pure as the
driven snow', and the association with
purity and chastity is borne out by *Cymbeline*, 2.5.13 ('As chaste as unsunned
snow') and *Kinsmen* 5.3.3–4 ('white as
chaste, and pure | As wind-fanned
snow'). Othello's physical obsession with
Desdemona's fairness is painfully complicated by the moral symbolism of colour
he has absorbed from Iago.
5 **monumental alabaster** Alabaster was
the preferred stone for tomb sculpture,
and Othello's simile draws attention to
the resemblance between the sleeping
Desdemona and the prostrate figures
displayed on the bed-like 'tester tombs'
fashionable at this time. For the proverbial whiteness and smoothness of
alabaster, see Dent A95.1–2.
7 **Put . . . and . . . light** First put out this
candle, and then snuff out her life. Apart
from the erotic associations of torches
noted at 1.2.28, the use of an extinguished candle, torch, or lamp as a symbol for death is an ancient one which
occurs in classical and neoclassical tomb

If I quench thee, thou flaming minister,
I can again thy former light restore,
Should I repent me; but once put out thine, 10
Thou cunning'st pattern of excelling nature,
I know not where is that Promethean heat
That can thy light relume. When I have plucked thy
    rose,
I cannot give it vital growth again,
It needs must wither: I'll smell thee on the tree— 15
    He kisses her
O balmy breath, that dost almost persuade

---

10 thine] Q; thy Light F   11 cunning'st] F, Q2; cunning Q1   13 relume] F; returne Q1;
relumine Q2   thy rose] F; the rose Q   15 needs must] F; must needes Q   thee] F; it Q   *He
kisses her*] Q2 (*subs.*); *not in* F, Q1   16 O] F (Oh); A Q   dost] F; doth Q

---

sculpture, as well as in scripture ('How oft
shall the candle of the wicked be put out?
and their destruction come upon them?',
Job 21: 17); cf. also *Macbeth*, 5.5.22 ('Out,
out, brief candle'), and see Dent CC1. The
gesture may also symbolize the extinction
of Othello's 'light of reason'.

8 **minister** servant; magistrate, minister of
justice (*OED n.* 1, 2c). Cf. also Psalms
104: 4 ('[God] maketh the spirits his messengers, and a flaming fire his ministers');
and Hebrews 1: 7 ('He maketh the spirits
his messengers, and his ministers a flame
of fire').

10 **thine** Most editors prefer F's *thy light*; but
apart from its metrical awkwardness, this
reading results in a somewhat inelegant
repetition at l. 13; it is quite possibly a
scribal or compositorial error produced
by contamination from 'the light . . .
thy . . . light' (7–9).

11 **cunning'st . . . nature** most exquisitely
formed example of nature's craftsman-
ship when she excels herself. But *cunning*
is inevitably also coloured by its negative
meanings; cf. 4.2.90, 'that cunning
whore of Venice'.

12 **Promethean** Prometheus was the
Greek hero who stole fire from the
gods and gave it to humans; he was
punished by Zeus who chained him up
in Hades where an eagle fed perpetually
on his liver. A second myth made him

creator of humankind (Mowat–
Werstine).

13 **relume** relight. Earliest citation in *OED*.

13–15 **When . . . wither** The withered rose
was a conventional emblem for death in
the *memento mori* tradition; but the pluck-
ing of a rose could also be a metaphor for
the taking of virginity, a *double entendre*
emphasized by F's '*thy* rose' (where Q
prints '*the* rose'). As numerous critics
have observed, part of the shock of Desdemona's murder depends upon the way
in which killing is elided with sexual
consummation.

15 **smell thee** An implicit stage direction.
Kemble insisted that Othello must bend
over Desdemona at this point (Hankey,
p. 311); and, in a detail later imitated
by Patrick Stewart, Olivier deliberately
anticipated the gesture when he made his
first entry inhaling the fragrance of a red
rose (Pechter, pp. 143–4). F's 'thee'
expresses a tenderness and intimacy
absent from Q's 'it'.

16 **balmy** deliciously sweet; soothing, healing. Various aromatic balms were used in
contemporary medicine; but the use of
such resins in embalming creates an
uncanny resonance with the mysterious
'mummy' in which Desdemona's handkerchief was dyed. See also 5.2.349–50 n.
Sweet breath was frequently eroticized in
the period, no doubt because it was such a
rarity.

Justice to break her sword—one more, one more!
⌈*He kisses her*⌉
Be thus when thou art dead, and I will kill thee
And love thee after—one more, and that's the last.
        He kisses her
So sweet was ne'er so fatal. I must weep,   20
But they are cruel tears: this sorrow's heavenly,
It strikes where it doth love. She wakes.

DESDEMONA

Who's there? Othello?

OTHELLO   Ay, Desdemona.

DESDEMONA

Will you come to bed, my lord?

OTHELLO

Have you prayed tonight, Desdemon?

DESDEMONA   Ay, my lord.   25

OTHELLO

If you bethink yourself of any crime
Unreconciled as yet to heaven and grace,
Solicit for it straight.

DESDEMONA

Alack, my lord, what may you mean by that?

OTHELLO

Well, do it, and be brief; I will walk by: 30
I would not kill thy unprepared spirit,
No—heavens forfend!—I would not kill thy soul.

---

17 Justice] F; Iustice her selfe Q   sword—one more, one more] F (Sword. One more, one
more); sword once more Q1; sword: one more Q2   *He kisses her*] This edition; *not in* F, Q
19 one more, and that's] F; once more, and this Q1; one more, and this Q2   *He kisses her*] Q1
(*next to ll.* 19–20); *not in* F, Q2   22 where it doth] F; when it does Q1; where it does Q2   She
wakes] F, Q; *as direction* CAMBRIDGE   25 Desdemon] F; *Desdemona* Q   29 Alack] F; Alas Q
32 heavens] F; heauen Q

---

17 **Justice ... sword** Alluding to the allegorical figure of Justice as a blindfold
woman with scales (for weighing the
truth) and a sword (for punishment).

20 **fatal** ominous; destructive, deadly;
doomed (*OED a.* 4c, 6, 2)

21–2 **sorrow's ... love** A recurrent theme
in Scripture: see e.g. Psalms 94: 12
('Blessed is the man, whom thou chastis-
est'), Proverbs 3: 12 ('For the Lord cor-
recteth him, whom he loveth'), Hebrews

12: 6 ('whom the Lord loveth, he chas-
teneth'), Revelation 3: 19 ('As many as I
love, I rebuke and chasten').

25 **Desdemon** By forcing a heavy stress on
the second syllable, the metre brings out
the dangerous pun latent in the name.

27 **grace** The property in God which allows
him to grant forgiveness to penitent
sinners.

28 **Solicit** plead (for absolution)

32 **forfend** forbid

DESDEMONA
  Talk you of killing?

OTHELLO   Ay, I do.

DESDEMONA   Then heaven
  Have mercy on me.

OTHELLO   Amen, with all my heart.

DESDEMONA
  If you say so, I hope you will not kill me.   35

OTHELLO Humh!

DESDEMONA
  And yet I fear you, for you're fatal then
  When your eyes roll so. Why I should fear I know not,
  Since guiltiness I know not; but yet I feel I fear.

OTHELLO Think on thy sins.   40

DESDEMONA They are loves I bear to you.

OTHELLO Ay, and for that thou diest.

DESDEMONA
  That death's unnatural that kills for loving.
  Alas, why gnaw you so your nether lip?
  Some bloody passion shakes your very frame: 45
  These are portents; but yet I hope, I hope,
  They do not point on me.

OTHELLO Peace, and be still.

DESDEMONA I will so. What's the matter?

---

35 so] Q; *not in* F   42 Ay] F; *not in* Q   46 I hope, I hope] F; I hope Q   49 will so. What's] F
(will so: What's); will, so, what's Q1; will so, what's Q2; will. So: what's HONIGMANN

33–4 **heaven . . . me** Honigmann compares the liturgical response from the Anglican prayer book, 'Lord have mercy upon us'.

36 **Humh** (regarded as extra-metrical)

38 **eyes roll so** For an account of the extravagant physical symptoms expected of the jealous man, see Robert Burton's *Anatomy of Melancholy* (1621): 'Besides those strange gestures of staring, frowning, grinning, *rolling of eyes*, menacing, ghastly looks, interrupt, precipitate half-turns, [he] will sometimes sigh, weep, sob for anger . . . curse, threaten, brawl, scold, fight; and sometimes flatter again and speak fair . . . and then . . . rave, roar, and lay about him like a madman, thump her sides, drag her about

perchance' (3.3.2, pp. 840–1; emphasis added). These are almost exactly the symptoms that an actor seeking to represent jealousy is advised to display by Aaron Hill's *Thespian Praeceptor* (1734), which cites Othello as a case in point (Potter, p. 25).

41 **They . . . you** 'An allusion to the sin of loving a human being more than God' (Sanders). Metrically amphibious.

44 **why . . . lip** Cf. *Richard III*, 4.2.28: 'The king is angry. See, he gnaws his lip.'

47 **point on me** indicate my fate

48 **Peace . . . still** Metrically amphibious. The words spoken by Christ to calm a storm at sea (Mark 4: 39).

OTHELLO

That handkerchief which I so loved and gave thee,   50
Thou gav'st to Cassio.

DESDEMONA   No, by my life and soul—
Send for the man, and ask him.

OTHELLO   Sweet soul, take heed,
Take heed of perjury: thou art on thy death-bed.

DESDEMONA

Ay, but not yet to die.

OTHELLO   Yes, presently.
Therefore confess thee freely of thy sin;   55
For to deny each article with oath
Cannot remove nor choke the strong conception
That I do groan withal: thou art to die.

DESDEMONA

Then Lord have mercy on me.

OTHELLO   I say, Amen.

DESDEMONA

And have you mercy too. I never did   60
Offend you in my life; never loved Cassio,
But with such general warranty of heaven
As I might love. I never gave him token.

OTHELLO

By heaven I saw my handkerchief in's hand.
O perjured woman, thou dost stone my heart,   65
And makes me call what I intend to do

---

54 Ay, but] F, Q (I, but); I? But HONIGMANN   Yes] Q; *not in* F   57 conception] F, Q2; conceit
Q1   59 Then Lord] Q; O Heauen F   61 my] F, Q2; thy Q1   66 makes] F; makest Q

52–3 **Sweet . . . perjury** To commit such a
sin at the point of death would ensure her
damnation.

54 **presently** immediately

55, 59, 67 **confess . . . Amen . . . sacrifice**
As the agent of heavenly sorrow (ll.
21–2), Othello casts himself in a priestly
role.

55 **freely** without reservation

56 **article** item or count in a criminal
indictment

57 **conception** (a) belief; (b) plan; (c)
embryo, baby (*OED n.* 7, 9, 3). Sense (c)
together with 'groan' in the following
line, picks up the recurrent figure of
obscene pregnancy and parturition as a

metaphor for Iago's plot and Othello's
jealousy (cf. 1.3.392–3; 2.1.127–8,
3.4.137, 151, 156–7; 4.2.96).

59 **Then . . . me** See ll. 33–4 n. Cf. Giraldi,
App. C, p. 444.

61 **Offend** sin against

62 **warranty** authorization, allowance

63 **token** keepsake, love-token

65 **stone** turn to stone (*OED v.* 2; earliest
citation); 4.1.176 (see note) suggests that
F's 'my heart' is correct, though Johnson
defended Q's 'thy heart' on the grounds
that Desdemona by hardening her heart
undermines Othello's priestly role as con-
fessor and sacrificer.

A murder, which I thought a sacrifice.
I saw the handkerchief.
DESDEMONA   He found it then;
I never gave it him—send for him hither;
Let him confess a truth.
OTHELLO   He hath confessed.   70
DESDEMONA
What, my lord?
OTHELLO   That he hath—'ud's death!—used thee.
DESDEMONA
How? Unlawfully?
OTHELLO   Ay.
DESDEMONA   He will not say so.
OTHELLO
No, his mouth is stopped—
Honest Iago hath ta'en order for't.
DESDEMONA
O, my fear interprets—what, is he dead?   75
OTHELLO
Had all his hairs been lives, my great revenge
Had stomach for them all.
DESDEMONA
Alas, he is betrayed, and I undone.

---

70 Let] F, Q2; And let Q1   hath] F; has Q   71 hath . . . used thee.] ALEXANDER; hath vs'd thee. F; hath—vds death. Q1; hath—vsde thee. Q2   75 O] F; *not in* Q   interprets] F; interprets then Q

---

70 **a truth** Honigmann amends to 'the truth' on the grounds that F's *a* represents a 'common error' deriving from Q (which once again prints *a truth* at l. 128); however, 'a truth' was good idiomatic usage (see e.g. *LLL*, 2.1.65; *Romeo*, 4.1.33; *Merry Wives*, 4.4.37; *All's Well*, 5.3.210), and the indefinite article gave it a slightly different nuance: 'Let him admit to *what we know to be true*.'

71 **'ud's death** Corruption of 'God's death'. Ridley suggests that Q's violent oath represents a misreading of the manuscript's 'usde the' (i.e. 'used thee'). But the lineation adopted by Honigmann makes a conflation of the Q and F readings metrically attractive. The burst of mid-line emotion marks the fact that it is now

Othello, in his priestly role, who cannot bear to speak the obscene words that similarly upset Desdemona in the brothel scene (4.2.118–23, 161–2); the struggle for linguistic control registered here will make his explosion at l. 79 ('Out, strumpet!') even more violent.
used i.e. sexually

74 **ta'en order for't** seen to that

76 **Had . . . lives** Cf. Dent H30, 'As many as there are hairs on the head'; Psalms 40: 12 ('My sins . . . are more in number than the hairs of mine head'); and Luke 12: 7 ('all the hairs of your head are numbered: fear not therefore').

77 **stomach** (a) appetite, capacity; (b) courage (*OED n.* 5, 8a)

OTHELLO

  Out, strumpet!—Weep'st thou for him to my face?

DESMONA ⌈*grasping him in supplication*⌉

  O banish me, my lord, but kill me not!   80

OTHELLO Down, strumpet!

DESDEMONA

  Kill me tomorrow, let me live tonight!

    ⌈*She struggles with him*⌉

OTHELLO Nay, if you strive—

DESDEMONA

  But half an hour? But while I say one prayer?

OTHELLO It is too late.

    He smothers her

                     Being done, there is no pause.   85

DESDEMONA O Lord, Lord, Lord!

EMILIA (*within*)

  My lord, my lord! What ho! My lord, my lord!

OTHELLO

  What noise is this? Not dead? Not yet quite dead?

  I that am cruel am yet merciful:

  I would not have thee linger in thy pain—   90

  So, so.

---

79 Out] F; O Q   79.1 *grasping . . . supplication*] This edition; *not in* F, Q   82.1 *She . . . him*]
This edition; *not in* F, Q   83 if] F; *not in* Q   84 hour? But] Q1 (houre, but); hour. | *Oth.* Being
done, there is no pawse. | *Des.* But F, Q2   85 *He smothers her*] F (*Smothers her*); *he stifles her* Q
Being . . . pause] *as here* This edition (*conj.* Amneus); *after* 'houre' (*l.* 87) F, Q2; *not in* Q1
86 O . . . Lord, Lord] Q1; *not in* F, Q2   87 EMILIA . . . *within*)] *after* F (*Æmilia at the doore.*), Q
(Emillia *calls within.*)   88 noise] F; voyce Q   89 that am] F (*corr.*), Q; am that F (*uncorr.*)

85 **Being . . . pause** Editors have struggled
to make sense of this line in its original
location (after 'hour', l. 83) when Othello
is so evidently not 'done'. But since it does
not appear in Q, it is possible that it
appeared as an addition in the margin of
the manuscript from which F derives (perhaps to replace Desdemona's *O Lord, Lord,
Lord*) and that whoever was responsible
for the transcription misplaced it. The
same suggestion has been made by Daniel
Amneus, *The Three Othellos* (Alhambra,
Calif., 1986), p. 6. For other examples of
such transpositions, see Kellner, pp.
152–3.

86 **O . . . Lord** Q's exclamation may represent Desdemona's cries as Othello smoth-

ers her (on which account Dyce omitted it
as a 'disgustingly vulgar' addition 'foisted
into the text by the players', and Furness
dismissed it as a tasteless 'supererogatory
horror'); or it may be meant as a moan,
coinciding with Emilia's line, which
prompts Othello's 'Not . . . quite dead'
(l. 88); in which case his 'What noise is
this?' can be played as a response either
to Emilia's shouts or to Desdemona's
moaning. For a subtle analysis of the
alternative possibilities, see Kerrigan,
p. 11.

91 **So, so** Some Othellos, rather than smoth-
er Desdemona again, choose to stab her at
this point: a tradition that, according to
Furness, apparently goes back to Garrick.

⌈*He smothers her again*⌉
EMILIA (*within*) What ho, my lord, my lord!
OTHELLO   Who's there?
EMILIA (*within*)
O good my lord, I'd speak a word with you.
OTHELLO
Yes—'tis Emilia—(*calling*) by and by!—She's dead.
'Tis like she comes to speak of Cassio's death: 95
The noise was high. Ha! No more moving?
Still as the grave. Shall she come in? Were't good?
I think she stirs again—no. What's best to do?
If she come in, she'll sure speak to my wife—
My wife, my wife! What wife? I have no wife.   100
O insupportable! O heavy hour!
Methinks it should be now a huge eclipse
Of sun and moon, and that th'affrighted globe
Should yawn at alteration.

91 *He smothers her again*] This edition (*after* DELIUS); *not in* F, Q   *within*] F; Q *omits*   92,
103 *within*] MALONE; F, Q *omit*   92 I'd] Q; I would F   93 Yes—'tis] SANDERS; yes: 'Tis F; yes,
tis Q   *calling*] OXFORD (*after* ROWE) F, Q *omit*   Emilia—by and by!—She's] ROWE (*subs.*);
Aemilia: by and by. Shee's F; *Emillia*, by and by: shee's Q   95 high] F; here Q   97 again—
no. What's] This edition; againe. No, what's F; againe; no, what's Q   best to do] F;
the best Q   99 What wife] F, Q2; my wife Q1   100 insupportable!] F; ~: Q1; ~; Q2; ~,
HONIGMANN   103 Should] Q; Did F

It has no warrant in the text and contradicts Othello's vow at l. 3. Furness devotes
several pages to an inconclusive debate
between medical experts as to whether
Desdemona's brief revival is technically
possible after smothering, or only if stabbing were the real cause. But the existence of an exactly similar episode in
Webster's *Duchess of Malfi* (4.3.343–9),
not to mention Roderigo's reported
revival (ll. 326–7), indicates that audiences were unlikely to be bothered about
such niceties.

93 **by and by** soon, in a minute
94 **like** likely
95 **high** loud. Presumably referring to the
noise of the brawl in which Cassio and
Roderigo were stabbed, though it is sometimes taken to refer to the Desdemona's
cries.
96 **Still . . . grave** Cf. Tilley D135, 'As silent
as death', and Dent D133.1, 'As dumb
(silent, still) as death (the grave)'.
100 **insupportable** unbearable

heavy sorrowful; burdensome
101–3 **huge . . . alteration** As Theobald
recognized, Othello's vision almost certainly owes something to the portents
which follow Christ's crucifixion in the
gospels: eclipse (Luke 23: 44–5) and
earthquake (Matthew 27: 51–2), as well
as perhaps to the similar apocalyptic
events of Revelation 6: 12–13. Hart cites a
suggestive observation in Pliny, where
earthquakes are said to occur 'when the
Sun and Moon are eclipsed' (2.80; sig.
E1ᵛ).
102 **affrighted globe** This quibble on the
name of the theatre for which the play
was written creates an image of the audience gaping in terror at the spectacle of
Desdemona's murder. First recorded use
of 'affrighted' (*OED*).
103 **yawn** gape; split open
alteration At the unnatural change represented by the eclipses; that is, by the
death of Desdemona, itself imaged as an
eclipse (ll. 7–13).

EMILIA (*within*)   I do beseech you
  That I may speak with you—O good my lord.
OTHELLO
  I had forgot thee—(*Calling*) O come in, Emilia!—   105
  Soft—(*calling*) by and by!—let me the curtains draw.
     He closes the bed curtains
  (*To Emilia*) Where art thou?
     He unlocks the door. Enter Emilia
               What's the matter with thee now?
EMILIA
  O, my good lord, yonder's foul murders done.
OTHELLO What? Now?
EMILIA But now, my lord.   110
OTHELLO
  It is the very error of the moon:
  She comes more nearer earth than she was wont,
  And makes men mad.
EMILIA   Cassio, my lord, hath killed
  A young Venetian called Roderigo.
OTHELLO
  Roderigo killed? And Cassio killed?   115
EMILIA
  No, Cassio is not killed.
OTHELLO   Not Cassio killed?
  Then murder's out of tune, and sweet revenge
  Grows harsh.
DESDEMONA O falsely, falsely murdered.
EMILIA O Lord! What cry is that?
OTHELLO   That? What?

---

104 That] F; *not in* Q   O] F; *not in* Q   105 thee—O . . . Emilia!—] OXFORD; thee:
oh . . . *Æmilia*. F, Q (*Emillia*)   *Calling*] This edition (*after* OXFORD)   106 Soft—(*calling*) . . . by—
let] This edition; Soft, by and by, let F; Soft, by and by; let Q   106.1 *He . . . curtains*] OXFORD;
not in F, Q   107.1 *He unlocks the door*] THEOBALD (*subs.*); *not in* F, Q   *Enter Emilia*] WALKER; *after*
'now' F; *after* 'draw' (*l.* 106) Q   109 What? Now?] F, Q2; What, now? Q1   112 nearer] F;
neere the Q   113 hath] F; has Q   119 O Lord] Q1; Alas F, Q2

106.1–107 *He . . . curtains . . . door* The
  extensive business in this scene, involving
  repeated openings and closings of the bed
  curtains and (to a lesser extent) lockings
  and unlockings of the door, literalizes the
  motif of discovery in a play obsessed with
  hidden iniquity and unbearable secrets.

111 **error** wandering, deviation from its
  proper orbit
113 **mad** The supposed power of the moon to
  induce madness is embedded in the term
  'lunatic' (from Latin *luna* = moon).

EMILIA

Out and alas! That was my lady's voice.   120

 She opens the bed curtains

Help, help, ho, help! O lady, speak again!

Sweet Desdemona, O sweet mistress, speak!

DESDEMONA

A guiltless death I die.

EMILIA   O, who hath done this deed?

DESDEMONA

Nobody—I myself. Farewell—

Commend me to my kind lord—O, farewell! *She dies* 125

OTHELLO

Why, how should she be murdered?

EMILIA   Alas, who knows?

OTHELLO

You heard her say herself it was not I.

EMILIA

She said so: I must needs report the truth.

OTHELLO

She's like a liar gone to burning hell:

'Twas I that killed her.   130

EMILIA

O, the more angel she, and you the blacker devil!

OTHELLO

She turned to folly, and she was a whore.

---

120 That was] F; it is Q1; it was Q2 120.1 *She . . . curtains*] WALKER (*subs.*) *after* BOOTH *in* Furness (*Emilia rushes to the bed and throws back the curtains*); *not in* F, Q 123 hath] F; has Q 125 *She dies*] Q; *not in* F 127 heard] Q; heare F 128 the] F; a Q

120 **Out** Exclamation of lament, often intensifying *alas*.

123 **A . . . die** Cf. Giraldi, App. C, p. 444.

124 **Nobody—I myself** Desdemona's exculpation of Othello is, like Cordelia's 'No cause, no cause' (*Trag. Lear*, 4.6.68), an act of self-abnegation, but one so extreme that—though fully in accord with the Victorian image of 'the sweet, dear sufferer' (Furness)—it can sound to modern ears painfully like self-cancellation, as though *I myself* were simply another way of saying *nobody*.

125 **kind** (a) lawful, rightful; (b) natural (behaving as a husband should); (c) loving; (d) kindly, generous, gentle (*OED a.* 3b, 1, 6, 5); as at 4.2.159–60, a play on

the question of Othello's paradoxical 'kind' or 'nature', as both Christian and Moor, may also be involved.

126 **Why . . . murdered** Booth, moved by Desdemona's speech, delivered this line as 'a half-choked utterance', whilst Fechter spoke it with 'steady effrontery' (Furness).

129–30 **She's . . . her** Fechter's Othello showed 'a burst of triumph' here, where Booth registered 'deep emotion' (Furness).

131–3 **O . . . a devil** Cf. Tilley D297, 'Though I am black, I am not the devil'.

132 **folly** wickedness; wantonness, unchastity (*OED n.*[1] 2–3)

EMILIA
Thou dost belie her, and thou art a devil.

OTHELLO
She was false as water.

EMILIA   Thou art rash as fire
To say that she was false. O, she was heavenly true!   135

OTHELLO
Cassio did tup her: ask thy husband else.
O, I were damned beneath all depth in hell
But that I did proceed upon just grounds
To this extremity. Thy husband knew it all.

EMILIA
My husband?

OTHELLO   Thy husband.

EMILIA   That she was false to wedlock?   140

OTHELLO
Ay, with Cassio. Nay, had she been true,
If heaven would make me such another world
Of one entire and perfect chrysolite,

---

133 art] F, Q2; as Q1   136 tup] POPE 1728; top F, Q   141 Nay] Q; *not in* F

133, 134 **Thou** Emilia's use of the singular
pronoun to Othello, who is both her
immediate master and a representative of
Venetian authority, is as defiant and
insulting as her more obvious gibes.

134 **false as water** Cf. Dent W86.1, 'As
unstable (false) as water'; *false* =
unfaithful.
   rash as fire Cf. Dent F246.1, 'As hasty as
fire'.

135 **heavenly true** Cf. Dent G173, 'As false
as God is true'.

136 **tup** Cf. 3.3.398. Othello once again ven-
triloquizes Iago's language.
   else if you don't believe me (idiomatic;
OED adv. 4c)

138 **But that** if it were not for the fact
that

139 **extremity** extreme violence; utmost
penalty; extreme rigour; the utmost point
of severity or desperation (*OED n.* 4, 3b, 6,
9).

143 **chrysolite** 'A name formerly given to
several different gems of a green colour,
such as zircon, tourmaline, topaz, and

apatite' (*OED*). Shakespeare could have
learned about this stone in Pliny: 'the
Topaz or Chrysolith hath a singular green
colour . . . for which it is esteemed very
rich, and when it was first found sur-
passed all others in price' (37.8, sig.
Ggg3ᵛ). Lynda Boose has suggested, however, that the dramatist is more likely to
have known it from the Geneva version of
the Song of Solomon, 5: 14. Her argument that this text imagines a white stone
(consistent with the play's emphasis on
Desdemona's whiteness) is less than
decisive, but it is certainly possible that
Shakespeare associated *chrysolite* with the
purity of 'crystal'; and the passage she
cites from Francis Meres's *Palladis Tamia*
(1598), which asserts that a chrysolite
will crack when placed on the finger of an
adulteress, seems highly suggestive, and
may help to explain Othello's emphasis on
the 'entire and perfect' gem ('Othello's
"Chrysolite" and the Song of Songs
Tradition', *Philological Quarterly*, 60
(1981), 427–37).

I'd not have sold her for it.

EMILIA   My husband?

OTHELLO

Ay, 'twas he that told me on her first;   145
An honest man he is, and hates the slime
That sticks on filthy deeds.

EMILIA   My husband?

OTHELLO

What needs this iterance, woman? I say, thy husband.

EMILIA

O mistress, villainy hath made mocks with love:
My husband say that she was false?

OTHELLO   He, woman;   150
I say thy husband—dost understand the word?—
My friend, thy husband, honest, honest Iago.

EMILIA

If he say so, may his pernicious soul
Rot half a grain a day! He lies to th' heart:
She was too fond of her most filthy bargain.   155

OTHELLO Ha?

EMILIA Do thy worst:
This deed of thine is no more worthy heaven,
Than thou wast worthy her.

OTHELLO   Peace, you were best.

---

145 on her] F; *not in* Q   148 iterance, woman? I] F; iteration? woman, I Q   149–52
EMILIA . . . Iago] F, Q2; *not in* Q1   150 that] Q2; *not in* F

---

144 **sold . . . it** Cf. Emilia's 'The world's a
huge thing: it is a great price | For a small
vice' (4.3.64–5). For all the splendour of
Othello's 'entire and perfect chrysolite'
there is something disturbing about the
commercial calculus of this speech.
Othello's recollection of being himself
'sold' (1.3.138) may deepen the ironic
colouring.

146 **slime** moral pollution; semen or vaginal
fluid (*OED n.* 2a, and Williams,
Dictionary, pp. 1254–5).

148 **iterance** iteration, repetition (first
recorded use in *OED*).

149–52 EMILIA . . . Iago A plausible cut
and most unlikely addition, since the
danger of Emilia's 'iterance' is that the

scene may tip over into comedy at this
point.

149 **made mocks with** made a mockery of.
Perhaps also suggesting 'made a mocking
counterfeit of' (*OED, mock, n.* 3).

154 **lies . . . heart** Cf. Dent T268, 'To lie in
one's throat'.

155 **filthy bargain** Emilia picks up both Othello's commercial language (ll. 142–5)
and his contemptuous *filthy* (l. 147), but
here associates it with the supposed 'foulness' of his black skin (cf. 'ignorant as
dirt', l. 162). Ironically Iago will use the
same language of her ('Filth, thou liest',
230).

159 **Peace . . . best** be quiet, if you know
what's good for you

EMILIA

   Thou hast not half that power to do me harm   160
   As I have to be hurt. O gull, O dolt
   As ignorant as dirt, thou hast done a deed—
      Othello threatens her with his sword
   I care not for thy sword, I'll make thee known,
   Though I lost twenty lives: help, help, ho, help!
   The Moor hath killed my mistress! Murder, murder!   165
      Enter Montano, Gratiano, and Iago

MONTANO

   What is the matter? How now, general?

EMILIA

   O, are you come, Iago? You have done well,
   That men must lay their murders on your neck!

GRATIANO What is the matter?

EMILIA

   Disprove this villain, if thou be'st a man: 170
   He says thou told'st him that his wife was false;
   I know thou didst not—thou'rt not such a villain.
   Speak, for my heart is full.

IAGO

   I told him what I thought; and told no more
   Than what he found himself was apt and true.   175

EMILIA

   But did you ever tell him she was false?

IAGO I did.

EMILIA

   You told a lie, an odious damnèd lie,
   Upon my soul, a lie, a wicked lie:
   She false with Cassio? Did you say with Cassio?   180

160 that] F; the Q   162.1 *Othello . . . sword*] HONIGMANN (*subs.*); *not in* F, Q   163 known] F;
know Q   164 ho] F (hoa); O Q   165.1 *Enter . . . Iago*] F; *Enter* Montano, Gratiano, Iago, *and
others.* Q   168 murders] F (Murthers); murder Q   169 GRATIANO] F, Q2; *All.* Q1

161 **As . . . hurt** as I have the capacity to
   endure pain
  gull dupe
162 **dirt** excrement, filth (*OED n.* 1–2); cf.
   l. 155.
168 **on your neck** to your charge

(*neck* because murder is a hanging
offence)
173 **heart is full** i.e. bursting with emotion,
   about to break
175 **apt** Cf. 2.1.278.
177 **I did** metrically amphibious

IAGO

With Cassio, mistress—go to, charm your tongue!

EMILIA

I will not charm my tongue; I am bound to speak:
My mistress here lies murdered in her bed.

MONTANO, GRATIANO *and* IAGO O heavens forfend!

EMILIA

And your reports have set the murder on.   185

OTHELLO

Nay, stare not, masters, it is true indeed.

GRATIANO 'Tis a strange truth.

MONTANO   O monstrous act!

EMILIA

Villainy, villainy, villainy! Now
I think upon't, I think I smelled a villainy—
I thought so then. I'll kill myself for grief.   190
O villainy, villainy!

IAGO

What, are you mad? I charge you get you home.

EMILIA

Good gentlemen, let me have leave to speak:

181 mistress—] *after* Q (mistresse;); Mistris? F 183–91 My . . . O, villainy, villainy] F, Q2;
not in Q1 184 MONTANO . . . IAGO] This edition; *All.* F, Q2 185 murder] F; murderer Q2
188 Now] This edition; *not in* F, Q2 189 I think I smelled a villainy] This edition; I thinke: I
smel't: O Villany F; I think, I smell a villany Q2

181 **charm your tongue** be silent. A common idiomatic expression (*OED, tongue,
n.* 4), but here resonating with the play's
recurrent language of magic.
182 **bound** duty bound
183–91 **My . . . villainy, villainy** Since they
add little of substance to the exchange,
these lines are more likely to represent a
cut from Q than revision of F; but the evident confusion in ll. 189–90 could suggest
a hastily written and less than legible
addition to the F copy.
187 **strange truth** Cf. Dent S914, 'It is (no)
more strange than true'. The phrase had
a sharper, more oxymoronic ring than
modern clichés might suggest, since truth
was proverbially 'plain', 'innocent',
'naked' and essentially familiar or 'natural', whilst *strange* referred to the alien,
unnatural, and uncanny. The connotations of Gratiano's *strange*, in fact,
closely resemble those of Montano's
'monstrous'.

188–9 **Now . . . smelled** Since the F wording of these lines has no independent confirmation in Q, it seems quite possible that
some errors may have crept in at this
point, resulting from difficulties in deci-
phering the copy text. The Q2 editor
clearly thought so, but his attempt at
emendation is not particularly satisfactory either. Because Emilia appears to be
recalling her earlier suspicions of Iago's
part in Othello's jealousy (3.3.317–20,
4.2.130–3–6), F's *smell't* is probably a
misreading of *smelt* (easy, since apostro-
phes were very inconsistently used in
this period); while (as the Q2 editor
recognized) F's *O* could easily result from
a confusion of *a* with lower case *o*. In F
line 188 is one syllable short, which may
indicate a missing word; and *now* most
readily completes the sense. It may, however, be that the speech was meant to
sound incoherent.

'Tis proper I obey him, but not now.
Perchance, Iago, I will ne'er go home.   195

OTHELLO

O, O, O!

He falls on the bed

EMILIA   Nay, lay thee down and roar,
For thou hast killed the sweetest innocent
That e'er did lift up eye.

OTHELLO ⌈*rising*⌉   O, she was foul!
I scarce did know you, uncle: there lies your niece,
Whose breath, indeed, these hands have newly stopped: 200
I know this act shows horrible and grim.

GRATIANO

Poor Desdemon, I am glad thy father's dead:
Thy match was mortal to him, and pure grief
Shore his old thread in twain; did he live now,
This sight would make him do a desperate turn,   205
Yea, curse his better angel from his side

---

196 *He . . . bed*] Q (Oth. *fals on the bed.*); *not in* F   198 *rising*] THEOBALD (*subs.*); *not in* F, Q   201
horrible] F; terrible Q   202 Desdemon] F; *Desdemona* Q   204 in twain] F (in twaine), Q2;
atwane Q1

194 **proper I obey** In the marriage liturgy
wives promised to *obey* their husbands, a
doctrine widely reiterated in homilies, ser-
mons, and treatises on household government; but in *Othello*, as in his next major
tragedy, *King Lear*, Shakespeare is interested in testing the limits of obedience
and service. Emilia's defiance of both husband and master parallels Desdemona's
defiance of her father in 1.3, and also
looks forward to the servant's defiance of
Cornwall over the blinding of Gloucester
(*Trag. Lear*, 3.7.70–3).

195 **ne'er go home** Since the household is
imagined as a locus of masculine authority and a carefully hierarchized 'little
commonwealth', Emilia's refusal to go
home amounts to an absolute repudiation
of her social 'place': an insurrectionary
gesture that resonates ironically with
Iago's rebellious resentments over his
subordinate 'place' at the beginning of
the play.

198 **lift up eye** 'i.e. to heaven in purity of
spirit and prayer' (Sanders); 'perhaps
implying that she usually kept her eyes

modestly down' (Honigmann); it may be,
however, that nothing more than an attitude of decorous submission, literally
'looking up to' her husband, is implied.

199 **uncle** Cf. l. 253. Evidently Gratiano is
the 'brother' referred to by Brabantio at
1.1.174 (hence his inheritance of the
estate at 5.2.364–6). Honigmann notes
how Othello's insistence on the family
relationship pathetically emphasizes his
sense of isolated alienation (p. 23).

204 **Shore . . . thread** Classical mythology
imaged human life as a thread, spun,
measured, and cut by the three Fates
successively charged with these tasks:
Clotho, Lachesis, and Atropos.

205 **do . . . turn** commit an act of despair.
Despair, itself a mortal sin, frequently
issued in suicide, for which orthodox
Christian doctrine offered no forgiveness.

206 **better . . . side** Cf. Sonnet 144 where
despair 'Tempteth my better angel from
my side'. Gratiano imagines his brother as
the protagonist of a morality play like *Dr
Faustus*, where Good and Bad Angels
compete for Faustus's soul.

And fall to reprobance.

OTHELLO
'Tis pitiful; but yet Iago knows
That she with Cassio hath the act of shame
A thousand times committed—Cassio confessed it,   210
And she did gratify his amorous works
With that recognizance and pledge of love
Which I first gave her: I saw it in his hand,
It was a handkerchief, an antique token
My father gave my mother.   215

EMILIA   O God, O heavenly God!

IAGO   'Swounds, hold your peace.

EMILIA   'Twill out, 'twill out! I peace?
No, I will speak as liberal as the north;
Let heaven and men and devils, let them all,   220
All, all, cry shame against me, yet I'll speak.

IAGO
Be wise, and get you home.

---

207 reprobance] F; reprobation Q   212 that] F, Q2; the Q1   216 O . . . heavenly God]
Q1; Oh Heauen! oh heauenly Powres! F, Q2   217 'Swounds] Q1 (Zouns); Come F, Q2
218–19 'twill out . . . speak] F; 'twill: I hold my peace sir, no, | I'le be in speaking Q1; 'twill
out: I hold my peace sir, no, | Ile be in speaking Q2   219 north] F, Q2; ayre Q1

---

207 **reprobance** reprobation (a coinage,
OED; cf. *iterance*, l. 148). A sinner in a
reprobate condition was cast off from God
and condemned to damnation.
208 **pitiful** According to Aristotle's *Poetics*,
pity and terror were the emotions that
tragedy ought to arouse in its audience.
210 **A thousand times** An obvious hyperbole, but an important detail for those
who believe in the 'double time scheme'
(see Introduction, p. 34).
211 **gratify** reward
   works doings; perhaps also with the
sarcastic sense of 'masterpieces' (*OED*
n. 1, 14).
212 **recognizance** token, badge
215 **father . . . mother** Contradicts 3.4.54–
64. Some critics argue that the inconsistency indicates that the earlier account
was concocted in order to frighten Desdemona, or to conceal the real reason for
the passion stirred up by the loss of this
seemingly trivial item. Others offer a
psychoanalytic reading of the apparent

transformation of the handkerchief from
a badge of maternal power to an emblem
of paternal authority. But the inconsistency may be a simple oversight, or perhaps even result from an inadvertent
transposition of *father* and *mother* in the
copy from which both F and Q seem ultimately to derive (cf. 2.3.168, 207, 4.2.55).
217 **'Swounds . . . peace**   Metrically
amphibious.
218 **'Twill out** the truth must come out.
'But is there a hint that Emilia has bottled
up a guilty secret . . . which now bursts
forth?' (Honigmann).
219 **as . . . north** as freely as the north
wind (blows); one of numerous Shakespearian variations on a common
proverb, 'As free as the air' (Dent A88): cf.
e.g. *Henry V*, 1.1.49, 'The air, a chartered
libertine'; *Troilus*, 1.3.250, 'Speak frankly
as the wind'. Because of its closeness
to the standard formulation, Q's 'liberal
as the air' may represent memorial
corruption.

EMILIA

  I will not.

    Iago threatens Emilia with his sword

GRATIANO   Fie, your sword upon a woman?

EMILIA

  O thou dull Moor, that handkerchief thou speak'st of

  I found by fortune, and did give my husband: 225

  For often, with a solemn earnestness—

  More than indeed belonged to such a trifle—

  He begged of me to steal't.

IAGO   Villainous whore!

EMILIA

  She give it Cassio? No, alas, I found it,

  And I did give't my husband.

IAGO   Filth, thou liest!   230

EMILIA

  By heaven I do not; I do not, gentlemen:

  O murderous coxcomb, what should such a fool

  Do with so good a wife?

    Othello runs at Iago, but is disarmed by Montano; Iago

    kills his wife

OTHELLO   Are there no stones in heaven

  But what serves for the thunder? Precious villain!

GRATIANO

  The woman falls: sure he hath killed his wife.   235

---

223 *Iago . . . sword*] *after* ROWE (*Iago offers to stab his wife.*); *not in* F, Q 224 *of*] F; *on* Q
225 *give*] F; *gaue* Q 233 *wife*] F; *woman* Q *Othello . . . wife*] *after* Q (*The Moore runnes at*
Iago. Iago *kils his wife.*), DYCE 1864 (*but is disarmed by Mont.*); *not in* F 234 *Precious*] F, Q1
(*pretious*); *pernitious* Q2 235 *hath*] F; *has* Q

224 **dull Moor** A complicated quibble depending on the resemblances and (supposed) etymological links between Med. Latin *Morus* = 'Moor', Latin *morus* (from Greek μωρός) = 'dull, stupid', and Latin *morus* = blackberry or black mulberry. Greek *moros* (μόρος) = 'fate, doom, death' may also be part of this tightly enfolded word-play. See also 2.1.221, and cf. 4.3.37.

228 **whore** Iago, like Othello, bewhores his wife before killing her.

230 **Filth** Cf. l. 155.

232–3 **O . . . wife** Presumably directed at Othello, though it would be possible for Emilia to play it as aimed at Iago.

232 **murderous coxcomb** A *coxcomb* was the cap, resembling a rooster's comb, worn by jesters; hence a metonymy for *fool*. By thus acknowledging the element of brutal farce in its plotting, the play seeks to pre-empt and disarm neoclassical criticisms of cuckoldry as an indecorous subject for tragedy.

232–3 **what . . . Do** what has he done to deserve

fool Cf. 2.1.134–5.

233 **stones** thunderbolts

234 **Precious** out-and-out (a sarcastic intensifier)

EMILIA

Ay, ay. O, lay me by my mistress' side.   *Exit Iago*

GRATIANO

He's gone, but his wife's killed.

MONTANO

'Tis a notorious villain. Take you this weapon

Which I have here recovered from the Moor;

Come guard the door without, let him not pass,   240

But kill him rather. I'll after that same villain,

For 'tis a damnèd slave.

Exeunt Montano and Gratiano

OTHELLO   I am not valiant neither:

But every puny whipster gets my sword.

But why should Honour outlive Honesty?

Let it go all.

EMILIA   What did thy song bode, lady?   245

Hark, canst thou hear me? I will play the swan,

And die in music: (*sings*) 'willow, willow, willow'.

Moor, she was chaste, she loved thee, cruel Moor—

So come my soul to bliss, as I speak true!

So speaking as I think, alas, I die.   250

She dies ⌈and falls on the bed⌉

236 *Exit Iago*] Q; *not in* F   238 you this] F; your Q   239 here] Q; *not in* F   242 *Exeunt . . . Gratiano*] Q (*Exit Mont. and* Gratiano.); *Exit.* F   245–7 What . . . willow] F, Q2; *not in* Q1   247 *sings*] DYCE (*subs.*); *not in* F, Q   250 alas] F; I die Q   250.1 *She dies*] Q; *not in* F   *and falls on the bed*] This edition; *not in* F, Q

238 **notorious** conspicuous, obvious (*OED n.* 3, 1608)

you this Q *your* may reflect a piece of stage business in which Othello snatched Gratiano's sword in his effort to kill Iago, though ll. 242–4 would seem to make this inappropriate.

243 **puny** inferior, subordinate; raw, inexperienced; feeble, undersized (*OED a.* 1, 3, 4)

whipster insignificant or contemptible person (*OED n.* 1c; earliest recorded use)

244 **But . . . Honesty** Usually glossed 'why should reputation outlive integrity?' But if Othello is already contemplating suicide, he may be casting himself as the allegorical figure of Honour and his wronged wife as Honesty.

245–7 **What . . . willow** Cf. 4.3.24–9. This passage would logically have been cut from Q following the removal of the Willow Song in 4.3.

246–7 **swan . . . music** Cf. Dent S1028, 'Like a swan he sings before his death'.

250 **So . . . die** Cf. Dent S725, 'To speak as one thinks'.

250.1 **falls . . . bed** Emilia's request to 'lay me by my mistress' side' (l. 236) seems to constitute an implicit stage direction (though it is not clear exactly how and when her body should be placed on the bed); this direction was invariably ignored in the 18th- and 19th-century theatre (Pechter, p. 149), but has been honoured in some more recent productions, including the Olivier version, where Gratiano helped Emilia on to the bed.

OTHELLO

I have another weapon in this chamber,
It was a sword of Spain, the ice-brook's temper—
O, here it is: uncle, I must come forth.

GRATIANO (*within*)

If thou attempt it, it will cost thee dear:
Thou hast no weapon, and perforce must suffer.   255

OTHELLO

Look in upon me then, and speak with me,
Or, naked as I am, I will assault thee.

    Enter Gratiano

GRATIANO

What is the matter?

OTHELLO   Behold, I have a weapon—

A better never did itself sustain
Upon a soldier's thigh: I have seen the day   260
That with this little arm and this good sword
I have made my way through more impediments
Than twenty times your stop. But O vain boast!
Who can control his fate? 'Tis not so now.
Be not afraid, though you do see me weaponed: 265
Here is my journey's end, here is my butt
And very sea-mark of my utmost sail.

---

252 was] F; is Q ice-brook's] F (Ice brookes); Isebrookes Q 254 *within*] Q (Gra. *within*), *after*
'forth' (*l.* 255); *not in* F 256 with] F; to Q 257.1 *Enter Gratiano*] THEOBALD; *not in* F, Q 263
your] F, Q2; you Q1 265–71 Be . . . wench] F, Q2; *not in* Q1

---

252 **sword of Spain** The quality of Spanish
blades (especially those from Toledo and
Bilbao) was legendary; Spanish weapon-
makers had perfected their craft, ironically enough, in the course of the long
struggle to expel the Moors from Spain.
  ice-brook's temper 'Steel is hardened
[tempered] by being put red-hot into very
cold water' (Johnson). *OED, temper, v.*
14a cites Palsgrave (1530): 'They have a
great advantage in Spain to temper their
blades well because of the nature of their
rivers.'
257 **naked** unarmed, unprotected (*OED n.*
4)
260 **I . . . day** Proverbial phrase: Dent
D81.1.
263 **your stop** your efforts to impede me
264 **Who . . . fate** Cf. Dent F83, 'It is impossible to avoid fate'.

265–71 **Be . . . wench** It is difficult to
account for these lines as a deliberate cut
from Q, let alone as an addition to F, since
the Q text does not really make sense as it
stands. An exceptionally careless omission (perhaps connected with the repeated 'now' in ll. 264 and 271) seems to be
involved; or perhaps (as Ridley conjectured) a cut was confusingly marked, and
was meant to begin and end one line
earlier.
265 **Be not afraid** Cf. John 6: 20: 'But
[Jesus] said unto them, It is I: be not
afraid.'
266 **butt** terminal point, goal; mark for
shooting, target (*OED n.*[4] 1, 2a)
267 **sea-mark** object serving to guide sailors
at sea, beacon; boundary or limit of the
sea's flow
  utmost sail furthest point of my voyage

Do you go back dismayed? 'Tis a lost fear:
Man but a rush against Othello's breast,
And he retires. Where should Othello go?   270
    He goes to the bed
Now: how dost thou look now? O ill-starred wench,
Pale as thy smock, when we shall meet at count,
This look of thine will hurl my soul from heaven,
And fiends will snatch at it. Cold, cold, my girl?
Even like thy chastity. O cursèd, cursèd slave!   275
Whip me, ye devils,
From the possession of this heavenly sight,
Blow me about in winds, roast me in sulphur,
Wash me in steep-down gulfs of liquid fire—

---

270 And] F; The Q2   270.1 *He . . . bed*] WALKER (*subs.*); *not in* F, Q   271 Now: how] F; How
Q2   272 count] Q (count), F (compt)   274 girl?] F; girl, Q   275 cursèd, cursèd] F; cursed Q
276 ye] F; you Q

268 **dismayed** stripped of your courage; defeated
    lost wasted, groundless
269 **Man . . . rush** use a mere reed
271 **ill-starred** ill-fated, governed by an unlucky star (first recorded use in *OED*)
272 **Pale . . . smock** Cf. Dent C446, 'As pale as a clout [piece of cloth or clothing]'.
    count accounting (i.e. the Day of Judgement, when souls are weighed and the damned consigned to hell, a common motif in the painting and sculpture of medieval churches and cathedrals). F's *compt* was a common variant spelling. In 1563, Shakespeare's father John authorized the over-painting of the chancel arch 'Doom' in the Guild Chapel, Stratford (near New Place, the house Shakespeare bought in 1597); see Wells, *All Time*, p. 25.
274–5 **Cold . . . chastity** Cf. Dent I11, 'As chaste as ice (snow)'.
274 **Cold . . . girl** An implied stage direction: Othello presumably feels Desdemona's hand or face.
275 **Even . . . slave** This line can be scanned either as a pentameter or as a hexameter, depending on whether *cursed* is treated as monosyllabic or disyllabic (as here).

cursèd slave Othello probably curses himself (in which case *slave* will recall his being 'sold to slavery', 1.3.138), but (as Edwin Booth, for example, assumed) the words could also be aimed at Iago, denounced as a *slave* by Montano at l. 242; in either case the word further emphasizes the ironic parallels between the two.
276 **Whip . . . devils** The half-line suggests a significant pause after an emotional breakdown in the previous line; but some editors prefer to re-align, taking the pause after 'chastity', as Othello absorbs the full impact of her cold flesh.
277 **possession . . . sight** Othello feels that in his damnable state he no longer deserves to possess the 'heavenly' Desdemona; but, in a play where *sight* is so painfully obsessive, the phrase can also suggest that he is possessed by the sight of her, as if by an evil spirit; even here, then, 'possession' and 'heavenly' continue to register the angel/devil split in Othello's response to Desdemona.
278–9 **sulphur . . . liquid fire** Sulphur (brimstone) and a lake of fire figure in Revelation's description of the torments of hell (20: 10, 14).
279 **steep-down** precipitous

O Desdemon! Dead Desdemona! Dead! O, O!   280
   Enter Lodovico, Montano, Iago with officers guarding
   him, and Cassio in a chair

LODOVICO
Where is this rash and most unfortunate man?

OTHELLO
That's he that was Othello: here I am.

LODOVICO
Where is that viper? Bring the villain forth.

OTHELLO
I look down towards his feet—but that's a fable:
If that thou be'st a devil, I cannot kill thee.   285
   He wounds Iago

LODOVICO
Wrench his sword from him.

IAGO   I bleed, sir, but not killed.

OTHELLO
I am not sorry neither: I'd have thee live,
For in my sense 'tis happiness to die.

LODOVICO
O thou, Othello, that was once so good,

280 O Desdemon . . . O!] This edition *after* F (Oh *Desdemon*! dead *Desdemon*: dead. Oh, oh!);
O *Desdemona, Desdemona,* dead, O, o, o. Q1; O *Desdemona, Desdemona*; dead, O. o, o. Q2
280.1–2 *Enter . . . chair*] *after* Q (*Enter* Lodouico, Montano, Iago, *and Officers* | Cassio *in a
Chaire.*), ROWE (. . . *Iago prisoner, with Officers.*); *Enter Lodouico, Cassio, Montano, and Iago, with
Officers.* F   281 unfortunate] F; infortunate Q   283 that] F, Q2; this Q1   285.1 *He wounds
Iago*] ROWE (*subs.*); *not in* F, Q   286 Wrench] F, Q2; Wring Q1   287 live] F, Q (*corr.*); loue Q
(*uncorr.*)   289 was] F; wert Q

284 **I . . . fable** The devil supposedly had
cloven feet (Tilley D252); there may be an
echo of Faustus's 'I think hell's a fable'
(*Dr Faustus*, 2.1.516).
288 **sense** opinion (*OED n.* 18)
   happiness to die Booth noted the echo
of 2.1.184–5 ('If it were now to die, |
'Twere now to be most happy'): 'The
same sad refrain first heard in the very
heaven of his happiness. Let it be faintly
heard wherever possible through your
performance of this character' (Furness).
289 **O . . . Othello** Lodovico's exclamation
seems to draw a kind of punning attention to the repeated 'o' in the Moor's
name. For a discussion of the significance
of the play's repeated 'O's, see Joel Fineman, 'The Sound of "O" in *Othello*: The
Real of the Tragedy of Desire', in

280.1–2 ***Enter . . . chair*** At this point
Booth's Othello drew the bed-curtains in
order 'that Desdemona's corpse [might]
not be polluted by Iago's gaze' (Furness).
282 **That's . . . am** Othello's renunciation
of his name acknowledges the effective
cancellation of his Venetian identity. His
name is used only twice by other characters in this last scene: once by a confused
Desdemona as she awakes ('Who's there?
Othello?', l. 23), and once by a regretful
Lodovico ('thou, Othello, that was once so
good', l. 289); otherwise he has reverted
to the anonymity of 'the Moor' (cf. l. 365).
With Othello's disintegrating sense of
identity compare Iago's 'I am not what I
am', and Antony's self-dissolution: 'Here
I am Antony, | Yet cannot hold this
visible shape' (*Antony*, 4.15.13–14).

Fallen in the practice of a damnèd slave,   290
What shall be said to thee?

OTHELLO   Why anything—
An honourable murderer, if you will,
For naught I did in hate, but all in honour.

LODOVICO
This wretch hath part confessed his villainy:
Did you and he consent in Cassio's death?   295

OTHELLO Ay.

CASSIO
Dear general, I never gave you cause.

OTHELLO
I do believe it, and I ask your pardon:
Will you, I pray, demand that demi-devil
Why he hath thus ensnared my soul and body?   300

IAGO
Demand me nothing: what you know, you know;
From this time forth I never will speak word.

LODOVICO What, not to pray?

GRATIANO Torments will ope your lips.

OTHELLO Well, thou dost best.   305

290 damnèd] Q (damned); cursed F   291 shall] F; should Q   293 I did] F; did I Q   297 never gave] F; did never giue Q   298 your] F; you Q   299 I] F, Q2; *not in* Q1

Anthony Gerard Barthelemy (ed.), *Critical Essays on Shakespeare's 'Othello'* (New York, 1994), pp. 104–23, and Daniel J. Vitkus, 'The "O" in *Othello*: Tropes of Damnation and Nothingness', in Kolin, pp. 347–62. For Vitkus, Othello's name 'beginning and ending in "O", becomes a cipher signifying nothing' (p. 360).

289–91 **thou . . . thee** Lodovico's use of these singular pronouns is probably condescending and aggressive; but either or both could also be played as markers of regretful intimacy.

290 **Fallen . . . practice** victim to the treacherous plotting
  damnèd F's *cursed* is probably a result of contamination from l. 275, but may be a deliberate alteration by whoever was responsible for purging and softening the oaths in F.

292 **honourable murderer** Another version of the 'civil monster' oxymoron (4.1.60), which (on one reading of the

play) is latent in the very idea of a 'Moor of Venice'.

295 **consent in** agree in planning

299–300 **Will . . . body** Cf. Giraldi, App. C, p. 446: 'It appeared astonishing to everybody that a human heart could harbour such malice.'

300 **ensnared** Cf. 1 Timothy 3: 7; 2 Timothy 2: 26: 'the snare of the devil'.

301 **what . . . know** Cf. Tilley K178, 'I know what I know'.

302 **From . . . word** Honigmann compares Iago's refusal to speak with the similar defiance of Aaron the Moor in *Titus* (5.1.58), and of Hieronimo in Kyd's *Spanish Tragedy* (4.4.182) who bites out his tongue rather than submit to his accusers' interrogation.

304 **Torments . . . lips** Metrically amphibious.

305 **Well . . . best** Might be addressed to Lodovico or (in sarcastic approbation) to Iago.

LODOVICO

Sir, you shall understand what hath befallen,
Which, as I think, you know not: here is a letter
Found in the pocket of the slain Roderigo,
And here another—the one of them imports
The death of Cassio, to be undertook   310
By Roderigo.

OTHELLO

O villain!

CASSIO   Most heathenish and most gross!

LODOVICO

Now here's another discontented paper
Found in his pocket too; and this it seems
Roderigo meant t'have sent this damnèd villain,   315
But that, belike, Iago in the nick
Came in and satisfied him.

OTHELLO   O thou pernicious caitiff!

How came you, Cassio, by that handkerchief
That was my wife's?

CASSIO   I found it in my chamber;

And he himself confessed it but e'en now   320
That there he dropped it for a special purpose
Which wrought to his desire.

OTHELLO   O fool, fool, fool!

---

310 undertook | By] F, Q2; vndertooke—by Q1   316 nick] Q1; interim F, Q2   317 thou] F;
the Q   318 that] F; a Q   320 it but e'en] F (euen), Q2; it euen Q1; but even CAPELL

306–28 **Sir ... set him on** Like the
Friar's speech at the end of *Romeo*, this
extended piece of retrospective explanation can easily seem very clumsy in
performance, not least because of the
over-elaborate use of the revelatory letters. In so far as the latter belong to a predominantly comic convention, the effect
is to emphasize the ironies of Othello's
deception by underlining the grossly
theatrical and mechanical nature of
Iago's plotting.
312 **heathenish** barbarous, abominable
(*OED a.* 3a–b)
    gross monstrous, flagrant, obvious (*OED
a.* 3, 4)
313 **discontented** full of resentment

316 **in the nick** at the critical moment
(Dent N160). As Honigmann suggests, F's
interim seems likely to be a sophistication
by someone who thought the vivid colloquial phrase inappropriate to the dignified
emissary of Venice.
317 **satisfied him** gave him a satisfactory
explanation
    caitiff wretch
320 **it but e'en** The F reading is satisfactory
if *even* is meant to be contracted in this
way; otherwise Malone may have been
right in supposing that *it* was erroneously
imported from the following line.
322 **wrought to his desire** produced the
effect he wanted
    fool Cf. 2.1.134–5.

CASSIO

    There is besides in Roderigo's letter
    How he upbraids Iago that he made him
    Brave me upon the watch, whereon it came   325
    That I was cast; and even but now he spake—
    After long seeming dead—Iago hurt him,
    Iago set him on.

LODOVICO (*to Othello*)

    You must forsake this room and go with us:
    Your power and your command is taken off,   330
    And Cassio rules in Cyprus. For this slave,
    If there be any cunning cruelty
    That can torment him much and hold him long,
    It shall be his. You shall close prisoner rest
    Till that the nature of your fault be known   335
    To the Venetian state. Come, bring away!

OTHELLO

    Soft you, a word or two before you go:
    I have done the state some service, and they know't—
    No more of that. I pray you in your letters,
    When you shall these unlucky deeds relate,   340
    Speak of me as I am; nothing extenuate,
    Nor set down aught in malice: then must you speak
    Of one that loved not wisely, but too well;
    Of one not easily jealous, but being wrought,
    Perplexed in the extreme; of one whose hand,   345

---

336 bring away] F; bring him away Q   337 before you go] F, Q2; *not in* Q1   341 me as I am]
F, Q2; them as they are Q1

---

325 **Brave** insult, defy
    upon during
325–6 **whereon . . . cast** as I result of
    which it came about that I was
    cashiered
333 **hold him** keep him alive (for prolonged
    suffering)
334 **close** closely guarded
337 **Soft you** wait a minute
338 **state . . . service** Perhaps recalling
    Contarini's remarks about the adoption
    of 'foreign men and strangers' into the
    ranks of Venetian citizens 'either in
    regard of their great nobility, or that they
    had been *dutiful towards the state*, or else
    had done unto them *some notable service*'

(Lewkenor, p. 18; italics added). In its
concern for the rewards of service, the
last big speech of the play returns to
the theme of Iago's opening diatribe
(1.1.10–60).
340 **unlucky** unfortunate, resulting from
    unhappy chance
343 **loved not wisely** 'So Ovid, *Heroides*,
    2.27 "non sapienter amavi" (I loved not
    wisely)' (Honigmann).
344 **wrought** fashioned (by someone else);
    worked up, agitated. Used esp. of the sea,
    OED p. ppl. 5; cf. Knolles, p. 368, 'The
    billows of a wrought sea'.
345 **Perplexed** bewildered, distracted;
    tormented

Like the base Indian, threw a pearl away
Richer than all his tribe; of one whose subdued eyes,
Albeit unusèd to the melting mood,
Drops tears as fast as the Arabian trees
Their medicinable gum. Set you down this;   350
And say besides that in Aleppo once,
Where a malignant and a turbaned Turk
Beat a Venetian and traduced the state,
I took by th' throat the circumcisèd dog
And smote him—thus.
                    He stabs himself   355

---

346 Indian] Q, F2; Iudean F1   349 Drops] F, Q1; drop Q2   350 medicinable] F; medicinall Q
352 malignant and] Q (*Malignant* and); malignant, and F   355.1 *He . . . himself*] Q; *not in* F

---

346 **base** dark-coloured; lowly, vile; degraded, unworthy (*OED a.* 5, 6, 10)
   Indian A much debated crux. See App. F(iii) for discussion of the textual arguments.
346–7 **pearl . . . Richer** An ironic echo of the sarcastic 'jewel' with which Brabantio dismissed Desdemona (1.3.194); and cf. also Cassio's 'The riches of the ship is come on shore' (2.1.83). In the Marian tradition, the Virgin is associated with Matthew's 'pearl of great price'.
348 **melting** being overwhelmed with grief; dissolving into tears. In the context of Othello's eroticized suicide, the common sense of sexual dissolution or ecstasy may also be present (see Williams, *Dictionary*, pp. 872–3).
349–50 **Drops . . . gum** Shakespeare seems to be remembering Pliny's account of the medicinal resins produced by certain Arabian species, including myrrh trees which 'sweat out of themselves a certain liquor called stact, which is very good myrrh' (12.15, sig. Ii4ᵛ), and goes on to describe opobalsamum (probably from the true Balm of Gilead), which 'issueth out of the wound . . . which cometh forth by small drops; and as it thus weepeth, the tears ought to be received in wool' (12.25, sig. Kk3). One type of so-called 'mummy' was obtained in this fashion.
350 **medicinable** ('med'cinable') medicinal
351 **Aleppo** A city in Turkey known as an important centre of the Venetian-dominated trade with the Orient.
352 **malignant** Either an adjective meaning 'malevolent', or more probably (as the F punctuation and Q's capitalization and italics suggest) a noun meaning 'one who is ill-disposed towards true religion'.
352–4 **turbaned . . . circumcisèd** Ritual signs of Islamic allegiance; apparently echoing the 'circumcised turbaned Turks' of James I's *Lepanto* (l. 11); see Emrys Jones, '*Othello*, *Lepanto*, and the Cyprus Wars', *SS* 21 (1968), 47–52. Vitkus sees this as the moment that symbolically confirms Othello's damnation as a renegade, a 'baptized Moor turned Turk . . . [who] becomes the enemy within' (' "Turning Turk" ', p. 176).
355 **smote him** Hart cites Sir Antony Sherley's *Travels* (1599; ed. 1825, p. 32): 'they have a law in Turkey, that if a Christian do strike a Turk, he must either turn Turk or lose his right arm'. Many 19th-century Othellos, from Kean (1831) to Irving (1881), used this as the curtain line. As many critics have recognized, Othello's suicidal re-enactment of this killing perfectly embodies the contradictions of his position as both Moor and Venetian Christian. David Harewood (National, 1997) stabbed himself with a blade hidden in the cross he wore (see Introduction, p. 86 n. 1).

LODOVICO

O bloody period!

GRATIANO   All that's spoke is marred.

OTHELLO

I kissed thee ere I killed thee—no way but this:
Killing myself, to die upon a kiss.

He kisses Desdemona, falls on the bed and dies

CASSIO

This did I fear, but thought he had no weapon,
For he was great of heart.

LODOVICO   O Spartan dog,   360
More fell than anguish, hunger, or the sea,
Look on the tragic loading of this bed:
This is thy work. The object poisons sight—

358.1 *He . . . dies*] *after* WALKER (*falls on the bed, and dies*), OXFORD (*He kisses Desdemona and dies*);
Dyes F; *He dies.* Q   362 loading] F; lodging Q

356 **period** termination; issue, outcome; death; appointed end, goal (*OED n.* 5a, b, d; 8, 9). Gratiano's 'All that's spoke . . .' also suggests a quibble on the rhetorical and grammatical meanings: a periodic (or syntactically complex) sentence, and the pause or full stop that marks the end of a sentence (10a, 11a–b).

357–8 **I . . . kiss** A popular curtain speech from the mid 18th century (John Palmer, 1766) to the Edwardian productions of Frank Benson (1900) and Oscar Ashe (1907), and used as late as Robert Atkins's 1945 production at Stratford-upon-Avon, this provided the inspiration for Verdi's ending, with its harrowing repetition of Othello's earlier cry, *Un bacio, ancora un bacio* ('A kiss, one more kiss'). Victorian productions frequently added an expiring sigh of 'O, Desdemona!' at the end of the speech; by contrast, Patrick Stewart, in an extraordinary touch, punctuated it with a laugh before 'no way but this', suggesting both ironic self-recognition and wry triumph over Iago.

358 **die . . . kiss** Those who favour *Iudean* at l. 346 read this as a Judas-kiss; but like the last kisses of Romeo ('Thus with a kiss I die'), Juliet, and Antony (*Romeo*, 5.3.120, 164–7; *Antony*, 4.16.20–2, 39–41), Othello's is an erotic *mors osculi* that transforms literal dying into the 'death' of sexual consummation.

360 **great of heart** proud, high-spirited; magnanimous. Balz Engler, however, has argued (citing e.g. 5.2.173) that Cassio means only that Othello's heart was swollen with grief to the point of bursting ('Othello's Great Heart', *English Studies*, 68 (1987), 129–36).

Spartan dog A kind of bloodhound (cf. *Dream*, 4.1.112–13, 118–19). But in the context of 'circumcisèd dog' (l. 354), and in the light of the fact that Roderigo calls Iago 'inhuman dog' (5.1.62), a sarcastic quibble on his display of 'Spartan' courage is probably involved.

361 **fell** savage, cruel, ruthless; cunning (*OED a.* 1, 5)

362 **tragic loading** Although one or the other is likely to result from compositorial (or scribal) misreading, both the F and Q readings seem attractive here: *tragic* suggests a subdued word-play on the metaphorical sense of *load* ('weigh down, burden, oppress'; *OED v.* 6a); but *lodging* would also involve a quibble on the specialized sense of *lodge* favoured by Ridley ('throw on the ground, lay flat . . . beat down crops', *OED v.* 5), a 'countryman's word' and authentically Shakespearian (cf. *Contention* (2 *Henry VI*), 3.2.176; *Richard II*, 3.3.161; *Macbeth*, 4.1.71).

363–4.1 **The object . . . bed-curtains** The Dexter/Olivier film (like some critics) interpreted 'object' as referring contemptuously to Iago as a mere 'thing'; but it is difficult to parallel such a usage in the

Let it be hid.
⌈*They close the bed-curtains*⌉
            Gratiano, keep the house   365
And seize upon the fortunes of the Moor,
For they succeed on you; (*to Cassio*) to you, lord
    governor,
Remains the censure of this hellish villain—
The time, the place, the torture, O enforce it;
Myself will straight aboard, and to the state   370
This heavy act with heavy heart relate.   *Exeunt*

---

364 *They . . . curtains*] WALKER (*subs.*); *not in* F, Q   366 on you] F; to you Q

early 17th century, and the word is more likely to mean 'spectacle of horror' (as in *Trag. Lear*, 5.3.213: *OED n.* 3b), so that (as in many productions) Lodovico's 'Let it be hid' is to be interpreted as a command to close the curtains around the four-poster bed. For the meaning of this theatrical gesture see Neill, ' "Unproper Beds" ', pp. 258–9, 267–8.

363 **poisons** Although Othello is accused by the First Senator of poisoning Desdemona's affections (1.3.113), it is Iago whom the play persistently associates with diabolic poison, beginning at 1.1.68, when he promises to 'poison [Brabantio's] delight' with his libels on Desdemona and the Moor (see also 2.1.288; 3.3.327–8, 391; 4.1.196–200). The venomous 'aspics' tongues' that torment Othello's bosom in the temptation scene belong to Iago (3.3.450), giving a special appropriateness to the biblical 'serpent's curse' that Emilia calls down upon her husband (4.2.16).

364–5 **keep . . . fortunes** A parallel construction; *keep* = seize, take possession of.

365 **the Moor** Lodovico's dismissive reference conclusively returns Othello to the anonymity of the opening scene.

366 **they . . . you** you inherit them.

367 **censure of** the task of passing judgement on

368 **the torture** Cf. Giraldi, App. C, p. 445.

APPENDIX A

THE DATE OF THE PLAY

As with many plays of this period, it is difficult to establish the date of *Othello* with any certainty. The earliest record of its performance consists of an entry in the Accounts Book of Sir Edmund Tilney, Master of the Revels from 1579 to 1610. Tilney noted that on Hallowmas Day (1 November), 1604, 'the King's Majesty's players . . . [acted] a play in the Banqueting House at Whitehall called The Moor of Venice [by] Shaxberd' (i.e. Shakespeare).[1] The 1604 court performance provides a *terminus ad quem* for the play; and a *terminus a quo* can be deduced from the fact that much of *Othello*'s exotic geographical detail appears to derive from Philemon Holland's translation of Pliny's *Historie of the World* [*Naturalis Historia*], published in 1601.[2]

Until recently, most scholars have been inclined to assign the play to the latter part of this span, *c.*1603–4, at the very beginning of James I's reign. In practice this would almost certainly mean that it was first staged in mid-1604, since the theatres were closed during the final illness of Queen Elizabeth in March 1603, and seem to have remained closed through the terrible plague that ravaged London for the rest of the year, not reopening until April 1604. So, although a prior season at the Globe is much more likely, it is just possible that *Othello* was a completely new play when it was staged at Whitehall.[3] Certainly there are indications that it may have been written with an eye to the tastes of the company's new royal patron and his queen. The King's interest in the conflict between Turkey and Christendom had been proclaimed in a poem celebrating the naval victory over the Turks at Lepanto (1571), first published in 1591. James's poem was reprinted in 1603, following his accession to the English throne, and might well have provided a stimulus for Shakespeare's decision to write about the Cyprus wars.[4] At the same time the choice of a Moorish protagonist was well calculated to appeal to a passing fascination with blackface exoticism amongst the Queen's circle; for it is surely a telling coincidence that the

---

[1] The authenticity of this document has been challenged on a number of occasions since its discovery in the nineteenth century—most recently by Charles Hamilton, *In Search of Shakespeare* (1985)—but is nevertheless accepted by the majority of modern scholars, including Sanders and Honigmann.

[2] See Commentary, 3.3.331; 5.2.143, 348–9; App. F(ii–iii).

[3] This position is argued, for example, by the *Textual Companion*, p. 93.

[4] See Emrys Jones, '*Othello, Lepanto* and the Cyprus Wars', *SS 21*, 47–58; and Sanders, Introduction, p. 2.

programme of court entertainments in the winter of 1604/5 also included Ben Jonson's masque *Blackness,* an African fantasy written at the request of Queen Anne, in which she and her ladies appeared as the dusky 'daughters of Niger'. However, a possible reference to *Othello* in Dekker and Middleton's *The Honest Whore* (Part 1), first performed in 1604 and entered in the Stationers' Register on 9 November in the same year, makes it probable the play had already made its public debut, and that the players (as they typically did) were simply presenting the Court with an established popular success—albeit one well tailored to current royal fads.

The idea that *Othello* might be Shakespeare's first Jacobean tragedy has received additional support from its links with a second play which his company contributed to the royal revels in the winter of 1604/5: *Measure for Measure,* which is usually dated to that year, was offered at court on 26 December; and because it derives its plot from the same source as *Othello*—Giambattista Giraldi Cinthio's collection of *novelle, Gli Hecatommithi* (1565)—it is entirely possible that the dramatist worked on the two plays at about the same time. The mysterious recurrence in *Othello* (1.3.16) of the name given to *Measure for Measure*'s protagonist, Angelo, might be taken as a further pointer in this direction.[1] However, the dating of *Measure for Measure* itself is by no means secure; and in any case (as the example of Shakespeare's Roman plays indicates) years might sometimes intervene between the dramatist's various uses of the same source work.

By an odd coincidence, however, the name Angelo, given to the commander of the galleys whose report the Sailor delivers to the Venetian Senate in 1.3, has also been used to link *Othello* with another text that seemed to point to a composition date of *c.*1604—Richard Knolles's *The Generall Historie of the Turkes* (1603). Dedicated to the King, Knolles's work makes its own appeal to James's interest in the Turkish wars. It gives a complete account of the prolonged struggle for control of the eastern Mediterranean that provides the backdrop for *Othello*; and some of its details suggest that Shakespeare might have consulted it. Knolles, for example, mentions a Venetian commander called Angelus Sorianus (Angelo Soriano) who may be the 'Signor Angelo' of the Sailor's report (1.3.16), and (in a passage that might have shaped the Messenger's account of Turkish tactics at 1.3.34–6) he describes how, prior to the siege of Nicosia in 1570, two Turkish fleets met at Rhodes before sailing on to Cyprus.[2] The fact that Knolles's prefatory epistle is dated 'the last of September, 1603' might seem to establish late 1603 as the earliest possible date of composition.

---

[1] The name in *Measure for Measure* derives from Giraldi, where, however, it belongs not to the protagonist, Juriste, but to his sister, Angela.

[2] Bullough includes Knolles as a 'probable source', and the case for supposing that Shakespeare made use of the *Generall Historie* has been supported by Stanley Wells in a letter to *TLS*, 20 July 1984; see also *TC*, p. 126.

Nevertheless the parallels between the two texts are not sufficiently precise or extensive to put Shakespeare's use of Knolles beyond dispute; and in any case, given that the dramatist clearly moved in circles that gave him access to private manuscripts,[1] it is not impossible that he might have read the *Generall Historie* before it went to press.

That said, there is a certain amount of circumstantial evidence to suggest that *Othello* may actually have been written as early as 1601–2; and this receives some support from recent work on vocabulary and metrics which offers significant clues to the chronology of Shakespeare's oeuvre. The most telling hints of this possibility are to be found in a number of apparent echoes of *Othello* found in the 1603 'bad quarto' of *Hamlet* (Q1)—turns of phrase whose appearance is most easily explained as the result of memorial error by someone familiar with both plays;[2] and since Q1 *Hamlet* is a patchwork text that seems to have been assembled by an actor or reporter prepared to eke out the deficiencies of his memory in any way possible, the borrowing can only have been in one direction. Thus the Ghost's 'to my unfolding | Lend thy listening ear' (Q1 *Hamlet*, C3^v–4) seems to derive from Desdemona's 'To my unfolding lend your prosperous ear' (1.3.243); Q1's ending probably adapts 'look upon this tragic spectacle' (I4) from Lodovico's injunction at the end of *Othello* 'Look on the tragic loading of this bed' (5.2.362); while the expression 'Olympus-high' (Q1 *Hamlet*, I1^v) sounds like another unconscious borrowing from *Othello* (2.1.183). Finally, it seems possible that the mysterious substitution of the unusual name 'Montano' for 'Reynaldo' in Q1 may simply have resulted from these two minor parts being played by the same actor.[3] Since the Q1 title-page refers to *Hamlet*'s performance 'by his Highness' servants', it must have been published after 19 May 1603, when Shakespeare's company, formerly the Lord Chamberlain's Men, were taken under the patronage of the new king. But Honigmann believes that its text was probably in existence nearly a year before this; for he argues that news of plans to publish an 'unauthorized' text of *Hamlet* must have reached the ears of the company by 26 July 1602.

---

[1] The numerous echoes of Florio's Montaigne in *Hamlet*, and of Strachey's *True Reportory of the Wracke* in *The Tempest*, for example, make it plain that Shakespeare must have had access to these texts in manuscript form.

[2] First noted by Alfred Hart in 'The date of *Othello*', *TLS*, 10 October 1935, and subsequently amplified by J. C. Maxwell in '*Othello* and the Bad Quarto of *Hamlet*', *N&Q* 21 (1974), 130, and Ernst Honigmann, 'The First Quarto of *Hamlet* and the Date of *Othello*', *RES* 44 (1993), 211–19. See also Honigmann's edition, Appendix 1, 'Date', pp. 344–5.

[3] This possibility is compromised, however, by the even more peculiar replacement of Polonius with 'Corambis'—a name otherwise known only (in the form 'Corambus') from a casual reference in *All's Well* (4.3.167). It may be that both names were simply remembered from an earlier (possibly non-Shakespearian) version of *Hamlet*.

On that date James Roberts (who would print the presumably 'authorized' Q2 in late 1604) entered the play in the Stationers' Register. This Honigmann thinks was a 'blocking entry' designed to inhibit a publication of which the players disapproved.

If Honigmann is right in the latter conjecture, then the company's manoeuvre was not successful for long; and the apparent echoes of *Othello* in Q1 *Hamlet*, though more convincing than the *Textual Companion* was prepared to allow, are insufficient in themselves to be decisive.[1] But Honigmann finds further evidence for an early date in the casting requirements of *Othello* and *Twelfth Night* (*c.*1601–2), which he sees as 'remarkably alike' (Arden, p. 346); and he goes on to suggest that the parts of Viola and Desdemona were both originally written for a boy actor with a good singing voice, further proposing that the cutting of the Willow Song from Q might have been due to the same circumstance (presumably the breaking of the boy's voice) that seemingly required the transfer of the song 'Come away, death' from Viola to Feste in *Twelfth Night* (p. 347). If he is right, then the most likely date for the first performance of *Othello* will have been in the first half of 1602—or perhaps even late 1601.

As indicated above, there is some internal evidence to support such a dating: for, while the metrical tests and those for colloquialism-in-verse analysed by the *Textual Companion* seemed to place *Othello* with (or soon after) *Measure for Measure* (1603) and a little before *All's Well* (1604–5), its tests for word rarity brought the play closer to *Henry V* (1598–9), *Hamlet* (1600–1), and *Troilus and Cressida* (1602). The links with *Hamlet* and *Troilus* have subsequently been supported by MacDonald Jackson, citing a number of metrical and vocabulary tests. In a careful statistical analysis of the metrical indices compiled by Ants Oras, Jackson has shown that, at least as far as pause-patterns are concerned, *Othello*'s closest correlations are with *Hamlet*, *Troilus*, *Merry Wives*, *Twelfth Night*, and *Measure for Measure*, in that order.[2] Jackson notes that the average date of this group is 1601, close to *Hamlet*; however, if we exclude *Merry Wives* (statistically problematic, as he admits, because so much of it is in prose), the average is 1602, exactly Honigmann's preferred date.

Such tests, while highly suggestive, can never be decisive, however—as Jackson's wildly diverse correlations for *Troilus and Cressida*

---

[1] *Textual Companion*, p. 126.

[2] See Ants Oras, *Pause Patterns in Elizabethan and Jacobean Drama* (Gainesville, Fl., 1960); and MacD. P. Jackson, 'Pause Patterns in Shakespeare's Verse', *Literary and Linguistic Computing*, 17 (2002), 37–46. Other evidence for this probability is cited in Jackson's earlier essay, 'Another Metrical Index for Shakespeare's Plays: Evidence for Chronology and Authorship', *Neuphilologische Mitteilungen*, 4 (1994), 453–8: particularly persuasive are the figures for percentages of unstopped lines, which again place *Othello* very close to *Hamlet*.

reveal;[1] and there are grounds for a degree of scepticism about some parts of Honigmann's argument too. The evidence he cites for associating *Othello* with *Twelfth Night* seems especially shaky, for the casting patterns he detects sometimes depend on rather tendentious descriptions of the actorly 'lines' or specialisms involved in particular roles; and, since there is little sign of similar patterns in other plays thought to be written at about the same time (*As You Like It, Hamlet, Troilus and Cressida*), the seeming resemblances may be purely accidental. Moreover, Honigmann's conjectures about the boy actor's singing voice become irrelevant if, as I argue in my discussion of the text, the text of Q *Othello* derives from a later revival of the play. Honigmann himself admits that there are 'steps in [his] reasoning that cannot be proved' (p. 350); and the acceptance of 1601–2 as the most likely date for the play has the effect of creating a rather odd gap in the dramatist's chronology. Whereas for most of his working life Shakespeare produced (on average) two plays a year, Honigmann's proposal would appear to make 1603—just when the extended closure of the theatres might have given the dramatist more leisure for writing than usual—an exceptionally unproductive year.

So, while the apparent echoes of *Othello* in Q1 *Hamlet*, combined with the internal evidence compiled by Jackson and others, point strongly towards 1602, we still cannot rule out the possibility that Shakespeare worked on this play, and perhaps on *Measure for Measure*, in 1603. Given that the players could not know when playing would be resumed in London there is no reason why they might not have begun rehearsing a new play in the course of that year; and (given that we know little of how the King's Men survived during the long closure) it is even possible, as the *Textual Companion* proposes, that *Othello* was first staged as part of a provincial tour—perhaps during their sojourn at Oxford in 1603–4.[2] Moreover, it remains entirely conceivable that Q1 *Hamlet* was assembled and published towards the end of 1603; and, if that were the case, then its text could still have been contaminated by a play written earlier in that year. On that basis, it would remain entirely possible for Shakespeare to have consulted Knolles's *Generall Historie*—at least in manuscript—whilst writing *Othello*.

The one thing we can say with some certainty was that *Othello* was the next tragedy that Shakespeare wrote after *Hamlet*. In mood, if not perhaps in strict chronology, these two plays belong with the darker 'Jacobean' Shakespeare; and the action of *Othello* centres on the relationship between

---

[1] The closest correlations for this play are with *Merry Wives* (1597–8), *Richard II* (1595), *Othello*, *2 Henry IV* (1597–8), and *Contention* (*2 Henry VI*; 1591).

[2] *TC*, p. 126. See also MacD. P. Jackson, 'Editions and Textual Studies', *SS 38* (1985), 245–6.

two figures who are infected with a more extreme version of the misogyny and sexual nausea that taints the hero of the earlier tragedy—qualities that are equally conspicuous in two of the plays that have most in common with *Othello* stylistically and that are probably closest to it in time, *Troilus and Cressida* (1601–2), and *Measure for Measure* (1603–4). All things considered, then, a date of 1602–3 is as close as we are likely to get—at least in default of some hitherto unsuspected evidence for more precise dating.

THE TEXTS OF THE PLAY

The Textual Problem

Othello presents an editor with daunting textual problems. The play, despite its great popularity, remained unpublished until six years after Shakespeare's death, when two significantly different editions appeared in quick succession—a separate Quarto text (Q) in 1622, and a slightly longer version included as part of the First Folio of Shakespeare's plays (F) in 1623. F contains approximately 160 lines that are absent from Q, including a number of extended passages and some well-known set-pieces; while Q has generally fuller and more elaborate stage directions, and includes a scattering of lines and phrases missing from F, as well as 63 oaths and profanities either purged or diluted in the later version. In addition, there are over a thousand small variations in wording, lineation, spelling, and punctuation—some of which involve significant adjustments of tone and nuance; whilst scattered press correction of each text has produced a small number of minor variants both within and between the two. With only a few exceptions, there has been broad agreement amongst editors and textual critics that both Q and F derive from a manuscript (or from separate manuscripts) in Shakespeare's own hand—either directly or from scribal transcripts of the original. Thus each has claims to authority; but, after more than seventy years of intense debate, the exact nature of their relationship with one another and with Shakespeare's original version (or versions) remains, in the words of one editor, 'a . . . mystery'.[1]

A third text, the Second Quarto of 1630 (Q2), while it has no independent authority, also demands serious attention, since it offers a carefully corrected version of Q, produced by an editor who made extensive use of F. Not only did this editor incorporate several passages completely absent from Q, he frequently preferred F's individual variants, and sometimes even ventured emendations of his own. It is difficult to understand why any publisher should have gone to the trouble and expense of so far-reaching a revision, unless Q were recognized as being in some respects defective; moreover, as Thomas L. Berger has argued, any modern scholar seeking to adjudicate between the different readings of Q and F is well

---

[1] Scott McMillin, 'The *Othello* Quarto and the "Foul-Paper" Hypothesis', *SQ* 51 (2000), 67–85 (p. 67). An expanded version of McMillin's essay appears as his introduction to *The First Quarto of Othello* (Cambridge, 2001), and its ideas are further developed in 'The Mystery of the Early *Othello* Texts', in Kolin, pp. 401–24.

advised to pay attention to the decisions of this thoughtful and often meticulous editor—not because he had access (as was once supposed) to any independent manuscript source of his own, but because his privileged position as the playwright's near contemporary, combined with his evident intelligence, makes him a uniquely well-informed witness.[1]

So far, the most elaborate attempt to solve the vexed relationship between Q and F is E. A. J. Honigmann's study, *The Texts of 'Othello' and Shakespearian Revision* (1996), to which readers are referred for a full account of the play's textual difficulties. The work of a formidable textual scholar, this book represents the fruit of many years' meditation and research, stretching back to the author's earlier study *The Stability of Shakespeare's Text* (1965); yet its arguments, based as they are on the New Bibliographical methods developed by Pollard, Greg, and Dover Wilson, have proved at least as contentious as those of earlier scholars—especially in the light of current scepticism about the narrative assumptions on which New Bibliographical methodology was constructed. Moreover, Honigmann's telling reluctance to apply the full logic of his conclusions to his own Arden edition of the play is evidence of the continuing intractability of the problems he addresses.[2] Consensus, unfortunately, seems as far away as ever.

Quarto and Folio

'The Tragedie of Othello, the moore of Venice' was entered in the Stationers' Register on 6 October 1621 by Thomas Walkley, the bookseller for whom Q was printed early in the following year. Walkley's title-page proudly advertised his text as reproducing the play '*As it hath beene diuerse times acted at the* | Globe, and at the Black-Friers, by | *his Maiesties Seruants*'; and the Q text, as we shall see, has characteristics that suggest derivation from a fairly reliable playhouse manuscript. According to Honigmann, however, it appeared under somewhat suspicious circumstances. Arguing, like his New Bibliography predecessors, that the acting

[1] Berger, 'The Second Quarto of *Othello* and the Question of Textual "Authority"', in Virginia Vaughan and Kent Cartwright, *Othello: New Perspectives* (Madison, Wisc., 1991), 26–47 (pp. 30–2). An earlier form of Berger's essay appeared in *Analytical and Enumerative Bibliography*, NS 2 (1988), 141–50.

[2] Whilst stressing that any modern editor will be driven to some degree of textual conflation when faced with two texts, neither of which is wholly trustworthy, Honigmann concludes, somewhat nervously, that Q (despite being less reliable with regard to substantive variants) should nevertheless be regarded as the marginally more dependable text because of its allegedly greater fidelity to a Shakespearian original. However, he immediately backs away from the conclusion that Q should therefore be employed as a copy text, declaring that (for unexplained reasons) it would be undesirable 'at this point in time' (*Texts*, p. 146).

companies needed to protect their financial interest in their own plays by keeping them out of the hands of unscrupulous stationers,[1] Honigmann makes much of the fact that, with the exception of the so-called 'Pavier quartos'—all of them reprints—not one of Shakespeare's plays had found its way into print between 1609 and 1621; he attributes this to steadfast protection of their own interests by the King's Men, whose right to dispose of their own playscripts had been reasserted as recently as 1619 in a letter from the Lord Chamberlain to the Court of the Stationers' Company. Moreover, he maintains that the imminent appearance of the ambitious and expensive First Folio collection, under the aegis of two leading members of the King's Men, would have given Shakespeare's old company a more immediate incentive for maintaining their exclusive control over the text of a tragedy as popular as *Othello*. Nevertheless Walkley somehow managed to acquire ownership of his copy—thereby ensuring that the players would have to negotiate with him before this play could be included in the Folio.

Although there is no way of knowing exactly how Walkley came by his copy, Honigmann's own researches and those of Peter Blayney have cast a somewhat dubious light on the character of this bookseller and of his printer, Nicholas Okes: the often unscrupulous Walkley (dubbed a 'fascinating rogue' by Honigmann) turns out to have been in severe financial difficulties in 1621, whilst Okes was a notoriously sharp operator who had already been in trouble for printing pirated work.[2] Consequently Honigmann has conjectured that corrupt practice was probably involved when these two obtained their manuscript copy of *Othello*. Nevertheless, as Scott McMillin has pointed out, Walkley's position seems to have been strong enough to enable him to exert continued rights over his own version of the text: he successfully entered the play in the Stationers' Register on 6 October 1621, in spite of the staying order recently secured by the actors; and he thus retained publication rights until 1628, when he sold the tragedy (along with three more of the company's plays, which he had published between 1619 and 1625) to Richard Hawkins, who produced a second quarto edition two years later. All of this suggests that some sort of understanding was reached with Shakespeare's company, preserving Walkley's

---

[1] See e.g. A. W. Pollard, *Shakespeare's Fight with the Pirates and the Problems of the Transmission of his Text* (1917).

[2] Honigmann, *Texts*, pp. 22–9, and Peter W. M. Blayney, *The Texts of 'King Lear' and their Origins*, vol. I (Cambridge, 1982), pp. 298–9. In addition to *Othello*, Okes was employed to print a pair of Beaumont and Fletcher plays, which Walkley had somehow acquired from the King's Men at about the same time. It is probably significant, as the *Textual Companion* points out, that of the other King's Men plays published by Walkley between 1619 and 1625, all four seem to have been printed from private transcripts.

interest in the play while publication of the Folio went ahead (McMillin, *Q*, p. 16).

The precise circumstances under which Walkley acquired his manuscript have been regarded as important because they might have implications for the reliability of the Q text. However, as Honigmann acknowledges, stolen goods are not necessarily inferior or damaged goods, and it remains possible that 'a wicked stationer may "procure" a good text'.[1] Moreover, there were perfectly legitimate ways in which Walkley could have acquired his copy: he might have bought one of the 'private' manuscripts which the players sometimes made for patrons and friends, or he might even have obtained a manuscript from the company itself—for the recent work of Blayney has shown that, since the publication of plays was much less profitable than Pollard and others supposed, it was actually the acting companies, keen to advertise their wares by any means possible, who had the greatest interest in getting plays into print.[2] But even if Walkley's manuscript was of entirely respectable provenance that would not guarantee its authority; for just as stolen copy could be good copy, even impeccably acquired manuscripts might be defective. Indeed, as the theories of Alice Walker and (more recently) Scott McMillin would indicate, manuscripts acquired from company sources were especially liable to be compromised by their playhouse origins: they might, that is to say, incorporate alterations made in the course of performance by someone other than the dramatist; and, if a manuscript were then assembled (as some of Q's readings suggest) by dictation, it might also reproduce memorial errors on the part of the actors.

Of course, to those like Andrew Gurr who have begun to think of early modern plays as essentially collaborative products, for which the dramatist's original script supplied no more than the necessary groundwork, such alterations are a necessary part of the play-making process; and it follows that a demotic performance-based script, incorporating cuts and other alterations made (with or without the author's approval) should arguably be credited with greater authority than a fuller, but necessarily more 'literary', text closer to the author's original. From this perspective, the New Bibliographical ambition to reconstruct a text representing as accurately as possible what Shakespeare actually wrote is dismissed as part of a post-Romantic fetishization of the author, entirely inappropriate to early modern conditions of dramatic production. This edition assumes, however, that because any playhouse version, by its very nature,

---

[1] Honigmann, *Texts*, p. 28.
[2] See Peter W. M. Blayney, 'The Publication of Playbooks', in John D. Cox and David Scott Kastan, *A New History of Early English Drama* (New York, 1997), 183–422.

represents a series of choices that foreclose on other possibilities latent in the dramatist's 'maximal' script, there are sound practical reasons for producing a text as close as we can make it to that more expansive version—even if the idea of re-creating an ideal 'original' now looks hopelessly chimerical.

Whatever its history of transmission, the Quarto text differed in important respects from the version that would appear little more than a year later in the Folio volume assembled by Shakespeare's fellow actors John Heminge and Henry Condell for the stationers William and Isaac Jaggard.[1] In an implicit challenge to previously published versions, the Jaggard title-page presented the plays in this collection as 'Published according to the True Originall Copies'. Heminge and Condell similarly boasted that the new texts, 'cured and perfect of their limbs', would replace the 'stolen and surreptitious copies' now in circulation, which they dismissed as 'maimed and deformed by the frauds and stealths of injurious impostors'. In point of fact the Folio actually made use of existing quarto editions as copy for some plays; but for others (including some that, like *Othello*, had previously appeared in 'good' quartos) they clearly had access to independent manuscript copy.

Modern bibliographers and textual critics, whilst acknowledging that in some cases quarto texts might be closer to the autograph manuscript originally supplied to the players, have recognized that the compilers of the Folio, as senior members of the King's Men, were uniquely placed to obtain what they thought were the best copies of their colleague's work. F has thus been granted a particular claim to textual authority—even if the material circumstances of its production created the potential for various kinds of error and sophistication. However, this consensus has been complicated in recent years by a growing belief that, in some instances at least, divergences between Quarto and Folio versions may represent significant revision of the original work, presumably by the dramatist himself. This has been most persuasively argued with respect to *Hamlet* and *King Lear*. In the case of *Hamlet*, the situation is further complicated by the existence of no fewer than three different texts—including the truncated First Quarto with its oddly discrepant character names and markedly different arrangement of the text. The effect of current textual scholarship has been to suggest that the text of a popular Renaissance play was a much more fluid thing than author-centred, print-oriented literary and textual criticism have been prepared to allow—so that rather than imagining an ideal version of any given play, its form fixed at the point where the dramatist's

---

[1] William Jaggard is described by Honigmann as the printer of F; but by 1623 illness had forced him to hand over the running of his printshop to his son, Isaac, whose name appears (along with that of Edward Blount) on the title-page.

'final intentions' were realized, or even at the point of 'original perform-ance', we might do better to think of a theatrical work as an infinitely vari-able diachronic phenomenon, of which the surviving printed texts represent more or less arbitrarily chosen cross-sections.[1]

In the course of its lifetime a play could be changed in a variety of ways: additions and alterations might be made by the original author, they might be commissioned from another playwright (as we know to have hap-pened with *The Spanish Tragedy* and *Dr Faustus*, and as seems to have hap-pened with *Macbeth*), or they might be imposed by the actors themselves.[2] A script might be cut or revised for a wide variety of reasons: some of these might be trivial—to suit the changing composition of the company, to match the needs of particular venues, to bring the play up to date by adding or removing topical allusions, or to accommodate the pressures of occasional censorship; others might be more significant—to incorporate actors' suggestions, to respond to the experience of performance, or to allow for the playwright's second thoughts about his own dramatic design. In the case of *King Lear*, it is now widely accepted that the F text, with its frequent omissions and occasional amplifications, its re-assignment of speeches and altered stage directions, and its omission of the Doctor's part, is sufficiently transformed to constitute an alternative version of the play—and one that seems distinctively Shakespearian. The decision to revise was perhaps prompted by the dramatist's experience of working on the play in the theatre, since a number of changes seem designed to tighten the dramatic action at key points, while others involve significant modifications to the treatment of such key characters as the Fool and Cordelia. Taken together, they are sufficiently extensive to have persuaded a number of editors to publish separate or parallel-text editions of what they regard as discrete versions of the play.

In the case of *Othello*, however, although the New Cambridge Shakespeare has published a separately edited text of the First Quarto, the differences between Q and F are by no means so great as those between Q

---

[1] Thus Gurr, in 'Maximal and Minimal Texts: Shakespeare v. the Globe' (*SS* 52 (1999), 68–87) and in his introduction to *The First Quarto of Henry V* (Cambridge, 2000), argues that the 1986 Oxford editors' quest for a text approximating as close-ly as possible to that performed by Shakespeare's company in his own lifetime was necessarily chimerical. 'When we recognize', Gurr writes, 'what a high-speed process it was to produce the plays for original performance, how irregular those original performances were, how liable to change the conditions of playing, and how flexible the text had to be as it was taken from page to stage, we can see that there is little hope of retrieving from the text much of the original performance, and that a concept of a fixed "performance text" is a misconception' (Introduction, p. 2).

[2] See Eric Rasmussen, 'The Revision of Scripts', chap. 23 of Cox and Kastan (eds.), *New History of Early English Drama*.

and F *Lear*, or even between Q2 and F *Hamlet*; and, whilst Q may represent something closer to a performance text, there is no real suggestion that distinct alternative versions of the play are at issue. Nevertheless, the unusually large number of variations—together with the generally accepted superiority of F's substantive variants—has led some scholars to suppose that the play was subject to a measure of authorial revision. As we shall see, there are several objections to this hypothesis. Not the least of these is the fact that—in striking contrast to *Lear*, where revision seems to have involved substantial cutting—the Folio text of *Othello* makes significant *additions* to an already lengthy play. These include such important set-pieces as Othello's Pontic Sea speech in 3.3, and Desdemona's Willow Song in 4.3—the last of which is added at precisely the point in the action where (because of the danger of flagging pace) one might more easily expect cuts to be applied.

The Scholarly Debate

The first serious attempt to account for the divergences between the two texts was made by the distinguished bibliographer and theatre historian E. K. Chambers, who argued in 1930 that Q and F must rest substantially upon the same original, even though they had clearly been printed from separate manuscripts—an early and somewhat careless scribal transcript in the case of Q, and the dramatist's holograph in the case of F.[1] Both F and Q were to be thought of as 'good' texts, though F was generally more authoritative, except where it had been sophisticated by the expurgation of swearing and profanity—presumably in response to the 1606 Act to Restrain Abuses. Chambers's theories, which provided ample warrant for the extensive editorial conflation underlying most modern editions, won general acceptance. But in 1952 Alice Walker, co-editor of the New Cambridge *Othello* (1957), published a provocative essay calling the received narrative into question. In this paper, and in the book-length study of *Textual Problems* that followed, Walker argued that F was in fact printed from a corrected copy of Q.[2] This, she maintained, was consistent with F's general practice of working from printed copy wherever it was available ('Texts', p. 18). She based her argument principally on the presence of a number of common errors in the two texts, and on some orthographical anomalies seemingly incompatible with the two-manuscript theory. In the

---

[1] *William Shakespeare: A Study of Facts and Problems*, 2 vols. (Oxford, 1930).
[2] 'The 1622 Quarto and the First Folio Texts of *Othello*', SS 5 (1952), 16–24; *Textual Problems of the First Folio* (Cambridge, 1953).

case of *Othello*, she supposed, the F compilers were aware of deficiencies in the Q text which made extensive correction from a company manuscript desirable.

Walker proposed that Q itself derived from a prompt-book, already marred by performance cuts, which had been further mutilated by its transcriber, a book-keeper who relied extensively on his memory, thereby introducing 'not only some corruptions which had established themselves on the stage . . . but also some nonce readings of his own'. This would account for the very high number of variants between Q and F, and for what Walker saw as the 'quite shocking inferiority' of so many Q readings. While Walker's arguments in some ways confirmed 'the general superiority of the Folio text', her conviction that F derived substantially from Q suggested that 'neither text may be as good as it seems', thereby licensing an even greater margin of editorial discretion in responding to 'the many baffling problems of this text'.[1]

Walker's case for the prompt-book origins and memorial corruption of the Q text proved controversial, partly because Q, especially in its inconsistent and sometimes offhand treatment of stage directions, did not bear the supposedly characteristic marks of playhouse origins; consequently the influential W. W. Greg preferred to suppose that the Q printer's copy had been a late and rather hastily made transcript of Shakespeare's first draft (or 'foul papers') that was itself difficult to read.[2] Greg's arguments concerning the foul-papers origin of Q proved so persuasive that they became the basis for most editorial approaches to that text; but Walker's central idea concerning F's use of Q copy won wide acceptance, attracting the support of such textual luminaries as Greg himself, Fredson Bowers, and Charlton Hinman.[3] Before long, however, this new consensus faced a number of challenges—from the editorial conclusions of M. R. Ridley,

---

[1] *Problems*, pp. 152–3; 'Texts', p. 23; *Problems*, p. 138; 'Texts', p. 24; *Problems*, p. 161.

[2] Greg, *The Shakespeare First Folio*, pp. 357–74. One deficiency of Greg's position was that it failed to account for the presence of cuts in Q. Latterly, the whole status of 'foul papers' as a significant element in textual transmission has been called in question by Paul Werstine. Pointing out that 'no example of Greg's idealized "foul papers"—the author's original and ultimate draft much corrected—has yet been identified', Werstine maintains that there is no good evidence for supposing that playwrights ever delivered their work to the players in anything less than a fair copy—see his 'Narratives About Printed Shakespeare Texts: "Foul Papers" and "Bad" Quartos', *SQ* 41 (1990), 65–86 (esp. p. 81), and 'Post-theory Problems in Shakespeare Editing' (unpublished manuscript).

[3] Fredson Bowers, *Bibliography and Textual Criticism* (Oxford, 1964), chap. 6, 'The Copy for the Folio *Othello*'; Charlton Hinman, *Othello 1622* (Oxford, 1975), p. xiv, and Hinman, *The Printing and Proof-Reading of the First Folio of Shakespeare*, 2 vols. (Oxford, 1963), i. 4.

from the theatrically-based examination of F's 'additions' by Nevill Coghill, and from the more rigorous bibliographical analysis of J. K. Walton.

In his 1958 Arden edition, Ridley offered a serious objection to Walker's belief in quarto copy for the Folio; this took the form of a simple but unanswerable question involving the reduced number of stage directions in F: 'why [would] any sane person, preparing a copy of Q1 to serve as copy for F, deliberately *delete* a number of stage-directions, including almost all those which illuminate business?' (p. 218). Ridley went on to maintain that nearly all of the 'vulgarizations' by which Walker purported to demonstrate the supposed inferiority of Q could, depending on one's aesthetic perspective, be justified as more effective readings, sophisticated away by the enfeebling interference of the F editor(s). He concluded that Greg was right in thinking that Q derived fairly directly from Shakespeare's 'foul papers', probably via a transcript made for a private collector, while F was based on a second transcript, deriving from a prompt-book that included 'a good deal of Shakespeare's second thoughts', but that also probably exhibited memorial contamination from the prompter, and sophistication from the editorial work of Heminge and Condell. He therefore departed from accepted practice by making Q the copy-text for his edition.

Whilst Ridley's belief in the superior authority of Q has not been widely accepted, the notion that F might incorporate elements of authorial revision received additional support from Nevill Coghill in *Shakespeare's Professional Skills* (1964): Coghill proposed that the F passages whose absence from Q had been interpreted by Greg and others as evidence of theatrical cutting were more readily explained as additions made in the course of Shakespeare's own revision of the play—one immediately occasioned, he conjectured, by the need to respond to the Act to Restrain Abuses, but which conveniently allowed the dramatist to answer his own 'dissatisfaction with certain features of the play as it was first written' (p. 167). Coghill could see no reason why the company would have allowed a transcript of the play to have been made in around 1620, when Heminge and Condell were already preparing the Folio edition, nor why they should have allowed any authority to the fruit of such a transcript. Ignoring the possibility that Walkley might have obtained access to a private transcript, he accordingly maintained that Q must have been printed from the original prompt-copy 'made (with the usual mistakes) from Shakespeare's "foul papers" by the book-keeper in, or shortly before, 1604'; F, on the other hand, will have been printed from 'a second prompt copy, made (also with the usual mistakes) from a revised set of foul-papers, in or not long after 1606'; the common errors he accounted for by supposing that, when making the second transcript, the book-keeper might have dealt with the notorious difficulty of Shakespeare's handwriting by consulting the earlier prompt-book.[1]

Coghill's belief in discrete manuscript origins for F and Q received powerful bibliographical support from J. K. Walton in 1971; whilst his arguments for revision were enthusiastically taken up in the 1980s, when interest in the idea of Shakespeare as reviser reached a peak with Gary Taylor's and Michael Warren's influential collection of essays on the two texts of *Lear*.[2] In his extensive study of the use of quarto copy by the Folio printers, Walton challenged the whole basis of Alice Walker's case, arguing that the number of unmistakable common errors in the two *Othello* texts was no greater than could be accounted for by chance,[3] and maintaining that the large number of indifferent variants could only be explained by derivation from separate manuscripts—especially since a high proportion of them were of a kind unlikely to be introduced by simple compositorial carelessness. Walton could see no reason why, if Heminge and Condell had good manuscript copy at their disposal, it would have been thought worthwhile to undertake the laborious task of collating it with a printed text—especially since the amount of correction involved would often have produced copy that was messier and harder to read than the manuscript itself.[4] More recently, however, Ernst Honigmann has revived Walker's theory in a modified form, proposing that the scribe responsible for the manuscript behind F must have consulted Q at some points where his own copy had become illegible (*Texts*, p. 94).

However, the notion that F could actually have been set from a marked-up copy of Q was finally laid to rest by the work of Gary Taylor (1983) and MacDonald Jackson (1987). Building on the compositorial analyses of Charlton Hinman and Trevor Howard-Hill, which showed that printing work on the Folio *Othello* had been divided between the experienced

---

[1] Coghill, p. 167. A difficulty with Coghill's argument is that it requires the book-keeper to have transcribed nonsense from the original, on the grounds that 'he was accustomed to hearing it' on the stage (p. 168); but it seems improbable that such stuff would have survived in the theatre, given that the dramatist was himself a performing member of the company.

[2] Gary Taylor and Michael Warren (eds.), *The Division of the Kingdoms: Shakespeare's Two Versions of 'King Lear'* (Oxford, 1983).

[3] J. K. Walton, *The Quarto Copy for the First Folio of Shakespeare* (Dublin, 1971). Statistically speaking, Walton's argument seems quite plausible; but if, for example, 'exufflicate' at 3.3.185 results from a misreading (as it seems to do), it is hard to explain how this otherwise unknown word could have found its way into both Q and F; and if 'place of sense' and 'time of scorn', printed by both Q and F at 2.3.158 and 4.2.54, are accepted as accidental transpositions (as they are by most editors), it is difficult to believe in anything other than a common origin for such errors.

[4] Walton, pp. 38–41, 117–19, 124–41, 183–227; for obvious reasons, variants introduced by a compositor tend to be similar in form as well as sense, whilst those in the *Othello* texts are generally of a more divergent character.

Compositor B and the novice Compositor E, Taylor demonstrated a divergence in spelling and punctuation between Q and F quite incompatible with the usual practice of E who normally followed his copy fairly closely in these matters.[1] Taylor was able to conclude, therefore, that F 'cannot have been set from printed copy' (p. 60); and his thesis is borne out by Jackson's analysis of F misreadings: since these are overwhelmingly concentrated in the stints of Compositor E, '[t]he only convincing explanation . . . is that both compositors were setting from manuscript, and that the naïve and inept Compositor E misread his copy far more often than the experienced Compositor B'.[2]

Taylor's explanation for the substantive variations between Q and F was that F was printed from a manuscript that (as Coghill had argued) incorporated the dramatist's own revisions of the Q version. The patterns of spelling and punctuation, however, indicated that another scribal hand must have intervened between Shakespeare's revised manuscript and the printed text. This is the position elaborated in the *Textual Companion* (1987), where Wells and Taylor further argue that while 'F . . . brings us closer to Shakespeare's final text than Q1', nevertheless 'Q1's scribe obliterated fewer authorial characteristics than F's'. Accordingly, in their Oxford *Complete Works*, Wells and Taylor elected to follow Ridley in taking Q1 as 'the basic copy-text', while 'graft[ing] on to it passages found only in F' and observing what they took to be Shakespeare's subsequent revisions by 'follow[ing] F in all readings which make acceptable sense' (*TC*, pp. 477–8). Taylor himself went on to refine this position by proposing, chiefly on the basis of F's expurgated oaths and profanities, that F must derive (via a literary transcript) from a late prompt-book—thus putting it at up to three removes from the revised authorial manuscript from which its authority derived.

Nevertheless, while the effect of textual criticism since Ridley has undermined confidence in the superiority of F, it is significant that of recent scholarly editions only the complete Oxford has been willing to follow Ridley in taking Q1 as copy-text for *Othello*. This is partly because Coghill's theatrically based arguments for authorial revision in F—especially since their vigorous development by Ernst Hongimann (1982), John Kerrigan (1987), and John Jones (1995)—have proved so persuasive.[3] Each of these

---

[1] Gary Taylor, 'The Folio Copy for *Hamlet, King Lear*, and *Othello*', *SQ* 34 (1983), 44–61.
[2] MacD. P. Jackson, 'Printer's Copy for the First Folio Text of *Othello*: the Evidence of Misreadings', *The Library*, 6th ser., 9 (1987), 262–7 (p. 264).
[3] E. A. J. Honigmann, 'Shakespeare's Revised Plays: *King Lear* and *Othello*', *The Library*, 6th ser., 4 (1982), 142–73; John Jones, *Shakespeare at Work* (Oxford, 1995); and John Kerrigan, 'Shakespeare as Reviser (1987)', in *On Shakespeare and Early Modern Literature* (Oxford, 2001), 3–22. Ironically, Honigmann's own position has subsequently shifted, so that at the end of *The Texts of 'Othello'* he concludes that, in

critics pays close attention to small verbal substitutions as well as to the significant additions in F, and concludes that, while some variants illustrate nothing more than the seemingly pointless tinkering to which writers are prone when revisiting their texts, much of the detail shows the dramatist as an intensely purposive reviser, 'visibly busier', in Kerrigan's estimate, 'than everywhere else except Q and F *King Lear*' (p. 16). None of the three, however, develops convincing new textual reasons for believing in Coghill's hypothesis; and their arguments remain overwhelmingly aesthetic. With great subtlety, Kerrigan seeks to uncover a Shakespeare 'work[ing] along fault lines in the story, ambiguating afresh points at which the audience's sympathy seems too readily assured' (p. 11). But this is only another way of registering the difficulty of discerning a single controlling intention behind supposed 'revisions' that often seem to pull in different directions; and one reason for the controversial status of F and Q *Othello* is the problem of constructing an explanation that will account for all the divergences between two texts, each of which has strong claims to authority. For this reason the most recent New Cambridge editor, Norman Sanders, adopts an even more eclectic practice than most of his predecessors, basing his text on a thorough conflation of Q1 and F in which 'each pair of variants [is treated] as a separate entity' (pp. 203–6). Sanders believes that Q and F must 'reflect two stages of composition for both of which Shakespeare himself was responsible', with the F-only passages representing 'Shakespeare's amplification of his own text'; but he concludes that while each text is 'superior to the other in many respects', each—as a result of the carelessness of scribes and compositors in the case of Q1, and of both compositorial carelessness and editorial sophistication in the case of F—is also defective.

A similar view of the relative authority of Q and F underlies Ernst Honigmann's Arden edition; but it is based on a rather different assessment of the probable relationship between the two. In his extended study of the two texts, Honigmann finds himself having to discard the theory of revision of which he was once a strong proponent. Whilst clinging to the belief that 'Q and F reflect two authorial strains in some shorter passages', Honigmann now thinks that Q and F 'are examples of textual instability, not of large scale revision', with F offering at best a scattering of small alterations that represent the author's 'second thoughts' (*Texts*, pp. 21, 144). However, Coghill's argument for regarding the longest and most important of the F-only passages as an authorial 'addition' is unsustainable; for it seems inconceivable that Shakespeare would have written

view of the apparent scribal sophistication in F, Q should probably be chosen as the 'parent text'—only to excuse his own Arden from that imperative by invoking St Augustine's 'Let me live chaste, Lord! but not yet' (p. 146). The new *Variorum*, however, will apparently follow his prescription.

Desdemona's lines about Barbary and her 'Song of Willow' (4.3.24–31) unless he had intended the song itself to be sung;[1] and if the song was excised from Q, then it seems likely that the same must be true of the other substantial F 'additions'. Indeed, there are signs of even more inexpert cutting elsewhere: for example, Q's omission of sixteen lines from Roderigo's speech describing Desdemona's elopement (1.1.120–36) is almost certainly a cut, since Brabantio is made to refer back to it at ll. 162–6. The probability of cutting is further increased by the fact that most of the relevant passages in Q exhibit metrical disturbance, suggesting that rather hasty patching was involved.[2]

However, these excisions are insufficient to reduce the play's running time to any great extent; and since Q, with its incomplete and sometimes rather literary stage directions, lacks what are usually regarded as convincing marks of prompt-book origins, Honigmann argues that its cuts are unlikely to be theatrical in origin. Instead, he concludes that the deficiencies of its text are best explained by the history of its transmission. Like Sanders, he concludes that Q must derive from Shakespeare's earliest holograph—his so-called 'foul papers'. This will have been a messy, much overwritten, and sometimes illegible manuscript inviting all kinds of misreading and misconstruction—not least where it may have been subject to revision or marked for cutting. But the printer did not have access to this manuscript at first hand; for Q, as a succession of scholars from Greg onwards have argued, bears a number of marks of scribal intervention—notably the frequent use of the un-Shakespearian abbreviations *'em, ha'*, and *tho'*. Thus Shakespeare's manuscript was exposed to two kinds of corruption: first as it was copied by 'one or more scribes who misread Shakespeare's hand repeatedly', and then as 'one or more compositors manhandled the [resulting] text in other ways'.[3] However, given that some

---

[1] John Jowett, reviewing Honigmann's book in *SS* 50 (1997), 281–4, argues that '[Q's] dash after "that Song to night / Will not goe from my minde" is authorial shorthand for "She sings" ' (p. 281), but offers no corroborating examples.

[2] Honigmann, *Texts*, pp. 10–14.

[3] Ibid, p. 49. In a long and thoughtful review of Honigmann's book, MacDonald P. Jackson provides supporting evidence for the likelihood that two different scribes (and perhaps more than one compositor) worked on the text that became Q (*Shakespeare Studies*, 26 (1998), 364–72; p. 367). By contrast, Pervez Rizvi, while agreeing that 'most F-only passsages are much better explained as cuts than as additions', argues, not entirely convincingly, that 'it is F which represents a transcript of foul papers . . . [while] Q represents a transcript of Shakespeare's fair copy, with cuts, revision of many words and phrases and the elimination of false starts' ('Evidence of Revision in *Othello*', *N&Q* NS 45 (1998), 338–43; p. 343). Unfortunately, Rizvi's thesis depends in part on the improbable notion that Shakespeare himself was the reviser responsible for the somewhat clumsy cuts in Q, and upon some rather strained arguments for the superiority of a number of doubtful readings in Q.

of the longer omissions from Q are clearly deliberate and systematic,[1] the printer's copy may have been marked up for cutting 'by someone asked to shorten the play'; but 'either the printer overlooked some of the intended cancellations, or, more probably, the person marking the cuts made a start, saw he was damaging the play and gave up in disgust'.[2] In the case of some of the more arbitrary-seeming omissions, however, Honigmann guesses that the compositors may simply have decided to 'save themselves time and trouble by omitting bits of text'.[3] Because Q was set by formes,[4] this was especially likely to happen when the compositor, as he approached the bottom of a page, found himself running out of space, and could not resolve the difficulty (as he often did) by converting verse to prose. By the same token, Honigmann conjectures, the compositor might even have inserted lines of his own when he found himself with excess space at the end of a page.

If Honigmann's account of its transmission points to the unreliability of Q, the narrative he constructs for F renders that text equally suspect. He argues that this too must derive from a non-theatrical manuscript— probably Shakespeare's own fair copy of the play, not extensively revised, but incorporating some authorial second thoughts in its minor variants. Such a manuscript would have been generally more legible than the foul papers, but still liable to some misreading because of obscurities in Shakespeare's handwriting, which Honigmann suspects deteriorated over the years. But the most conspicuous deficiency of F lies in the fact that it has been stripped of the oaths and profanities that litter the Q text, and that are particularly characteristic of Iago's speech. It has generally been supposed that they were purged in response to the 1606 Act to Restrain Abuses of Players. Since the Act sought to control only the uttering of oaths in public performances and did not extend to published material, such expurgation must either have been part of a revision aimed at a revival of the play, or derive from a suitably cleaned-up prompt-book. With significant revision now an unlikely possibility, we seem to be left with the latter explanation; and indeed Gary Taylor has insisted that in default of strong counter-evidence, we should assume that all heavily expurgated Folio texts

[1] For example, whoever removed Desdemona's Willow Song from 4.3 was careful to cut Emilia's plangent recollection of it at 5.2.245–7.

[2] Honigmann, *Texts*, p. 13.

[3] Ibid, p. 49.

[4] Honigmann, who once thought that Q had been set by three different compositors, now edges towards Charlton Hinman's position (in the introduction to his 1975 facsimile of Q) that Q was set by formes, apparently using only a single set of cases; but Honigmann is understandably puzzled as to why setting by formes would be employed, if not to allow simultaneous work on the text by more than one compositor; and, where Hinman thought that his evidence argued for a single compositor, Honigmann (pp. 45–6) continues to think that more than one compositor may have been involved—a view supported by Jackson in his review (366–7).

must derive from late prompt-books.[1] No mere scribe, he believes, would take it on himself to purge the text of profanity, since that would amount to an interference with the author's meaning. However, since the provisions of the 1606 Act were confined to explicit blasphemy, they can hardly have been responsible for F's removal of such mild expletives as 'tush', 'by this hand', and 'by my troth'; nor would they explain the strange inconsistency whereby F typically replaces Q's 'God' with 'heaven', whilst frequently replacing 'heaven' itself with even weaker exclamations. Moreover, Taylor's argument is further weakened by the fact that F, with its scanty stage directions, looks even less like a theatrically derived text than Q.

In fact, as Honigmann shows, it was by no means uncommon for expurgation to occur in manuscript transcriptions that were never intended for theatrical use (pp. 77–81); and Barbara Mowat has pointed out that such alteration could sometimes be authorial (as in the case of Jonson's 1616 *Works*), or even editorial—as in the case of Q2 *Othello*, which accepts F's replacements for many of Q1's oaths, but allows others to stand, while sometimes making different substitutions of its own.[2] Honigmann, however, believes that certain oddities of spelling and punctuation in F enable him to identify the man responsible—Ralph Crane, a scribe with strong links to the King's Men, whose practice elsewhere suggests that he was well capable of significant interference with an author's text. Honigmann's main evidence lies in F's frequent use of 'swibs' (single words in brackets)—an idiosyncrasy which he is able to show was a characteristic of Crane's punctuation (pp. 59–62, 161–5). Honigmann conjectures that Crane may have been 'a senior figure in the Folio's editorial team' (p. 73), and that, since his transcript of Middleton's *A Game at Chess* shows him willing to take all sorts of liberties with the text, 'eliminating colloquialisms and profanity, changing words and omitting words, lines and longer passages' (p. 75), he may well have sophisticated his copy in other ways too.

Much of Honigmann's argument is, of course, highly speculative, laying him open to criticism not simply on points of detail, but to attack by those like Jowett who continue to advance the case for revision, and by others like Paul Werstine who challenge the basic New Bibliographical assumption behind Honigmann's procedures—namely that it is an editor's business to recover a text as close as possible to the author's final

[1] Gary Taylor, ''Swounds Revisited: Theatrical, Editorial, and Literary Expurgation', in Gary Taylor and John Jowett, *Shakespeare Reshaped 1606–23* (Oxford, 1993), pp. 51–106.

[2] Barbara Mowat, 'Q2 *Othello* and the 1606 "Acte to restraine Abuses of Players"', forthcoming in *Varianten–Variants–Variantes*, ed. Christa Jansohn and Bodo Plachta, *Internationales Jahrbuch für Editionswissenschaften*, 22 (Tübingen, 2005).

intention.[1] Honigmann's pessimistic conclusions about the dependability of F depend partly on the supposition that a significant number of its errors resulted from scribal misreading of an authorial manuscript. But MacDonald Jackson has shown that 'a disproportionate number of F's most clearly identifiable misreadings' (including a majority of those involving confusion of final s, which Honigmann attributes to Shakespeare's scrawled endings) fall within the stints of the inexperienced and often careless Compositor E (see 'Copy' and '*Texts* review'). This, of course, is strong evidence for believing that the copy for F must have been manuscript and not (as Alice Walker believed) an annotated version of Q; but, if the printer received a text much freer of scribal errors than Honigmann imagines, and if the scribe's transcript was as clean and legible as one would expect of a fair copy, it means that the possibility of invisible corruption in other F readings is also much reduced.

Jackson is similarly uneasy about Honigmann's attempt to account for errors that are common to Q and F by proposing that Crane had available a copy of Q which he occasionally consulted when faced by obscurities in the manuscript. This in itself is not improbable; but Jackson finds it hard to believe that, if that were the case, Crane would 'so often prefer his own nonsensical misreading of Shakespeare's hand to the meaningful Shakespearian reading . . . in Q' ('*Texts* review', p. 369). One could, of course, reverse the question and ask why, if his copy were as difficult to decipher as Honigmann argues, Crane would *not* have availed himself of the readily available and relatively inexpensive printed text? The answer must presumably be that Crane had confidence in his text and in his own ability to make sense of it—however odd some of the results may seem to us. How then are the common errors to be explained? Walton's belief that they are few enough to have been generated by accident may be well founded; but his case (Jackson argues) is ultimately sustainable only if we assume that F and Q derive from a single authorial archetype. This is because of another perplexing piece of evidence cited by Walker: namely the distribution of -t and -'d/-ed endings in F and Q. Although all Shakespeare texts make arbitrary use of both forms, quarto texts show a preference for -t where it is phonetically appropriate, whereas the Folio has a marked tendency to substitute modernizing -d endings. These preferences are clear in the two *Othello* texts: F has approximately half Q's number of -t endings, but the fact each of them is anticipated in the earlier text is difficult to explain as pure coincidence. Walton accordingly argued that the -t endings in F, though some had been changed in the process of transmission, were reproduced from a common Shakespearian original. Jackson rightly points out that the pattern is difficult to reconcile with Honigmann's idea that Q and F

[1] See Jowett (above, p. 421 n. 1) and Paul Werstine, review of *The Texts of 'Othello' and Shakespearian Revision*, *SQ* 51 (2000), 240–4.

derive from two different Shakespearian manuscripts, given the notorious irregularity of the poet's spelling (pp. 370–1); yet the distribution of these endings through the F text means that they can hardly be accounted for either by the idea that Crane made occasional use of Q.

Whatever the weaknesses of Honigmann's case, his repudiation of the revision theory seems well founded; and his arguments against it have received powerful support from Scott McMillin's introduction to his edition of the Quarto. McMillin, however, subscribes to an entirely different explanation for the peculiarities of Q, reverting to the idea that it is, after all, a theatre-derived text. His arguments are, in many respects, persuasive; and crucial to them is the evidence of cutting. Coghill argued that Q's omissions were too few to be of any practical value, since he calculated they would reduce the play's running-time of nearly three hours by a mere eight minutes (pp. 177–9). But this is hardly decisive: cutting need not be aimed at a radical reduction in running time, but can be made for a whole variety of practical reasons—some of which may be quite local to the scenes in which they occur;[1] and it is instructive that in the 1997 National Theatre production, for example, the director, Sam Mendes, chose to excise no more than 170 lines—coincidentally almost exactly the same amount of material as seems to have been cut from Q.[2] McMillin, noting the heavy concentration of cuts in Act 4,[3] argues that Q bears every sign

[1] Chambers, for example, suggested that the Willow Song might have been cut simply because at some point the voice of the boy playing Desdemona had broken, making it impossible for him to perform it (ii. 261).

[2] At the RSC in 1985, Terry Hands chose to cut only about a hundred lines; yet the performance struck Michael Ratcliffe as 'quite short' (*Observer*, 29 Sept. 1985). While Coghill's estimate of an eight-minute saving for the Q omissions is conservative, given that they included the Willow Song, it is probably about right for Mendes's cuts, which did not. Andrew Gurr's arguments tend to support Honigmann's belief that the Q cuts are too limited to produce a version 'that was ever performed' (Honigmann, *Texts*, p. 13). Gurr believes that the evidence of surviving 'minimal texts' indicates that plays were normally cut to fit something close to the 'two hours' traffic of the stage' referred to in the *Romeo and Juliet* prologue, and corroborated by a number of contemporary claims (Gurr, pp. 81–2). Whatever one might think about the practice of dramatists like Jonson and Webster, anxious about the literary status of their 'poems', Gurr's thesis fails to explain why a playwright as experienced as Shakespeare, himself an actor, and apparently unconcerned with publication of his plays, would routinely squander his energies producing texts that were much too long for ordinary performance. More recently, however, Lukas Erne has proposed that Shakespeare typically thought in terms of two versions of his plays—a longer 'literary' version designed for reading, and a shorter 'theatrical' text whose extensive cuts were designed to fit it to the customary 'two hours traffic of the stage'. Arguing that 'at 3,055 lines Q1 *Othello* is still substantially too long to have been performed in its entirety', he suggests that it was set up from a transcript of 'an only partly abridged' text, not yet fully prepared for performance—*Shakespeare as Literary Dramatist* (Cambridge, 2003), pp. 183–4.

[3] According to McMillin's calculations, nearly 50 per cent of the cuts are from Act 4, and nearly 67 per cent from Acts 4 and 5 together. Perhaps significantly,

of tactical pruning, aimed at ensuring that the pace of the action was maintained at key points in the play, rightly pointing out even 'eight minutes saved *in the right place* can . . . help' (p. 13). Coghill maintained that the supposed cuts, involving as they did some of the play's most compelling set-pieces, were simply too 'stupid' and 'destructive' to be credible. But (as even Honigmann felt bound to protest) stupid cutting is by no means unheard of in the theatre.[1] Moreover, one might ask: destructive to what, exactly? Coghill thought it inconceivable that anyone would have decided to remove such an exceptional *coup de théâtre* as the Willow Song; but in nineteenth-century productions it was common to do so, and the reason is obvious: however effective Act 4, Scene 3 may be, considered purely on its own theatrical and poetic merits, it does little or nothing after the first ten lines to advance the plot—and this at a point where some directors might feel that the play's drive towards its tragic catastrophe cannot be allowed to slacken.

Thus the case for regarding the F-only passages missing from Q as theatrically-based cuts begins to appear, by comparison with Honigmann's rather strained conjectures, much more plausible. But if this points towards a playhouse origin for Walkley's copy, is it possible to account for the other peculiarities of Q in the same way? McMillin thinks that it is. Once the possibility of significant revision is discarded, the greatest problem for any editor is to explain the innumerable small variations between the two texts. They are far too numerous to be plausibly blamed on a scribe or compositor; and, in the absence of more serious revision, the likelihood that they represent the author's first thoughts is significantly diminished. In some few variants Q seems superior to F, in many more F is clearly superior, whilst in a very substantial number of cases the alternative readings seem (at least as far as meaning is concerned) equally viable. This would be consistent with authorial fiddling, except that in many instances the Q version is marked by disturbance in the verse that (unless we think that Shakespeare was an incompetent metrical craftsman) suggests that corruption may be involved —or perhaps even revision by some other hand.[2] Moreover, it seems telling

more than half are excised from the parts of Desdemona (45 lines) and Emilia (36 lines), suggesting that the boy actors concerned may also have been inadequate to the demands of their parts, especially in the Willow Scene (McMillin, p. 9).

[1] *Texts*, p. 10. Several critics of the 1930 Robeson/Ashcroft *Othello*, for example, complained of the insensitive abbreviation of the text; whilst James Agate, reviewing Michael Horme's heavily pruned production at the Arts Theatre Club in 1931 (*Sunday Times*, 8 Nov. 1931), declared that most of the cutting 'was merely foolish': it included Othello's demented 'I had been happy . . . nothing known' (3.3.347–9), the resonant closing lines of the temptation scene 'Damn her, lewd minx . . . your own for ever' (3.3.475–9), as well as most of Iago's reflections on his own motives, 'That Cassio loves her' (2.1.277–303).

[2] For evidence that 'complex revision' of this sort is not necessarily authorial (as was once assumed) see Rasmussen, pp. 452–3.

that a number of the Q variants can be explained as the result of mishearing. Aural confusion of this sort is often attributed to piracy by an unscrupulous publisher—such as may account for the existence of the so-called 'bad quartos' of plays such as *Romeo and Juliet, Henry V,* and *Hamlet.* Copy in such cases, it is supposed, would have been secured either by shorthand transcription during a performance, or through the memorial efforts of actors disloyal to the company's interests. Piracy hardly seems a probable explanation in this case, however; for, not only does Q lack the gross corruptions normally associated with what the Folio editors called 'stolen and surreptitious copies', but (as we have seen) Walkley seems to have been entirely successful in establishing and sustaining his claim to ownership of the play, even after the publication of F.

If the peculiarities of Q are attributable neither to sharp practice on Walkley's part, nor to scribal or compositorial intervention, nor to Q's preservation of an early authorial version, then it is logical to turn to the theatre for an explanation. Following the propositions advanced by Andrew Gurr, McMillin thinks that two kinds of manuscript would have been available in the theatre: a 'minimal' script embodying the text as currently performed, including cuts and other alterations made in the course of production; and a 'maximal' script, the company's precious 'allowed book', a full-text version, typically in the dramatist's own hand, bearing the licence of the Revels office (Gurr, p. 70).

McMillin's analysis of Q leads him to believe that its origins must lie in a 'minimal' script, prepared for a later revival of the play, and assembled (in whole or in part) by dictation from the actors, after they had mastered their parts. Such a transcription might have become necessary if the players' working copy had been lost or damaged in some way—especially if (as McMillin conjectures) the company's master copy were in the Revels office awaiting re-licensing. McMillin thinks that such 'minimal' copies would have been made quite frequently in the life of a play as popular as *Othello* (Gurr, p. 42), so that Walkley's copy could have been either a theatrical playbook, or a scribal transcript—either one made for a private patron, or one commissioned specifically for the printing shop. Such an origin would help to account for most of the variants in Q, because a manuscript compiled in this way would probably include, as well as theatrical cuts and other changes deliberately made in the course of rehearsal, actors' interpolations (including a significant number of extrametrical 'o, o, o' exclamations), substitutions, accidental omissions, and aural errors made by the scribe in the course of dictation.

McMillin rebuts the usual case against a theatrical provenance for the Q copy, by appealing to evidence from surviving authorial and playhouse manuscripts which suggest that the New Bibliography's long-accepted distinction between the characteristics of foul-papers and 'prompt-books' is no longer sustainable. Indeed, it might be better to abandon the hallowed term 'prompt-book' altogether, in favour of 'playscript', or Andrew Gurr's 'minimal text'—since the idea that the book-holder acted as a 'prompt' in the modern fashion is almost certainly anachronistic. According to Gurr, experience at the newly rebuilt Bankside Globe suggests that the physical structure of the Elizabethan stage and tiring-house would have made prompting impossible; and, significantly, the markings in surviving play-house copies seem concerned only with backstage business, such as noises off and cueing entrances.[1] It has generally been supposed that vague or inaccurate stage directions are incompatible with playhouse copy: according to this theory, directions like '*Exit two or three*' (1.3.121.1), or '*Enter Desdemona . . . and the rest*' (1.3.170.1) would necessarily have been made more precise in a prompt-book, whilst a detail like the mistaken entry of Desdemona at 1.3.48.1 would certainly have been corrected. But it is conceivable, as McMillin argues, that a 'plot' hanging backstage was more important than the prompt-book as a device for regulating entrances. For all of these reasons, a less than perfect text might have been quite adequate to the book-holder's purposes (p. 14). Thus he concludes that, so far from reflecting an authorial manuscript or even a scribal transcript of such an original, Q 'comes from a theatre-script on which Shakespeare may never have left a mark of his own'—an 'acted version of the play' that was preserved in 'a prompt book legitimately prepared once the actors [had] memorized their roles' (pp. 3, 7–8).

The strongest evidence that dictation has played a part in the transmission of a text consists of errors that appear to be the result of mishearing. Probable examples of aural confusion cited by Honigmann and McMillin include: 'Weele' for 'Will' at 1.2.17; 'Ha, with who' for 'Ha[ve] with you' (1.2.53); 'mindes of sulphure' for 'mines of sulphur' at 3.3.331; and to these one can add 'an excellent courtesy' for 'and excellent courtesy' (2.1.172); 'slow unmoving' for 'slow and moving' (4.2.55); and possibly 'offence' for 'of sense' (2.3.258). It is hardly an overwhelming list; and one might expect to find more numerous instances of apparent mishearing in an aurally constructed text. Moreover, it is not impossible, as Honigmann points out, for errors of this kind to be generated by a kind of internal 'mishearing' on the part of a tired compositor.[2] However, McMillin strengthens his case by drawing attention to a number of passages in which

---

[1] See Gurr, pp. 70–3, and his introduction to *The First Quarto of Henry V*, pp. 2–4. The anachronistic implications of the term 'prompt-book' are also discussed by Werstine, ' "Foul Papers" and "Bad" Quartos', pp. 68–9, and William B. Long, ' "A bed for woodstock": A Warning for the Unwary', *Medieval and Renaissance Drama in England*, 2 (1985), 91–118 (esp. p. 93).

[2] Such mishearing, as McMillin concedes, might even have been of a literal kind, if (as seems quite possible) seventeenth-century compositors read their copy aloud (p. 33).

confusions of syntax and punctuation seem to have resulted from aural mistakes (pp. 33–5); and goes on to argue (pp. 37–41) that much of the mislineation in Q—usually attributed to inexpert casting-off, or to lack of clarity in the manuscript—might well have been similarly produced. Line endings can be difficult even for a practised ear to pick, and are especially so in verse with a good deal of enjambement. Furthermore, in many instances the mislineation involves the appearance of half-lines in the middle of long speeches; and McMillin suggests (pp. 38–41) that these are likely to reflect the scribe's effort to anticipate the shared line that (reflecting an increasingly well-established convention) ends most speeches in Q.

There are also a number of passages in which Q prints verse as prose, or vice versa. Sometimes this can be explained as a compositorial device to cover up faulty casting-off on a page which had proved to be either too crowded or too sparse; but this will not explain Q's printing as prose Iago's blank verse at 4.1.41–4. Even more telling is the passage at 2.3.253–6, where Q converts Cassio's prose lament to verse, despite the fact that on this page (F2^{v}) the compositor seems to have been trying to save space:

> Reputation, reputation, I ha lost my reputation:
> I ha lost the immortal part sir of my selfe,
> And what remaines is beastiall, my reputation,
> *Iago*, my reputation.

McMillin attributes this to the scribe's having 'missed the change of mode' and so feeling his way for imaginary pentameters ('Mystery', p. 418). But the listening ear may not have been entirely at fault here: the excision of F's third 'reputation' and following 'O' in the first line, and the insertion of 'sir' in the second, sound very much like adjustments an actor might make when taking advantage of the pentameter beat for mnemonic purposes.[1]

If, then, there are enough signs of possible actors' alterations and aural confusion on the part of a scribe to make it seem likely that dictation played some part in the transmission of the earlier text, how is it possible to account for the fact that Q is nevertheless a demonstrably better text than the 'stolen and surreptitious' playscripts generally thought to have been assembled by this method? Part of the answer may be, as McMillin suggests, that in the case of a transcription carried out for company purposes the entire cast will have been involved, rather than one or two maverick actors. But is it conceivable that the scribe might also have had access to a manuscript with which he could piece out the imperfections of what the actors dictated? If that were so, it is difficult to see why dictation would have been necessary in the first place. There was, however, one kind of theatrical manuscript that could readily have been called on when a new

---

[1] Cf. also Commentary, 1.3.249.

copy of the play was required, but which would have been inconvenient as a source of direct transcription—namely an assemblage of the 'parts' into which the text had to be divided when the play was first cast.[1] Each 'part' consisted of a roll of paper (from which the modern term 'role' derives) on which were written out all of the character's speeches, together with the necessary cue lines. In the Elizabethan repertory system such 'parts' would presumably have belonged to the actors to whom they were first assigned, and (when they retired, left the company, or grew too old for a particular role) would have been passed on to their successors.[2] By their nature, individual 'parts' could not easily be reassembled into a version of the script coherent enough for simple copying, but they would have been available for consultation at any point where the actors' memories were uncertain, or where the scribe might have felt the need to confirm the accuracy of his dictated text. A text produced in this fashion, though still liable to corruption from the actors' imperfect memories, would have made up a generally reliable version of the tragedy, and one that (in the absence of any true equivalent to the modern prompter with his carefully annotated script) was likely to be closer to the play-as-performed than anything the book-keeper would need to possess. Produced originally by careful scribal transcription from the fair copy that served as the players' master-text, 'parts' would presumably have been subject to alteration or revision and marked up for cutting during the process of rehearsal and performance in successive stagings of the play. In the case of the King's Men, this process might well have involved the dramatist's second thoughts, but could also have included interpolations and changes made by the actors themselves.

The notion that printing-house copy might have originated in this way is not entirely fanciful, for it fits the process that Humphrey Moseley had in mind when, in his prefatory epistle for the 1647 folio of Beaumont and Fletcher, he compared the versions in his collection with others in circulation: 'When these comedies and tragedies were presented on the stage, the actors omitted some scenes and passages (with the author's consent) as occasion led them; and when private friends desired a copy, they then (and justly too) transcribed what they acted.'[3] It seems entirely possible, then, that Q represents just such a transcription of 'what they acted'; and, given

---

[1] McMillin himself does not consider the possibility that the 'parts' themselves might have been made available to the scribe, but there seems no reason in principle why this should not have been done—especially when the actors had good reason to require as accurate a transcript as possible.

[2] For a useful discussion of 'parts' and other theatre scripts, see McMillin, 'Mystery', pp. 409–12.

[3] 'The Stationer to the Reader', in Francis Beaumont and John Fletcher, *Comedies and Tragedies* (1647), sig. A4.

that the King's Men had good reasons to resist publication of any Shake-speare play in 1622, Walkley is likely to have acquired his transcript from one of those 'private friends' to whom Moseley refers. The large number of contractions suggested to Greg that this manuscript was compiled at a relatively late date—probably after Shakespeare's death in 1616—although this conjecture sits a little uneasily with the text's unexpurgated oaths and asseverations which might point to a date prior to the Act to Restrain Abuses in 1606.

Clearly the best evidence for Q's supposed playhouse origins (apart from the various kinds of scribal error detected by McMillin) is to be found in textual variants that are readily explained as actors' interpolations, substi-tutions, or omissions—whether deliberate or accidental. The problem here lies in the danger of circularity, since any theory of Q's provenance is itself partly designed to account for the existence of such variants. What, from the perspective of an editor committed to a theory like McMillin's, will look like an actor's substitution in Q, can equally be explained as the product of authorial fiddling; alternatively, an editor persuaded by Honigmann's ideas about Crane's practice might wish to explain the F reading as a result of 'improvement' by an interfering scribe. Inevitably the case for favouring one explanation or the other must usually depend on aesthetic—and therefore subjective—criteria, so that not all of McMillin's examples will seem equally persuasive to every reader. However, there are a number of variants that it is difficult to explain in any other way.

At 3.3.148–54, for example, F reads:

> I do beseech you,
> Though I perchance am vicious in my guesse
> (As I confesse it is my Natures plague
> To spy into Abuses, and of my iealousie
> Shapes faults that are not) *that your wisedome,*
> From one, that so imperfectly conceits,
> Would take no notice . . .

whereas Q prints:

> I doe beseech you,
> Though I perchance am vicious in my ghesse,
> As I confesse it is my natures plague,
> To spy into abuses, and oft my iealousie
> Shapes faults that are not, *I intreate you then,*
> From one that so imperfectly coniects,
> You'd take no notice . . .

It is difficult to imagine the author deliberately complicating Iago's already knotty syntax to produce the F reading; but Q's 'I intreate you then', which effectively begins the sentence anew, reads like exactly the kind of substitution an actor (failing to see how Iago's syntax functions as deliberate mystification) might choose when attempting to make his meaning clear to the audience. By the same token at 2.1.65, Q's rather lame 'Does bear all excellency' seems like an easy actor's substitution for Cassio's characteristically flowery hyperbole in F—'Does tire the ingener'; at 3.3.321 Q's 'Be not you known on't' looks like a probable substitution for F's unusual and somewhat antiquated phrasing 'Be not acknown on't'; 'reputation' at 1.3.272 and 'catch you' at 2.1.167 seem likely to be actors' replacements for F's more striking 'estimation' and 'give [i.e. gyve] thee'. The substitution of the conventional honorific 'his Worship' at 1.1.32 for Iago's witty coinage 'his Moorship' is just the kind of memorial slip an actor might easily make. In addition, the large number of casual variants and small omissions in extended prose passages—notably in Iago's speeches at 2.1.208–75—may reflect actors' difficulties in accurately mastering extended speeches without the mnemonic advantages of verse. Finally, while the stage directions in Q may not be as full and accurate as normally expected of so-called 'prompt-books', there are at least two instances (3.4.93, 102 and 4.2.86, 89) where Q seems to anticipate actors' entries in the fashion associated with such texts. This is important because the proper organization of entrances was the one aspect of performance over which the book-keeper could be expected to exercise some control.

Whilst the theory that Q is (at least in part) a memorially reconstructed text helps to account for the widely accepted superiority of a high proportion of F variants, it will not explain all the differences between the two—especially in those cases where the Q reading seems demonstrably better. Some of these can be ascribed to simple error—to misreading or carelessness on the part of the F scribe or compositor, or to problems with illegible copy. There are, however, a number of variants that are not so easily explained away. At 1.3.342, for example, Q's *acerb* (a rare word, otherwise unrecorded before 1657) not only seems like a characteristically vivid Shakespearian coinage, but apparently derives from a passage in the source, where the Moor's love for Desdemona is described as turning to bitterest hate (*acerbissimo odio*). It must, therefore, be authorial; and it is difficult to imagine why Shakespeare would ever have chosen to substitute F's more pedestrian *bitter*. The latter could, however, be explained as a scribal or compositorial sophistication. The same might apply to F's substitution of *sorry* for *sullen* at 3.4.49. As soon as such possibilities are admitted, then the integrity of F is put in question. This is especially so in light of the fact that someone (not necessarily Shakespeare) was responsible for purging the F version of oaths and profanities—a decision that has significant dramatic consequences, since in Q profanity is such an important feature of Iago's bilious idiolect. As we saw, this bowdlerizing has generally been explained as a response to the 1606 Act to Restrain Abuses; but since the Act applied to performed rather than to printed material, it is difficult to explain why the same process was not applied to Q, the text that bears the clearest signs of playhouse origins—unless (despite its late date) it derives from a very early playscript.[1] This would seem to support Honigmann's argument that the purge was an editorial decision taken by the scribe responsible for the transcript behind F.

If Honigmann is right in identifying this man as Ralph Crane, then the scribe was someone capable of taking considerable liberties with the texts he was transcribing.[2] It is not necessary, however, to subscribe to Honigmann's complex and sometimes rather tenuous arguments about Crane to admit the possibility of non-authorial interference in F; and this might have worrying implications for the status of some passages that are often thought to reflect authorial 'second thoughts' in the later text. There are, for example, a number of passages in the F version of Act 1, Scene 3 that depart from Q in ways that significantly affect our understanding of Desdemona's character. Taken as a group, these F variants suggest systematic alteration by someone troubled at the apparent boldness of Desdemona's behaviour as Q represents it. At 1.3.248–9, where F has Desdemona's heart 'subdued | Even to the *very quality* of my lord', Q has her talk more suggestively of his *utmost pleasure*. The F reading fits better with the following lines ('I saw Othello's visage in his mind . . .'), and it might be tempting to account for the Q variant as a memorial vulgarization, were it not for a more elaborate discrepancy at ll. 258–9, where Othello seeks permission for Desdemona to join him in Cyprus. In Q he begs the Senate to 'let *her will,* | *Haue a free way*', while in F he simply asks them to 'Let *her haue your voice*', thereby excluding the suggestions of both wilfulness and sexual desire in *will* and *free*. Q hardly reads like an easy actor's substitution, and the fact that F's l. 258 is metrically incomplete strongly suggests that some tampering has occurred in the later text—especially in view of the slightly awkward way in which 'Let her haue your voice'

---

[1] It has often been argued that the presence of act divisions in Q must reflect its origins in a version of the play performed after 1610, when (following their acquisition of the indoor Blackfriars theatre as a winter house) the King's Men began to follow the private theatre practice of punctuating their performances with breaks between the acts. The supposed allusion to the heraldry of the new order of baronets, founded in 1612, at 3.4.44–5 would be an insertion supporting a later date. But the allusion is dependent on an unnecessary emendation of this passage; and the act divisions, which are also to be found in all five of the Walkley–Okes King's Men quartos, might have been inserted by someone making a private transcript (as McMillin suggests)—or even by the publisher himself—to conform with the expectations of late Jacobean readers and playgoers.

[2] Honigmann, *Texts*, chaps. 6 and 7.

repeats the syntax of Desdemona's preceding 'Let me go with him' (l. 257). On the other hand, whilst Q is metrically complete, Othello's 'I therefore beg it not' (l. 259) constitutes a rather abrupt switch of direction unless introduced by F's asseveration 'Vouch with me, heaven', so that (as the Q2 editor seems to have felt) neither version may be fully satisfactory. Other metrical disturbances occur in F at ll. 240 and 276: in the first of these F again seems to soften Desdemona's character by omitting her repetition of Othello's defiant 'Nor I'; and in the second F's omission of Desdemona's 'Tonight, my lord?' at l. 276 (though explicable as eye-skip) appears to belong to the same pattern, since it makes Desdemona appear more passively accepting of the men's arrangements, and perhaps (as Honigmann suggests) less openly concerned about losing the pleasure of her wedding night.

F's failure to adjust the metre at these points could suggest (even in a play marked by as much metrical irregularity as *Othello*) that someone lacking Shakespeare's facility with verse was responsible for the alterations. Nevertheless the proximity of another small but significant F variant at l. 159, with quite opposite implications for Desdemona's character, makes it unlikely that they were made by an editorializing scribe. Where Q's Desdemona is so moved by Othello's stories that she gives him 'for [his] pains a world of *sighs*', in F she overwhelms him with 'a world of *kisses*'. Since it seems improbable that Shakespeare would have described such an extravagant expression of emotion as 'this hint', the most plausible explanation is that the scribe's manuscript had become illegible at this point, and that 'kisses' represents his conjectural substitution. It is highly unlikely that anyone responsible for the systematic moderation of Desdemona's behaviour at ll. 240–57 would have arrived at such a conjecture. Accordingly, while F is certainly not the product of wholesale revision, it remains entirely possible that here (and elsewhere) the manuscript from which it derived incorporated the author's 'second thoughts'—even if these were often somewhat hastily executed and inserted.

Conclusion

The one conclusion we can safely draw from this protracted history of debate is that the textual mystery of *Othello* is unlikely ever to be resolved to general satisfaction. Its problems have attracted the attention of the most distinguished minds in the pantheon of bibliographers, textual scholars, and editors; yet none has succeeded in arriving at a watertight and self-consistent theory of the copy for the two texts, and of their relationship to one another. It may well be true that, as Paul Werstine has argued, the quest is chimerical: 'it is only our desire for New-Critical unity', he argues, 'that may have caused us to . . . fix the origins of the early printed versions upon single agents', when the evidence suggests that agency may well have been 'multiple and dispersed'. After all

these texts were open to penetration and alteration not only by Shakespeare himself and by his fellow actors but also by multiple theatrical and extra-theatrical scriveners, by theatrical annotators, adapters and revisers (who might cut or add), by censors, and by compositors and proofreaders.[1]

If early modern play-texts were indeed the fluid, infinitely variable artefacts suggested by much of what we know about contemporary stage practice, then the guiding star by which even the radical Oxford editors set their compass—the author's *'final* intentions'—may be a fiction of the modern imagination. Yet even those editors who are most sceptical about the possibility of establishing an authoritative text of *Othello*, are forced, sooner or later, to make judgements not just about the merits of individual variants but about the relative reliability of F and Q; and, in default of conclusive empirical evidence, such judgements (whatever the scholarly arguments adduced in their support) must often be, in the last analysis, critical—that is to say idealist.[2]

This edition is no different. It proceeds from the assumption that F is in most respects the more reliable of the two texts. Whilst there can be no certainty about the nature of the manuscript copy for either Q or F, the evidence in the former of cutting, memorial corruption, probable actors' substitutions, omissions, and interpolations, together with possible aural mistakes, is sufficient to point to the likelihood of a theatrical origin—perhaps in a scribal transcription of a text assembled, with occasional memorial assistance, from actors' parts. The transcription may well have been made for a private patron, and obtained from him by Walkley. Act divisions were probably inserted as part of the process of preparing the script for a reading public. Of course the fact that some of the peculiarities of Q may be theatrical in origin does not necessarily discredit its variants, since it is quite conceivable that changes introduced in the course of production could have included minor authorial revisions, as well as other alterations made, as Moseley put it, 'with the author's consent'. Nevertheless, as nearly all editors have agreed, F seems to offer the better reading in the case of the great majority of substantive variants; and there are good reasons for supposing that *Othello* was one of the texts that Heminge and Condell had in mind when they claimed to be offering the best available versions of Shakespeare's plays 'cured and perfect of their limbs; and all the rest . . . as he conceived them' (A3). The fact that F includes material

---

[1] Werstine, ' "Foul Papers" and "Bad" Quartos', p. 86.

[2] Thus Werstine and Barbara Mowat chose to use F as the basis for their New Folger edition on the grounds that it is 'the more accurate' of the two. See Barbara A. Mowat and Paul Werstine (eds.), *Othello* (New York, 1993), p. xlv.

that appears to have been cut from Q suggests that the printer's manuscript derived from the players' 'maximal' script, via a scribal copy commissioned expressly for the purpose. Honigmann's researches make it likely that the scribe introduced some changes of his own, notably the purgation of oaths and profanities, but there are no compelling reasons for believing that his interventions otherwise went much beyond the usual liberties with punctuation, spelling, and lineation. Perhaps because of the greater technical difficulties involved in casting off a folio sheet, F is generally more cavalier than Q in its treatment of versification: I have collated 186 instances of mislineation; in 33 of these neither F nor Q appears to lineate correctly, suggesting confusion in the original manuscripts; Q lineates correctly in 99 instances, however—twice as often as F (54).[1]

We have no means of knowing whether or not the King's Men received (as Honigmann argues) more than one autograph manuscript from the dramatist; but since he was a member of the company, it is entirely conceivable that he might have supplied separate copies for use in the theatre and for submission to the Revels office. In that case, some at least of F's variants may have resulted from the kind of authorial fiddling suggested by Honigmann in *The Stability of Shakespeare's Text*. But given the possibility of authorially sanctioned changes in the course of production, and the probable theatrical origins of Q, we cannot rule out the possibility that each text contains variants that represent Shakespeare's second thoughts. Either way Honigmann's insistence that F and Q represent a history of 'textual instability' rather than of systematic revision seems well founded. However, the fact that F not only reproduces a fuller text, but is therefore likely to be the product of a rather less problematic transmission history, makes it appear generally the more reliable of the two. Accordingly this edition, like the majority of its predecessors, takes F as its copy-text, correcting it wherever necessary by reference to Q. Like nearly all modern editors, I have usually restored the expletives and profanities missing from F, and have included all significant Q-only passages, noting in the commentary wherever they do not fit easily into the F text. I have carefully compared both texts with Q2, and have often been guided by its choices, especially when it deliberately abandons its Q1 copy to follow F, or where it departs from both originals. In one or two instances I have also been influenced by the corrections in F2. That said, any serious student of the play should be cautioned that the text of *Othello* printed here (like any other—including Q and F themselves) is to some extent a synthetic creature, shaped by editorial judgements and aesthetic preferences that are inevitably the product of a particular place and time. It is most unlikely to

---

[1] It is probably significant that a disproportionate number (62) of the mislineations peculiar to F occur in the stints of the otherwise more careful Compositor B, suggesting that they may well derive from the copy.

correspond in every detail to any version of the play actually performed in Shakespeare's lifetime—much less to the dramatist's 'final intention' (assuming he ever arrived at such a thing). For that reason the collations should be regarded for what they are—not as a mere scholarly accessory, but as a reservoir of poetic and theatrical possibility.

GIOVANNI BATTISTA GIRALDI CINTHIO: *GLI HECATOMMITHI* THIRD DECADE, SEVENTH NOVELLA
Translated by Bruno Ferraro

Like many collections of novelle, *Giraldi's are placed within a frame narrative, involving a group of friends who debate a number of moral and social issues, using stories to illustrate their arguments. The stories in this decade are linked by their common concern with 'the infidelity of husbands and wives'.*

In the text below, passages of particular relevance to 'Othello' are printed in italics, and references to the play are included in brackets where appropriate.

A Moorish Captain takes a Venetian citizen as his wife; his Ensign accuses her of adultery to her husband; he solicits the Ensign to kill the adulterous man; the Captain kills his wife and is accused by the Ensign. The Moor does not confess but, given clear proof of his guilt, he is banished. And the wicked Ensign, thinking to harm others, brings a miserable death upon himself.

The ladies would have felt great pity for the fate of the Florentine woman had her adultery not made her appear worthy of the severest punishment. They considered that the gentleman's patience had been overly great. They were of the opinion that it would have been very difficult to find any other gentleman who, upon discovering his wife in such a compromising situation, would not have killed both parties. After considering every aspect of the affair, they decided that he had acted in the wisest possible way. Among those who shared these opinions was Curzio, on whom all eyes were turned since he was about to start his story: 'I believe,' said he, 'that neither men nor women can ever escape the passion of love since human nature is so disposed to it that (even against our will) our souls cannot but feel its effects. But nevertheless I think that it is in the power of a virtuous lady, when she is overwhelmed with passion, to prefer to die rather than tarnish herself with that shame from which women must defend themselves if they wish to remain blameless and pure as white ermine. And I believe that those women who, free of the sacred bond of matrimony, offer their bodies to the delights of every man, err less than married women who commit adultery, even if only once. But as this woman suffered a punishment proportionate to her sin, so it *sometimes happens that a faithful, loving woman, guilty of nothing, is put to death by her faithful husband because of the insidious plots hatched by a wicked mind or because of the weakness of one who believes more than he need*—as will be evident in the story which I am about to relate.

There was once in Venice a very valiant Moor who, because he was very brave and had given proof of his courage and prudence in warfare and of his energy and skill [1.3.48, 221–7], *was dear to those lords who in rewarding great deeds surpass those of all other republics in their actions.* [1.1.151–2; 1.2.18] *It happened that a virtuous and extraordinarily beautiful lady, called Disdemona, drawn not by her womanly appetite but by the Moor's mettle, fell in love with him.* [1.3.246–53, 259–63] *The Moor, overcome by her beauty and noble mind, likewise fell in love with her. So favourably did their love proceed that they were joined in marriage, even though her family tried all they could to make her wed somebody else.* [1.2.67–8; 3.3.233–4; 4.2.125] *They lived in harmony and tranquillity while they were in Venice and never exchanged a word that was not sweet and amorous.*

It happened that the Venetian lords made a change in the forces which they are accustomed to maintain in Cyprus and they dispatched the Moor as captain of those soldiers. The Moor, though flattered by the honour (since *such an office is usually given to noble, brave, and faithful men who have had a chance to display their valour* [1.3.221–7]), was rather saddened by the prospect of having to undertake such a long and uncomfortable journey, since he thought that Disdemona might be troubled by it. The Lady, *who had no other love in the world but the Moor* and was delighted at the honour which so noble and powerful a Republic had bestowed upon her husband for his prowess, *could not wait to see her husband set off with his aides and to accompany him soon after* [1.3.246–57]; but she was upset to see that the Moor was worried; and as she did not know the cause of this, one day while they were dining she said to him: 'Why is it, Moor, that despite the great honour which the Lords have bestowed upon you, you are so disconsolate?' The Moor replied to Disdemona: 'The love which I feel for you clouds my happiness at the honour I have received, because I envisage one of two things happening: either I take you with me and expose you to the perils of the sea or, to avoid such discomfort, I leave you behind in Venice. I would feel very sad if I chose the first alternative because I would suffer to see you endure discomfort and be exposed to danger. I would find the second alternative even more unpleasant, since to be separated from you is tantamount to death for me.' After hearing these words, Disdemona said: 'My husband, why do you entertain such thoughts? Why do you let yourself be burdened by these worries? I want to follow you wherever you go, even if it means walking through fire in my chemise, rather than travelling with you by sea in a safe and well-equipped ship, as I am about to do. If there are going to be dangers and exhausting trials, I want to share them with you; *I should consider myself little loved by you if, in order to spare me this sea voyage, you were to leave me in Venice, or if you thought that I would rather stay safely here and not share the same dangers as you.* [1.3.253–7] So I want you to prepare yourself for the trip with all the cheerfulness befitting the rank you hold.' The Moor then threw his arms joyfully around his wife's neck and said to her with an affectionate embrace: 'May the Lord grant us this love for ever, my dear wife.' After a short while, having gathered his apparel and prepared himself for the trip, he embarked upon the ship with his wife and all his train; and having given the order to set sail, he set off on the journey to Cyprus, aided by a very calm sea.

In his company he had a very handsome *Ensign who, however, harboured the most wicked disposition. He was much loved by the Moor, who had no inkling of the Ensign's ugly character. For, although he was very wicked, he concealed the wickedness which he harboured in his heart with lofty words and a proud manner* [1.1.61–5; 3.3.110–11] to such an extent that he appeared to resemble a Hector or an Achilles. This *vile man had also brought with him his wife,* a beautiful and virtuous young woman; because she was Italian, *she was dearly loved by the Moor's wife* and spent a good part of the day with her.

In the same company there was also *a Corporal who was very dear to the Moor. He often visited the Moor at home and dined with him and his wife.* [3.3.71–4, 96–102] Since the Lady knew him to be so well liked by her husband, she gave him proofs of her greatest kindness. This was much appreciated by the Moor. *The wicked Ensign, disregarding the word he had given his wife and the friendship, loyalty, and obligations he owed the Moor, fell passionately in love with Disdemona* [2.1.282] and put all of his efforts into possessing her carnally; but he did not dare show his hand, fearing, should the Moor notice anything, that he would be put to death. He tried, in many ways and as covertly as possible, to make the Lady aware of his love. But the Lady, who thought only of the Moor, did not heed the Ensign or any other man. Everything he tried in order to make her fall in love with him had as little effect as if he hadn't tried anything at all. *It then occurred to him that she might have behaved in this way because she was in love with the Corporal; he therefore decided to get rid of him and devoted all his efforts to that end.* [2.1.229–41, 277–8, 296–8] However, the love he felt for the Lady changed to hatred and he concentrated all his efforts into working out how, once the Corporal had been killed, he could—should he fail to conquer the Lady—prevent the Moor from enjoying her favours. After considering various wicked and treacherous plans, *he decided in the end to accuse her of adultery and to make her husband believe that the culprit was the Corporal.* [1.3.381–7] But, since *he was aware of the special love that the Moor had for his wife* [2.1.279–82] and of his friendship with the Corporal, he realized that, unless he managed to concoct a particularly cunning trick, he wouldn't be able to convince the Moor of either misgiving. For this reason he decided to wait for the right time and place in order to put his wicked plan into action.

Not long afterwards the Moor stripped the Corporal of his rank for having drawn his sword and wounded a soldier while on guard duty. [2.3] *This immensely displeased Disdemona who tried on various occasions to mend the rift between her husband and the Corporal.* [3.3.41–84; 3.4.46–8, 86–93] Whereupon the Moor told the wicked Ensign that his wife importuned him so much on the Corporal's behalf that he feared that he would be compelled to reinstate him. The depraved man, hearing this, decided to put his plan into action and said: *'Maybe Disdemona has a reason to look upon him so favourably.'* [3.3.232–42] *'Why?'* asked the Moor. *'I do not want to come between husband and wife,'* said the Ensign, *'but if you keep your eyes open, you will see for yourself.'* [3.3.200–1] *Despite all the Moor's entreaties, the Ensign was unwilling to do anything further. Nonetheless his words remained such a sharp thorn in the Moor's side that he tormented his brain wondering about their meaning and became very melancholic.* [3.3.111–19, 158, 165, 246–7]

Then one day, as his wife was trying to tone down the Moor's anger towards the Corporal by saying that he should not ignore his thirty years of service and friendship for such a small fault—especially since there had been a perfect reconciliation between the Corporal and the wounded soldier—the Moor burst out into anger and said to her: 'There must be a very good reason, Disdemona, for you to take such a matter to heart and worry about him: it is not as if he were your brother or a kinsman.' The Lady answered in a very polite and humble manner: 'I do not want you to become angry with me; the only reason which moves me to speak is that I am aggrieved to see you deprived of such a good friend as (by your own admission) the Corporal has been to you. He has not committed a grave enough fault to deserve such hatred. But you Moors have such a hot temperament that any little matter moves you to anger and vendetta.'

Further enraged by these words, the Moor answered: 'Anyone who does not believe that may easily have proof of it! I shall take revenge for any wrongs done to me until I am fully satisfied!' The Lady was astounded at these words and, observing her husband's unprecedented fury with her, said humbly: 'I was prompted to speak for a good purpose; but, rather than have you angry, I shall speak no more.' The Moor, surprised by his wife's intervention in favour of the Corporal, guessed that the words uttered by the Ensign were meant to suggest that Disdemona was in love with the Corporal. Deeply disturbed by this realization, the Moor went to talk to the rascal and *tried to convince him to speak more openly about the matter.* [3.3.135–7] *The Ensign, who was eager to bring about the Lady's downfall, at first feigned not to want to say anything that might upset the Moor, but, after pretending to have been persuaded by his entreaties, said: 'I cannot deny that it grieves me greatly to have to tell you something which will cause you enormous distress; but since you urge me to talk, and because of the great regard I have for your honour as my lord, I do not want to fail you or fall short of my duty to you.* [3.3.137–40, 196–9] You must, therefore, know that it is painful for your wife to see the Corporal punished in disgrace with you, for the simple reason that she takes her pleasure with him whenever he comes to your house, *as if she had already grown tired of your blackness.'* [3.3.232–7]

These words penetrated deeply into the Moor's heart; [3.3.261 ff.] but in order to learn more (and to ascertain, because of the suspicion already awoken in his mind, that what the Ensign had said was true) he said with a fierce look: *'I do not know what is holding me back from cutting out that audacious tongue of yours, which has dared to utter such calumny against my wife.'* [2.3.212; 3.3.361–75] Then the Ensign replied: *'Captain, I did not expect any tangible reward for my loving service; but since my duty and care for your honour have carried me as far as they have* [3.3.120, 196–8, 463–9], I tell you that the affair stands exactly as you have just heard. If your Lady, by pretending to love you, has so blinded your eyes that you have not seen what you should have, that does not mean that I am not speaking the truth. The Corporal himself has confessed to me, like someone whose happiness is not complete unless he has confided in someone else.' He then added: 'If I had not feared your wrath, *I would, when he revealed it to me, have given him the punishment he deserved—death.* [1.2.4–5] But since letting you know what concerns you more than anyone else brings me such undeserved reward, *I wish I had kept quiet* [3.3.394] so as not to have fallen into disfavour with you.' Then the Moor, in a most distressed voice, said *'If you do not help me to see with my own eyes what you have just told me, rest assured, I shall make you realize that it would have been better for you to have been born dumb.'* [3.3.361–8] 'When he used to come to your house, it would have been easy to prove,' replied the villain, 'but now that you have driven him away—not for the reason he deserved but for a trivial one—*it will be very difficult for me* [3.3.399]; for although I think that he still takes his pleasure with Disdemona whenever you give him a chance, *he has to act much more cautiously now that he has fallen foul of you than he had to before.* [3.3.420–1] But I do not lose hope of being able to show you what you do not want to believe.' And with these words they parted.

The wretched Moor, as if he had been stabbed by the very sharpest of knives, went home, waiting for the day when the Ensign would be able to show him the thing that would make him miserable for ever. But the Lady's chastity caused the accursed Ensign no less anxiety, for it did not seem possible to find a way to convince the Moor of the truth of what he had falsely told him. After turning over various thoughts in his mind, the rascal came up with a wicked new stratagem. As I have said, the Moor's wife frequently went to visit the Ensign's wife and spent a great part of the day with her; and because the Ensign noticed that the Lady often took with her a *handkerchief—a gift from the Moor—which was most delicately embroidered in the Moorish fashion* [3.3.434–6; 3.4.62–7] *and much treasured by the Lady and the Moor alike* [3.3.310–12, 320–21; 3.4.21–4, 54–74; 5.2.50], *he plotted to steal it from her and set the last deceitful trap.* [3.3.310–18; 5.2.224–8] He had a three-year-old daughter, who was much loved by Disdemona, so he took the child in his arms one day when the wretched Lady had gone to the rascal's house, and placed her in the arms of the Lady, who drew her to her bosom. This deceitful scoundrel, who was very deft with his fingers, very carefully took the handkerchief out of her belt, without her noticing anything, and, in high spirits, took his leave of her. Disdemona, unaware of this, went home and, busy with other thoughts, did not miss the handkerchief. But a few days afterwards, as she was looking for it and could not find it, she became anxious in case the Moor should ask her about it, as he was accustomed to do. *The vicious Ensign, choosing a suitable time, went to the Corporal's house and left the handkerchief* [3.3.323–4; 3.4.175] at the head of the bed. The Corporal noticed nothing until the following day when, as he was rising from bed, he knocked the handkerchief to the ground and put his foot on it. Since he could not fathom how it came to be in his house and recognized it as being Disdemona's, he decided to return it to her. He waited for the Moor to leave the house, went to the back door and knocked. Fortune seemed to have conspired with the Ensign to bring about the death of the unfortunate Lady, since at that very moment the Moor came home. When he heard knocking at the door, he went to the window and angrily demanded 'Who is that knocking?' The Corporal, having heard the Moor's voice and fearing that he might come down to harm him, ran away without uttering a word. The Moor went downstairs, opened the outside door into the street and looked around, but saw no one. *Having gone back into the house, filled with bitter anger, he asked his wife who had been knocking at the door. The Lady answered truthfully that she did not know.* [3.3.36–40] But the Moor replied 'It looked to me like the Corporal.' The Lady responded that she did not know whether it was him or somebody else.

The Moor checked his rage, despite the fact that he was fuming. He decided not to act until he had first talked to the Ensign, whom he sought out straight away, told him what had happened, and entreated him to find out from the Corporal all he could about the incident. The Ensign, rejoicing at this latest turn of events, promised he would do so. *He talked to the Corporal one day when the Moor was in a place where he could see them conversing. While talking to the Corporal about every other matter except that concerning the Lady, the Ensign burst into loud laughter and, feigning great surprise, moved his head and gesticulated as if he were listening to extraordinary things.* [4.1.89–163] The moment the Moor saw them part company, he went to the Ensign to learn what they had said to each other. The Ensign, after making the Moor beg him for a while, finally said: 'He concealed nothing from me, telling me that he took his pleasure with your wife every time your absence gave him the chance and saying that the last time they were together she gave him the handkerchief that you gave her as a present when you married her.' The Moor thanked the Ensign and *thought that if the Lady did not any longer have the handkerchief, then it was obvious that things must be just as the Ensign said.* [3.3.440–2] *One day after dinner, therefore, while discussing various matters with his wife, he asked her for the handkerchief. The poor woman, who had greatly feared this, grew red in the face at the request and, to conceal her blushing (which, however, did not escape the Moor's eyes), she ran to the chest pretending to look for it. After searching for a while, she said 'I don't know why I can't find it; perhaps you have had it.' The Moor replied: 'If I had it, why would I ask you for it? You can look for it at your own leisure some other time.'* [3.4.30–95]

Once he had left, he began thinking of how he might murder his wife and the Corporal too in such a way that he wouldn't be accused of it [4.1.164–86]; and since he thought about this day and night, *the Lady could not help noticing that his attitude towards her had changed. She enquired about this several times:* 'What is it that is troubling you and has altered you from the most cheerful person in the world into the most melancholic of men?' [3.4.118–21; 4.2.42–3, 99–102] The Moor tried to answer his wife in several ways, but none of them satisfied her; and although she knew that no action of hers could have upset the Moor to such an extent, she nevertheless thought that, because of their inordinate lovemaking in the past, he might have grown bored with her. Sometimes she would tell the Ensign's wife, *'I do not know what to make of the Moor. He used to be all-loving towards me, but in the last few days he has changed.* [3.4.120–1] I very much fear that I shall be held up as an example to young girls who wish to marry against their family's wishes, and to Italian girls so that they may *learn not to choose a man whom nature, God and manner of life make so different from us.* [3.3.233–7] Since I know that he is such a good friend of your husband's and opens his heart to him, I beg you, if you have heard anything from him which you can tell me, to come to my help.' She uttered these words in a rush, weeping as she spoke. The Ensign's wife, who was au fait with everything (that is, with the way in which her husband had tried to use her as an instrument in his plan to kill the Lady), but who had never wanted to become part of it, did not wish to say anything for fear of her husband. She said only: 'Be careful not to arouse your husband's suspicion, and try as hard as you can to make him recognise the love and loyalty you feel for him.' 'That is exactly what I do, but to no avail,' answered the Lady.

In the meantime *the Moor tried to find confirmation for what he actually did not want to uncover; he begged the Ensign to find a way for him to see the hand-*

kerchief in the Corporal's possession. *Although this was a difficult undertaking for the villain, he nevertheless promised that he would do his best to provide such proof.* [3.3.366–8, 399–410] *The Corporal kept a woman in his household who made the most beautiful embroidery on lawn fabric; when she saw the handkerchief and learned that it belonged to the Moor's wife, she set out to make one just like it before it was to be returned.* [3.4.183–6] The Ensign noticed that she was doing this while sitting near a window and that she could be seen by anyone going past in the street. *So he arranged for the Moor to see this, and as a result the latter was fully convinced that this most virtuous woman was an adulteress.* [4.1.70–171] *Accordingly he arranged with the Ensign to have her and the Corporal killed, and they discussed the ways in which this might be done. The Moor implored him to kill the Corporal personally, promising that he would be eternally grateful to him.* [4.1.164–76, 192–205] The Ensign, claiming that this would be a very difficult and dangerous task to carry out because the Corporal was skilful and courageous, initially refused; but after the Moor had begged him insistently and offered him a large sum of money, he extracted a promise from the Ensign that he would tempt Fortune.

One dark night, soon after they had taken this decision, as the Corporal was leaving the house of a whore with whom he used to take his pleasure, he was accosted by the Ensign, sword in hand; first aiming a blow at his legs to knock him down, he cut through the poor man's right thigh making him fall to the ground, and then set upon him to finish him off. But the Corporal was courageous and used to bloody deeds and to facing death; he drew his sword and, despite being wounded on the legs, set about defending himself and shouted at the top of his voice 'I am being murdered!' When the Ensign, who knew that there were soldiers quartered nearby, heard people come running, he took to his heels so that he would not be caught; and then, turning back, he pretended he was running to where the commotion was taking place. He mingled with the others and, noticing that the Corporal's leg had been cut off, he thought that even if he wasn't dead, he would soon die of this blow. Despite the fact that he was very happy at this outcome, he commiserated with the Corporal as if he were his own brother. [4.2.226–41; 5.1.1–73] Next morning the whole city knew about the incident, which also reached Disdemona's ears; whereupon, since she was good-natured and did not imagine that harm would come of it, she showed great sorrow for what had happened. The Moor drew some very negative conclusions from this. He went to see the Ensign and said to him: 'You know that my fool of a wife is so distressed about what has happened to the Corporal that she is going crazy!' To which the Ensign answered: 'What else could you expect, since he is her very soul?' To which the Moor retorted: 'The very soul, eh? I shall tear her soul from her body; and I would not consider myself a man unless I were to rid the world of this wicked woman.' As *they were discussing whether the Lady should be poisoned or stabbed to death* [4.1.194–202], and were unable to agree on any method, the Ensign said: 'I have thought of something which would make you happy and not attract anybody's suspicion. Here is the plan: the house in which you live is very old and the ceiling of your bedroom has many cracks; I intend beating Disdemona to death with a stocking filled with sand—without, however, leaving any mark on her body. As soon as she is dead, we shall make part of the ceiling collapse; and we shall smash the Lady's skull, making it look as if it was a beam from the ceiling which did it; this way no one will suspect you, as every one will think she died as a result of the accident.'

The Moor appreciated this wicked advice [4.1.202–5] and waited for the appropriate moment. One night, having previously hidden the Ensign in a closet which opened on to the bedroom, he was in bed with her, when the Ensign, as per the agreed signal, made a big commotion in the closet. Drawing his wife's attention to it, the Moor asked: 'Did you hear that noise?' And she replied: 'Yes, I heard it.' 'Get up,' the Moor went on. 'Go and see what it is all about.' The wretched Disdemona got out of bed and, as soon as she approached the closet, the Ensign jumped out and, being strong and muscular, hit her with the stocking which he had ready, giving her such a blow in the middle of her back that she collapsed, with the breath knocked out of her. But with the little voice she still had, she called out to the Moor for help; and, as he got out of the bed, he said to her: 'Most vicious of women, this is the reward for your unchastity. This is how those women should be treated who, pretending to love their husbands, put cuckold's horns on their heads.' Hearing this, the wretched woman, feeling that she was about to die (since the Ensign had inflicted another blow on her) *declared that she called on divine justice as a witness to her fidelity, since worldly justice was failing her. While invoking God's help she was struck for the third time* [5.2.33–4, 59–63, 85–6, 123] and was finished off by the wicked Ensign. After placing her in bed and breaking her skull, the Moor and the Ensign caused the ceiling to collapse, just as they had planned, and the Moor started crying for help, shouting that the house was falling down. *The neighbours soon arrived and found the bed with the Lady dead* [5.2.121, 183] under the rafters. Since she had led a good life, her death was lamented by one and all. The next day Disdemona was buried amid the universal mourning of the populace. But God, the just observer of men's souls, did not want such an iniquitous deed to go without the punishment it deserved. For this reason the Moor, *who had loved the Lady more than his own eyes* [3.3.91–3], *started mourning her death. He missed her so badly that he began to lose his mind* [5.2.99–103, 270–80], wandering all over the house and thinking that the Ensign had been the cause of his losing with his wife all the joy of his life and the very reason for his existence. *As a result he started to hate the Ensign so much that he could not bear even looking at him* [5.2.299–300]; and, if he had not feared the inviolable justice of the Ven-

etian Lords, *he would have surely killed him*. [5.2.285] But since he could not
safely do this, he relieved him of his post and did not want him any longer
in his company. As a result, such animosity developed between the two
that no one could imagine any deeper or more bitter feud. For this reason
the Ensign, the most wicked of criminals, turned all his thoughts to injur-
ing the Moor. When he found out that the Corporal had recovered and that
he was managing with a wooden leg instead of the one which had been
chopped off, he said to him: 'The time has come for you to avenge the loss
of your leg. The moment you are ready to come to Venice with me, I shall
tell you who was responsible for this crime (since I do not dare to reveal it
here for a number of reasons) and I'll testify on your behalf at the trial.'
The Corporal, who thought himself greatly wronged and did not know the
reason, thanked the Ensign and went to Venice with him. Once they got
there the Ensign told him that the Moor had been responsible for the loss of
his leg because he had convinced himself that he was Disdemona's lover;
and for this very reason, he was also the one who had killed her and had
then spread the rumour that she was killed by the collapsed ceiling. After
hearing this, the Corporal denounced the Moor to the Signoria both for the
severing of his leg and for the death of the Lady. He called as his witness
the Ensign who corroborated both pieces of information and said that the
Moor had confided everything in him, that he had tried to convince him to
carry out both crimes, and that, after he had killed his wife because of the
bestial jealousy that had bred in his mind, he had told him about the way
in which he had killed her. The Venetian lords, after learning of the cruelty with which the *Barbarian* [1.1.111; 1.3.349] had treated one of their
own citizens, *gave orders for him to be arrested in Cyprus and to be taken to
Venice, where they tortured him severely in order to squeeze the truth out of
him*. [Cf. Iago, 5.2.331–6] But the Moor was strong-willed and *resisted all
the tortures and denied everything so firmly that nothing could be extracted from
him*. [Cf. Iago, 5.2.301–4] Although by his steadfastness he escaped death,
after many days in prison, he was condemned to banishment for life; and
eventually he was killed, as he deserved, by the Lady's relatives. The Ensign
returned to his own country; and, as was his inveterate practice, he laid
accusations against one of his companions, saying that the latter had tried
to engage him to murder one of his enemies, who was a gentleman. For
this reason the man was arrested and tortured; since he denied that what
the accuser had said was true, *the Ensign too was arrested and tortured*
[5.2.301–4, 331–4, 368] so that they could weigh up the two conflicting
stories. He was tortured so badly that his intestines were ruptured. After
leaving the prison and going home, he soon died of his injuries; and thus
God avenged Disdemona's innocence. After his death the Ensign's wife,
who was aware of what had happened, told the whole story, just as I have
related it to you.'

The Third Decade, Story 8

. . . *It appeared astonishing to everybody that a human heart could harbour such malice* [5.2.299–300]; and the case of the unfortunate Lady drew tears from everyone. Remembering the unfortunate name that she had been given by her father, the party decided that, since the name is the first gift which a father bestows upon his son, he should give him a great-sounding and fortunate name as if he wanted to wish him wealth and greatness. *The Moor was no less blamed for being so gullible in his beliefs* [5.2.161–2, 224, 232], while everyone praised the Lord from whom the wicked had received their well-deserved punishment.

THE MUSIC IN THE PLAY
Linda Phyllis Austern

Othello is neither as musical as Shakespeare's late romances, nor as simply reliant on the realistic musics of state and battlefield as the history plays. Musically speaking, it is probably best known for the 'willow song' assigned to Desdemona in Act 4, Scene 3, whose oldest complete version has become one of the most performed extant pieces of early modern English music (see Discography below), and whose hauntingly lyrical melody remains memorable even apart from its theatrical context. *Othello* is a work in which each musical scene, and each musical piece, is highly significant to the unfolding of the narrative, or to the establishment of setting, or to revelation of the psychological states and motivation of the characters—or to some combination of these. Even the most seemingly casual piece of music can serve to establish a sense of social reality and location on the relatively bare Elizabethan stage.[1]

(i) *Trumpet Signals*

Trumpets at 2.1.174.1, 4.1.205, and 4.2.169.1 announce the arrival of important personages or summon guests to a ceremonial meal, as they would have done in the world outside the theatre. Each of these will have consisted of a fairly simple, primarily rhythmic call, for the early modern trumpet was more limited in its range and melodic capacities than its descendants. Each, however, must also be distinctive; for not only is Iago able to identify Othello by the sound of his trumpet before he enters (2.1.174.1), but to speculate that an unfamiliar trumpet heralds 'something from Venice' (4.1.206). The final use of the instrument is doubtless

---

[1] A comprehensive listing of all extant musical settings from performances of *Othello* from the seventeenth century to the late twentieth is included in Brian N. S. Gooch and David Thatcher (eds.), *A Shakespeare Music Catalogue*, 6 vols. (Oxford, 1991), ii. 1200–82. For the use of music in the Shakespearian theatre, including *Othello*, see Ross W. Duffin, *Shakespeare's Songbook* (New York, 2004); Richmond Noble, *Shakespeare's Use of Song, with the Text of the Principal Songs* (Oxford, 1923); F. W. Sternfeld, *Music in Shakespearean Tragedy* (London and New York, 1963); Peter J. Seng, *The Vocal Songs in the Plays of Shakespeare: a Critical Study* (Cambridge, Mass., 1967); John H. Long, *Shakespeare's Use of Music: the Histories and Tragedies* (Gainesville, Fla., 1971); John S. Manifold, *The Music in English Drama from Shakespeare to Purcell* (1956). The settings printed below are adapted from Sternfeld (1, 3, 5) and Long (2, 4).

the most intricate, for the dialogue indicates that multiple trumpets— 'these instruments'—perform (4.2.170). They do not herald the imminent arrival of military or political officials, but instead call invitees to a formal state supper, the sort of occasion famous for the elaborate use of music.

(ii) **Drinking song fragments** (Act 2, Scene 3)

The first fully musical episode in the play occurs in Act 2, Scene 3, in which Iago sings fragments of two songs as part of his drunken revelry with Cassio and Montano. These belong to the stylistically simple repertoire of ballads and tavern songs, a body of orally circulating works condemned for their desultory style of performance and negative moral effect by many of the same Elizabethan writers who censured stage plays. Music for both songs has been reconstructed several times. The original tune for the first, 'And let me the cannikin clink', has yet to come to light; it has been suggested that the song may have been specially written for the play in the style of the era's drinking songs, but the text is simple and metrical enough to be fitted to several extant popular tunes. Two are given here.

Ex. 1

Ex. 2

The second, 'King Stephen was a worthy peer', is the seventh of eight stanzas from the ballad 'Take Thy Old Cloak About Thee', whose text was collected as part of Thomas Percy's *Reliques of Ancient English Poetry* (1765), and is probably originally from Scotland or the north of England. The same section of the same song is alluded to in *The Tempest* (4.1.221–2), when Trinculo says 'O King Stefano, O peer! O worthy Stefano, look what a wardrobe here is for thee!', which attests to its popularity. The tune (or at least a later variant that works with the text Shakespeare uses) was also collected in Percy's era, and is given here.

Ex. 3

Apart from contributing to the social realism of the carousal scene, and altering the audience's sense of the passage of time, these songs help to shape the relationship between Iago and Cassio, suggesting that Iago is (no doubt deliberately) drinking less than his companions—since, after all, one cannot simultaneously drink and sing. Moreover, since many of Shakespeare's contemporaries considered music itself to be a potentially dangerous intoxicant, the songs may have helped the audience to sense the increasing 'rouse' that Cassio begins to feel even before Iago calls for wine by way of preface to his first song.

(iii) **Cassio's aubade and other musical references** (Act 3, Scene 1)

Act 3 opens with Cassio's misguided morning serenade to Othello and Desdemona. This scene, often omitted in performance, is predicated as much on an understanding of the multi-level early modern meanings of music as on the evidently opposed social customs of the serenade and the charivari.[1] Dialogue makes clear that the music in this scene is performed on wind instruments by hired professional musicians. The Clown's bawdy puns draw attention to the phallic shape and nasal timbre of the instruments. Early modern town bands, known in England as waits, performed predominantly on such loud 'outdoor' instruments as shawms or hautbois

---

[1] See Bristol, 'Charivari'.

(hoboys), which had a nasal resonance not unlike the modern oboe. Thus the band available to Cassio is entirely in keeping with cultural custom; presumably, they are the municipal waits of Shakespeare's imagined Cyprus, paid for a one-off job in the manner of their English counterparts. However, the Clown's punning references to a hanging tail and to a bag imply that at least one of the instruments may be a more rustic bagpipe, age-old butt of phallus-and-flatulence jokes across literary and visual media, and an equally obvious and venerable signifier of male impotence. The original music probably belonged to the classic and widespread morning genre of the aubade (or hunts-up); one such example, from a manuscript of *c.*1588–1609 in the Folger Shakespeare Library (Folger MS 1610.1), is given here:

Ex. 4

Although the Folger arrangement is for lute, the piece is readily playable by up to five musicians; and in this case a bagpipe drone should probably be added to three or four shawms.

Even more important than audible music in this scene are the references to 'music that may not be heard' and to Othello's lack of interest in musical art. In addition to the contrast between the sounding music meant to induce love and the silent music of love itself, any mention of unheard music would have suggested the perfect, eternal music of the spheres—the ultimate concord of true harmony so conspicuously absent from the world of this play whose clumsy musicians cannot evoke it. At the same time, the Clown's statement that 'to hear music the general does not greatly care' resonates both with Castiglione's portrait of the early modern professional soldier as one who eschews music as effeminate artifice, and with Lorenzo's chilling depiction of 'The man that hath no music in himself' in *The Merchant of Venice* (5.1.83–8).[1] The idea that unmusical individuals were untrustworthy, savage, and possessed of 'affections dark as Erebus' was so widespread in Shakespeare's England that the earliest full-length English-language treatise on music (1586) prominently cites Polydore Virgil's statement that 'if I made any one which cannot brook or fancy music, surely I erred and made a monster'.[2] Thus Othello's indifference to music, especially when taken in conjunction with his own description of Desdemona as 'an admirable musician [who] will sing the savageness out of a bear' (4.1.182–3), may hint at one of the underlying causes of their tragedy.

(iv) The Willow Song (4.3.37–52)

It is, in fact, that admirable musician's performance that stands at the heart of the most famous musical scene of the play: the 'willow song' of Act 4, Scene 3. No song from any of Shakespeare's works has attracted

[1] See Baldassare Castiglione, *The Courtyer*, trans. Thomas Hoby (1561), sig. Jii.
[2] *The Praise of Musicke* (Oxford, 1586), p. 74.

more attention or inspired more composers. New settings of it have been written by many from the late seventeenth century onwards, among them Pelham Humphrey, Jean-Jacques Rousseau, Arthur Sullivan, Percy Grainger, and Ralph Vaughan Williams, as well as Giuseppe Verdi in his magnificent operatic version of Shakespeare's play.

During the sixteenth century and early seventeenth there were so many English laments for lost love with refrains evoking the willow tree as to constitute a distinct genre, of which Shakespeare clearly took advantage in *Othello*—though his is the only known example in which the lamenting lover is a woman. There is no evidence that any previously existing song-text or music served as a direct model for the one assigned to Desdemona, but Shakespeare's lyric may have subsequently inspired a number of broadsides. Some willow songs were disseminated as poetry without musical notes, while others were preserved in versions for instruments alone with only a 'willow' title. Several early modern English music manuscripts include willow songs that music scholars have modified with varying degrees of success to fit Shakespeare's lyrics. However, only one roughly contemporary tune fits Shakespeare's text with minimal alteration—'The poore soule sate sighing' from British Library MS Add. 15117 (fol. 18).[1] This musical miscellany, dating from *c*.1614 to 1616, preserves a significant quantity of music from the final quarter of the sixteenth century as well as newer pieces, including a number of other songs used in the Elizabethan and Jacobean theatre; and, since the nineteenth century, its willow song setting has been the one most often considered 'authentic', becoming traditional in modern productions with period music, as well as on recordings of Shakespearian songs. The first stanza, refrain, and several other lines of 'The poore soule' show marked resemblances to Desdemona's lyric (albeit using the conventional masculine narrative voice); however, this may simply reflect the fact that the two versions (as well as the famous broadsides later included in the Percy and Roxburghe ballad collections) made use of a common (lost) source. Shakespeare's version, with the music from the British Library manuscript, follows:

Ex. 5

```
The    poor   soul  sat   sigh - ing              by a
The    fresh  streams ran   by   her,              and
Let    no - bo - dy   blame him,              his
I      call'd my    love  'false love';              but
```

---

[1] Available in facsimile as the first manuscript in Elise Bickford Jorgens (ed.), *English Song 1600–1675: Facsimiles of Twenty-Six Manuscripts* (New York, 1986), vol. i.

The dramaturgical effect of this song is carefully calculated: not only does the music itself contrast in every way possible with that used elsewhere in the play, but the circumstances of its performance help to emphasize Desdemona's chaste propriety. Othello has already spoken of her excellence as a musician, suggesting how intensely the exquisite sound of her voice, distracted though she is, can be expected to move the audience. At the same time, by linking her musicianship to her skill with the needle (4.1.182–3), he places it firmly in the world of feminine decorum. According to early modern English social codes, public musical performance of any sort by a woman was a sign of whoredom; and even to play or sing in front of a man in private was perceived as an invitation to dangerous erotic pleasure. In marriage, however, it could stand for the harmonious bond between husband and wife. Thus Desdemona, the 'admirable musician', whose music, like that of the unfortunate Orpheus, can tame a savage beast, restricts her skill to the culturally appropriate confines of feminine domesticity; yet even in this innocent display of musical propriety, the melancholy tone of Desdemona's song seems heavy with foreknowledge of her own death.

Select Discography

'A Distant Mirror—Shakespeare's Music'
Delos DDD
Performers: The Folger Consort
Music from *Othello*: 'Willow Song'

'As You Like It—Shakespeare in Music'
Sony Classical NPR SMK 61874
Performers: various
Music from *Othello*: 'Othello: The Willow Song'

'The English Lute Song'
Dorian DOR-90109
Performers: Julianne Baird (soprano) and Ronn McFarlane (lute)
Music from *Othello*: 'The Willow Song'

'Music of Shakespeare'
Channel Classics CCS 11497
Performers: Alba Musica Kyo
Music from *Othello*: 'Willow Song'

'Shakespeare's Music'
Dorian DOR-90017
Performers: various (this is a compilation CD from other Dorian recordings)
Music from *Othello*: 'The Willow Song'

'Shakespeare's Musick: Songs & Dances from Shakespeare's Plays'
Philips 446 687–2
Performers: Musicians of the Globe (directed by Philip Pickett)
Music from *Othello*: 'The Poor Soul Sat Sighing (The Willow Song)'

'Shakespeare Songs'
Harmonia Mundi Musique d'abord HMA 195202
Performers: Alfred Deller (counter-tenor) and Desmond Dupré (lute)
Music from *Othello*: 'Willow Song'

'Songs & Dances from Shakespeare'
Saydisc CD-SDL 409
Performers: The Broadside Band (directed by Jeremy Barlow)
Music from *Othello*: 'The Poor Soul Sat Sighing (The Willow Song)'

ALTERATIONS TO LINEATION

MISLINEATION is common in both F and Q. For a discussion of the problems
and principles involved in realigning improperly set verse, see Appendix D
in my edition of *Anthony and Cleopatra* (Oxford, 1994), pp. 370–4. The
most comprehensive recent treatment of Shakespeare's versification is
George T. Wright, *Shakespeare's Metrical Art* (Berkeley, Calif., 1988); but
lineation issues are best explored in Paul Werstine's 'Line Division in
Shakespeare's Verse: An Editorial Problem', *Analytical and Enumerative
Bibliography* 8 (1984), 73–125.

1.1. 4–7	'Sblood . . . city] This edition; F *divides after* 'dream', 'abhor me', 'told'st me', 'hate', 'despise me', *but probably assumes that* 'Of . . . told'st me' *and* 'Thou . . . Despise me' *constitute shared lines*; Q *divides after* 'hear me', 'abhor me', 'hate'; STEEVENS *and many eds. divide after* 'hear me', 'matter', 'Abhor me', 'hate'
16–17	I have . . . he] POPE; *as one line* F, Q
34	Why . . . service] ROWE; F, Q *divide after* 'remedy'
37	Stood . . . yourself] F; Q *divides after* 'first'
49–52	Whip . . . lords] F; Q *divides after* 'knaves', 'forms', 'hearts', 'throwing'
53–4	Do well . . . soul] ROWE; F, Q *divide after* 'them', 'coats', 'homage'
79	Awake . . . thieves!] F; Q *divides after* 'Brabantio'
82–3	What summons . . . there] Q; F *divides after* 'terrible'
91–2	Or . . . say] F; *as one line* Q
105–6	What . . . grange] Q; F *divides after* 'robbing'
156–7	Which . . . search] F; Q *divides after* 'surely'
168	O . . . blood] Q; F *divides after* 'out'
1.2. 8–9	Against . . . have] POPE; *as one line* F, Q
34	The servants . . . lieutenant] Q; F *divides after* 'Duke[s]'
59–61	Keep . . . weapons] Q; *as prose* F
62	O . . . daughter] Q; F *divides after* 'thief'
1.3. 18–19	This . . . pageant] F; Q *divides after* 'reason'
47	Write . . . dispatch] Q; F *divides after* 'us'
92	Of . . . charms] Q; F *divides after* 'love'
95–6	A . . . motion] F, Q2; Q1 *divides after* 'spirit'

122	Ensign . . . place] Q; F *divides after* 'them'
198	Let . . . sentence] Q; F *divides after* 'sentence'
366–70	Where . . . land] This edition; *as prose* F, Q
390–1	And . . . are] F; *as one line* Q
2.1. 22–3	That . . . sufferance] F; Q1 *divides after* 'seen'; Q2 *divides after* 'halts', 'Venice'
26–7	The ship . . . Cassio] Q; *as one line* F
31	I . . . governor] Q; F *divides after* 'on't'
37	Like . . . ho!] F; Q *divides after* 'soldier'
74	She . . . captain] Q; F *divides after* 'of'
81	Give . . . spirits] F; Q *divides after* 'fire'
91	O . . . company] *as one line* Q; F *divides after* 'feare'
109–13	Come . . . beds] *as verse* Q; *as prose* F
112–13	Players . . . beds] This edition; *as one line* Q
117	What . . . praise me] *as one line* F; Q *divides after* 'of me'
120	Come . . . harbour] *as one line* Q; F *divides after* 'assay'
125–8	I . . . delivered] *as verse* Q; *as prose* F
131	Well . . . witty] Q; F *divides after* 'praised'
137–8	These . . . foolish] *as prose* F; Q *divides after* 'alehouse', 'her'
159–64	O . . . scholar] *as prose* F; Q *divides after* 'conclusion', 'husband', 'liberal', 'counsellor', 'him'
175	The . . . trumpet] *as verse* F, Q2; *as prose* Q1
179	To . . . joy] *as one line* Q; F *divides after* 'me'
189	But . . . increase] *as one line* Q; F *divides after* 'loves'
194–6	O . . . am] *as verse* Q; *as prose* F; HONIGMANN *begins new line with* 'O', *divides after* 'down', 'honest'
197	News . . . drowned] Q; F *divides after* 'done'
2.3. 21–4	What . . . love] *as prose* Q; F *divides after* 'has', 'provocation', 'eye', 'modest', 'speaks'
47	As . . . Roderigo] Q; F *divides after* 'dog'
55	And . . . drunkards] Q; F *divides after* 'too'
57	That . . . come] F; Q *divides after* 'isle'
61–2	Good . . . ho] *as verse* Q; *as prose* F
65–6	A . . . span] CAPELL; *as one line* F, Q
122–3	It . . . it] F; *as one line* Q
132–3	It . . . Moor] F; *as one line* Q
142–4	Nay . . . mazard] *as prose* Q; F *divides after* 'lieutenant', 'hand', 'sir'
155–6	'Swounds, I . . . dies] *as one line* F, Q (F *omits* ' 'Swounds', Q *omits* 'He dies')
243–5	All's . . . off] *as* F, Q; POPE *divides after* 'bed', 'surgeon', 'off'; SANDERS (*treating* 'Lead him off' *as a direction*) *divides after* 'bed', 'surgeon'

253–6	Reputation . . . reputation] *as prose* F; Q *divides after* 'lost my reputation', 'myself', 'my reputation', 'My reputation'
321	And . . . villain] Q; F *divides after* 'then'
324	To . . . easy] Q; F *divides after* 'again'
347	That . . . Roderigo] *as one line* POPE; F, Q *divide after* 'all'
367	Nay . . . done] *as one line* Q; F *divides after* 'gone'
369–70	I'll . . . apart] Q; *as one line* F
3.1. 22	No . . . you] *as prose* Q; F *divides after* 'friend'
31–5	Why . . . access] CAPELL; F *divides after* 'parted', 'wife', 'Desdemona'; Q *divides after* 'parted', 'her', 'Desdemona'; SANDERS *divides after* 'parted', 'Iago', 'her', 'Desdemona'; HONIGMANN *divides after* 'parted', 'in', 'will', 'me'
35–6	Procure . . . presently] F, Q; *as one line* RIDLEY; 'Some . . . presently' *as one line* HONIGMANN
46–7	And great . . . loves you] F, Q; HONIGMANN *divides after* 'affinity', 'but'
3.3. 3	Good . . . husband] Q; F *divides after* 'do'
96–7	Did . . . love] *as one line* Q; F *divides after* 'Cassio'
97–8	He . . . ask] F; *as one line* Q
105–6	Honest . . . I honest] F; *as one line* Q
161	Who . . . nothing] *as one line* Q; F *divides after* 'trash'
206	They . . . conscience] *as one line* Q; F *divides after* 'husbands'
214	He . . . blame] *as one line* Q; F *divides after* 'witchcraft'
220	Comes . . . moved] *as one line* Q; F *divides after* 'love'
227	Which . . . friend] *as one line* Q; F *divides after* 'not'
230	Long . . . think so] *as one line* Q; F *divides after* 'she so'
232	Ay . . . you] *as one line* Q; F *divides after* 'point'
242–4	Farewell . . . Iago] ROWE; F *divides after* 'farewell', 'know more', 'observe'; Q *divides after* 'if more', 'set on'
246	Why . . . doubtless] *as one line* Q; F *divides after* 'marry'
285–6	Why . . . well] F; *as one line* Q
305	You . . . common thing] *as one line* Q (*omits* 'You have'); F *divides after* 'me'
317–18	What . . . filch it] Q1; *as prose* F; Q2 *divides after* 'with it'; 'What . . . earnest' *as one line* THEOBALD *and many eds.*
321–2	Be . . . me] F; *as one line* Q
374–5	For . . . that] F; *as one line* Q
416–19	And . . . Cassio] F; Q *divides after* 'sleep', 'soul', 'affairs'
425–7	That . . . Moor] *as* Q; F *divides after* 'thigh', 'fate'
446	All . . . gone] *as one line* F, Q; POPE *divides after* 'heaven'
453	Never . . . Sea] F; Q2 *divides after* 'Iago'
474	'Tis . . . live] *as one line* Q; F *divides after* 'request'
475	Damn . . . her!] *as one line* Q; F *divides after* 'minx'

478	For . . . lieutenant] *as one line* Q; F *divides after* 'devil'
3.4.30–1	I . . . lord] STEEVENS–REED; F *divides after* 'be'; Q *divides after* 'now'
34	Give . . . lady] *as one line* Q; F *divides after* 'hand'
46	I . . . promise] *as one line* Q; F *divides after* 'this'
50–4	Lend . . . that handkerchief] This edition; F, Q divide after 'handkerchief', 'lord', 'you', 'me', 'Not', 'lord'
88	Fetch . . . misgives] *as one line* Q; F *divides after* 'handkerchief'
141–4	Though . . . gods] F; Q *divides after* 'object', 'ache', 'members', 'think'
150–2	Pray . . . you] F; Q *divides after* 'think', 'toy'
183	I . . . chamber] *as one line* Q; F *divides after* 'neither'
4.1. 1–2	Will . . . kiss] CAPELL; F, Q *divide after* 'so', 'Iago', 'private'
22	Ay . . . What] *as one line* DYCE; F, Q *divide after* 'that', 'now'
41–4	Work on . . . Othello] *as verse* F; *as prose* Q
41	Work . . . caught] *as one line* CAPELL; F *divides after* 'on'
110–11	Now . . . said] F; Q *divides after* 'o'er [on]'
116–18	I . . . ha!] *as prose* POPE; F *divides after* 'bear', 'it'; Q1 *divides after* 'wit'; Q2 *divides after* 'customer', 'wit'
124–6	This . . . promise] *as prose* Q; F *divides after* 'out', 'marry her'
134–5	So . . . ha!] *as prose* Q; F *divides after* 'upon me'
136–8	Now . . . it to] *as prose* F; Q *divides after* 'chamber'
151–2	How . . . now? How now?] *as prose* Q; F *divides after* 'Bianca'
172–3	I . . . woman!] *as prose* Q; F *divides after* 'killing'
186–7	O . . . condition] *as prose* Q; F *divides after* 'times'
189–90	Nay . . . Iago!] *as prose* Q; F *divides after* 'certain', *then prints* 'but . . . Iago!' *as prose*
200–4	Do . . . midnight] *as prose* Q; F *divides after* 'her bed', 'contaminated', 'Good, good', 'very good', 'undertaker'
205	Excellent . . . same] *as one line* F; Q *divides after* 'good'; *as prose* SANDERS
206–8	I warrant . . . him] F; Q *lines* 'Something . . . Lodovico | Come . . . him'; CAMBRIDGE 1891 *lines* 'I warrant . . . Lodovico | This . . . him'; *as prose* SANDERS
214–15	I . . . Cyprus] F, Q2; *as prose* Q1
255	You . . . monkeys] *as one line* Q; F *divides after* 'Cyprus'
4.2.25–6	Let . . . face] CAPELL; *as one line* F, Q
35–8	Come . . . honest] Q; *as prose* F
40	To . . . false] *as one line* Q; F *divides after* 'lord'
67–8	That . . . sweet] F; Q *divides after* 'blowing', 'fair'
69	That . . . born] *as one line* CAPELL; F, Q *divide after* 'thee'
80–1	And . . . strumpet] CAPELL; *as one line* Q
99	Good . . . lord] *as one line* Q; F *divides after* 'madam'

110	What . . . you] *as one line* POPE; F, Q *divide after* 'madam'
128–9	Beshrew . . . upon him] F; *as one line* Q
136–8	A . . . likelihood] Q; F *divides after* 'him', 'bones', 'whore', 'company', 'time'
151	I know . . . kneel] *as one line* F; Q2 *divides after* 'him'
174	I . . . me] *as one line* Q; F *divides after* 'find'
176–81	Every . . . suffered] *as prose* F, Q2; Q1 *divides after* 'Iago', 'from me', 'least', 'it', 'already'
183–4	Faith . . . together] *as prose* F; Q1 *divides after* 'words'; Q2 *divides after* 'much', 'performance[s]'
220–7	Sir . . . Cassio] *as prose* F; Q1 *divides after* 'Venice', 'place', 'Desdemona', 'Venice', 'him', 'lingered', 'so'; Q2 *divides after* 'Venice', 'place', 'Desdemona', 'Venice', 'lingered', 'determinate'
229–30	Why . . . brains] *as prose* F; Q *divides after* 'place'
4.3.4–5	Will . . . Desdemona] CAPELL; *as one line* F, Q
5–7	Get . . . done] HONIGMANN; *as prose* F, Q
53–4	So . . . weeping] F, Q2; Q1 *divides after* 'night'
64–5	The . . . vice] *as* Q; F *divides after* 'thing'
79–80	Yes . . . for] *as verse* THEOBALD; *as prose* F, Q
99	Good night . . . send] *as one line* Q; F *divides after* 'good night.'
5.1. 1	Here . . . come] *as one line* Q; F *divides after* 'balk' ('Barke')
27	I . . . murder] *as one line* Q; F *divides after* 'ever'
38	What . . . murder] *as one line* Q; F *divides after* 'passage'
49	Who's . . . murder] *as one line* Q; F *divides after* 'there'
57	O . . . this] *as one line* Q; F *divides after* 'lieutenant'
61–2	O murd'rous . . . villain] This edition; *as one line* F, Q
63	Kill . . . thieves] *as one line* Q; F *divides after* 'dark'
75–6	O . . . Cassio, Cassio.] F; *as one line* Q
80	I . . . seek you] *as one line* Q; F *divides after* 'thus'
81–2	Lend . . . hence] This edition; F *divides after* 'chair'; *as prose* Q2
85–7	To . . . no] F; Q1 *divides after* 'Cassio'; Q2 *divides after* 'Cassio', 'light'
97	He . . . chair] *as one line* Q; F *divides after* ' 'tis he'
108–9	Do . . . use] Q; F *divides after* 'speak'
110	'Las . . . husband] *as one line* Q; F *divides after* 'matter'
120–2	I am . . . me] HONIGMANN; F, Q *divide after* 'honest'
123	Kind . . . dressed] *as one line* Q; F *divides after* 'gentlemen'
5.2.13	That . . . rose] Q; F *divides after* 'relume'
29	Alack . . . that] *as one line* Q; F *divides after* 'lord'
33–4	Then . . . me] SANDERS; *as one line* F, Q

38	When . . . not] *as one line* Q; F *divides after* 'so'
50–1	That . . . Cassio] Q; F *divides after* 'handkerchief'
51–2	No . . . him] Q; F *divides after* 'man'
60–1	And . . . Cassio] F; Q *divides after* 'too'
76–7	Had . . . all] F; Q *divides after* 'lives'
84	But half . . . prayer] *as one line* Q1; F, Q2 *print* 'OTHELLO Being . . . pause' *after* 'hour'
87	My . . . lord!] *as one line* Q; F *divides after* 'ho'
103–4	I . . . lord] F; *as one line* Q
113–14	Cassio . . . Roderigo] F; Q *divides after* 'Venetian'
116–18	Not . . . harsh] HONIGMANN; F, Q *divide after* 'tune'
131	O . . . devil] F; Q *divides after* 'she'
134–5	Thou . . . true] Q; F *divides after* 'say'
148	What . . . husband] Q; F *divides after* 'woman'
149	O . . . love] *as one line* Q; F *divides after* 'mistress'
174	I told . . . more] *as one line* Q; F *divides after* 'thought'
176	But . . . false] *as one line* Q; F *divides after* 'him'
180	She . . . Cassio] *as one line* Q; F *divides after* 'false with Cassio'
181	With . . . tongue] *as one line* Q; F *divides after* 'mistress'
182	I . . . speak] *as one line* Q; F *divides after* 'tongue'
186	Nay . . . indeed] *as one line* Q; F *divides after* 'masters'
192	What . . . home] *as one line* Q; F *divides after* 'mad'
202	Poor . . . dead] *as one line* Q; F *divides after* 'Desdemon'
224	O . . . of] *as one line* Q; F *divides after* 'Moor'
234	But . . . villain] *as one line* Q; F *divides after* 'thunder'
235	The . . . wife] *as one line* Q; F *divides after* 'falls'
275–6	Even . . . devils] F, Q; CAPELL *divides after* 'chastity'
283	Where . . . forth] *as one line* Q; F *divides after* 'viper'
306	Sir . . . befallen] *as one line* Q; F *divides after* 'Sir'
310–11	The . . . Roderigo] F; *as one line* Q
342	Nor . . . speak] *as one line* Q; F *divides after* 'malice'
363	This . . . sight] *as one line* Q; F *divides after* 'work'

LONGER NOTES

(i) **Military designations** (Persons of the Play)

Shakespeare's use of military designations calls for comment, both because they are of some significance in the play and because they can be confusing to modern readers. For more detailed discussion of the various ranks in the play, see Charles Edelman, *Shakespeare's Military Language*: *A Dictionary* (2000), Henry J. Webb, 'The Military Background in *Othello*', *Philological Quarterly*, 30 (1951), 40–52, and Paul A. Jorgenson, *Shakespeare's Military World* (Berkeley, Calif., 1956), pp. 100–18.

general 'General' (originally 'captain-general') was a relatively novel designation for the commander of an army: *OED*'s earliest citation is 1576, but it had become standard by the turn of the century. It appears more frequently in *Othello* than in any other Shakespeare play, despite the fact that Giraldi's Moor is described merely as a 'captain' (*capitano*), a term which might describe anything from the commander of a company to a general, depending on its context. However, the original Moor's commission to Cyprus as *Capitani de' soldati* (Commander of the troops) will have suggested 'general' as the equivalent rank—though, as with 'lieutenant' and 'ensign', it also provides an occasion for significant wordplay (see 2.3.302–3; 3.3.347).

lieutenant Giraldi's character is simply described as 'un Capo di Squadra': *capo* is variously translated by modern editors as 'captain' or 'corporal'; while *capo di squadra* is glossed by Florio (p. 82) as 'a ring-leader or chief', and *squadra* as 'a part of a company of soldiers of twenty or five and twenty whose chief is a corporal'. The period's terminology of military rank is rendered confusing by the fact that senior officers could hold different staff and company ranks; Cassio's designation, however, is evidently not that of a modern subaltern, but equivalent to 'lieutenant-general'; it thus represents a significant change, since it clearly elevates Cassio above Iago, giving the latter a motive for envy of his fellow officer that is lacking in Giraldi. The use of 'lieutenant' (like 'general') to designate a particular military office was something of a novelty (*OED*'s earliest example is dated 1578)—and a controversial one at that, since a number of commentators, citing widely admired Spanish practice, argued that this rank should never have been inserted above that of 'ensign' ('ancient'), the captain's traditional deputy. Thus Digges's military treatise *Stratioticos* (1590) notes that the rank had no equivalent in Roman times, when the ensign (*signifer*) was 'next their captain of greatest reputation—as at this day he is with the Spaniards, who admit no other lieutenant in their band. . . . neither see I any cause why in these days we should need them, if the ensign and other officers sufficiently knew their duty' (sigs. P1–P1ᵛ). The citation of Spanish practice is interesting in the light of Iago's Spanish name; but in any case tension between holders of this new rank and their ensigns seems to have been common, for Digges takes care to emphasize that the lieutenant 'ought brotherly and friendly to use the ensign' (sig. P1ᵛ), while in *The Art of War and Englands Traynings* (1620), Edward Davies warns every lieutenant to take special care to 'observe great affability and fraternity with the alfierus [ensign]' and 'to avoid all stomaching and strife that might arise betwixt him and the alfierus, for thereby oftentimes great scandals have fallen out, and the division of the company, a thing above all other to be carefully foreseen and shunned' (sigs. O1ᵛ–O2).

The French derivation of the word (from *lieu tenant* = [one] holding [another's] place or position; deputy) gives it important resonances in this tragedy of displacement, usurpation, and corrupt substitution (see Neill, 'Places', and Julia Genster, 'Lieutenancy, Standing In and *Othello*', *ELH* 57 (1990), 785–805).

ensign In both F and Q Iago is described as Othello's 'ancient' or 'auncient', Shakespeare's preferred spelling of the more usual 'ensign' (cf. Ancient Pistol in *2 Henry IV* and *Henry V*), and thus a literal translation of Giraldi's *alfieri* ('a standard-bearer'). The pronunciation of the two forms was closer than their orthography might suggest, and they should simply be regarded as variant spellings of the same word; *OED* gives 'ensine' as the standard pronunciation, but 'ensin' (adopted in many recent productions, including the Burge/Olivier film) is at least equally common and perhaps better indicates the relation with *ancient*. For further discussion of this issue see Gary Taylor, 'Ancients and Moderns', *SQ* 36 (1985), 525–7. Like Cassio's lieutenancy, Iago's seems to be a staff rather than a company rank. As the general's personal standard-bearer he would be an officer of some importance (Webb, p. 45), a long way from the disgruntled NCO represented in some modern productions (see Introduction, pp. 77, 86, 91–9). According to *Stratioticos*, 'the value and virtue of the ensign setteth forth the virtue and valour of the captain and whole band' (sig. O4ᵛ); thus, ironically enough, Iago (whose sobriquet 'honest' can also mean 'honourable') is entrusted with the honour of his commander. His rank acquires a deepened ironic significance when he speaks mockingly of his 'flag or sign of love— | Which is indeed but sign' (1.1.155–6). The Digges treatise, in a suggestive passage, compares the ensign's concern for his function to that of a careful husband, 'above all other [he should] have honourable respect of his charge, and to be no less careful and jealous thereof than every honest and honourable gentleman should of his wife' (sig. O1).

(ii) **Othello's traveller's tales** (1.3.143–5)

143 **Cannibals . . . eat** Cannibals appear amongst the names of tribal peoples in Ralegh's *Discoverie of Guiana* (1595), and amongst the legends delineating tribal territories in the map illustrating de Bry's 1599 edition of the *Discoverie* (see fig. 2). An anagram of the word is used to name Caliban, the 'salvage and deformed slave' of Shakespeare's colonial fantasy *The Tempest*. Othello's travels, then, may have taken him to the New World; perhaps after he was 'sold to slavery'.

144 **Anthropophagi** A legendary tribe first described by the Roman writer Pliny, and here presumably distinct from *Cannibals*. Pliny includes a list of monstrous peoples, many of them belonging to the African continent, among them 'the Anthropophagi, that feed of man's flesh' who appear in Book 6 between 'the Pomphagi, who eat all things whatsoever' and 'the Cynamolgi, who have heads like dogs' (sig. O5). Book 7 offers a lengthy catalogue of human oddities, including Indian and African cave-dwellers (*Troglodytae*), 'Indians [who] engender with beasts, of which generation are bred certain monstrous mongrels, half beasts and half men', and 'Scythians called Anthropophagi . . . or eaters of men's flesh' (sig. O5ᵛ). Pliny's catalogue of monsters would be expanded by later writers, notably the author of Sir John Mandeville's *Travels*, a book whose fantastical qualities did not prevent its being regarded by Hakluyt and others as a foundational text of English voyaging.

144–5 **men . . . shoulders** Cf. also *Tempest*, 3.3.46–7, 'men | Whose heads stood in their breasts'. Pliny's Book 7 describes an Indian people known as *Blemmyae*, 'without heads standing upon their necks, who carry eyes in their shoulders' (sig. O6ᵛ), whilst Mandeville follows his account of anthropophagy in the East Indian island of Dondun with a list of the 'diverse folk' in adjacent islands, including 'folk of foul stature and of cursed kynde, that han non hedes. And here [their] eyen ben in here scholdres, and here mouth is croked as an hors schoo, and that is in the myddes of here brest. And in another yle also ben folk that han non hedes, and here eyen and here mouth ben behynde in here schuldres' (cited from M. C. Seymour, *Mandeville's Travels* (Oxford, 1969), p. 147). Similar figures of *Blemmyae* or *Acephali* are illustrated on the outer margins of the *orbis terrarum* in a number of medieval *mappae mundi*. The belief in such monstrous races died hard: Richard Eden in material attached to the account of John Lok's voyage to Guinea (published in his *Decades of the New World* (1555) and reprinted in Hakluyt) describes Anthropophagi and headless 'Blemines' among the peoples of the African interior; and early modern explorers from Columbus onwards reported the existence of similar peoples in the New World (see Introduction, pp. 19–21).

(iii)   **Textual cruxes** (3.3.185, 5.2.346)

3.3.185   **exsuffilate** Although both Q and F read *exufflicate*, it is impossible to exclude the possibility of common error (see App. B; Honigmann, chap. 9). Most editors (following Malone) emend to *exsufflicate*, glossed by *OED* (citing only this example, and conjecturing an arbitrary formation from *exsufflate* = blow out, blow away) as 'puffed up, inflated, windy'. Since the word appears to form a doublet with *blown*, this is not impossible, but the etymology seems strained. *Exsuffilate*, the reading proposed here, would mean 'hissed, whispered'. Hanmer first suggested a possible coinage from Italian *suffolare* (= whistle, hiss), which Florio lists in the form *suffilare*. If this conjecture is correct, then *blown* would mean either 'whispered' or 'rumoured' (see below). Mowat and Werstine guess that *exsufflicate and blown* may mean 'spat out and fly-blown'. Other possibilities include *exuscitate* (= awakened), or *exulcerate* (= ulcerated, diseased, corrupted).

5.2.346   **Indian** Both Q's *Indian* and F's *Iudean* (Judean) have their defenders; but they are most unlikely to be true alternatives (as Andrews, taking F as a possible revision, supposes), since they are too suspiciously alike. See App. F(iii) Both Q's *Indian* and F's *Iudean* (Judean) have their defenders; but they are unlikely to be true alternatives (as Andrews supposes), since they are too alike. Those who prefer *Iudean* have either (like Theobald) taken it to allude to Herod's repudiation of his wife Mariamne, or (more plausibly) accepted Halliwell's suggestion that it refers to Judas Iscariot, Jesus's Judean disciple. Through his treachery, Judas deprived himself of the Kingdom of Heaven, described by Matthew (13: 46) as a 'pearl of great price'; the parallel is arguably supported by the kiss with which Judas betrayed Christ ('I kissed thee ere I killed thee'). Moreover, 'tribe' had not yet acquired the association with 'primitive' peoples fostered by 19th-century ethnography, but was habitually applied to the twelve biblical divisions of Israel. Cf. also 3.3.178 for Lewkenor's use of the term to describe the division of the Venetian people in six 'tribes'.

However, as Richard Levin has argued (*SQ* 33 (1982), 60–7), Othello would be unlikely to identify himself with Judas in his speech of self-exculpation. The ignorance of the Indian, by contrast, is consistent with the hero's notion of himself as 'one that loved not wisely', and whose 'unlucky deeds' result not from malice but extreme perplexity. Travellers' tales repeatedly stress the careless ignorance of pearls and precious stones manifested by 'Indian' savages; and Levin cites numerous literary parallels. Not only does this image of barbaric profligacy recall the exotic scenes of Othello's travels in 1.3, but Indians and Moors were often conflated with one another, as in Marlowe's reference to 'Indian Moors' (*Faustus*, 1.1.48), or in the description of the black Moor Eleazar as an 'Indian slave' in *Lust's Dominion* (3.4.18–19). Moreover, while pearls characteristically adorn black Africans in contemporary portraiture, as well as in e.g. *Titus* (2.1.19) and Jonson's *Masque of Blacknesse* (ll. 59–60, 76–8), Sanders notes an instance in George Gascoigne's satire *The Steel Glass* (1575) where indifference to the value of pearls is approvingly credited to Moors them-selves: 'How live the Moors that spurn at glistering pearl, | And scorn the costs, which we do hold so dear?' (sig. D2). Pliny associates pearls with India: 'The Indian ocean is chief for sending them' (9.35, sig. Z1^v).

Textually the balance of evidence favours Q. The fact that *Indian* not only seemed the better reading to the editor of Q2, but was independently substituted by the conservative editor of F2 (1632) indicates that contemporaries were puzzled by *Iudean*, a rare word before the 19th century, though instances occur in the anonymous tragedy *Tiberius* (1607) and in Elizabeth Cary's *Tragedy of Mariam* (1613). So *Iudean* is unlikely as a misreading of *Indian*, though the opposite error is entirely possible. But 'Indean' (though rare and not found elsewhere in the Folio) was an alternative spelling for 'Indian', so the simplest explanation would be that *Iudean* resulted either from a scribal or compositorial misreading or from a turned letter *n*—of which there are six other examples in F *Othello* alone. Macdonald Jackson ('Editing, Attribution Studies, and "Literature on Line"', (*Research Opportunities in Renaissance Drama* 12 (1998), 1–15 (12)) notes that *Indean* was apparently misread as *Iudean* in Thomas Jordan's poem *Love's Dialect* (1646); and a similar error seems to have affected the key passage from Jeremiah that played a shaping role in early modern constructions of race (see Introduction, p. 126): where the Geneva Bible (the version most often echoed in Shakespeare) asks whether 'the blacke More' can change his skin, all previous translations had spoken of a 'man of Inde'; however, at least two early texts—a 1540 edition of the Great Bible, and a 1549 version of the Matthew Bible—print 'man of Iude'. In both cases a turned *n* seems likely to have been the culprit—though other occurrences of 'Iude' in Jeremiah 13 may have confused the compositors. Conceivably F's *Iudean* was influenced by an associative recollection of the erroneous 'man of Iude'—but the overwhelming preponderance of texts printing 'man of Inde' makes simple coincidence more likely; and Shakespeare's appropriation of that phrase in *Love's Labour's Lost* (4.3.220) and *A Midsummer Night's Dream* (2.2.58) shows his familiarity with a context in which Indian and black Moor appeared to be interchangeable categories, rendering Othello's identification with a 'base Indian' even more apposite. Finally, as Honigmann points out, the case for *Indian* is strengthened by the metrical desirability of a stress on the first, not the second, syllable of the word (as in *Judean*).

(iv) **Other long notes** (3.4, 5.2)

3.4.28–9 **sun . . . him** Othello describes himself as 'one not easily jealous, but being wrought, | Perplexed in the extreme' (5.2.344–5). By contrast, Giraldi's Disdemona claims that 'Moors have such a hot temperament that any little matter moves [them] to anger and vendetta' (see App. C, p. 439). As Floyd-Wilson points out, contemporary opinion was divided on this issue: against the simple notion that hot climates naturally produced hot temperaments, humoral theory had traditionally maintained that excessive exposure to the sun in southern climes drew out the body's natural heat and moisture, leaving it cool and dry, but with an excess of black bile that darkened the skin and induced a melancholic disposition. Theorists disagreed, however, as to whether this would render southern peoples more or less liable to jealousy: Desdemona echoes the traditional view that their 'complexion' made southerners typically constant and dispassionate; but this ran counter to the supposedly first-hand observation of travellers such as Leo Africanus, who remarked on the extraordinary jealousy of Moors and other Africans. Shakespeare may also have been aware of the influential work of Jean Bodin, who modified humoral theory to accord with Leo's observations. Remarking that 'southerners, who are full of bile, are said to be more inclined to passion', Bodin argued that whilst their emotions were slow to waken, once aroused they were difficult to mollify and inclined to excess: 'Because self-control was difficult, particularly when plunging into lust, they gave themselves over to horrible excesses. Promiscuous coition of men and animals took place, wherefore the regions of Africa produce for us so many monsters. *Hence is derived that unbelievable jealousy of the southerners . . . referred to in Leo*' (Bodin, pp. 105–6; emphasis added). By 1621, Robert Burton could cite Bodin and Leo together in support of the claim that 'Southern men are more hot, lascivious, and jealous, than such as live in the North; they can hardly contain themselves in these hotter climes, but are most subject to prodigious lusts. Leo Afer [Africanus] telleth incredible things almost of the lust and jealousy of his Countrymen of Africa' (*Anatomy*, 3.3.1.2, p. 827).

3.4.73 **mummy** Originally prepared from the bituminous remains of mummified corpses, but by Shakespeare's time frequently concocted from other sources, including the bodies of condemned criminals. It was credited with both medical and magical properties, notably by Paracelsus, who believed that good quality *mumia* could restore the failing spirits of the sick by infusing them with the life-power of the deceased. Though prescribed for a wide variety of ailments, it was (interestingly, in view of Othello's fit in 4.1) celebrated for its anti-epileptic virtues. Shakespeare's son-in-law John Hall records its use in a 'fume' to be inhaled at the onset of a fit (*Select Observations on English Bodies*, Observation 29). See also Louise Noble, 'The *Fille Vièrge* as Pharmakon: The Therapeutic Value of Desdemona's Corpse', in *Disease, Diagnosis and Cure on the Early Modern Stage*, ed. Stephanie Moss and Kaara Peterson (Burlington, 2004), pp. 115–31; and ' "And make two pasties of your shameful heads": Medicinal Cannibalism and Healing the Body Politic in *Titus Andronicus*', ELH 70 (2003), 677–708.

69 **maidens' hearts** The high demand for mummy meant that it was no longer derived exclusively from ancient mummies, but could be prepared from any human remains; those of saints or healthy young people were especially effective, according to Paracelsus. Several authorities vouched for the peculiar efficacy of mummy extracted from the corpses of virgins, the magical power of whose virginity was presumably concentrated in their pure hearts. In John Davies of Hereford's *Microcosmos* (1601) jealousy is described as 'A sore which nought that's good for aught recures, | That's mummy made of the mere heart of love' (*Complete Works*, ed. Grosart, p. 77); so, ironically enough, the embroidery on the handkerchief may contain a charm against jealousy. Cf. also 3.3.436.

5.2.0.1 *in her bed* The fullest account of the staging of this scene is in Siemon. Various suggestions have been made as to what may have happened at the Globe: the bed could have been 'discovered', either (a) in a curtained 'discovery space' let into the tiring-house wall, or (b) inside a curtained booth which might also have served as a 'bulk' in the previous scene (see 5.1.1), as L. J. Ross suggested ('The use of a "fit-up" booth in *Othello*', SQ 12 (1961), 359–70). Alternatively, as Richard Hosley argued in rebuttal, it could have been 'put forth' on to the stage through one of the tiring-house doors, like the bed in *Contention* (*2 Henry VI*), 3.2.146.1 ('The staging of Desdemona's bed', SQ 14 (1963), 57–65). Dessen and Thompson's study of more than 150 examples leads them to conclude that '[m]ost signals are for beds to be brought onstage', although at least twenty call for the bed to be 'discovered'. Nowhere is a booth explicitly called for, however, and though its use in scenes of 'discovery' cannot be excluded, it would create unnecessary staging difficulties, interfering with the sightlines of a significant portion of the audience in the galleries. Alan C. Dessen and Leslie Thompson, *A Dictionary of Stage Directions in English Drame*, 1580–1642 (Cambridge, 1999).

INDEX

This is a selective guide to words and phrases glossed in the Commentary, and to names and topics in the Introduction, Commentary and Appendices A, B, D and F. Information supplementary to *OED* and citations of first recorded use are indicated by asterisks. Biblical, liturgical, and theological allusions are grouped together, as are proverbial usages.

a 4.3.38
abhor 4.2.142
abode 4.2.225
abuse 5.1.122
abused 1.1.172; 2.1.226; 3.3.203
abuser 1.2.78
accident(s) 1.1.141; 5.1.94
accomodation 1.3.237
account 1.3.5
accountant 2.1.284
accumulate 372
Acephali p. 463
acerb 1.3.342; p. 428
achieved 2.1.61
acknown 3.3.322
acquaintance 2.1.198; 4.2.190
act 3.3.330
act divisions pp. 429, 431
Act to Restrain Abuses pp. 411, 413,
    418, 427, 429
action 1.3.71; 2.3.56
actors' alterations pp. 425, 427–8, 431
addiction 2.2.6
addition 3.4.189; 4.1.100; 4.2.163
additons (to the play) *see* cuts
Adelman, Janet p. 120; 2.1.287
Adler, Doris p. 63
adultery pp. 145–6
advantage 1.3.295; 3.3.315; 4.2.179
advocation 3.4.119
aerial 2.1.40
affection 2.1.234; 4.3.93
affects 1.3.261–2
affined 2.3.209
affinity 3.1.46
after 1.3.36
against 2.3.361
Agate, James pp. 54–5, 78, 82
agnize 1.3.230
aim 1.3.6

alabaster 5.2.5
alarum 2.3.24
Albanese, Denise p. 67
Alchemist see Jonson
Aldridge, Amanda p. 54
Aldridge, Ira pp. 10–11, 15, 42, 43,
    50–2, 54, 57
Aleppo 5.2.351
alfieri p. 194
allowance 1.1.126; 2.1.50
allowed 1.3.223
All's Well that Ends Well 1.3.255;
    4.1.116; pp. 401, 402
Almain 2.3.75
alteration 5.2.103
amazed 3.3.373; 4.2.238
amiable 3.4.58
Amneus, Daniel 5.2.85
anagnorisis p. 135
anatomy 3.3.119
and 2.3.81
Angelo 1.3.16
Angelus Sorianus p. 400
Anikst, Alexander p. 105
Anne, Queen p. 400
anon 4.1.76; 4.3.45
answer 1.1.118; 1.3.275
answerable 1.3.339
antres p. 140
Anthropophagi 1.3.144; p. 463
Antony and Cleopatra pp. 2, 131;
    1.1.65; 3.3.450; 3.4.34–6, 54–64;
    4.1.237; 4.2.61; 5.2.282
apartheid pp. 63–4
Aphrodite 2.1.200
appeared 4.2.209–10
appetite 2.3.332
apprehensions 3.3.143
approve 1.1.78; 2.1.45; 2.3.58; 4.3.10
approved in 2.3.202

469

apt 2.1.278; 2.3.307
Arden of Faversham pp. 114, 174
argues 3.4.36
Ariosto, Ludovico p. 17; 3.4.71
Aristotle 5.2.208
arithmetician 1.1.18
Armin, Robert p. 72; 3.3.447
Armstrong, Louis p. 59
arrivance 2.1.43
article 3.3.22; 5.2.56
As You Like It 3.3.24; p. 403
ashamed 2.3.153
Ashcroft, Peggy pp. 53, 55, 104
Ashe, Oscar 5.2.357–8
aspics 3.3.450
ass 1.1.47
assay 1.3.19; 2.1.120
assigned 1.1.38
at a time 2.3.301
at fortune 3.3.266
at stake 4.2.13
Atkins, Robert 5.2.357–8
atone 4.1.225
attach 1.2.77
Attenborough, Michael pp. 66, 99, 100
attend 3.4.188
attending 1.1.51
attends 3.1.24
aubade pp. 448–9
Auden, W. H. p. 92
avaunt 3.3.337
away 4.2.44–5

baboon 1.3.312
Bacon, Francis pp. 127, 149, 1.2.213
Baker, Sean p. 111
balk 5.1.1
Balm of Gilead 5.2.349–50
balmy 5.2.16
Balthasar (of the Three Magi) pp. 26, 127
Bandello, Matteo p. 20
Bannen, Ian p. 85
banning 2.1.11
barbarian 1.3.349
Barbary 1.1.111; 1.3.349; 4.3.24
Barber, John pp. 60, 62, 93, 94
Barry, Spranger pp. 10, 80
Bartels, Emily p. 115
Barthelemy, Anthony pp. 115, 122
Barton, John pp. 60–1, 89–90, 111
base 2.1.210; 5.2.346

Bate, Jonathan p. 8
bauble 4.1.130
Baughan, E. A. p. 54
bawd 4.2.20
Beale, Simon Russell pp. 88, 95, 96–9; 4.1.43
beam 1.3.322
Bear 2.1.14
bear it out 2.1.18
Beattie, Maureen p. 109
Beaumont and Fletcher pp. 407, 426
bed pp. 131, 173–4; 3.3.415; 4.1.247–8; 4.3.20; 5.2.0.1, 106.1, 250.1, 363–4.1; p. 467
bed and board 3.3.24
before 2.1.106
before me 4.1.140
begrimed 3.3.389
beguile pp. 1.3.67, 156; 2.1.122
Behn, Aphra pp. 15, 41
belch 3.4.102
beleed 1.1.29
bending 1.3.234
benefit 3.4.115
Benson, Frank pp. 11, 74
Benthall, Nichael p. 79
Berbers 1.1.111
Berger, Harry pp. 133–4
Berger, Thomas L. pp. 405, 406
Bernard, John pp. 10, 80
Bertish, Suzanne pp. 105, 106
beshrew 3.4.146
besort 1.3.237
Best, George p. 126
better angel 5.2.206
betimes 1.3.367
Betterton, Thomas pp. 45, 47, 74, 79
*bewhored 4.2.115
Bible, Geneva 1.1.112; p. 465
    Great p. 465
    Matthew p. 465
biblical, liturgical, and theological
    allusions (including homilies)
        1.1.47, 112; 1.2.59; 1.3.342;
        2.1.85, 290; 2.3.66, 284–5;
        3.3.120, 269, 462.1; 3.4.108;
        4.1.8, 137, 226; 4.2.16, 47–53,
        57–62; 4.3.69–70; 5.2.21–2, 41,
        48, 55, 76, 101–3, 194, 205,
        278–9, 346–7, 349–50, 363;
        pp. 464–5
big 3.3.351

Billington, Michael pp. 64, 91, 93, 95, 99, 100, 105, 107
birdlime 2.1.126
black 1.3.288; 2.1.131, 132–3
blackness (*see also* colour) 1.1.88, 112, 139; 1.2.63, 66; 1.3.250; 2.1.132–3; 3.3.447; 4.2.74–5; 5.2.155; p. 400
Blackfriars playhouse pp. 2, 406, 429
Blake, Peter p. 37
Bland, Joyce p. 104
Bland, Sheila Rose p. 71
blank 3.4.124
Blayney, Peter pp. 407, 408
blazoning 2.1.63
Blemmyae p. 463
blotted 5.1.36
blown 3.3.185
blood 1.1.168; 1.3.105, 124, 323; 2.3.196; 3.3.330, 451–78; 4.1.267; 5.1.37
Boaden, James p. 80
board 3.3.24
boarded 1.2.50
bobbed 5.1.16
Bodin, Jean p. 145; 1.3.340–1; p. 466
Bohler, Danielle Régnier p. 130
Boitard, François Boitard p. 37–8
Boito, Arrigo p. 15
bold cure 2.1.51–2
bolster 3.3.401
bombast 1.1.12
bondslaves 1.2.99
Boose, Linda pp. 123, 136, 155; 5.2.143
Booth, Edwin pp. 75–7, 82, 96, 113; 4.2.130–44; 5.2.126, 129–30, 5.2.280.1–2, 288
Booth, Junius Brutus p. 75
bootless 1.3.208
Bosch, Hieronymus p. 155
bound 3.1.55; 3.3.216; 5.2.182
Bowers, Fredson p. 412
Boy Musician 3.1.5
Boyd, Michael p. 69
Boydell, Josiah pp. 39, 135–6
brace 2.3.27
Bradley, A. C. pp. 7, 40, 103–4, 114, 117, 118, 171
Bradshaw, Graham pp. 6, 34–5, 137; 1.1.20; 3.3.332–5; 4.1.112
Branagh, Kenneth pp. 68, 88, 89
Brathwait, Richard p. 166

brave 5.1.32
brave *v.* 5.2.325
bravery 1.1.101
Brayton, Lily p. 104
breed 3.3.16
breeding 2.1.98
Brewster, Yvonne p. 68
bridal 3.4.146
Brien, Alan pp. 58, 59, 77, 87, 88
brimstone 4.1.116
bring 3.4.194
bring you in 3.1.50
Bristol, Michael pp. 5, 448
Brome, Alexander 2.1.132
Brown, Ivor pp. 55, 77, 78
Brown, John Russell p. 36
bruised 1.3.218
Bryant, Michael p. 91
Bryden, Ronald pp. 58, 60, 61, 62, 90
Buchowetski, Dmitri p. 53
bulk 1.3.0.1; 5.1.1; p. 467
Bullough, Geoffrey pp. 18, 22
Bulwer, John 2.1.216
Burbage, Richard pp. 47, 71
Burge, Stuart pp. 59, 88
Burke, Kenneth p. 143
burlesques, *see* travesties
Burnett, Mark Thornton p. 139
Burton, Robert 5.2.38; p. 466
Burton, Richard p. 79
business 1.3.269
busy 3.3.257; 4.2.131
but 3.4.24
but that 5.2.136
Butler, Robert p. 98
butt 5.2.266
by and by 2.1.274; 5.2.93
by my troth 4.3.66
by this hand 4.1.130–1; 4.1.169
Byron, Lord pp. 10, 130

cable 1.2.17
Caesar, Julius 2.3.113
caitiff 4.1.105
Calder, David pp. 94–5, 111
Calderwood, James pp. 136, 140, 1.1.157
Callaghan, Dympna p. 70
callet 4.2.121
Canada, Ron pp. 67, 89, 110
cannibals pp. 20, 145; 1.3.143; p. 463
cannikin 2.3.63
capable 3.3.459

Capell, Edward 1.3.45, 48.1–2
capo di squadra p. 194
caps 4.3.69
Caribs 1.3.143
Carlin, Murray pp. 1, 11–12
Carné, Marcel p. 9
carrack 1.2.50
Carrington, Ethel p. 104
carry 1.1.67
carve 2.3.164
Cary, Elizabeth p. 465
cashiered 1.1.48; 2.3.360
Cashin, Fergus p. 59
cast 1.1.148; 2.3.14; 5.2.325–6
cast water 2.1.14
castigation 3.4.39
Castiglione, Baldassare p. 450
catechize 3.4.15
cause 1.2.95; 3.3.28; 3.3.413;
    5.2.1–2, 1
Cavell, Stanley pp. 5, 134, 135
censorship p. 410
censure 2.3.184; 4.1.262; 5.2.367
centaur 1.1.57
certain 2.2.2
certes 1.1.15
chair 5.1.82
Chakravarti, Paromita p. 13
challenge 1.3.187; 2.1.206
chamberers 3.3.268
Chambers, E. K. p. 421
chaos 3.3.93
charge 5.1.119
Charles I, King p. 3
charm your tongue 5.2.181
charmer 3.4.56
charms 1.1.170; 5.1.36
charter 1.3.244
check(s) 1.1.147; 3.3.67–8; 4.3.18
choler 2.1.263
christened 1.1.29
chuck 3.4.47
Churchill, Sir Winston p. 62
chrysolite 5.2.143
Cibber, Colley pp. 72, 78, 79
Circe 2.3.280–1
circumstance 1.1.12; 3.3.356, 408
circumstanced 3.4.196
cistern 4.2.61
civil 2.3.181; 4.1.60
Clapp, Susannah pp. 97, 99, 109
Clark, Austin p. 68
Clarke, Mary Cowden 4.1.338

clime 3.3.234
clip 3.3.464
close 3.3.127; 5.2.334
closet 4.2.22
Cloutier, Suzanne p. 104
clown 3.1.0
clyster-pipes 2.1.174
coat(s) 1.1.53; 5.1.25
Cockpit playhouse p. 9
coffers 2.1.203
cogging 4.2.132
Coghill, Nevill 4.3.24–9; pp. 413–14,
    416, 421–2
Cohen, Derek p. 137
'collaring scene' 3.3.362.1
coldness 2.3.373
Coleridge, S. T. pp. 31, 42, 45, 47, 54,
    98, 113, 114, 146, 152; 1.3.377;
    4.1.100
collied 2.3.197
Collier, J. P. pp. 72, 194
coloquintida 1.3.343
colour (*see also* blackness) pp. 1, 16,
    23, 40–71, 85, 113–30, 142–3,
    146–7, 178; 1.1.202; 1.2.99
Columbus, Christopher 1.3.224;
    p. 464
come in 5.1.45
Comedy of Errors p. 33
comforts 4.2.190
comic convention pp. 4–6, 28–9;
    4.1.70, 122–204
committed 4.2.70
common thing 3.3.305
commoner 4.2.73
commonly 3.4.41
companions 4.2.141
compass 2.1.234; 3.4.19; 4.2.219
compasses 3.4.70
compassing 1.3.353
complete 2.1.240
complexion 3.3.234; 4.2.62
comply 1.3.261
composition 1.3.1
Compositor B pp. 415, 432
Compositor E p. 415
compulsive
conceit 3.3.118; 328
conceive 4.2.96
conception 5.2.57
conclusion 1.3.325; 2.1.159; 3.3.429
confine 1.2.27
congregated sands 2.1.69

Index

conjects 3.3.153
conjunctive 1.3.360
conjured 1.3.106; 3.3.295
conduct *n.* 2.1.75
Conrad, Joseph p. 69
consent in 5.2.295
construe 4.1.97
consuls 1.1.24, 1.2.43
Contarini, Cardinal Gasparo pp. 18, 158
content 2.3.1; 3.3.450
continuate 3.4.173
contrived 1.2.3
conveniences 2.1.225–6
conveniency 4.2.178
conversation 3.3.267
conveyance 1.3.283
convinced 4.1.27
Cooke, George Frederick p. 74
Cooke, William p. 79
cope 4.1.82
corner 3.3.275
Cornwallis, Sir William 3.4.44–5
corrigible 1.3.321
corrupted 1.3.61
Coryat, Tomas p. 194
couch 4.3.52
Couling, Barbara p. 94
counsel 3.3.114; 4.2.95
count 5.2.272
counter-caster p. 30
country 3.3.241
country forms 3.3.241
course(s) 1.2.86; 1.3.112; 3.4.69–70; 4.1.271; 4.2.94
coursers 1.1.112
court of guard 2.1.212; 2.3.207
courtesans p. 194
courtesy 2.1.99, 172
courtship 2.1.168
cousins 1.1.112
Coveney, Michael pp. 62, 69, 93, 95, 96, 107
covered 1.1.111
Cowhig, Ruth p. 41
coxcomb 5.2.232
cozening 4.2.132
crack of 2.3.322–12
Crane, Ralph pp. 193, 419–21, 427, 429
creature 2.3.297
credit 1.3.2, 98; 2.1.278; 2.3.344
cries 1.3.274

cries on 5.1.49
crocodile 4.1.237
crusadoes 3.4.24
cry 2.3.349; 5.1.45
cry you mercy 4.2.89; 5.1.68
Cukor, George p. 8
Cumaean sibyl 3.4.69–70
cunning 3.3.49
cunning'st 5.2.11
Cupid 1.3.266–7
Curtis, Nick p. 100
Cusack, Niamh p. 106
Cushman, Robert pp. 60, 92
Cushman, Charlotte p. 102
*customer 4.1.116
cuts and additions 1.3.25–31; 3.3.327, 3.3.385–92, 453–60; 4.1.44–177; 4.2.151–64; 4.3.24–9, 29–48, 81–98, 100; 5.2.245–7, 265–71; pp. 410, 417, 421, 426, 431
Cymbeline 1.3.166; 3.3.460; 5.2.4
Cyprus p. 148, 1.1.28; 2.1.200; p. 400

daily 5.1.19
Dale, Janet pp. 107, 109
dam 4.1.143
D'Amico, Jack pp. 121–2
Danaë 4.3.83
Daniel, Samuel p. 130
Danson, Lawrence 2.3.161–2
Darlington, W. A. pp. 82, 85
Davenant, Sir William p. 47
David, Richard p. 58
Davies, Andrew p. 7
Davies, Edward p. 32; 2.3.130, 254–5; p. 462
Davies, John ('of Hereford') p. 467
Davis, Willy p. 13
daws 1.1.65
Day, Angel 4.2.22
Day of Judgement 5.2.272
dear 2.1.282
de Botton, Alain p. 150
de Bry, Theodor pp. 20, 21, 463
defend 1.3.264
defunct 1.3.259–63, 262
degree 3.3.234
de Jongh, Nicholas pp. 93, 94, 99, 100
Dekker, Thomas 3.4.5–6; p. 400
delicate 1.3.347; 2.1.226; 3.3.272
delighted 1.3.287; 4.2.155
Delius, Nicolaus 2.1.11, 208–9
demerits 1.2.22

demonstrable 3.4.138
demonstrate 3.3.432
Dennis, John p. 72
denote 4.1.171
denotement 2.3.305
Dent, Alan pp. 77, 83, 84, 87
deputing 4.1.229
Desdemon 4.2.41; 5.2.25
deserve 1.1.182
designment 2.1.22
desired 2.1.199
desperate 2.1.21; 5.2.205
despite 4.2.116
Dessen, Alan C. p. 467
determinate 4.2.227
de Vigny, Alfred p. 10
device 4.2.176
Dexter, John pp. 5, 57–8, 85, 88, 89,
    90, 117
diablo 2.3.151
dial 3.4.170
Dickins, Richard p. 77
dictated scripts pp. 424–5, 431
diet 2.1.285
Digges, Leonard (*Stratioticos*) pp. 71;
    1.1.18, 41–65; 2.3.130, 254–5;
    p. 462
Digges, Thomas 1.1.18
dilate 1.3.153
dilations 3.3.127
dilatory 2.3.358
dinner 3.3.59
direction 1.3.297
directly 2.1.213; 4.2.208
dirt 5.2.162
discipline 2.1.259
discontented 5.2.313
discords 2.1.194
discover 1.1.177
discovery pp. 130–8, 178; 3.3.409
discreet 2.1.219
discretion 3.3.32
Disdemona p. 194
disembark 2.1.203
dislikes 2.3.43
dismayed 5.2.268
displanting 2.1.267
displeasure 3.1.42
disports 1.3.269
dispose *n.* 1.3.386
disposition 1.3.235
disproportion p. 147; 3.3.296
disproportioned 1.2.2

disrelish 2.1.227
distaste 3.3.329
distempering 1.1.100
distinctly 3.3.239
distract it with 1.3.319
divesting 2.3.172
divine p. 211
divinity of hell 2.3.335
division of a battle 1.1.22
do 2.3.309; 3.3.1; 3.3.433
do my duties 3.2.2
Doctor Faustus see Marlowe,
    Christopher
Dod, John and Cleaver, Robert p. 162
does 4.2.166
doffest 4.2.176
domestic 2.3.206
Domingo, Placido p. 65
done 4.3.67
done our course 4.2.94
Donne, John p. 162
dotage 4.1.26
dote 2.1.201
double 1.3.383
double negatives 3.4.183
'double time' *see* time scheme
doubt 3.3.19, 182–3, 191, 430
Downes, Cathy p. 69
dram 1.3.106
dreadful 2.3.166
drinning songs pp. 446–8
driving in (*sd.*) 2.3.135.1
Drury, Alan p. 91
Dryden, John 4.3.68
Duberman, Martin N. p. 56
Ducis, François pp. 10, 14, 41–2
dull 1.1.122; 2.1.221; 5.2.224
dull *v.* 2.3.373
dullness 1.3.267
Dumas, Alexandre (*père*) pp. 10, 87
Dunderdale, Sue pp. 69, 106
duties 4.3.82
Dutch 2.3.69–76
Dyce, Alexander 3.3.388; 5.2.86

easily 5.1.82
ecstasy 4.1.75
Eden, Richard p. 463
edified 3.4.13 education 1.3.181
Edwardes, Jane p. 97
Edwards, Christopher p. 69
Egyptian 3.4.55
elements 2.3.53, 326–7; 3.3.464

Eliot, T. S. pp. 60, 74
Elizabeth, Princess p. 3
Elizabeth, Queen p. 399
Ellis, Ruth pp. 10, 84
else 5.2.136
embarked 1.1.148
embayed 2.1.18
*encave 4.1.77
enchafed 2.1.17
enchanted 1.1.63
endues 3.4.142
enemy 2.3.279
*enfettered 2.3.330
engage 3.3.462
engines 4.2.216
Engler, Balz 2.1.153; 5.2.360
English 2.3.69–76
English Courtier, The p. 161
engluts 1.3.58
*enmesh 2.3.347
ensign pp. 30, 151; 1.1.32, 155;
    pp. 461–3
ensteeped 2.1.70
entertainment 2.3.32; 3.3.254
enwheel 2.1.87
epilepsy 3.3.287; 4.1.47
epithets of war 1.1.13
equinox 2.3.115
equivocal 1.3.216
Erne, Lukas p. 421
err 1.3.63
erring 1.3.348
error 5.2.111
estimation 1.3.272
eternal 4.2.130
ethic dative 1.1.49; 2.3.74; 3.4.175;
    4.2.133
evades 1.1.12
Evans, Gareth Lloyd pp. 60, 62, 90, 91
Evans, K. W. p. 122
Evans, Robert C. p. 168
Everett, Barbara pp. 115, 116, 150, 194
ever-fixed 2.1.15
ewe 1.1.89
execute 2.3.219
execution 3.3.466
exercise 3.4.39
exhibition 1.3.236; 4.3.69
expectancy 2.1.42
expedition 1.3.227
expostulate 4.1.198
exquisite 2.3.18; 2.3.73
exsufflate 3.3.185; p. 464

extend 2.1.98
extincted 2.1.81
extravagant 1.1.135
extremity 5.2.139
eyes (*see also* ocular proof) 1.1.27;
    1.3.268; 4.2.35–6; 5.2.38
Eyre, Ronald pp. 90, 105, 107, 111
Eyres, Harry pp. 95, 96

fain 4.1.160
faintly 4.1.109
fair 1.1.66; 1.3.114–15; 2.1.129;
    3.3.478
fall 4.3.82
fall into 3.3.226
fall to match 3.3.241
fall out 4.2.235
false 5.2.134
false gaze 1.3.20
familiar 2.3.297
fancies 3.3.89; 3.4.62
fancy 4.2.26
fantasy 3.3.302
Farjeon, Herbert pp. 54, 55
fast 1.2.11; 1.3.355
fasten 2.3.44
fatal 52.20
Fates 5.2.204
fathom 1.1.151
favour 2.1.223; 3.4.121
Fay, Gerard p. 54
fear 1.2.71
Fearon, Ray pp. 57, 64, 99–100
Fechter, Charles pp. 49, 108;
    4.2.130–44; 5.2.129–30
fell 5.2.361
fellow 4.2.140
fellowship 2.1.93
Fenton, Geoffrey pp. 20, 92
Ferrer, José pp. 9, 141
field 1.3.135
fig 1.3.315
fig's end 2.1.244
fills it up 3.3.250–1
filthy 5.2.155
fineless 3.3.176
Fineman, Joel 5.2. 289
Finlay, Frank pp. 36, 59, 86–8
Fishburne, Laurence p. 68
fitchew 4.1.141
flag and sign 1.1.155
fleers 4.1.78
Fletcher, John 3.3.446

Fletcher, Phineas p. 165
flood 2.1.2
flood-gate 1.3.57
Florentine 1.1.19; 3.1.40
Florio, John pp. 194, 464
Floyd-Wilson, Mary pp. 127, 128, 129;
    1.3.316, 340–1; 2.3.197; p. 466
foaming 2.1.11
follow 1.1.40
folly 2.1.136; 5.2.132
fond 1.3.314; 3.3.446; 4.1.191
foolish 2.1.134–5
footing 2.1.76
fopped 4.2.195
for 1.3.266; 3.3.156
for that 1.3.25; 2.3.303
Ford, John p. 14; 3.3.166
foregone 3.3.429
forehead 3.3.287
forfend 5.2.32
forswear 4.2.159
fortitude 1.3.221
forth 5.1.36
found him 2.1.241
fountain 4.2.61
fordoes 5.1.128
forked 3.3.279
form 4.2.155
Forrest, Edwin pp. 8, 44, 49, 102, 110
Foucault, Michel p. 123
foul 1.2.62; 1.3.118; 1.3.139–40
'foul papers' pp. 412, 413,
frail 2.1.152
frailty 4.3.94
frankly 2.3.286
fraught 3.3.449
free 1.3.42, 211–12, 263, 388;
    2.3.307, 322; 3.3.188, 202, 259,
    342
freely 2.3.315; 5.2.55
Freeman, Morgan p. 98
fresh 3.3.388
friend 3.3.146, 382; 3.4.176
frieze 2.1.126
from 1.1.130
full 4.1.256
full soldier 2.1.37
fulsome 4.1.34
function 2.3.333; 4.2.27–9
Furness, H. H. pp. 8, 45, 47, 72, 114,
    135, 142; 1.1.20; 1.3.259–63;
    5.2.76, 91
fustian 2.3.270

*futurity 3.4.113
Fyfe, Christopher p. 9

gained 1.3.373
Galenic medicine 1.3.340–1; 3.4.139;
    p. 466
gall 1.1.147; 1.3.215
galls 4.3.87
game 2.1.222; 2.3.19
Gandhi, M. K. p. 62
garb 2.1.297
Garrick, David pp. 73, 79; 5.2.91
Gascoigne, Bamber p. 83–4, 84–5, 88,
    89
Gascoigne, George p. 465
gastness 5.1.105
Gautier, Théophile p. 57
gay 2.1.148
Geary, David p. 13
Geelan, Christopher p. 61
gender 1.3.319
gender v. 4.2.62
general p. 194; 1.3.50, 55; 2.3.302–3;
    p. 461
general camp 3.3.347
generous 3.3.283
Genster, Julia pp. 32, 462
gentle 1.2.25; 1.3.51; 4.1.187
Gentleman, Francis pp. 38–9, 101, 102
Gerard, John 1.3.342, 343
Germans 2.3.69–76
germans 1.1.113
gesture 4.1.83
get 1.3.190
Ghazoul, Ferial p. 13
Gielgud, Sir John pp. 57, 83, 84–6,
    88
Gildon, Charles pp. 72, 73, 124
Giraldi Cinthio, Giovanni Battista
    pp. 20–32, 33, 158, 179, 183, 193,
    194; 1.3.253–8, 383–5; 2.1.16,
    279–82, 282; 2.3.240; 3.3.0,
    42–75, 186–8, 196–200, 233–7,
    361–5, 399–410, 434–6; 3.4.28–9,
    49–95, 68; 4.1.89–163, 164–206,
    193–202; 5.1.71; 5.2.59, 123,
    299–300, 368; pp. 400, 461, 462,
    465
give away 3.3.28
Globe playhouse p. 2; 1.1.139;
    5.2.102; pp. 399, 406
Globe (rebuilt) p. 424
glorious 3.3.356

go to 1.3.367; 4.1.163; 4.2.148
go to *v.* 4.2.193
goat 3.3.182–3, 405
goats and monkeys 4.1.255
God bless the mark 1.1.32
God by you 3.3.377
Godwyn, Morgan p. 124
Goethe, J. W. von p. 1
gone 3.3.270
good 2.1.96–9
goodbye 1.3.88
good morrow 3.1.2
Gouge, William pp. 161, 163, 164, 165, 167
government 3.3.260; 4.1.229
gown 1.1.86
grace 3.3.46; 4.3.87; 5.2.27
grace and favour 4.3.19
graces 2.3.305
Grainger, Percy p. 451
grange 1.1.106
Grant, Ulysses S. p. 15
Gratiano 1.1.174; 5.2.199
gratify 5.2.211
*graze 4.1.260
great of heart 5.2.360
grece 1.3.199
green-eyed 3.3.169
Greene, Robert 2.3.81–8; 3.3.331
Greg, W. W. pp. 412, 427
grievance 1.2.15
Griffin, Eric p. 116
gripe 3.3.422
gross 1.1.133; 1.1.72; 3.3.406
Gross, John pp. 97, 98
grows to waste 4.2.241–2
guardage 1.2.70
Guazzo, Steffano p. 162
guinea-hen 1.3.311
gull 5.2.161
gum 5.2.349–50
Gurr, Andrew pp. 408, 410, 421, 423, 424
Guthrie, Tyrone p. 78
guttered 2.1.69
gyve 2.1.167

Hagen, Uta pp. 9, 36
haggard 3.3.263
Haines, Charles pp. 137, 155
Haines, Richard Haddon p. 64
Hakluyt, Richard p. 463
Hale, J. R. 3.4.124

half asleep 4.2.98
Hall, John p. 466
Hall, Joseph p. 120
Hall, Kim p. 123
Hall, Peter pp. 90, 91–2
halter 4.2.136
halts 2.1.23
Hamilton, Charles p. 399
Hamlet pp. 1, 36, 132, 160; 1.1.46;
    1.3.6, 188; 2.3.69–76, 144;
    3.1.16–17; 3.3.204, 331, 446,
    447; 4.1.20–1, 249; 4.2.54;
    4.3.26–7, 83; pp. 400, 401, 402,
    403, 409, 411, 423
hand and heart 3.3.466; 3.4.34–6,
    44–5
handkerchief pp. 4, 23, 98, 155, 174;
    3.4.54–64, 89–91, 99–102;
    5.2.215
Hands, Terry pp. 17, 62, 91, 93–4, 107,
    421
hang clogs p. 227
Hankey, Julie pp. 8, 9, 10, 14, 15, 36,
    47, 48, 49, 50, 51, 58, 71, 72, 73,
    75, 76, 79, 80, 94, 102
Hanmer, Thomas p. 464
haply 2.1.263
happily 3.3.242
happy 1.2.66
hardness 1.3.231–2; 3.4.32
Harewood pp. 57, 64, 65, 98–9, 100;
    1.2.22; 5.2.355
harlotry 4.2.233
harmony pp. 450, 453
Harris, Bernard p. 116
Harrow, Lisa p. 36, 105
Hart, Alfred p. 401
Hart, H. C. 3.4.5–6; 5.2.355
Harvey, Brian pp. 83, 89
Havens, Richie p. 15
have with you 1.2.53
having 4.3.86
Hawkins, Richard p. 407
Hazlitt, William p. 80
head and front 1.3.81
heart *see* hand and heart
heart-strings 3.3.264
hearted 1.3.359
heat 1.2.40; 1.3.261
heathenish 5.2.312
heave the gorge 2.1.227
heavy 1.3.256; 2.1.142; 4.2.116;
    5.1.43; 5.2.100

Hedgecock, Frank p. 79
hell 4.2.92–3
Hellespont 3.3.453–6, 456
helped 2.1.136
Heminge and Condell pp. 409, 413, 431
Hendricks, Margo p. 123
Henrietta Maria, Queen p. 3
2 Henry IV 1.3.363; p.462
Henry V 1.2.28; pp. 402, 423, 462
1 Henry VI 1.3.188, 255; 2.3.135.1
2. Henry VI (Contention) 5.2.362
Heywood, Jasper 3.3.447
Heywood, Thomas p. 26
hideous 3.3.111
hie thee 4.3.45
hies 5.1.35
high 2.3.226; 4.1.183; 5.2.95
high supper time 4.2.241
high-wrought 2.1.2
Hill, Aaron p. 80; 5.2.38
hinge 3.3.367
Hinman, Charlton pp. 181, 412, 414, 418
hint 1.3.142, 166
Histrio-mastix see Marston, John
Hobson, Harold pp. 58, 59, 83, 84, 89; 3.3.460
hoppy-horse 4.1.149
Hodgdon, Barbara pp. 64, 68
hold him 5.2.333
Holinshed, Raphael p. 114
Holland, Philemon pp. 19, 399
hollow mine 4.2.79
homage 1.1.54
home 2.1.163
honest pp. 160–2, 178; 1.3.292; 2.3.132, 322, 326; 3.3.104, 229, 386; 4.2.142; 5.1.120–2
honesty 1.3.282; 5.2.244
Honigmann, Ernst pp. 17, 22, 34, 37, 111, 116, 193; 1.1.4–7, 19, 130–26; 1.2.49–53, 59, 83; 1.3.166; 1.3.247, 316, 329–30, 367–71; 2.1.0.1, 3, 11, 15, 27, 85, 85–7, 96–9, 101; 2.1.129–47, 153, 290; 2.3.153–6, 280–1, 362; 3.3.158, 166, 283–4, 361–5, 447; 468; 3.4.69–70, 89–91; 4.1.3–4, 61, 70, 124, 206.1, 214–16; 4.2.2, 21–3, 64, 74–5, 112; 4.3.20, 33, 47–8, 60–2, 79–80; 5.1.60; 5.2.33–4, 70, 72, 199, 218;

pp. 399, 401, 402, 403, 406, 407, 409, 414, 415, 416–22, 424, 427, 429, 430, 432, 464, 465
Hope-Wallace, Philip p. 57
Hopkins, Sir Anthony pp. 60, 92
Horace (Quintus Horatius Flaccus) p. 41
Hornback, Robert p. 5
Horne, Michael p. 422
horned 4.1.58
Hosley, Richard p. 467
Hoskins, Bob pp. 89, 92
hot 3.3.405–6; 3.4.37
hotly 1.2.44
housewives 1.3.270; 2.1.112
Howard-Hill, Trevor p. 414
Hoyle, Martin p. 95
humane 2.1.233
humour 3.4.121
humours (*see also* Galenic medicine) 3.4.29
Humphrey, Pelham p. 451
hungerly 3.4.101
Hunt, Marsha p. 108
Hunter, G. K. pp. 62–3, 117, 119–20, 121, 146; 3.4.71
hurt your head 4.1.55
hussy 4.1.90
hypocrisy against the devil 4.1.6
Hydra 2.3.292

ice-brook's temper 5.2.252
*idle 1.2.95; 1.3.140
ill-starred 5.2.271
'I.M.' p. 165
import 3.3.319; 4.2.31
imports 4.1.133
importing 2.2.3
imposition 2.3.260
impudent 4.2.81
in 3.3.341
in position 3.3.238
in the nick 5.2.316
incline 1.3.146
inclining 1.2.82; 2.3.325
incontinently 1.3.301
incontinent 4.3.10
incorporate 2.1.254
index 2.1.249
Indian(s) p. 115; 5.2.346; pp. 464–5
indign 1.3.271
infectious 4.1.20
inference 3.3.186

ingener 2.1.65
ingraft 2.3.132
injointed p. 216
innovation 2.3.36
inordinate 2.3.295
insinuating 4.2.131
instruction 4.1.38
insupportable 5.2.100
intendment 4.2.202–3
intentively p. 224
inversion errors 2.3.158
invisible 2.3.271
Irving, Sir Henry pp. 71, 75–8, 102;
    5.2.355
issues 3.3.222
iterance 5.2.148
Iyengar, Suajata pp. 11, 55

Jackson, C. Bernard pp. 13, 71
Jackson, Henry pp. 1, 9, 36, 71, 100–1,
    135
Jackson, Macdonald pp. 402, 403,
    414–15, 417, 418, 420, 465
Jacobi, Derek p. 111
Jaggard, Isaac p. 409
Jaggard, William p. 409
James, Emrys pp. 36, 90, 95
James, Henry pp. 49, 83, 95
James I (King) p. 18; 3.4.44–5;
    5.2.352–4; p. 399
Jannings, Emil p. 53
Janus 1.2.33
jealousy 3.3.151
jennet 1.1.113
jesses 3.3.264
Jew of Malta see Marlowe
John, Errol pp. 57, 86
Johnson, Patrice pp. 67, 110–11
Johnson, Samuel pp. 8, 135; 1.1.122;
    3.4.69–70, 99
Johnson-Haddad, Miranda p. 67
joint-ring 4.3.68
Jolson, Al p. 59
Jones, D. A. N. p. 106
Jones, Eldred Durosimi pp. 62–3, 119,
    121
Jones, Emrys 5.2.352–4; p. 399
Jones, Ernest p. 78
Jones, James Earl pp. 4, 36, 40, 49, 92,
    115
Jones, John pp. 415–16
Jonson, Ben pp. 32, 72, 128, 145, 193;
    1.3.62; 2.1.216; 3.3.93, 361–5;

3.4.5–6; 4.1.124; 5.1.0; pp. 421,
    465
Jordan, Thomas p. 465
Jove (Jupiter) 2.3.17; 3.3.358
Jowett, John pp. 417, 420
Judas 1.2.59
Judean pp. 464–5
judgement 1.3.9
Julius Caesar 3.3.310
jump 1.3.5; 2.3.371
just 1.3.5
Justice 5.2.17
justly 1.3.125

Kani, John pp. 63, 94
Kean, Edmund pp. 10, 47, 54, 57, 73,
    75, 80–1, 87, 113, 114; 3.3.174;
    4.1.0; 5.2.355
Kee, Robert p. 59
keep 5.2.364–5
keep time 4.1.88
keeps her company 4.2.137
Kellner, Leon 1.1.57; 1.3.329–30;
    2.3.271; 5.2.85
Kelly, Jude pp. 66–7, 89, 109–10
Kemble, Fanny pp. 49, 102
Kemble, John Philip pp. 45, 47, 72, 74,
    79–80
Kendall, Felicity p. 105
Kermode, Frank p. 6
Kerrigan, John 5.2.86; pp. 415–16
kind 1.3.378; 2.3.307; 5.2.125
King, Francis p. 62
King John 4.2.71–2
King Lear pp. 1, 36, 156, 170, 171, 176;
    3.3.331, 405, 464; 4.2.92–3, 190,
    193; 4.3.19; 5.2.124, 194,
    363–4.1; pp. 409, 410, 411
King's Men p. 399, 401, 403, 407,
    426–7, 429, 432
Kingsley, Sir Ben pp. 11, 17, 62, 93–4
Kingston, Jeremy pp. 60, 90
kiss(es) 1.3.159; 5.2.358
Kittredge, George L. 2.1.109; 3.3.127
knave p. 45; 1.1.45; 2.1.231; 4.2.140
knee-crooking 1.1.45
kneels (sd.) 3.3.450.1, 462.1;
    4.2.31–40, 151;
Knight, Charles p. 45
Knight, G. Wilson p. 24
Knolles, Richard pp. 17, 194; 1.3.16;
    5.2.344; pp. 400–1, 403
knot 4.2.62

know of 5.1.115
Knyvett, Henry 1.1.35–6
Kongo kingdom p. 26
Kretzmer, Herbert pp. 5, 58, 85
Kutkevich, Sergei p. 105
Kyd, Thomas 3.3.390–1; 5.2.302;
    p. 410

labours 2.1.127–8
Lacy, Thomas Hailes p. 47
lack 3.3.321
Lamb, Charles pp. 45, 113
languishes 3.3.43
Las Casas, Fra Bartolomé p. 124
Laslett, Peter p. 162
Laurenson, James p. 111
law-days 3.3.144
lawn 4.3.68
lay 2.1.256–7; 2.3.311
lay by 4.3.44
lay down 4.2.13
Le Tourneur, Pierre 4.3.24
leaden 172
leapt 2.1.287
learn 1.3.182
leave 105
Leavis, F. R. pp. 57–8, 60, 74, 117,
    128
leets 3.3.144
Leo Africanus, John p. 18; 1.3.129–45,
    140, 340–1, 349; p. 466
Lepanto, battle of pp. 18, 148; 2.1.27;
    5.2.352–4; p. 399
Lerner, Laurence p. 117
lethargy 4.1.49
Levin, Bernard p. 87
Levin, Richard pp. 464–5
Lewes, G. H. pp. 10, 45, 80, 86
Lewkenor, Sir Lewis pp. 18, 158;
    1.2.13–14, 43; 5.2.338
liberal 2.1.161; 3.4.36
liberal as the north 5.2.219
lie 3.4.1–11
lieutenant pp. 30, 151–2, 194;
    2.3.93–7, 130; 3.3.478, pp. 461–2
*lieutenantry 2.1.169
life 1.1.154
lift up eye 5.2.198
light 2.3.165; 4.1.98
lights and torches 1.2.28
like 5.2.94
lingered 4.2.225
Linschoten, Jan Huygen van 1.2.62

lip 4.1.67
lips 4.1.39–40
list 4.1.71
list *v.* 2.3.331
Lister, David p. 98
Lister, Moira p. 104
Little, Arthur p. 122
loading 5.2.362
locusts 1.3.342
Lok, John p. 463
Long, William B. p. 424
Loomba, Ania pp. 14, 115
loose of soul 3.3.418
lord 4.2.101
Lord Chamberlain's Men *see* King's
    Men
lose 1.3.210; 3.3.323
lost 5.2.268
Love's Labour's Lost 1.3.188;
    2.1.132–3, 170; 5.2.70; p. 465
love's sake 3.1.12
Lowin, John p. 72
lown 2.3.84
Lupton, Julia Reinhard p. 116
Lust's Dominion pp. 18, 465
lusty 2.1.286
'Lydford Law' 4.1.36–7

Macaulay, Alistair p. 99
Macbeth pp. 36; 1.1.122, 139;
    4.1.20–1, 124; 5.2.7, 362
McCabe, Richard pp. 88, 99
Macdonald, Joyce Green pp. 42,
    68
McGoohan, Patrick p. 15
Machavariani, A. p. 15
Machiavelli, Niccolò p. 197
McKellen, Ian pp. 66, 88, 89, 95–6,
    108, 109
McKern, Leo pp. 57, 86
Macklin, Charles pp. 71, 72
MacLiammóir, Micheál p. 88
McMillin, Scott p. 93; 2.1.0.1, 172;
    2.3.135.1; 4.2.67; 4.3.60–2;
    5.1.62.1; pp. 405, 407, 408,
    421–2, 423, 424–7, 429
McNulty, Charles p. 98
McPherson, James A. p. 68
Macready, William Charles pp. 10, 11,
    48, 57, 74, 75, 81, 82, 102;
    3.3.174
mad 4.3.25; 5.2.113
made mocks with 5.2.383

magic 3.4.68; 5.2.168
magnifico 1.2.12
maidens' hearts 3.4.74
main 2.1.254
make after 1.1.68
make waay 5.1.59
make head against 1.3.272
make proof of 5.1.26
makes 1.2.49
makes my gain 5.1.14
malignant 5.2.352
mamm'ring 3.3.71
man 1.3.330; 4.1.61
man but a rush 5.2.269
manage 2.3.206
Manawa Taua pp. 9, 13, 123
Mandeville, Sir John p. 463
mandragora 3.3.332
mane 2.1.13
mangled 5.1.78
Mannion, Tom p. 111
marble 3.3.460
Marcell, Joseph pp. 57, 64, 69
Marcus, Frank p. 90
Marcus Luccicos 1.3.45
mark 1.1.44; 2.3.305
Marks, Elsie pp. 9, 11, 54, 70
Marks, Peter p. 67
Marlowe, Christopher pp. 17, 32, 72,
    169; 3.3.295; 3.4.20–1; 5.2.206,
    284; pp. 410, 465
Marmion, Patrick pp. 61, 89
Marowitz, Charles p. 12
marry 1.2.53
Marston, John pp. 166; 1.1.46;
    3.3.460; 4.1.32
Marston, Westland p. 10
mask 4.2.10
Massing, Jean Michel p. 126
Mason, Brewster pp. 36, 60–1, 90
master 1.3.78; 2.1.204
Masters, Brian p. 95
Matar, Nabil pp. 116, 125
matter 1.2.38
Matthews, G. M. pp. 62–3, 138
Mauretania 4.2.224
Maurice (Saint) pp. 26, 27
Maxwell, J. C. p. 401
'maximal' and 'minimal' scripts
    pp. 409, 423–4, 432
mazard 2.3.144
mean 3.1.37
means 3.3.253

Measure for Measure 3.1.28; pp. 400,
    401, 402, 403, 404
mediators 1.1.15
medicinable 5.2.350
meet 1.1.144
melting 5.2.348
memorial corruption pp. 412, 413,
    428, 431
Mendes, Sam pp. 66, 96, 98, 99, 100,
    109, 111, 421
Merchant of Venice pp. 107, 115;
    1.1.80; 3.1.3; 4.3.87–98; p. 450
mere 2.2.3
Meres, Francis 5.2.143
Merivale, Herman Charles pp. 71, 94,
    95
Merry Wives of Windsor 1.3.363;
    5.2.70; p. 402
Meryman, Richard p. 85
messes 4.1.193
mettle 4.2.204
Meyerstein, E. H. W. 1.3.169
Middleton, Thomas pp. 400, 419
Middleton and Rowley pp. 14, 149–50
Midsummer Night's Dream, A pp. 131,
    149; 2.3.197; 4.2.71–2; p. 465
might not but 3.1.49
Miles, Bernard p. 77
Millard, Evelyn pp. 103–4
Miller, Jonathan pp. 89, 90, 92
Milton, John p. 165; 1.3.329–30
mince 2.3.238
minerals 1.2.74
minion 5.1.34
minister 2.1.263; 5.2.8
minx 3.3.475
Miola, Robert p. 193
mischief 1.3.203
misgives 3.4.88
mislineation p. 425
miuse 4.2.109
mock 3.3.169
molestation 2.1.16
Molière (Jean-Baptiste Poquelin) p. 85
Mondello, Bob pp. 67, 110
monkeys 3.3.405; 4.1.124
monsters and monstrousness
    pp. 138–47, 178, 1.1.88, 157;
    2.3.208; 3.3.110, 111, 393;
    3.4.156–7; 4.1.60
Monu, Nicholas p. 64
mood 2.3.263–4
moon 4.2.77

Moor(s) pp. 115–16, 157; 1.1.6–39, 57, 111; 1.3.340–1; 2.1.221; 3.4.28–9; 4.1.60; 4.2.224; 5.2.224, 352–4, 365; p. 466
Moorship 1.1.32
*moraller 2.3.287
more 3.3.402
Moriarty, Marcus J. p. 50
Morgan, Emily p. 106
Morley, Sheridan p. 61
Morris, Clara p. 49
mortal 3.4.111
mortal engines 3.3.357
mortise 2.1.9
Moseley, Humphrey pp. 426–7
moth 1.3.254
motion 1.2.75; 1.3.96, 326; 2.3.165
mountebanks 1.3.62
move 2.3.368
moved 3.4.18
Mowat, Barbara pp. 419, 431, 464
Much Ado About Nothing p. 131; 1.3.255; 4.1.70
much to do but 4.3.29–30
Muir, Kenneth pp. 18, 22; 3.3.453–6; 3.4.71
mummy 3.4.73; pp. 466–7
mutiny 2.3.147
mutualities 2.1.253

naked 5.2.257
napkin 3.3.293
Naples 3.1.2
Nathan, Norman p. 137
National Theatre (Royal) pp. 66, 96, 98, 99, 100, 109, 111; 1.2.22; p. 421
nature pp. 142–5, 221
necessaries 2.1.275
Neely, Carol Thomas pp. 39, 125
neigh 1.1.112
Neill, Michael pp. 32, 37, 41, 45, 115, 126, 127, 131, 136, 138, 139, 140, 145; 1.1.2, 41–65, 89; 2.1.200; 2.3.306–7; 3.3.119; 3.4.34–6, 155–6; 4.1.77; 5.2.363–4.1; p. 462
Neill, Juliet p. 69
Neilson-Terry p. 48
Nelson, Tim Blake p. 6
Nelson, T. G. A. pp. 137–8, 155
nephews 1.1.112
nettles 1.3.317–18

Neville, John pp. 79, 89
New Bibliography pp. 406, 408, 419, 423
*new-create 4.1.268
Newman, Karen pp. 115, 122, 126, 139
next 1.3.204
nice 3.3.15
Nicosia, siege of p. 400
Nightingale, Benedict p. 99
nightcap 2.1.298
nightgown 1.1.158.1
nightly wearing 4.3.14
Niven, Penelope p. 40
Nkrumah, Kwame p. 58
Noble, George pp. 39 (fig. 5), 135–6
Noble, Louise p. 467
noise 3.1.13
none such 3.1.18
nose 3.1.3; 4.1.39–40, 117
not this hour 2.3.13
not your way 4.1.180
nothing 3.3.433
notorious 5.2.238
Nunn, Trevor pp. 11, 64, 65, 95, 99, 106, 108, 109, 111

O 5.2.289
O me 5.1.57
oaths and profanities pp. 405, 411, 415, 418, 428, 432
obedient 3.3.90; 4.1.147–8
obey 5.2.194
object 363–4.1
objective genitive 3.3.220; 4.1.90
obsequious 1.1.46
observance 3.3.155
observancy 3.4.145
occasion 2.1.236; 3.1.49; 4.1.49
occupation 3.3.359
ocular proof (*see* eyes) 1.1.27; 3.3.361–5, 433; 4.2.1–4, 25–6
odd-even 1.1.122
odds 2.3.176
Odyssey 3.280–1
off-capped 1.1.9
offend(s) 2.3.190; 5.2.61
office (*see also* place, service) 1.1.16; 1.3.377; 3.3.377, 414; 3.4.109; 4.2.92–3
offices 2.2.8
officed 1.3.268
officer 1.1.16

officers of night 1.1.181
Ogude, S. E. p. 70
Okes, Nicholas pp. 407, 429
Okri, Ben pp. 113, 146
Oliver, Edith p. 49
Olivier, Laurence (Lord) pp. 5, 10,
    57–60, 62, 78, 85–8, 89, 94, 95,
    117, 1.3.159; 3.3.362.1, 460;
    5.2.15, 250.1
Olympus 2.1.183
O'Neill, Eliza p. 102
on the hip 2.1.296
on you neck 5.2.168
once 3.3.182–3
opinion 2.3.186
opposite 1.2.67
opposition 2.3.175
oppresses 1.1.142
Oras, Ants p. 402
Orkin, Martin pp. 63, 120–1, 123
Orgel, Stephen p. 5
Orr, Bridget p. 124
Otello p. 193
Othman p. 194
Ottoman Empire p. 194
Ottomites 1.3.34
out 4.1.109; 5.2.120
out of fashion 2.1.201
out o'th'way 3.4.79
out-sport 2.3.3
out-tongue 1.2.19
overt 1.3.108
Overton, Richard p. 167
Ovid 5.2.343
owe 1.1.66; 3.3.335
Oxenbridge, Faith p. 69
Oxford editors p. 431

Packard, Vance p. 150
paddle 2.1.246
pagans 1.2.99
pageant 1.3.19
pains 1.1.182; 1.3.159
painted 4.1.249
Palmer, John 5.2.357–8
Papp, Joe p. 49
Paracelsus pp. 466, 467
Paradise Lost see Milton
paragons v. 2.1.62
parcels 1.3.154
Parker, Oliver pp. 68, 88, 137–8
Parker, Patricia p. 139; 3.3.127;
    4.3.37

parlours 2.1.110
parrot 2.3.269
particular 1.3.56
part 1.3.75
Partridge, Eric 2.1.153
parts 1.2.31; 1.3.251; 2.3.305
'parts' (actors') pp. 425–6, 431
Pasolini, Pier Paolo p. 10
pass 2.3.237
passage 5.1.38
passing 1.3.160
passion 4.1.38, 249
Paster, Gail 2.1.192; 2.3.197;
    3.4.139
patent 4.1.191
patience 4.1.86
Paton, Maureen pp. 95, 106, 108
'Pavier quartos' p. 407
Payne, Henry Nevil p. 14
peace 5.2.159
pearl 5.2.346–7
Pechter, Edward pp. 1, 9, 36, 60, 71;
    3.3.204; 4.2.64
Peck, Linda Levy p. 161
Peck, Bob pp. 61, 91
peculiar 1.1.60; 4.1.65
Peele, George p. 18
peevish 2.3.176
Pepys, Samuel pp. 9, 101
peradventure 2.1.283
Percy, Thomas 2.3.81–8; p. 447
perdition 2.2.3
perdurable 1.3.332
period 5.2.356
perplexed 5.2.345
pestilence 2.3.341
Peter, John pp. 11, 95, 98, 99, 109
Peters, Clarke p. 64
Petrarch, Francesco 1.3.159
perdition 3.4.66
perfect 1.2.31
permission 1.3.329–30
person 1.3.386
Phillips, Caryl pp. 12–13
pictures 2.1.109
piece of work 4.1.146
pierced p. 1.3.218
pioneers 3.3.348
pipe 3.1.13
pirated texts p. 423
pitch 2.3.345
pith 1.3.84
pitiful 5.2.208

place (*see also* office, service) pp. 32,
135–58, 178; 1.1.10, 103, 144,
155; 1.3.54, 221, 236; 2.3.93–7,
306–7; 3.3.250–1, 415, 478;
4.1.253; 4.2.229; 5.2.195
plain 2.1.303
platform 2.3.111
play 2.1.114
play the sir 2.1.171
played 4.3.80
players 2.1.112
pleasance 2.3.280
please it 1.3.189
pliant 1.3.151
plies 2.3.339
Pliny the Elder pp. 19–20, 145;
2.1.153; 3.3.331, 453–6;
5.2.101–3, 143, 349–50; pp. 399,
463
plume up 1.3.382
Plummer, Christopher pp. 4, 36, 92–3
Plutarch p. 168
point on me 5.2.47
poise 1.3.322; 3.3.83
poison 2.3.341
poisons *v.* 5.2.363
Poitier, Sidney p. 40
policy 2.3.264
Pollard, A. W. pp. 407, 408
Polydore Virgil p. 450
Pontic Sea 3.3.453–6, 453
Pope, Alexander 1.3.159
poppy 3.3.332
portance 1.3.139
Porter, Thomas p. 14
Pory, John pp. 18; 1.3.129–45
position 2.1.230
possession 5.2.277
possible 2.3.276; 4.1.40; 4.2.87
Potter, Lois pp. 9, 17, 36, 49, 57, 62,
68, 71, 74, 75, 78, 81, 83, 88, 89,
94, 96, 99, 101, 102, 103, 104,
106, 108, 110
potting 2.3.70
pottle 2.3.50
practice 1.3.103; 3.4.137; 5.2.290
practised 1.2.73
practiser 1.2.78–9
practising 2.1.301
praise 5.1.66
pranks 1.3.141
prating 2.1.219
pray 3.3.221

precious 5.2.233
prefer 2.1.269
preferment 1.1.35–6
pregnant 2.1.229–30
preparation 1.3.14
preposterously 1.3.63
prerogatived 3.3.277
prescription 1.3.305
present 1.2.90, 1.3.125
presently 3.1.36; 5.2.54
pressed 3.4.172
Pressley, Nelson pp. 110–11
Prester John p. 26
Preston, Mary p. 114
price 1.1.10; 4.3.64
pricked 3.3.414
pride 3.3.356, 406
prime 3.3.405–6
Privedi, Poonam p. 13
probal 2.3.323
probation 3.3.367
process 1.3.142
proclaim 1.1.69
procreants 4.2.28
produced 1.1.145
profane 1.1.114; 2.1.161
profane *v.* 1.3.373
profit 3.3.80–1, 381
Promethean 5.2.11
prompt books pp. 412, 417, 424
proofs 3.3.431, 442
proper 1.3.70; 1.3.381; 4.3.33
property 1.1.171
Propontic (Sea) 3.3.456
propose 1.1.24
propriety 2.2.167
prospect 3.3.400
prosperity 2.1.271
prosperous 1.3.243
protest 4.2.202–3
proud 1.2.23
prove 3.3.193; 5.1.66
provender 1.1.48
proverbial usages 1.1.25, 42, 64;
1.3.139, 172, 201, 298, 362–3,
390, 392–3; 2.1.109–13, 114,
129–47, 180, 216; 2.3.59, 66,
69–76, 94, 161–3, 232, 234, 238,
254–5, 261–2, 265–6, 269, 292,
309–12, 336–8, 351–2, 355, 356,
362, 364; 3.1.8, 49; 3.3.130,
159–60, 161, 166, 175, 176–7,
178–9, 213, 278–9, 301, 303, 384,

405, 406, 478; 3.4.5.6, 34–6, 65;
4.1.32, 35–6, 36–7, 58, 88, 93,
141, 143, 176, 237; 4.2.25–6, 39,
144, 172; 4.3.43, 54; 5.1.3, 4, 66,
103, 124; 5.2.4, 5, 7, 96, 131–2,
134, 135, 154, 187, 219, 246–7,
250, 260, 264, 272, 274–5, 284,
301, 316
provocation 2.3.21–2
provulgate 1.2.21
psychomachia 3.3.447–9
public 4.2.73
puddled 3.4.139
puffed 3.4.133
puny 5.2.243
Purchase, Bruce 4.2.57–62
put 5.1.2
put away your pipes 3.1.19
put it to 3.3.394
put me to't 2.1.118
put on 2.3.336
put out the light 5.2.7
put up 4.2.180
putting on 2.1.295

qualification 2.1.266–7
qualified 2.3.36
qualities 3.3.362
quality 1.3.249; 3.3.355
Quarshie, Hugh pp. 5, 69–70, 106
quarter 2.3.171
quat 5.1.11
Quayle, Sir Anthony pp. 57, 58, 83, 89
quick 2.1.80
quicken 3.3.280; 4.2.67
quillets 3.1.23
Quin, James pp. 47, 79
quirks 2.1.63
quite 5.128

race, *see* colour
raised 1.2.29, 43
Ralegh, Walter (Sir) pp. 20, 463
ram 1.1.88
rank *a.* 2.1.297; 3.3.236
rank *n. see* place
rash 3.4.78
Rasmussen, Eric pp. 410, 422
Ratcliffe, Michael pp. 93, 94, 421
raven 4.1.20–1
reach 3.3.222
reason 3.3.65
rebuke 2.3.200

reckoning 3.4.171
recognizance 5.2.212
recoiling 3.3.240
recover 2.3.263
refer 1.2.64
Reisch, Walter p. 9
relish 2.1.163–4
relume 5.2.13
remembrance 3.3.294; 3.4.181
remorse 3.3.468
repeals 2.3.342
reprobance 5.2.207
re-stem 1.3.38–9
resolved 3.3.182–3
respect 4.2.190
Revels office pp. 423, 432
Revenger's Tragedy 3.1.179
reverend p. 203
revision, theories of pp. 409, 410–11,
416, 422, 429, 431
rheum 3.4.49
Rhodes 1.1.28; p. 400
Richard II 5.2.362
Richard III pp. 32, 72; 1.1.65; 1.2.28;
1.3.255; 2.3.321; 3.3.274; 4.3.19;
5.1.115; 5.2.44
Richards, David p. 94
Richardson, Sir Ralph p. 78
Richardson, Tony p. 104
Ridley, M. R. pp. 34, 37, 118–19;
1.2.72–7; 1.3.166, 342; 2.1.14,
165; 2.3.345; 3.3.120; 3.3.388;
4.1.231; 5.2.265–71; pp. 412, 413,
415
rise 2.1.115; 2.3.152
rites 1.3.255
Rizvi, Parvez 1.1.14; 2.3.153–6; p. 417
Robeson, Paul pp. 9, 11, 36, 53–7, 61,
94, 114, 141
Robinson, Henry Crabb p. 80
Robson, William p. 80
Roderigo 1.1.56
Roman 4.1.115
Romeo and Juliet pp. 112, 131, 1.3.166,
255; 4.2.71–2; 5.2.70, 306–28;
pp. 421, 423
rose 5.2.13–15
*rose-lipped 4.2.63
Rose, Lloyd p. 67
Rosenberg, Marvin pp. 10, 14, 47, 48,
73, 75, 76, 77, 78, 80, 83, 102
Ross, Lawrence J. pp. 155, 467
Rossi, Ernesto pp. 48, 49, 81–2

Rossini, Gioachino p. 15
round 1.3.91
rouse 2.3.60
Rousseau, Jean-Jacques p. 451
rout 2.3.201
Rowe, Nicholas pp. 37–8, 45, 47;
  1.3.247; 3.3.362.1
royal 3.3.355
rude 1.3.82; 3.3.357
ruffianed 2.1.7
Rushdie, Salman pp. 13, 123
Rymer, Thomas pp. 3–6, 8, 15, 24–5,
  34, 35, 36, 37, 41, 45, 74, 91, 113,
  124, 136, 146, 179

sadly 2.1.33
Saggitary 1.1.157
Salih, Tayeb pp. 13, 117–18, 123
salt 2.1.234; 3.3.405–6; 3.4.49
Salvini, Tommaso pp. 10, 48, 49, 81–2,
  83, 95; 4.1.44–177
sanctimony 1.3.348
Sanders, Norman pp. 34, 58, 93, 117;
  1.3.247; 2.1.0.1, 11, 27;
  2.3.69–76, 158; 4.1.262–4;
  4.2.57–62; pp. 399, 416
Sandford, Samuel pp. 72, 74
sans 1.3.65
Sant'Iago Matamoros p. 194
satisfaction 4.2.200
satisfied him 5.2.317
satisfy 3.3.385–92, 392
satisfying 5.1.9
satisfied 4.2.244
saucy 1.1.127
Saunders, Ben 2.1.174
'Sblood 1.1.4
scant 4.3.86
scapes 1.3.136
scattering 3.3.155
Schlegel, A. W. p. 117
Schröder, F. L. p. 14
scion 1.3.327
Scofield, Paul pp. 60, 61, 91–2, 112
score 3.4.174
scored 4.1.123
scorn of fortunes 1.3.247
scorn of time 4.2.54
scurvy 1.2.7
sea-mark 5.2.267
seals 2.3.329
Sears, Djanet p. 13
sea-bank 4.1.129

seamy 4.2.146
seat 2.1.287
seated (*sd.*) 1.3.0.1
second 2.3.130
sect 1.3.327
secure 4.1.67
seel 1.3.267; 3.3.213
*segregation 2.1.10
self-bounty 3.3.203
self-charity 2.3.193
sennight 2.1.77
sense 1.2.64, 72; 1.3.258; 3.3.240;
  4.3.89; 4.3.288
sentence pp. 227, 228
Sepulveda, Fra Juan Ginés de p. 124
sequester 3.4.38
sequestration 1.3.339
sequent 1.2.41
seriously 1.3.146
serpent's curse 4.2.16
serve 1.1.42
service (*see also* office, place)
  pp. 149–50, 158–69, 178; 1.1.34,
  47, 57; 1.2.4; 3.1.55; 3.2.2;
  3.3.18, 467, 479; 5.2.194, 338
servants 2.3.138; 3.2.6; 3.3.9
session 1.2.86
set 1.3.318
set down the pegs 2.1.195
set the watch 2.3.111
several 1.2.46
Seymour, Alan pp. 59, 88
shadowing 4.1.38
Shakespeare, John 5.2.272
shambles 4.2.66
shape him for 2.1.56
Shaw, Bernard pp. 5–6, 7, 11, 83,
  179
Sherley, Sir Antony 5.2.355
shifted 4.1.74
Shirley, James 5.1.25
shirt 5.1.48
Shorter, Eric p. 91
shot of courtesy 2.1.57
should be 3.3.384
shouldst me 3.3.383
shrewd 3.3.430
shrift 3.3.24
Shulman, Milton pp. 79, 84, 105, 106
sibyl 3.4.69
Siddons, Sarah p. 102
siege 1.2.22
Siemon, James R. pp. 8, 135

sighs 1.3.159
sign 1.1.155, 156
Signory 1.2.18
silliness 1.3.304
silly 1.3.303
simple 1.1.107
simpleness 1.3.245
Simpson, O. J. pp. 67, 68, 123
Sinden, Donald pp. 60, 61, 90–1
sink 2.3.200
Singh, Jyotsna p. 14
sir 2.3.157; 3.4.85
sirrah 3.4.1
sith 3.3.382
skillet 1.3.270
slave 5.2.275
slavery 1.2.99
slime 5.2.146
slip 4.1.9
slipper 2.1.235
slubber 1.3.225
small beer 2.1.158
smell thee 5.2.15
Smith, Maggie pp. 36, 59, 104, 105
Smith, Peter p. 5
Smythe, John p. 69
snipe 1.3.374
snorting 1.1.90
Snow, Edward A. p. 155
Snyder, Susan pp. 5, 28
so 3.3.349; 5.1.22
Sodkhanskaya, N. S. p. 52
soft 1.3.83; 3.3.267
soft you 5.2.227
sold 5.2.144
solicit 5.2.32
solicitor 3.3.27
Sonnets (Shakespeare) 1.1.65; 5.2.206
sorry 3.4.49; p. 428
soul 1.2.31
soundly 3.3.173
Southam, Brian p. 14
Southerne, Thomas p. 41
Spanish Tragedy see Kyd, Thomas
Spartan dog 5.2.360
Speaight, Robert p. 77
speak your bosom 3.1.55
speculative 1.3.268
Spencer, Charles pp. 97, 98, 99, 100
spends 1.3.208
Spenser, Edmund 2.3.280–1; 3.3.93, 390–1
spirits 3.4.61

splinter 2.3.310
Spivack, Bernard pp. 31, 72
spirit 1.1.103
*spirit-stirring 3.3.354
spleen 4.1.84
sport 2.1.222; 4.3.92
spotted 3.3.436; 5.1.37
Sprague, A. C. pp. 9, 10
speed 4.1.104
spoiled 5.1.55
*squabble 2.3.269
squadron 1.1.21
squire 4.2.145
Stack, William p. 53
stamp 2.1.236
Stanislavski, Konstantin p. 90
stands in act 1.1.150
start 1.1.102
startingly 3.4.78
state 1.3.234; 3.4.136
Stationers' Company p. 407
stay you 5.1.104
stead 1.3.333
Steele, Richard p. 79
steep-down 5.2.279
Steevens, George 1.1.4–7; 3.3.127; 4.1.68–9
Stendhal (Henri Beyle) p. 8
Stephenson, Sarah p. 105
Stewart, Ian pp. 61, 91
Stewart, Patrick pp. 64–5, 66–7, 94, 110–11; 3.3.93; 4.2.41; 5.2.15, 357–8
Stewart-Dorn, Franchelle p. 110
stick 4.2.108–9
still 1.3.129; 2.1.105
stillness 2.3.182
stirring 3.1.28
stomach(s) 3.4.100; 5.2.77
stone 5.2.65
stones 5.2.233
stop 2.3.2, 293; 5.2.263
stops 3.3.124; 4.2.77
stops me 2.1.192
store 4.3.80
stoup 2.3.27
straight 1.3.49; 3.3.88
strain 3.3.221; 3.3.254
strange 5.2.187
stranger 1.1.135
strangeness 3.3.12–13
Stratford-upon-Avon 1.1.76; 5.2.272
Stratioticos see Digges, Leonard

strawberries 3.3.436
Strier, Richard p. 176
strike 3.4.174
Stuart, Lady Frances p. 174
stubborn 1.3.226
Stubbes, Philip 3.3.144
Stubbs, Imogen p. 106
stuff 1.2.2
*stuffed 1.1.13
subdued 1.3.248
substitute p. 228
subtle 1.3.349; 2.1.235
subirned 1.3.149
success 3.3.226
such another 4.1.141
Suchet, David pp. 88, 91, 93–4
sudden 2.1.263; 4.2.190
sufferance 2.1.23
sufficiency 1.3.223
sufficient 3.4.89; 4.1.257
*suffocating 3.3.391
suggest 2.3.337
sullen p. 428
Sullivan, Arthur p. 451
sulphur 3.3.331; 5.2.278–9
*supervisor 3.3.397
supplied 4.1.27
support 1.3.256
surety 1.3.379
Suzman, Janet pp. 63–4, 110, 123
swag-bellied 2.3.71
sweating 3.4.40
swelling 2.3.51
sword of Spain 5.2.252
'swounds 1.1.86
sycamore 4.3.37
sympathy 2.1.113

tail 3.1.8
tainting 2.1.259
ta'en order for't 5.2.74
take exception 4.2.206–7
tall 2.1.79
Talma, Joseph pp. 10, 42
Taming of the Shrew 3.3.23; 4.3.69
taper 1.1.140
tarras 1.1.81–1
task *v.* 2.3.38
tasks 4.2.112
Tasso, Torquato p. 17
taste 2.1.266–7
Taylor, Gary pp. 181, 414–15, 418–19, 462

Taylor, James H. p. 118
Taylor, Joseph p. 72
Taylor, Paul pp. 97, 99
Tearle, Godfrey pp. 83–4, 94, 111
teem with 4.1.236
tell's another tale 5.1.124
tells 3.3.172
Tempest, The pp. 33, 125, 171; 1.2.28; 2.3.135.1; pp. 401, 447, 463
temptation scene pp. 132–3
tenderly 1.3.390
tenderness 2.1.226
*tented 1.3.86
term 1.1.38
Terreblanche, Eugene p. 64
Terry, Ellen pp. 75, 102, 104
test 1.3.108
Thacker, David p. 65
that 1.3.269; 4.2.154
thee *see* thou
Theobald, Lewis p. 124; 2.3.271, 305; 5.1.26.1; 5.2.101–3
theoric 1.1.23
thick-lips 1.1.66
thicken 3.3.431
thief 1.2.57
thinly 3.3.432
Thomas, Ben p. 64
Thomas, Siân p. 105
Thomas, William 1.2.13–14
Thompson, Leslie p. 467
Thorello p. 193
thou (*and* you) pp. 193; 1.1.117; 1.3.297; 2.1.208–9, 255–7; 3.3.9; 5.1.120; 5.2.133; 5.2.289–91
thrice-driven 1.3.230
throwing 1.1.52
Tiberius p. 465
Tierney, Colin p. 111
Tilney, Sir Edmund p. 399
time scheme pp. 33–6; 3.3.312; 3.4.99, 168–9; 4.2.44–5; 5.2.210
Timon of Athens 3.3.460
timorous 1.1.75
tinder 1.1.139
Tinker, Jack pp. 95, 96
tire 2.1.65
title 1.2.31
Titus Andronicus pp. 18, 45, 115, 126; 3.3.447; 5.2.302; pp. 465, 467
to 1.2.56
to do 3.3.74
to the sense 5.1.11

to th'vantage 4.3.79
toad 3.3.273; 4.2.61
toga'd 1.1.24
token 5.2.63
told 2.2.10
tongue 2.1.101
Took, Barry p. 91
touch 2.3.211; 3.3.82; 4.1.191
touching 2.1.33
town of war 2.3.204
toy 1.4.152
Toynbee, Arnold p. 59
trace 2.1.294–5
Tracy, Susan p. 107
*tranquil 3.3.350
trash 2.1.294; 3.3.161
travailous 1.3.139
Travels of Sir John Mandeville p. 20
traverse 1.3.363
travesties (of *Othello*) pp. 42–4
Tree, Sir Herbert Beerbohm pp. 47–8, 49, 81
trespass 3.3.65; 4.2.152
Trewin, J. C. pp. 84, 85, 104
tribe 3.3.178
trick 4.2.129
tricks of custom 3.3.126
Troilus and Cressida pp. 154; 1.3.247; 2.1.175; 3.3.23, 273; 4.1.141; 5.2.219; pp. 402, 403, 404
truly 4.2.38
trumpets pp. 445–6
truncheon 2.1.264
tup 5.2.136
tupping 1.1.89
tupped 3.3.398
turbaned 5.2.352–4
Turk(s) pp. 115–16, 147, 194; 2.1.114; 2.3.161–3; 5.2.352–4
turn 4.1.244; 4.2.62
turn Turk 2.3.161–3
turned your wit 4.2.146
tush 1.1.1
Tutin, Dorothy p. 104
Twelfth Night pp. 112; 1.3.166; 2.1.170; 4.1.32; 4.3.26–7; pp. 402, 403
twiggen bottle 2.3.139
'twill out 5.2.218
Two Noble Kinsmen 5.2.4
Tynan, Kenneth pp. 58, 59, 77, 79, 85, 86, 87, 104, 105; 3.3.362.1, 460

'ud's 4.3.70
'ud's death 5.2.71
unbitted 1.3.326
unblest 5.1.35
unbonneted 1.2.23
*unbookish 4.1.97
uncapable 4.2.229
undertake 2.3.316
undertaker 4.1.203
unfolding 1.3.243
unfold(s) 3.3.247; 4.2.141; 5.1.21
unforced 2.1.230
unhandsome 3.4.147
unhappy 2.3.30–1; 3.4.98; 4.1.224
unhatched 3.4.137
unhoused 1.2.26
unkind 4.1.219
unkindness 3.4.148; 4.2.159
unlace 2.3.185
unlucky 5.2.340
unpin 4.3.19
unprovide
unquietness 3.4.129
*unshunnable
unvarnished 1.3.91
unwholesome 4.1.117
*unwitted 2.3.173
upon 2.2.2; 5.2.325
Ure, Mary p. 104
use 2.1.130; 4.1.266; 4.3.97
uses 4.3.99
used 5.2.71
utmost 4.2.51
utmost sail 5.2.267

*vale of years 3.3.269
Valk, Frederick pp. 77, 82
Van Volkenburg, Nellie p. 55
Vandenhoff, George p. 75
vanity 4.2.164
Varma, Indira p. 109
vast 1.3.140
Vaughan, Virginia Mason pp. 10, 14, 36, 75, 83, 106, 108, 122–3
Vaughan Williams, Ralph p. 451
Venice pp. 148–9, 211; 1.3.62; 2.3.265–6
Venus and Adonis 3.3.93; 3.4.34–6
venture 4.3.72
Verdi, Giuseppe pp. 6, 7, 15, 65, 95, 99; 5.2.357–8
Veronese 2.1.27
very 1.2.2

very much 4.1.234
very nature 2.1.227
vessel 4.2.83
vesture 2.1.64
Viganò, Salvatore p. 15
villain 1.1.117
villainous 1.3.307
violence 1.3.247; 2.1.217
Virgil 3.4.69–70; 4.2.79
virtue 1.3.287, 315; 3.3.352;
    4.1.258
visage 1.1.50; 1.3.250
Vitkus, Daniel pp. 21, 115, 116, 122,
    124, 157; 5.2.289
Vogel, Paula pp. 4, 41
voice 1.3.258
Volpone see Jonson
Voltaire, François-Marie Arouet de
    p. 14
voluble 2.1.232
voluntary 4.1.26
votarist 4.2.188
vouch 1.3.259

wait upon 3.2.6
Waith, Eugene M. p. 74
Wallack J. W. 4.1.0
Walker, Alice pp. 114, 408, 411–14,
    420
Walker, Rudolph pp. 57, 64
Walkington, Thomas 3.4.139
Walkley, Thomas pp. 158, 406,
    407–8, 413, 421, 423, 427, 429,
    431
Walton, J. K. pp. 414, 420
Wambu, Onyekachi p. 70
Wanamaker, Sam p. 78
Wanamaker, Zoë pp. 108–9
wanting 3.3.344
wanton 1.3.267
Warburton, William 3.4.44–5
Warren, Michael p. 414
Wardle, Irving pp. 60, 62, 63
warrant 2.1.274; 3.3.20
warranty 5.2.62
watch him tame 3.3.23
watches 2.1.212
watching 3.3.288
waterish 3.3.15
wayward 3.3.295
wear 3.3.201
*wear my heart upon my sleeve 1.1.64
web 3.4.68

Webster, John pp. 72, 150; 5.2.71;
    p. 421
Webster, Margaret p. 56
wedding sheets 4.2.105
well 1.3.379
well met 2.1.207
well said 2.1.165; 4.1.111
Welles, Orson pp. 57, 58, 88, 104
Wells, Stanley pp. 181, 400, 415
Werstine, Paul pp. 412, 419, 420, 424,
    430, 431, 464
what you will 4.1.32
Wheatcroft, Geoffrey p. 65
wheeling 1.1.135
whereon 3.3.85
Whitehall, Palace of p. 399
Whitney, Geoffrey p. 155
Whitworth, Philip p. 89
white 2.1.132–3
White, Willard pp. 57, 64, 95, 96, 106
Whitelaw, Billie p. 105
Whitney, Lois p. 18
whore 5.2.228
Whythorne, Thomas p. 167
wider 1.3.108
Wickham, Rupert p. 89
Wiest, Dianne p. 36
wight 2.1.156
wild 2.3.205
wild fame 2.1.62
will 1.3.256, 329–30, 341; 3.3.236
Williams, Gordon p. 154
willow 4.3.26–7
Willow Song pp. 101, 175; 4.3.24–9;
    5.2.245–7; pp. 411, 417, 418, 421,
    445, 450–3
Wilson, John p. 34
Wilson, John Dover p. 114
Wilson, Richard pp. 65–6
wind instrument 3.1.10
window (*sd.*) 1.1.81.1
*wind-shaked 2.1.13
Wine, Martin L. p. 36
winks 4.2.77
Winter, William pp. 50, 76, 113–14
Winter's Tale 3.3.220, 392
wisdome 3.1.46
wit 2.1.129, 132; 2.3.353; 3.3.466
witchcraft 3.3.214; 3.4.68–74
with your earliest 2.3.7
within door 4.2.144
witty 2.1.131
wived 3.4.63

womaned 3.4.190
women pp. 169–77
wonder 3.4.97
wont 2.3.181
work 2.1.115; 3.3.299
works 3.2.3; 5.2.211
worse and worse 2.1.134
Worsley, T. C. p. 104
would 3.4.110
wretch 3.3.91
Wright, Abraham pp. 2, 36
wrought 5.2.344
wrought to his desire 5.2.322
wrought upon p. 107

yawn 5.2.103
yerked 1.2.5
yet 3.3.433–4; 4.2.156
you *see* thou
you have said 4.2.201
you talk 4.3.23
Young, Al p. 13
Young, B. A. pp. 58, 90, 105
Young, Charles p. 75
Young, Edward p. 15

Zadek, Peter p. 10
Zeffirelli, Franco p. 84
Zvantsev, K. p. 52